JACK BEATTY

AGE *of* BETRAYAL

Jack Beatty is a senior editor of *The Atlantic Monthly* and news analyst for *On Point*, a National Public Radio news and public affairs program. He is the author of *The Rascal King*, winner of an American Book Award, as well as the editor of *Colossus: How the Corporation Changed America*. He lives in Hanover, New Hampshire.

AGE *of* BETRAYAL

AGE
of
BETRAYAL

THE TRIUMPH OF

MONEY IN AMERICA, 1865–1900

JACK BEATTY

VINTAGE BOOKS

A DIVISION OF RANDOM HOUSE, INC.

NEW YORK

FIRST VINTAGE BOOKS EDITION, APRIL 2008

Copyright © 2007 by Jack Beatty

All rights reserved. Published in the United States by Vintage Books,
a division of Random House, Inc., New York, and in Canada by Random House
of Canada Limited, Toronto. Originally published in hardcover in the United States
by Alfred A. Knopf, a division of Random House, Inc., New York, in 2007.

Vintage and colophon are registered trademarks of Random House, Inc.

The Library of Congress has cataloged the Knopf edition as follows:
Beatty, Jack.
Age of betrayal : the triumph of money in America, 1865–1900 / Jack Beatty.—1st ed.
p. cm.
Includes bibliographical references and index.
1. United States—Politics and government—1865–1900.   2. Political corruption—
United States—History—19th century.   3. Democracy—United States—History—
19th century.   4. United States—Economic conditions—1865–1918.   5. Capitalism—
Social aspects—United States—History—19th century.   6. United States—
Social conditions—1865–1918.   I. Title.
E661.B37 2007   973.8—dc22   2006048729

Vintage ISBN: 978-1-4000-3242-6

Book design by M. Kristen Bearse
Author photograph © Mary Mead

www.vintagebooks.com

FOR AARON

Oligarchy is when the men of property have the government in their hands.

—ARISTOTLE, *Politics*

Each age writes the history of the past anew with reference to the conditions uppermost in its own time.

—FREDERICK JACKSON TURNER

Contents

Introduction

> Reason and right feeling on any public subject has a better chance of being favorably listened to, and finding the national mind open to comprehend it, than at any previous time in American history. This great benefit will probably not last out the generation which fought the war, and all depends on making the most of it before the national mind has time to get crusted over with any fresh set of prejudices.
>
> —John Stuart Mill, 1870

This book tells the saddest story: How, having redeemed democracy in the Civil War, America betrayed it in the Gilded Age.

The twenty-fifth anniversary of the battle of Gettysburg fell at the start of the 1888 presidential election campaign. Ten days before the veterans of the Army of the Potomac and a disappointing representation from the Army of Northern Virginia met to pledge devotion to "enduring peace, brotherhood, and union," the Republicans nominated former Indiana senator Benjamin Harrison, a Civil War general, to run against Grover Cleveland, the first Democratic president since James Buchanan.[1] Into the 1880s sectional politics had discouraged blue-gray reunions.[2] Reconstruction ruled them out for southerners; the southern rebellion for northerners. Republicans fanned the memory of the war, "waving the bloody shirt" to distract northern voters from the moral shipwreck of the postwar. In an 1866 speech, Oliver P. Morton, the Republican boss of Indiana, set the standard of verbal atrocity:

> Every unregenerate rebel . . . calls himself a Democrat. . . . Every man who murdered Union prisoners . . . who contrived hellish schemes to introduce into Northern cities the wasting pestilence of yellow fever, calls himself a Democrat. . . . [E]very one who shoots down negroes in the streets, burns

"To him who hath borne the battle . . ."
This man's courage and sacrifice helped to cauterize the evil of slavery.
All he stood for was lost in the sordid decades after Appomattox.
Thomas Waterman Wood, A Bit of War History: The Veteran *(1866)*

negro school houses and meeting houses, and murders women and children by the light of their flaming dwellings, calls himself a Democrat. . . . In short, the Democratic party may be described as a common and loathsome receptacle, into which is emptied every element of treason North and South, and every element of inhumanity and barbarism which has dishonored the age.[3]

Even when, in 1880, the Democrats nominated one of the highest ranking officers in the Union army, "many stories connect[ed]" Winfield Scott

Hancock, whose Second Corps held the high ground at Gettysburg, with "rebels." "They hug the war, and fondle the war," a Democrat complained in 1879, "as a loving mother does her first-born babe." Democrats to a man, Confederate veterans shunned fraternity with their former enemies so long as they stirred to Republican calls to "vote as you shot" and so long as Republican politicians like Representative James A. Garfield, addressing a convention of the Lincoln Battalion of the Boys in Blue, castigated southerners for "bloody[ing]" more "shirts by killing unoffending [Negro] citizens." The southern Democracy, in turn, waved the bloody shirt of the "Lost Cause" and fanned fears of "Negro domination" should the Republican Party take power.[4]

In 1888 the candidates' biographies invited bloody shirting. The *Chicago Tribune* identified Cleveland as "a political associate of ex-rebels and secessionists" and contrasted General Harrison's "charge at Peachtree Creek" with the young Cleveland's failure "to respond to [the] call" during the "period of the country's awful peril." The commander of the Grand Army of the Republic scarified Cleveland for returning captured battle flags to their original Confederate units: "May God palsy the hand that wrote that order! May God palsy the brain that conceived it, and may God palsy the tongue that dictated it." Such splashes of venom aside, the 1888 election, "the last campaign of the post–Civil War era," would be fought out not over the bloody shirt but the tariff—"the vicious, inequitable, and illogical source of unnecessary taxation" to Democrats, and the "constitutional, wholesome, and necessary" guardian of prosperity to Republicans.[5]

At Gettysburg the heat was reminiscently "fierce."[6] James Longstreet, worn from commanding the mostly black Metropolitan Police of New Orleans under the biracial Republican state governments of the 1870s, was the senior general present.[7] Yes, the South's leading "scalawag" told a northern interviewer, he'd warned Robert E. Lee against assaulting the Federals on Cemetery Ridge. Nonetheless, Lee had ordered Longstreet to lead the attack on the second day, which, partly because of his sluggish start, failed to turn the Federal flank. That evening Longstreet again urged Lee to maneuver *around* the Federals, and Lee, seeking a victory that would stun the war-weary North into "a recognition of our independence," again refused.[8] Twenty-five years later, at the end of a day of commemorations of the July 2 attack on the Federal left, Longstreet received a telegram from the widow of the man whose Virginians charged the Federal center on July 3: George Pickett was dead.[9]

The doomed devotion to an idea of right singed in fame by Pickett's division and matched by the 262 men of the First Minnesota Volunteers who charged the 1,600 of an Alabama brigade on the second day of the battle must have seemed incredible to the Gettysburg alumni living into the fall of the postwar, "days," the *New York Tribune* observed, "full of fraud, corruption, bargain, and sale."[10] The thought had to be in some minds: Did their comrades die for *this* country? Die for the "Corrupt Union Pacific," as a headline appearing during the Gettysburg anniversary labeled that deep frisk of the public pocket? Die that Jay Gould, "the Mephistopheles of Wall Street," who corrupted whatever and whomever he touched—the Erie Railroad, the gold market, President Ulysses S. Grant's brother-in-law, possibly the president's wife—might flourish rankly? In his notes for *The Gilded Age,* the 1873 novel that named the era, Mark Twain wrote that recent gold rushes and Gould-led railroad speculations were "the worst things that ever befell Amer; they created the hunger for wealth when the Gr[eat] Civ[ilization] had just completed its youth & ennobling WAR—strong, pure, clean, ambitious, impressionable—ready to make choice of a life-course."*

From the rostrum at the National Cemetery, General Dan Sickles, who, commanding the Federal left on the second day, lost a leg and won a Medal of Honor, spoke for the North, followed by General John B. Gordon, governor of Georgia, and a founding father of the Ku Klux Klan in that state, for the South. "This meeting is an historical event," Sickles said.

> We dedicate here on this battlefield today an altar sacred to peace and tranquility and union. . . . The war of 1861–65 was our heroic age . . . the heroic age of the Republic. We fought until the furnace of war melted all our discords and molded us into an homogeneous Nation. Let us all be devoutly thankful that God has spared us to witness and share the blessings of Providence upon our country, and the compensation for countless sacrifices made to establish on a just and firm foundation a government of the people, by the people, and for the people.[11]

For Sickles's former comrade-in-arms, Rutherford B. Hayes, "Hayes of the Twenty-third," the generation after glory had traduced those sacrifices. He had traduced them himself, becoming president in 1876 only by

---

* After the exposure of his 1869 conspiracy to corner the gold market, Jay Gould "became invested with sinister distinction as the most cold-blooded corruptionist, spoliator, and financial pirate of his time. . . . For nearly half a century the very name of Jay Gould was a persisting jeer and byword . . . the signification of every foul and base crime by which greed triumphs." Gustavus Myers, *History of the Great American Fortunes* (New York: Modern Library, 1936), p. 542.

agreeing to end Reconstruction. (A year earlier, after white terror and voter fraud had overturned the biracial government in Mississippi, its last Republican Congressmen despaired that "[t]he war was fought in vain.") Writing two years before the Gettysburg anniversary, the ex-president agreed with the radical Henry George about "the rottenness of the present system"—"the excessive wealth in the hands of the few" coexisting with the "extreme poverty, ignorance, vice, and wretchedness of the many, a maldistribution of property" sealed by the "influence of money . . . growing greater and greater . . . in Congress, in state legislatures, in city councils, in the courts, in the political conventions." "This is a government of the people, by the people, and for the people no longer," he wrote. "It is a government by the corporations, of the corporations, and for the corporations."[12]

Hayes confided those thoughts to his diary. Had he made them public they would possess more authority. But, according to his biographers, they *were* Hayes's considered, post-presidential views. How did Hayes come by them? What had he seen since the war to make him sound like a radical? How had "the corporations" supplanted representative government? Why had "the people" allowed themselves to be shouldered aside? And where was Hayes when that regime change occurred? For that matter, where are *we*? "[E]xcessive wealth in the hands of the few," a "maldistribution of property" secured by the "influence of money" on politics—Hayes could be describing public life today.*

Inequality achieved a style in the Gilded Age, "conspicuous consumption," illustrated by the New York millionaires who, the literary historian Andrew Delbanco tells us, "hosted treasure hunts at their country estates,

---

* Hayes's diagnostic applies to an energy bill John McCain called "No Lobbyist Left Behind" containing $14 billion in tax breaks for energy companies, a $1 trillion prescription drug bill of which an estimated 61 percent will go as profits to drug companies, a $190 billion farm bill lavish with subsidies for agribusiness, a "clean skies" initiative lenient on polluters, a bankruptcy "reform" bill shaped by credit card companies, and a bill to eliminate an estate tax paid by .1 percent of Americans pushed by heirs of the Mars Candy, Gallo Wine, Campbell Soup, and Krystal fast food fortunes. For details on the "Paris Hilton" lobby, see the excellent scholarly study by Michael J. Graetz and Ian Shapiro, *Death by a Thousand Cuts: The Fight over Taxing Inherited Wealth* (Princeton: Princeton University Press, 2005), especially pp. 1–17, 27. For figures on subsidies and tax breaks, see Peter Beinart, *The Good Fight: Why Liberals—and Only Liberals—Can Win the War on Terror and Make America Great Again* (New York: HarperCollins, 2006), p. 205. According to an Associated Press–Ipsos poll published in late 2005, "88 percent of adults find American political corruption a 'very serious' or 'somewhat serious' problem," *The New Republic* reported in December 2005. "House Rules," *The New Republic*, December 26, 2005–January 9, 2006.

"The Bosses of the Senate"
In this 1889 cartoon, Puck, *the satirical weekly, captures the essence of public life*
in the Gilded Age. The sign above the swag-bellies reads "This is a Senate of the
Monopolists by the Monopolists!" The "Peoples' Entrance" is "CLOSED."
Joseph Keppler, Puck, *January 23, 1889.*

burying diamonds in the lawn and furnishing their friends with golden trowels." But, brazen as it was, inequality then conformed to the pattern of the unequal past. Not so inequality in what publications from *The Atlantic Monthly* to *Seattle Weekly* have denominated the "New Gilded Age," when for every additional dollar earned by the bottom 90 percent of the income distribution, the top .01 percent earn $18,000. From 1950 to 1970, they earned $162.

And today the bottom 90 percent is not earning many additional dollars. Nonsupervisory "workers have sometimes gained ground, sometimes lost it, but they have never earned as much per hour as they did in 1973," Paul Krugman notes. "Not since the Gilded Age," the *Economist* asserts, "has America witnessed a similar widening of the income gap." Americans then lived *before* equality, before progressive income, inheritance, and corporation taxes; a generous minimum wage; unemployment insurance; Social Security, and the other egalitarian interventions in the market economy made during the Progressive and New Deal eras—the twentieth-century response to nineteenth-century industrialism. We live *after* equality; and like Rutherford B. Hayes in the first Gilded Age, Americans increasingly see not merely an economics but a politics of inequality behind that result.

"Would you say the government is pretty much run by a few big interests looking out for themselves or that it is run for the benefit of all the people?" a CBS/*New York Times* poll asked in July 2004. Sixty-four percent said government was run by big interests, nearly double the percentage who gave that answer in the 1960s. Over the same period, an earlier poll found, the number who believed that "public officials don't care about what people think" rose from 36 to 66 percent. In the judgment of two experts on Congress, Norman Ornstein and Thomas Mann, today's House of Representatives, in its responsiveness to business lobbyists, "more closely resembles the House of the 19th century than that of the 20th, of the Gilded Age more than the Cold War era." A 2004 report from the American Political Science Association, "American Democracy in an Age of Rising Inequality," found that "Recent research strikingly documents that the votes of U.S. senators far more closely correspond with the policy preferences of each senator's rich constituents than with the preferences of the senator's less-privileged constituents." The APSA report describes a system in which "inequalities in political voice" augment economic inequality. Campaign contributions and lobbying enable access to politicians, access leads to voice, voice to policy—to tax breaks, subsidies, "earmarks," regulatory relief, and the power to set the agenda. Meanwhile the voice of Americans who "sweep floors, clean bedpans, or collect garbage" is not heard, discouraging them from voting. Their civic withdrawal enhances the voice of the already advantaged, the 12 percent of American households with incomes over $100,000 who make 95 percent of all political contributions. "Our government," the political scientists conclude, "is becoming less democratic, responsive mainly to the privileged and not a powerful instrument to correct disadvantages or to look out for the majority." To which the student of the first Gilded Age can only add, We been here before.[13] The APSA's verdict on "our government" echoes the populist James B. Weaver's 1892 verdict on *his* government. "Public sentiment is not observed," the People's Party presidential candidate declared. "The wealthy and powerful gain a ready hearing, but the plodding, suffering, unorganized complaining multitude are spurned and derided."

"Contemporary history," according to the British historian Geoffrey Barraclough, "begins when the problems which are actual in the world today first take visible shape." This book is an essay in contemporary history. It attends the birth of *our* nation.[14]

AGE *of* BETRAYAL

Chapter One

ANNIHILATING SPACE

There have been two great dispensations of civilization, the Greek & Christian and now comes the railroad.

—William Cregg,
southern textile mill owner, 1853

Julius Caesar regularized the calendar in 46 B.C. Pope Gregory XIII reformed it in 1582. King George III subtracted eleven days from the British calendar nearly 200 years later. On November 18, 1883, America's railroad corporations stopped time.

In the 1850s Americans set their watches to eighty local times—thirty-eight in Wisconsin alone, twenty-seven in Indiana, twenty-three in Illinois. Noon in Chicago was 11:27 A.M. in Omaha, 11:50 A.M. in St. Louis, 12:09 P.M. in Louisville, and 12:31 P.M. in Pittsburgh. An 1883 railway gazetteer included time conversion tables for over 8,000 stations. Fingers plowed the ink off dark columns of type, plotting a route across the temporal Babel.

Yet, perhaps because few Americans traveled far, most of them tolerated this time quilt, to judge by the letters column of the *New York Times,* which printed seven letters of travelers' complaints in fifteen years. Basically, Americans took nature's word for time: Noon arrived when the sun looked nearest to being overhead, at times that differed with locations. ("A movement of one degree around the earth's surface—about 48 miles due east or west in the United States—changes local time four minutes," according to one authority.) Town clocks, to be sure, were set not by sundials but by almanacs that averaged the sun's variations over months and years. A scattering of localities rented astronomically precise time from observatories, which wired them through Western Union.

These innovations, however, only welded time more firmly to place. "[I]t would appear to be as difficult to alter by edict the ideas and habits of the people in regard to local time," a U.S. Senate report concluded in 1882, "as it would be to introduce among them novel systems of weights [and] measures." The Senate failed to reckon with a self-sovereign power that, having "annihilated space"—a railroad-boomer verb phrase—sought dominion over time. The sun told time from Genesis to 12:01 A.M. on November 18, 1883, when the railroads dispensed with it. "The sun," the *Indianapolis Centennial* commented, "is no longer to boss the job." Fifty-five million people "must eat, sleep, and work as well as travel by railroad time. . . . The sun will be requested to rise and set by railroad time. The planets must, in the future, make their circuits by such timetables as railroad magnates arrange."[1]

Those magnates rode the mystique of progress. The founding of the Greenwich observatory in 1848 stimulated a worldwide movement to standardize time in zones of longitude. That Greenwich promoted itself as the "prime meridian" consternated the French, who urged Paris.[2] American time chauvinists likewise objected to "John Bull's time." The railroads themselves only slowly came around to the idea. Rate wars undermined their will to cooperate. As competition yielded to consolidation, resistance weakened.

At an 1883 railway time convention, William F. Allen, the editor of the *Traveler's Official Guide* to railways, used two maps to show railroad managers the advantages of standardizing time. One depicted the prevailing forty-nine different times in a fling of colors; the other, four broad bands, north to south, fifteen degrees of longitude apart. The old map, in the clashing hues of competition, represented "the barbarism of the past"; the new map, a consolidated rainbow, "the enlightenment we hope for in the future."[3] The delegates left persuaded, and with cosmic presumption set out to reform time.

When Britain adopted the reformed Gregorian calendar in 1752 a mob gathered outside Parliament demanding "Give us back our eleven days!" By contrast, the railroads' imposition of standard time on the United States occasioned anxiety but not protest. On November 17 city jewelers, the *New York Times* reported, "were busy answering questions from the curious, who seemed to think that the change in time would . . . create a sensation . . . some sort of disaster, the nature of which could not be exactly entertained."[4] On the eighteenth, the master clock at Chicago's West Side Union Depot was stopped at 12:00, waiting for the railroad-decreed noon, which arrived, via telegraph, nine minutes and thirty-two seconds later. "Have you the new time?" strangers inquired of one another. In Washington the attorney general ordered federal employees to conduct business in the old time. The railroads could not force their standard on the U.S. government. That would take an act of Congress. Popular disquiet over the issue delayed legislation until 1918, when government surrendered time to the railroads.[5]

Railroads had long since accelerated the *tempo* of life, and a book, *American Nervousness: Its Causes and Consequences* (1883), traced that condition partly to this source. The author, George Beard, introduced a new term, "neurasthenia," to describe the "nervelessness" or "lack of nerve power" brought on by "modern civilization" in its most emotionally invasive form, the railroad. Its shrieking whistle, the historian Barbara Young Welke observes, "shattered the traditional division between public and private," and making the train on time quickened dictatorial anxiety. Using a new word, a Cincinnati paper feared that "the longer a man is a commuter the more he grows to be a living timetable." "Today a nervous man cannot take out his watch and look at it when the time for an appointment or train is near," Beard asserted, "without affecting his pulse." He listed depression, dyspepsia, inability to concentrate, uterine irritability, and impotence as symptoms of neurasthenia. The diagnosis caught on. By 1888 a magazine editor could call "neurasthenia . . . almost a household word."

Until the 1880s, when total railroad trackage and passenger usage both doubled over the decade, the speed-up captured by watchwords like "on time" and "on the tick" and "on the clocker" had occurred gradually, and under cover of celebration. Standard time focused a pent-up ambivalence.[6] "Damn Vanderbilt's time! We want God's time," one old party fleered at a railroad time consultant. Many pre-codgers felt the same way. Told that his train left at eight o'clock "standard" time, a Pennsylvania Irishman, thinking of Standard Oil yet making a railroad-resonant point, replied, "Well that settles it." Settles what, asked the conductor? "Why, the whole of it. They'll be gittin' the wind next, they've got the time now."[7]

Pittsburgh banned standard time until 1887. Augusta and Savannah held out until 1888. City after city balked in Ohio. When the Bellaire school board voted to adopt standard time, the city council had the board arrested.[8] The mayor of Bangor, Maine, vetoed a time-altering resolution passed by its city council.* Any change "that disarms the customs of people handed down from time immemorial," he argued, "should at least have the sanction of the State legislature."[9]

---

* For which *Railway Age* lampooned him in an editorial that began "A Dogberry who holds the office of mayor" and built to this: "[R]emember what Leonidas was at Thermopylae to Greece, what Bruce was to Scotland, what all great leaders have been to the liberties of the people in all ages, he is to the town clocks of Bangor." In fact, people in easternmost

Standardizing time challenged both nature *and* democracy. "The system adopted by you," editor Allen boasted to the railroad managers at their next meeting, "now governs the daily and hourly actions of at least fifty million people."[10]

But who elected the railroads to *govern?* "Today the 75th meridian is standard because the railroad kings have ordered it," one congressman declared. "Tomorrow the railroads may make it the 76th, or the 80th." Let the people decide, he said. Put time to a vote.

Private enterprise had done more than upend a convention rooted in millennia of observation and agreement. Standard time, the *New York Herald* observed, "goes beyond the public pursuits of men and enters into their private lives as part of themselves." In his fascinating book *Keeping Watch: A History of American Time,* source of much of the detail above, Michael O'Malley explains: "Once individuals experienced time as a relationship between God and nature. Henceforth, under the railroad standards, men and women would measure themselves in relation to a publicly defined time based on synchronized clocks."[11]

Already they measured distance in time, translating miles into minutes. "[T]he real distance between New York and Philadelphia," a writer in *Niles Weekly Register* noted in 1848, "is just the same as it was a hundred years ago—but the relative distance is changed from seven days to seven hours."[12]

To a Nebraska editor, the conquest of space and reordering of time offered "signal proof" that railroads were "the most potent factors of our progressive civilization." He marveled that, "In a quarter of a century, they have made the people of the country homogeneous, breaking through the . . . provincialisms which marked separate and unmingling sections."[13] The railroads had knit back together a broken Union—but in their time and on their terms. Those twenty-five years yielded up a new dispensation. From November 18, 1883, the phrase "corporate America" meant most of what it suggested.

The railroad pierced horizons. Just before sleep young Richard Nixon would hear the whistle of a train cutting the night, inviting him to dream.

Maine felt they lost time on the new clock because the sunsets arrived earlier than under the old local time. Ian R. Bartky, "The Adoption of Standard Time," *Technology and Culture,* vol. 30, no. 1 (January 1989), pp. 51–54.

Where might those tracks lead? The yearning the whistle spoke to, the train alone could satisfy. You could go *anywhere*. Track led on to track; possibility to possibility. The railroad formed a network; and, like the Internet, it drew investors with the prospect of "network effects"—the Golconda of connectivity, things joined multiplying the value of the same things apart.

America's railroads often "built ahead of demand," laid tracks to people-less places. "Railroads in Europe are built to connect centers of population," Horace Greeley reflected, "but in the West the railroad itself builds cities." Build it and they will come. European observers viewed this strategy as incipiently suicidal. What if they did *not* come? If investors had similarly interrogated schemes for laying broadband cable ahead of broadband demand, they might have saved billions in the telecom bust of 2000–2001. Regarding Americans, it's not enough to say, with John Kenneth Galbraith, that speculation buys up the available intelligence. The romance of big recruits them for ventures of scale.[14]

"By the 1840s," the railroad historian James A. Ward writes, "promoters and railway financiers discovered that isolated lands had a pecuniary worth they could extract even before their railroads gave them any market value"—by securing land grants from governments, then selling the land to speculators and settlers to pay for construction. Ralph Waldo Emerson likened "[r]ailroad iron" to "a magician's rod in its power to evoke the sleeping energies of land and water."[15] Railroad corporations routinized the magic. Government provided the land, 155 million acres of it—in Minnesota the equivalent of two Commonwealths of Massachusetts, in California of two New Hampshires.[16] And men so ruthless that one who wrested millions from this marriage of powers, Jay Gould, was reputed to be "the worst man on earth since the beginning of the Christian era."[17]

By 1800 a half-million Americans had migrated from the original colonies across the Appalachian barrier. They might have gone to the moon.

"Nowhere did eastern settlements touch the western," Henry Adams writes in his history of the United States during the first administration (1801–1804) of Thomas Jefferson. "At least one hundred miles of mountainous country held the two regions everywhere apart." Snaking through gaps in the mountains in Pennsylvania and Virginia, three wagon roads, unimproved since the French and Indian War of the 1750s, formed the only land link between the regions. A journey up one of the few rivers to the interior might end wetly in a waterfall.

The river systems turned their backs on each other. "The valley of the Ohio had no more to do with that of the Hudson, the Susquehanna, the Potomac, the Roanoke, and the Santee, than the valley of the Danube with that of the Rhone, the Po, or the Elbe." Nearly a quarter of a century before the Erie Canal, Albert Gallatin, secretary of the treasury under Jefferson and James Madison, had outlined plans to link the valleys by canals. But by land, Americans believed, it would take "centuries of labor" to "conquer those obstacles which Nature permitted to be overcome."

Without a bridge able to bear the weight of an industrializing economy the sundered regions might evolve into separate countries.

"Whether we remain in one confederacy," Jefferson wrote in 1804, after completing the Louisiana Purchase, "or form into Atlantic and Mississippi confederations, I believe not very important to the happiness of either part." Jefferson was ready to concede to geography, in Adams's words, "the experiment of embracing half a continent in one republican system."[18]

Even along the seaboard, after nearly 200 years of expanding settlement, Adams wrote, distance barred larger integrations: "Each group of states lived a life apart." As late as 1812, a wagon pulled by four horses took seventy-five days to go from Worcester, Massachusetts, to Charleston, South Carolina.[19] Between Boston and New York stagecoaches ignobly competed with fast walkers. The road from Philadelphia to Baltimore was "tolerable" but a driver "rejoiced if in wet seasons he reached Washington without miring or upsetting his wagon." On his hundred-mile journey north from Monticello to the new capital in Washington, D.C., Jefferson wrote his attorney general, five of the eight rivers he had to cross had "neither bridges nor boats." South of Petersburg, Virginia, "even the mails were carried on horseback."[20] When you had taken the stagecoach from Charleston to Savannah, you had exhausted the public transportation of the South.

If American geography mocked the presumption of the *United* States, it vetoed a united economy. Coastal towns barely tapped their hinterlands. Privately operated turnpikes supplied the only considerable point-to-point transportation. Their tolls, however, discouraged wide use; a survey of the records of western Massachusetts farmers between 1750 and 1855 found only one entry for a turnpike toll in 1,827 trips to market. Inclemency and season often rendered impassable the alternative "shunpikes," poorly maintained by embarrassed citizens working off their taxes.[21]

Transportation costs—for wagon, team, feed, teamster, and lodging—

meant that farmers could not profitably ship corn more than forty miles or wheat more than eighty. By land, in 1815, it cost an estimated 30 cents "to carry one ton of goods a distance of one mile," Jeremy Atack and Peter Passell write in *A New Economic View of American History*. By boat upstream, the cost fell to 6 cents; by raft downstream to 1.3 cents; by ocean to less than one cent.[22] These economics suggest why the ship, not the covered wagon, dominated trade to the first West. Using technology essentially unchanged for centuries, traders sailed down the Atlantic coast, into the Gulf of Mexico, and up the mouth of the Mississippi to New Orleans.[23]

Over 1,800 flatboats arrived in that port in 1807, carrying whiskey, pig iron, lumber, and nonperishable agricultural goods from as far north as Pittsburgh, but only a hundred boats departed upstream.[24] On flatboats descending the inland rivers shipping costs were conscionable; on keel-boats pulled upstream by as many as thirty hands they could mount to $100 a ton.[25] And the pace upstream—New Orleans to Louisville in four months—was of a man staggering.[26]

For want of transportation the western economy stagnated. With farmers unable to ship their goods east, surpluses accumulated. Prices fell. Subsistence farming persisted. Producing for use not sale, western farm-ers did not have the money to buy eastern goods priced to cover the cost of transporting them. Meanwhile, relative scarcity inflated food prices in coastal America.

Without western customers, merchants plowed the sea. As in the colo-nial economy of 1700, commerce ruled. Profits of 250 percent could be made on a single voyage to Asia. The wars following the French Revolu-tion increased European demand for American exports and encouraged American merchants to *re-export* sugar and coffee from Britain's Carib-bean islands, a trade the Royal Navy, busy elsewhere, could no longer sup-press. Re-exports rose in value from $300,000 in 1790 to $46 million in 1801 and imports doubled.[27]

The fillip in trade was adventitious—peace in Europe, or war between the United States and a European power, could end it. "Experience has evinced the precarious and fluctuating nature of foreign markets," De Witt Clinton, the New York governor, told the legislature five years be-fore the completion of a canal that would join the separate domestic markets—by when both contingencies had occurred.[28]

Success dissuaded merchants from becoming manufacturers, delaying the industrial revolution in America. America's "first millionaire," the

Salem merchant Elias Derby, built a waterfront mansion crowned by a glass-walled cupola where he could watch his ships come in. Carrying-trade prosperity yields a Holland, not a U.S.A. "Foreign commerce may cooperate in creating flourishing Atlantic cities," Governor Clinton maintained, "but internal trade must erect our towns on the lakes and rivers and our inland villages; and internal trade must derive its principal aliment from the products of our agriculture and manufacturers."[29]

"As yet, my friend, we only crawl along the outer shell of our country," the Framer Gouverneur Morris wrote in 1800, recounting a visit to western New York. "The interior excels the part we inhabit in soil, in climate, in everything." The future spoke to Morris when, at a turn in a forest road, Lake Erie hove into view, and a gateway to the western rivers opened before him: "At this point commences a thousand miles of navigation."[30] Morris caught fire with the idea of a route to the west through the lowest gap in the Appalachians; the 363-mile Erie Canal begun in 1817 and completed a decade later realized Morris's dream. By joining the Hudson to the Mississippi, Alexis de Tocqueville wrote, Americans had "changed the whole order of nature to their advantage."[31]

The Erie Canal transformed the economics of distance; the cost of shipping a ton of grain from Buffalo to New York fell from $100 to $5 and the time from around twenty to six days.[32] Not even the railroad would reduce ton-mile costs so precipitously.

The canal enabled the farmers of Ohio, Indiana, Illinois, and Michigan to provision eastern dinner tables, cutting the price of potatoes in New York City in half, and opened the interior to eastern-made goods.[33] Manufacturing employment in New York and Pennsylvania doubled in twenty years as the value of merchandise sent west ten-tupled.[34]

The overspill of the canal, Nathaniel Hawthorne wrote, "causes towns with their masses of brick and stone, their churches and theatres, their business and hubbub, their luxury and refinement, their gay dames and polished citizens, to spring up."[35] This pattern of indirect benefits would be replicated by the railroads that would outmode canals, which froze, and their mule-pulled barges, which averaged two to the railroad's twelve miles per hour.[36]

New York taxpayers financed the Erie Canal, through borrowing, and its success spread a mania of imitation. States moved rapidly to subsidize "several thousand" internal improvements, chiefly turnpikes, canals, and railroads. Such "developmental" projects were too expensive to build and yielded benefits too diffuse to justify private investment.[37] William H.

Seward, the New York senator, advanced the rationale for state intervention: "A great and extensive country like this has need of roads and canals earlier than there is a private accumulation of capital within the state to construct them."

Barely had the states approved their internal improvement projects than in 1837 the economy entered a years-long depression. With their tax receipts plummeting, state and local governments were left holding a profoundly empty bag: They could neither afford to finish the improvements nor pay interest on the tens of millions borrowed to make them. Five states defaulted on interest; one on principal.[38] Publicly financed improvements fell from public favor. The depression looms, according to William G. Roy, as a "watershed in the development of the modern American business corporation" partly because it discredited state sponsorship of economic infrastructure projects. This "revolt against internal improvements" favored privately financed railroads, which cost roughly $17,000 per mile to build, a 50 percent advantage over canals; and so did a second watershed development.[39]

The riddle of American business history is why "incorporation for business was commonly denied long after it had been freely granted for religious, educational, and charitable purposes." In his dissent in *Liggett Co. v. Lee* (1933), Supreme Court Justice Louis D. Brandeis answered the riddle he posed:

> It was denied because of fear. Fear of encroachment upon the liberties and opportunities of the individual. Fear of the subjection of labor to capital. Fear of monopoly. Fear that absorption of capital by corporations, and their perpetual life, might bring evils similar to those which attended mortmain. There was a sense of some insidious menace inherent in large aggregations of capital, particularly when held by corporations.

That fear coiled in America's Revolutionary heritage, its republican DNA. "Drawing largely on the work of seventeenth-century republican theorist James Harrington," the historian James L. Huston writes, "Americans believed that if property were concentrated in the hands of a few in a republic, those few would use their wealth to control other citizens, seize political power, and warp the republic into an oligarchy."[40]

Fear that corporations, enacting an ancient pattern, would form *imperia in imperio*—states within a state—motivated legislatures to reserve incorporation for public ventures. Chartering corporations to build bridges and turnpikes and granting them the right to charge users tolls for a period long enough to reap handsome returns, state governments fielded public works without taxing the public. Politicians esteemed this feature highly. For investors "franchise corporations" provided certainty of reward. They were monopolies—only one bridge spanned the river and it was all yours.

Icarian punishment awaits the monopoly. As the three representative corporations of their eras—the Second Bank of the United States, Standard Oil, and Microsoft—discovered, a company can succeed *too* well. William Leggett, the editor of New York's *Evening Post,* articulated a running complaint in Jacksonian America: "We cannot pass the bounds of the city without paying tribute to monopoly; our bread, our meat, our vegetables, our fuel, all pay tribute to monopolists. Not a road can be opened, not a bridge can be built, not a canal can be dug, but a charter for exclusive privileges must be granted for the purpose. . . . The bargaining and trucking away chartered *corporation* privileges is the whole business of our lawmakers." "Business" indeed: charters were often the fruit of biddable favor.[41]

Popular anger focused on the unbreakable nexus between state and corporation and demanded that it be broken. Andrew Jackson's moment had come.

To the despair of socialists, the reform tradition descended from Jackson eschews fundamental changes in the economic system; insisting, rather, that everyone play by the same rules *within* the system. *Equal freedom,* not equality, is its goal; the political magnification through which capitalists raise up "natural" inequality on public stilts is its target, not capitalism. In his 1832 veto message on legislation that would have rechartered the Bank of the United States, an 80 percent privately owned franchise corporation awarded the keeping of government deposits and protected from competition by government fiat, Jackson took aim at the stilts: "The rich and powerful too often bend the acts of government to their selfish purposes. . . . Many of our rich men have not been content with equal protection and equal benefits, but have besought to make themselves richer by act of Congress." Opposed by politicians like Daniel Webster on retainer from the bank, Jackson well knew how such "corporations" sought "power to control the Government and change its character." By its conduct during the presidential election campaign of 1832, when its existence was at stake in the choice between Jackson and Henry Clay, the bank confirmed Jackson's fears. In the months before the election it extended loans and discounts of $28 million, "an extraordinary sum," according to one historian. Blatantly electioneering, it spent $80,000 to print and circulate anti-Jackson literature; its president, Nicholas Biddle of Philadelphia, sequestered $20,000 in a secret fund "to bribe the press" and "pollute the public elections," Jackson charged. Calling for the bank's deposits to be disbursed to state banks, Jackson told his cabinet, "The Bank of the United States is itself a Government."[42]

The wave of Jacksonian reform next swept into the states. Jackson's war on the bank, Senator Thomas Hart Benton, a Missouri Democrat, told a Cincinnati audience in 1835, forecast local battles to come: "[T]he states abound with other monopolies, just as much at war with the Rights of the People as that great one was. . . . Chartered companies, with exclusive and extraordinary privileges, are the legislative evil and opprobrium of the age in which we live." To remedy privilege, democratize it.[43]

"By a general law of incorporation," William Leggett argued, "the good effects of private corporations would be secured, and all the evils avoided. The humblest citizens [can] associate together, and wield . . . a vast aggregate of capital, composed of the little separate sums which they could afford to invest in such an enterprise, in competition with the capitals of the purse-proud men who almost monopolize certain branches of business."[44] Starting with Connecticut in 1837 and New York a decade later, states enacted the spirit of Jacksonian reform by replacing special legislative charters with general incorporation laws that treated "the act of incorporation as nothing more than a mere license to exist" and a cheap one at that—a Connecticut button maker with $600,000 in capital and 200 employees paid only 50 cents for the privilege. And no longer did corporations have to serve a public purpose. Any enterprise satisfying minimal capital requirements could incorporate, even for exclusively "private" ends. As a "respectable farm couple might feel on receiving into the household a flashy successful son-in-law of uncertain character," the state cut the corporation loose.[45]

Pacing the changes in politics, law, and the climate of opinion toward corporations, from the mid-1840s the economic climate, too, turned propitious for railroads. King Cotton still ruled, but the Erie Canal was rotating the axis of the economy from north–south to east–west. "The discovery of gold in California in 1848," Douglas North writes, "created a third source of expansion outside the South. The Far West was not only a major market for the goods and services of the Northeast, but its one export, gold, played a vital role in the whole expansion of the 1850's."[46]

Rarely have the financing and necessity of a new technology been so aligned. The railroad was poised to annihilate American space.

It began in New England. In 1841 goods shipped from Concord, New Hampshire, via the Merrimack River and the Middlesex Canal, took four days to reach Boston. In 1842, via the just opened extension of the Boston and Lowell Railroad, they took four *hours*. A decade later, with the completion of the four east–west trunk lines, the travel time between New York and Chicago fell even more dramatically, from three weeks to three *days*.[47]

America sped up in the 1850s. An economic historian conveys the moment's thrust in the language of rocketry: "The American version of entrance into sustained modern growth, breakthrough, takeoff— whatever you will—seems to have occurred almost simultaneously with the introduction and diffusion of the railroad."[48] The railroad and its sentinel, the telegraph, stimulated the rise of big business, the factory, and mass production, "critically alter[ing] the conditions of supply and demand," Alfred D. Chandler writes. "They did so directly, by providing a new market for the iron industry. And they did so indirectly, on the demand side by lowering the cost of transportation and opening up new areas to high-volume overland movement, and on the supply side by making possible a continuous flow—winter and summer—of raw and semi-finished material to the factory."[49]

The railroad also revolutionized finance. Wall Street was invented to build railroads, the first business enterprises in America too big for individuals or local investors to finance on their own.

In the 1850s, according to Chandler, "only a few of the largest textile mills or iron-making and metalworking factories were capitalized over $1 million." But by 1859, investment in railroads rose above $1 billion—$17 to $35 million in the east–west trunk lines, the Erie, the Pennsylvania, the Baltimore & Ohio, and the New York Central; $10 to $17 million in western roads like the Michigan Southern and the Illinois Central.[50] The traders of the New York Stock Exchange had only come indoors from Wall Street in 1817, and as late as 1830, on "one day in March only thirty-one shares were traded."[51] By the 1850s, however, hundreds of thousands of railroad stocks traded every week. The mystifying jargon of Wall Street—"puts," "calls," trading "short" and "long" and "on margin"—entered the language, and the speculator became synonymous with the crook.

Finally, the railroad revolutionized organization, launching the career of management, one of the biggest contributions big business made to American life.

Plantation slaves constituted America's largest workforce in 1850, yet fewer than 1,500 plantations worked more than one hundred slaves, nine more than 500, and only two more than a thousand. For the most part their resident-owners ran these plantations themselves, aided by "the first salaried manager in the country," the 18,859 overseers listed in the 1850 census.[52] At the other end of the cotton economy, the largest textile factories in New England employed fewer than 500 hands. The factory owners had "incorporated these manufacturing enterprises in order to pool capital," Chandler writes in *The Visible Hand: The Managerial Revolution in American Business,* but "continued to run them as partnerships," often with only two full-time administrators, a treasurer-stockholder who kept the books, and a salaried agent in charge of the factory.[53]

In simplicity of organization the first railroads resembled the plantation and factory. A fifty-mile road might employ fifty men under a single superintendent. "A superintendent of a road fifty miles in length," Daniel C. McCallum, one of the pioneers of business administration, wrote, "can give its business his personal attention, and may be constantly on the line engaged in the direction of its details." However, "In the government of a road five hundred miles in length a very different state exists. Any system which might be applicable to the business and extent of a short road would be found entirely inadequate to the wants of a long one."

A long road needed more employees, required a more complicated division of labor, and had more intricate functions—operations, maintenance, finance, procurement, administration—to coordinate. Making the trains run on time took a "system perfect in its details, properly adapted and vigilantly enforced." Organization determined success or failure: "[The] disparity in cost per mile in operating long and short roads is not produced by *difference in length,* but is in proportion to the perfection of the system adopted."

In 1854, McCallum, the general superintendent of the New York & Erie, included a diagram in his annual report showing the lines of authority and communication connecting the Erie's departments. Henry Varum Poor, the editor of the *American Railroad Journal,* lithographed it and sold copies for a dollar apiece. Demand was strong. The organization chart entered history, and efficiency began its unwaning war on equality.[54]

To Tocqueville, writing before the deluge, the separation of thinking

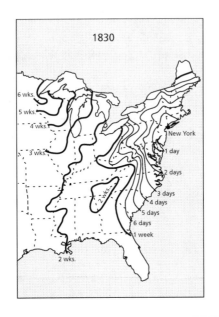

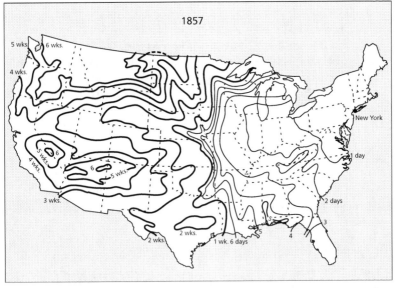

Rates of travel from New York City, 1830 and 1857.

and doing in industrial labor leaped out as "the monstrous exception" to American egalitarianism: "When a workman is unceasingly and exclusively engaged in the fabrication of one thing . . . his thoughts are forever set upon the object of his daily toil; his body has contracted certain fixed habits, which it can never shake off; in a word, he no longer belongs to himself, but to the calling he has chosen."[55] The lines on the chart separating the mechanic from the manager were mute. They said nothing of the one's stimulation by work and the other's stultification; of the one's initiative and the other's obedience; of the deference accorded the one and the surrender of pride demanded of the other. The manager's work sustained his life; the laborer's could kill him. Between 1890 and 1917, to jump ahead to the evolved system, 158,000 mechanics and laborers were killed in repair shops and roundhouses, another 72,000 workers on the tracks, and close to two million were injured. That mayhem owed much to the railroad lobby, which fought off installing safety devices like the air brake until the 1890s and defeated legislation to limit the continuous hours worked by railroad employees to a sybaritic sixteen. The railroad executive and the mechanic stood equal only at the ballot box.[56]

American democracy posed a more formidable barrier to American industrialization than American geography. "[T]he new economic order needed . . . part-humans: soulless, depersonalized, disembodied, who could become members, or little wheels rather, of a complex mechanism," Werner Sombart, the German sociologist, wrote, but in America the part-humans were full citizens. This regime-effect complicated the training of men and women habituated to task-driven work in agriculture, husbandry, or spinning and weaving at home under the putting-out system of manufacture to "renounce their desultory habits . . . and identify themselves with the unvarying regularity of the . . . automaton." Charles Dickens's Mr. Gradgrind, the factory owner in *Hard Times,* keeps "a deadly statistical clock . . . which measured every second with a beat like a tap upon a coffin-lid." The image evokes the ghosts of lives throttled by the mechanical yoke.*

---

* The prison inspired the design of the early factory—its walls and watchtowers kept the world out and the worker in. Freedom stayed *outside.* It remains there. "When you enter the low-wage workplace . . . you check your civil liberties at the door," Barbara Ehrenreich writes in *Nickel and Dimed: On (Not) Getting By in America* (New York: Metropolitan,

The language of economics muffles the cries of the full humans broken to the machine; and elides the politics of their breaking. For example, quoting from a book written by four economists, "An economy enters the industrial age when the rate of gross capital formation attains a substantial chain reaction in which a significantly larger amount of capital is available each period to increase output more than is necessary to sustain the old level and composition of output." To trigger and sustain this chain reaction "a community must convert 5% savers into 12% savers." That *sounds* anodyne. But how do you induce people to forgo enough consumption to double savings? They won't do it voluntarily; at any rate, they haven't. For "consumption" means wages and what wages buy—more life. "Savings" comes down to getting paid less than you earn by your productivity and your employer plowing the difference into investment, less the sift for himself. Imagine saving half your earnings. You'd have half your life. And the "savings" would not go to buy a better one for your children, but preserve in leisure a dividend-collecting gentleman.

To accumulate the "savings" to launch the industrial revolution, Britain despoiled its independent rural peasantry. Enclosure, first by landlord violence, then by legislation, cleared the land of people to make room for sheep. "[Y]our shepe that were wont to be so meke and tame, and so small eaters," Thomas More wrote in *Utopia*, "now, as I heare saye, become so great devourers and so wylde that they eate up, and swallow downe, the very men themselfes." "Clearing" continued into the nineteenth century. When the Duchess of Sutherland entertained Harriet Beecher Stowe to show sympathy for America's slaves, Karl Marx unearthed for readers of

2001) an account of a journalist's experience as a low-wage worker. "[You] leave America and all it stands for behind, and learn to zip your lips for the duration of the shift." And not only your lips. Until 1998 you had no federal right to pee. A passage from *Void Where Prohibited: Rest Breaks and the Right to Urinate on Company Time* (Ithaca: Cornell University Press, 1997) lights up the risk of humiliation in the time-driven workplace. "The right to rest and void at work is not high on the list of social or political causes supported by professional or executive employees, who enjoy personal workplace liberties that millions of factory workers can only dream about," the labor historian Marc Linder and the physician Ingrid Nygaard write. "While we were dismayed to discover that workers lacked an acknowledged right to void at work, [the workers] were amazed by outsiders' naïve belief that their employers would permit them to perform this basic bodily function when necessary." One such employer, the nation's largest, is Wal-Mart. According to an internal audit leaked to the *New York Times*, it violated state laws by denying thousands of its employees mealtimes and breaks—with humiliating results. A former Wal-Mart cashier, Verette Richardson, told the *Times* that in a Kansas City, Missouri, store, "it was sometimes so hard to get a break that some cashiers urinated on themselves" (January 13, 2004).

the *New York Tribune* the un-bleeding heart of an earlier duchess who between 1814 and 1820 cleared a Scottish county of its 15,000 inhabitants, using British soldiers to evict those who refused to go: "The whole of the stolen clan-land she divided into 29 great sheep farms, each inhabited by a single family, for the most part imported English farm servants. In the year 1835 the 15,000 Gael were already replaced by 131,000 sheep." The Duchess relocated the families "who for centuries had shed their blood for her family" to the barren seashore, where she charged them rent while they "tried to live by catching fish."

Many of those cleared off the land migrated to the cities, creating a surplus population of laborers—six for every unskilled factory job available in London in 1840—that held wages close to sustenance. "The force of the physical sanction being sufficient," Jeremy Bentham wrote of hunger, "the employment of the physical sanction would be superfluous." The state then passed laws giving laborers freedom to choose: they could sell their labor at market rates or, the state having abolished England's version of "welfare," starve. Karl Polanyi called this turn of history the Great Transformation. "The road to the free market [in labor] was opened and kept open," he writes, "by an enormous increase in continuous, centrally organized and controlled [state] interventionism. . . . [L]aissez-faire itself was enforced by the state." In Britain, as in Europe generally, feudal habits of deference and the restriction of the franchise until well past 1850 protected the coercive processes of industrialization from what Theodore Roosevelt called the "crushable elements" beneath it.*

In Russia the Communist Party led the Great Transformation. "Primitive socialist accumulation" outstripped its capitalist precursor in brutality and intensity. Joseph Stalin terrorized Russia's peasants into collective farms, then emptied their lives into the capital fund to industrialize the Soviet Union overnight. In a totalitarian state monopolizing the means of violence, rebellion was hopeless against "revolution from above."

---

* The economic historian Robert Heilbroner distinguishes five "waves of invention" that have lent "developmental thrust" to capitalism: "The first of these waves was the Industrial Revolution of the late 18th and early 19th centuries that brought the cotton mill and the steam engine, along with the mill town and child labor; a second revolution gave us the railroad, the steamship, and the mass production of steel, and along with them new forms of instability—business cycles; a third revolution introduced the electrification of life and the beginnings of a society of mass semi-luxury consumption; a fourth rode in on the automobile that changed everything from sex habits to the locations of population; a fifth electronified life in our own time." From *21st Century Capitalism* (New York: Norton, 1993), pp. 35–36.

To save their discipline from justifying cruelty in newly industrializing countries, economic historians have reanalyzed the "trade-off" model of accumulation illustrated above, a verity to economists from Adam Smith to John Maynard Keynes. "The immense accumulation of fixed capital, which, to the great benefit of mankind, was built up during the last half century before the Great War, could never have come about in a society where wealth was divided equally," Keynes wrote in 1920. "The railways of the world, which that age built as a monument to prosperity, were, not the less than the pyramids of Egypt, the work of labour, which was not free to consume the full equivalent of its efforts." A search of *The Journal of Economic History* turns up fifteen pages of entries debating that thesis since 1965. Economic historians produce numbers showing that industrialism benefited Britain's rural poor, with real incomes rising and infant mortality rates falling. Others, the Marxist historian E. J. Hobsbawm for one, dismiss this new view of industrialism as so much algebraic parsing of misery, marveling at "the ways in which people try to argue that black is white, or at least that it isn't black, or possibly that if it is, it is nobody's fault." Yet others, like E. P. Thompson, in *The Making of the English Working Class*, concede the facts: "By 1840 most people were 'better off' than their forerunners had been fifty years before," yet insist that those same people "had suffered and continued to suffer this slight improvement as a catastrophic experience." Mostly the debate is over the balance sheet of the industrial revolution in Britain. But does the trade-off model of equality for growth describe *American* reality?

"America inequality rose sharply in the decades after 1820," the economic historian Jeffrey Williamson observes in his *Inequality, Poverty, and History.* "At the same time, the net investment rate in national product doubled or tripled. . . . It is exactly the kind of correlation—rising inequality with rising savings and accumulation during industrial revolutions— that reinforced the trade-off postulate among classical economists who developed their growth models while the process was under way in Britain between 1780 and 1860." According to Williamson's research, in the United States "more inequality did not raise conventional accumulation by much." More important was investment in technology and immigration. On immigration, a noneconomist might wonder if that isn't a distinction without a difference. After all, immigration piled up unskilled surplus workers, which by keeping wages down increased inequality—as Williamson himself demonstrates in a 1998 paper. But if the question is, Were New England factory operatives "better off" than Iowa farm laborers?, the answer is yes—by the numbers. E. P. Thompson's point crosses the Atlantic: "A per capita increase in quantitative factors may take place at the same time as a great qualitative disturbance in people's lives." The historian must credit people's felt experience—for those caught up in industrialism, one of dislocation and exploitation.

In his short story "The Tartarus of Maids" Herman Melville evokes "a great qualitative disturbance" in the lives of farm girls new to their work in a New England paper mill. "At rows of blank-looking counters sat blank-looking girls, with blank, white folders in their blank hands, all blankly folding blank paper," the narrator reports of the sight that greeted him on entering the mill. In one corner "stood some huge frame of ponderous iron," a "tall girl . . . feeding the iron animal with half-quires of rose-hued paper. . . . I looked from the rosy paper to the pale cheek, but said nothing." He notices other figures tending other machines. All are "maids." "[M]arried women . . . are apt to be off-and-on too much," the proprietor, "an old bachelor," explains. "We want none but steady workers; twelve hours to the day, day after day, through the three-hundred and sixty-five days, excepting Sundays, Thanksgiving, and Fast-days." All are silent. "Nothing was heard but the low, steady, overruling hum of the iron animals. Machinery—that vaunted slave of humanity—here stood menially served by human beings, who served mutely and cringingly as the slave serves the Sultan." The narrator has come to buy paper, and a young supervisor explains how the machines make it. After asking a few desultory questions, the narrator sinks into reverie. "Something of awe now stole over me, as I gazed upon this inflexible iron animal. . . . [W]hat made it so specially terrible to me was the metallic necessity, the unbudging fatality which governed it." He watches as "the thin gauzy veil of pulp" on its parturition to paper disappears into the machine, yet like the pulse of industry through the century of progress, "it still marched on in unvarying docility to the autocratic cunning of the machine." Then, in an epiphany, the narrator glimpses the sacrifice at the base of the industrial pyramid: "I stood spell-bound and wandering in my soul. Before my eyes—there, passing in slow procession along the wheeling cylinders, I seemed to see glued to the pallid incipience of the pulp, the yet more pallid faces of all the pallid girls I had eyed that heavy day. Slowly, mournfully, yet unresistingly, they gleamed along, their agony dimly outlined on the imperfect paper, like the print of the tormented face on the handkerchief of Saint Veronica."

The young man calls him back from this vision: "Halloa! The heat of the room is too much for you." The narrator replies: "No—I am rather chill, if any thing." Of young women like these, the shock troops of industrialism, Hobsbawm writes: "They do not as yet grow with or into modern society; they are broken into it."

Before General Electric's Toledo bulb works, Melville's imagination might have failed for want of mythic analogy. Like the maids of the paper mill, nearly all the workers in this cutting-edge industry in 1914 were women. At the Toledo plant, working in teams, they attached wire filaments to the bulbs. A team once turned out 3,500 bulbs in one day; "that is to say, each minute for ten hours they flared and sealed between four and six lamps," the labor historian David Montgomery writes, for which General Electric paid each of them $1.58. The work demanded exacting attention—a government investigator sounding the complaints that led to a strike in 1914 described it as tantamount to threading several thousand "very fine cambric needle[s]" a day. In order to sleep, strikers told a local minister, they were "obliged to place wet cloths over their eyes nights to stop the aching." The highest pay went to those "who could exhaust (the operation that completed the vacuum) 900 bulbs per day with the aid of roaring-hot gas ovens." According to the strikers, only four of the 200 women who had begun that job that year remained; "six had died of tuberculosis and two were recuperating in a fresh-air camp." The bulb made, it was tested by being placed against an electrified plate—thirty-three bulbs per minute. "At the start of each day [the testers] felt a shock with each one, but soon, in the rush to earn 6.5 cents per thousand, they no longer felt anything."

So America had its "dark satanic mills." The difference between Britain and the United States was social and political more than economic. America had no Duchess of Sutherland; and no institutions to insulate industrialization against popular challenge. Deference to one's "betters" was not the American way, not after the birth of mass politics in the age of Jackson, and the nearest native approximation to a modernizing party dictatorship was the government of the Confederacy. Industrialization was an extra-democratic revolution unfolding in a democracy. Walter Dean Burnham puts that historic tension at the center of his seminal analysis of the nineteenth-century American electorate. While "industrialization adds immensely to national power, and may also promote the long-term betterment of the material conditions of the mass of the population . . .

it also involves the creation of structures of power, and, indeed, conquest," he writes. "This in turn requires the economic and cultural subordination of the mass of the population and the redefinition of the terms of their social and cultural existence." *But,* in the United States, "[T]he institutions of mass democratic politics and universal suffrage uniquely came into being *before* the onset of full industrialization." Its existential casualties (even if "better off") could mitigate its punitive terms at the ballot box.

New York's business elite had an answer for that: disfranchisement. To escape Tammany Hall's taxes on their property and contain the growing threat posed by striking workers who unreasonably resented pay cuts during the long depression of the 1870s, the *New York Times, Harper's Weekly, The Nation,* the Stock Exchange, the Chamber of Commerce, Governor Samuel Tilden, and the city's best people lobbied one session of the New York state legislature to pass a constitutional amendment taking the vote away from all non-property-holding or high-rent-paying citizens, 69 percent of the city electorate—but Tammany Hall and the city's Workingmen's Party, joined by upstate farmers, campaigned on the franchise in the 1877 election, and in the next session of the legislature turned back this attempted coup against democracy.

It wasn't necessary to assault democracy so frontally. The American "party-system provided America's industrializing elites with the insulation they needed against the challenges to which the prior establishment of democratic institutions made them vulnerable," writes Andrew Martin, an interpreter of Burnham's work. The party system—the structure and terms of political competition—insulated industrialism from democracy through a politics of distraction, based on the manipulation of real hatreds and sham issues. "Parties as they exist today are bellowing imposters and organized frauds," a former Populist lieutenant governor of Kansas asserted in 1898, when his own party had decayed into an unorganized fraud. "They are either reliable machines of plutocracy and the corporations, or they are the handy tools of hypocrites and harlequins, and are as much responsible, through the deceptions they have practiced and the corruption they have defended, for the servitude of the masses to plutocratic usurpers, as are the lawless exactions of organized capital for their plundering." Distraction, deception, corruption—the editor omitted only force.

As any reader of period newspapers quickly sees, industrial capitalism was up for debate in Gilded Age America; it had not achieved "cultural hegemony," a concept introduced by the Italian Marxist thinker Antonio Gramsci to elucidate how regimes rule without force. Hegemony, for Gramsci, is "the 'spontaneous' consent given by the great masses of the population to the general direction imposed on social life by the dominant fundamental group; this consent is 'historically' caused by the prestige (and consequent confidence) which the dominant group enjoys because of its position and function in the world of production." In an illuminating essay in the *American Historical Review,* the nineteenth-century Americanist Jackson Lears describes hegemonic rule's subtle sway: "Gramsci realized that 'every language contains the elements of a conception of the world.' The available vocabulary helps mark the boundaries of permissible discourse, discourages the clarification of social alternatives, and makes it difficult for the dispossessed to locate the source of their unease, let alone remedy it." In the United States, historians stress, the vocabulary of the corporate state, its "conception of the world," attained cultural authority only after 1900. The "great merger wave" of 1895–1904 created megacorporations in industries from steel to tobacco; massive corporate public relations campaigns were mounted to persuade Americans that bigness was good for them—that it increased efficiency and lowered prices—despite its diminution of competition.* Before then, the economic argument for bigness could not still the ancestral republican aversion to it. General incorporation laws had not discouraged the postwar growth of monopolies; competition had led to the same place as state-sponsored privilege. Big business reinvigorated Americans' fears of concentrated wealth corrupting government and legitimated popular resistance to the emergent order. "Both in word and deed, the late nineteenth century . . . provided ample evidence of popular opposition to the consolidation of control over economic and political life by a corporate elite," according to the labor historian Leon Fink. The counter-hegemonic culture of republicanism had not yet yielded to corporate liberalism. "At particular times and places, one can argue that the dominant historical bloc had not established a hegemonic culture and therefore turned to violence to protect its

---

* Reflecting the views of his adviser Louis D. Brandeis, Woodrow Wilson, in the 1912 presidential campaign, turned that contention on its head. "A trust does not bring efficiency to the aid of business; it *buys efficiency out of business.*" He distinguished between a trust, "an arrangement to get rid of competition," and a "big business . . . that has survived competition by conquering in the field of intelligence and economy." Thomas Goebel, "The Political Economy of American Populism from Jackson to the New Deal," *Studies in American Political Development,* vol. 11 (Spring 1997), p. 139.

interests," Lears writes. "[R]uling groups resort to force when their hegemony breaks down or when it has not yet been established." In Lears's view, the period from 1877 to 1919 was such a time.

High theory suggests the why of violence; low politics explains the how. The parties placed the coercive machinery of the state—Gatling guns, anti-"tramp" legislation, Supreme Court rulings—at the disposal of the industrializing elites who, in a quid pro quo, underwrote the costs of Gilded Age electioneering. What Henry George called "government by campaign contribution" produced the most violent strikes in the industrializing world.

In a quantitative study of strikes in France and the United States, Gerald Friedman documents the decisive role of the state. In France, "State intervention was associated with strike success." Partly from fear of strikes igniting revolutionary disorder, partly motivated by republican ideals of equality and fraternity, partly influenced by the socialist bloc in the Chamber of Deputies, the French government pressured employers to settle strikes by exhortation and action—for example, by threatening to lift their tariff protection or withdraw the police guarding their plants. State arbitration of strikes also helped labor, which requested "nearly half the cases of state mediation" between 1890 and 1914 compared to the 3 percent requested by employers. In the United States, arbitration was largely "a dead letter." "Repression, rather than conciliation, was the method chosen by most American government officials to deal with large strikes and with rising labor militancy." Between 1870 and 1903, state militia, the National Guard, or federal troops intervened over 500 times in labor disputes or civil disturbances stemming from them. "Domestic militarism," is the label affixed to this policy by the author of a comparative study of nineteenth-century nation-states, who also applies it to Bismarck's Germany. "The police in the United States," a Frenchman observed, "have become another of the armed bands of the Middle Ages which were found in the service of the barons." And whereas in France politicians and strikers were all Frenchmen together, in the United States the barons and the politicians were native white Protestants, the bulk of strikers immigrants—over 54 percent by 1903—Catholics, or African-Americans. "An American mob . . . contains all the vice, ignorance, and criminality of every country of the globe," the commander of the New York National Guard declared after the Haymarket bombing in 1886, in which an anarchist's bomb killed several Chicago policemen. Fellow feeling did not run to *these* fellows, nor inhibit shooting them. "American exceptionalism," Friedman concludes, "reflected the readiness of the American political elite to support the economic elite in the quick and efficient repression of radical labor organizations."

Under the stress of economic depression in the 1890s, the insulation the party system conferred on the merger of state and business frayed, and a revolt from below challenged the revolution from above.[57]

Chapter Two

ROME OF THE RAILROADS

> The western and middle western parts of the U.S. were, economically speaking, created by the railroad.
>
> —Joseph Schumpeter

No single railroad operated more than 250 miles of road in 1849, when trackage in the United States totaled 7,500 miles. By 1860, sixteen railroads exceeded that limit and 30,000 miles of track spidered the map from Maine to Missouri. The intervening decade witnessed the fastest growth powered by the inland engine of the nineteenth-century economy—a city.[1]

When Mark Beaubien was born in 1822, his was one of only two American families living at the trading post outside Fort Dearborn local Indians had named Chigagou, meaning "the wild-garlic place," and which they regarded as too marshy for habitation. When Beaubien died in 1907, two and a half million people lived there. Most of his fellow Chicagoans of 1907 owed their presence in the city to the train—"nearly *all* foreign born reached the midwest by train," an economic historian notes—or to the commotion of prosperity it generated.[2]

Nature endowed Chicago with a location promising a Cincinnati—a lake and river highway connecting North and South. The east-flowing Chicago River ended in a swamp that offered portage to rivers flowing into the Mississippi. But it took the magician's wand of railroad iron, waved over a frontier town, to quicken the metropolis of the "Great West."

The "City of Big Shoulders" was the first in history born of big business—or business that got big keeping up with it. With a hinterland stretching to the Rockies, Chicago demanded bulging enterprise—warehouses and fleets sized to carry Nebraskas of grain, lumberyards equal to the forests of the Old Northwest, slaughterhouses able to process meat for the millions, mail-order houses scaled to service a vast dispersion of customers, and railroads long enough to carry their sons and daughters to a city big enough to hold them, various enough to tempt them, and hard enough to break their hearts.

As William Cronon documents in *Nature's Metropolis: Chicago and the Great West,* great expectations flavored Chicago's propaganda from village-hood. Boosters of the pre-railroad era saw the Sears Tower rising from streets, marked with signs warning "No Bottom Here; Shortest Route to China," that marooned wagons in mud. The romance of Chicago was for the ears of auslanders with migratory cash. Within the city limits, Chicagoans leveled with each other. Their instinct to sell warred with the cut-the-crap realism befitting the eventual "Hog Butcher to the World."[3]

Addressing a crowd on an occasion inviting rodomontade, the start of construction on a canal linking Lake Michigan to the Mississippi, certain to sluice a vibrant commerce through the city, Judge Theophilus Smith, of the Illinois Supreme Court, meant to think Chicago-big. Chicago's popu-lation then, in 1836, numbered 3,820, a tenfold increase in less than a decade: Soldiers sent through Chicago in the Black Hawk War (1832–33) had returned home bearing news of cheap, well-sited land. Chicago would have a population of 20,000 in twenty years, Judge Smith predicted, 10,000 short of reality; and 50,000 in fifty years.

How about in a hundred years, a scoffer interjected? "In a hundred years from this time," the judge, standing atop a barrel, prophesied, "you will have a city of 100,000!"

"This," a witness recalled, "was too much for the boys. They took him off the barrel and threw water in his face. 'Arrah,' one said, 'if we hadn't stopped you, you'd have made it a million.' " Judge Smith may have been the last Chicagoan punished for civic exaggeration.[4]

Though the canal that buoyed the judge's soon exceeded forecasts took more than a decade to build, the prospect of Chicago as the nexus of inter-regional trade at once attracted eastern capital. A gold rush in real estate broke out over a ditch, with lots purchased for $150 in the morning selling for $5,000 in the afternoon. "A prevalent mania seemed to have infected the whole people," wrote Harriet Martineau, the English social observer, who visited Chicago at the height of the land boom.[5]

The bubble burst with the depression of 1837. European lenders demanded payment from eastern financiers, who squeezed their western creditors, who called in loans whose only collateral was a rising market. Construction halted on the canal. Growth stuttered—then stopped.[6]

A post-crash visitor described financial desolation. Residents "possessed at present the means of earning their sustenance, but little more," and "having lost all their capital" were "obliged to begin the world again." Chicago, incorporated as a city in 1837, seemed to be slipping back into a frontier town. On empty lots lately worth tens of thousands, Chicagoans revived farming. Travelers heard wolves "howling continually" at night; bears reconnoitered Michigan Avenue in daylight. Within flimsily built boardinghouses, at temperatures of minus twenty-eight degrees, cups froze to their saucers at breakfast and ink congealed in the act of writing.[7]

"Chicago is indebted for its unprecedented growth chiefly to its geography," a nineteenth-century historian reflected. A twentieth-century historian, Allan Nevins, elucidates: "The great north–south wall of Lake Michigan, jutting three hundred miles into the heart of the prairies, forced all east–west traffic to pass around its southern tip; and this tip was the natural point for breaking all lake-and-land traffic." But with the advantages of geography went its liabilities.[8]

Cold was one. All merchandise came to Chicago by lake, icebound from November to May.

Rain was another. The prairie soil, "so entirely vegetable," a British visitor observed, that it "makes no dust," owed its richness to a climate where rain could fall for sixty days straight.[9]

Mountains had barricaded trans-Appalachia. Mud "slued" Chicago, the local verb for immured. Missing persons were thought to have vanished in a slough off State Street. "On the outskirts of town," a farmer wrote of the approaches to Chicago in the 1840s, "the highways were impassable, except in winter when frozen, or in summer when dry and pulverized into the finest and most penetrating of dust. At all other seasons they were little less than quagmires." To keep them from disappearing in the State Street slough cattle rode into Chicago in wagons.[10]

After harvest, farmers enjoyed a dry sprint, and between September and November wagon trains filled the city streets and tailed into the prairie. Chicago exported its first shipment of wheat across the Great Lakes (to New York City via Buffalo and the Erie Canal) in 1839. By 1841 so much wheat poured into the warehouses along the Chicago River that "there were not vessels enough to carry it."[11]

A wagon, however, holds only so much wheat; farmers needed to make several round-trips, from distances of up to a hundred miles, to clear their fields. As in trans-Appalachia in 1800, so in northern Illinois and Indiana in

the 1840s—transportation costs skinned profits, discouraging production
for sale. "Most Illinois and Indiana farmers in the 1840's, therefore,"
Robert G. Spinney writes in his history of Chicago, "remained subsistence
farmers."[12]

With its "unbroken surface" extending for "hundreds of miles," an eastern
projector reflected, the prairie seemed "formed by nature to receive . . .
Rail Roads." Chartered in 1836 to run from Chicago 182 miles west to
Galena, Illinois, a prosperous lead-mining center, the Galena and Chicago
Union Railroad succumbed to the depression. A decade passed before
the venture regained plausibility. Eastern lenders, chary from their losses
in the land bubble, found the reorganized Galena and Chicago of 1846
resistible.[13]

So the new owners, public men from the two cities, sought local financing. At a railroad convention held in Rockford, a two-day ride from both
Chicago and Galena, over 300 delegates from ten Illinois counties came
out in support of the railroad—rapid, all-weather, and mudproof transportation. Hoping "[t]hat the value of farms along the route would be
doubled by the construction of the road," they resolved, "That in order to
accomplish the object of this convention . . . the inhabitants and owners
of property between Galena and Chicago should come forward and sub-
scribe to the stock of the proposed railroad to the extent of their ability."[14]

The railroad's new president, William B. Ogden, Chicago's first mayor
and foundational capitalist, spent the dry window of 1847 on horseback,
riding from Chicago to Galena, peddling stock door-to-door to farmers
who often "had to borrow the first installment of two dollars and fifty
cents on a share," an associate who rode with Ogden remembered, "and
get trusted 'till after the harvest' for the same."[15]

After weeks of spreading the gospel of the railroad to an amen chorus
of farmers in the Rock River Valley, Ogden and a fellow director, a
Chicago lawyer named J. Young Scammon, reached Galena, where they
got bad news. The Galena directors on Ogden's board had failed to persuade their townsmen to buy the road's stock.

The Galenans viewed the railroad's success with as much apprehension
as its failure. Proximity to the Mississippi River had made Galena "the
leading city of the west," and the railroad might undermine the basis of its
prosperity, perhaps even redirect it to Chicago. The Galenans also feared,
Scammon wrote, that "before the road should be completed the enter-

prise would break down, the small stockholder would be sacrificed and the road would pass into the hands of large capitalists." In fact the capitalists who declined to invest in the Galena anticipated its bankruptcy—and looked forward to feeding on its bones.[16]

"Go home," William F. Weld, "the Railroad King" of Boston, told Ogden and Scammon when they approached him for financing. "[R]aise what money you can, expend it upon your Road, and when it breaks down, as it surely or in all probability will, come and give it to us, and we will take hold of it and complete it, as we are completing the Michigan Central."[17]

Thanks to Ogden's missionary work, the Galena did not need Galena's capital, or Boston's. Farm families covered the shortfall, "depriving themselves of the means to educate their children," in the admiring words of a Chicago historian, "that the railroad might be built for the good of that and future generations." Their sacrifices combined with Ogden's industry—in one day he sold $20,000 worth of subscriptions to farmers in the city to sell grain—raised $351,800, enough to start laying track. Ogden located the terminal on the north side of the city, of which, the other directors observed, he owned a "large part."[18]

William B. Ogden, born in 1805, represented a new social type, the "businessman," a word invented in America in the 1830s. "In the period when he first appeared," the historian Daniel Boorstin informs us, "his primary commodity was land and his secondary commodity was transportation." The businessman entered history in the "upstart cities" of the Midwest. Unlike the merchant or manufacturer, the businessman had no fixed business.[19]

He was, *par example,* an entrepreneur. "The entrepreneur," as defined by the eighteenth-century French economist J. B. Say, who coined the term, "shifts economic resources out of an area of lower into an area of higher productivity and yield." Ogden specialized in mobilizing and shifting capital even if he had to scrape it off the prairie.[20]

A former New York legislator and champion of state aid to railroads, Ogden came to Chicago as an agent for his brother-in-law's land-buying company and from the first conceived for it a prescient zeal. "He saw in 1836, not only the Chicago of today, but in the future the great city of the continent," a friend recalled. "From that early day, his faith never wavered." Another observer of his career remarked on the identity of interest Ogden achieved with his city: "He could not forget that everything which benefited Chicago, built up the Great West, benefited him."[21]

Ogden's $20,000 day came on October 22, 1848, when the Galena's first locomotive, *Pioneer*, arrived at the Clark Street Dock. Purchased from the New Buffalo, Indiana, terminus of the Michigan Central, *Pioneer* was painted a glistening black, with polished brass and copper fittings and 24,000-pound wheels "sand-papered until they resembled steel." Crowds gathered watching as a team of horses towed *Pioneer* across town to the Galena's Kinzie Street depot. Ogden had a captive audience for his stock subscriptions. Three days later, *Pioneer* made a five-mile run into the prairie, the westmost point of whistle-heard.[22]

On November 20, *Pioneer* pulled one passenger car and one freight car from the Kinzie terminal to Oak Ridge, ten miles west. The directors and their guests, who'd gone along for the ride, alighted for refreshments. Among the onlookers they picked out a farmer with a wagonload of grain under him and asked if he was going to Chicago. He was. Would he like to load his bags of wheat on the freight car and enjoy a free trip to market? He would. Neptune's first tear began the sea.[23]

A week later the directors learned that thirty *carloads* of wheat were waiting at Oak Ridge.

The Galena reached Elgin in 1850, Rockford in 1852, and Freeport in 1853, where the line ended, seventy-five miles short of Galena. Along its shores land values spiked, in some locations from $1.25 to $25 an acre. Population increased, towns sprang up, stores opened. "Where a few months before," a county history notes, "there was nothing but an undisturbed prairie . . . all became hustle and bustle." By 1852, this single line carried more than half the wheat shipped to Chicago. With fifty-six locomotives pulling 1,200 freight cars over 260 miles of track, the Galena soon paid yearly dividends of 16 percent.

For eastern capitalists the Galena confirmed a delightful hypothesis: You could build a railroad without paying for it. Ogden and his associates contributed some capital but mainly entrepreneurial stamina and can-do confidence. ("At fourteen," he once boasted, "I fancied I could do anything I turned my hand to, and that nothing was impossible, and ever since . . . I have been trying to prove it, with some success.") The Galena's customers financed its construction. In no other business would such heroics be expected of customers. Railroads could pay for themselves, even in lightly peopled northern Illinois—or so the Galena taught the incorporators of the Illinois Central.[24]

Farmers escaping mud financed the Galena. Pursuing one of the best deals in American business history—the chance to own the longest railroad in the world without, in the hyperbole of a nineteenth-century historian, costing themselves "a cent"—Boston and New York capitalists financed the Illinois Central.

The Central was prairie gold for its incorporators, who staked their claims in Washington, D.C., and Springfield, Illinois, the state capital. They did not even have to journey to Springfield themselves. They sent lobbyists instead.

Jacksonian reformers may have denounced using government for "the private gains [of] a busy few," but political chastity had not ensued. The "busy few" purchased politicians. Politicians commanded government, the economy's key actor. Through subsidy, government paid off the busy few. The Mississippi editor who wrote, "We can stand a pretty big 'steal' if we can get railroads in the state," read corruption as a preface to progress. The indebtedness of local governments multiplied from $25 million in 1840 to $840 million in 1880, "much of which flowed into the coffers of private corporations," most of them railroads; *and* achieved developmental ends. Such was the trade-off involved in the federal land grants, subsidies, and tax breaks awarded railroads for two decades beginning in 1850.[25]

Stephen A. Douglas, the "Little Giant," won congressional backing for the Central by spreading the steal around. Douglas, who stood five feet four inches tall, earned his sobriquet by his resource as a legislator. Irony stalked his career. His achievements made his failures. He sought the presidency three times, and might have won on his last try, in 1860, if the "great central railroad" he brought to his region had not peopled it with Republicans. On what posterity regards as the transcendent issue of the time, Douglas cuts a poor figure. "To a man who, as Lincoln observed, had 'no very vivid impression that the Negro is a human,' " David M. Potter writes, "slavery did not appear as a great moral issue or as an agonizing dilemma. The most important thing about it was to avoid a violent national quarrel about it, and that could be done best by treating it as a local question." Douglas's orchestration of the Compromise of 1850, which admitted California as a free state in exchange for the Fugitive Slave Act—which required northerners to actively pursue renegade slaves and return them to their masters—reflected that outlook.[26]

For Douglas the Illinois Central formed the second act of the Compromise. It fit into a design of interregional comity: a Mississippi Valley railroad running from Chicago to Mobile, connecting North and South with iron bands, forging an identity for the area from the Great Lakes to the Gulf and from the Alleghenies to the Rockies that Douglas called "The Great West," "the resting place of the power that is not only to control, but to save, the Union."[27]

As a freshman member of the Illinois state legislature in 1836–37, Douglas championed a $10.5 million internal improvement bill that contemplated state construction of three railroads: a central railroad running north–south from Cairo to Galena, and two east–west lines. In the event, only twenty-four miles of one of the latter got built, connecting Meredosia to Jacksonville, where Douglas, coincidentally or not, lived.

Fourteen years later, Douglas took time away from weaving the Compromise to win congressional approval for a nearly three-million-acre land grant to Illinois. Along with a 200-foot right-of-way for its tracks, the grant awarded the central railroad tracts of adjacent land, which it could sell to finance its construction. Douglas encountered constitutional objections to giving a state a swath of the federal domain but overcame them, and he neutralized sectional jealousy by spreading the steal around.

To win the backing of an Iowa senator he moved the terminus from Galena to Dubuque, where the senator owned land the railroad would enhance in value. Galena, jilted by two railroads, lost the terminal that Illinois (and Iowa) might gain.[28]

Douglas brought Gulf state senators aboard (13–0) by extending the railroad from southern Illinois to Mobile and securing land grants for rights-of-way through Alabama and Mississippi.

A branch line to Chicago captured the votes of thirty-eight eastern senators—who saw Chicago as a potential transit point for north–south commerce via the central railroad—and bolstered Douglas politically in northern Illinois.

It helped that the most influential eastern senator, Daniel Webster, owned land worth $100,000 in La Salle.[29]

It helped that eastern investors held millions of dollars in bonds issued to fund the stillborn projects conceived in the Internal Improvement Act. Illinois had nearly defaulted on these bonds after 1837, failing to pay interest on its debt for five straight years. The bonds, however, would gain in value as the state's finances improved. That prospect forged the bondholders into a lobby for the land grant, which, Douglas maintained, would permit Illinois "to fulfill its obligations [to the bondholders] and extinguish its debt without being compelled to resort to . . . oppressive taxation."[30]

It especially helped that the chairman of the House Ways and Means Committee, Thomas H. Bayly of Virginia, motivated by a farsighted investment of $17,000 in Illinois bonds made, at Douglas's suggestion, a month before the bill became law, put the land grant ahead of all other pending bills on the House calendar. Douglas himself instructed his banker to buy "as many [bonds] as you are willing and able to purchase for me." He also bought up lakefront property in Chicago in the likely path of the Chicago branch, and the certainty of selling it at a good price helped, too.

There was no end of steal to spread around.

Under the Illinois Central charter, the state of Illinois received 7 percent of the railroad's gross profit annually, which enabled a settling of its accounts with eastern bondholders.

A holder of a charter issued in the 1840s to revive the Cairo–Galena line of 1836 was bought off with 1,000 shares of the Illinois Central. Cairo, no longer the southern terminus, was promised funds to build a levee.

To secure the backing of the capital newspaper, the Whig *Springfield News,* a Boston lobbyist lent the editor $2,000; the *News's* subsequent editorials on behalf of the Boston–New York group helped sway Whig legislators uneasy over the Democratic provenance of the land grant.

The chief lobbyist in Springfield for the Boston–New York group, George Billings, received a certified map of the Central's route a year before the information became public, allowing him to buy land cheap and, after the Central located a station nearby, sell it dear.

As for Douglas, he sold sixteen of his Chicago lakefront acres to the Central even though thirteen of them lay underwater.[31]

The financing of the Illinois Central disproved the ex nihilo theorem. "It would be a rather singular thing," one of the incorporators wrote a friend, "if it should turn out that this Company should own a Road about 670 miles long and cost the stockholders (the present ones) nothing or not over $4[00,000] or 500,000 [to cover calls on the stock] and would be worth 12 or 13 millions—wouldn't it?" He ended with the wholly understandable counsel: "Please keep this to yourself."[32]

The incorporators planned to use the land grant as collateral for a bond issue; to use the bonds to fund construction; and to sell land to pay off the bonds. The land was better than free. The directors knew where the tracks would go, so they bought up prime land ahead of demand and then sold it at profit to retire the company's debt and enrich themselves.

The Illinois Central transformed central Illinois. There were only ten towns along its right-of-way in 1850, but forty-seven in 1860 and eighty-one in 1870. Before the Central the route eventually taken by the Chicago branch ran through three settlements. Twenty years later, twenty-eight cities and towns had grown up around the Central's stations on that line.

To prevent the Central from speculating on land given value by its tracks, the charter conferred by the Illinois legislature forbade it to lay out towns. So, pioneering in railroad finance legerdemain, the Central spun off a new company, which proceeded to lay out thirty-three towns—Centralia, Tolono, Kinmundy, Elmwood—using a standard plat: streets running east–west from the station were named for trees in the order Mulberry, Walnut, Chestnut, Oak, Locust, Poplar, and Ash. North–south streets were numbered.

Build it and they will come. Dunleith surged from five people in 1850 to 2,000 in four years. Centralia, open prairie in 1850, had a population of 2,500 in 1860. In Champaign County, Livingston's population increased from 1,552 in 1850 to 11,637 by 1860, Piatt's from 1,606 to 6,127, McLean's from 10,163 to 28,772. Most towns grew; station towns burgeoned. Before it got a station, West Urbana was "nothing." Then, in a single year, 500 people settled there, construction started on 300 buildings, two hotels opened, along with six stores, nearly as many lumberyards, and a Presbyterian church. Altogether, the state's population doubled in a decade, greater in percentage and more in numbers than any other state in the Union.[33]

The people came in waves, first to build the railroads, for the Central was only the longest of ten roads under construction in Illinois—then to settle their shoulders. Statewide, ten miles of track were laid in 1848, 100 in 1852, 900 in 1854. Building the 700-mile-long Central took 10,000 men. With native labor scarce, agents recruited immigrants in New Orleans and New York.[34]

One contractor went directly to the most abundant source, Ireland. The Irish mixed combustibly with German and Scandinavian laborers, and it was said "that 'a murder a mile' was committed on the Illinois Central."[35]

Since its business plan depended on land sales, the Central mounted a publicity campaign to attract émigrés. It printed ads and circulars headed "Homes for the Industrious in the Garden State of the West" and depicting a family threshing a wondrous flat field, eye-bait for hill-weary New England farmers. Beneath the illustration ran a promise of happiness on the installment plan:

> The Illinois Central Railroad Co., Have for Sale
> 1,200,000 ACRES OF RICH FARMING LANDS.
> In Tracts of Forty Acres and upward on Long Credit and at Low Prices[36]

The Central placed these ads in farm journals like *The Rural New Yorker* and the *Albany Cultivator,* but also in *Putnam's Monthly* and *The Atlantic Monthly.* In New York City its sylvan pitches appeared on the sides of the Second Avenue cars. The Central brought German travel writers to Illinois, commissioning books and articles for a German-speaking audience. British investors in the Central subsidized literary enthusiasm to spur emigration, one of its authors panegyrizing Illinois as "the greatest tract of fertile land on the surface of the globe," which was too much even for a local press known to boast that Chicagoans inhaled more oxygen than New Yorkers.[37]

The advertising campaign helped touch off a migration dwarfing the Gold Rush. The *New York Herald Tribune* estimated that 300,000 people would leave New England in 1857, bound for Illinois and beyond. For the Central had competitors for settlers. Borrowing its template, the Fort Des Moines Navigation Company, the Dubuque and Pacific, and the Burlington and Missouri advertised to recruit immigrants for Iowa, the Galena and Fond du Lac for Wisconsin, and the Hannibal and St. Joseph for Missouri. Publication of a sixty-page pamphlet helped the Hannibal sell 14,000 acres in the last five months of 1859 alone. Noting a falloff in immigration to Canada, the *Toronto Leader* blamed the selfishness of British railroad investors for diverting British and Irish emigrants to the United States. Eastern newspapers, echoing themselves during the Gold Rush, lamented the loss of people. Concerned to hold on to their workers, eastern employers dispatched whisperers to Chicago to plant doubts about the validity of the land titles the Central conveyed to buyers.[38] But the Central could withstand slander because Illinois could—skeptics could view its agricultural riches on model farms set up by the Central to persuade them, and because men didn't need Illinois to be Eden, only a better place than home.

Since the opening of the Erie Canal, New York and New England farmers had been losing local markets to western foodstuffs. Pushed west by economic forces, pulled west by advertising, rumor could not discourage them, any more than it could Europeans escaping the repression that ended the revolutions of 1848. By the mid-1850s colonies of Vermonters, Englishmen, Germans, Norwegians, and French Canadians had settled along the line of the Central. The railroad had labored and produced Illinois.

The soil of the Illinois prairie was black from millennia of silt-bearing winds. Grain fairly grew itself. And now it poured forth, as if by a wave of the railroad wand, and flowed toward Chicago. "With the use of a map any person can see that all the [rail]roads and branches . . . aim at Chicago," the editors of the *Daily Democratic Press* wrote. "From the east and west, north and south, it is the great center which they seek. Let them come!"[39]

The tracks all led to Chicago because rail met water there. Before the Civil War nearly all grain shipped east from Chicago went by sail or steamship, and more than half of it after the war. Rail was faster: Grain got to New York in five and a half days instead of ten and a half by steamship across the Great Lakes to the St. Lawrence River. But water was cheaper, and the time differential insignificant for grain. By 1854 New Orleans had yielded to Chicago its long-held place as the chief port of east–west trade. Two years later the steamer *Dean Richmond* left Chicago with 14,000 bushels of wheat bound for Liverpool, which feted captain and crew for inaugurating the cross-ocean grain trade.[40]

Grain arrived in Chicago as nature and departed as commodity. The steam-powered grain elevators, which by 1848 had replaced "Irish power," scooped grain out of the cars in buckets, stored it in four-story warehouses holding up to four million bushels, and poured it into ships in efficient cascades. The Board of Trade regulated the quality of grain and sorted it by grade—"No. 2 spring," "No. 2 white winter"—restructuring "Chicago's market in a way that would forever transform the grain trade of the world." After the telegraph reached the city in 1848, the futures market rationalized grain pricing, Chicago was no mere urban warehouse. It added value. It managed grain into capital.[41]

Beyond Illinois, the circumambient Great West paid tribute to Chicago; indeed, as William Cronon argues, city created country. Frederick Jackson

Turner's frontier was not "an isolated rural society" but the "expanding edge of the . . . urban empire." City–country "commerce was the motor of frontier change."[42]

The novelist Frank Norris evokes Chicago's economic carry in a much quoted passage from *The Pit* (1902):

> For thousands of miles beyond its confines was its influence felt. Out, out, far away in the snow and shadow of Wisconsin forests, axes and saws bit the bark of centuries-old trees, stimulated by the city's energy. Just as far southward pick and drill leaped to the assault of veins of anthracite, moved by her eternal power. Her force spun the screws and propellers of innumerable squadrons of lake steamers crowding Sault Sainte Marie. For her and because of her all the Central States, all the Great Northwest roared with traffic and industry; sawmills screamed; factories, their smoke blackening the sky, clashed and flamed; wheels turned, pistons leaped in their cylinders; cog gripped cog; beltings clasped the drums of mammoth wheels; and converters of forges belched into the clouded air their tempest breath of molten steel.[43]

A British visitor, who'd had Chicago thrown up to him as "the great feature of [the] new western world" from the moment he landed, found that reality surpassed publicity: "It is a city not in growth, in revolution." The population tripled in the 1850s—by 60 percent in 1853 alone. Ballyhooing Chicago's "miraculous" growth, an 1856 city directory warned scoffers that "our city is one of the manifest destinies, and all the croaking in the world will not impede her march a single day."[44]

Chicago was an immigrant city: As early as 1850 half the residents of Cook County, which includes Chicago, were foreign-born compared to an immigrant population of 12.8 percent for Illinois as a whole.[45]

It was a city in "golden subjugation" to eastern capital. "Chicago build railroads! Nonsense! We have permitted others to build them sometimes provided they would make Chicago a terminal point," the *Chicago Times* editorialized, "and give us all the benefits resulting from their construction, without expense or trouble."[46]

It was a railroad city, the "Rome of the Railroads," with trunk lines connecting Chicago to the rest of the country, twenty branch lines linking Chicago to the rest of Illinois, and a hundred trains pulling in and out of four stations every day.

It was a city sprouting buildings—2,700 under construction in September 1857—like so much urban wheat. Thanks to a young engineer named George Pullman, they were firmly planted. Buildings had been sliding down beneath their first floors in soil tenuously interrupted from mud. Pullman jacked the city up and put new dirt under it, a feat that garnered worldwide publicity for Chicago.

It was a city "mad after money," where commercial values ruled—"I tell you God don't do business that way," a Chicago preacher was heard to remark—and where, over suspender-stretching dinners, men talked money with guiltless quantitative relish.[47]

Pervasively, Chicago was also a city of mass death: By the mid-1850s meatpacking ranked as the leading industry, the largest employer of men and women, mostly immigrants, who spat blue phlegm from laboring in chilled hells. The twentieth-century assembly line began in the disassembly line of the slaughterhouse. "If they can kill pigs and cows that way," Henry Ford reportedly said, "we can build cars that way."[48]

By the 1860s, attracted by the charisma of industrial death, 10,000 tourists annually visited the slaughterhouses at the Union Stockyards, there to witness, William Cronon writes, "something never before seen in the history of the world."[49] On his 1889 tour Rudyard Kipling saw something *he* had never seen before:

> And there entered that vermilion hall a young woman of large mould, with brilliant scarlet lips, and heavy eyebrows. . . . She was dressed in flaming red and black and her feet were cased in red leather shoes. She stood in a patch of sunlight, the red blood under her shoes, the vivid carcasses tackled round her, a bullock bleeding its life away not six feet away from her, and the death factory roaring all around her. She looked curiously, with hard, bold eyes, and was not ashamed.
>
> Then, said I, "This is a special Sending. I have seen the city of Chicago."[50]

Contemporaries rightly sensed something dark about the slaughterhouses, among modernity's axial institutions. The industrial warfare of the First World War would inflict death in numbers and with a rapidity matched only by the destruction of animals in Chicago's slaughterhouses. The omnipresent stench of burning flesh—"the sky is a stain; the air is streaked with runnings of grease and smoke," Waldo Frank wrote in 1919, prefigured a worse horror.[51]

Chicago transmuted cattle and hogs into exotic products, given their natural telos. The hog, for example; his parts made surprising things—pork and bacon, of course, but also "lard, glue, brushes, candles, soaps." Everything hog was used, in the local boast, "except the squeal." "Everything— without particularizing too closely—every single thing that appertains to a slaughtered beef is sold and put to use," a nineteenth-century visitor wrote.

> The horns become the horn of commerce; the straight lengths of leg bone go to the cutlery-makers; the entrails become sausage-casings; their contents make fertilizing material; the livers, hearts, tongues, and tails, and the stomachs, that become tripe, all are sold over the butchers' counters of the nation; the knuckle-bones are ground up into bone-meal for various uses; the blood is dried and sold as powder for commercial purposes; the bladders are dried and sold to druggists, tobacconists, and others; the fat goes into oleomargarine, and from the hoofs and feet and other parts come glue and oil and fertilizing ingredients.[52]

These by-products made the steer pay. Philip Armour, the pioneer meatpacker, calculated that a 1,260-pound steer yielded 710 pounds of beef. Bought at the stockyards for $40.95, the steer, in table-ready pieces, sold in New York for $38.17. Without cashing in on knuckle bones and the like, Armour would go out of business. And harvesting knuckle bones was lucrative because he slaughtered so many steers.[53]

The packers had made a defining discovery of our civilization—the economies of scale *and* scope. Scale and scope are to industrial capitalism what gasoline is to an automobile. To borrow Alfred D. Chandler's concept, they constitute its dynamics. They make it go. By processing herds of cattle, the meatpackers reduced the cost of processing each steer—scale. By producing more than one product from the same system that primarily processed beef, they achieved economies of scope.

They could not have done it without the railroad. Mud-moated Chicago was a microcosm. The industrial revolution in America was inhibited so long as transportation depended on animals, wind, and current, which were "too slow, too irregular, and too uncertain to maintain a level of throughput necessary to achieve the economies"—throughput being Chandler's shorthand for the amount of goods "actually processed within a given time period." Without unflagging throughput, the volume of production would fall beneath "the minimum efficient scale"—the volume needed to cover the fixed costs of building and running a plant. Unit costs would rise: It would cost more to make more.

The railroad opened the gates of throughput. It carried so much, so far, so fast that factories could at last begin to pace American demand. Raw materials reached the factory in quantities and with a reliability hitherto unimaginable, while finished goods leaving it could travel by train to customers previously lost to distance. At the same time, throughput-contingent economies of scale lowered the price of goods, which attracted new customers. In the railroad-altered economic environment, "The critical entrepreneurial act was not the invention . . . of a new or greatly improved product or process," Chandler writes. "Instead it was the construction of a plant of the optimal size required to exploit fully the economies of scale and scope, or both." *Big* became the first law of American economic life.[54]

For Chicago, thinking big meant the construction of a huge stockyard for throughput on the hoof. In the 1850s, the stockyards, having sprung up around boardinghouses that provided libidinal relief to drovers, were scattered across the southern part of the city. The Civil War forced concentration: The 1.5 million men in the Union army consumed half a billion pounds of meat. In 1864, with torrents of steers and 2 million hogs running through the streets from stockyard to stockyard, Chicago's nine largest railroads joined with the Chicago Pork Packers Association to found the Union Stock Yard and Transit Company. They bought a half-square-mile lot four miles from the city center, and wrought upon it engineering marvels—three miles of water troughs, ten miles of feed troughs, thirty miles of drainage pipes.[55]

The externalities, however, were frightful. The drainage pipes emptied into Dantean sewers that discharged nearly half a million reeking gallons daily into the South Branch of the Chicago River. The packers had to look elsewhere for the ice to chill their plants and, after Gustavus Swift's successful experiments of the late 1870s, their refrigerated railway cars. Swift calculated they needed "as many tons of ice as you expect to ship tons of dressed beef." Frank Norris's inventory of Chicago's economic instigations could have included the lake at Pewaukee, Wisconsin, where Armour built a 1,200-foot-long ice shed and employed hundreds of workers, "harvesting the winter."[56]

Because their fixed costs were so high, the Big Four—Armour; Swift; Nelson Morris; Libby, McNeil and Libby—were among the pioneers of oligopolistic competition. Such businesses could not survive price wars, as the railroads would learn. So they fixed prices among themselves. Since the Big Four controlled 90 percent of the Chicago market, farmers and stockmen sold at their price or not at all. Using their economies of scale to undersell local markets, they destroyed eastern competition. Cronon magisterially sketches a picture of disparate economic actors—Montana cowboys, Iowa feed lot operators, Cleveland butchers—drawn into a system that "standardized" and made them "fungible." The sempiternal rhythms of their physical geography yielded to the hectic imperatives of economic geography: "Once within the corporate system, places [too] lost their particularity and became functional abstractions on organization charts." Nature answered to industrial capitalism now.[57]

The Rome of the railroads ruled through economic magnetism, drawing things and people to it and transforming them—grain into capital, farmers into wage laborers, immigrants into Americans. Economic power translates, inevitably, into political power. In 1860 Illinois furnished two presidential candidates: one a Democrat, Stephen A. Douglas; the other the second nominee of a new party, the Republicans. The Republicans were the Chicago of politics. At the end of a decade that saw both emerge, the city drew the party to it, and together they changed America. "Chicago exhibited a great party springing to life and power, every motive and force compelling cooperation and growth," a visitor recalled. "The rush and spirit of the great city, and the enthusiasm and hope of the visitors, blended and reacted upon each other as if by laws of chemical affinity."

More people may have attended the Republican National Convention in Chicago, held between May 16 and 19, than had gathered in one place at one time in the United States before—as many as 50,000. Chicago's population stood at 100,000, so it was as if a tidal wave of 3.5 million had washed over New York for the 2004 Republican National Convention.[58]

The conventioneers were the vanguard of a mass movement fueled by northern frustration over the South's expanding political hegemony. In the decade since the Compromise of 1850, the Democratic Party, the Senate, the presidency, and the Supreme Court had all gone south, giving political and judicial impetus to "the Slave Power." Three years earlier, in the *Dred Scott* decision, the Court had ruled that Congress could not ban slavery from the territories and neither could their citizens. Slaves were property; the Fifth Amendment banned state limitations on the right to property without due process. The Missouri Compromise, the Compromise of 1850, popular sovereignty as a brake against slavery—all dead. The territories were open to slavery, and many Republicans feared it would not stop there.

In the "House Divided" speech that kicked off his 1858 Senate campaign against Douglas, Abraham Lincoln voiced a crystallizing suspicion when he wondered if "ere long," "We shall lie down pleasantly dreaming that the people of Missouri are on the verge of making their state free, and we shall wake to the reality instead that the Supreme Court has made Illinois a slave state."[59]

IN THE GARDEN STATE OF THE WEST.

WATERS & SON sc.

THE ILLINOIS CENTRAL RAILROAD CO., HAVE FOR SALE

1,200,000 ACRES OF RICH FARMING LANDS,

In Tracts of Forty Acres and upward on Long Credit and at Low Prices.

THE attention of the enterprising and industrious portion of the community is directed to the following statements and liberal inducements offered them by the

ILLINOIS CENTRAL RAILROAD COMPANY.

which, as they will perceive, will enable them, by proper energy, perseverance and industry, to provide comfortable homes for themselves and families, with, comparatively speaking, very little capital.

LANDS OF ILLINOIS.

No State in the Valley of the Mississippi offers so great an inducement to the settler as the State of Illinois, There is no portion of the world where all the conditions of climate and soil so admirably combine to produce those two great staples, CORN and WHEAT, as the Prairies of Illinois.

EASTERN AND SOUTHERN MARKETS.

These lands are contiguous to a railroad 700 miles in length, which connects with other roads and navigable lakes and rivers, thus affording an unbroken communication with the Eastern and Southern markets.

RAILROAD SYSTEM OF ILLINOIS.

Over $100,000,000 of private capital have been expended on the railroad system of Illinois. Inasmuch as part of the income from several of these works, go to diminish the State expenses ; the TAXES ARE LIGHT, and must consequently every day decrease.

THE STATE DEBT.

The State debt is only $10,106,398 14, and within the last three years has been reduced $2,959,746 80, and we may reasonably expect that in ten years it will become extinct.

PRESENT POPULATION.

The State is rapidly filling up with population ; 868,025 persons having been added since 1850, making the present population 1,723,663, a ratio of 102 per cent. in ten years.

AGRICULTURAL PRODUCTS,

The Agricultural Products of Illinois are greater than those of any other State. The products sent out during the past year exceeded 1,500,000 tons. The wheat-crop of 1860 approaches

35,000,000 bushels, while the corn crop yields not less than 140,000,000 bushels.

FERTILITY OF THE SOIL.

Nowhere can the industrious farmer secure such immediate results for his labor as upon these prairie soils, they being composed of a deep rich loam, the fertility of which is unsurpassed by any on the globe.

TO ACTUAL CULTIVATORS.

Since 1854 the Company have sold 1,300,000 acres. They sell only to actual cultivators, and every contract contains an agreement to cultivate. The road has been constructed through these lands at an expense of $30,000,000. In 1850 the population of forty-nine counties, through which it passes, was only 335,598 since which 479,293 have been added ; making the whole population 814,891, a gain of 143 per cent.

EVIDENCES OF PROSPERITY.

As an evidence of the thrift of the people, it may be stated that 600,000 tons of freight, including 8,600,000 bushels of grain, and 250,000 barrels of flour were forwarded over the line last year.

PRICES AND TERMS OF PAYMENT.

The prices of these lands vary from $6 to $25 per acre, according to location, quality, &c. First class farming lands sell for about $10 to $12 per acre ; and the relative expense of subduing prairie land as compared with wood land is in the ratio of 1 to 10 in favor of the former. The terms of sale for the bulk of these lands will be

ONE YEAR'S INTEREST IN ADVANCE,

at six per cent per annum, and six interest notes at six per cent., payable respectively in one, two, three, four, five and six years from date of sale ; and four notes for principal, payable in four, five, six and seven years from date of sale ; the contract stipulating that one-tenth of the tract purchased shall be fenced and cultivated, each and every year, for five years from date of sale, so that at the end of five years one-half shall be fenced and under cultivation.

TWENTY PER CENT. WILL BE DEDUCTED

from the valuation for cash, except the same should be at six dollars per acre, when the cash price will be five dollars

Pamphlets descriptive of the lands, soil, climate, productions, prices, and terms of payment, can be had on application to

J. W. FOSTER, Land Commissioner,
CHICAGO, ILLINOIS

For the name of the Towns, Villages and Cities situated upon the Illinois Central Railroad, see pages 188, 189 and 190 Appleton's Railway Guide.

HOMES FOR THE INDUSTRIOUS

(Advertising cut widely used by the Illinois Central Railroad in 1860 and 1861)

The struggle had been one-sided. After California's admission to the Union in 1850 disturbed John C. Calhoun's "equilibrium" of fifteen free and fifteen slave states to the advantage of freedom, the South had more than righted the balance. *Dred Scott,* the Kansas-Nebraska Act, the mob violence and intersectional terrorism in "Bloody Kansas," the backing given by the southern-dominated administration of James Buchanan to a pro-slavery constitution adopted in defiance of that territory's majority, the caning in the Senate chamber of a defenseless Massachusetts Republican by a South Carolina congressman and the laudations his villainy received in the South: These assertions of southern power had fused northern factions into a party united, James Russell Lowell wrote in *The Atlantic Monthly,* by "a common resolve to resist the encroachments of slavery everywhen and everywhere." Republicans sensed, one newspaper reported, that the "long-wished for contest between freedom and slavery" was about to be joined. In Chicago freedom would strike back.

As the front-runner for the nomination, New York senator William H. Seward had swept all the presidential straw polls taken on the convention-bound trains except one, on the New Albany & Salem from Indiana, which he lost to Lincoln, the region's favorite son.

Lincoln's debates with Douglas, reprinted in four editions, had gained national attention—though not enough to make Lincoln a target of rival candidates. He was not even listed in a political booklet identifying twenty-one possible candidates for the nomination; newspapers still "spelled his first name Abram." Unlike the leading candidates—Seward, Pennsylvania senator Simon Cameron, Ohio governor Salmon P. Chase, New Jersey senator William L. Dayton, and Missouri judge Edward Bates—office did not confine Lincoln, a private citizen. In the last year he had out-traveled and out-talked them, journeying 4,000 miles to give twenty-three speeches. Publicly coy about his ambitions, seemly in a former one-term congressman, privately he was game. "The taste *is* in my mouth a little," he confided to an associate.[60]

His strategy was to be "available" as a second choice for delegates should the convention deadlock over their first choices. "Our policy," he instructed his political managers at the convention, "is to give no offense to others—leave them in a mood to come to us, if they shall be compelled to give up their first love."[61]

To house the convention, Chicago built the nation's largest assembly hall, the Wigwam, a two-story wooden structure at the corner of State and Market near the Chicago River that could hold 15,000. The Wigwam

went up in a few weeks; the "Republican ladies of Chicago" were still dec-
orating it, wreathing the pillars supporting the second-floor gallery in
evergreens and hanging red, white, and blue drapes between pillars, as the
first delegates arrived.

Chicago's forty-two hotels bulged with Republicans—sleeping five or
six to a room, underneath stairs, in storage rooms, on billiard tables—but
the delegates numbered only 466. In a reverse of today's convention
layout, the delegates sat on the stage behind the podium. In front of the
stage stood the candidates' cheering sections—thousands of broad-bellies
primed to hoot and stomp when their man's name was called; also curious
Chicagoans hoping for Lincoln's nomination; also some of the 900 journalists who'd applied in vain for the sixty seats assigned to the press, one
occupied by the first woman to cover a national political convention, Mary
A. Livermore.[62]

Only escorted "ladies" could sit in the three galleries above the convention floor, a category elastic enough to accommodate Chicago schoolgirls
to whom gentlemen paid 25 cents to accompany them inside and an Irish
washerwoman carrying a bundle of laundry, but not an Indian "squaw,"
lately selling moccasins outside, with whom one gentleman-rooter tried
to enter the Wigwam. *She,* the policeman at the gate ruled, was no lady.[63]

Anti-slavery united Republicans only negatively. What were they *for?*

They were for the thing in American life that allowed a child laborer
in a textile factory to work his way up to mechanic at age twenty-four; that
spurred him to read books from the company library and attend company-
sponsored lectures by eminences like Daniel Webster and Theodore
Parker; that promised him if he applied his character to his ambition he
could leave the machine shop, read the law, enter politics, and climb the
ladder of office until it reached speaker of the House of Representatives.
Republicans were for what the life of their first speaker, Nathaniel P.
Banks, the "Bobbin Boy" of Massachusetts politics, proclaimed possible in
the free states and there alone in the world. Lincoln—rail-splitter, river-
boat pilot, country-store clerk, merchant, postmaster, surveyor, small-
town lawyer, state legislator, U.S. congressman, corporate lawyer, Senate
nominee, contender for the highest office in the land—Lincoln called it
"the right to rise."[64]

Republicans were for the right to rise.

That right crowned the free labor system, which Richard Yates, the

Republican candidate for governor in Illinois, called "the great idea and basis of the Republican Party." Lincoln defined free labor as: "the just, and generous, and prosperous system," in which the "prudent, penniless, beginner in the world, labors for wages for a while, saves a surplus with which to buy tools or land for himself; then labors on his own account another while, and at length hires himself another new beginner to help him." For Republicans, free labor was no mere ideal; it described the existing economy of the North—economic independence was a goal any man could and most men did reach. And free labor was about more than getting and spending. "Proprietorship, as Americans understood it," Christopher Lasch explains, "tended to elicit qualities essential to democratic citizenship—initiative, self-reliance, foresight, independence of mind."[65]

The Republicans meant to defend the right to rise. Here what they were for merged with what they were against. For two alternative economic orders threatened free labor: slave labor and industrial capitalism.

"The Slave Power" challenged free labor frontally—"Recent scholarship," James M. McPherson writes, "sustains Lincoln's apprehension that the [Roger B.] Taney Court, which in the Dred Scott decision of 1857 opened the territories to slavery, would have sanctioned 'some form of slavery in the North.' "—and through ideological unmasking. Looking at the North, southern apologists for slavery did not see Lincoln's paradise of free labor. They saw a system moving toward wage labor: by 1860 over 60 percent of Americans were employees. Wage labor, the southerners charged, was "wages slavery"; northern workers "slaves without masters," "slaves of the community." As for the Bobbin Boy, he was a hero of the economics of anecdote. The genus Bobbin Boy spent the rest of his working life as an operative, and when too old to work could die, for all his employers cared. That was the gravamen of a well-circulated southern poem, "The Hireling and the Slave," which drew freedom as anarchy— "No mobs of factious workmen gather here / No strikes we dread, no lawless riots fear"—and slavery as paternalism, "No paupers perish here for want of bread."[*][66]

In his *Pro-Slavery Argument*, the South Carolina jurist William Harper offered a Dixie-Marxist definition of slavery that crossed racial with class

---

[*] "The territorial aristocracy of former ages was either bound by law, or thought itself bound by usage, to come to the relief of its serving-men and to relieve their distresses. But the manufacturing aristocracy of our day first impoverishes and debases the men who serve it and then abandons them to be supported by the charity of the public." Alexis de Tocqueville, *Democracy in America,* vol. 2 (New York: Random House, 1990), p. 161.

domination, slavery with capitalism: "[W]here man is compelled to labor at the will of another, and to give him much the greater portion of the product of his labor, there Slavery exists; and it is immaterial by what sort of compulsion the will of the laborer is subdued." Free labor, unmasked, was wage labor, the defining feature of industrial capitalism, of scale and scope production, of big.[67]

When the average workplace still employed fewer than ten workers, industrial capitalism was an accelerating destiny, the railroad-borne future. Nevertheless, free labor was already a nostalgic ideal. It looked back to the world before scale and scope.

The age weighed against small. Consider an Akron butcher who spent years working for wages, finally putting enough money by to set up a shop of his own—thus far, an imago of the free labor system. But now comes Armour & Co. to dash his dream. Armour dispatches a "peddler car" of beef to the Akron railway station, selling its contents right off the car at "never-before-heard-of prices." Next Armour opens a refrigerated warehouse. "Dodgers were scattered, like leaves of the forest, stating the time of the first opening to be at 6 A.M. on Saturday," our Akron butcher relates. "Long before that hour people were waiting for the doors to open." Scale and scope put the butcher out of business. Lucky for him Armour was hiring.[68]

The Republicans, in line with pre-industrial economic opinion, identified freedom with the Akron butcher's dream—economic independence. By that standard, the roughly 90 percent of us who work for wages are not free. Lincoln would have contemned our dependence. "If any continue through life in the condition of the hired laborer," he said, "it is not the fault of the system, but because of either a dependent nature which prefers it, or improvidence, folly, or singular misfortune."[69]

For Republicans, Eric Foner writes, "A man who remained all his life dependent on wages for his livelihood appeared almost as unfree as a southern slave." Unfree because economically and *politically* dependent. Opponents of universal manhood suffrage had argued, to quote a delegate to the 1821 New York constitutional convention, that it would mean "a turning over the votes . . . of day laborers, poor mechanics, & co into the hands of the rich man who feeds and employs them. . . . The influence which the employer possesses is sufficient to prostrate our republican institutions." That was Tory republicanism. Working from democratic premises, mid-century voices of working-class republicanism like the labor editor and organizer George McNeill came to the same conclusion, positing "an inevitable and irresistible conflict between the wage-system of labor and the republican system of government."[70]

The equation of wage labor with slave labor shared by slavers, Republicans, and northern labor radicals alike affronted the ex-slave Frederick Douglass. Men would be "ashamed to be reminded" of such "flimsy nonsense," he wrote, once slavery was abolished.* W.E.B. Du Bois engraved the difference between the hireling and the slave in stone: "No matter how degraded the factory hand, he is not real estate."[71]

In *The Story of American Freedom*, Foner traces our idea of freedom to the abolitionists, not the Republicans. The abolitionists redefined American freedom from "propertied independence" to "self-ownership," and defended wage labor as a contract freely entered into. Republicans would come to this new understanding of freedom reluctantly; deep into the postwar era of ever-bigger business their hearts still belonged to the Bobbin Boy, improbably rising.

"Vociferous cheering" greeted the announcement of the "historic name of David Wilmot" as temporary chairman of the convention. A former Democratic congressman from Pennsylvania whose 1846 proviso calling for the exclusion of slavery from the territories then being seized in the war with Mexico had ignited a country-splitting debate, Wilmot was the John the Baptist of the Republicans, party of free soil, free labor, and free men. During the platform reading that afternoon, two planks raised "the longest and loudest cheers"—the Homestead Act (providing free land to settlers) and the protective tariff. These core economic doctrines of Republicanism, along with a bill to construct a railroad to the Pacific, had been voted down by southern Congresses or vetoed by James Buchanan.

The planters ruled politics, law, *and* economic policy. In 1854 the House passed a homestead bill granting 160 acres to settlers on the public lands,

---

* After Emancipation a Mississippi freedwoman remembered her grandmother being flogged, "wid her clothes stripped down to her waist, her hands tied 'hind her to a tree . . . it just made an impression on my childest mind." A freedman from the Yazoo delta described the beatings meted out to his father: "My pa an' ma wasn't owned by de same masters. . . . At night pa would slip overt to see us an' ole Masrse wuz mos' always on de look out fer everything. When he would fetch him he would beat him so hard 'till we could tel which way he went by de blood. But pa, he would keep a comin' to see us an' takin' de beatins." David M. Oshinsky, "Worse Than Slavery: Parchman Farm and the Ordeal of Jim Crow Justice," http://www.historyisaweapon.org/defcon1/oshinsky .html, p. 7.

but southern senators, afraid their region's farmers and poor workmen would migrate to the soil-rich west, defeated it. Internal migration would cost the South House seats, weakening the political struts of slavery.[72]

The Homestead Act, as we will see, filled a gap in Republican ideology between free labor and wage labor: By enabling dependent wage workers to become independent farmers, the "safety valve" of western settlement would check the growth of a permanent working class in the North. Interests not ideology attached the Republicans to the tariff. As late as 1860 the manufacture of cloth ranked as the second leading industry in the North, but with the passage of the Corn Laws, which eliminated all duties on cotton and grain, Britain competed with the North for cotton's favor. By the mid-1850s, the South supplied four-fifths of Britain's cotton. That trade would not continue, the planters realized, unless Americans reciprocated by buying British goods—"woolens, the finer cotton textiles, railroad iron, and miscellaneous manufactures." The chronic demand of northern manufacturers for tariff protection against these goods must be and, from 1853 when the presidency passed to the Democrats, was resisted.[73]

With tariff schedules favoring the importation of British iron for American railroad tracks while Pennsylvania iron mills closed for lack of business, the southern grip on government held back the northern industrial economy. Cotton throttled iron.

The alliance between government and business remained the lever of private fortune and economic development. Southern politicians and planters held the lever in the 1850s. The Civil War broke their grip. For this reason, the Progressive historian Charles Beard called it the "Second American Revolution" and Barrington Moore, Jr., "the last revolutionary offensive on the part of what one may legitimately call urban or bourgeois capitalist democracy." To work the great transformation in American history, government had to pass into northern hands. For forty-nine of the seventy-two years between 1789 and 1861, southern slaveholders held the presidency. Twenty-three of the thirty-six House speakers, twenty-four of the thirty-six Senate presidents, and twenty of the thirty-five justices of the Supreme Court were southerners. After the war southerners were shut out of the presidency for one hundred years; no southerner would serve as speaker or Senate president for fifty years, and of the twenty-six justices named to the Court in that span only five would be from the South.[74]

Representing the frustrated hopes of a decade, the Republican platform planks were also strokes of electioneering: "Vote yourself a farm—vote yourself a tariff" made a potent slogan in the 1860 campaign. Horace Greeley, seated as a delegate from Oregon, described the politics of these policies in a candid letter: "Now about the Presidency: I want to succeed this time, yet I know the country is not anti-slavery. It will only swallow a little anti-slavery in a great deal of sweetener. An anti-slavery man per se can't be elected; but a *tariff,* river and harbor, pacific railroad, free homestead man may succeed *although* he is anti-slavery." The sweeteners were regionally flavored. Oregon and California were to be brought on board with the Pacific railroad; the Great Lakes states with the pledge to clear rivers of snags and improve harbors; the Northwest with the Homestead Act; and Pennsylvania with the tariff.[75]

Nothing would sweeten the cup of William Seward. Party professionals feared that his identification with the cause of anti-slavery—condemning the *Dred Scott* decision, he invoked "a higher law than the Constitution"— would cost the Republicans the border states and the election. At 6:00 P.M. on the evening before nomination day three representatives from each of the key states of Indiana, Pennsylvania, Illinois, and New Jersey met in David Wilmot's rooms in the Tremont Hotel to concert behind a candidate to stop Seward. Lincoln's manager, Judge David Davis, made the case for his man. Caleb Smith, governor of Indiana, seconded Davis. Indiana had secretly agreed to support Lincoln on the first ballot. Ignoring Lincoln's telegram to "Make no Contracts that will Bind me," Davis had secretly promised Smith a seat in Lincoln's cabinet. Dangling a cabinet post before Simon Cameron helped swing Pennsylvania to Lincoln. William Dayton of New Jersey, along with his campaign manager, would ornament Lincoln's diplomatic service. The two states would come over to Lincoln if their favorite sons failed to advance after the first ballot. By the time the meeting broke up at 11:00 P.M., Lincoln was the Republican candidate for president.[76]

Accounts of the next day recur to its sounds. Before the convention convened, shouting matches broke out between the Lincoln and Seward claques. So much noise greeted Seward's nomination, one reporter noted, that "hundreds of persons stopped their ears in pain."

When an Ohio delegate seconded Lincoln's nomination as "a man who can split rails and maul Democrats," a Lincoln handler on the platform drew his handkerchief, at which signal Lincoln "howlers" commenced to be heard across Lake Michigan. Murat Halstead, a correspondent for the *Cincinnati Commercial,* rendered the sound that now engulfed the hall in a Chicagoesque metaphor: "Imagine all the hogs slaughtered in Cincinnati, giving their death squeals together and you can conceive something of the same nature."[77]

On the first ballot Lincoln received 102 votes, Seward 173½. On the second, as agreed in Wilmot's room, Lincoln gained votes from favorite-son candidates in Pennsylvania and New Jersey. By the third he grazed victory.[78] "Profound stillness gripped the room," according to a memoirist, as the clerks tallied the results. Ladies' fans were audible, and "one could distinctly hear the scratches of pencils and the tick of telegraphs on the reporter's [*sic*] tables."

Lincoln appeared to be within two votes of the nomination, but before the counting could be completed, an Ohio delegate ("If you can throw the Ohio delegation behind Lincoln," a Lincoln man had told the Ohio spokesman, "[Governor Salmon P.] Chase can have anything he wants") stood on his chair to announce a change of four of Ohio's votes to "Mr. Lincoln." Murat Halstead had shot his bolt with the slaughtered hogs. "It is ever memorable to those who witnessed it," he wrote of the ensuing pandemonium, "and no more can be said." As one delegation after another lined up behind the winner, "the Lincoln river became an inundation."[79]

A charcoal portrait of "Honest Old Abe" appeared on the stage followed by Judge Davis holding a moss-covered rail with a sign affixed reading "split by Lincoln." This campaign emblem debuted at the Illinois state convention held in Decatur the last day of April. John Hanks, first cousin of Lincoln's mother, had strode onto the stage carrying two fence rails putatively from a lot of 3,000 he and Lincoln had cut in the summer of 1830. Lincoln was carried to the stage on the shoulders of his rooters, who shouted, "Identify your work!" Blushing, he complied. "It may be that I split these rails," he ventured tentatively; then, after inspecting them, added, "Well, boys, I can only say that I have split a great many better ones."[80]

The Illinois delegation set up a shrine to the right to rise in the lobby of the Tremont House: a fence rail lit by candles and decorated with flowers.[81]

When a cannon installed on the roof of the Wigwam roared out, signaling Lincoln's victory, the crowd of between 20,000 and 30,000 outside the hall began a duel of roars with the 11,000 inside. Nearby another cannon went "bang . . . every thirty seconds for the next 17 minutes steady." With one hundred guns atop the Tremont firing salutes, Chicago went "wild with joy."

"Go to the devil—what do I want to eat for?" a Lincoln stalwart in the Tremont's dining room replied to a waiter's query. "Abe Lincoln is nominated . . . and I'm going to live on air—the air of Liberty." That night, a bonfire thirty feet high illumined the front of the hotel and rockets "clove the air like fiery telegrams to the stars."[82]

Chapter Three

"VOTE YOURSELF A TARIFF"

[T]he protective system of our day is conservative while the free trade system is destructive. It breaks up old nationalities and pushes the antagonism of the proletariat and the bourgeoisie to the extreme point. In a word, the free trade system hastens the social revolution. It is in this revolutionary sense alone, that I vote in favor of free trade.

—Karl Marx, in an 1848 speech[1]

The Civil War subtracted an estimated $6 billion from the American economy, including the $3 billion the two governments spent fighting it, the $1 billion in property it destroyed, and the $2 billion worth of "human capital," shorthand for the lost contribution of the more than 620,000 soldiers killed and the myriads wounded, it consumed.[2] The forgone earnings of the dead—they included as many as 50,000 southern civilians killed by war-related causes—and the curtailed earnings of the maimed may have reduced consumption by as much as $14 billion. That for the year 1866 Mississippi devoted 20 percent of its budget to prosthetic limbs suggests the intimate metrics of lost productivity.[3]

Against this catastrophic subtraction, government purchases weighed lightly. Between 1861 and 1865 small arms production, for example, accounted for 1.1 percent of U.S. iron output while the "shortfall in [railroad] mileage built during the war below the 1856–60 level was seven times that amount." Commodity output grew by 60 percent in the 1850s but by only 23 percent in the 1860s.[4]

To reach the multibillion estimate of the war's costs cited above, the authors of an influential paper "created a hypothetical north and south which did not fight a war during the years 1861 to 1865" and compared the "consumption stream of persons in th[is] warless economy" to "that actually achieved" by persons in the real economy.[5] Those real persons did not know what they were missing in the hypothetical economy. Many might not have cared.

For paradoxically as it may seem, "the North flourished," Allan Nevins writes in *Ordeal of the Union* in a chapter titled "The Great Boom in the North." Though "it came gradually and unevenly and . . . not all the populace benefited by any means," the "boom was beyond all question real." Northern businesses turned profits of 10 to 15 percent. On the farm, crop values soared by 103 percent. Gold streamed into the northern economy from California, silver from the Comstock Lode in Nevada, oil from newly discovered fields in Pennsylvania. By 1865 petroleum ranked sixth among northern exports. Railroads that never paid dividends before paid them now. Goods that would have gone down the Mississippi in boats before the war instead came east in railroad cars belonging to the Illinois Central (whose share price rose $80 in one year), the Michigan Central, the Baltimore & Ohio, the Pennsylvania, and the Erie. "Money is pouring into Wall Street from all over the country," the *New York Herald* reported in 1863, in the midst of a post-Gettysburg rally in railroad stocks. "So busy were the brokers," John Steele Gordon relates, "that the lunch counter was invented to afford them a quicker meal than could be had by going home." Congress passed legislation to curb speculation in gold—but its quick repeal signaled its instant failure. Asked what to do about the speculators, Lincoln said, Shoot their heads off.[6]

During the war's first years social sobriety prevailed. Clubs disbanded. News of a Federal defeat would curtail evening plans. Men and women dressed plainly. By 1864, however, those who had it, spent it. "Foreign finery" was all the vogue, especially, according to popular prejudice, among the "shoddy people," parvenus of profiteering who had grown rich making uniforms from inferior materials. "We are clothed in purple and fine linen, wear the richest laces and jewels and fare sumptuously every day," the *Chicago Tribune* editorialized on the "wealth effect" in that city. Washington was swept by an "epidemic" of "gayety," according to Fred Seward, the brother of the secretary of state: "A year ago the Secretary of State was 'heartless' or 'unpatriotic' because he gave dinner; now the only complaint of him is he don't have dancing." The *Springfield Republican* offered its readers "a shocking picture of life in Washington," a city of vice and corruption, where politicians put their mistresses on the public payroll, a bureau of the Treasury doubled as a bordello, and, though it would not shock children today, contractors bribed congressmen. A report to Congress found "gigantic and shameless fraud on the government" among contractors—guns of "very inferior quality," adulterated oils, false weights on foodstuffs. In 1878 a former army quartermaster estimated that at least 20 percent of wartime expenditures totaling "over 700 million dollars" were "tainted with fraud." The greed stood out the fouler next to the sacrifice of self to country seen on the battlefield and in places like the Jackson Hospital in Memphis when its patients heard that Vicksburg had fallen. "[T]he whole great building filled with the terribly wounded," a nurse recalled, "rang for an hour with cheers and songs. Some sang and shouted who never had strength to speak again, and many who knew they should never hear of another victory on earth."[7]

What accounts for the discrepancy between the dour picture of the war's costs presented by the economic historians and the boom times enjoyed by the North?

The condition of the South; the subtraction occurred there. Its agent was the Union army. During a month-long raid into Alabama in early 1865, General James H. Wilson's cavalry destroyed seven iron works, two rolling mills, five collieries, three factories, four niter plants, one military university, one navy yard, five steamboats, thirty-five locomotives, 565 railroad cars, and three railroad bridges. "I can make the march and make Georgia howl!" General William T. Sherman wrote General Ulysses S. Grant from Atlanta, asking permission to ignore the rebel army in his rear, break free of his supply umbilical from eastern Tennessee, and embark on a 285-mile "march to the sea" feeding his army by "forag[ing] liberally upon the countryside," to quote his general order of November 1864. "War is cruelty and you cannot refine it," he told the mayor of Atlanta, in extenuation of his order to expel its civilian population. "[W]e are not only fighting hostile armies," he added, "but a hostile people, and must make young and old, rich and poor feel the hard hand of war."[8]

Atlanta felt it first. Sherman ordered that everything of military value be put to the torch, a distinction lost on the flames. "All the pictures and verbal descriptions of hell I had ever seen," a major who had just emerged from the inferno wrote in his journal, "never gave me half so vivid an idea of it as did this flame-wrapped city tonight." "I had a noble field of corn not yet harvested," a farmer who felt the hard hand of war told a postwar visitor from the North. "Old Sherman came along and turned his droves of cattle right into it, and in the morning there was no more corn than there is on the back of my hand." Horses, mules, pigs, chickens, even dogs felt it—the soldiers shot bloodhounds, a species corrupted by its role in hunting escaped slaves. ("But this is not a bloodhound!" a poodle owner protested. "Well, Madam," came the reply, "we cannot tell what it will grow into if we leave it behind.") Columbia, capital of South Carolina, the cynosure of rebellion, felt war's hand. Drunken soldiers, flinging "turpentine-soaked" rags into buildings and cutting the hoses of the civilian fire department with their bayonets, started fires that consumed eighty-four of the city's 124 blocks. Richmond, made "a vista of desolation" by fires started by retreating Confederates, felt it. "For a quarter of a mile one passes nothing but toppling walls, forlorn cooking chimneys, heaps of bricks," a correspondent for *The Nation* wrote of the business district two months after Appomattox, "with here and there a ruined safe lying in the midst, warped and red from the effects of the intense heat." The once lush Shenandoah Valley felt war's hand. Burn it, Grant ordered *its* Sherman, Philip Sheridan, so that "a crow could not fly over it without carrying his own rations." The Tennessee Valley felt it, an English writer finding plantations in "a state of semi-decay" or "plantations of which the ruin is total and complete." Far-off Arkansas, two-thirds of its counties destitute, felt it. So did Galveston, "a city of dogs and desolation." The South's rice plantations, covered with salt water, felt it. Many of the largest cotton fields, flooded by broken levees—they, too, felt the hand of war. From Chattanooga to Atlanta a postwar traveler did not see a single smiling face.[9]

Southern farmers entered the postwar with half the farm machinery they possessed before the war. Southern livestock would not reach its 1860 levels until 1910. The South accounted for 7.2 percent of U.S. manufacturing in 1860 and 4.7 percent in 1870. In 1860, six out of the ten states with the highest wealth per capita were in the South; in 1880 not one southern state ranked in the top thirty. In 2003 dollars $68.4 billion was invested in slaves, representing all but 20 percent of the gross national product in 1860, which as a share of today's GNP would total an estimated $9.75 trillion—this wealth melted away when the slaves who survived the war won their freedom.

"Disease, want, and migration" wrought "demographic devastation" on the freed people. "At least 25% of the negro population is gone," Wisconsin senator James Doolittle reported from Louisiana after the war. An 1866 census found an absolute decrease since 1860 in the black and white populations in fifty of Mississippi's sixty counties. On the verge of freedom, "a great human tragedy had occurred."[10]

Southern elites pursued two strategies to restore the region's economy. They coerced the freedman back into the fields of his servitude with terror and law, and, ambivalently, against the grain of sectional prejudice and politics, they drew northern railroads and capital to the South with sales of state-owned railroad lines and land grants and with tax exemptions for manufacturers. A letter printed in the *Manufacturers' Record* from a Massachusetts man warned southerners not to expect too much from their neocolonial strategy: "Our capitalists are going into your country because they see a chance to make money there, but you must not think that they will give your people the benefit of the money they make. That will come North and enrich their heirs, or set up public libraries in our country towns." Books appeared with titles like *How to Get Rich in the South*. The formula was not secret. The Arkwright Club of New England saw only one reason why textile manufacturers should build plants in the South: "[L]abor is cheaper in the South . . . the hours of labor are longer; and . . . there is neither any of the restrictive legislation urged among us by the labor unions, and very generally placed upon our statute books, nor any prospect even of an early agitation in behalf of such restrictions." In 1900, North Carolina's commissioner of labor also worked as a cashier in the Dime Savings Bank in Raleigh; the budget for his bureau was $1,100 and he was its only employee. Asked about North Carolina's labor laws, he replied that aside from one minor law affecting railroad labor, "we have got none in the State at all. . . ." Between 1881 and 1900, 1,253,685 people went out on strike in Pennsylvania, 238.5 strikers per 1,000 of population; in North Carolina, 786 people went out on strike, 0.5 strikers per 1,000 people. As in New England in the 1820s, women, girls, and boys constituted the majority of the mill workforce in the New South. Wages, their level set by what desperate African-Americans would work for, were as much as 40 percent below New England rates, as low as 2.3 cents an hour for adults in the South Atlantic states in the 1890s. By the first decades of the twentieth century, though the wage gap had narrowed in manufacturing, per capita income in the South still ranked 40 percent below the national average. Southern banks held only $1 billion of the nation's $16 billion in deposits. "The locomotive passed through nearly a thousand southern counties," Edward L. Ayers writes, "but it belonged to none of them."[11]

The Civil War launched "the modern American state," Eric Foner writes. Prior to the war, "one could live one's life without ever encountering an official representative of the national authority." During the war the federal government expanded into the nation's largest employer (with 53,000 workers). After the war Washington overrode the authority of southern state governments by enfranchising the freedmen, expanded its powers of taxation and regulation, managed the nation's first social welfare program—the pension system for Union veterans that by 1893 directed benefits totaling 41 percent of the federal budget to nearly one million pensioners—and fashioned an industrial policy analogous to "Japan Inc.," the development strategy pursued by Japan after World War II, to transform an agrarian Arcady into an industrial power. Whether the Civil War spurred or retarded industrialization remains in dispute. "But there can be little doubt that the war decisively affected the *political economy* of industrialization," Steven Hahn observes. The "fostering hand" of government, long constrained by constitutional scruples masking southern fears of national power, could now be employed freely to sculpt the future. "The war has taught us some valuable lessons of constitutional law, which plain men who are not lawyers can understand," avowed a Republican pamphlet issued for the 1864 campaign. "It has taught us that the government must have power to save the nation; that whatever is necessary to that end is constitutional . . . that the Constitution exists for the people . . . and we have a right to modify it to suit our needs according to our will." For Republicans, Illinois representative Owen Lovejoy said, "the government is simply an agency through which the people act for their own benefit."[12] With southern Democrats absent from Congress, some until 1870, and northern Democrats stigmatized as "disloyal" for their wavering support of the war, the unobstructed Republicans drew up what one historian calls "the blueprint for modern America." Whereas the Thirty-fifth and Thirty-sixth Congresses, the last elected before the war, respectively passed 129 and 157 public acts and resolutions, the Thirty-seventh Congress (1861–62) passed 428 and the Thirty-eighth, 411. These included income, inheritance, sales, and corporate tax bills; a legal tender act; and the establishment of a national banking system. The master blueprint was the protective tariff.[13]

The Democratic administrations of the 1840s and 1850s lowered tariff duties first imposed after the War of 1812. By the late 1850s there was talk of following England's example and abolishing them. But a recession in 1857 spurred northern manufacturers to demand protection against imports. Southern Democrats made their last stand in 1860, defeating a tariff increase. They had gone home when, a month before the attack on Fort Sumter, Congress passed and President Buchanan signed the Morrill Tariff Act. Congress would raise the tariff three more times to finance military operations. These "war tariffs" long survived the war, lasting until 1913, when the Democrats, controlling the White House and both Houses of Congress for only the second time since the 1850s, rolled them back. They proved to be the Civil War's outstanding economic legacy. "We lead all nations in agriculture; we lead all nations in mining; we lead all nations in manufacturing," President William McKinley declared in 1900. "These are the trophies which we bring after twenty-nine years of the protective tariff." Posterity welcomes the trophies, not their instrumentality. The tariff is a subversive subject. It challenges a shibboleth of our time—free trade.[14]

In *An Inquiry into the Nature and Causes of the Wealth of Nations* (1776), Adam Smith expressed an insight heretical in his mercantilist world of "beggar thy neighbor" trade: "All commerce that is carried on betwixt any two countries must necessarily be advantageous to both." Consequently, "all duties, customs, and excise should be abolished, and free commerce and liberty of exchange should be allowed with all nations." Smith's followers have reduced his logic of free trade to a formula of felicity—"win-win." Smith arrived at it by reasoning from family to nation. Just as it is "the maxim of every prudent master of a family, never to attempt to make at home what it will cost him more than to buy," so "if a foreign country can supply us with a commodity cheaper than we . . . can make it," then "better buy it of them with some part of the produce of our own industry, employed in a way in which we have some advantage." Surely, "what is prudence in the conduct of every private family, can scarce be folly in a great kingdom."

The founders of the Republican Party would not hazard America's future on that analogy. They projected a protective family onto the nation, not a calculating one. "The principle of protection is as old as man," Pennsylvania congressman Washington Townsend declared during a tariff debate. "It is that instinct which induces the head of a family to succor and protect his offspring in their early helplessness and to aid and encourage them into adolescence . . . [A] nation is but an aggregate of families living under one government, and the principles of protection which govern families and tend to their advancement and prosperity should govern the nation." Republicans believed in making winners, not waiting for the "hidden hand" of the world market to select them. "Free trade is a fiction," Rhode Island's Benjamin Eaves maintained. "It is based upon the idea that the nations of the earth are one, not separate . . . ; and that what may be for the interest of one is for the interest of all." The Republicans' object was to increase the wealth of *a* nation, a point William McKinley painted in red, white, and blue: "The people of this country want an industrial policy that is for America and Americans." Especially for that majority-making member of the Republican coalition, the American workingman. Free traders would have him compete with Malthusian foreign wages. Protection, James G. Blaine averred, rescued him "from the servitude of poverty." Amos Townsend of Ohio allowed that, "capital can always take care of itself, but the labouring-man needs the fostering care of the Government, that he may have constant work and good wages." The Republicans wrapped the tariff in their free-labor ideals—through its benign instrumentality the wage earner "move[s] onward and upward until the laborer of yesterday is the capitalist of today." Beyond its economic benefits, protection was good for women. "Protection maintains the women of America in their proper sphere," William Russell of Massachusetts claimed. Their well-paid spouses could afford having them stay home to provide "mind-culture" to the children. And protection preserved republican virtue. "How," Maine's William P. Frye wanted to know, "can a half-paid, half-fed, half-educated citizen rightly and intelligently understand and perform the duties of citizenship?"[15]

Back on earth, though Republicans posited "multiplier effects" across the economy, manufacturers were the primary gainers from protection. So long as it fostered *them,* the industrial and financial interests the Republicans spoke for grasped the "fostering hand." The view that the Age of Enterprise was "dominated by 'conservatism,' 'rugged individualism,' and *laissez-faire . . .* fl[ies] squarely into the face of the facts," John P. Roche wrote a generation ago.

> There was clearly an elite of businessmen, but it was neither ruggedly individualistic . . . nor "conservative" in any acceptable definition of that much-abused term. On the contrary, this elite lived at the public trough, was nourished by state protection, and devoted most of its time and energies to evading Adam Smith's individualistic injunctions. In ideological terms, it was totally opportunistic: It demanded and applauded vigorous state action in behalf of its key values, and denounced state intervention on behalf of its enemies.[16]

When Adam Smith was an old man much revered, he met with William Pitt, the British prime minister, and other government officials. They rose when he entered the room. "Be seated, gentlemen," he said. "No," Pitt came back, "we will stand until you are first seated, for we are all your scholars."[17] The Republicans who drew up the future's blueprints would have stayed in their seats.*

"[T]wenty men can enter a room as friends," Will Rogers joked, "and someone can bring up the Tariff and you will find nineteen bodies on the floor with only one living that escaped." The wonder is that they did not fall asleep. The tariff is a Canada of a subject—ignored, massive, *there*. How could an issue so technical—involving distinctions among rates formal, nominal, effective, average, and ad valorem; bilateral, reciprocal, and equal trade; conditional and unconditional most-favored-nation treatment —roil congressional debate, decide presidential elections, and foment agrarian protest? In *The Great Tax Wars: Lincoln to Wilson,* Steven R. Weisman builds a bridge for our comprehension when he writes: "Tariffs were not called taxes per se, but that is what they were, and what Americans understood the tariff system to be." Woodrow Wilson called the tariff "very sly": People knew when they paid a property or excise tax but "very few of us ever taste the tariff in our tea." Southerners tasted it. Because it increased domestic prices and thus producers' costs, by one estimate the tariff leveled "an implicit . . . tax" of 11 percent on agricultural exports. Indeed, the tariff imposed a double tax on the southern and western nonindustrial agricultural "periphery," Richard Franklin Bensel writes. "[W]ealth was redistributed from the periphery to the core [industrial regions] in the form of higher prices for manufactured goods and from the periphery to the national treasury in the form of customs duties." During the war "Wanted, Dead or Alive" posters appeared in rebel-held Virginia for Justin Morrill, the Vermont congressman accused of being "the author of the infernal tariff of 1861." For the next half-century the southern-dominated Democrats assailed the "sacred temple of the Republican party" as "a tremendous system of legislative rapine and robbery."[18]

The battle lines formed as early as 1866, when the Special Commissioner of the Revenue, David Wells, a Republican, issued a report urging Congress to cut tariffs generally but especially to cut $6 from the nine-dollar-a-

---

* Citing the tariff, railroad land grants, "easy availability of an immigrant labor force from Europe," low taxes, and little regulation, among other "felicities, " David R. Mayhew asks, "In the history of the world, when has a governmental environment ever favored private capitalism more than America did during the 1860s through the mid-1890s?" David R. Mayhew, *Electoral Realignments: A Critique of an American Genre* (New Haven: Yale University Press, 2002), pp. 112–13.

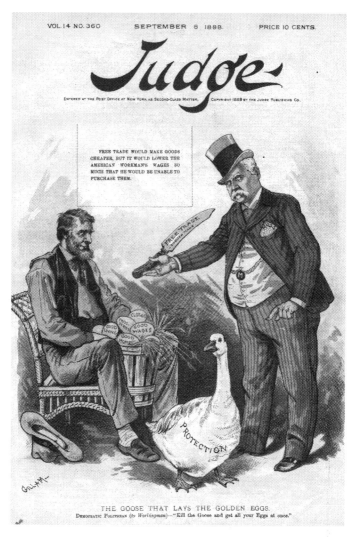

VOL. 14 NO. 360   SEPTEMBER 8 1888.   PRICE 10 CENTS.

Judge

ENTERED AT THE POST OFFICE AT NEW YORK AS SECOND-CLASS MATTER.   COPYRIGHT 1888 BY THE JUDGE PUBLISHING CO.

FREE TRADE WOULD MAKE GOODS
CHEAPER, BUT IT WOULD LOWER THE
AMERICAN WORKMAN'S WAGES SO
MUCH THAT HE WOULD BE UNABLE TO
PURCHASE THEM.

THE GOOSE THAT LAYS THE GOLDEN EGGS.
DEMOCRATIC POLITICIAN (to Workingman)—"Kill the Goose and get all your Eggs at once."

The Tariff Is Good for the Workingman

"Kill the Goose and get all your Eggs at once," the "Democratic Politician" says to the "Workingman." The politician is Roger Q. Mills, a Texas congressman and champion of "tariff reform," a euphemism for tariff reduction. The Democrats ostensibly favored a "tariff for revenue" only, but in practice accepted a milder version of protection. They did not advocate free trade. Yet the message in the box reads, "Free trade would make goods cheaper, but it would lower the American workman's wages so much that he would be unable to purchase them." Judge, *September 8, 1888.*

ton tariff on pig iron, "a striking illustration of an instance where a duty originally levied for revenue and protection . . . has been continued long after its object has been fully attained, for the interests of the few, but to the detriment of the many." Pig iron—made in blast furnaces and used "by rolling mills to produce iron sheets, rails, and bars"—cost $26 a ton to produce domestically. The tariff, however, added $11 to the price—government-secured profit to the pig iron makers but an addition to the costs of "the rolling mill interest . . . and [to] every consumer of iron from rail to a ploughshare, and from a boiler plate to a tenpenny nail." Wells dismissed "the usual and almost the only argument offered in reply to such [criticisms]"—that they maintained employment. The tariff on pig iron cost jobs in industries like railroads and construction that consumed pig iron. Lower the tariff, he argued, and shipbuilders could sell 600 additional iron ships and employ 30,000 more workers, a prognostication that scanted the nontariff impediments to selling U.S. ships abroad. Protectionist congressmen tried to stop publication of the report—and payment of Wells's salary. The Republican majority on the House Committee of Manufacturers did not "conceive the promulgation of special theories to have been part of the duty imposed on the commissioner." Pennsylvania congressman William D. "Pig Iron" Kelley earned his cognomen, declaring, "The day the telegraph announces that we have reduced the duty on pig and railroad iron will be the day on which the price of British iron will go up." With variations, Wells and Kelley wrote the script followed by critics and defenders of protection into the twentieth century. The debate continues today, with mainstream economists arguing Wells's case and economic heretics, enlisting history to advocate managed trade, arguing Kelley's.

One side in the debate views the protective tariff as the most successful industrial policy in U.S. history; the other says you cannot argue from the success—America's industrial preeminence by 1913—to the tariff as its cause. At best the evidence supports a "correlation" between the tariff and good economic outcomes generally, though even correlation scandalizes orthodoxy. If, in the 1880s, the Wharton School of Finance and Commerce at the University of Pennsylvania, established by the ironmaster Joseph Wharton, required aspirant instructors of economics to sign a contract not to teach free trade, today's academy as effectually bans the teaching of protection. "If you don't accept the views derived from Adam Smith—that free competition is ultimately best for all participants, that 'protection' and 'interference' are inherently wrong—," James Fallows writes of orthodoxy's grip, "then you are a flat-earther." Paul Bairoch found that "the dogma of free trade was so strong that I have not found any research published before the 1980s showing the impact of protectionism on U.S. industry in the nineteenth century to be positive." Beyond history, the protective tariff haunts the lean banquet of globalization. Echoing in anti-globalization protests, in calls for managed, fair, or bilateral trade, protection belongs to a past with a future.[19]

By the early 1860s, Britain had abandoned the infant-industry protection, export subsidies, import tariff rebates, and other policy distillates of mercantilism through which it rose to industrial preeminence, and adopted unilateral free trade. The United States followed Britain's practice not its preachment. "After two centuries, England found it convenient to adopt free trade because it thinks that protection can no longer offer it anything," President Grant declared. "Very well, Gentlemen, my knowledge of our country leads me to believe that within 200 years, when America has gotten out of protection all that it can offer, it too will adopt free trade."*[20]

After displaying the trophies of the tariff, William McKinley asked, "Can any other system furnish such evidences of prosperity?" Friends of protection then and managed trade today have taken up McKinley's challenge by setting the U.S. record against Britain's.

Free trade theory predicts higher growth for economies practicing it than for those under protection. Did Britain's performance vindicate the theory? From 1870 to 1913, Britain's gross domestic product grew an average of 1.9 percent a year; the protected U.S. economy at 4.1 percent. These facts "constitute real paradoxes for the supporters of free trade," Bairoch writes. Defenders of free trade like Douglas A. Irwin stress that the "underlying sources" of U.S. growth were the "rapid increase in population" and a pace of "capital accumulation" three times as fast as Britain's. "[T]he effects of trade policy on growth are probably swamped by other policies and unrelated factors so that one cannot isolate the true impact of trade policy," Irwin argues.[21]

---

* By conditioning aid on the adoption of free trade policies, the developed world appears to have kicked away the ladder for the Third World. "It depends on the data we use, but roughly speaking, per capita income in developing countries grew at 3% per annum between 1960 and 1980 [when they followed "bad" managed trade policies], but at only about 1.5% between 1980 and 2000 [when they used "good" trade policies]. Even this 1.5% is reduced to 1% if we take out India and China, which have not pursued liberal ITT [trade and technology] policies recommended by the developed countries." Ha-Joon Chang, "Kicking Away the Ladder: Infant Industry Protection in Historical Perspective," *Oxford Development Studies,* vol. 31, no. 1 (2003), p. 28.

Free trade theory predicts that U.S. growth would have been greater *without* the tariff. Yet data standing that assumption on its head was "sufficiently surprising" to a recent investigator that he "ran equations relating tariffs and growth using many specifications in an attempt to see how robust this correlation was." It proved "surprisingly robust." His a priori view, based on the "late twentieth century evidence that tariffs should be negatively correlated with growth" was "not supported by the data," which showed that "tariffs boosted late 19th century growth."[22]

Free trade theory predicts that U.S. productivity should have flagged—since protected industries lack the spur of foreign competition to get more out of their plant, equipment, and workers—and British productivity, plenty spurred, surged. In fact it grew by an anemic 0.6 percent yearly, less than half the American rate.[23]

Under free trade, British prices fell, especially on imported food, helping Britain avoid the revolution that Marx, writing in the "hungry forties," prophesied as the end of free trade. Prices were a sore point for American protectionists. The worse they would concede were temporary price increases in a protected industry, until domestic competition drove them down. But some Republican statesmen invested America's relatively higher prices with patriotic import. "[N]o American citizen who enjoys the advantages of this country is entitled to cheaper commodities than can be produced by free labor in this country," Nevada Senator William Stewart boldly maintained. "The individual who has such desires should follow the logic of them and go where slavery is." Britain did not have slavery but its consumers paid 25 percent less than Americans for nontradable services—"housing, domestic service, and transportation." Douglas Irwin finds that protection was only "slightly harmful" to consumers overall because they spent most of their money on "exportable goods"—foodstuffs, mainly. And some prices of tariff-affected goods actually fell—in "heavily-protected" metal products, for example, by as much as 49 percent between 1870 and 1913.

But did the price of the protected article fall relative to the foreign price? That, the tariff historian Frank Taussig argued at the turn of the century, was the decisive question to ask about the tariff. For unless the domestic and foreign price converge, then the infant industry case for protection, first advanced by Alexander Hamilton in his 1791 "Report on Manufactures," collapses and the tariff is supporting a hungry dinosaur. By this test, did U.S. protection work? Taussig, "a man who ascribed positive moral virtues" to free trade, concluded that "protective duties in the great majority of cases" did not prop up dinosaurs.

Consider what Pennsylvania's "Pig Iron" Kelley termed "the muscles of our more modern civilization," iron and steel. From 1870 to 1897 the duty on steel rails for railroad tracks sometimes approached 100 percent—that is, a U.S. railroad seeking to buy British rails paid twice their value for the privilege. But as the industry grew, the tariff fell from $28 to $3.92 in 1909 before being eliminated in 1913. And as the tariff fell, U.S. prices converged with those of its chief foreign competitor, Britain, and even fell below them. "The object of the protection of young industries seems to have been attained," Taussig wrote. Convergence also occurred with pig iron. *And* the United States developed an iron and steel industry of its own. From a fifth of British production in 1870, when the tariff was first applied, U.S. iron production exceeded Britain's and Germany's combined by 1910. It would have happened without the tariff, Taussig thought, given America's natural resources, its abundant cheap imported labor, and the annihilation of American space by the railroad, among other factors—"but not so soon or on so great a scale."*[24]

The tariff also influenced the structure of American industry by reinforcing the economic logic of vertical integration. The business historian Thomas K. McCraw explains: "If a steel-maker located on the Atlantic coast had to pay a protected market price for pig iron coking coal from western Pennsylvania, rather than import it cheaply by ship from Canada, he would be more likely to integrate backward and acquire these inputs at their unprotected cost." Vertical integration tended to increase productivity, which lowered prices for consumers.[25]

Free trade theory predicts that wages fall under protection because tariff-inflated prices increase production costs at the expense of wages. But American wages rose under protection, though whether *because of* protection is a contentious debate. Woodrow Wilson had the preponderance of the evidence on his side circa 1912 when he asserted that "American wages

---

* "By means of such regulations," Adam Smith conceded of tariffs, "a particular manufacture may sometimes be acquired sooner than it could have been otherwise, and after a certain time may be made at home as cheap or cheaper than in the foreign country." But "it will by no means follow than the sum total" of a nation's wealth "can never be augmented by any such regulation." This was because "[t]he industry of a society can augment only in proportion as its capital augments, and its capital can augment only in proportion to what can be gradually saved out of its revenue. But the immediate effect of every such regulation is to diminish its revenue, and what diminishes its revenue is certainly not very likely to augment its capital faster than it would have augmented of its own accord, had both capital and industry been left to find out their natural employments." Protection was warranted, however, "when some particular sort of industry is necessary for the defense of the country." That rationale would seem to cover the protection of iron and steel in the late nineteenth century. *The Wealth of Nations* (New York: Modern Library, 2000), pp. 486–87, 492.

are established by competitive conditions, and not by the tariff. . . . I wish I might hope that our grandchildren could indulge in free trade."

His *great*-grandchildren are of mixed minds about it. Concerned over the effect of the "China price" on their wages today, they fear that under free trade low-wage countries set those "competitive conditions."

In his revisionist history of U.S. trade policy, the source of much of the data and argument cited in this discussion, *Opening America's Market: U.S. Foreign Trade Policy Since 1776,* Alfred E. Eckes, Jr., compares U.S. wages in the last period of protection to wages in the first period of free trade. Between 1909, when the Labor Department began to compute weekly earnings, and 1929, weekly earnings for production workers rose 1.5 percent a year, but over "the period 1970 to 1992," Eckes writes, "government data show a decline in real weekly earnings." The tariff on dutiable imports fell below 20 percent in only one year between 1909 and 1920—and wages rose. Duties averaged less than half that between 1970 and 1992, imports flooded the country—and wages fell.* The economist Richard Freeman calculates that trade accounts for 20 to 30 percent of the decline in real wages since 1970. "Average incomes will go up with free trade," the economist Lester Thurow assured us in 1989, but theory and reality have yet to converge. Fifteen years on, average American incomes remain stagnant.[26]

Rapid growth, increased exports, falling prices, rising wages, buoyant productivity—what's not to like about protection? A great deal. If protection "worked" by the numbers, it felt like extortion to many Americans. The prices of capital goods may have fallen, but, using data from the 1890 census, the House Ways and Means Committee documented that the tariff hurt the three-quarters of American families earning $600 or less a year, raising prices on the humblest props of daily life—dishes, cups, forks, clothing, "everything except air and water."[27]

Contemporary critics of the protective system assailed it for reducing politics to grab. Writing in 1866, David A. Wells found he had changed his

---

* "The selection of these dates stacks the deck against the free trade period. The twenty years after 1890 was a period of strong growth, yet the period 1870 and 1890—also part of the high-tariff period but not included in Eckes's sample—saw slower economic growth. The economically disappointing twenty years after 1972 are included in his sample, yet [not] the low-tariff, rapid growth period." Douglas A. Irwin, "Tariffs and Growth in Late Nineteenth Century America," January 2001, www.dartmouth.edu/~dirwin/papers.htm.

"ideas respecting tariffs and protection very much since coming to Washington . . . I am utterly disgusted with the rapacity and selfishness which I have seen displayed by Penn[sylvania] people, and some from other sections on the subject." Forty years later, in *The Tariff in Our Times*, Ida M. Tarbell delivered the same verdict: "[U]nder our operation of the protective doctrine, we have developed a politician who encourages the most dangerous kind of citizenship a democracy can know—the panicky, grasping, idealless kind." That species of politician was a Republican. "[T]he bills of the Republican party were paid by business men who wanted a high tariff," Woodrow Wilson charged, accurately, in the 1912 presidential campaign.

As a "Henry Clay Whig," Abraham Lincoln had mocked the idea that taxing British "pantaloons" would bother the "Illinois farmer, who never wore, nor ever expects to wear, a single yard of British goods in his lifetime." But, despite his confidence that "the consumer does not usually pay the tariff," consumers did pay it. As the first Democrat elected after Lincoln, Grover Cleveland, explained in a historic 1887 message to Congress calling for tariff "reform": "While comparatively few use the imported articles, millions of our people who never use or never saw any of the foreign products, purchase and use things of the same kind made in this country, and pay therefore nearly . . . the same enhanced price which the duty adds to the import." So long as American and foreign prices did not converge, the tariff differential constituted a transfer payment from consumers to American manufacturers—that is, to owners, managers, and stockholders.

"None of these tariffs go to the laborer," Roger Q. Mills, the Democratic chairman of the House Ways and Means Committee, contended during the tariff debate joined by Cleveland's message. On a pair of heavy blankets, Mills pointed out, the manufacturer's cost was $2.51, of which labor accounted for only 35 cents, the tariff for $1.90. The tariff added 80 cents above labor costs to a $1.38 per yard of cashmere, and $6.92 to the $11 price of a ton of foundry iron costing 29 cents to make. Tarbell's reporting in the *American Magazine* bore out Mills's verdict. Surveying wages and working conditions in the "tariff-made" state of Rhode Island, where 75 percent of the population depended upon factory work, she found that for the "boom year" 1907, average weekly earnings for fifty-eight hours of work in cotton factories ranged from $7.80 for carding room hands to $12.92 for mule spinners. These wages were for piecework. Men slowed at it over time. So their wives and children worked against the penury of the man's old age. Newborns were a miracle—"They give you heartbreaking figures on infant mortality in Rhode Island"—and a means of survival for "the old woman," the fifty-year-old widow from whom "the factory ha[d] got all it can," who for $2 a week would take in an infant or young child while the mother put in her ten hours in the heat and high humidity of shut-up rooms, her lungs thickening from the "fly," specks of cotton lint. In England laws forbade such working conditions; in Rhode Island the mill owners made the laws. Its rubber industry protected by a 35 percent tariff, its cheap jewelry manufacturers cocooned by one of 87 percent, Rhode Island, Tarbell wrote, was "high protection's most perfect work . . . the laborers in its chief industry underpaid, unstable, and bent with disease, the average employers rich, self-satisfied . . . an industrial oligarchy made by a nation's beneficence under the mistaken notion that it was working out a labor paradise." During the debate over Cleveland's proposed tariff revision, the Democrats underscored just how far from paradise: Seventy-five percent of the 22,336 strikes between 1881 and 1886 occurred in states "where protection is claimed to have wrought such wonders for the working man." Strikers, Democrats charged, were "oppressed laborers revolting against the exactions of merciless capital"—against the "condition in which the millions own nothing and the few own millions" created by the tariff, which they blamed for the new "civil war . . . between labor and capital."[28]

Workers' wages in tariff-protected industries partially offset the tariff-inflated prices they paid for the goods they made—but, in the country as a whole, such protected workers totaled 5 percent of the labor force. Otherwise, "It is doubtful whether any large percentage of laborers got any benefit from the tariff," Fred A. Shannon writes. "And it is certain that the farmer was a consistent loser."[29]

The farmer sold in free trade and bought in protection. According to an 1882 Tariff Commission report, the farmer paid a duty of 33 to 60 percent on "all articles consumed and on articles of farm implements used by him." The western farmer, a Democratic congressman argued

pays a tax of 20 per cent on the lumber his house is built of; a tax of 35 per cent on the paint it is painted with; of 60 per cent on his window glass; of 35 per cent on the nails; of 53 per cent on the screws; of 30 per cent on the door locks; of from 35 to 40 per cent on the hinges; of 35 per cent on the wallpaper; of from 60 to 70 per cent on his carpet . . . of 51 per cent on the common castile soap he uses. . . . Suffice it to say that the furnishings of his child's cradle and the coffin in which he is finally buried pay a direct tax or one enhanced in price by our tariff system.

. . . And Bad for the Farmer
"The Tariff cow—the farmer feeds her—the monopolist gets the milk." The legend in the
hay reads: "War Taxes," a reminder that the Republicans enacted the tariff as an
emergency revenue-raising measure during the Civil War, twenty-five years earlier.
Puck, May 2, 1889.

In an age of big business the farmer stood forth as the prototypical small businessman. Corporations might escape foreign competition through the tariff and domestic competition through monopoly and oligopoly, but the farmer could not escape it. Consistent with his individualism, he believed in competition. Meanwhile, the Adam Smith of American economic experience, John D. Rockefeller, a captain of an industry (oil refining) nearly destroyed by "ruinous competition," was inventing corporate capitalism, which substituted the "visible hand" of management for the "invisible hand" of marketplace competition. Gulled by the platitudes, fooled by the politicians, the farmer stuck by the old verities long after their date of expiration.[30]

Chapter Four

"VOTE YOURSELF A FARM"

> O wife let us go; oh, don't
> Let us wait.
> I long to be there, and I long
> To be great.
>
> Dear husband, remember, but those
> Lands are so dear
> They will cost you the
> Labor of many a year,
> Your horses, sheep, cattle
> Will all be to buy
> You will hardly get settled
> Before you must die.
> —From a nineteenth-century ballad

On January 1, 1863, the Republicans abolished slave labor for southern blacks and provided a ladder up from wage labor for northern whites: the Emancipation Proclamation and the Homestead Act both took effect on that day. Year by year, under the deepening shadow of 1900, racism and industrial capitalism whittled the promise of these measures—citizenship for the freedman, economic independence for the wage earner—down to their statutory husks. The nineteenth century left the twentieth what W.E.B. Du Bois, in 1901, called its defining burden—"the problem of the color line," and an economy organizing around mass production and dependent wage labor for the laborer's life. Not until the 1960s would the nation attempt to erase the color line; it would never address the problem of class so directly again.*

---

* Before the war Joseph Smith, the prophet of Mormonism, and later Ralph Waldo Emerson, advocated a program of compensated emancipation to be paid for by the sale of public lands. Richard Lyman Bushman, *Joseph Smith: Rough Stone Rolling* (New York:

Colonel Thomas W. Higginson, drilling black volunteers on a South Carolina island, preserved freedom's moment in his memoirs. On New Year's Day former slaves from the island joined the soldiers to hear a preacher read aloud President Lincoln's order proclaiming them "henceforth free." As soon as "the speaker ceased and just as I took and waved the flag," Higginson recalled, "there suddenly arose close beside the platform a strong male voice . . . into which two women's voices instantly blended . . . I never saw anything so electric. It made all the other words seem cheap; it seemed the choked voice of a race at last unloosed." "My country 'tis of thee," they sang, "sweet land of liberty, of thee I sing!"

Through sordid decades the Republicans took shine from Lincoln's luster. "We are the party of Lincoln—the Emancipator, the rail-splitter cum president, exemplar of the right to rise," they could boast, "not the 'tariff gang' of Democratic billingsgate—and not, at our core, the party of the Roscoe Conklings and James G. Blaines," the representative Republicans of the Gilded Age, men who sought office, in the shocked italics of Lord Bryce, *"as a means of gain."* Yet if Lincoln's twin legacies endowed the Republicans, they also saddled them with a new constituency and an old economics. Post-slavery, "free labor" was a tricky ideal to have on their hands; no longer needed to parry southern charges of moral equivalence between the "Hireling and the Slave," it lingered as an indictment of wage labor. An alternative economic system based on small proprietorships and producer cooperatives, free labor undermined the justification of industrial capitalism—that scale and scope production and wage labor under corporate management was *the* path to progress. Free labor was a mutinous dream.

Yet the party of "free soil, free labor, free men" was stuck with it. Embracing trade unions as a ladder to a higher standard of living for permanent wage laborers, the industrial age alternative to entrepreneurial mobility, was not in the political cards. The Republicans represented "the industrious farmers and mechanics, the independent men in comfortable circumstances in all the various walks of life," the Boston Brahmin Charles Francis Adams boasted; the Democrats, "the most degraded or the least

---

Alfred A. Knopf, 2005), pp. 4–5. Of the significance of the Civil War tariffs, the Land-Grant College Act, and the Homestead Act, one historian writes: "This was the nation's first positive use of the federal government's powers to combat the social ills that attended the rise of the factory system; it was the government's first positive response to industrialism." James L. Huston, "A Political Response to Industrialism: The Republicans Embrace Protectionist Labor Doctrines," *Journal of American History,* vol. 70, no. 1 (June 1973), p. 54.

intelligent of the population of the cities," code for laborers and Irish laborers in particular. Depending on business contributions to fund their campaigns and relieve the austerities of office, the Republicans could champion the immigrant workingman only when his interests coincided with his employer's, as they sometimes did with the tariff.

The Republicans, as well, were stuck with the freedmen. Once allowed to vote on the same basis as whites, the Negro helped Republican candidates win in the North. William Jennings Bryan, a Democrat, appealed for the Negro vote in the era's one critical election, 1896. "The Negro," he charged in the campaign, "has bestowed Presidents on the Republican party—and the Republican party has given the Negro janitorships in return." But the Republican managers paid $5 a vote to southern Negroes they imported into Louisville, Chicago, Philadelphia, and Baltimore, some casting as many as sixteen ballots for William McKinley; and another Republican went to the White House.[1]

In the South, however, the freedman became a wasting political asset for the GOP. Enfranchising blacks while disenfranchising former Confederates, Republicans hoped, would build a political base in the Democratic South. But once white southerners resumed voting in the early 1870s, white numbers reduced the freedman's share of the vote while white terrorism suppressed its volume. As Reconstruction met resistance in the South, support for it withered in the North. The thin federal occupation could not transform the South's political culture. White supremacy was an imperative of southern identity, a racial nationalism, and "foreign" occupations tend to inflame the nationalism of the occupied, not change their hearts and minds. Tenable today, when the war colleges studied the failed occupation of the South to preview the challenges likely to confront the U.S. forces occupying Iraq, that conclusion came easier to northerners of the 1870s for whom it provided a rationale to have done with the Negro.

The 1874 congressional elections revealed the depth of northern weariness with Reconstruction—and the price the Republicans paid for being identified with it. The "strumpet of corruption," the Democrats charged, had debauched the biracial state governments of Reconstruction and their allies in the Grant administration and the Republican Congress. The Democrats also blamed the Republicans for the depression of the 1870s. Ideologically laissez-faire, operationally late-nineteenth-century Americans were Keynesians. They expected government to maintain employment. The business cycle was a political wheel of fortune; and now it had stopped on the Democrats' number. In what Eric Foner terms "the greatest reversal of partisan alignments in the entire nineteenth century," the Republican majority of 110 seats in the House of Representatives switched to a Democratic majority of sixty.[2]

Though the federal occupation of parts of the South lasted until 1877, Reconstruction ended with the election of 1874; and the Negro's ordeal in freedom began. The eighty-one-year-old ex-slave who told WPA interviewers in the 1930s, "The Yankees helped free us, so they say, but they let us be put back in slavery again," testified to the blighted hope of Emancipation.[3] By the twenty-fifth anniversary of Lincoln's Gettysburg Address ("a new birth of freedom"), the Yankees had abandoned the four million former slaves to terrorism, disfranchisement, segregation, and peonage.

The war deprived planters of their human property not their land, the foundation of the southern economy. But the freedmen claimed the same land. As an ex-slave wrote to the *Philadelphia Press* in 1864, "[W]e wants land—dis bery land dat is rich wid de sweat ob we face and de blood ob we back." When blacks who had settled on land around Yorktown, Virginia, were evicted by the army, a freedman named Bayley Wyat protested, citing slavery's contribution to *national* prosperity as a justification for compensating ex-slaves with land: "We have a right to the land where we are located. For why? I tell you. Our wives, our children, our husbands, has been sold over and over again to purchase the lands we are now located upon. . . . And den' didn't we clear the land, and raise the crops ob corn, ob cotton, ob sugar, ob everything. And den' didn't dem large cities in de north grow up on de cotton and de sugar and de rice dat we made? . . . I say they has grown rich and my people is poor."[4]

Eric Foner's once-in-a-generation synthesis, *Reconstruction: America's Unfinished Revolution, 1863–1877* (1988), movingly evokes the freedmen's will never to pick the white man's cotton (or rice) again. "Freedom" signified self-dependence—racial and economic. The Republicans had not consulted slaves in developing free labor ideology. And from David Wilmot's "White Man's Proviso" of 1846 forward, "free soil" meant sparing free white labor from competing against slave black labor in some of the territories acquired in the Louisiana Purchase and all of the land seized from Mexico. The Union cracked over slavery extension to the "territories," not over slavery "where it already exists," in Lincoln's words, in the southern states. But free labor was a hunger in the hearts of slaves long before it was Republican doctrine, and to the freedmen free soil meant the land won by a northern victory for which 185,000 black troops had fought and died.

Free men would take up free labor on free soil confiscated from the planter cabal that had fomented the rebellion.

"Radical" Republicans earned the epithet because they shared the freedman's vision. As early as 1863 George W. Julian, an Indiana congressman and chairman of the Committee on Public Lands, argued that the government should fuse Emancipation and homesteading by "parceling out the plantations of the rebels in small farms for the enjoyment of the freedmen, who have earned the right to the soil by generations of oppression." Julian labeled Lincoln's resistance to such a policy "sickly magnanimity."[5] Though in its last public statement the Confederate Congress brandished the specter of confiscation if the North won, Lincoln did not enforce the confiscation acts passed by Congress.[6] General Sherman's Special Field Order No. 15—which granted the 40,000 freedmen who had accumulated behind his army 400,000 acres in the South Carolina rice lands and on the Sea Islands off the South Carolina and Georgia coasts, there to work forty-acre plots with government-issue mules—this combining of the dual legacies of January 1, 1863, free men and free labor, was not to be the model of a social revolution.[7]

"The industrial North instinctively recoiled" from an assault on property, W.E.B. Du Bois writes, especially when "the northern working man himself had not achieved such economic emancipation." Slavery was abolished but the slavers retained their slave-made property inviolate. Preserving the "plantocracy" ranks as among the most regressive steps ever taken in U.S. domestic policy. Following C. Vann Woodward's interpretation in *The Origins of the New South, 1877–1913* (1951), revisionist historians of the postwar South argued that "urban-oriented parvenus" supplanted the planters as the ruling class, but "recent state studies for the most part suggest that traditionalist, agriculturally-oriented elites grasped the New South as firmly as they had the Old South," James Tice Moore notes in the *Journal of Southern History*. Congress required only one group of former "masters" to turn over their land to the ex-slaves who worked it: slaveholding Indians who had sided with the Confederacy.[8]

After 1867 the struggle in the South was not over who owned the land but over who worked it and on whose terms. To get the freedmen to return to the fields as "gang labor" under the supervision of white overseers, the planters resorted to terrorism. Fresh from a three-month tour of the South, Carl Schurz, a Lincoln ally and "Fighting Politician" in the war, documented the terror in letters to Andrew Johnson. "Some planters held back their former slaves on their plantations by brute force," he reported.

Armed bands of white men patrolled the county roads to drive back the Negroes wandering about. Dead bodies of murdered Negroes were found on and near the highways and byways. Gruesome reports came from the hospitals—reports of colored men and women whose ears had been cut off, whose skulls had been broken by blows, whose bodies had been slashed by knives or lacerated by scourges. A number of such cases I had occasion to examine myself.[9]

With President Andrew Johnson's blessing, unreconstructed state legislatures had taken hold of the planters' whip by passing "Black Codes." These offered "idle," "vagrant," or "undomiciled" persons the choice of working or going to jail, and forbade one employer from "enticing" the workers of another with offers of better pay. "Almost every act, word, or gesture of the Negro," a turn-of-the-century historian not unfriendly to Johnson wrote, "not consonant with good taste and good manners as well as good morals, was made a crime or misdemeanor, for which he could be fined by the magistrate, and then be consigned to a condition of almost slavery for an indefinite time, if he could not pay the bill." The codes added up to "an astonishing affront to emancipation," in Du Bois's words.[10] No longer "the property of an individual master," Schurz explained to an unheeding president, "the freedman . . . is considered the slave of society, and all independent state legislation will share the tendency to make him such."[11]

Congress outlawed the Black Codes. So the planters tried contract labor. They tried wage labor. They dangled incentives. The freedmen and women clung to the free labor ideal. By November 1867, distilling the message of two years of failure, the *Southern Cultivator* concluded that to produce cotton profitably with free labor, the planters must give up on the plantation: "The first change that must occur . . . is the subdivision of landed estates." Together planters and freedmen evolved a labor system to replace slavery and preserve at least the form of free labor: tenant farming and sharecropping.

This new system of labor control was a global phenomenon. American slavery had made growing cotton uneconomic in otherwise conducive climates, such as India's, Egypt's, and Brazil's. Emancipation ended America's comparative advantage. Production soared worldwide. The *Revue de Deux Mondes* linked "the emancipation of the enslaved races" with "the regeneration of the people of the East." *They* might not have put it that way. Those who did not voluntarily quit sustenance farming to raise "the white gold" were driven to cotton by the necessity to pay taxes on their land. To set up as cotton growers, peasants and farmers from Berar in India to the Nile Valley in Egypt borrowed from moneylenders financed by European banks. "While cultivators were now nominally free, networks of credit in every cotton-growing region of the world captured them in an ongoing cycle of indebtedness that required them to grow cash crops," Sven Beckert writes in "Emancipation and Empire: Reconstructing the Worldwide Web of Cotton Production in the Age of the American Civil War." From India to North Carolina, governments moved to abolish customary hunting and grazing rights, forcing farmers into growing cotton to pay for their food. In 1877 and again between 1899 and 1900, bottoming cotton prices brought death by starvation to tens of thousands of one-crop cultivators in Berar. A half million starved in Brazil. Not lack of food "(indeed, food grains continued to be exported from Berar), but the inability of the poorest cotton growers to buy it" caused these famines. The privations of the "empire of cotton" sparked revolts on four continents. In the Quebra Quilos uprising of 1873–1874, Brazilian farmers refused to pay taxes. The Deccan riots in India a year later targeted moneylenders. In Egypt the Urabi revolt of 1882 drew recruits with its call to "banish the usurer." In the United States resistance took the form of a third-party insurgency, the Populist revolt of the 1890s, against debt servitude.

Sharecropping represented a symbolic victory for blacks: working for the white man's wages insulted their dear-won autonomy. "Sharecroppers were not 'coolie' laborers," Eric Foner points out, "not directly supervised wage workers."[12] For that reason, a planter complained, sharecropping "is wrong policy; it makes the laborer too independent; he becomes a partner, and has a right to be consulted." Yet the "partner" feature of sharecropping overcame the clash of interest between planters and freedmen, giving both sides a stake in production.[13]

It was hardly a win-win proposition. Forty years of sharecropping, the editor of the *Progressive Farmer* wrote in 1904, had shown it to be "a system not far removed from slavery." To plant their crops, sharecroppers had to borrow money to pay for supplies—plow points, hay, seeds. They turned to the planter or, more commonly, the local "furnishing" merchant, pledging the next year's crop as collateral and paying usurious interest on the loan. "It is the general opinion in many counties where inquiries have been made," a political scientist reported in 1893, "that the interest and profit on crop liens amount to not less than 25 percent yearly of the capital advanced, that the common proportion is from 40 to 80 percent and that even 200 percent is exacted in some places." Most years the cropper's or tenant's debts exceeded the value of the crops, a cycle of futility that could end in eviction and the attachment of the tenant's mule (if he had a mule) or the sale of his mean furnishings. "The pathos of the lien-farmer," the *Progressive Farmer* noted, "is that he is always only twelve months from freedom."[14] He was decades away from exercising the "right to rise." School, inferior where available, was a luxury survival could rarely afford. Since the size of a cropper's family determined the number of acres he could farm, all family members had to work all day.[15] Forty years after slavery nearly half of southern blacks remained illiterate; and, while five out of six black farmers were croppers or tenants, white sharecroppers outnumbered black and ate of the same bread of ignorance and futility.[16] Whereas before the war a third of farmers under thirty rented but nearly 90 percent of those over forty owned their farms, indicating considerable mobility, "There were simply no rungs on the agricultural ladder" in the postwar South.[17]

To keep blacks from *owning* land white men abandoned economic rationality—whites would accept a lower price from a white buyer rather than sell at a better one to a black. "The feeling against ownership of the soil by the Negro is so strong that the man who should sell small tracts to them would be in actual physical danger," the *New York Herald*'s Whitelaw Reid wrote from the South.[18] And, supposing a white man would sell him land and he had saved a downpayment, where would a black man get the money to finance a farm? Banks were few. Holding worthless currency, many had failed. In 1869 there were only 126 national banks in the former Confederacy compared with 829 in New York, Massachusetts, Pennsylvania, and Ohio. Spitefully, and at cross purposes with the avowed aims of Reconstruction, Congress gave the southern states "almost none" of the $80 million appropriated during the war as "start-up money" for the banking system established under the National Banking Act.[19] Planters and merchants, the only other sources of credit, would not lend money to blacks. Lenders rarely assayed individual merit; they went by the skin of incapacity. Citing a range of statistical evidence—that blacks, for example, owned only 7.3 percent of southern farms by 1880—two economic historians conclude, "Our analysis suggests that the freedman was systematically denied the opportunity to become an independent farmer *because of his race.*"[20] White farmers enjoyed a 60 percent higher return for their labor than blacks, because, while the whites borrowed to invest in animals, tools, fertilizer, and seeds, "Black access to capital was effectively curtailed." That is one reason the South lagged the country economically well into the twentieth century and why to get ahead blacks had to get out. Anti-enticement laws, prejudice against hiring blacks in the North, and foreign immigration kept them on the plantation until World War I cut off the supply of low-wage labor from Europe, and northern employers, desperate for help, no longer could afford to exclude them. Between 1910 and 1920 black emigration from the Deep South increased nearly threefold over the prewar period, with young men and women quitting the South at a rate "almost beyond belief."[*21]

The war destroyed property, but the South could recover from the physical damage. Emancipation made the difference between the surging economy of 1840, when cotton state income was at the national mean, and the stagnation of 1880, when it had fallen to 60 percent of the mean.[22] Emancipation had reduced total man-hours worked in the South to a third of "the quantity of labor which had been extracted by the coercion of slavery."[23] The lash had raised the South's numbers; peonage pulled them down.

The southern country store was emptying the southern country of its wealth. The furnishing merchant—whether Yankee, immigrant, or planter—attached a condition to his loans beneficial to him but destructive to the South. He got his lending money from northern investors who gave it only to back cotton, the one southern crop with an established if declining demand in world markets: The merchant-planter lent for cotton and for cotton only.[24] "The merchant was only a bucket in an endless chain by which the agricultural well of a tributary region was drained of its flow," C. Vann Woodward writes. The merchant could dictate terms because nobody else would extend credit to the farmer. Once the farmer was in debt to one merchant "no competitor would sell the farmer so much as a side of fat back, except for cash, since the only acceptable security, his crop, had been forfeited." The lender enjoyed a local monopoly. He drove the farmer to plant cotton to his doorstep not only to pay for the

---

* "With the persistence in the plantation way of life, the behavioral, as differentiated from the juridical, content of freedom was denied to the Black population of the United States. . . . Slavery had been abolished, but Northern policies and prejudice meant that Blacks remained entrapped in the South's plantation economy." Jay R. Mandle, "Continuity and Change: The Use of Black Labor After the Civil War," *Journal of Black Studies,* vol. 21, no. 4 (June 1991), p. 425.

loan but to keep the farmer from growing his own food, forcing him to borrow against his future crop to eat. Merchants "charged from 25 percent to grand larceny," according to a contemporary observer. For common items "credit price" markups ranged from 20 to 40 percent in North Carolina to 50 to 75 percent in Alabama; for medicine the premium could run to 250 percent. To borrow $800 a Georgia farmer might pay $2,800 in interest over five years. "When one of these mortgages has been recorded against the southern farmer," a researcher found, "he has usually passed into a state of helpless peonage to the merchant who has become his creditor. . . . Every mouthful of food that he purchases; every implement that he requires on the farm, his mules, cattle, the clothing for himself and family, the fertilizers for his land, must all be bought of the merchant who holds the crop lien, and in such amounts, as the latter is willing to allow." "Lien slavery" had replaced chattel slavery—for poor black *and* white farmers alike. "Judged by its economic results alone," Woodward concludes, "the new evil may have worked more permanent injury to the South than the ancient evil."[25]

Men recognized this, and saw the way out. "The first reform must be made in the system of farming," Henry Grady, the editor of the *Atlanta Constitution,* wrote in *Harper's* in 1881. That system rendered the most fertile region in the country a net importer of food. "The South must prepare to raise her own provisions, compost her own fertilizer, cure her own hay, and breed her own stock. Leaving credit and usury out of the question, no man can pay seventy-five cents a bushel for corn, thirty dollars a ton for hay, twenty dollars a barrel for pork, sixty cents for oats, and raise cotton for eight cents a pound."[26]

The system of southern farming was not reformed. Southern agriculture furrowed the same one-crop path until the 1930s, when the New Deal, seeking to increase prices by reducing the supply of cotton, paid benefits to cotton planters to take land out of production, displacing tenants and sharecroppers from the land of their privation into the cities of their discontent. The planters, true to their historical character, cheated many croppers out of their share of the "allotment" payment by hiring them as wage laborers, who were ineligible for the allotment. By 1930 more than half of all southern farmers, and in some places 80 to 90 percent of black farmers, were either tenants or sharecroppers, earning a dollar a day.[27] This penurious system ensnared about one in four southerners.[28] Reporting on the Depression South, an English journalist who "had traveled over most of Europe and part of Africa" maintained that she had "never seen such terrible sights as I saw yesterday among the sharecroppers of Arkansas." The writer Erskine Caldwell described visiting a sharecropper's cabin in Georgia and watching, horror-struck, while "on the floor before an open fire lay" two babies, neither a year old, sucking "the dry teats of a mongrel bitch."[29] The one-crop path led to that Georgia cabin. Could the South have taken a different path to a better place?

Lincoln's legacy of 1863, Emancipation and Homestead joined, the injuries of race and class addressed: Where would that path have led? We have clues. In an awkward White House meeting with a black delegation that included Frederick Douglass, Andrew Johnson said he was afraid favoritism toward the freedman would touch off "a war of races" pitting poor whites against blacks.[30] In that spirit he rejected his visitors' pleas for black suffrage. He also rescinded Sherman's Special Field Order No. 15, pardoned planters who had fought in or aided the rebellion, and, in a cruel cut to black hopes, authorized Federal troops to evict freedmen squatting on planter land. Sherman's legatees in the Carolina and Georgia lowlands, who had already received their forty acres, resisted. Fighting off armed attempts to dislodge them, they worked their own farms into the twentieth century.

As for the former slaves given land on the Sea Islands, General Rufus Saxton, appointed inspector of settlements and plantations by Sherman, hailed their early progress, crediting it to their "conviction that they were to have the lands of their former masters." He wrote:

> The greatest success attended the experiment, and although the planting season was very far advanced before the transportation to carry the colonists to the Sea Islands could be obtained, and the people were destitute of animals and had but few agricultural implements and the greatest difficulty in procuring seeds, yet they went out, worked with energy and diligence to clear up the ground run to waste by three years' neglect; and thousands of acres were planted and provisions enough were raised for those who were located in season to plant, beside a large amount of sea island cotton for market.[31]

A twentieth-century historian seconds Saxton's judgment: "In a short time they had made improvements on the land exceeding the previous valuation accumulated over two centuries of plantation improvement."[32] That observation—and it could be supplemented with testimony to the initiative shown by the 1,800 freedmen who, between 1864 and 1866, worked the confiscated Mississippi plantations of Jefferson Davis and his brother Joseph, earning profits of from hundreds of dollars to $5,000 apiece—frames the haunting might-have-been of Reconstruction. Thaddeus Stevens, the Radical leader in the House, calculated that 70,000 planters, "arch traitors," owned 394 million acres of the South's best land. Seize it, Stevens urged, sell it to loyal citizens, use it to retire war debt, above all homestead it out to the freedmen.[33] The "Emperor of Russia" had done as much for the serfs: "[W]hen that wise man set free twenty-two million serfs, he compelled their masters to give them homesteads on the very soil which they had tilled."

But neither the profits of slavery nor the guilt were the planter's alone; they belonged to the whole country. And the whole country should have paid. "The plantation land should have gone to those who worked it," W.E.B. Du Bois wrote in 1935, "and the former owner should have been compensated in some part for a lost investment made with the social sanction of the nation." Mindful of the tragic postwar history between poor whites and blacks, he added: "To this should have been added economic opportunity and access to the land for the poor whites."[34] Radical land reform would have been just; and, extended to poor whites, politic. But would it have made economic sense? Freehold farmers might have returned to sustenance farming, and the South's economic numbers been worse than under sharecropping. But even in that improbable scenario, George W. Julian's dream of "stud[ding] over" the South with "small farms tilled by free men" could not have produced a *worse* material outcome than infants suckling a dog on a Georgia cabin floor.

If the rungs were missing on the southern agricultural ladder, they were far apart on the northern industrial ladder. In a study of the working lives of 300 unskilled laborers in Newburyport, Massachusetts, between 1850 and 1880, Stephan Thernstrom found "not a single instance of mobility into the ranks of management or even into a foremanship." Upward mobility "*within* the working class" did occur; and "property mobility," though the latter rarely led to "real wealth."[35] A survey of 194 executives of the 1870s turned up sixteen former laborers. Thirty years later only 3 percent of business leaders had come up from the shop floor.[36] Rags-to-riches businessmen, Edward Pessen writes, "have always been more conspicuous in American history books than in American history."[37] John D. Rockefeller, a farm boy, and Andrew Carnegie, an immigrant Bobbin Boy who entered the factory at age thirteen, were first among the few exceptions to the rule. "The man at the bottom of the ladder leading up to the social heavens may yet dream there is a ladder let down to him," the Reverend Newman Smyth wrote in 1885, "but the angels are not seen very often ascending and descending; one after another, it would seem, some unseen yet hostile powers are breaking out the middle rungs of the ladder."[38]

It fell to the pioneer, then, to put them back. Just as the hierarchical "society of organizations" was hardening in the East, Americans sought a new beginning in the West. Under what Frederick Jackson Turner called the "sanative influences of the free spaces," the homesteading pioneer would restore the Jeffersonian predicate of economic democracy to a political democracy veering toward plutocracy.[39] The tide steadily making for inequality in the nineteenth century would thin out on the Great Plains and be thrown back by the Rockies.

Dying in his log cabin on the frozen Nebraska plain, John Bergson, the Swedish father in Willa Cather's *O Pioneers!*, reflects on nature's indiffer-

"The Westering"
Emigrants, circa 1860s, probably west of the ninety-eighth meridian, in the "dry."

ence to the homestead romance, the dream of starting over that still capti-
vates the American imagination:

> In eleven long years John Bergson had made but little impression upon the wild
> land he had come to tame. It was still a wild thing that had its ugly moods; and
> no one knew when they were likely to come, or why. Mischance hung over it.
> Its Genius was unfriendly to man. . . . Bergson went over in his mind the things
> that had held him back. One winter his cattle perished in a blizzard. The next
> summer one of his plow horses broke its leg in a prairie-dog hole and had to be
> shot. Another summer he lost his hogs to cholera, and a valuable stallion died
> from a rattlesnake bite. Time and again his crops had failed. . . . [T]he land was
> an enigma. He had an idea that no one knew how to farm it properly. . . . Their
> neighbors, certainly, knew even less about farming than he did. Many of them
> had never worked on a farm until they took up their homesteads. They had
> been *handwerkers* at home; tailors, locksmiths, joiners, carpenters. . . . Bergson
> himself had worked in a shipyard.[40]

Before 1890, two-thirds of all homesteaders failed. Unlike Bergson, Fred
A. Shannon notes, "the great majority of . . . these were persons who had
spent all their earlier years on the land."[41]

The proponents of homesteading diagnosed a condition homesteads
could not cure: a wage-labor economy. Scale and scope production hard-
ened a system in which employers had "little personal acquaintance" and
"took little personal interest" in their employees, the minister Josiah
Strong observed, "render[ing] it vastly more difficult to rise from the condition of employee to that of employer, thus separating the classes more
widely."[42] Social stratification came as an un-American surprise.

"[S]ocial barriers in this country are a violation of our national ideals,
and therefore the mere awareness of them impairs public morale," David
Potter explains in his study of the American character, *People of Plenty.*
Tripping over invisible class lines, some Americans "lose confidence in
themselves or rebel against a society which, as they feel, betrayed them
with a false promise." Others are "personally broken and defeated by a
system which sets one standard for what people shall attempt and another
for what they may attain." Nineteenth-century Americans dealt with this
double standard by ascribing failure to bad character, not bad luck. Nothing in the social medium held men back. America was not Britain.

With the Revolution less than a century behind them, Americans were
completing their separation from the parent country; and as they had no
king, they would have no classes. From the time of Francis Lowell, who

returned from a tour of British factories in 1812 with the secret of the power loom and a vow to build a city of industry on nobler lines than Birmingham and Manchester, Americans deplored Britain's road to industrialism. Britain had ground its independent rural yeomen into the social dust of an urban proletariat. Men cleared off the land, unable to grow or hunt their own food, forced by hunger to submit to the inhuman terms of industrialism; free to starve, bound to labor. "We make a nation of Helots, and have no free citizens," Adam Smith's teacher, Adam Ferguson, summed up the cost of British progress.[43]

An Abraham Lincoln was impossible in Britain. Rail-splitters stayed "Helots" there; they were presidents-in-waiting here. Only a churlish foreigner would point out that just one rail-splitter managed it, or that *his* father owned two farms of 600 acres, town lots, livestock, and horses at his son's birth. "Five years later," Edward Pessen reports in *The Log Cabin Myth,* Thomas Lincoln "belonged to the richest 1% of property owners in his area." Of the forty presidents from George Washington to Ronald Reagan, Pessen finds only one—Andrew Johnson, whose father worked as a janitor, bank messenger, and porter—from either the lower or upper lower classes to which half of Americans belong.[44]

Lincoln could not emerge from the toxic chrysalis of a youth spent in a New Jersey factory, though that state, no laggard in reform, passed a law in 1855 forbidding a "minor who has attained the age of 12 years, and is under the age of 15 years" from working "in any manufacturing establishment more than 11 hours in any one day, not before 5 o'clock in the morning, nor after 7:30 in the evening." Earlier ages would have branded cruel what the New Jersey lawmakers considered kind, for the exposure of children to wage labor, whatever their age or hours of work, was the innovation of industrial capitalism. "That which today, e.g., in the State of Massachusetts, until recently the freest state of the North American Republic," Karl Marx noted in *Capital,* "has been proclaimed as the statutory limit of the labor of children under 12, was in England, even in the middle of the seventeenth century, the normal working-day of able-bodied artizans, robust labourers, and athletic blacksmiths. . . . According to capitalistic anthropology, the age of childhood ended at 10, or at the outside, 11."[45]

Although the census did not distinguish between wage and salary workers until 1890, industrialism had long since solidified a two-class system—a lower class mostly of "unskilled" workers and a middle class of managers, professionals, merchants, clerks, skilled workers, successful farmers, and small producers. In his research on the two classes in Buffalo,

New York, and Hamilton, Ontario, before the onset of industrialism and after, Michael Katz shows how it shaped even their reproductive lives. *Before* industrialism, in 1855, the "capitalist class," the highest tier of the middle class, displayed the highest marital fertility; *after,* in 1871, the lower class did. Before industrialism the lower classes kept their children in school almost as long as the upper class, but not after, when factory work created jobs for children. The capitalist class families could have sent their children to work but sacrificed income for their children's education while the lower-class families sacrificed their children's education to income—with grim implications for future mobility. The toll of this decision on young lives comes through in an 1884 report on "work-children" in New Jersey that documented heartrending impairment. The 1855 curb on the hours children could work, though it may have spared their bodies the exactions required of adults, had not saved their minds. "There is no exaggeration in saying that three-fourths of the work-children know absolutely nothing," the report concluded. Over 95 percent had never heard of Abraham Lincoln, and "very few" of George Washington. ("He discovered America," one child ventured.) Immigration could not be blamed: Children from the British Isles and Germany knew more about America than the native-born. Asked the "part of speech" of the word "boy," one answered "comma." Many could not say whether New Jersey was in North or South America; some thought Pennsylvania was New Jersey's capital. More than half did not know what the "United States" or "Europe" was, though one fourteen-year-old girl guessed the latter "was in the moon."[46]

Americans had invested too much narcissism in the equality of all white men to accept inequality as intrinsic to industrial capitalism; easier to write off its blatancy in Britain, the birthplace of industry, as a feudal vestige that could not leap the ocean. Besides, a "special Providence" made America the great exception among nations. What had happened in other countries could not happen here.

Belief in American exceptionalism rose out of America's wide-open spaces. The land would confound Malthus *and* Marx; scarcity and socialism alike founder on America's "shoals of roast beef," the German socialist Werner Sombart's phrase for plenty's shield against want and radicalism. The land would suspend the perverse law of industrialism whereby progress fed on poverty, economic health on human debility. Adam Smith framed that law after observing what the division of labor in manufacture did to the laborer—and he wrote before machinery cracked the whip of speed over production. In *The Wealth of Nations,* after his famous observation that, "The man whose whole life is spent in performing a few simple operations, of which the effects too are, perhaps, always the same . . . generally becomes as stupid and ignorant as it is possible for a human creature to become," he exposed the win-lose truth of industrialism: "But in every improved and civilized society, this is the state into which the labouring poor, that is, the great body of people, must necessarily fall . . ."—*must,* because the increased productivity that lifted the flat line of economic growth for the first time in a thousand years rested on the division of labor. Then Smith adds a caveat that aligns him with twentieth-century liberals like John Kenneth Galbraith: ". . . unless government takes some pains to prevent it."[47]

Republican government would take pains; progress would lose its perversity in America. Before labor, in Smith's words, "corrupts the courage" of the "[laborer's] mind," before it "renders him incapable of exerting his strength with vigor . . . in any other employments than that to which he has been bred," the laborer would begin a new life on a government-supplied homestead in "the salubrious and fertile West," as the *Working Man's Advocate,* in an 1844 editorial, referred to the promised land.[48] In leaving the factory the laborer would reduce the labor supply in the East, raising the wages of the men, women, and children remaining behind. Better paid, they could save faster and end their servitude to the machine sooner. Free land would check the growth here of the population of surplus laborers that held down British wages and sowed misery in Britain's cities. Eden for depleted laborers, solvent of class, predicate of western economic development, free land was also a prophylaxis against revolution. "In Europe," Turner declared, "labor said, raise wages or we fight. In the United States labor said, raise wages or we will go West."[49]

This "safety valve" theory of the frontier fooled some of the best minds of the century. Hegel subscribed to it. Marx did: laborers were not "so dependent" in America "as in Europe" because of the availability of free land. John Stuart Mill would "never wish to see Protection abolished" if it explained why "the general level of [the] wages of labour in America" was above the English level. "But it is not because of Protection that wages in America are high," he added, with relief, "it is because there is an abundance of land, and every labourer is at liberty to acquire it."[50]

Horace Greeley was the leading publicist of the homestead "win-

win"—individual opportunity in the West and social peace in the East— and the probable drafter of the Homestead plank in the 1860 Republican platform.[51] "The public lands," he wrote, "are the great regulator of the relations of Labor and Capital, the safety valve of our industrial and social engine." He may not have coined the line posterity assigns him—"Go west, young man! Go west!"—but he preached that message, in editorials in the *New York Tribune,* and in public lectures, from the 1840s to his death in 1873.[52] In the midst of General George B. McClellan's doomed Peninsula campaign, the passage of the Homestead Act went uncelebrated in the *Tribune's* news columns. Greeley himself barely squeezed in an editorial salute: "Young men! Poor Men! Widows! Resolve to have a home of your own."[53] ("Widows" gestures toward the war's price.) But Greeley's clarion to free labor, fittingly, punctuates a discussion of the war's objectives—an America of free soil, free labor, free men, and free land. After the war, when the young men and widows were resisting his call, Greeley wondering what was wrong with them, Henry George invoked the safety valve, but had the empirical scruple to emphasize the *psychology* of free land: "[I]t has given a consciousness of freedom even to the dweller in crowded cities, and has been a well-spring of hope even to those who have never thought of taking refuge in it." The finding of the superintendent of the 1890 census that, in Turner's words, "the frontier is gone, and with its going has closed the first period of American history," brought a prediction from a Kansas writer of "unendurable distress" in eastern cities "in the absence of the safety valve heretofore existing in the public domain."[54]

The thinkers and prophets got it wrong: Actual homesteading, fewer than 400,000 claims filed between 1860 and 1890, disappointed theoretical homesteading. To counter their party's image as the political arm of the corporations, Republican politicians invested the Homestead Act with what Paul W. Gates, the preeminent student of land policy, calls "a halo of political and economic significance" it has never deserved.[55] The *significant* migration was not from the city to the country but from the country to the city. The churn of people through America's cities approaches the unbelievable. In their close analysis of Boston's population, Stephan Thernstrom and Peter R. Knights discovered that while between 1830 and 1890 "the city grew from 61,000 to 448,000, a net increase of 387,000 . . . the number of migrants entering Boston in those years was an amazing 3,325,000, eight and a half times the net population increase." Whereas the rural population increased sixteen-fold between 1860 and 1900, city dwellers increased 139-fold. Richard Oestreicher finds that "[e]ven within the native stock minority of the working class, rural-to-urban migrants generally outnumbered those who had been born and bred in urban working-class families"; as late as the 1950s former farmers headed a third of such households. Country-to-city migrants multiplied the population of Los Angeles from 5,000 to 100,000; of Denver from zero to 134,000; of Memphis from 23,000 to 100,000. One hundred cities doubled in size during the 1880s. Sioux City, Iowa, surged by 500 percent; Kansas City, Kansas, by 1,000 percent; Seattle, by 1,100 percent. "By 1880," Richard White notes, "the West had become the most urbanized region of the country."[56] Conversely, two-thirds of Pennsylvania and New York townships, and three-fifths of New England's villages, lost people. So did half or more of the townships in Illinois, Indiana, and Ohio.[57] "Millions of acres . . . solicit cultivation," Greeley lamented, "yet hundreds of thousands reject this and rush into cities."[58] The city was the safety valve for rural discontent that rose as commodity prices fell, a refuge for a surplus population of farmers, tenants, and farm laborers, as well as for European immigrants, many uprooted by the same economic forces impelling Americans to leave the country. By 1925 Turner, the father of the frontier interpretation of American history, was writing, "There seems likely to be an urban reinterpretation of our history."[59] Journalism knows the story that is too good to check; the frontier theory explained too much to be risked in an encounter with frontier fact. Turner's picture of the frontier derived from the "well-watered prairies and forests" and village-scale democracy of his Wisconsin boyhood, not from the trans-Missouri West, a region of hope-killing droughts dominated by national railroad corporations like the Northern Pacific, which presided over 60 million acres, a tenth of the land mass of the United States. As for Greeley, in his *New York Tribune* column, recording "many trips" west, he mentions only one "industrious mechanic" (a New Yorker) who had taken his advice.[60]

Turner's schema suggested that western settlement waxed as economic conditions in the East worsened. As he phrased it in the book that grew out of his canonical lecture, "The Significance of the Frontier in American History," delivered at the World's Columbian Exposition in Chicago, in 1893, "Whenever social conditions tended to crystallize in the East, whenever capital tended to press down upon labor . . . there was this gate of escape to the free conditions of the frontier."[61] That gate should have swung like a turnstile, then, during the longest economic contraction of the nineteenth century, the depression of the 1870s. In countercyclical fashion, employment and wages should have risen in the cities as more and more workers crowded through the gate of escape and social harmony reigned. The push driving emigration and the pull of now "free" western lands were never stronger. Unemployment in the eastern cities approached 25 percent, and the factory laborers, railway workers, and miners still in work suffered wage cuts of 10 to 30 percent.[62] There were strikes, violent demonstrations, incendiarism, scores of workers shot by state militia. Yet with the social temperature at the boiling point, the safety valve of western migration was "rusted solid."[63] When conditions were bitterest and the "promise of freedom and equality was theirs for the taking," very few wage earners took it.

How few? A study of newspaper listings of residents of two Massachusetts cities moving to other places, a feature of local journalism, found no mention of a "mechanic," shorthand for factory wage earner, heading west between 1836 and 1886—fifty years!—from two of the most industrialized cities in America, Fall River and Lowell. One hundred and twenty men, who "including doubtful cases . . . might have been wage earners," departed Fall River for the West. How many stayed is uncertain, but it can't have been many if twenty of the thirty men who left in 1877 and returned in 1878 were representative. For Lowell "there is mainly negative evidence" of worker migration. Doctors, lawyers, and merchants left for San Francisco during the Gold Rush, but no mechanics. Strikes punctuated every decade, yet the editorial columns did not once recommend western settlement for the hard-pressed wage earner. Even when, seeking to people Kansas with anti-slavery immigrants, the New England Emigration Society offered to pay the transportation and start-up costs of settlement, few responded—"almost all" its recruits came off the farms of New England and New York. After examining state and local histories, western as well as eastern newspapers, hotel registers, city directories, and the records of several other emigrant aid societies, the authors of the study concluded that "too few industrial workers reached the frontier to attract notice in the accounts of settlement . . . and too few wage-earners left the industrial centers to exert any marked influence on the labor situation." Writing in 1884, Henry D. Lloyd anticipated Turner's apprehensions a decade later over the closing of the frontier: "Our young men can no longer go west; they must go up or down."[64]

Three years after Greeley's death, a letter published in the *Tribune* under the heading "a failure and a delusion" breathes a realism about the safety valve of western emigration missing in Turner two decades later: "Most prominent of the legacies bequeathed to this country by Mr. Greeley is the Homestead law. But I must do his memory the justice of saying that in his zealous and persistent advocacy . . . he believed he was serving 'the toiling millions' for whose prosperity and elevation he ever labored. And yet how few, how very few, of these 'downtrodden millions' ever possessed themselves of what he regarded as the greatest boon and blessing."[65] To Turner, the "gift of free land . . . explain[ed] American development," but it was not a gift, because the land was not free.[66]

In 1788 the United States occupied 150 million acres. Later, the Louisiana Purchase and the Mexican Cession increased its size tenfold, all but 250 million acres belonging to the public domain.[67] Before the Civil War the federal government obtained 40 percent of its revenue from the sale of public lands, mostly to the forgotten man of the frontier. Turner bids us "Stand at Cumberland Gap and watch the procession of civilization, marching single file—the buffalo following the trail to the salt springs, the Indian, the fur trader and hunter, the cattle raiser, the pioneer farmer—and the frontier has passed by."[68] Missing is the speculator, without whom "it is difficult to imagine a frontier," Paul W. Gates writes. Often the speculator moved ahead of the pioneer farmer and just behind the Indian agent who by treaty or purchase cleared off the original inhabitants and the government surveyor who mapped out "wild" land into "sections" of one square mile, subdividing them into quarter sections of 160 acres for sale. The sales, at prices that fell from $2 an acre in 1800 to as little as 25 cents in 1854, were conducted at public auctions held at government land offices.[69] The phrase "land office business" was coined to describe the throngs who would line up outside the land office when new land was opened for settlement. A photograph in Everett Dick's classic *The Sod-House Frontier* shows land office officials using ladders to enter and leave the second-story back windows of their office in Garden City, Kansas, "to escape the constant crowd" on the front stairs.[70] The sales were held before a revisionist cast of frontiersmen.

There was the "capitalist estate builder," who made it his business to know the best land (and the government auctioneer). There was the land agent, buying tracts for eastern investors, land being the coin of wealth in the first half of the century. Between 1833 and 1837 one group of New Yorkers bought up over 350,000 acres in the Northwest and frontier South.[71] By 1862 speculators owned 10 million acres of Iowa, nearly two-thirds of the state, 5.5 million acres in Illinois, 5 million in Indiana. As late as 1900, thirty-four landlords owned 1,100 farms in Illinois; a single Washington, D.C., resident owned 322 farms there and 845 farms in Missouri, Kansas, and Nebraska; one man owned an Illinois county.[72]

And there was the ur-pioneer, the "squatter," who had gone before the surveyor, setting up a farm and improving land now being sold from under him. Squatters on land acquired by speculators fell from the status of independent farmers to tenants overnight, becoming vassals of Prairie Kings, Lumber Kings, and Cattle Barons, to use Gates's anti-Turnerian ideal types, ruling "imperial estates." The feudal resonance is unexpected on the frontier, fixed in our minds as the incubator of democracy by Turner; yet, as more and more of the public lands became private domains, the Jeffersonian dream of a seamless democracy between polity and economy faded. "Princely domains were acquired by individuals and groups who thereby forestalled and subsequently took tribute from actual settlers"[73]— and made them pay the taxes on their rented farms.[74]

Political influence, here as everywhere in this period, leveraged fortunes. Money sought power. Entrepreneurial genius consisted in strategic generosity toward public officials. Men like William W. Corcoran, of Washington's Corcoran and Riggs Bank, whose loans to congressmen helped pass the Compromise of 1850, made killings off the public lands. Corcoran obtained land held by the Treasury Department after the Panic of 1837 forced widespread forfeitures—though "stole" may be apposite for bids of 2 cents an acre for 45,000 acres in Texas, and 38 cents an acre for 15,800 acres in Mississippi and 22,000 in Illinois. Others bid higher for smaller lots, yet Treasury smiled on Corcoran—he had "large" loans outstanding to the secretary of the treasury.[75]

Under the Preemption Act of 1841, the squatter who wanted to buy his farm had the right to do so; but, having sunk his capital into cattle and fences, rarely had the cash. So he turned to the pathfinder of finance "present at every public auction . . . prepared to buy claims for squatters"—the loan shark. The loan shark would buy his land, then loan the squatter the funds to buy it from him for more than he had just paid for it. William B. Ogden got his start as a loan shark, lending eastern money to squatters at premium rates.[76] Debt haunted the settler who resorted to the loan shark. At one point three-fourths of the farms in Minnesota had liens on them.[77] If the crop failed and the settler could not meet his payment, the loan shark would extend him more credit at higher interest. Unable to pay, many settlers abandoned their farms, forfeiting the improvements they had made. Foreclosure awaited others. Horace Greeley complained that settlers had lost "Five or Six Hundred Millions, in the shape of usury, extra price, Sheriff's fees, cost of foreclosing mortgages, etc. . . . paying the Government price of their quarter sections twice or thrice over before they could call them their own."[78]

Half of the 1860 Republican campaign slogan, "Vote yourself a farm— vote yourself a tariff," promised a fresh start on the frontier.[79] It was an illusory promise when $500 was the minimum needed to transport a family to the homestead and plant the first year's crop and survive until the harvest and $500 was six months' wages for a skilled urban worker and, as late as 1900, a year's pay for a factory hand. Moreover, irregularity of employment, being laid off in slack months, was so common—of 800,000 employable persons in Massachusetts, 241,000, or 30 percent, were either idle or worked only a few months during the nondepression year 1884— that any savings the wage earner set aside went into tiding his family over until he had work again.[80] What Fred A. Shannon asserts of the promise of "cheap land" before the war was true of the promise of free land after it— "for the labourer it was as futile as a signboard pointing to the end of the rainbow."[81]

In 1877, responding to a memorial signed by 20,000 of his miner-constituents, a Pennsylvania congressman, Hendrick Wright, filed a bill to loan homesteaders $500 "to aid in the commencement of a permanent farming residence." The depression had idled many in his district and this premature New Dealer wanted government to help the unemployed help themselves. "It is not the part of wisdom for a great country to allow suffering among the people when there is ample means to prevent it," Wright argued. "The working men of this land are better entitled to the bounty of Government than aggregated wealth. . . . It is a wonder to me that they . . . still comply with the laws of this country." In a letter to Wright a workingman hinted that "they" might not comply for long: "It would seem as though this Republic was drifting from its foundations. This is no idle twadel. But there may come a time when patience ceases to be a virtue and farewell thou wreck of an American Republic."

Safety was at risk without a functioning safety valve, Wright maintained. When a proponent of a similar bill said he feared a permanent underclass forming unless the government settled the unemployed in the West, Representative James A. Garfield, the future president, exclaimed "Thank God, here in America, there are no classes!" That bill was defeated; as was Wright's, 274–35. The margin indicated how far Congress had retreated from the philosophy inspiring the Homestead Act. Congress was on the rebound from its wartime experiment in state capitalism; generosity toward railroads had given generosity a bad name—"paternalism." "These grants," a unanimous resolution passed by the House affirmed of the 100 million acres granted to railroads between 1868 and 1872, along with $100 million in loans, "have been made on the theory that government is an organized benevolence, and not merely a compact for the negative function of repelling a public enemy or suppressing disorder." Earlier that year, President Rutherford B. Hayes had abandoned the promise of Emancipation by withdrawing the last federal troops from the South. After 1877 white workingmen and southern blacks were on their own.

Two years later, Wright resubmitted his bill; this time only twenty-three congressmen, ten from Pennsylvania, voted with him. "There are not idiots enough in Congress to vote for Hendrick B. Wright's bill," the post-Greeley *Tribune* editorialized. The homesteader subsidy was "class legislation"—a handout to a clamorous constituency. That objection had not proved fatal to railroads. "Congress can grant railroads money and land," Wright argued, "but if it talks of relieving the poor and oppressed, the cry comes, 'We cannot reward idleness.' " In fact President Grant had proposed a program of public works construction for the unemployed earlier in the depression, but Garfield, as chairman of the Appropriations Committee, talked him out of it, maintaining, with Treasury Secretary Benjamin Bristow, that "it is no part of the business of government to find employment for people," nor settle them in the West. At the next election, Wright, tagged "the Pennsylvania Communist" by *The Nation*, lost his seat.[82]

In granting land to railroads Congress bracketed off much of the map for private sale. Following the template pioneered by the Illinois Central, the railroads would finance their construction by selling land along the railway corridor or borrowing against it.[83] Until the early 1870s, the Union Pacific, the Central Pacific, the Atchison, Topeka and the Santa Fe, the Atlantic and Pacific, and the Texas and Pacific, as well as a scattering of smaller roads, had received five times more land than homesteaders—the Northern Pacific alone an area larger than New England.[84] Congressmen harvested their gratitude. In return for a modest land grant, for example, a Kansas road spread $295,000 worth of stock among Thaddeus Stevens, the chairman of the House Ways and Means Committee, and nine other members of Congress.[85] Largesse to railroads contracted the land available for homesteaders. By the 1860s, prewar land speculation and railroad land grants had closed a third of Kansas to homesteading.[86] Even where abundant, "free" land was to be had only well beyond railroad land, and the farther from the tracks the poorer the land—in Kansas it was so poor that half of all homesteaders quit before "perfecting" their claims. "Under the Homestead law the settler must, in order to get a good location, go far out in the wild and unsettled districts," an advertisement for an Iowa land company truthfully represented, "and for many years be deprived of school privileges, churches, mills, bridges, and in fact all the advantages of society"[87]—all of which flowed from the railroad. Some could not bear the isolation, like the Texans who left this note on their cabin door: "Two hundred miles to nearest post office; one hundred miles from wood, twenty miles from hell. God bless our home. Gone to live with the wife's folks." Sundays, on his family's cotton farm in Bonham, Texas, young Sam Rayburn would "sit on the fence and wish to God that somebody would drive by in a buggy—just anybody to relieve my loneliness. . . . Loneliness," the speaker of the house recalled decades later, "consumes people."[88] Like Rayburn, ten farmers' sons left for the city for every one who stayed and took over the farm.[89] By 1890, when the superintendent of the census declared the frontier "closed," "free" homesteads occupied only 3.5 percent of the land west of the Mississippi.[90]

Intended to end speculation, the Homestead Act tended to stimulate it— in the homesteader. He could "commute"—sell—his claim after spending only fourteen months on it, as nearly 140,000 homesteaders did between 1882 and 1909.[91] The apostles of the homestead idea had wanted the grant made inalienable to keep farms in families and families on farms.[92] Instead: "On the mid-continent frontier almost all the early comers to any area were speculators first and homesteaders second or not at all."[93] Homesteaders could file for only one claim, and the law stipulated that they had to erect a dwelling "twelve by fourteen" on it. "Chronic settlers" whittled dollhouses, twelve by fourteen, so they could truthfully swear to have erected a house of those dimensions. Receiving title to their claim, they would sell it, carry the dollhouse to another site, and file under a new name. "A change of name was no inconvenience," Everett Dick notes, since "eastern prisons yawned in vain for many western pioneers."[94] In Nebraska an enterprising chap rented a portable house on wheels, which would be towed from site to site by teams of oxen. "Perhaps the majority who took up land never intended to live on the prairie," Dick writes.[95]

The homesteader could also turn perjurer, filing false claims on behalf of speculators. One study found a 60 percent discrepancy between the names listed on the original claims at local land offices and the names of the settlers who "perfected" the claim five years later.[96] To keep settlers out of the neighborhood, ranchers paid their cowboys to file homestead claims for timberland near rivers. The size of the homestead grant—160 acres, the Platonic farm unit established by the Land Ordinance of 1785—drove homesteaders to sell out or move on.[97] In the arid regions west of the ninety-eighth meridian, expecting a farm to succeed on a plot that size was "like expecting a fisherman to survive on just a little square of ocean."[98] Significantly, the sharpest spike in claims came in 1909, when Congress doubled the homestead size; a 1916 increase to 640 acres for stock-raising also boosted settlement.[99] But these adjustments came too late for the cycles of homesteaders defeated by the dry. "Some of the counties lying within the dry belt [of Kansas], have been populated and depopulated two or three times," an article in an eastern magazine noted of rainfall's effect on migration. "One or two years of exceptional rainfall brings in a fresh throng of settlers to take the place of others who have given up the struggle; they in turn are impoverished by the dry years that are sure to follow and abandon their farms."[100] Its individualist assumptions defeated homesteading in the West, where farmers could not survive on their own. Collective action—starting with federal water management—would be needed to sustain individualism.[101]

Beyond its statutory flaws, its incentives to greed, and the disincentives to long-term settlement built into its 160-acre limit, the Homestead Act was grafted onto an "incongruous" system of land disposal under which the government continued selling land while giving it away. As with railroad land grants, so with government land sales; the net effect was to leave poorer land for homesteaders.

The government sold land under old programs, like the Preemption Act, and new. Partly because of competition from parallel sales of preempted land, the Southern Homestead Act (1866) was adjudged a failure, and repealed. Under it freedmen and "loyal" southern whites could claim eighty-seven-acre homesteads in the southern public domain, 47 million acres stretching across five states. Only 46,000 claims were filed in ten years; many "dummy entries acting for . . . lumber companies."[102] Following repeal in 1876, Congress opened the South's public lands to unlimited sales, triggering a rush for riches. The Illinois Central ran special trains from Chicago to Mississippi and Louisiana for "land lookers," speculators representing the same families and interests that had carved up the prairie

states before the war. Now they set about carving up the South's timberlands. Two Pennsylvania men, for example, bought up 500,000 acres of
cypress forest in Texas and Louisiana. Altogether, 5 million acres of the
southern public domain were sold off between 1876 and 1886, when out-
cries against "land monopolies" ended sales.[103]

Outside the South land sales continued through the era of free land;
indeed more land was sold in the thirty years after the Homestead Act
than in the thirty-seven before.[104] Under the Land-Grant College Act
(1862) the federal government awarded the states—from Massachusetts to
Iowa—over 200 million acres of the public domain to sell and with the
proceeds build public colleges.[105] "Probably no other scrip or warrant act
was used so extensively by speculators to build up large holdings," according to Paul Gates.[106] Under the Timber and Stone Act (1878), the commissioner of the General Land Office stated in 1901, "Immense tracts of the
most valuable timber land, which every consideration of public interest
demanded should be preserved for public use, have become the property
of a few individuals and corporations."[107] A congressional investigation
revealed that the California Redwood Company ran "men into the land
office by the hundreds" to file claims to timberland. Some got $10 for the
fraud; others settled for free beer. Lumber companies sponsored excur-
sion trips to the redwoods for midwestern schoolteachers; "trainloads" of
them would arrive in California, file claims to some of the world's most
valuable timberland, and deed it to their sponsors.[108] In what Fred A. Shannon labels "the greatest timber raid of all," James J. Hill, of the Northern
Pacific Railroad, swapped the 450,000 acres he owned around Mount
Rainer in Washington state, which Congress wanted for a National Park,
for "an equivalent of richer timber lands elsewhere, from which [the
Northern Pacific] proceeded to drive out the homesteaders."[109] Under the
Desert Land Act (1877), cattle and sheep companies, through fraudulent
claims filed by serial perjurers, obtained 6 million acres of the Southwest.
Gifford Pinchot, the chairman of Theodore Roosevelt's National Conservation Commission and later chief of the Forest Service, said the "amount
of fraud in the administration of the land laws was almost incredible."
"I have seen desert claims [filed]," he said in a 1937 speech, "when the
law required that water be brought on the land. So the claimant put a
couple of his friends in a wagon and took along a barrel of water. Then
he emptied the water into a dry ditch, consisting of a single furrow; the
friends swore the water had been brought on the land and the title passed
to the thief."[110]

Under yet another program, the government permitted railroads to buy up immense swaths of land from Indian tribes. The Kansas City, Fort Smith, and Gulf Railroad obtained 800,000 acres of Kansas belonging to the Cherokee for $1 an acre.[111] The Leavenworth, Kansas, and Galveston Railroad bought 8 million acres from the Osage for 20 cents an acre. When he learned of the pending sale, the governor of Kansas denounced it as "one of the most infamous outrages ever before committed in this country." Public indignation forced Congress to cancel the deal.[112]

The scandal of the public lands grew too flagrant for politicians to ignore. The Democrats exploited it in the 1884 presidential election, distributing a map depicting railroad land grants in thick black stripes under a caption reading: "How the Public Domain Has Been Squandered—map showing the 139,403,026 acres of the people's land . . . worth at $2.00 an acre $278,806,052, given by Republican Congresses to railroad corporations." Add state and local land grants to that acreage, throw in land forfeited by the railroads for failure to build in the agreed time, and you arrive at the state of Texas, 233 million acres, or one-tenth the continental landmass—three-tenths if you include the "indemnity" lands the railroads were allowed to hold in untaxed perpetuity until President Cleveland opened them for homesteading in 1887. These percentages are for the United States as a whole; the railroads' footprint covered proportionately more of the land west of the Mississippi, where the major land grants began. Counting all forms of public aid—land, direct subsidies, bonds, credits—up to 1930 the U.S. taxpayer gifted the railroads with $1.4 billion. From the sale and other uses of their piece of the United States the railroads earned profits approaching $500 million. In return the railroads carried government shipments at reduced rates. According to "Public Aid to Transportation," a study published in 1940, land grants saved the federal government $168 million.[113] Yet, an authority on the land grants concludes, "[t]he inescapable fact remains that the generation which witnessed the operation of the land grants considered that the evils outweighed the benefits."[114]

The evils convened in the person of Jay Gould, who, speaking from the rear of his private car, could threaten the citizens of Columbus, Nebraska: Buy bonds in my railroad or grass will grow in your streets. Sometimes towns voted such bonds only to have the railroad run one train to them, collect the bonds, and never be heard from again. The evils went beyond bullying and bilking to encompass corruption. "To what extent," a land historian asks, "was the long prostitution of representative government to the railroads attributable to the land-grant policy?" Traveling to state party conventions or yearly meetings of cattlemen and farmers' associations on free passes, "The leaders of the people fed at the crib of the railroads, hence were favorable to them, making corrective legislation well-nigh impossible."

Revulsion over the handing over of the public domain to railroads, lumber, cattle, and mining interests helped elect Cleveland in 1884.[115] He appointed an energetic reformer as land commissioner; and in his first report to Congress, William Andrew Jackson Sparks sounded like Old Hickory flaying the "Monster Bank."

"The widespread belief of the people of this country that the Land Department has been very largely conducted to the advantage of speculation and monopoly, rather than in the public interest," Sparks wrote, "I have found supported by developments in every branch of the service."[116] The eighty-one federal and state railroad land grants not only left less desirable land for settlers. Many were "forced . . . to buy their homes of railroad companies or suffer eviction" if they stood in the path of rights-of-way that could shift as much as one hundred miles on either side of the original proposed line as surveyors encountered topographical obstacles.[117] Lines of "probable," "generally designated," and "definite" routes cross-hatched the map until, according to Sparks's boss, Secretary of the Interior L.Q.C. Lamar, "a settler seeking a home could scarcely find a desirable location that was not claimed by some, or perhaps two or three" roads.[118] If the "legal right of settlers . . . was cruelly denied" by land office and court rulings in favor of railroads, the inharmonious policy objectives enshrined in the laws were more culpable than their corrupt administration.

Corruption, Sparks's agents discovered, abounded in the other federal land programs. In the Dakota Territory, Nebraska, and Kansas, one of Sparks's agents reported, cattlemen used fraudulent entries under the Timber Culture Act of 1873, which made grants of land contingent on planting trees, to usurp "the best lands and practically all the waters" and dominate "entire townships."[119] They grazed cattle on public land, and bought off settlers who dared to file claims on such illegal annexations, or scared them off with "parties of armed men."[120] Though 4,300 homestead and preemption claims were recorded in Duluth, Minnesota, fewer than one hundred settlers lived in the area. "I have yet to find *one* person," the Duluth agent wrote Sparks, "who is making a farm or trying to make a farm."[121] The settlers had signed over their land to lumber companies. Citing estimates that 95 percent of preemption claims in California and 75 percent of those in Dakota and the Osage strip of Kansas were fraudulent, Sparks concluded, "The commutation feature of the law has undermined the homestead system."[122] Sparks called for an end to the sale of public lands, but before Congress could act a saturnalia of buying closed out history's greatest transfer of public wealth to private hands.[123]

The government had traded land for railroads, and the railroads peopled the land. The Burlington road alone spent $1 million on advertising to attract prospective settlers and the Union Pacific nearly as much on Nebraska. Railway agents in Europe placed brochures in the steerage compartments of transatlantic steamers. People like you are "living almost in affluence on their prairie farms," the copy informed prospective farmers in their native languages. Males so greatly outnumbered females in the West, a pamphlet intended for a domestic audience noted, that "when a daughter of the East is once beyond the Missouri she rarely re-crosses it except on a bridal tour."[124] A "chromatic triumph of lithographed mendacity" drew future Kansas senator John J. Ingalls from New England to Sumner, Kansas, a congeries of huts on footpaths depicted as avenues lined with churches, schools, libraries, and a university on the "engraved romance." About Dakota boosters an eastern investor complained, "[E]very townsite was a city, every creek a river, every crop a bonanza, every breeze a zephyr, and every man a damned liar."[125]

The people came: native-born and immigrants, merchants and lawyers (more on the frontier than members of any other profession).[126] And, most numerous of all, farmers and farm workers displaced by western crop yields. The scale and scope economies realized by the first waves reduced commodity prices in the nationalizing marketplace, sending more farmers west on a stream of failure and hope that rose in New England and New York State and flowed into the Ohio Valley, eventually reaching yesterday's west: Illinois, Wisconsin, Iowa. Altogether, between 1860 and 1900, 6 million people joined that stream. They came to North Dakota: population 2,405 in 1870 and 182,000 in 1890; to Nebraska: 17,000 to 719,000; to Kansas, which grew by 500,000 in the 1880s alone. They came all at once to Oklahoma—in twenty hours on April 22, 1884, 100,000 homesteaders rushed into the territory; by nightfall Oklahoma City had a population of 10,000.[127] Most sought more economic independence than they had known at home; few found it. "It must be remembered that monopolistic control was infinitely more potent in the West, in those days, than in the East," Gifford Pinchot recalled. "The big fellow had control of the little fellow to an infinitely greater extent west of the Father of Waters than east of it."[128] The big fellow not only included the cattleman, the lumberman, the banker, and the loan shark, but the bureaucrat. "In some basic way," Richard White writes, "the federal government created itself in the West."[129] The U.S. Geological Survey, the Bureau of Indian Affairs, the Land Office, and other agencies of the Interior Department with regulatory and administrative responsibilities for economic life pioneered the bureaucratic state. And, in some basic way, from land and loans for the railroads that opened the region to economic exploitation to land-grant colleges that trained the engineers who mined its natural resources, the federal government created the West.

Not just interests and officials, but *forces* ruled in the West. Nature, its caprices magnified, could decide a farmer's fate—but so could the prices set by a grain market that tapped Australia, India, Russia, Algeria, and Argentina.

The east–west flow of people was subject to eddies of reversal by biblical disasters like the grasshopper plague of 1874. Attracted by bountiful crops, grasshoppers ravaged the plains from Dakota to Texas. They arrived in Nebraska on a sunny day in late July. A Buffalo County family, sitting down for dinner, thought a cloud had produced the sudden dark until a boy fetching water from the well shouted "Grasshoppers!" and they struck the roof like hail and crashed against the walls. The grasshoppers stayed up to a week, or until "Every green thing except castor beans, cane, and the leaves of certain trees, was eaten."[130] They ate fence posts, tool handles, clothing. Piling up four to six inches deep, they broke tree limbs. Trains, unable to gain traction on their squish, stopped. Their droppings fouled wells. For months the water, the chicken, the pork tasted of grasshopper. Families who lost their stores to the grasshoppers survived that winter only through government- and charity-provided relief—food, clothing, blankets, shoes, as well as seeds to plant the new crop. Those who had the money to leave left, and the flow of immigration stopped.[131]

Few died of grasshoppers, but prairie fires carried by the wind could kill a man caught in the open. They killed animals and razed towns. "The sky is pierced with tall pyramids of flame, or covered with writhing, leaping, lurid serpents," a witness recorded. "Now a whole avalanche of fire slides off into the prairie, and then opening its great devouring jaws closes in upon the deadened grass."[132] On Theodore Roosevelt's North Dakota ranch the cowboys cut a steer in two and riders dragged the two halves, bloody sides down, along the line of fire, "men following on foot with slickers and wet horse-blankets to beat out any flickering blaze that was left."[133] That worked on short grass. Elsewhere fires, locustlike, tended to burn out only after consuming all possible fuel. Fortunately, the sod house, dark, leaky, prone to shed on the family meal, was not combustible.[134]

Blizzards were the worst killers. The blizzard of '88 is known as the "schoolchildren's storm" because, while the day began warm, by the time the children started for home the temperature had fallen forty degrees and the wind, blowing the snow in blinding horizontal sheets, whipped up to nearly sixty miles an hour. Despite the desperate efforts of their heroic teachers, some children never reached home. Some parents died searching for them. In Dakota a husband and his wife died while searching for each other in "their own dooryard." The blizzard of '86 killed 60 percent of the cattle in Montana. T.R. wintered in New York, but when he returned to his ranch in the spring and surveyed his dead cattle, like Winston Churchill's uncle and other émigré owners, he gave up ranching. "The winter of '86 was the end of all but a few of the giant investor-owned ranches," Ian Frazier writes. "It was also the end of people coming to the Great Plains in any numbers from far away for the sake of adventure or fun."[135] The blizzards gorged the rivers with ice, and when it melted floods swept the valleys of crops, animals, and buildings.

Next to drought as "a menace to populating the plains" ranked fear of the Indian.[136] For the most part Native Americans had been pushed onto reservations, where the reform policy was "kill the Indian"—destroy his culture, language, and tribal identity—to "save the man."[137] Some Indians resisted salvation. Atrocity stories triggered panics in the settled areas, where Indians were, at worst, irritants—begging for food and whiskey, stealing tobacco, scaring housewives by peering through cabin windows. In 1864, for example, reports of a Sioux massacre in eastern Colorado drove Colorado settlers into Denver and emptied Buffalo County into Omaha. State and territorial officials tried to minimize the damage to immigration, but could not contain rumors and sensational news. Indian panics made settlers give up and kept others from taking their place.[138]

Economic independence on the farm rested on the farmer's ability to feed his family; that secured, he need truckle to no man, and could enter or leave the market as he wished. After 1850, with costs, land values, and taxes rising, farmers could no longer afford sustenance farming. To eat, they had to produce for the market. "Now the object of farming is not primarily to make a living, but it is to make money," the *Cornell Countryman* editorialized in 1904. "To this end it is to be conducted on the same business basis as any other producing industry."[139] Until surpassed by manufacturing and mining in 1880, farming was the nation's leading industry. Aggregately, it boomed. Wheat production multiplied from 152 million bushels in 1866 to 675 million in 1898; corn from 730 million bushels to 2.33 billion; cotton from nothing to 4 billion pounds.[140] Two hundred twenty-five million acres of new land spread over nearly 4 million new farms produced this abundance.[141] New principles borrowed from manufacture enhanced it. "The old rule that a farmer should produce all that he required and that the surplus represented his gains is part of the past," the *Chicago Prairie Farmer* observed in 1867. "Agriculture, like all other business, is better for its subdivisions, each one growing that which is best suited to his soil, climate, and market, and with its proceeds purchase his other needs."[142] New tools harvested it. By hand, shelling a bushel of corn took nearly two hours; with a "steam sheller," less than two minutes. A combine cut the task of reaping, binding, and threshing a bushel of wheat from an hour and a half to four minutes. Investment in farm machinery, $6.8 million in 1850, totaled $101 million in 1900.[143] Manpower was saved; and money. For a basket of twenty-seven crops surveyed by the census in 1900, production costs had fallen 46 percent since 1850. These years witnessed "an unparalleled advance in the economic well-being of Americans engaged in farming," say the authors of *The Evolution of the American Economy,* a statistical claim abstracted from history but one that helps explain why more farmers did not join the "Agrarian Revolt" of the 1890s.[144]

America's cornucopia spilled over onto the world. From 1870 to 1892 wheat exports grew fourfold; by 1900 one-quarter of U.S. farm output went abroad.[145] As farm sizes grew, American farmers realized economies of scale unmatchable in Europe, excluding Russia, the chief competitor to the U.S. granary. Thanks to American imports Europeans paid less for food but, as with goods imported into the United States from China today, what consumers gained domestic producers lost. With wheat prices on the continent falling 30 percent and land values collapsing, "many European farmers were ruined and pressed down into the status of agricultural laborers," Carl Degler observes.[146] Between 1860 and 1900, Berlin tripled in population as displaced rural people migrated to the city.[147] Others "sought relief by flight to El Dorado itself, the source of their misery."[148]

Still others protested. "Almost everywhere, certainly in England, France, Germany, Italy, Scandinavia, and the United States," the *London Spectator* observed, "the agriculturalists, formerly so instinctively conservative, declare that they have gained less by [industrial] civilization than the rest of the community, and are looking about for remedies of a drastic nature."[149] An English writer blamed "the American railroad" for the "revolution in the food supply of European countries."[150] An Austrian minister called the flood of American grain "the greatest economic event of modern times."[151]

The source of the flood, America's farmers, felt like it was sweeping *them* away. They were early casualties of the productivity revolution. When, in 1798, Thomas Malthus prognosticated that population would outrun the food supply, one farmer could feed ten people; in 1898 one South Dakota wheat farmer could feed 120.[152] Censuring the "uncalled for expansion" of agriculture promoted by government policies that "let a man have a farm for a sou," *The Nation* stated the new problem of abundance: "The capacities to produce food stuffs [have] greatly outstripped the capacities to consume them."[153] There were too many farmers, *The Country Gentleman* declared in an 1890 editorial, "No More 'Development' Wanted," which noted "the strong and deep feeling that it is now quite time for the entire stoppage of the selling and giving away of the national domain."[154] American agriculture had entered the zero-sum world of overproduction from which it has not emerged.

The same forces that, between the 1870s and the 1890s, drove down the price of a seven-cottage, 639-acre British farm from $100,000 to $28,500 also littered Massachusetts towns with 1,500 abandoned farms and reduced land values in Ohio by as much as 50 percent.[155] Commodity prices plummeted as sharply. Wheat sold at 29 percent less a bushel in 1900 than in 1860, corn 25 percent less.[156] During the 1880s alone cotton fell 26 percent, wool 30 percent, barley 20 percent. Cotton costing 6 or 7 cents a pound to produce sold for 4 or 5 cents; "fifty-cent wheat," for 25 cents.[157] Volume production, farmers concluded, was the only way to survive such price deflation. The siren of expansion tempted many onto the rocks of mortgaged debt, which increased 71 percent in fifteen years.[158] Terms were demanding—payment in full within three years—and foreclosures frequent. Freeholders slipped down the ladder to tenants; tenants to farm laborers; farm laborers to migrant workers.[159] The finding of the 1880 census that a fourth of all farmers were tenants disturbed Congress and led to Commissioner Sparks's report on the reasons why. By 1890 a majority of farmers farmed mortgaged land, or rented.[160]

On the bottom rung of the western agricultural ladder stood the farm laborer, as unexpected on the farm of ideality as the speculator on its frontier. To be sure, the "hired man" had been a fixture of farm life for generations; he ate with the family, had a place in the community. But mechanization allowed farm families to dispense with his services. In 1891 a Massachusetts farmer found evidence of his passing in farmers' help-wanted ads: "The old-fashioned term, 'help,' has been dropped, and the word 'labor' used with a peculiar significance."[161] As farmers specialized to realize economies of scale, they needed seasonal, not permanent, labor; and as western farms expanded—farms of 500 or more acres increased 43 percent between 1880 and 1900—they required quantities of seasonal labor.[162] A mass workforce was needed to produce for a mass market consuming 213 million cans of tomatoes by 1900.[163] The "Bonanza" wheat farms of North Dakota's Red River Valley, developed by bondholders of the Northern Pacific Railroad after its failure, employed as many as 1,000 laborers, city boys hauled out by the flatcar from Detroit and Chicago and professional harvesters who followed the growing season up from Tennessee, operating crop binders pulled by 800 horses.[164] "Wage labor un-Americanizes them," a Dakota farmer said of migrant laborers. Rather than factory workers, the factory had come to the farm.[165]

And child labor followed. With the development, in 1888, of a refrigerated railroad car able to keep fruits and vegetables fresh over transcontinental distances, the Imperial Valley of California employed a mass seasonal labor force first of Anglo, then of Japanese, and finally of Mexican laborers. And, "Wherever there were berries, fruit, or vegetables to pick," the agricultural historian La Wanda Cox writes, "women and children were employed."[166] These were farm families without farms, and no prospect of getting them. As a Department of Agriculture official noted, "There are a great many men who start on the farm and are good workers and continue to be farm hands all their lives."[167] Although their purchasing power had increased, the average wage of farm laborers in 1900, $13.90, was lower than it had been in 1860. In the Midwest nearly four in ten people who derived their livings from agriculture were laborers, and nearly three out of four, when a pound of beefsteak cost 15 cents, earned less than sustenance.[168] In a 1910 study of American agriculture, V. I. Lenin saw in the growth of farm labor the "principal earmark and index of capital-

ism in agriculture," a judgment one economic historian terms "substantially correct for its time" and about "the underlying forces."[169]

Returning to the past to escape the lowering horizon of the industrializing present, Americans had found the future. Pursuing free labor in the West, the "underlying forces" enmeshed many in wage labor. In 1860 they voted themselves a farm but they also voted themselves a railroad, and that had made all the difference. The tracks brought progress but at a price. The railroad lured the homesteader with a vision of prosperity; he went into debt to reach it, but it eluded him. For the Iowa farmer who complained that it took "one bushel of corn to pay the freight on another," prosperity was a treadmill.[170] Areas where that perception was "often . . . no exaggeration and sometimes . . . an understatement" were the strongest centers of agrarian protest.[171] Once a touchstone of republican virtue, the farmer gathered subversive associations. "The agrarian element" became a conservative fright-word, synonymous with "nihilist," the equivalent of "communist" for striking railroad workers. Farming's historic fall to number two among American industries was paralleled by the farmer's fall from the cultural pantheon. Despite his attachment to progressive causes—railroad regulation, the income tax, tariff reform—in city dwellers' eyes the farmer seemed more and more a reactionary figure; his once hallowed farm a locus of frustration and confinement; his small town a hive of bigotry, gossip, and resentment. President Theodore Roosevelt's Country Life Commission heard testimony about the pervasion of drink on the farm. "Intemperance is largely the result of the barrenness of farm life, particularly the lot of the hired man," the commissioners found. Writing in the mid-1890s a sociologist remarked the erosion advertising had made in rural contentment. Confronting daily the "impossibility" of living as well as the people pictured in the Montgomery Ward catalogue, the farmer's "embittered life . . . in many cases, destroys his mental balance."[172] At once beneficiary and victim of postwar policies and transformations, caught between competition and cooperation, rising production and falling income, conservative in ideology, increasingly radical in politics, the farmer suffered a loss of status in urbanizing America as painful to his pride as low prices to his pocket. The representative American of 1860, the farmer, in a Gilded Age coinage, had become the "hayseed" of 1890.*[173]

---

* "Among the interpretative conventions that historians would do well to reconsider is the characterization of the post–Civil War decades as a 'Gilded Age,' " Richard R. John writes. "Although the phrase was coined in 1873 by Mark Twain and Charles Dudley Warner, it was never embraced by contemporaries. . . . [L]ate nineteenth-century social commentators almost never used the phrase 'Gilded Age' to describe the period in which they were living—unlike, for example, the 'Progressive Era,' which *was* embraced by contemporaries. As it happens, the phrase 'Gilded Age' would not be popularized until the 1920s, when social critics Van Wyck Brooks and Lewis Mumford adopted it as part of a broader critique of American industrialism." Richard R. John, "Ruling Passions: Political Economy in Nineteenth-Century America," *Journal of Policy History*, vol. 18, no. 1 (2006), p. 18, n. 36.

Chapter Five

THE INVERTED CONSTITUTION

All persons born or naturalized in the United States, and subject to the jurisdiction thereof, are citizens of the United States and of the State wherein they reside. No State shall make or enforce any law which shall abridge the privileges and immunities of citizens of the United States; nor shall any State deprive any person of life, liberty, or property, without due process of law; nor deny to any person within its jurisdiction the equal protection of the laws.

—The Fourteenth Amendment, Section 1

"That these dead shall not have died in vain," Lincoln resolved at Gettysburg, death still scenting the air four months after the battle. Cleansed of slavery by their blood, the nation would experience a "new birth of freedom." Lincoln was prophetic. Constitutionally, the United States had a new founding after the Civil War, with three "Freedom Amendments" as its new charter—at last, an "Everyman's Constitution" for all "persons born or naturalized in the United States" codifying what John Hope Franklin called "one of the basic social revolutions in the history of humanity." The Congresses that passed these amendments—the Thirteenth ending slavery, the Fourteenth extending equal protection of the laws to the nearly 4 million freedmen, and the Fifteenth establishing that the right to vote shall not be "denied or abridged . . . on account of race, color, or previous condition of servitude"—knew the demobilizing Union army could not enforce them against the resistance of the South, where more than 500,000 men had served recently in the Confederate armed forces, so they looked to the federal courts to protect the rights of the freedmen. Yet, exercising its power, in Chief Justice John Marshall's words, to "say what the law is," the Supreme Court refused the part Congress assigned it. In an 1883 opinion overturning the Civil Rights Act of 1875 banning racial discrimination in public accommodations, Justice Joseph P.

Bradley voiced the Court's prevailing sentiment: "Blacks must cease to be the special favorite of the laws."[1] The laws had a new favorite. "There is nothing which is lawful to be done," Stephen J. Field, one of five justices appointed by Lincoln, wrote in a later opinion that reads like an introduction to St. Francis of Assisi, "to feed and clothe our people, to beautify and adorn our dwellings, to relieve the sick, to help the needy, and to enrich and ennoble humanity, which is not to a great extent done through the instrumentalities of corporations."[2] The new Constitution, as interpreted by the Court, applied to economic, not civil rights. The "person" whose "life, liberty, or property" the Fourteenth Amendment secured was not the freedman but the corporation. Within fifteen years of its ratification, Everyman's Constitution gave way to the "Inverted Constitution."[3]

Agreed truth rarely represents truth in its mottled grain.[4] That the Supreme Court admitted corporations to the constitutional company of "persons" is well known, even if few recall the case, *Santa Clara County v. Southern Pacific Railroad* (1886). Generations of state, federal, and Supreme Court opinions have cited *Santa Clara* as establishing that proposition, weaving it into the texture of constitutional law. Legal scholars have concurred. Here, for example, is Morton Horwitz, in his authoritative history *The Transformation of American Law*: "The *Santa Clara* case held that a corporation was a person under the Fourteenth Amendment and thus was entitled to its protection." He goes on:

> [F]or such a momentous decision, the opinion in the Santa Clara case is disquietingly brief—just one short paragraph—and totally without reasons or precedent. Indeed, it was made without argument of counsel. It declared:
>
> The court does not want to hear argument on the question whether the provision in the Fourteenth Amendment to the Constitution, which forbids a state to deny to any person within its jurisdiction the equal protection of the laws, applies to these corporations. We are all of opinion that it does.[5]

In fact those words do not appear in the *opinion*, which, at nineteen pages, is not "disquietingly brief," mentions the Fourteenth Amendment only to dismiss the railroad's claims that it was "essential to the disposition of the case," and says nothing about the corporate personhood it did not confer. Professor Horwitz has conflated the court reporter's "headnotes," a précis of the opinion, with the opinion, a technical discussion of a trivial question—whether the fences running beside the Southern Pacific's railroad tracks are "property" taxable by the state or "improvements" taxable only by the county of Santa Clara.[6] One hundred and twenty years of Court decisions citing *Santa Clara* partake of that long since mooted error. Time has washed away the political scandals of the Gilded Age—Crédit Mobilier, the Whiskey Ring, the Tweed Ring, and the rest. The scandal of *Santa Clara* remains the law of the land.

History is not a conspiracy, but historical acts often seem concerted to a pattern as if by a directing power. Hegel called it "the cunning of reason," the hidden hand that sculpts events, actions, accident, and the passions of men to the contours of inevitability, the petrifaction of what happened.[7] In the Age of Enterprise the cunning of the corporation framed a constitutional home for its subject from anything to hand: the imprisonment of a former Supreme Court justice as a suspect in Lincoln's assassination; the tragic blindness of a sitting justice who, meaning to save Reconstruction, expelled the freedman from the Constitution; and the social hysteria of a third justice who saw "anarchy" and "communism" where reality disclosed economic regulation and democracy. Anything: the *Dred Scott* decision, offal, cholera, yellow fever, a massacre in Louisiana, a revolution in France, a wave of anti-Chinese bigotry in California, even a case called "The Twenty-Two Prostitutes"—all became clay. No one present at Abraham Lincoln's inauguration on March 4, 1861, could have foreseen the finished design.

In his inaugural address Lincoln summoned the "mystic chords of memory" to restore "bonds of affection" "strained by passion." Gossamer ties were all Lincoln could appeal to by then, for between his election and inauguration, seven lower South states had seceded, snapping the bonds of the union. After Lincoln finished speaking, Chief Justice Roger B. Taney administered the oath of office.

Ten days after Taney handed down the *Dred Scott* decision, in early 1857, the Washington correspondent of the *New York Tribune* struck off an acidic portrait of Taney that the passage of four years, taking him to age eighty-four, had rendered truer: "It is a singular, but not wonderful fact in nature, that the body to some extent intimates the character of the soul that inhabits it. That is the case with Judge Taney. He walks with inverted and hesitating steps. His forehead is contracted, his eye sunken and his visage has a sinister expression." A reporter watching the ceremony on the East

Portico of the Capitol noted that, as he took the new president's hand, Taney's hand "shook very perceptibly with emotion." That betrayed more than an old man's tremor. Lincoln's election repudiated *Dred Scott*—and the authority of the Taney Court.[8]

In his 1858 debates with Stephen Douglas, Lincoln had posited a conspiracy among "Stephen and Franklin and Roger and James" (Stephen Douglas, Franklin Pierce, Taney, and James Buchanan) to extend slavery into the territories and beyond. With the Kansas-Nebraska Act Douglas and Pierce had overthrown the Missouri Compromise's ban on slavery north of the line 36 degrees 30 minutes.[9] But a future Congress could repeal that act. It remained to rule the ban unconstitutional, which was where Roger and James came in.

Four years to the hour before Taney swore in Lincoln, he and Buchanan had exchanged whispers on the inaugural platform. Then, in his inaugural address, Buchanan had hinted at an imminent Court resolution of the question that had polarized the nation since the war with Mexico— whether slavery should be extended to the territories annexed in the war and acquired through the Louisiana Purchase. Taney, William Seward charged, gave the president advance word on *Dred Scott* two days before handing down the decision. In fact the "conspiracy" entailed more than these "whisperings," Seward's word for them. Buchanan pressured Robert Grier, a fellow Pennsylvanian, to give Taney the northern justice he needed to put a national face on the decision. In the "House Divided" speech opening his Senate campaign, Lincoln said nothing could stop the conspiracy from extending slavery to the free states—except the people.[10]

Speaking in Cincinnati, Lincoln invoked the people's right to "overthrow" not the Constitution, "but the men who would pervert the Constitution." He meant Roger B. Taney and the six other Supreme Court justices, one described as "a brooding pro-slavery fanatic" and three others as "unreserved defenders of slavery" voting with him on *Dred Scott*. Distorting the Framers' views, they denied citizenship to the Negro—in Taney's words, blacks possessed "no rights that the white man was bound to respect"—even though black men in five free states could vote when the Framers drafted the Constitution.[11] The justices perverted the Constitution by holding that Congress could not prohibit slavery in the territories, even though Article IV, Section 3 assigned that power to it. Under the proscenium of the Senate campaign, Lincoln used *Dred Scott* to separate northern Democrats like Douglas, who championed "popular sovereignty," the right of the people of the territories to decide whether they should be slave or free themselves, from southern Democrats, for whom *Dred Scott* required the territories to accept slavery no matter what their people decided. Lincoln's forensic surgery on the Democrats helped him win the Republican nomination in 1860.

Sitting on one of the Senate's red leather armchairs carried out to the platform erected for the ceremony, Taney may have sensed posterity's contempt when Lincoln, in his inaugural address, touched on the lesson of *Dred Scott*. While the Court's rulings should be respected, "[a]t the same time, the candid citizen must confess that if the policy of the Government is to be irrevocably fixed by the decisions of the Supreme Court . . . the people will cease to be their own rulers, having to that extent practically resigned their Government into the hands of that eminent tribunal."

If Lincoln thought his election would end the unelected branch's usurpation of the people's role, he was mistaken. Taney died in 1864. ("The Hon. Roger B. Taney has earned the gratitude of his country by dying at last," George Templeton Strong, the Samuel Pepys of the Gilded Age, wrote in his diary, reflecting northern opinion, which blamed the war on *Dred Scott*.) But Taneyism lived. Lincoln appointed four justices and, on Taney's death, a new chief justice to the court; and the "candid citizen" could as justly lodge Lincoln's complaint against the Taney Court against the postwar Republican court. Taneyism lived in its opinions and rulings limiting government's power to regulate business under a doctrine adumbrated in *Dred Scott* and based on the postwar amendment to the Constitution that repealed the decision. Taneyism lived, too, in rulings on civil rights for the freed slaves, white property no longer and so exposed to white violence as never before, now sentenced to the American South.[12]

How could justices appointed by the party of Emancipation abandon the emancipated? How could men zealous to defend the economic rights of railroad corporations refuse to defend the civil rights of freedmen? "Stronger evidence of national failure, inertia, and inversion," the archaeologist of the Fourteenth Amendment, Howard Jay Graham, writes, "more striking evidence of judicial bias and historical error, could hardly be found or imagined."[13] The Court that constitutionalized segregation in *Plessy v. Ferguson* (1896) also exempted manufacturing corporations from prosecution under the Sherman Antitrust Act while sanctioning it for labor unions. On civil rights, "separate but equal" stood until struck down by the Warren Court in the 1950s and 1960s. On economic rights, "laissez-faire constitutionalism" ruled from 1890 to 1937, and ended then only because Franklin D. Roosevelt threatened to pack the Court to save the New Deal from justices who had ruled much of it unconstitutional and were preparing to strike down the Wagner Act's protection of labor rights as a violation of the Fourteenth Amendment rights of corporations.[14] Like Macbeth his destiny, the law's future could be "seen in the instant" one weekend in 1873.

In the white cemetery of Colfax, Louisiana, above the headstones, stands a marble obelisk bearing this inscription:

> IN LOVING REMEMBRANCE
> ERECTED TO THE MEMORY OF
> THE HEROES
> STEPHEN DECATUR PARISH
> JAMES WEST HADNOT
> SIDNEY HARRIS
> WHO FELL IN THE COLFAX
> RIOT FIGHTING FOR
> WHITE SUPREMACY
> APRIL 13, 1873[15]

Accounts differ on the details but the inscription captures the bottom truth of that day in Colfax, a village on the high east bank of the Red River, 225 miles northwest of New Orleans. White supremacy was the cause for which more than 200 whites, Ku Klux Klansmen among them, shot, bayoneted, and burned to death "at least" 105 African-Americans.[16]

The Colfax Massacre ranks with the bloodiest acts of terrorism—of political violence—in our history. White Democrats and Republicans of both races claimed victory in the November 1872 Louisiana state elections. The outgoing governor, Henry Clay Warmoth, started out as a Republican committed to biracial government but, pandering to white resistance to Reconstruction, fused his wing of the party with the all-white Conservatives, the name postwar southern Democrats adopted to differentiate them from Radical Republicans. Warmoth controlled the election machinery, and his returning board, the official vote counters, declared the Conservative-Democratic candidate for governor, a Confederate veteran named John D. McEnery, the winner by 8,000 votes. The Republicans, refusing to accept the official count, claimed they would have won if 10,000 blacks had not been denied ballots on election day. A Republican-appointed federal judge declared the Republican William Pitt Kellogg, an Illinois "carpetbagger" and one of Louisiana's United States senators, the winner.[17] The Democrats refused to concede. Mounting a coup on behalf of the Republicans, President Grant ordered federal troops to seize the New Orleans statehouse to prevent them from taking power. Criticized in the North for interfering in a state election, Grant reversed himself a month later, refusing to send troops to disperse the Democrats meeting elsewhere in the city to set up *their* legislature and install their governor. Louisiana had two governments.

Across the state the parties mobilized their supporters to seize power in their localities. Violence spread outward from New Orleans. Colfax saw the worst. Named for Grant's vice president Schuyler Colfax and the county seat of the recently created Grant Parish in the state's Black Belt, Colfax consisted of a few plantation buildings—its courthouse was a converted stable. In January the Democrats installed their candidates for sheriff and county judge. In late March, on the authority of the Republican governor, Republican officials steamed upriver from New Orleans to dislodge the opposition from the Colfax courthouse. Helped by a black boy, who climbed through a window and unlatched the door, the Republican sheriff and judge got inside and evicted the Democrats, who fled Colfax. After hearing rumors that the Democrats wanted them hung, these white Republicans deputized local blacks to defend the government they had elected. While three black ex-Union soldiers drilled the deputies, bands of whites menaced the village, and shots were traded. "Nobody died in these exchanges (the only injury reported was that a white man had had his thumb shot off)," Nicholas Lemann writes in his searing book *Redemption: The Last Battle of the Civil War* (2006), "but the effect on the whites of encountering successful black armed self-defense, a thing constantly feared through centuries of slavery but hardly ever realized, would be hard to overstate." In early April, just outside Colfax, a black farmer fencing his property was shot through the head. At word of Jesse McKinney's murder, black families fled to Colfax for safety.[18]

On the thirteenth, "a very considerable" force of white men in military formation, towing a small cannon, and led by Columbus Nash, the Democratic sheriff, descended on Colfax. The white Republican judge had gone to New Orleans for help. The white sheriff stayed in Colfax, but "as soon as he saw the fight was impending he left and got out of the way,"

Henry C. Beckwith, the U.S. attorney for New Orleans, told a congressional committee later that year, adding: "I believe there was a schoolteacher, a white man, at or about the courthouse . . . but he left and got out of the way; so that at the time the attack was made there was no person in the crowd around the courthouse . . . that [was] not colored. The negroes were there relying solely upon their own strength for protection." Perhaps half were armed, a few with Enfield rifles, the rest with shotguns. In a parley with Levin Allen, one of the former soldiers in charge at the courthouse, Nash demanded, Surrender your arms and disperse. Allen refused. "We are goin' to get 'em," Nash said. "I'll see you when you get 'em," Allen replied. He was given a half-hour to evacuate the women and children. Just past noon Nash's men deployed in a skirmish line and, from beyond the range of the defenders' shotguns, opened rifle fire on the low earthworks the blacks had thrown up in front of the courthouse.[19]

The two-and-a-half-inch-bore cannon decided the battle. The whites flanked the earthworks with the cannon and raked the line of black defenders with hot iron shards. The line broke, some of the blacks falling back on the courthouse, others retreating toward the riverbank. Whites on horseback pursued them and, as Beckwith put it in his testimony, "slaughtered all within their reach." The whites told a prisoner, Pinckney Chambers, they would spare his life if he set fire to the courthouse roof. With both sides shooting over him, he worked his way up to the courthouse and, "using a bundle of fodder tied to a long pole," fired the roof. Some of the men inside tried to knock the burning shingles free, but bullets drove them to cover. Soon, the fiery roof collapsed onto the ceiling above the defenders. Men on fire began leaping from the windows. With minutes to go before the fire consumed them all, one man flapped the white page of a record book, another a patch of white sleeve, to signify surrender. Come out, we won't shoot, the whites shouted. The blacks came out in waves and were shot down, and the wounded were bayoneted and their bodies hacked with knives. The whites marched the survivors into a nearby cotton field. The battle over, the massacre was about to begin.*

---

* The Colfax cannon added a new weapon to the armory of southern Redemption, the drive by white Democrats to restore white supremacy. In the Mississippi elections of 1874, as a federal district attorney informed the attorney general, cannon fire, supplementing murder and ballot stuffing, helped disfranchise blacks: "Cannon were purchased and used [prior to the election] as the *loudest argument*. In Lowndes, Colfax, and Monroe cannon fired day and night, were carried to different places in the country where there was to be

That night, forty-seven prisoners "were called by name, two at a time, and taken out into the road that ran through the plantation and past the ruins of the court-house, and several white men, mounted, formed behind them," in Beckwith's words. Benjamin Brinn, an old man who had played dead to escape the fusillade at the courthouse door, stood toward the rear of the line. He heard gunfire. The whites were shooting their way up the line, putting a bullet in the back of each black head. "The firing had reached back near to his vicinity when he heard a pistol cocked, and as he turned around to beg for his life, the man behind him shot him." Once again he played dead as Sheriff Nash's men emptied their revolvers on his comrades. The bullet went in under Brinn's left eye, flooding his sinus cavities with blood. Gagging, unable to breathe, he blew it out. Dead men don't make noise. "This nigger ain't dead yet," a white man on horseback shouted and shot Brinn in the back.

It started to rain, and the whites sought shelter. Thus ended what Eric Foner has called "the bloodiest single act of carnage in all of Reconstruction." It was Easter Sunday.[20]

When the deputy U.S. marshal arrived from New Orleans on Tuesday morning, he counted fifty-nine bodies, many mutilated, others burned beyond human trace.

Early on Monday morning, Brinn inched to a nearby ditch. Covering himself with weeds, he bled through the day, listening as crowds of whites "plunder[ed] the dead of all that was on them."[21]

While Brinn fought off death in a Colfax ditch, that same morning in Washington the Supreme Court handed down a tragic decision that would deny justice to the Colfax dead. The case before the Court arose from the actions of a Louisiana corporation—a slaughterhouse.

"Offal": In nineteenth-century novels that genteelism defeats imagination. The reader doesn't get the picture. He doesn't see "intestines and portions of putrefied animal matter lodged around [the drinking pipes] . . . being sucked into the reservoir," as New Orleans residents did when the tide fell on the Mississippi. Offal—animal entrails, dung, urine, and blood—laced

public speaking, or gatherings, and often fired on route. The effect of this kind of *argument* on the colored voters . . . who are naturally peaceable, timid, and cowardly as the result of slavery can be more readily imagined than understood." C. Peter McGrath, *Morrison R. Waite: The Triumph of Character* (New York: Macmillan, 1963), pp. 113–14.

their drinking water. Though they did not know and medical opinion only suspected it, offal bred "plague"—cholera—and the mosquitoes feeding on it spread yellow fever. Between 1832 and 1869 cholera struck New Orleans eleven times. Yellow fever epidemics killed thousands every year of the 1850s—a tenth of the city's population in 1853. Dr. Edward H. Barton, an ignored voice for sanitary reform, called his city "a great Golgatha"; outsiders knew it as "America's Necropolis." Wealthy residents decamped in the summer, leaving the annual *danse macabre* to "the ignorant and dissolute poor," to Negroes auctioned at its infamous slave market, and to luckless visitors—local lore deemed yellow fever "a stranger's disease" to which their "seasoning" rendered natives immune.

The history of public health in New Orleans constituted "one long, disgusting story of stagnant drainage, foul sewerage, environing swamps, ill and unpaved streets . . . and filth, endless filth every where," a postwar investigator wrote. The "filth"—offal—floated down the Mississippi from abattoirs, located a mile and a half upstream from the two intake pipes that took in the city's water supply, where a thousand butchers gutted over 300,000 animals every year. During the Federal occupation of New Orleans, as part of a campaign to protect unseasoned Yankee soldiers from plague, the upriver slaughterhouses were closed—and, between 1862 and 1865, only one or two cases of cholera were reported. As soon, however, as the occupation ended, the slaughterhouses began disgorging offal again, and the plague returned, killing 3,000 in 1867.

They died miserably. Cholera, a comma-shaped bacterium still ranked as one of the "top ten" scourges in the world by the World Health Organization, is, the medical historian Howard Markel writes, "one of the most feared (and disgusting) killers known." The toxin "unleashes a veritable Niagara of foul-smelling, mucous-flecked, watery diarrhea. . . . [N]ineteenth century physicians who did not yet have access to modern means of intravenous fluid replacement simply placed their patients on a 'cholera bed,' a canvas cot with a hole cut out in the center and a large bucket directly below it. The clear expectation of these doctors was that the patient would soon die of dehydration." Death often came within hours of swallowing cholera-bearing water.

New Orleans could not close the slaughterhouses and get its meat elsewhere. Hoping (in vain) to recoup its prewar pre-Chicago standing as "the beef capital of the United States," the city sought to exploit its proximity to Texas, its plains thick with 5 million steers kept off northern dinner tables by the war and "dying for want of a market" that would pay as much as $86 a head for cattle bought in Texas for as little $2. Offal was an externality of an industry thought vital to the city's prosperity.[22]

A New Orleans grand jury, investigating the link between offal and disease, recommended that the slaughterhouses be moved south of the city, but since many lay beyond the city limits it lacked jurisdiction over them. So New Orleans appealed to the state legislature, the first elected by the votes of freedmen and with one of the highest percentages of blacks (thirty-five out of 101 in the House; seven out of thirty in the Senate) among its members of any Reconstruction legislature.[23] Generations of anti-Reconstruction historians caricatured it as an assembly of vulpine Yankee carpetbaggers and illiterate freedmen, and the slaughterhouse statute as a "corrupt job," the product of bribes paid out by "the seventeen," a cabal of landowners who stood to gain from it.[24] "The fundamental underpinning of this interpretation," Eric Foner writes of this school's verdict on "negro governments" like Louisiana's, "was, to quote one member of [it], 'negro incapacity.' "[25] Since the civil rights movement pushed through the "Second Reconstruction" in the 1960s, historians have fumigated the magnolia narrative of Reconstruction, exposing the race-inflected evidence for its racist conclusions, and revised the reputation of "Negro governments." In a 1991 book, Herbert Hovenkamp challenged the received portrait of the Louisiana legislature. Conceding "lobbying," he found no "credible evidence" of bribery in the litigation surrounding the *Slaughter-House Cases,* and termed the statute "a work of great genius."[26]

"An Act to Protect the Health of the City of New Orleans, and to Locate the Stock Landings and Slaughter Houses" belonged to the national movement of sanitary reform begun by New York City in 1866, when the board of health confined butchers to a central slaughterhouse below Fortieth Street, helping eradicate cholera in the city. San Francisco, Boston, Milwaukee, and Philadelphia adopted similar measures.[27] Following the New York model, the Louisiana statute chartered a private corporation, the Crescent City Live-Stock Landing and Slaughter-House Company, to build and run a "Grand Slaughterhouse" at the southern edge of the city and on the opposite bank of the Mississippi. The statute gave Crescent City exclusive rights not to slaughter beef itself but to rent space to the city's butchers for a period of twenty-five years, required government inspection of meat, and ordered the slaughterhouses north of the city to be shut down. The butchers displaced could continue to practice their trade in the new facility by paying modest storage and slaughtering fees. Crescent City was a franchise corporation. Presiding over an economy recovering from four years of war and facing white tax resistance, the Louisiana legislature could not raise the revenue to build or rebuild needed infrastructure, so it chartered corporations to construct a new waterworks, repair the levees along the Mississippi, clean the city's privies—and to build and operate a central slaughterhouse. That northerners invested in these enterprises, though by no means exclusively, and that they provided jobs to blacks won them few local friends. The Grand Slaughterhouse opened an industry dominated by a clique of Gascon butchers to freedmen who had learned butchering as slaves. In past years the Gascon butchers drove black competitors out of their business with violence. This time they used the law. Joined 400 strong in the Butcher's Benevolent Association, they sued to stop Crescent City from engrossing the meat business.[28]

The butchers had long befouled the city, and conspired to keep meat prices high. "But admitting the butchers may have practiced a monopoly," the *New Orleans Bee* editorialized, "you do not destroy a monopoly by setting up another as bad or worse. . . . The butchers are not only fighting their own battle, they are fighting the battle of the community." That battle advanced a wider war to roll back laws "of no more binding force than if they bore the seal of a Haytian Congress of human apes" making it a crime to exclude blacks from public accommodations and integrating Louisiana's schools.[29] Not the butchers' lost business or the $40,000 they had raised to pay counsel, but the lost honor of white Louisiana drew to the butchers' cause a former candidate for governor, a later state chief justice, and John A. Campbell, a U.S. Supreme Court justice from 1853 to 1861.[30] An Alabama lawyer said to possess "tremendous intellectual power," Campbell had written a concurring opinion in *Dred Scott,* and if he could discredit a potentially popular public health measure of a government that included a black lieutenant governor, treasurer, secretary of state, and superintendent of public education he might do as much for white supremacy in the New South as he had done for slavery in the Old.[31]

In 1869 John A. Campbell was a bitter man with a lot to be bitter about. He had had a bad war. He participated in misbegotten schemes to head it off and end it prematurely; both failed; both tarnished his reputation. Eager to be known as a peacemaker, he was made a fool of peace by William Seward, Abraham Lincoln, and Jefferson Davis. His trial of pride began in the secession spring of 1861.

In early March the new rebel government in Montgomery, Alabama, sent three commissioners to Washington to seek diplomatic recognition for the Confederacy and to assure Lincoln that the South would fight only if the North "tried to exercise the erstwhile power of the Federal government within the Confederate states."[32] As the southern states left the Union beginning in late December, they commandeered the federal property—post offices, customs houses, arsenals, and forts—within their reach. By March only Fort Pickens in Pensacola and Fort Sumter in Charleston remained in Federal hands. Negotiating the peaceful transfer of the two forts was part of the Confederate commissioners' brief.[33]

Since the commissioners represented a government he would not recognize, Lincoln refused to meet with them. By some accounts he forbade William Seward, his secretary of state, to contact them; others say Seward merely kept Lincoln in the dark as he commenced a "deep and devious game."[34]

Abandon Sumter, he advised Lincoln. That placatory gesture would reawaken Unionist sentiment in the states of the upper South that had not yet seceded and in border states like Virginia, then debating secession. Seward was a giant first of Whig then of Republican politics; Lincoln a former one-term congressman who, distracted by patronage appointments and hoarding responsibility, seemed unable to scale up his abilities to his office. After conferencing with Seward, the diplomat Charles Francis Adams reflected something of the secretary's private view when confiding to his diary, "The man is not equal to the hour." Seward wanted peace, he wanted to preserve the Union, and on the strength of correspondence from friends in the South he believed surrendering Sumter would isolate secession in the Deep South and perhaps weaken it there—but, like Secretary of State Alexander Haig on the day President Ronald Reagan was shot, he also wanted to show that, "As of now, I am in control here." So he disobeyed the man who was by opening a back channel to the Confederate commissioners.[35]

The channel ran through John A. Campbell. His walk-on role in history began with a chance meeting on Pennsylvania Avenue with Samuel Nelson, a fellow justice. Seward, Nelson told him, was anxious to slow the drift to war, would "spare no effort to maintain peace." Confederate commissioners were in Washington to arrange a peaceful separation between the sections, and if Seward met them it might offset the hard line Lincoln had taken toward the South in his inaugural and open vistas of conciliation. The commissioners had sent a formal diplomatic note to Seward asking to negotiate with him, but the secretary had not answered it. Unless he did, the justices agreed, southern opinion would force the Montgomery government to attack Sumter. They sought Seward out at the State Department, Campbell later wrote, "to enforce these views upon him."[36]

Meet with the commissioners—now, in the name of peace—the justices urged. "I wish I could do it," Campbell recalled Seward replying. "See [Postmaster General] Montgomery Blair, see [Attorney General] Bates, see Mr. Lincoln himself; I wish you would; they are all *southern* men, convince them—no there is not a member of the Cabinet who would consent to it. If Jefferson Davis had known the true state of things he would not have sent those commissioners." Then he let slip a bombshell: "[T]he evacuation of Sumter is as much as the Administration can bear."[37] Earlier that day, March 15, Lincoln had polled his cabinet on Sumter, and only two members had voted to "relieve" the fort, whose commander, Major Robert Anderson, estimated could hold out only a few weeks without supplies.[38] No decision had been taken, which was not what Seward represented to the startled justices. Why, evacuating Sumter, Campbell said, might transform the whole situation in the South, discrediting the fire-eaters' propaganda that Lincoln was bent on aggression and giving Unionists a chance to come forward and be heard. He volunteered to carry Seward's news to the commissioners. Davis he would write immediately. "What should I say to [him] on the subject of Fort Sumter?" he asked. "You may say to him," Seward replied, with what part guile and what braggadocio we can only guess, "that before that letter reaches him—how far is it to Montgomery?" "Three days," Campbell supplied. "You may say to him that before that letter reaches him, the telegraph will have informed him that Sumter will have been evacuated."[39]

Campbell was elated. Lincoln's election, he'd argued in letters to an Alabama lawyer published in Mobile, did not "afford sufficient ground for the dissolution of the Union," and the Constitution, as interpreted by the Taney Court, would check the Republicans from touching slavery in the South (like Taney, Campbell had freed his own slaves). Secession was unwarranted and unnecessary. In a January letter to his Mississippi "kinsman," L.Q.C. Lamar, Campbell said that the seizure of U.S. forts in Georgia and Alabama "seem[ed] to be dictated by the insane sentiment that the North will stand anything." He doubted whether "a cotton Confederacy would console the world for the loss of the American Union or furnish the same security to ourselves as we now have." *"Peace, peace, peace"* remained his hope—and here Seward was telling him that if his mission succeeded he "might prevent a Civil War."[40]

Seward and Campbell, the latter's biographer, Robert Saunders, Jr., shrewdly remarks, shared an "overblown perception of their importance" that blended badly with the salvific aura of their mission—leading Campbell to oversell it.[41] To Davis he expressed "perfect confidence" that Sumter would be evacuated. Thus assured, the commissioners held off issuing an ultimatum over their unanswered note. Days passed. A week. Two weeks. Nothing happened. Three times over the next sixteen days Seward told Campbell that Sumter's surrender was imminent and three times Campbell assured the commissioners of his "entire confidence" or "unabated confidence" or that he was "still confident" the fort would be evacuated. While Campbell was writing Davis, "I counsel inactivity in making demands on this government," word of ships weighing anchor in northern ports and other warlike preparations reached Montgomery, which now feared Campbell had been taken in by what one historian calls "Seward's mesmeric dissembling."[42] On the thirtieth the commissioners showed Campbell a telegram from the governor of South Carolina, Francis W. Pickens, reporting that a Lincoln emissary, Ward Hill Lamon, had recently met with him, promising to return to Charleston soon to expedite the fort's evacuation. Where was Lamon, the governor asked? And when would the evacuation take place? When Campbell showed the telegram to Seward, who may not have known that Lincoln had sent Lamon, a former law partner, to South Carolina to test Seward's hypothesis about latent southern Unionism, his coolness matched the need: Lamon could not return, the fort could not be handed over, until after the Rhode Island and Connecticut elections in two days, on April 1. Campbell showed up at Seward's office on April Fool's Day, expecting to receive a timetable for the fort's surrender. Pickens's telegram, Seward said, disturbed Lincoln; Lamon, a notorious tippler, had engaged in loose talk. Seward then wrote something on a slip of paper and handed it to Campbell. "The President," it read, "may desire to resupply Fort Sumter, but will not do so without first giving notice to Governor Pickens." When Campbell recovered his powers of speech, he asked "What does this mean? Does the president attempt to supply Fort Sumter?" Don't believe your eyes, Seward told him. "No, I think not. His ears are open to everyone, and they fill his head with schemes for its resupply. I do not think he will adopt any. There is no design to reinforce the fort." Reinforce not "resupply," a nuance lost on Campbell. Desperate to save face from his collapsing diplomacy, he clung to Seward's verbal (and deniable) avowals ignoring his written communication. "I do not doubt," he wrote Davis, "that Sumter will be evacuated shortly, without any effort to *supply* it."[43]

Shortly, a messenger from Lincoln informed Pickens that, as General

P.G.T. Beauregard wired the Confederate commissioners in Washington, "Sumter to be provisioned peaceably; otherwise, forcibly."

As rumors of an approaching Union fleet strained nerves in Charleston, the burden of decision shifted from Abraham Lincoln to Jefferson Davis. Lincoln's note, carried by the messenger, promised that the ships en route to Sumter contained provisions only, but Seward's devious game had eroded Lincoln's credibility with Davis. "Like the oral and written pledges of Mr. Seward given to Judge Campbell," he wrote after the war, "it seemed to be perfectly divested of every attribute that could make it binding and valid, in case its authors should see fit to repudiate it." Absent Seward's deceit and Campbell's credulity, Davis might have accepted Lincoln's word, and the militarily insignificant fort been allowed to stay in northern hands. In that case, the war would have begun at Fort Pickens or some other obscure place name. Instead, the Civil War began at Fort Sumter. When Davis, fearing the relief expedition masked a land-sea attack on Charleston, ordered the fort reduced, the onus for beginning the Civil War fell on the South. "The plan succeeded," Lincoln told a White House visitor after Major Anderson surrendered the battered fort. "They attacked Sumter—it fell, and thus, did more service than it otherwise could."[44]

The attack on Sumter provided a moral tonic to the Union cause. The South answered with "Seward's perfidy," which rubbed off on John A. Campbell. "[I]t scarcely seems possible now," a colleague later wrote of Campbell's folly, "to conceive of a more embarrassing, and at the same time, more humiliating, position."[45]

After Sumter was attacked, Campbell resigned from the Court. "Resigned," Mary Chestnut, the wife of a Confederate senator, wrote in her diary, "—and for a cause he is hardly more than half in sympathy with. His is one of the hardest cases."[46] Hardest, because though he put loyalty to his state above loyalty to his country, his state wanted no part of him.[47] He returned to Mobile in May—where he had practiced law, raised his children, and which he considered his home—but months of attacks by Alabama papers on his doubtful zeal for secession and imputations of treachery in the Seward debacle had made him reviled in Mobile. After threats of lynching reached him, he moved to tolerant New Orleans in July.

It would have meant something to Campbell to have seen the salute given him by Edwin Stanton, President Buchanan's attorney general and Lincoln's second secretary of war, in a letter to Buchanan: "[T]he *New York Evening Post* is very severe on Judge Campbell, and very unjustly so, for the

Judge has been as anxiously and patriotically anxious to preserve the Government as any man in the United States, and he has sacrificed more than any other Southern man, rather than yield to the Secessionists."[48]

Campbell's eventual service to the Confederacy, as assistant secretary of war, was controversial—he administered the draft—and the end of the war went worse for him than the beginning. In early February 1865, as a member of a three-man Confederate peace delegation, he met with Seward on a Union steamer in Hampton Roads, Virginia—and with Abraham Lincoln, who joined them at the last minute.[49]

How can the war be ended, the commissioners asked Lincoln? By your surrender, he replied. That ended the parley. "When the Confederate emissaries were returning to their steamer, which was to take them back to Richmond," Lincoln biographer David Donald tells us, "Seward sent a freedman in a rowboat with a basket of champagne, and the Southerners waved their handkerchiefs in acknowledgement. Speaking through a boatswain's trumpet, Seward called out: 'Keep the champagne but return the negro.' "[50]

His nemesis War had not done with John Campbell, and neither had Abraham Lincoln. In early April, with the last big fight over, Lincoln accompanied Grant's troops into Petersburg, Virginia, just hours after Robert E. Lee abandoned it. The plan was for him to return to Washington through City Point on the James River, but on April 4, having come up the James by steamer and barge, Abraham Lincoln materialized in Richmond. Holding his son Tad's hand, Lincoln walked uphill from Ricketts Landing on the James toward the Confederate White House vacated thirty-six hours earlier by Jefferson Davis. He visited Libby Prison. One reporter saw "tears pouring down his cheeks" in that infamous keep for Union prisoners of war. Mrs. George Pickett said he stopped by her townhouse to see her new baby. Black citizens got past the dozen blue-coated marines guarding him to touch Lincoln's garments—some, as incredulous as posterity to see him in Richmond, shouting "Glory Hallelujah! Come to free his children from bondage."[51] He took a glass of water on the porch of the Confederate White House, then moved into the cool parlor. Directly he sent for the highest-ranking Confederate in the capital, John A. Campbell.[52]

At Hampton Roads, Campbell had pressed the issue of reconstruction: How would the North treat the conquered South? Among other hints of leniency, Lincoln said he might consider compensating slave owners for their lost property.[53] Campbell recurred to the postwar in Richmond, asking Lincoln to adopt "a long, liberal and magnanimous policy" toward the

South. He could begin right here: Make Virginia a model for its sister states of how to rejoin the Union. Would the president allow the leading citizens of Virginia to meet to discuss "the renewal of her relations as a member of the Union?" Lincoln seemed receptive, and at a second meeting the next day, Campbell later claimed, said he wanted "the same legislature that had been 'sitting up yonder'—pointing to the Capitol—to come together and to vote to restore Virginia to the Union, and recall her soldiers from the Confederate army."[54] When, days later, Campbell published an open letter "To the People of Virginia" outlining this plan, Lincoln rejected it. Bending to Edwin Stanton's argument that recognizing a legislature still led by the secessionists who voted Virginia out of the Union would undermine Reconstruction before it began, he rescinded his call for the legislature to convene. Campbell misrepresented his views, Lincoln wrote the Federal commander in Richmond. Campbell broadcast that "I have called the insurgent Legislature of Virginia together, as the rightful Legislature of the State, when I have done no such thing." Half in the wrong and knowing it—he had "perhaps made a mistake," he privately admitted—Lincoln equivocated. "I spoke of them not as a Legislature, but as the gentlemen who have acted as the Legislature of Virginia in support of the rebellion."[55] Campbell shouldered the other half of the wrong. "There can be no question," Robert Saunders, Jr., concludes in his generally sympathetic biography, "that Campbell exceeded his authority."[56] Once again he had sought to be at the center of events, and once again he had been exposed as on the margins, the Zelig of the Civil War.

A month after Lincoln's assassination, an armed guard entered Campbell's home and, with his wife looking on, clapped him in irons hand and foot and led him away. Initially charged with distorting Lincoln's views to cloak a rebel assembly with legitimacy, he became a suspect in the "conspiracy" to assassinate Lincoln when a letter turned up that had passed through his office containing a soldier's wild offer to "rid my country of some of its deadliest enemies" and that bore the signature, "By Order, J. A. Campbell." He was held in a fort off the Georgia coast while Anne Campbell pled his case in Washington. Campbell himself wrote the new president, Andrew Johnson, from Fort Pulaski. He "did not resign to aid the rebellion," "had served the Confederacy only half-heartedly," had spoken to Davis only six times since 1862—and knew nothing of any plot to kill Lincoln.[57] Convinced that Campbell routinely stamped all correspondence to the War Department as he had the "Austin Letter," Johnson freed him in October, five months after being taken from his home at the end of a chain.[58]

Ill-used by politicians, held without trial, his pride shamed, his reputation tattered, scorned in the North, distrusted in the South, John A. Campbell, former associate justice of the Supreme Court, returned to New Orleans, confined to that city by the Republican Congress, "held as one of the selected hostages of the southern states," as he wrote Anne, explaining why he could not join her in Baltimore. Having lost over $100,000 in property during the war and without resources until he could build up his

John A. Campbell

law practice, he lived with his daughter Mary Ellen and her husband. In 1870 Mary Ellen died of yellow fever, the scourge meant to be ended by the Grand Slaughterhouse. The statute John Campbell fought all the way to the Supreme Court might have saved his daughter's life.[59]

"Hello massa; bottom rail top dis time!" exclaimed a black Union soldier on recognizing his former master in a group of military prisoners. Bottom rail top: The Civil War wrought social revolution in the South. The freed people had no firm purchase on power, no material resources—"nothing but freedom," in the words of the treasurer of the American Cotton Planters Association. But in Washington men were saying it was "the Negro's hour" with the Radical Republican Congress framing constitutional amendments to give content to his freedom and the Lincoln-appointed justices of the Supreme Court ready to protect his new rights.[60] The freed people, as well, could rely on themselves. Under the new state constitutions drawn up across the South, they could and did vote, electing two U.S. senators, sixteen black congressmen, and more than 600 state legislators during Reconstruction and forging biracial governing majorities with white Republicans.[61] Against them weighed history, the 240 years of white over black in America. Bottom rail would not stay top for long.

White masters, the conservative *New Orleans Picayune* lamented, "have been subject to the terrible humiliation of seeing hordes of their former slaves, ignorant, brutal, and savage, placed above them in the political scale, and united with hordes of carpet-bag adventurers and robbers, coming down from the North, and now clothed with the law-making power."[62] "Let every decent white man consider himself sworn," the *New Orleans Bee* intoned, "that the 'white man's flag' shall be upheld." Under that ensign the defeated white South launched a counterrevolution, transforming "peace," a historian of Reconstruction notes, "into war carried on by other means."[63]

The counterrevolution advanced by terror and law. Between 1868 and 1871, the Ku Klux Klan lynched 400 black men in the southern and border states and brutalized—whipped, beat, dragged—thousands.[64] The Klan was not alone in targeting delegates to the postwar constitutional conventions. The Louisiana convention, held in New Orleans in July 1866, ended in what General Philip Sheridan called "an absolute massacre" as a mob led by white policemen broke through the door of the assembly hall and began shooting black delegates and their supporters. After the whites used up their bullets, the blacks drove them out with chairs and clubs. Twice more the whites attacked; twice more the blacks repulsed them. Blacks who tried to surrender were shot dead. Blacks who fled into the streets were chased down, pulled out of streetcars and shops, and shot dead. "[T]hrown in like sacks of corn," the dead filled four furniture wagons.[65]

Campbell blamed the mayhem on radicals for encouraging black hopes. "Discontent, dissatisfactions, murmurings, complaints even insurrection," he later brooded, would be preferable to a state of affairs in which, he complained to his surviving daughter, "We have the Africans in place all around us."[66] Identifying his humiliation with the white South's, he pursued the counterrevolution in court, becoming the barrister of southern Redemption, the terrorist campaign to end Reconstruction and nullify the amendments passed to protect black civil rights, that triumphed after 1877, when the Republicans gave up on Reconstruction—and the freedman.*[67] For three years Campbell mounted dozens of lawsuits against the policy initiatives of the biracial regime of the Illinois-born governor, Henry Clay Warmoth, tying them up with "obstructionist

* Of "Redemption" Nicholas Lemann writes: "The name implied a divine sanction for the retaking of the authority of the whites who had lost in the Civil War, and a heavenly quality to the reestablishment of white supremacy in the post-Reconstruction South." Nicholas Lemann, *Redemption: The Last Battle of the Civil War* (New York: Farrar, Straus, and Giroux, 2006), p. 185.

injunctions" issued by friendly judges. Taxes went uncollected; projects stalled. Warmoth downplayed civil rights to court white businessmen with Yankee-style economic modernization. But Campbell's injunctions stymied Warmoth's delivery of railroads and canals to the businessmen while rising black impatience split his party behind him. Conservatives came to rely on "God and Mr. Campbell." So long at the edge of events, Campbell at last stood at center stage.[68]

Campbell conducted his longest campaign against Warmoth's most promising bridge to New Orleans's businessmen tired of losing profits to quarantines and children to plague—the slaughterhouse statute. Campbell fought it in the state courts, in the lower federal courts, and finally, in February 1873, four years after taking the case, in the U.S. Supreme Court.[69]

Tall, bald, with wisps of white hair beneath his chin, at his temples, and tufting out from the thick eyebrows hooding his sad gray eyes, Campbell, in his first appearance before the Court since resigning in 1861, spent two days delivering his oral argument. Justice Samuel F. Miller, hostile to his views, remarked Campbell's research and eloquence.[70] His colleague, Joseph P. Bradley, more sympathetic, said he had "never heard an advocate who brought to his aid so much learning and breadth." Bradley added: "The esteem in which [Campbell] was held by the members of the Supreme Court anointed him to reverence."[71]

Campbell's argument still resonates. It ranged constitutional law on the side of business well into the twentieth century, but it also sounds in *Brown v. Board of Education* and *Roe v. Wade*.[72] Yet the same argument seeded with decisions expanding personal liberty had roots in *Dred Scott*, not in Campbell's concurrence but in a doctrine Roger B. Taney dropped into his lengthy opinion, which took him over two hours to read, the pages shaking in his hands.*[73]

In banning slavery from the territories, Taney held, Congress had

---

* Campbell's views on slaves as property and on the authority of Congress to control slavery in the territories evolved. In an 1848 letter to John C. Calhoun, a friend of his father's, Campbell wrote that the Constitution assigned the government of the territories to Congress and it did not provide that "the rights of slave owners shall be protected in all the territories of the U.S. or that the master should be free to carry them as slaves to those territories." Two years later, at a southern convention called to protest the then terms of the Compromise of 1850, he drew up a document that repudiated his earlier views. Did this shift represent a sincere change of heart? James M. McPherson finds it "highly improbable." Campbell wanted a seat on the Supreme Court and it "would have been

violated the Fifth Amendment's guarantee that persons could not be "deprived of life, liberty, or property without due process of law." Quoting Taney, "[A]n act of Congress which deprives a citizen of the United States of his liberty or property . . . could hardly be dignified with the name due process of law."[74] That sentence marks the first Court appearance (in a majority opinion) of "substantive due process." According to this doctrine, the due process clauses in the Constitution give the Court the power to review not simply the judicial procedures that must be observed before a person's liberty or property can be abridged but the "substance" of legislation—in *Dred Scott,* an act of Congress; in the postwar cases, acts of state legislatures—impinging on liberty or property. Justice John Harlan offered a clear definition of substantive due process: "The courts are at liberty—indeed, are under a solemn duty to look at the substance of things," he wrote in *Mugler v. Kansas* (1887). "If, therefore, a statute purporting to protect the public health, the public morals, or the public safety, has not a real or substantial relation to these things, or is a palpable invasion of rights secured by the fundamental law, it is the duty of the courts so to judge."[75] Taney found substantive due process in the Fifth Amendment, which applied against the federal government. Campbell was the first to find it in the freshly ratified Fourteenth Amendment, which applied against the states.

"Your petitioners," Campbell wrote in his submission to the Louisiana court, "represent that the first clause of the 14th amendment . . . prohibits the States to abridge the privileges and immunities of citizens of the United States, and secures to all protection from State legislation that invades the rights of property, the most valuable of which is to labor freely in a chosen occupation." He expanded on this idea before the Supreme

---

political suicide to have made public his beliefs as expressed in the letter to Calhoun." In his *Dred Scott* concurrence, Campbell looked "in vain" in the debate over the Constitution for "the assertion of a supreme sovereignty for congress over the territory then belonging to the United States, or that they might thereafter acquire." In his *Slaughter-House* brief, Campbell reversed course again, holding that the "fourteenth amendment struck down and forever destroyed" the doctrines he had espoused in the 1850s. "Having emerged from the storm and fury of the political pressure of the years before and during the Confederate War," McPherson concludes, "Campbell returned to the spirit of his former beliefs." In fact, despite his avowal in the *Slaughter-House* brief that the Fourteenth Amendment made the United States *"one people,"* states' rights—above all the right of the southern states to do as they liked with the freedmen—was his overriding cause. James M. McPherson, "The Career of John Archibald Campbell: A Study of Politics and Law," *Alabama Review,* January 1966, pp. 53–63.

Court. The new amendment protected "conscience, speech, publication, freedom or whatever else is essential" to personal liberty. Protected them from what? From newly enfranchised blacks and a "growing population" of (Catholic) immigrants with "a perceptible influence over" state governments; from the actions of polities in which people "without education in the laws and constitution of the country" predominated; from multiracial, multiethnic democracy. The Fourteenth Amendment was a charter of white Anglo-Saxon freedom passed not to protect blacks from whites but whites from blacks. In a case heard at the same time as the *Slaughter-House* appeals, Campbell made precisely that argument: A state law forbidding segregation of Negroes in New Orleans opera houses violated the Fourteenth Amendment rights of their white owners.[*76]

This upside-down reading cleaved the amendment from its history: A Radical Republican Congress passed it in 1866 to protect the 4 million freedmen not to fence business off from state regulation, nor curb assemblies representing racial or ethnic minorities. To the Republicans, the Unionist Democrat Andrew Johnson, after succeeding to the presidency following Lincoln's assassination the year before, had repudiated the results of the Civil War, vetoing a Freedmen's Bureau bill and a civil rights bill, passed to make good on the Thirteenth Amendment's guarantee of freedom to former slaves. "What does the veto mean?" Johnson asked in an April 1866 speech. A shout from the crowd answered: "It is keeping the nigger down." The country showed little sentiment for letting him up. In a December 1865 referendum to enfranchise blacks in the District of Columbia, thirty-five voted for, 6,951 against. Congress overrode the wishes of D.C. voters, but, in 1867–68, voters in Colorado, Connecticut, Kansas, Michigan, Minnesota, Missouri, New York, Wisconsin, and, by 40,000 votes, Ohio, rejected black suffrage amendments.[77] "The real trouble is that we hate the negro," Indiana congressman George Julian conceded of the North in 1866. An avowed motive of the protections embodied in the Civil Rights Act was to prevent an exodus of blacks into the North. "A just

---

* And so the amendment was long construed, according to Associate Supreme Court Justice Stephen G. Breyer. "May 17, 1954, was a great day in Supreme Court history," Breyer wrote on the fiftieth anniversary of *Brown v. Board of Education*. "Before May 17, the Court read the 14th Amendment's words 'equal protection of the laws' as if they protected only members of the majority race. After May 17, it read those words as the framers who wrote them after the Civil War meant them to be read, as offering the same protection to citizens of every race." Stephen G. Breyer, "A Decision That Changed America," *New York Times*, 5/17/2004, p. A25.

policy on our part leaves the black man in the South where he will soon be happy and prosperous," Representative George Boutwell, an architect of the Civil Rights Act, declared. "An unjust policy [in the South] forces him from home and into those states where his rights will be protected, to the injury of the black man and the white man both of the North and South." Presidential vetoes, white resistance to black equality, and the political necessity of keeping the freed people in the South, moved the Republicans, Eric Foner writes, toward "fixing in the Constitution . . . their understanding of the fruits of the Civil War."[78] The Fourteenth Amendment was intended, Senator John Sherman told his Ohio constituents, to be "an embodiment of the Civil Rights Bill, namely: that everybody . . . without regard to color, should have equal rights before the law."[79]

Campbell's application of the amendment to the property rights of white butchers, in short, had no lineaments in its intent. The counsel for Crescent City, Charles Allen, a former attorney general of Massachusetts, argued as much in his submission to the Court. "Have Congress and the whole nation," he asked, "been deceived, misled, mistaken?"[80] The Fourteenth Amendment according to Campbell would destroy federalism, make the Court the arbiter of state legislation, overthrow democracy for nine-man rule. If the Court endorsed Campbell's revolutionary argument, Allen presciently warned, laws regulating the hours and conditions of employment, child labor, and women's labor could be voided.

By a 5–4 vote the Court agreed with Allen. The author of the opinion was Samuel Freeman Miller, a former physician who wrote his medical school dissertation on cholera and who, in his native Kentucky, had traced an outbreak in the Cumberland Valley to the Cumberland River, and the stream of hogs filling the Wilderness Road as it passed through the nearby Gap. Though "[n]early all" his "blood relations" owned slaves, he wrote, and though he regarded them "as the warmest personal friends and the purest men on earth," his "horror" at seeing his black nursemaid whipped left the deeper mark.[81] One of ten children, he tried running the family farm after his father's death, but, a heavy boy, the work tried him. At fourteen he quit school to apprentice in the town drugstore. The pharmacist encouraged him to study medicine at Transylvania University in Lexington. He opened a practice in Barbourville, a hill town on the western side of the Gap, and wed Lucy Ballinger, who brought five slaves into the marriage with her. Miller, who considered slavery "the most stupendous wrong . . . that the sun shines upon in his daily circuit around the globe," subsequently freed one a year.[82]

Traveling by horseback to remote villages and farms, Miller wearied of medicine. So, in his early thirties, he took up the law. An advocate of gradual emancipation, in 1850 he ran as a delegate to the Kentucky constitutional convention; when it adopted a new charter more favorable to slavery than the old, Miller knew he could not stay in Kentucky. A conviction migrant, he settled in Keokuk, Iowa, which, as that state's "Porkopolis," contained cholera with stringent public health ordinances, and became active in the state's emergent Republican Party. Stressing his politics, legal reputation, and character, Iowa politicians commended

Justice Samuel F. Miller

him to President Lincoln to fill one of the vacancies on the Supreme Court created by the death of Justice Peter F. Daniel and the resignation of John A. Campbell.[83]

Miller's medical background inclined him to uphold the Louisiana statute as a constitutional exercise of "the most necessary and frequent" of a state's police powers, "[t]he regulation of the place and manner of conducting the slaughtering of animals."[84] A Massachusetts case, *Commonwealth v. Alger* (1851), had established the principle informing a state's exercise of police powers: "[E]very holder of property, however absolute and unqualified may be his title, holds it under the implied liability that his use of it may be so regulated, that it shall not be injurious to the equal enjoyment of others . . . nor injurious to the rights of the community." Miller's anti-slavery principles and his commitment to Republican Reconstruction also swayed his decision to uphold a law passed by a biracial legislature. "Fiendish hatred . . . for the Negro," Miller wrote his Texas brother-in-law just after the war, necessitated the federal presence in the South. "We cannot . . . trust the South with the power of governing the Negro and the Union White Man without such guarantees in the federal constitution as secure their protection." He put the point even plainer: "Show me a single white man that has been punished for murdering a Negro. . . . If I could be able to say tomorrow, 'See here, they have hung a rebel in Texas for killing a Negro,' it would be the most effective speech that has been made since the war ended." Miller did not mention Texas idly or to chivvy his brother-in-law. Between June 1865 and June 1868 white Texans killed an estimated 373 blacks; blacks killed ten whites. Yet the *only* person hung for murder in these years was a Houston freedman. "Civil law east of the Trinity River," the officer in charge of the Fifth Military District reported, "is almost a dead letter. . . . Murder of Negroes is so common as to render it impossible to keep an accurate account of them."[85]

Miller's contempt for John A. Campbell also inflected his opinion. "I have neither seen nor heard of any action of Judge Campbell's since the rebellion which was aimed at healing the breach he contributed so much to make," he wrote in an 1877 letter. "He has made himself an active leader of the worst branch of the New Orleans democracy. Writing their pronunciamentos, arguing their cases in our Court, and showing all the evidence of a disconcerted and bitter old man. I think no man that has survived the rebellion is more saturated today with its spirit . . . he deserves all the punishment he . . . can receive, not so much for joining the rebellion as for the persistency with which he continues the fight." Of course, as we have seen, Campbell only reluctantly joined the rebellion. What "saturated" him with the rebellion's spirit was the war—its cruel usage of him.[86]

"The overriding and efficient cause" of the rebellion, Miller contended in his opinion, was "African slavery, which perished as a necessity of the force and bitterness of the conflict."[87] But in a flight of audacity, Campbell had pronounced slavery revived in Louisiana. Requiring the butchers to work at the Grand Slaughterhouse, he argued, violated the Thirteenth Amendment's ban on "involuntary servitude." That elicited Miller's sarcasm: "a microscopic search" to find slavery in the butchers' plight "requires an effort, to say the least of it."[88] Nor could the Fourteenth Amendment's guarantee of equal protection of the laws shelter the butchers. Campbell's brain-spun reading ignored its legislative history. Its "pervading purpose" was to protect "the unfortunate race who had suffered so much" from laws passed by the southern state governments installed in 1865 by Andrew Johnson—laws "which curtailed their rights in pursuit of life, liberty, and property to such an extent that freedom was of little value."[89] Miller, a Lincoln appointee, doubted whether any state action *not* of the Black Codes type—discriminating against Negroes "on account of their race"— would ever be held to come within the amendment's purview.*[90] "Yet," as

---

* "It was simply wrong of Justice Miller to suggest that the 14th amendment could be limited only to cases of discrimination against blacks." William E. Nelson, *The Fourteenth Amendment: From Political Principle to Judicial Doctrine* (Cambridge: Harvard University Press, 1988), p. 163. Indians, Chinese, women, and Unionist whites in the South all were mentioned during the congressional debate over the amendment.

Justice Hugo Black noted in 1938, "of the cases in this Court in which the Fourteenth Amendment was applied during the first fifty years after its adoption, less than one-half of one percent invoked it in protection of the Negro race, and more than fifty percent asked that its benefits be extended to corporations."[91]

Miller's *Slaughter-House Cases* opinion ranks among the most criticized in Court history, and most consequential. Miller at once confined the Fourteenth Amendment to the rights of the freedmen *and* narrowed that application to the vanishing point. Even when blacks won they lost in the Gilded Age Court.

To Miller the first sentence of the Fourteenth Amendment—"All persons born and naturalized in the United States and subject to the jurisdiction thereof, are citizens of the United States and of the State where they reside"—recognized two citizenships, and the second sentence, forbidding the states from making "any law which shall abridge," confined the amendment's protection to federal rights only. Adding unnecessary dicta, Miller enumerated some of them: access to ports and navigable waterways, the ability to run for federal office, and to be protected while on the high seas.[92] ("Clearly," Eric Foner comments, "few of these rights were of any great concern to the majority of freedmen.")[93] They did not include what we call "civil rights." Campbell, Miller wrote, wrongly maintained that the "citizenship is the same, and the privileges and immunities guaranteed by the clause are the same. . . . The language is, 'No State shall make or abridge the privileges and immunities of the *United States.*'" The clause was not "intended" to protect "the citizen of a State against the legislative power of his own State." State constitutions protected the rights of their citizens, and with these the Fourteenth Amendment "has nothing to do." But states' rights, thus understood, comprehended civil rights, and if the Fourteenth Amendment had "nothing to do" with them, what good was it?

Writing four years before the last federal troops withdrew from the South, Miller trusted that Reconstruction would continue and that civil rights enforcement could be left to biracial governments sustained by black votes. And he accepted the argument mounted by the lawyers for Crescent City that Campbell's expansive reading of the Fourteenth Amendment would make the Court "a perpetual censor upon all legislation of the States." "Dual federalism"—"an indestructible Union composed of indestructible States," as the Court expressed it in an 1868 case—formed the keystone of the American constitutional system. Miller would not see it dislodged. So, to preserve federalism from Campbell's revolution, Miller gelded the Fourteenth Amendment. "A good man can do much good on the court," Miller wrote in an 1870 letter. "I hope I have done some good and not much ill." A tragic figure, intending good to "the unfortunate people who have suffered so much," he did them harm.[94]

A friend of Reconstruction had emboldened its enemies. Southern Democrats cited Miller's opinion against northern proponents of a new civil rights bill outlawing discrimination in public accommodations. "It amounts to this," Alexander Stephens, the Georgia congressman and former vice president of the Confederacy, declared in the House. "That these amendments do not change the nature and character of the Government."[95] Justice Stephen J. Field agreed, but in a prophetic dissent deplored the fact. Miller's opinion rendered the Fourteenth Amendment "a vain and idle enactment."[96] How vain would be revealed fourteen months later, when *U.S. v. Cruikshank*, a case arising from the Colfax Massacre, reached the court.

Bodies lay in the village streets and in the fields and woods and floated on the river. The deputy marshal missed the submerged bodies. He missed the ones carted off for burial. He missed the wounded dying with their families. The fifty-nine bodies he directed a working party of Colfax residents to bury "in a ditch—this little trench they had thrown up for their protection" were at least forty short of the total known to be killed. Short, too, of the number bragged about by a young white man, "armed to the death," who boarded a Red River steamer on Easter Sunday evening and "informed us," one of the passengers recalled, " 'that if we wanted to see dead niggers, here was a chance, for there were a hundred or so scattered over the village and surrounding fields,' and he kindly offered to guide us to the scene of action."[97] In a letter published by the *New Orleans Times*, a Democratic newspaper, R. G. Hull of Marshall, Texas, described what the passengers saw in Colfax after taking the young man up on his offer:

> Almost as soon as we got to the top of the landing, sure enough, we began to stumble on them, most of them lying on their faces, and, as I could see by the dim light of the lanterns, riddled with bullets.
>
> One poor wretch, a stalwart looking fellow, had been in the burning courthouse, and as he ran out with his clothes on fire, had been shot. His clothes to his waist were all burned off, and he was literally broiled.
>
> We came across bodies every few steps, but the sight of this fellow, who was burned, added to the horrible smell of burning human flesh—the remains of

those who were shot in the courthouse, which was still on fire—sickened most of us and caused a general cry of "Let's go back."[98]

As Hull's party retraced their steps to the landing, they noticed "some twenty or thirty" black prisoners being held in a storehouse. Hull had arrived after the battle but *before* the massacre. The full butcher's bill awaited the deputy marshal on Tuesday morning.

His report sickened U.S. Attorney Beckwith. He had never seen a crime "so revolting and horrible in the details of its perpetration and so burdened with atrocity and barbarity," he wrote Attorney General George Williams. The Grant administration had created the Justice Department and, under Georgia's Amos Akerman, it energetically prosecuted Klansmen. Under Williams, a former Oregon politician of flexible convictions, Justice had pulled back from civil rights enforcement, offered clemency to Klansmen, and extended patronage to "respectable" Democrats—all to woo southern votes. But Colfax shocked a public souring on Reconstruction—the *New York Times* branded it "a fiendish deed"—and Williams responded to this last reveille of northern indignation by instructing Beckwith to "spare no expense to cause the guilty parties to be arrested and punished." Yet, informed by Beckwith that at least 150 federal troops would be needed to hunt down the 300 to 400 potential defendants, many formed into armed bands, others fled to Texas, Williams shied from the expense. Bowing to congressional pressure to cut spending, he budgeted justice, letting hundreds get away with murder. Beckwith was to try only "the leaders."[99]

On June 16, 1873, Beckwith indicted ninety-eight whites for "murder in commission of offenses punished by the 6th and 7th sections" of the Enforcement Act of 1870, which criminalized conspiracies to deny blacks their constitutional rights, notably the right to public assembly and the right to vote.[100] In the event, only nine were arrested. They did not include Sheriff Nash, last seen (by the marshals shooting at him) swimming his horse across the Red River to the safety of Sabine County, or so runs the *white* version of his escape.[101] *United States v. Columbus C. Nash* was renamed *United States v. Cruikshank,* after William Cruikshank, who had not gotten away.

White witnesses furnished alibis for each of the defendants. It took courage for blacks to testify, but scores came forward, including Benjamin Brinn and a man perforated with buckshot, to identify the perpetrators. In fear of their lives, other witnesses, white and black, remained silent. For two months the trial absorbed New Orleans. From the Catholic bishop to the establishment pillars known as the "Seventy," civic worthies urged leniency. Swayed by respectability and fearful of retaliation yet confronted with eyewitness testimony of murder, the jury deliberated for weeks before throwing up its hands—convicting one man but failing to reach a verdict on the others.[102]

The first trial was heard by Judge William B. Woods, who, ignoring the distinction made in the *Slaughter-House* decision between federal and state rights, instructed the jury that "every right mentioned in the indictment was secured by the Constitution and laws of the United States." At the request of the defense counsel, the retrial was heard before Woods and the Supreme Court justice who sat on the Fifth Circuit Court as, in a practice ended only by the Federal Circuit Court of Appeals Act, in 1891, his brethren did on the other circuits.[103] This was Joseph P. Bradley, who had so admired John Campbell's judicial demeanor before the Court in the *Slaughter-House* arguments. The defendants were mass murderers; if they went free, fear would multiply terror in the South. Blacks would be kept from voting, bearing arms, or exercising the right of assembly. To raise money in support of a case that could restore white supremacy, New Orleans staged a benefit opera, which raised enough funds to hire well-connected lawyers, including Justice Field's brother, David Dudley Field—and John A. Campbell.[104]

For the butchers Campbell taught it round—federalism must yield to the Fourteenth Amendment, which brought "conscience, speech, publication, security, freedom" and the right to practice one's calling under national protection. For the killers, Campbell taught it flat—the national government must yield to federalism. "The subject matter of the counts and the nature of the offenses they describe," Campbell wrote, using Miller's federal-state dichotomy, "are not within the jurisdiction of the United States or the departments of their government but belong to the states and their tribunals under their own constitution and laws." Campbell's tactical arguments against states' rights in his *Slaughter-House* brief had forced Miller to vindicate Campbell's strategic objective—states' rights. Quoting from a New York State Supreme Court decision, the man who denied the supremacy of the state police power in his *Slaughter-House* argument now championed it: In matters affecting "order, tranquility . . . *[t]he authority of the state is complete, unqualified, and exclusive.*" Campbell prepared one of the briefs in *Cruikshank*; he did not make oral arguments before either the Circuit or Supreme Court. Perhaps he could not face Samuel Miller.

Arguing Campbell's brief in court, R. H. Marr, who had participated in a massacre of Republicans in New Orleans, asked that the indictment be thrown out on the grounds that the Enforcement Act (under which it was brought) trespassed on matters assigned to the states by Justice Miller. Justice Bradley would not go that far. But, should the jury find the defendants guilty, he promised to hear Marr's argument on appeal. Three defendants were found guilty—of conspiracy, not murder. The others got off. On the appeal, Bradley embraced Marr's argument, ruling that the provisions of the Enforcement Act the government cited in its indictments were unconstitutional. Judge Woods disagreed. An "arrest in judgment" was declared, and the case went to the Supreme Court.[105]

As with Campbell, the Bradley of *Cruikshank* was a stranger to the Bradley of *Slaughter-House*. In his *Slaughter-House* dissent and in an 1871 advisory to Judge Woods in a case that "raised questions almost identical to those presented by *Cruikshank*," Bradley was a nationalist—the Fourteenth Amendment protected the "fundamental" rights enumerated in the Constitution against government, federal and state, and not only against state action but inaction: *"[D]enying* the equal protection of the laws," he instructed Woods, "includes the omission to protect as well as the omission to pass laws for protection."[106] But, a majority of justices having since held for federalism, Bradley reversed himself before the Court could. The post-*Slaughter-House* Fourteenth Amendment, he held, did *not* protect the rights the defendants allegedly violated. Only racially motivated state action—like the Black Codes—could justify federal intervention to protect black rights. The acts of private individuals like the accused were not federally punishable.[107]

Bradley's opinion, the *Picayune* exulted, "virtually annuls and arrests all the proceedings in the Grant Parish prosecutions." "It was an ill-starred hour for this state when [Bradley] put in his appearance in this circuit in time to meddle with the trial," Beckwith complained to Washington. Fearful that Bradley's opinion would send the message that political murder could escape federal as well as state prosecution, Beckwith predicted that it would "cost five hundred lives between this time and November," when the Supreme Court would hear the case.[108] In Colfax, whites celebrated the decision by murdering two blacks. His own life in danger, Beckwith resigned in December. A new terrorist group, the White League, came to violent life, shooting white Republican elected officials, hanging blacks to keep its members' spirits up, and "barbarously wounding" Levin Allen, the former Union soldier who defied Sheriff Nash prior to the battle at the

Colfax courthouse and survived the massacre, before throwing him upon a pile of brush and burning him to death.[109]

The Klan reappeared in Alabama, where, the U.S. attorney wrote Williams, the belief gained currency that "any man may murder a Republican, for political reasons without the slightest reason to fear that he will be punished, but with every reason to believe that he will be applauded for the act."[110] As for Mississippi, where the Klan's anthem went: "Niggers and [Republicans], get out of the way / We're born of the night and we vanish by day / No rations have we, but the flesh of man—And love niggers best—the Ku Klux Klan / We catch 'em alive and roast 'em whole / And hand 'em around with a sharpened pole"—Mississippi, its U.S. attorney reported, "was in a condition of more thorough and effective armed resistance against the Constitution and laws of the United States than in 1861 when she raised the flag of rebellion." This new rebellion had one goal—to keep blacks from voting. It succeeded. Terror dramatically suppressed the Republican vote in the 1874 elections. In Louisiana's Sabine Parish, 432 Republicans and 347 Democrats voted in 1870—and two Republicans and 762 Democrats in 1874.[111] The next year, while the justices lucubrated on *Cruikshank*, the Republican vote in Columbus, Mississippi, fell from 1,200 before Bradley to seventeen.[112] "The only hope" the federal attorney for the Columbus area confided in a letter, "is the office and Court of the United States. If these fail, then a large mass of the people here are without remedy or protection by reason of the practical nullification of the Constitution and laws of the country."[113]

A new chief justice led the Court. After six others had either rejected the honor or been found unworthy of it, President Grant nominated Morrison R. Waite, a Toledo lawyer, to replace Salmon P. Chase, the prewar abolitionist and member of Lincoln's cabinet, who died a month after dissenting in *Slaughter-House*.* Samuel Miller, who was not asked, was men-

---

* Attorney General Williams was among those Grant canvassed for the job. Unlike the others he agreed to take it. The Senate, though, rejected him. Williams learned of his nomination, if a letter from a reporter to Charles A. Dana, the editor of the *New York Sun* can be believed, in a singular way: "Williams's appointment [to replace Chief Justice Chase] . . . is more horrible perhaps than even you know it to be. He, Williams, has said within two days that *his wife* knew of Grant's purpose to nominate him on a Saturday night—that he did not learn it till Monday morning.—Who is his Wife? She was a handsome adventuress in San Francisco known as Kate George—publicly kept as a mistress by one George, a prosperous stage proprietor. She has a son in the Maryland penitentiary, a

tioned for the appointment, but "it is said that my, or rather our, opinion in the Slaughterhouse Cases is to be used with effect against me," he wrote to his fellow Justice David Davis. "If so it will not be the first time that the best and most beneficial act of a man's life has stood in the way of his political advancement."[114] Miller's editing of the Fourteenth Amendment had armed the Democrats' attack on Republican Reconstruction. Waite carried no such baggage. In 1872, at the suggestion of Columbus Delano, his Ohio-born secretary of the interior, Grant had chosen Waite as one of three lawyers to represent the United States at the Geneva Tribunal, an international arbitration board weighing Ameri-

*Chief Justice
Morrison R. Waite*

can claims against Britain stemming from the depredations on commerce wrought by British-built cruisers sailing under the Confederate flag.[115] Geneva marked Morrison Remick Waite's lone foray from obscurity. John Sherman, the Ohio senator, on learning of his nomination, had to ask a Toledo congressman who he was. "M. R. Waites [*sic*] age 57," the congressman wrote back. "Born at Lyme, Conn't. Graduated at Yale 1837. Commenced practice law Toledo 1839."[116] Justice Field poured sarcasm on the general estimate of Waite: "He is a man that would never have been thought of for the position by any person except for President Grant."[117] Others were relieved that Grant had not named his cook.[118]

Precedent bound the Court. As the facts of *Cruikshank* proclaimed, the freedmen desperately needed the federal protection promised in the Fourteenth Amendment—but Miller's *Slaughter-House* opinion denied it to them. Marr, the defense lawyer, quoted Miller's own words back at him in oral argument. Campbell would not have dared that. In a stirring summation, David Dudley Field declared that the progress of American liberty would be reversed if Cruikshank and his fellow murderers did not go free.

---

convict for the crime of robbery, his second offense. The old Senators and Representatives who 'know' things in Washington believe that Kate 'screwed' her husband into the Attorney Generalship—one of the shrewdest of the old Senators said yesterday in conversation about this appointment—'Mrs. W. has the most profitable c . . t that has been brought to Washington in my day.' " Margaret Susan Thompson, "Corruption—or Confusion? Lobbying and Congressional Government in the Early Gilded Age," *Congress and the Presidency*, vol. 10, no. 2 (Autumn 1983), p. 189, n. 3.

Writing for an 8–1 majority, Chief Justice Waite sought to inoculate the *Cruikshank* decision against its moral absurdity: "If a hundred white men could massacre sixty black citizens without anyone being convicted of a crime against the United States, the reasons certainly should be made clear." Indeed the *New York Times* praised Waite's "admirable clearness," but clarity won't cleanse *Cruikshank* of its consequences.[119]

Cruikshank pivoted on Miller's distinction between state and federally protected rights. The defendants, it seems, did not violate the Fourteenth or Fifteenth Amendment rights of the Negroes they massacred because twenty-four hours before Miller issued his opinion, they had possessed the constitutional clairvoyance not to do their killings on navigable waterways or upon the high seas. In a centennial volume on the Fourteenth Amendment, Chief Justice Earl Warren described the opinion's claustral serenity: "The court held that several of the rights alleged infringed— including the right of peaceable assembly with others, the right to petition for redress of grievances, and the right to bear arms—were not rights secured by the federal constitution, and, therefore, could not come under the protective umbrella of federal legislative power. Although the indictment alleged interference with the right to vote, the court ruled the indictment was defective because it did not allege that the interference was racially motivated." That Attorney General Williams and his solicitor general, S. F. Phillips, committed such an elementary mistake on procedure while, on substance, failed to offer a "legal theory of civil rights enforcement," prompts one historian to ask whether "they may have welcomed a Supreme Court decision that precluded the civil rights enforcement efforts that had become so politically debilitating."[120] Warren coupled *Cruikshank* with an accompanying case, *U.S. v. Reese,* in which the Court, siding with a white Kentucky electoral official who had refused to register the vote of an African-American in a municipal election, cut the constitutional ground out from under black voting rights. Together, "These decisions offered little solace to the Negroes who would be required ultimately to look to the federal courts for the [protection] of their rights." *No* solace was more like it, and "ultimately" took until 1954. *Reese* gutted the Fifteenth Amendment—the Court refusing to extend the amendment to nonfederal elections. Waite's opinion fusses over the wording of the Enforcement Act. Eventually the fog lifts: "The Fifteenth Amendment does not confer the right of suffrage upon any one." That unnecessary dictum was accurate so far as it went. The amendment merely prohibited the federal government or the states from denying "the right of citizens of the United States to vote . . . on account of race color, or previous condition of servitude." But Waite's reading of the amendment, in the context of the white counterrevolution against Reconstruction, was as narrow as it was desolating. Self-help through the ballot was now a dead letter. Placed beyond the reach of the Reconstruction amendments, the freedman faced a season of terror followed by sixty years of court-blessed segregation and disfranchisement. Earl Warren canceled the blessing, when, within two months of becoming chief justice, he united a divided court behind the school desegregation decision, *Brown v. Board of Education,* that launched the civil rights era. The *Chicago Defender,* a leading black newspaper, called Brown the "second emancipation proclamation," white America having long since forgotten the price of the first.*[121]

Cruikshank was substantively unanimous—Justice Nathan Clifford wrote a concurrence, not a dissent—and seemed to displease nobody white. The *Reese* and *Cruikshank* decisions "meet with the most unexpected encomiums," Waite wrote his brother a week after issuing them. "The papers in N.Y., both Rep. and Dem. are to a certain extent enthusiastic." The *New York World* compared Waite to Jay, Marshall, and "Taney," which must have brought the Chief Justice up short. To a judge on the Fourth Circuit who teased him about "that *Dred* decision of the enforcement case," Waite wrote back: "Sorry about the '*Dred,*' but to my mind there was no escape." No escape from the *Slaughter-House Cases'* confinement of federal citizenship. Waite apologized to Miller for not citing his decision in *Cruikshank*: "I am so little accustomed to citing cases as authority, except when I quote, that I too often omit it when I should not," adding, "I am glad the opinion merits your approbation."[122]

This bipartisan applause echoed northern opinion on Reconstruction, which had outlived the mood of its gestation. "The cheering in the hall and densely packed galleries exceeded anything I ever saw and beggared description," George W. Julian recalled of the exultancy in the House

---

* "[B]y insisting on proof of racial intent, perhaps even of racial hostility, Waite was making it much more difficult to obtain convictions. If over 100 dead black bodies did not prove racial animosity, what would?" J. Morgan Kousser, *Colorblind Justice: Minority Voting Rights and the Undoing of the Second Reconstruction* (Chapel Hill: University of North Carolina Press, 1999), p. 50.

chamber on January 31, 1865, at passage of the Thirteenth Amendment banning slavery. "Members joined in the shouting and kept it up for some minutes. . . . I have felt, ever since, as if I were in a new country." Belief in a unifying American nationality, and in the necessity of a strong central government, ran high. "The tide of Union," a British journalist wrote in *The New America* (1867), "had replaced the rage for separatism, for independence, for individuality." But as the "weight of the war" lifted, the pre-war political culture reasserted itself. Surveying postwar policy on race, women's rights, public health, crime, charity, and education, Morton Keller traces a pattern of retreat: "First, in the wake of the war, there was an outburst of rhetoric and action designed to implement the war-born ideal of a unified more egalitarian nation. And then there followed the resurgence—and usually the triumph—of countering nineteenth-century American values, laissez-faire, individualism, assumptions of racial and sexual inferiority."

Northerners were torn between anti-slavery and the Union before the war; Reconstruction and Reunion after. They had accepted slavery "where it already existed" to preserve the Union; they would accept the freedman's disfranchisement to achieve Reunion. When, at a public meeting at Boston's Faneuil Hall called by "highly respectable citizens" to protest General Sheridan's use of federal "bayonets" to evict Democrats from five disputed seats in the Louisiana assembly, the abolitionist Wendell Phillips declared, "My anxiety is for the hunted, tortured, robbed, murdered" blacks of Louisiana, a heckler shouted, "That's played out, sit down." By this time, Keller observes, *"Uncle Tom's Cabin* was not a spur to popular indignation over the mistreatment of blacks by whites, but a half-minstrel, half-circus theatrical entertainment."[123]

The publicity given to "corrupt carpetbag" governments by the *New York Tribune* and influential liberal journals like *The Nation* had eroded the moral capital of Reconstruction. Northern reformers judged southern politics on an absolute scale—as if high-living black spoilsmen were the only corrupt pols in an otherwise Iowa of good government. In fact from the cities to the statehouses, from the Capitol to the Grant White House, the "Great Barbecue" of northern politics hosted by railroad money— one Republican Party chairman was simultaneously in the pay of four railroads—surpassed anything not only in the South but in American history. Between 1866 and 1872, the Union Pacific spent $400,000 on bribes; the Central Pacific, between 1875 and 1885, as much as $500,000 annually. Appalling the readers of the *North American Review* with the story of how

Daniel Drew, Jim Fisk, and Jay Gould looted the Erie Railroad and, competing dollar for dollar with their rival Cornelius Vanderbilt, turned the New York State legislature into "the worst assembly of official thieves" in state history, Henry Adams and Charles Francis Adams, Jr., saw portent in the crapulent particulars of the Erie: "The belief is common in America that the day is at hand when corporations far greater than the Erie—swaying power such as has never in the world's history been trusted in the hands of mere private citizens, controlled by single men like Vanderbilt, or by combinations of men like Fisk [and] Gould . . . after having created a system of quiet but irresistible corruption—will ultimately succeed in directing government itself." Next to the challenge to "the popular institutions which are spreading so rapidly over the whole world" posed by the "corporation . . . in its nature," the elite crusade against carpetbag graft—the bribes taken by Republican governors and politicians, the printing contracts let out by Reconstruction legislatures, the "costly table delicacies" black and white lawmakers lavished on themselves—looks like the politics of distraction. "[G]ranting all their mistakes," Kenneth Stampp concludes a discussion of the progressive measures enacted by the Reconstruction governments, "the radical governments were by far the most democratic the South had ever had."[124]

Accounts of "ignorant" blacks being "voted" by Republican bosses in one Florida precinct after another, a perceptive historian notes, of "the bellowings and physical contortions" of black delegates at state party conventions peopled with "baboons," "ragamuffins," and "jailbirds" expressed in racist terms "an underlying fear, which few dared to express . . . of the danger involved in the rising movement of the lower classes throughout the country." The labor militancy growing out of the hard times of the 1870s raised class anxiety among erstwhile abolitionists and reformers, quickening an "us" against "them" mentality. "Them" embraced northern workers organizing in unions, midwestern farmers protesting the rates railroads charged to ship their crops, and southern blacks.[125]

An earlier generation of historians conjured business support for Radical Reconstruction from evidence like this letter to Charles Sumner, the senator once caned at his desk by a southern Democrat, from a Rhode Island Republican: "In a selfish point of view free suffrage to blacks is desirable. Without their support, southerners will certainly unite again, and there is much reason to fear successfully, with the Democrats of the North, and the long train of evils sure to follow their rule is fearful to contemplate . . . a great reduction of the tariff doing away with its protective feature—perhaps free trade."[126] To protect the tariff many northern businessmen did support black suffrage, but "[m]ore influential" were "merchants engaged in the southern trade and eastern industrialists" who "contended that if the Negro theme were dropped from politics southern high-tariff advocates would join the Republican party for business reasons." Concerned over the falling supply of cotton, the *United States Economist* deplored the "idleness" of the freedmen and endorsed the Black Codes to force them back to work; the Radical program amounted to "revolution." *The Stockholder* attacked Thaddeus Stevens's "forty acres and a mule" plantation confiscation scheme, as "a thing unheard of since the days of Tamerlane." And the *Industrial American* hoped the return of southerners to Congress would prove a "sedative to the political excitement of the times" and looked forward to the day when "the valuable southern market" would "be open to the products of our factories." What the trade journals termed the "uncertainty," "doubt," "excitement," and "ferment" generated by the "race issue" aligned most business opinion against Reconstruction from its inception.[127]

A decade after the rebellion, the romance of blue and gray joined at the marriageable daughter had induced a fraternal amnesia about the war's *causes*.[128] Even "realists" like Henry James and William Dean Howells indulged the romance of Reunion.[129] Only the "foreign occupation" of the South held it back—and the Negro.

His "hour" was over. His political cover vanished in 1874, when the Democrats won control of the House of Representatives for the first time since secession.[130] His military protection ended with the Compromise of 1877, when, to hold on to the White House, his own party betrayed him. With *Cruikshank* the Court issued a constitutional pass to terrorism. State courts had refused to prosecute political murder from the moment blacks ceased to be property.[131] Between 1866 and 1875, General Sheridan estimated, 3,500 people had been killed in Louisiana, "and the civil authorities, in all but a few cases, have been unable to arrest, convict, and punish [the] perpetrators."[132] With *Reese* the Court stripped blacks of their only remaining weapon against terror—self-help through the ballot box. In the year before *Reese* federal attorneys brought more than 200 voting rights prosecutions; two years after *Reese* only twenty-five. Upon giving "Reese et al and Cruikshank et al my severest study," the federal attorney in Charleston wrote a friend, he'd concluded that "federal election laws are a delusion and a farce." Referring to bands of white vigilantes, he went on: "If red shirts break up meetings by violence, there is no remedy, unless it can be proved to have been done on account of race &c, which can't be proved; because the people can only peaceably assemble under the Constitutional guarantees, to petition Congress &c. It is hard to sit quietly and see such things, with the powerful arm of the Government . . . tied behind its back by these decisions." State officials from the governor to the precinct managers "reject and refuse to permit colored men to register" to vote. He had not bothered to register himself—what was the point? "Suppose I vote, will it be counted and if I can't protect myself, how can I protect my friend of African descent?"[133]

John A. Campbell died in 1889, having left the mark of Taney upon the postwar Republican Court. He was seventy-seven. After *Slaughter-House,* he had confined his practice to the Supreme Court, which held a memorial meeting to honor him. Few pleaders before the Court left a deeper impass on law—and history. Perversely refracted through Samuel Miller's opinion, Campbell's *Slaughter-House* brief pried Reconstruction from its constitutional foundations. Stephen J. Field set the corporation in its place.

Chapter Six

THE SCANDAL OF *SANTA CLARA*

Jurisdiction has been seized on casuistic pretenses; the right of trial by jury has been set aside in vast reaches of the country; the by-laws of corporations have overtopped in judicial estimation the legislation of States which were once called sovereign; and constitutional ordinances earned on the field of battle as charters of human liberty, have been turned into the shield of incorporated monopoly.

—Seymour D. Thompson, Annual Address to the
Ninth Annual Meeting of the Bar Association
of the state of Kansas (1892)

Not all legal propositions that are true of man will be true of a corporation. For example, it can neither marry nor be given in marriage.

—Frederick Maitland,[1]
nineteenth-century English Jurist

The inverted Constitution rests on Stephen J. Field's dissent in the *Slaughter-House Cases,* the dissent on a life rimmed by austere New England religion and the get-and-grab of Gold Rush California. Born in Haddam, Connecticut, in 1816, Stephen Johnson Field grew up in Stockbridge, Massachusetts, where his Yale-educated father, the Reverend David Field, preached from the same Congregationalist pulpit as Jonathan Edwards, the eighteenth-century Puritan divine, and adopted his scalding theology— "The smoke of your torment shall still ascend up forever and ever; and . . . your bodies, which shall have been burning and roasting all this while in the glowing flames, yet shall not have been consumed"—as Stephen did his delivery system, the jeremiad.[2] The nine Field children (their mother's given name was Submit)[3] suffered their father's sermon three times every Sunday, performances that taught Stephen language's power to make abstractions—cosmic estrangement, damnation, hellfire— realer than realities. "If the creed of the Puritans was an iron creed,"

Stephen's brother Henry wrote of his father, "it formed an iron character."[4] That fits Justice Field, creed and character alike. "Field did not
believe something to be right—he knew it to be," one of his biographers
observes. "[S]elf-righteousness was a dominant feature of his juridical personality."[5] And made him a trial to his fellow justices.[6]

Among the young Fields competition eased Puritan constraint and
energized Puritan striving. There were seven brothers; two set the bar at
fame. Stephen's younger brother Cyrus and older brother David Dudley
won "worldwide reputations," the one for being the promoter of the
Atlantic cable, the other for drafting a code of civil law for New York state
and writing a two-volume code of international law.[7] At Williams College,
Mark Hopkins, a moral philosopher, steeped Stephen in secular certainty.
For Hopkins, a Field biographer writes, "All human problems could be
deduced systematically and intelligibly from a few simple theorems."[8] He
lent Field a tool and a method of truth. Natural law furnished a lever to
upend laws enacting the fallible will of the people; and like his mentor's
teaching, Stephen Field's opinions descend from "right," "principles of
morality," and "eternal verity."[9]

After graduation, Stephen read law in David Dudley's Manhattan office,
eventually becoming partner. David's eminence, though, remained inex-
orable. Travel was called for, and in 1848 Stephen and his father embarked
on a year-long Grand Tour. In the "year of revolutions," they witnessed
fighting in Rome and Vienna, exciting but a memory of fear later, and
reached Paris in time for the overthrow of Louis Philippe but apparently
before the "June Days," when 50,000 government troops put down a rising
of unemployed workers and over 4,000 died. In Paris, Field read President
James K. Polk's message to Congress confirming rumors that had wafted
over the Sierras: gold in California![10]

"The Puritan treats himself as if he were a firm," the sociologist David
Riesman once observed, "and, at the same time, the firm's auditor."[11]
Stephen Field's auditor reported an overdraft on his expectations. At
thirty-two he lagged the pace of Field achievement. A pre-economic phenomenon, a kind of beachcombing, the Gold Rush dangled instant success before him and thousands of other young men like him, the first
American generation facing a lifetime's work in organizations. Eastern
clergymen warned "the merchant, the sailor, the clerk, the idler hastening
toward the shores of the Pacific" against the moral consequences of casting family and community aside. The Reverend Elisha Cleaveland, of New
Haven, preached a sermon on that folly, taking Proverbs, Chapter 28,

Verse 20, as his text: "The faithful man abounds with blessings; but he that maketh haste to be rich, shall not be innocent." Riches cursed men as conquest nations. Seized from Mexico in a predaceous war, the Golden State—the thirty-first star—as we have seen, disturbed John C. Calhoun's "equilibrium," the balance of fifteen free and fifteen slave states. At the beginning of the war, Ralph Waldo Emerson foresaw a tainted victory. "[T]he United States will conquer Mexico," he wrote in his journal, "but as the man swallows the arsenic, which brings him down. Mexico will poison us." California proved the fatal cup. "The truth will have to be acknowledged," the premier historian of California, Hubert Howe Bancroft, wrote in 1888, "that the admission of California as a free state led to the war of the rebellion."[12]

Within weeks of landing in New York, Field sailed for San Francisco. In Panama he contracted cholera, but recovered quickly. On the Panama City–San Francisco leg yellow fever broke out among the passengers on his steamer; Stephen, avoiding infection, nursed the sick. He arrived in late December 1849, with $10. Providently he had brought along bundles of New York newspapers, which he sold for a dollar apiece, along with a dozen chamois skins, to carry gold dust; he sold them, too. He would not find his fortune but, as a lawyer in a lawless land, make it.[13]

Field began as justice of the peace in a mining town, holding court in a saloon, a setting that brought out the brawler in defendants and attorneys alike. To persuade one attorney *not* to shoot the jury Field clamped a Bowie knife between his teeth and thrust a Navy Colt's revolver against counsel's temple.[14] Field may be the only Supreme Court justice to have ordered a man whipped—250 lashes, fifty every twenty-four hours, for five straight days—on *humane* grounds: to satisfy "the sense of justice of the community" that would hang him otherwise. Dispensing justice in a town containing "many desperate persons," as Field put it in a California memoir written to advance his presidential ambitions, made him fear for his life. He felt safer once he learned to shoot from his pockets, from which he can have rarely taken his hands, his enemies being many and ferocious. Years later, a California desperado deprived of his land by a Field ruling sent "a veritable infernal machine!" to Field's office at the U.S. Supreme Court in a package plausible as a Christmas present. "It is often a matter of wonder to me," Field reflected, "how it was that some good angel whispered to me not to open the box."[15]

In 1889 that seraph delegated to Field's bodyguard, a federal marshal who shot dead an inveterate political opponent of Field's, a Democratic lawyer and former California Supreme Court justice named David Terry. The year before Terry had brandished a knife at Field in a San Francisco courtroom for ruling against his client—and wife—Sarah Althea. As the former $400-a-month mistress of a deceased U.S. senator and silver magnate from Nevada, Sarah had sought a share of his estate by claiming a secret marriage, producing a certificate as proof. Field declared it a forgery and sentenced both Terry and Sarah Althea ("I could have killed the old villain") to jail for contempt. To protect Field on his return to California for his Ninth Circuit duties, the federal government assigned a bodyguard, David Neagle, who had won a reputation as a quick-draw shootist in Tombstone. *Terry* himself had killed a man in a duel but in the 1850s; in 1889 he was a fierce seventy-seven. Chance brewed the fatality. Field boarded a Southern Pacific train in Los Angeles en route to San Francisco. Somewhere along the line Terry and Sarah came aboard. When the train stopped at Lathrop Station in the San Joaquin Valley, all four alighted and entered the station restaurant. Field was eating breakfast when Terry approached and struck him what Neagle called "a violent blow in the face." (Some witnesses testified to a light slap, others to a gesture.) Neagle drew his pistol and shot Terry twice, in the head and stomach. Neagle told the sheriff that Terry had a knife; none was found. He was arrested and jailed in Stockton. He faced murder charges if the Supreme Court, Field abstaining, had not ruled that California lacked jurisdiction over a federal guard performing his duty, which may have saved David Neagle from hanging.[16]

Somebody up there liked Stephen Field. And just as the Puritans read their prosperity as a sign that they were "God's people in America,"[17] Field could feel he belonged to His preferred American family. In the Puritan dispensation, the Fields' fame testified to their "election"—to being bound for glory. And if their achievements could bear that interpretation, so could the good luck of others. For Stephen Field, if God did not make millionaires, he rooted for them. With this meld of religious and material values in mind Max Weber defined the Puritan sect as "a powerful, unconsciously refined organization for the production of capitalistic individuals."[18] Field might have said as much about the America of his wish and striving.

Puritanism's version of the holy sinner is the antinomian. "Antinomianism . . . teacheth men freedom from the law of Moses," its opponent John Cotton wrote of the heresy, "and if they commit any sin, they plead they are not bound by the law."[19] To the elect, all things are permitted. Stephen

Field was upright by his lights, but they shone dimly on his juristic faults: an end-justifies-the-means approach to jurisprudence and lax ethics. To a railroad lawyer arguing a case before the Court Field passed a confidential

memo from the other justices; he invited conflicts of interest by investing in urban street railroads and mines; he circumvented court rulings with which he disagreed; and he campaigned for president while on the High Court, giving the appearance of deciding cases with a view to winning votes. In an 1878 case that shaped subsequent American law on the power of states to attach private property, *Pennoyer v. Neff,* he cited nonapplicable cases, misstated precedents, mischaracterized existing law, created a difference of opinion on the facts that did not exist in the case or in the lower court ruling, and addressed issues not raised by that court, going miles beyond the facts to assert the doctrine of substantive due process, salting the record with a citation he could use in future cases.[20]

Justice Stephen J. Field

Though his ambitions were intellectual, Field met God more than halfway. He invested wisely in land; served a term in the California legislature, where he introduced his brother's legal code; practiced law lucratively; married a woman twenty years his junior; and won a seat on the California Supreme Court.[21] As a justice and chief justice of the California Supreme Court, Field evinced no appetite for judicial review. "Frequent elections by the people" would check legislative abuses. "It is not for the judiciary to assume a wisdom which it denies to the legislature, and exercise a supervision over the discretion of the latter." He wrote this in a dissent to a ruling striking down a Sunday closing law for business on the ground that it "prohibited the pursuit of a lawful occupation" (an argument that, advanced by John Campbell, Field made his own). The Sunday day-of-rest bill, Field maintained, protected workers who would not get a day off without it: "The law steps in to restrain the power of capital. To protect labor is the highest office of our laws." That sympathy for the unelect vanishes in his Supreme Court opinions.[22]

Stephen Field was a Democrat, David Dudley a Republican and a "large contributor" to Lincoln's campaign. "Does David want his brother to have it?" Abraham Lincoln reportedly asked, when, seeking a westerner for the Supreme Court, someone suggested Stephen. Assured David wholeheartedly did, he said, "Then he shall have it."[23] As on the California bench, Associate Justice Stephen Field "was less disposed than his colleagues to overturn state legislation" under the commerce and contract clauses of the Constitution.[24] The father of "laissez-faire constitutionalism" emerged only after 1871.

The Paris Commune of 1871 changed the social direction of Field's jurisprudence and sympathies, one Field commentator contends.[25] That conjecture gains cogency if one takes the Commune as a violent manifestation of bottom rail top, an inversion of the Puritan scenario of election. Thanks to Cyrus Field's cable, the revolutionary sequel to the Franco-Prussian War received more coverage in the United States than any foreign event to that point in history. Anxious for the safety of his brother David and his wife, who were in Paris at the time and for all he knew trapped by the fighting, Stephen Field followed the news obsessively and with conflicting emotions—fear for David, pride in Cyrus.[26]

The rising of Paris workers against a National Assembly in Versailles that had capitulated to Germany; the election and two-month rule of the Commune, a government more nationalist than socialist, formed to preserve France's newly won republic; the bombardment of Paris by troops from Versailles; the slaughtering of hostages, including the archbishop of Paris and fifty priests, by the Communards; and the eight-day battle for Paris ending in the massacre of over 20,000 Communards, many after they surrendered, by the forces of order—this convulsion was written up by American newspapers as a text of fear, and they spent "tremendous sums for cable tolls and correspondence" doing so.[27] "Communism" rampant in Paris "produced a hysteria in conservative circles in the United States which caused such current indigenous forms of radicalism as the Granger and labor movements to be attacked as conspiracies against the institution of property," Howard Jay Graham writes.[28] Paris, the *Cincinnati Gazette* editorialized, was "a den of wild beasts," given over to "mob rule"—(the *Wisconsin State Bulletin*), and "violent reds"—(the *Morning Bulletin* of San Francisco). In France, "Commune" evoked not only the "Paris Commune of 1793" but the independent communes of the Middle Ages, an ambiguity lost in translation. Just as the *Communist Manifesto* of 1848 was making its first English appearance, the American press rendered the Commune syn-

onymous with communism and communism with strikes. One paper stigmatized a coal miner's strike in Pennsylvania as "The Commune of Pennsylvania," a preview of the headlines—the "Commune in Chicago," the
"Commune in St. Louis," the "Commune in New York"—in store for the
Great Railroad Strike of 1877. The *Chicago Times* printed the "confession"
of a "Communist incendiary" dispatched from Paris to set the great
Chicago fire. The *Washington Star* blamed the Commune on the International Workingmen's Association, or First International, a group whose
5,000 American members loomed as a revolutionary underground. The
detective Alan Pinkerton warned against "agents of the Commune" infil-
trating labor unions. Noting that one of every thirteen New Yorkers was
on relief, the *New York Times* feared "the unreason and caprice of the gentlemen of leisure in the gutters" and warned that socialist organizers
among the poor and in the trade unions could set off "a communistic revolution . . . such as would astonish all who do not know these classes."[29]

Anti-slavery had consumed the available pity. Respectable opinion had
little left over for the freedmen, less for the striker, and none for the unemployed, the "tramp" of the era's journalism. Work relief and the construction of public works "seemed the obvious palliative for the plight of the
unemployed" during the Panic of 1857, but not in the depression beginning
in 1873, post-Commune. After a conference of charities charged that
20,000 "imposter paupers" had cadged free soup in New York City, *The
Nation* insisted, "Free soup must be prohibited, and all classes must learn
that soup of any kind, beef or turkey, can be had only by being paid for"—
this when "some weeks" as many as 14,000 homeless people slept in New
York's police stations. Editorials slurred the unemployed as "disgusting,"
"crazy," "loud-mouth gasometers," and "ineffable asses." Jane Grey Swiss-
shelm, "a prominent journalist," hoped that "cholera, yellow fever, or any
other blessing" would sweep them away. Responding to calls to relocate
the unemployed on western homesteads, the *Denver News* said it did not
want "the refuse of the great city" deposited in the West: " 'Be it ever so
humble, there is no place like home' to starve in." "Little can be done," the
New York Times concluded; "the natural laws of trade" must be allowed to
work themselves out. The *Times's* endorsement of firing squads for captured Communards suggested a tolerance for savagery against underclass
Americans. Unemployed New Yorkers got a taste of it in January 1874
when, goaded by conservative opinion demanding "order," mounted
policemen charged into a peaceful labor assembly at Tompkins Square,
bashing heads, trampling demonstrators, riding down "poorly dressed

people" anywhere in the vicinity. Samuel Gompers, who dove into a cellar-way to save his skull from a clubbing, called the "Tompkins Square Riot" an "orgy of brutality."[30]

The contagion of fear loosed by the Commune leaped the Rockies. Field presided over the Ninth Circuit Court in San Francisco when the *California Alta* ran a sensational series on a miners' strike in Amador County. The "Amador Communists" shared the front page with the Paris Commu-nards. One day's headlines: "More Trouble in Amador. Reign of Terror in Sutter Creek. Masked Miners Hunting for Mine Owners." In an editorial, "The Federal Authority and the Amador Conspiracy," the *Alta* called on the federal courts to use the Fourteenth Amendment and the Ku Klux Klan Act to suppress the miners, revolutionists demanding a $3-a-day wage and a twelve-hour day.[31]

If reading the Fourteenth Amendment—intended primarily to protect freed people from state laws like the Black Codes—as a bulwark of prop-erty had not occurred to Field before, it may have now, and for a personal reason: the Amador Mine belonged to an "intimate friend,"[32] a category encompassing an elite known to invective as the "Pacific Club Set" after the San Francisco club whose members included Leland Stanford and Col-lis P. Huntington, two of the "Big Four" who launched the Central Pacific Railroad in 1861, as well as their lawyers and fixers. An 1885 cartoon in a California newspaper caught the public face of the relation between Field and Stanford. "The Return of the Prodigal" depicts a ragged Field bowing before Stanford, garbed in a Supreme Court justice's robe.[33] Stanford appointed Field as a trustee of the university named for his deceased son, Leland Jr. Field reciprocated with service beyond the grave. Following Stanford's death, the federal government sought to recoup some of the millions loaned to the Central Pacific, but Field gave Mrs. Stanford "every possible assistance" in keeping every penny of her estate.[34] When, writing his opinions in his singular Capitol Hill home, a former prison and the house where John C. Calhoun died, Stephen Field thought of Property, he saw faces, he sensed friends.[35]

That may account for the "pervading tone of anxiety" in his opinions over "angry menaces against order."[36] For Field laissez-faire was order's guarantor, regulatory legislation, mob rule. Thirty men owned Chicago's fourteen grain elevators, fixing prices to gouge farmers. Nevertheless, a Granger law establishing maximum rates for the elevators was "subversive of the rights of private property," including the right to monopoly profits. Privately Field fulminated against the "agrarian and nihilistic element," meaning the Patrons of Husbandry, the formal name of the Grange.[37] He even detected revolution in the 2 percent federal income tax on the affluent, which, in an 1895 opinion, he decried as an unconstitutional "assault upon capital . . . the stepping stone to others, larger and more sweeping till our political contests . . . become a war of the poor against the rich; a war constantly growing in intensity and bitterness."[38] From the second-floor office he had built over the place where blindfolded prisoners once awaited the report of the firing squad, Field wrote fear of democracy and of the people—the poor, workers, farmers, blacks—into law.[39]

Samuel Miller's sympathy with Reconstruction colored his majority opinion in the *Slaughter-House Cases;* Stephen Field's scorn, his dissent. From bench and bar, the Field brothers fought Reconstruction with a passion lacking a Campbell-like backstory of humiliation. Ideologically David Dudley traveled further. An enthusiastic backer of the Wilmot Proviso, barring slavery from the territories, like David Wilmot he passed through the Free Soil Party before joining the Republicans. But since the war he had gone over to the Democrats and embraced the cause of home rule for the South. Stephen did not support the Proviso, adopting the point of view of hard-line southerners on extending slavery to the territories.[40] A year after he pled for the *Cruikshank* defendants before Stephen's Court, *Harper's Weekly* ran a cartoon of David Dudley taking Satan for a client, though, in Jay Gould, many might have thought he already had. Recanting his Republicanism, David Dudley served the white counterrevolution pro bono. "I had rather receive nothing but the thanks of my clients," he declared of the Colfax defendants, "and the consequences of doing what I could to avert a public calamity and wrong."[41] Answering for massacre was the "calamity." "[T]he people will not stand bayonet rule much longer in Louisiana," he wrote in an 1877 letter. "The vile wretches, who have fattened on the life-blood of that state, must be driven from their places, and its people be allowed to govern themselves, like the people of other states." Justice Field regarded racial injustice as the broken glass of federalism. Did a county judge violate the Civil Rights Act by discriminating against black jurors? In *Ex parte Virginia,* the Court majority thought so. Field, arguing that Congress had no right to interfere in local matters, dissented. Was a West Virginia law banning blacks from juries unconstitutional? In *Strauder v. West Virginia* the Court said yes. Invoking federalism, Field said no. Black defendants, the Court ruled in *Virginia v.*

Rives, had no right to demand that blacks serve on their juries—and this time Field voted with the majority.

When Stephen Field first felt the itch presidential is unclear, but by the end of the decade, as a justice favorable to states' rights in civil rights cases and brother to John A. Campbell's co-counsel in *Cruikshank,* he owned the name of a northern man with southern principles, like Franklin Pierce and James Buchanan, the last two Democratic presidents, in the 1850s.

Fatal to his fledgling candidacies, in 1880 and 1884, was his opposition to states' rights in *corporate* cases. As we will see, Field used the Fourteenth Amendment to deny California's right to tax his friends' railroads as it saw fit. Reacting to reports in the San Francisco papers that Field's name would be placed in nomination at the 1884 Democratic National Convention, the California Democratic Party, at its convention in Stockton, inserted a platform plank "expressly repudiating the Presidential aspirations of Stephen J. Field" for serving as the railroads' shill. Each delegate pledged to support "Tilden first, Thurman second and Field never." Before the vote on Field, the convention chairman, Delphin M. Delmas, a San Francisco lawyer, wanted no California Democrats "licking the hand that smites them and accepting from the railroad corporations their chosen candidate, Stephen J. Field." The anti-Field plank passed 453–19. Though not a delegate, David Terry, a Stockton resident and local hero, was "said to be" behind Field's repudiation.[42]

A group of "Field Fighters" showed up at the national convention in Chicago, but Field's name was not put before it. Field blamed "the very strange action of California" in a letter to an associate. "[H]ad I received the cordial support . . . of that State, my candidacy, according to the judgment of my friends, would have stood a chance of success." He had harbored "some ambition to carry out certain measures which I believed would be of great advantage to the country," but "[n]ow my political life will be considered substantially at an end." To a fellow judge on the Ninth Circuit, Field regretted that "it seems to be an established rule with [politicians], that a candidate must have the support of his own state before he can expect the support of a National Convention."[43] Still, he retained his seat on the High Court, where "I may do some good, and after all position is only desirable as a means of doing good."

Field was for the New Orleans butchers and against the state of Louisiana, for the railroads and against the state of California, for varying constitutional reasons—but constant political ones. The *Slaughter-House* dissent staked out the ground he fought on for the rest of his twenty-three years on the Court, that his nephew, Justice David Brewer, fought on, that a Fieldian Court fought on from the mid-1890s until the New Deal, and that a new conservative Court may fight on into the twenty-first century: property over community. Field sounded Jacksonian in denouncing Crescent City's "monopoly," yet four years later, in *Pensacola Telegraph v. Western Union Company,* he taught it flat: "Florida possesses the absolute right to confer upon a corporation created by it exclusive privileges for a limited period." He went on to all but plagiarize Miller's rationale for Crescent City's slaughterhouse monopoly: "[T]he exclusive privilege often constitutes the only inducement for undertakings holding no prospect of immediate success." In his *Slaughter-House* dissent Field conceded that states might grant exclusive rights to "franchises of a public character appertaining to government"—like those held by ferry operators. Meat-cutting, however, was "an ordinary trade." The Louisiana statute violated the Fourteenth Amendment by depriving the butchers, echoing Campbell, of the "right to pursue" this "lawful and necessary calling."

The Constitution being silent on that right, Field turned to the Declaration of Independence. The Fourteenth Amendment "was intended to give practical effect to the declaration of 1776 of inalienable rights, rights which are the gift of the Creator, which the law does not confer, but only recognizes." The right to pursue a "lawful calling" is among these inalienable rights. In a footnote he cites Adam Smith: "The property which every man has in his own labor, as it is the original foundation of all other property, so it is the most sacred and inviolable."

That workers have property rights in their labor was at the core of "artisan republicanism," the historian Sean Wilentz's coinage for the anticapitalist worldview of tradesmen and labor publicists in antebellum New York. In its name they challenged employers' rights to dictate working hours and condemned low wages as property theft. During the years of Field's apprenticeship and early practice in his brother's Manhattan office, these arguments were in the air. They had since found their way into the rhetoric of free labor and antimonopoly, of which Field's dissent is a powerful example. As social theory, the views Field expressed in the dissent were unexceptionable, even, invoked against monopoly, progressive; but they had no standing as law.[44]

No constitutional authority inheres in the Declaration, much less in *The Wealth of Nations.* "Constitutional doctrine must judge ordinary law as a matter of course—whether the subject is federalism, separation of powers, speech or religion, but in each of these areas there is a constitutional text somewhere in the vicinity to offer guidance (or at least cover) for the development of doctrine," Charles Fried writes, explaining "untethered judicial power." "Due process is cut adrift from such textual guides." With procedural due process, a long practice of adjudication had established standards of fairness that must be observed in trials. "But when due process becomes a rubric for judging the *substance* of law, the guidance of professional norms . . . is no longer available and the judges appear to be cast adrift on a sea of subjective preference and unbounded specula-tion."[45] Fried cites *Dred Scott,* but his strictures apply to Field's *Slaughter-House* dissent and subsequent majority opinions that wielded substantive due process against state laws for violating a right invented by John A. Campbell.

Field anchored substantive due process in a state of nature with surprising amenities, and his epigones liked the view. Here, in an 1891 lecture, "Pro-tection to Private Property from Public Attack," is David Brewer: "From the earliest records when Eve took loving possession of even the forbidden apple, the idea of property and the sacredness of the right of its possession has never departed from the race. When, among the affirmatives of the Declaration of Independence, it is asserted that the pursuit of happiness is one of the unalienable rights, it is meant that the acquisition, possession and enjoyment of property are matters which human government cannot forbid and which it cannot destroy." Chief Justice Melville W. Fuller, in an address to Congress on the Court's centennial in 1889, affirmed that "the rights to life, to use one's faculties in all lawful ways and to acquire prop-erty, are morally fundamental rights antecedent to constitutions which did not create but secured and protected them." In *A Treatise on the Limitations of the Police Power* (1886), which became "a rich source . . . for citations jus-tifying judicial invalidation of state regulation," the legal scholar Christo-pher G. Tiedeman joined the conservative migration to Nature: "The private rights of the individual . . . belong to man in a state of nature; they are natural rights, recognized and existing in the law of reason." The Founders had invoked natural rights to overleap the rule of a king and jus-tify self-rule; the laissez-faire jurists of the Gilded Age, to overleap the Constitution and negate self-rule.

Writing in 1909, Roscoe Pound, the Progressive legal scholar, identified Field's dissent as "the fountain head" of a "reactionary line of decisions" in the New York state courts that cited the descendant of Field's "right to

pursue lawful callings" to strike down social legislation. This was "the liberty to contract," a figment of the judicial mind "not only unheard of, but
even undreamed of, in the nearly six hundred years since . . . the Magna
Carta" that treated workers and employers as equals in bargaining over
what meant life to one and profit to the other. In the pioneer case, *In re
Jacobs* (1885), the New York Supreme Court voided a statute prohibiting
the manufacture of cigars in tenement dwellings for violating of the cigarmakers' right to contract for the terms of their own labor. The immigrant
cigar roller smearing the nicotine off his fingers with the family tablecloth
was a self-dependent entrepreneur. "Paternalistic" legislation like the New
York ban on tenement labor denied him his free labor right to pursue a
lawful calling, "the distinguishing privilege of all citizens of the United
States," as Stephen Field wrote in his *Slaughter-House* dissent, cited in *In re
Jacobs.* Free labor lent liberty of contract its economics and its vision of a
classless America. In the name of preserving the phantasmal economic
independence of the American worker, it denied him, her, and the kids the
rudiments of economic security.

Samuel Gompers, then a vice president of the Cigarmakers International Union, had spent "years of educational work" tutoring New York
state legislators in the evils of the "sweating system" in the "Bohemian
tenements." But "securing the enactment of a law does not mean the solution of the problem," Gompers wrote in his autobiography. An imperial
judiciary had blocked the legislative path to reform. Labor could not look
to the state; only to "strikes and agitations." *In re Jacobs* had given *Gompers*
an education; the anti-statist turn the American Federation of Labor subsequently took, its embrace of laissez-faire logic and language, and the
narrowing of its social ideal to "more" was its fruit. Judge-made law
"shaped" the distinctive feature of the American labor movement: Just
when England's unions were forming the Independent Labour Party to
push "a political programme" including the eight-hour day, American
labor rejected politics.[46]

Roscoe Pound's *Yale Law Review* article, "Liberty of Contract," includes
a roll call of similar decisions from other states, all tending to the judicial
suppression of labor. The California Supreme Court found that a city ordinance requiring city contractors to grant their employees an eight-hour
day violated *their* freedom to contract; and, in an 1899 decision citing the
Slaughter-House dissents, it struck down a law requiring employers to pay
employees at least once a month. A law mandating that coal should be
weighed to fix compensation for miners was, in the opinion of the Illinois

high court, an "undue interference" with the miners' "liberty of contract."
An Illinois mandate on iron mills to pay money wages rather than in
goods at the company store was "degrading and insulting" to the laborers
because it prevented them "from making their own contracts." An eight-
hour-day law for women and children employed in Illinois's factories and
mines denied the right of ten-year-old "breaker boys" to negotiate their
own hours of work with the downstate coal companies. Courts in Kansas,
Missouri, Colorado, and West Virginia rejected anti–company store laws
on the same socially unconscious grounds.[47]

"The restraining effect of judicial pronouncements is conjectural,"
Robert McCloskey writes in *The American Supreme Court*.[48] But going without pay for months or being paid in scrip cashable only at company stores
or having to work four more hours a day were not conjectural harms. In
an 1899 article in the *American Sociological Review*, Jane Addams traced the
roots of trade unionists' cynical realism about the law: "The one symp-
tom among workmen which most definitely indicates" their alienation
from political society "is a growing distrust of the integrity of the courts,
the belief that the present judge has been a corporate attorney, that his
sympathies and experiences and his view of life is on the corporate side."
Pound linked the violence of the era's strikes to workers' despair of finding justice in the courts. Exhibit A was Colorado. After the Colorado
Supreme Court turned back the state legislature's eight-hour bill for mining and smelter workers, the miners turned to "militant action." The leaders of the Western Federation of Miners, Charles Moyer and Big Bill
Haywood, helped found the anarchist International Workers of the
World. "The men now realize that they will never get relief by legislation,
and that they must get it through their own action," Moyer said after 80
percent of the miners voted to join the IWW in 1905. Colorado became
the scene of warfare between state militia acting for the "Smelter Trust"
and miners radicalized by government by the judiciary.[49]

Rufus Peckham, the New York State Supreme Court justice who issued
In re Jacobs, took liberty of contract with him to the Supreme Court in
1895, and wrote the unanimous opinion that first extended its reach to the
nation in a case testing a state's right to regulate a private business; the
state, fittingly enough, was Louisiana. In the federal courts liberty of contract jurisprudence came into its own after Field retired in 1897. Its cynosure is *Lochner v. New York* (1905), "still shorthand in constitutional law for
the worst sins of subjective judicial activism," "a symbol of everything
that is to be avoided in constitutional adjudication"; this is a view shared

by the liberal William O. Douglas and the conservative William Rehnquist. In *Lochner* a closely divided court, with David Brewer in the majority, held that a New York state law setting a ten-hour day and sixty-hour week for bakery workers violated the "liberty of person and freedom of contract . . . of master and employe[e] alike." For, Peckham wrote for the court, "[T]he general right to make a contract in relation to his business is . . . protected by the 14th Amendment of the Federal Constitution."[50]

Liberty of contract, Progressive critics charged, belonged to "the heaven of legal concepts." Roscoe Pound located that heaven in the colleges. The chapter in John Stuart Mill's *Principles of Political Economy* (1852) entitled "On the Grounds and Limits of the Laisser Faire or Non-Interference Principle" "was studied by every liberally educated lawyer of the last fifty years." The relevant passage: "The great majority of things are worse done by the interference of the government, than the individuals concerned in the matter would do them, or cause them to be done, if left to themselves. Even in those portions of conduct which do affect the interest of others, the onus of making a case always lies on the defenders of legislative prohibition. Laisser-faire, in short, should be the general practice; every departure from it, unless required by some great good, is a definite evil." The edition of Mill used in the schools omitted the chapters on the limits of laissez-faire and on government's positive role in the economy. The editor, Harvard economist J. Laurence Laughlin, who "is said even to have objected to the use of the word 'social,' " wanted only pure doctrine disseminated. Whether under Laughlin or his colleague Francis Bowen ("Things regulate themselves . . . which means, of course that God regulates them"), Arthur Latham Perry at Williams, Francis Amasa Walker at Amherst, the political scientist John Burgess at Columbia, or Arthur Twining Hadley and William Graham Sumner at Yale, young men learned contempt for government that *does*. The newly formed American Bar Association became a temple of this faith, lawyers its priesthood, judges its enforcers. In 1892 ABA president John Forbes Dillon, in his annual address, declared his profession pleased that, through the Constitution, the people had "effectually protected themselves against themselves." That view of their work would have surprised the Framers, who, Pound noted, "intended to protect the people against their rulers, not against themselves."[51]

For Stephen Field the Fourteenth Amendment was a set of keys to open the lock fastened on property by legislatures besotted with communism.

He tried the key labeled "privileges and immunities" in *Slaughter-House* and the "due process" key in the Granger cases, but neither fit. He tried again with "equal protection of the laws," and that key went in.

State courts had long "presumed" public corporations to be "freemen" or "persons," but private corporations did not seek that status until the Fourteenth Amendment made being a person worthwhile.[52] Starting in the 1870s, corporate lawyers pursuing the prized status for their clients encountered two barriers: Miller's *Slaughter-House* ruling that the Negro was the "person" whose rights the amendment protected; and the opinion of Judge Woods, in an 1870 New Orleans Circuit Court case, *Continental Insurance Co. v. New Orleans,* that only natural "persons" can be "born and naturalized"; corporations, which cannot be born and naturalized, cannot be citizens.[53] But Justice Field, taking a constitutional back channel, steadily eroded Miller's "persons of the Negro race" standard; not on the Supreme Court, where precedent controlled, but in a series of rulings in the Ninth Circuit Court in San Francisco. Field could escape precedent there thanks to the Reconstruction Congress, which had denied the Supreme Court jurisdiction in habeus corpus cases as a hedge against Taneyism. From such unappealable cases Field wrote his own "Ninth Circuit law": the Pacific beachhead of the corporate person.[54]

At issue in these cases were the rights of Chinese immigrants, as hated on the West Coast as blacks were in the South. In *The Twenty-Two Chinese Prostitutes,* officially *In re Ah Fong* (1874), Field held that a California law barring entry to persons deemed "lunatic, idiotic . . . crippled . . . lewd and debauched" not only infringed on the right of Congress to set treaty policy, but violated the equal protection clause of the Fourteenth Amendment, which protected the rights of "persons," not just the "citizens" covered by the privileges and immunities clause he had invoked the year before on behalf of the New Orleans butchers. The California Commissioner of Immigration had prohibited the prostitutes carried on the U.S. steamship *Japan* from landing unless bonds were posted for each of them. Field found the bonds violative of the Civil Rights Act of 1870, "which was passed under and accords with the spirit of the Fourteenth Amendment." That amendment's guarantee of equal protection of the laws "implies . . . equal exemption with others of the same class from all charges and burdens of every kind." Yet "foreigners of the same classes entering the state in any other way, by land from the British possessions in Mexico, or over the plains by railway" were not made to post bonds. Field "had little respect for that discriminating virtue which is shocked when a frail child of China is landed upon our shores, and yet allows the bedizened and painted harlot of other countries to parade our streets and open her hells in broad daylight without molestation and without censure." At heart, *Ah Fong* was an economic, not a civil rights, case. The bonding requirement, like the Crescent City monopoly for the New Orleans butchers, debarred Ah Fong and her associates from practicing their all-too-ordinary trade. When another of the prostitutes, Chy Lung, appealed a similar case to the Supreme Court, it struck down the California bonding law solely for trespassing on Congress's authority over immigration. Field joined the decision, but "passed on the opportunity to write a concurrence to Justice Miller's opinion and thereby promulgate his *Ah Fong* theory," Thomas Wuil Joo notes. "To do so might have drawn unwelcome attention to the maverick nature of Justice Field's west coast jurisprudence."[55]

Humanitarianism toward the Chinese flowed over onto corporations when Field's circuit court colleagues struck down an article in the California Constitution forbidding corporations to hire Chinese: in denying *both* "persons" rights to "pursue lawful callings" it violated the Fourteenth Amendment. Field's *Slaughter-House* dissent was the law if not of the land then of the Ninth Circuit, where corporations were "persons" just like Chinese laborers and southern Negroes. Corporation lawyers picked up on these welcome rulings and began citing Ninth Circuit law, not the *Slaughter-House Cases,* as the authoritative word on the Fourteenth Amendment. But the path to corporate personhood still led through the Supreme Court and Field needed a test case to take there. California, in the words of a turn-of-the-century commentator, was about to "place the corporation in an almost impregnable constitutional position."[56]

Hard times had betrayed the California dream. Burdened by mortgages, afflicted by drought, kept from markets by high railroad tariffs on their shipments, farmers were losing their farms and falling to farm laborers. As early as 1869 farms in Merced County, in the San Joaquin Valley, had annual payrolls nine times the national average. Chinese immigrants—"Those mudsills at the bottom of our success," one farmer called them—and white "bummers," transient laborers, harvested the fruit and vegetables of these vast farms, "though how . . . after [the harvest] they maintain themselves is not known," the state bureau of labor observed. By 1860 surface mining had played out in California. Miners might now work 2,000 to 3,000 feet underground, digging out quartz in one-hundred-degree temperatures—for mining corporations. "Instead of having the lure of wealth before them like the 49ers," a California historian writes, "these workers had nothing to hope for but their wages and nothing to lose but their jobs." Meanwhile, nearly 300,000 migrants seeking to escape the depression in the East had arrived. The depression followed them. Unemployment increased. Many blamed competition from California's 70,000 Chinese immigrants, who comprised 10 percent of the population but 20 percent of the workforce, and the railroad that recruited them to break through the Sierras by legendary feats of courage like carving through the cliffs above the American River by "lowering one another in wicker baskets to drill holes, set powder, and fire it off." Dennis Kearny, the sinister Irish-born organizer of the Workingmen's Party, harangued crowds of unemployed men gathered on the sandlots across from San Francisco's new city hall with cries of "The Chinese. . . . The Corporations. . . . The Southern Pacific Railroad . . . must go!"[57]

Farmer, miner, and urban worker discontent found vent in the California Constitutional Convention of 1878–79, which drew up a new constitution merciless toward the Chinese and tough on the railroads. In this new climate, being known as a champion of Chinese rights would destroy Field's chances of winning the Democratic presidential nomination in 1880: He called for a federal law banning further immigration from China. "We are alarmed upon this coast at the incursion of the Chinese," he told a reporter. "We declare that it is our conviction that the practical issue is, whether the civilization of this coast, its society, morals, and industry shall be of American or Asiatic type." The Chinese prostitutes and laundry men had done their work, riding constitutional interference for the railroads. Or rather railroad, for by the late 1870s, with the Southern Pacific under lease to the Central Pacific, one system spanned California, the two-million-mile "Octopus" of Frank Norris's 1901 novel. "Nowhere in the country is there a corner on transportation so complete as this," Henry Demarest Lloyd reported. "One company in which half a dozen families own practically all the stock holds in its grip every ironed highway by which you enter or leave the State of California or ship your goods in or out." Hatred of the Octopus extended beyond sandlot radicals to merchants paying monopoly rates to ship or receive goods and to farmers lured into the barren southern San Joaquin Valley by the railroad's broken promises of cheap land. Passion writes punitive laws. Shifting the tax burden from individuals to railroads, the constitution denied them "the right to deduct the amount of their debts [i.e., mortgages] from the taxable value of their property, a right which was given to individuals," the Field biographer Carl B. Swisher writes.[58] And passion can be manipulated. In his account of the convention Swisher finds it "plausible" that lawyer-delegates representing the railroad encouraged that invidious provision to shape an equal protection challenge to the Supreme Court. Another stresses the role played by Field's nemesis and victim, David Terry, in framing the tax article. Anti-monopolist Democrats like Terry saw railroad mortgages as a device for raising capital while avoiding paying taxes.[59]

In the event, the Southern Pacific refused, on constitutional grounds, to pay taxes based on the new scheme. Deprived of the railroad's tax revenue for 1880–82, which ran into the millions, San Mateo and its sister counties closed schools and cut back on other public services. The counties filed suits against the railroad to recover the withheld taxes. In *San Mateo County v. Southern Pacific Railroad Company* the state Supreme Court sustained the county. That should have ended the litigation, but the Inverted Constitution came to the aid of the Southern Pacific. Under the Jurisdiction and Removal Act of 1875, black litigants could appeal to the federal courts if denied justice by southern state courts. The railroad had a friend on the federal bench, so it put on blackface and appealed for removal. The law limited removal to cases raising an issue of "citizen's rights under the Constitution." The constitutional issue, the state argued, had been raised only in the railroad's briefs not by the facts of the case.[60] But Justice Field, presiding over the Ninth Circuit, said his hands were tied by a statute he'd opposed, and granted removal to his own court, where a lawyer he recommended to the Southern Pacific argued its case.[61]

With its two-tier tax scheme, Field held in *San Mateo v. Southern Pacific Railroad Company*, California transgressed the Fourteenth Amendment, which "forbids the State to lay its hand more heavily upon one than another under like conditions." If a farmer could deduct the value of his mortgage from his tax bill, why couldn't a railroad? "All the guarantees and safeguards of the Constitution for the protection of property possessed by individuals may . . . be invoked for the protection of property of corporations."[62] But this equation worked only if individuals and corporations partook of the same legal essence.[63] Citing his own "Ninth Circuit law," Field put the historic words in double apposition, as if they were uncontroversial, needing no assertion: "The defendant, being a corporation, a person within the meaning of the 14th amendment," should be "entitled, with respect to its property, to equal protection of the laws."[64] While it was true that the "occasion of the amendment was the supposed denial of rights to newly made citizens of the African race . . . the generality of the language used extends its provisions to persons of every race and condition against discriminatory and hostile state action of every kind." After all, Chief Justice Marshall had laid it down that, "The case being within the words of the rule, must be within its operation likewise." But, even granting elasticity to the word, how did *corporations* qualify as "persons"? Field conceded that "[p]rivate corporations are artificial persons." Still, "they consist of aggregations of individuals united for some legitimate business purpose. . . . It would be a most singular result if a constitutional provision intended for the protection of every person against partial and discriminating legislation by the states, should cease to exert such protection the moment a person becomes a member of a corporation." Field would have us "look beyond the name of the artificial being" to the real persons who own it. California's invidious taxation scheme abrogated the corporations' Fourteenth Amendment rights to equal protection of the laws.

This "associational theory" of the corporation broke new judicial ground. Building on Marshall's classification of the corporation as "an artificial being . . . possessing only those properties which the charter of its creation confers on it" in the *Dartmouth College* case of 1819, Chief Justice Taney, in *Bank of Augusta v. Earle,* ruled in 1839 that whenever a corporation makes a contract it is a contract of that "legal entity" and "not a contract of the individual members." The associational theory would "make a corporation a mere partnership in business, in which each stockholder would be liable to the whole extent of his property" for corporate debts, forfeiting limited liability protection. Field's theory opened that can of worms. Field's colleague, Judge Lorenzo Sawyer, endorsed the theory, quoting as Field did not from its source, the brief presented by John Norton Pomeroy, counsel for the Southern Pacific. But Sawyer also asserted that "A corporation, *itself* [my italics] . . . is a person," adumbrating the "natural entity" theory adopted by the Supreme Court in *Hale v. Henkel* (1905). From artifice of the state "existing only in contemplation of the law" to association of persons to organic entity or "group person"—such was the metaphysical progress of the corporation. Beginning as an institution that could do only "those things specifically allowed by its charter," it evolved into "one . . . which . . . could do anything not specifically prohibited to it."[65]

San Mateo was not a habeas corpus case, so California appealed Field's ruling to a reconstituted Supreme Court.

Through the 1870s, Waite and Miller had rallied the Court to uphold state regulation of railroads and grain elevators, businesses "affected with a public interest," in the phrase Waite borrowed from Lord Chief Justice Matthew Hale, a seventeenth-century English jurist, and subject to a measure of public control. "It's beginning to look Pretty Certain that a RR entering the Supreme Court of the U.S. leaves hope behind," the president of the Illinois Central complained.[66] But by 1882 the composition of the Court had changed. Since 1877, five justices had left, four of whom had made the majorities in the *Slaughter-House, Granger,* and *Sinking Fund* decisions, the latter requiring Field's friends at the Central Pacific to pay into the Treasury early installments on the interest charges for the millions borrowed from the government.[67] The cunning of the corporation had worked the wires of mortality, political ambition, and senescence.

The argument from paternity made by the Southern Pacific's lead counsel before the Supreme Court in *San Mateo* may rank as the strangest pleading in court history. Never before had an author of a constitutional provision testified to its meaning. The founding father of the Fourteenth Amendment called on in *San Mateo* was former New York senator Roscoe Conkling, who had been President Grant's first choice to succeed Salmon P. Chase as chief justice in 1874 and earlier in the year had declined President Chester A. Arthur's nomination as associate justice. Conkling was a spoilsman—the *New York Times* suggested that he turned down Arthur's appointment because a justice has no patronage to dispense—notorious for his lavender vests, his japes ("the snivel service"; "Rutherfraud B. Hayes"), and, in the words of James G. Blaine, "his haughty disdain, his grandiloquent swell, his majestic, super-eminent, over-powering turkey-gobbler strut." Collis P. Huntington was paying Conkling $5,000 for fraud not flair—but got both.

"I come now to say that the Southern Pacific Railroad Company and its *creditors* and *stockholders,*" Conkling began his argument, "are among the persons protected by the Fourteenth Amendment." For proof, in a piece of stage business that captured the attention of the justices, Conkling produced the hitherto secret "Journal of the Joint Committee on Reconstruction," the committee that drafted the amendment and of which he was a member; and by selective quotation insinuated that its framers had used "person" instead of "citizen" in Article 1 to make room for corporations, who "at the time the Fourteenth Amendment was ratified . . . were appealing for congressional . . . protection against invidious and discriminating state and local taxes."[68] One historian finds "no contemporary evidence—nothing in the records of the Joint Committee" to support that farrago, which struck Field as "great." It *was* clever: a way of rebutting the *Slaughter-House* presumption that Congress's "particular purpose" in framing the amendment was to protect African-Americans against the punitive actions of southern state governments. Field's "Ninth Circuit" grant of personhood to corporations, a head-on assault, was unlikely to prevail.[69]

Conkling may have sensed skepticism in the chamber: The justices might ask to examine the journal. So he argued in the alternative—and turned up the flair. Forget the intentions of its framers. Consider the protean vagueness of the amendment's wording—the capacious invitation extended by "persons." Construe the amendment in that light and "how minor and needless become conjectures about what the actors in a past scene knew or 'believed' . . . as to incidents in the future which might invoke the aid of a principle of law." Whether he was wearing it or not, he spoke in lavender:

> Man being human, and his vision finite, it is well that saving ordinances need not be shrunken in their uses or duration to the measure of what the framers foresaw. . . . A tree, a fountain, a lamp set in the public way—a beacon on the cliff—a buoy on the sea . . . becomes the common property of wayfarers, whoever they may be. . . .
>
> To the Mongoloian and the Caucasian, as well as to the African, the Constitution says,
>
> *"Humani nihil a me alienum puto."*

And here Roscoe Conkling, in another Supreme Court first, *sang* a stanza from an Emerson poem:

> The hand that rounded Peter's dome
> And groined the aisles of Christian Rome
> Wrought in a sad sincerity.
> *He builded better than he knew!*

"Those who devised the Fourteenth Amendment wrought in grave sincerity," he concluded. "They may have builded better than they knew." The future belonged to that reading not to Samuel Miller's. Until the Second Reconstruction of the 1960s the Fourteenth Amendment protected the rights of all persons, animate and corporate, against arbitrary state action—*except* Miller's "unfortunate race who had suffered so much."[70]

Following the conclusion of argument in the case, Field attended a dinner given by Leland Stanford at a prominent Washington restaurant in honor of Conkling and his co-counsels. Editorials criticized his indiscretion, and a cartoon appeared that "accused [Field] of making a mockery of justice," one of Waite's biographers writes. Waite, who valued the judicial proprieties, clipped and marked it "Judge Field's Dinner at Chamberlin's."[71]

Field's railroad affinities had embarrassed the Court before. Waite precipitated a row with Field over the issue, asking him not to write the majority opinion on an earlier railroad case, even though it was his turn in the rotation. "There was no doubt of your intimate personal relations with the managers of the Central Pacific," the chief justice explained, "and it would tend to discredit the opinion if it came from someone known as the personal friend of the parties representing these rail road interests."[72] Given their history with Field, the justices had reason to doubt the statistics in his *San Mateo* opinion. Borrowing from the railroad's brief, Field asserted that the mortgage on the Southern Pacific "exceeds $3,000 a mile," when the real figure exceeded $40,000, a figure that would have brought home to the justices the magnitude of the tax exemption contended for and imparted a touch of the risible to Field's argument that California had imposed "unequal burdens" on the Southern by treating its mortgage differently from a farmer's mortgage on his lettuce patch. Putting off their decision, his colleagues asked Field to hear more of the railroad tax cases to compile more (and more accurate) evidence.[73]

San Mateo dragged on for three more years—time for the railroads to find a sturdier vehicle raising the same equal protection issues in a group of cases from Santa Clara County. In 1885, "fake messages" purportedly from San Mateo county officials were sent to the Supreme Court, claiming that the railroad had settled with the county and asking for dismissal of the case. In fact a settlement "bearing the mark of legality," according to an early-twentieth-century authority on California's financial history, would not be reached "until many years later."[74] Meanwhile San Mateo County agreed to take whatever the railroad condescended to give it. Noting that the Southern Pacific had "essentially dictate[d] the terms of its own taxation," the *Los Angeles Times* drew the political moral of the age: "[There can] be no more forceful illustration of the fact that a power had grown up in the State greater than the State itself."[75]

Before oral arguments in *Santa Clara County v. Southern Pacific Railroad Company*, speaking from the bench Chief Justice Waite addressed the attorneys for the railroad. What Waite said, on January 26, 1886, should be among the most controverted dicta in Court history.[76]

In the triangular system of checks and balances the Court fights its corner on the page. Its opinions reach the legal fraternity in book form, in *United States Reports*. For most of the nineteenth century the volumes were named after the court reporters who edited them—Wheaton, Wallace, Otto. Citations to an opinion might read 33 Wallace 54, designating the volume number, reporter, and page of the cite. A section in small type known as a "headnote" in which the reporter-editor summarized the opinion, usually followed by a "syllabus" outlining the main facts and arguments, prefaced each case. In *U.S. v. Detroit Timber and Lumber* (1905), the Court defined headnotes as "simply the work of the Reporter, given his understanding of the decision, and is prepared for the convenience of the profession." That last phrase gives away the secret of headnotes. When seeking a glancing citation to support their arguments or situate their opinions in the chain of precedent, lawyers and judges relied on the summaries in the headnotes. In preparing them the reporter employed sources ranging from the unimpeachable, the written record, to the doubtful, his memory, aided by shorthand notes taken in court, to recapture colloquies between the justices and lawyers in oral argument. The reporter, clearly, was no mere stenographer. The Court chose men of standing for the job, which, in salary and royalties from the sale of the *Reports*, could earn the reporter $2,000 a year more than the justices.[77]

In 1886 the reporter was John Chandler Bancroft Davis, a former assistant secretary of state and minister to Germany under Grant, who had served with Waite in the *Alabama* claims litigation at Geneva in 1871 and remained his friend. As early as his first full year on the Court, Waite tried to make Davis reporter, but, in an embarrassment for the chief justice, a majority of the justices voted instead for William Otto, a former Indiana judge supported by Stephen J. Field. When Otto retired, in 1883, the Court voted unanimously to appoint Davis.[78]

Davis's first headnote to *Santa Clara County v. South Pacific Railroad Co.* reads: "The defendant Corporations are persons within the intent of the clause in section 1 of the Fourteenth Amendment to the Constitution of the United States, which forbids a state to deny to any person equal protection of the laws."[79] He summarizes the Court's additional findings, which, given the constitutional stakes, baffle expectations. The syllabus, too, leaves the reader at a loss: How could these facts yield *that* declaration? The facts did *not* yield it. After noting that counsel for the defense had argued "at length" that California's system of unequal taxation—one standard for individuals, another for railroads—was unconstitutional under the equal protection clause of the Fourteenth Amendment, the reporter elucidates the mystery:

"Before argument, Mr. Chief Justice Waite said: 'The Court does not want to hear argument on the question whether the Fourteenth Amendment to the Constitution, which forbids a State to deny any person within its jurisdiction equal protection of the laws, applies to these corporations. We are all of the opinion that it does.' "

That is Davis's rendering of Waite's statement to the Southern Pacific attorneys. To make sure he had it right, while compiling material for Volume 118 of *United States Reports,* Davis sent Waite this note, dated May 26, 1886:

> Dear Chief Justice
>   I have a memorandum in the California Cases
>   Santa Clara County
>   v.
>   Southern Pacific &c
>   As follows.
>   In opening the Court stated that it did not wish to hear argument on the question whether the Fourteenth Amendment applies to such corporations as are parties in these suits. All the Judges were of the opinion that it does.

To which Waite, in a less legible hand, replied on May 31: "I think your mem. in the California Railroad Tax cases expresses with sufficient accuracy what was said before the argument began. I leave it with you to determine whether anything need be said about it in the report inasmuch as we avoided meeting the constitutional question in the decision."[80]

"In other words, to the Reporter fell the decision which enshrined the declaration in the *United States Reports,*" writes C. Peter Magrath, who discovered this exchange in the Davis papers while researching his *Morrison C. Waite: The Triumph of Character.* "Had Davis left it out," Magrath adds, "*Santa Clara County v. Southern Pac[ific] R[ailroad] Co.* would have been lost to history among thousands of uninteresting tax cases."[81]

In fact it *is* an uninteresting tax case. Justice Harlan's (unanimous) opinion decides the fate of fences. It finds that the fences running beside the tracks of the Southern Pacific Railroad in Santa Clara County are not taxable by the state of California, which illegally included them in its assessment of the total value of the railroad's property, which assessment it used to tax the railroad, prorating the revenues collected to each county crossed by the railroad according to the length of track it contained. Fences are not "property"; under the California constitution, they are "improvements," and as such taxable only by the county, which cannot collect damages from the railroad for withholding taxes it should not have been required to pay. Polonius was a lawyer.[82]

True, Harlan notes, counsel for the railroad avoided the issue that decided the case. As Davis reports in the headnotes, "The main—almost the only—questions discussed by counsel related to the constitutionality of the taxes."[83] But the Court, Harlan says, avoided *that* argument. "These questions are of a class which the court should not decide," involving as they do "construction of the recent National Amendments" and California's "system of taxation, unless their determination is essential to the disposal of the case in which they arise."[84] In a concurrence to a second railroad tax case with the same facts as *Santa Clara, San Bernardino County v. Southern Pacific Railroad,* and decided in tandem with it, Justice Field agreed with the Court's verdict, but regretted "that it has not been deemed consistent with its duty to decide the important constitutional questions involved" that Harlan seemed relieved were not essential to decide *Santa Clara.*[85]

"Thus without argument or opinion on the point," Justice William O. Douglas wrote in 1949, "the *Santa Clara* case becomes one of the most momentous of all our decisions. . . . Corporations were now armed with constitutional prerogatives." And all thanks to a "fluke," the pondered word chosen a generation ago by Howard Jay Graham, in a paper on the roots of corporate personality, to describe this historic episode of reporter-made law.[86]

Why did the chief justice issue his dictum? Why did he leave it up to Davis to include it in the headnotes? After Waite told him that the Court "avoided" the issue of corporate personhood, why *did* Davis include it? Why, indeed, did he begin his headnote with it? The opinion made plain that the Court did not decide the corporate personality issue and the subsidiary equal protection issue. Did Davis, like so many judges, lawyers, and law professors since, even bother to read it? And, since Waite's dictum represented a victory for Stephen Field (though not the one—on equal protection and taxes—he wanted), did he play a backstage role in the scandal of *Santa Clara*?

———

Magrath's interpretation of his subject's most consequential judicial act is deflationary. Corporate personality was no big deal, accepted for centuries in common law. "Matter-of-factly" used in a bill passed by Congress in 1871: "[I]n all acts hereafter . . . the word 'person' may extend and be applied to bodies politics and corporate." Implicitly assumed in at least four Supreme Court opinions since 1874. Stated explicitly by Waite himself in his *Sinking-Fund Cases* opinion—viz, "[E]qually with the states they [the United States] are prohibited from depriving persons or corporations of property without due process of law."[87] Waite, in sum, took corporate personhood for granted, and saw no conflict between it and his belief in the constitutionality of corporate regulation. McGrath continues: "For unless Waite regarded it as a fairly routine instruction to counsel, it seems almost inconceivable that he would have delegated the announcement of a major constitutional doctrine to the Court Reporter." But if the corporate "person" was so casually assumed, why did Huntington need to hire Conkling to go behind *Slaughter-House* to the intentions of the amendment's framers?[88]

Magrath loses perspective in trying to gain it. Waite's dictum in the *Sinking-Fund Cases*—the state cannot deprive "persons or corporations" of property without due process of law—does not establish that Waite believed "corporations *are* persons" entitled to equal protection of the laws. Assent to the one does not require assent to the other. They say different things. The *Sinking-Fund* dictum (which, Graham suggests, Field may have "pressured" Waite to include or which he may have included as a gesture of comity to Field, who lost the decision on substance) chiefly refers to due process rights under the Fifth Amendment, which applies against the federal government, whose actions were at issue in that case. Due process means nonarbitrary: Corporations, like persons, could not be abused by "partial and discriminating" legislation—an unexceptionable point. But the history of the Waite Court suggests the unlikelihood of Waite's endorsing "equal protection" for corporations. Under Waite the Court consistently restricted the meaning of equal protection, rendering ten decisions involving that clause of the amendment and striking down a law for violating it only once, in *Yick Wo v. Hopkins,* handed down the same day as *Santa Clara.*[89] A San Francisco ordinance invidiously restricting the operations of Chinese laundries, the Court unanimously ruled, violated equal protection, which "extends to all persons within the territorial jurisdiction of the US without regard to differences of race, color, or nationality."[90] In any case, Waite did not sign off on "equal protection." The phrase does not appear in Davis's memo to him; only in the "*Santa Clara* decision."

Graham's analysis starts with that routine instruction. He terms it an "informal request" to the defense lawyers "designed to expedite argument." And thinks Waite said "something to this effect":

> The Court does not wish to hear further argument on whether the Fourteenth Amendment applies to these corporations. The point was elaborately covered in 1882 [by Conkling, in his *San Mateo* argument], and has been recovered in your briefs. We all presently are clear enough there. Our doubts run rather to the substance. *Assume,* accordingly, *as we do* [italics added], that your clients are persons under the Equal Protection Clause. Take the cases on from there, clarifying the California statutes, the application thereof, and the merits.[91]

But who is the "we" in Graham's "as we do"? Not the man sitting beside Waite while he spoke; not Samuel F. Miller. As counsel for the Southern Pacific in the San Mateo oral argument pointed out to Miller, his *Slaughter-House* opinion left room for "persons" other than southern Negroes to come under the protection of the Fourteenth Amendment. Miller agreed. Securing the rights of southern Negroes was its "pervading" not exclusive "purpose." He quoted the relevant lines from his opinion: "And so, if other rights are assailed by the States which properly and necessarily fall within the protection of these articles, that protection will apply, though the party interested may not be of African descent."[92] In *Barbier v. Connolly,* a case heard during the same term as *San Mateo,* the Court had moved toward embracing the dissents in the *Slaughter-House Cases*; at any rate Miller did not object to an expansive dictum Field inserted into the unanimous opinion: The Fourteenth Amendment "undoubtedly intended not only that there should be no arbitrary deprivation of life or liberty, or arbitrary spoilation of property, but that equal protection and security should be given to all under like circumstances in the enjoyment of their personal and civil rights. . . . Class legislation discriminating against some and favoring others, is prohibited." Nevertheless, except for Field's Ninth Circuit, no court had yet challenged the restrictive *Slaughter-House* rules for admission to the amendment or invited corporations to come in under them.[93]

Graham's concessive "as we do" may put the wrong words in Waite's mouth. It's as possible, and consistent with the record of his Court, Waite said something like this: *For the sake of argument,* let's assume your clients are persons under the Fourteenth Amendment. That will speed things up. Take the case from there . . . But if that is what Waite said (or meant to say), why didn't he object to Davis's twist on what he said? Why let Davis turn a rhetorical device into a landmark dictum? Waite *may* have read the words in Davis's note through the sense he had originally given them, overriding his perception of the difference between them and Davis's version of them.

Not conjectural is Waite's unsteady hand in his reply to Davis. Morrison Waite's labors on the Court had worn him down; the justices' workload, splitting their time between the circuit courts and the Supreme Court, was man-crushing—especially for the chief justice and more especially for Waite. He shouldered the burdens of leading the Court and harmonizing its strong personalities, and he had to write opinions—for him, an ordeal. Writing came hard, and it showed in his work. Felix Frankfurter complained of his "total want of style" and believed it kept Waite from receiving due recognition. "The difficulty with me," Waite once confessed to Field, "is that I cannot give the *reasons* as I wish I could." Emblematically, his most cited phrase, from *Munn v. Illinois,* that private businesses like grain elevators at the nodes of commerce are "affected with a public interest" he borrowed from Justice Bradley (who borrowed it from Lord Hale). (And, in Frankfurter's words, this "[v]ague and mischievous language . . . was readily adaptable to the restricting of government powers with rigid and unreal categories.") Finally, Waite had been ill. A little over a year earlier, Davis had worried that "he might break down before Spring comes"; Waite went to Florida for three months to restore his health. He may not have been dying when he left corporate personality up to Davis, but he would soon be dead.[94]

Davis may have gotten it right, may have misunderstood what Waite said or meant, or may have understood yet gone ahead to make constitutional law on his own. According to Karl Marx (!), Davis was a man to alter official records. During a December 1878 interview with Marx in London, an unnamed correspondent for the *Chicago Tribune* praised a report that Davis, when minister to Germany, had written of a convention of German socialists at Gotha as one of "the clearest and most concise expositions of socialism that I have seen." Davis's rendition of the Gotha platform contained a twelfth plank calling for "state aid and credit to industrial societies, under democratic direction" that was not in the convention platform; and the correspondent asked Marx to account for the discrepancy. "The 12th point was not placed [in] the platform," Marx explained, "but in the general introduction by way of concessions to the Lassalleans," a faction friendly to Bismarck's reich. "Afterwards, it was never spoken of. Mr. Davis does not say it was placed in the program as a compromise having no particular significance, but gravely puts it in as one of the cardinal principles of the program." This was a sensitive subject, because Mikhail Bakunin, the anarchist writer and radical celebrity, had exposed a socialist sore: their attraction to state power under the dictatorship of the proletariat—which the Davis-inserted twelfth point, in English language versions of the Gotha convention, could be taken to confirm. Davis handled the *Santa Clara* headnote similarly: He took a statement made in the "introduction" to the oral arguments and "gravely [put] it in as one of the cardinal principles" of the decision.[95]

The legal community echoed Marx's criticisms of Davis's procedures. "Many of Davis's headnotes were so vague that they gave no impression of the decision of the Court and sometimes they were quite misleading," Willard L. King, Chief Justice Fuller's biographer, writes. "The Harvard Law Review sharply criticized his headnotes on this score." Davis's character got a bruising in a case handed down the same day as *Santa Clara*. The shadow of Jay Gould darkens Davis in *Graham & Another v. Boston, Hartford, & Erie Railroad Company & Others*. Graham & Another, former stockholders in a defunct railroad, accused its former officers of mortgaging its assets to cover losses they incurred from speculating in the stock of other railroads, including, it appears, Gould's Erie. One of the trustees of the Boston, Hartford, they alleged, was at the same time "legal counsel and adviser" to the Erie, which, in transactions unfathomable to an honest man, wound up with the assets of the Boston, Hartford. The trustee-lawyer's conflict of interest breathed "collusion" and "fraud." That trustee, that lawyer, was John Bancroft Davis. The Court, as state and federal courts had done previously, not only turned *Graham & Another* down; it approved the assessment of laches—fines for delay—on them for bringing suit fourteen years after "the making of the mortgage, ten years after the commencement of the bankruptcy proceedings . . . and seven years after the foreclosure became absolute and the road was conveyed to a new corporation." So a headnote, written by John Bancroft Davis, (accurately) summarizes the opinion, which leaves the charge of collusion un-rebutted. The justices suffered Davis's résumé as a former assistant secretary of state turned Court reporter. (He "took a condescending attitude toward his work as Reporter and toward the Justices of the Court," King notes.) But the allegations made in *Graham & Another* undercut the impression he conveyed that he was too good for the job.[96]

Graham omits these Davis elements from his investigation of *Santa Clara*. He points the finger of suspicion beyond Davis—to Field. Davis, he surmises, "queried" Field to "determine whether anything need be said . . . in the report" and Field urged him on.[97] Consulting Field would have been a natural thing to do, since Waite's statement seemed to endorse Field's known position on corporate personality, and prudent on Davis's part, given Field's obsession with headnotes.

Supreme Court records reveal a shower of hectoring letters from Field to Davis about headnotes. The year before *Santa Clara*, Field criticizes one as "singularly defective"; another as "too broad." "I throw out these suggestions for what they are worth," he remarks of yet another headnote. "I am afraid you will think me a fault-finder." He not only scolds, he suggests variant wordings: "Of course it is only a suggestion. You will alter it, add to it, take from it as you like." In a bitter exchange, Field insisted that Davis change his headnote in the case of a Vermont man convicted of illegally selling liquor in that state even though he transacted his business in New York. Davis's note had stipulated: "No point on the commerce clause of the Constitution . . . was considered by the Vermont Supreme Court, or called to its attention." The defense *had* raised the commerce clause, Field insisted, and had brought it to the attention of the Vermont court; "at the first opportunity," Field would declare the headnote "to be an incorrect statement." In *O'Neil v. Vermont*, as in *Pennoyer v. Neff*, Field is trying to enshrine in the headnotes a constitutional issue avoided in the opinion, to win in the official record an argument discarded as irrelevant in the deliberation. To settle matters, Davis sent the correspondence to Chief Justice Fuller, who wrote Field that Davis was in the right. "The correctness of a head-note," he explained to Field, "depends on what is held in the opinion." By that standard, Davis's headnote to *Santa Clara*—the "*Santa Clara* decision" to the world—is incorrect.[98]

Obiter dicta—remarks made in passing—are not precedential. They solidify into "holdings" only when cited in subsequent opinions. Waite's *Santa Clara* dictum was first cited in a Supreme Court opinion in the obscure case of *Pembina Mining v. Pennsylvania*—by Stephen J. Field. He delivered it in the Court chamber on March 19, 1888, a poignant day in Court history, when Waite, stricken with pneumonia, had to break off reading his lengthy opinion in the Bell Telephone cases and leave the bench. "It was evident to the observer that death had placed its hand on him," one witness recalled. He died four days later. "The period of Waite's Chief Justiceship," Felix Frankfurter wrote, "is in large measure the history of a duel between him and Field." Field called Waite "His Accidency," after the manner of his ascent, but he was above all a necessary Chief Justice. With Samuel Miller, he had stood against Field's judge-made law, resisting the oligarchical temptations of the un-elected branch. Against the climate of advanced opinion, which, in Frankfurter's words, treated Adam Smith "as though his generalizations had been imparted to him on Sinai," Waite had defended the people's right to make the corporation answer to democracy.[99]

If there was a battle for the headnotes in *Pembina,* Field won it. "For the convenience of the profession" they enshrine a duplicity in his opinion. Pembina Mining Company, a Colorado firm, sued Pennsylvania for requiring it to pay a $250 license tax as a condition of maintaining an office in Philadelphia. The Pennsylvania Supreme Court upheld the tax. According to the reporter's summary of the case, Pembina argued that the tax was unconstitutional on two grounds: It violated the commerce clause by trespassing on Congress's power to regulate interstate commerce and Article 4, Section 11, which says that the citizens of each state are entitled to the privileges and immunities of the citizens of the several states. Field rejects those grounds as inapplicable and sustains the Pennsylvania Supreme Court. But Field adds a third ground to Pembina's case against the tax that Pembina did *not* argue: that the tax also violated "the [clause] embodied in the 14th amendment declaring that no state shall deny to any person within its jurisdiction the equal protection of the laws." Pembina was wrong on that one, too, he says, adding a gratuitous dictum to a factitious argument: "Under the designation of person, there is no doubt that a private corporation is included." That issue—not raised by the plaintiff in the Pennsylvania case and dismissed by Field in the opinion—is enshrined in the third headnote: "A private corporation is included under the designation of 'person' in the Fourteenth Amendment to the Constitution of the United States, Section 1." The first two headnotes are in the negative, stipulating that the "exaction of fees" from "foreign" (out-of-state) corporations does not violate the commerce clause and that corporations are not "citizens" within the privileges and immunities clause. *Pembina,* like *Pennoyer,* was a Potemkin ruling. Portia, in *The*

Merchant of Venice, knew how carelessly law can grow: "Twill be recorded for a precedent / And many an error, by the same example / Will rush into the State."[100]

Pembina lent *Santa Clara* the momentum of settled law. Corporate personality rolled—rolls—on. The corporate "person," Graham writes, became "the linchpin of judicially-sanctioned 'liberty to contract' and laissez faire."[101] Justice William O. Douglas, in a dissent in *Wheeling Steel v. Glander* (1949), cited twenty-eight cases in which "the Court has struck down state legislation as applied to corporations" for violating the rights of their persons. *Santa Clara* was judge-made (actually reporter-made) law in an area in which legislatures should rule. "It may be most desirable to give corporations this protection from the operations of the legislative process," Douglas argued. "But that question is not for us. It is for the people."[102] Douglas echoed the earlier critique of Justice Hugo Black. "The judicial inclusion of the word [corporation] . . . has had a revolutionary effect on our form of government," Black wrote in *Connecticut General Life Insurance v. Johnson* (1938). "The states did not adopt the Amendment with knowledge of its sweeping meaning under its present construction. No section of the Amendment gave notice to the people, that, if adopted, it would subject every state law and municipal ordinance, affecting corporations . . . to censorship of the United States courts." The inverted Constitution amounted to a judicial coup.*[103]

The Great Depression discredited laissez-faire; laissez-faire constitutionalism—"Lochnerism"—discredited itself. In the space of thirteen months during FDR's first term, the Court "struck down more important laws, federal and state, than at any time over its two centuries' history, before or since," according to William E. Leuchtenburg, among them "the foundation stones" of the New Deal, the National Industrial Recovery Act and the Agricultural Adjustment Act. On one occasion the old-guard justices harried FDR's solicitor general, Stanley Reed, "so relentlessly from the bench that he fainted in the courtroom." "The most indefensible decision, on any Court, in my lifetime," Felix Frankfurter, then a Harvard Law School professor, called the Court's ruling in *Colgate v. Harvey,* which marked the first time the Court had adopted John A. Campbell's reading of the "privileges and immunities" clause of the Fourteenth Amendment

---

* The *New York Times* headlined Black's dissent: "Only Justice Ever to Hold That Corporation Is Not a Person Under the Due Process Clause." Bernard Schwartz, *Main Currents in American Legal Thought* (Durham, North Carolina: Duke University Press, 1993), p. 510.

to strike down a state law. Of another decision Frankfurter, writing to Justice Harlan Stone, quoted Justice Oliver Wendell Holmes, "It makes me puke." Between 1935 and 1937 a frustrated Democratic Congress introduced more "Court-curbing" bills than in any *thirty-five-year* period. Legal scholars see an "internal" evolution in the Court away from Lochnerism (not apparent to the untenured eye), which, accelerated by "external" pressures from Congress, law professors, and notoriously from FDR's February 1937 threat to "pack" the Court, confirmed key justices in their evolved survival instinct to uphold legislation they had voted to strike down or, like the Wagner Act and the Social Security Act, seemed certain to strike down—in short, to let the elected branches *govern.* Thus ended the era of judicial supremacy opened with John A. Campbell's brief in the *Slaughter-House Cases.* For nearly half a century, as Samuel Miller feared if the New Orleans butchers won their case, the Court had served as "a perpetual censor . . . on all legislation of the States" *and* Congress. With the "Constitutional Revolution of 1937," it seemed, liberty of contract and economic due process had passed into history. The key decision, like the *Slaughter-House Cases* handed down on Easter Monday, came in *West Coast Hotel v. Parrish,* a case testing the constitutionality of Washington state's 1913 minimum wage law. Elsie Parrish, standing for the generations of workers denied simple justice by the High Court, was a hotel maid owed $216.19 in back pay by West Coast Hotel Corporation, which munificently offered her $17 to drop the suit. Speaking for a Court that had voided New York's minimum wage law just one year earlier, Chief Justice Charles Evans Hughes, in what an observer called "the greatest constitutional somersault in history," wrote: "In each case the violation alleged by those attacking minimum wage regulation for women is deprivation of freedom of contract. What is this freedom? The Constitution does not speak of freedom of contract."[104]

The corporate person weathered liberal attack. Though both Justices Black and Douglas called for *Santa Clara* to be overturned, it stood. In a *Columbia Law Review* article, "Stare Decisis," Douglas wrote that overruling precedents kept "one age unfettered by the fears and limited vision of another."[105] Still, *Santa Clara* stands. It undergirds *Buckley v. Valeo*'s 1976 holding that money in political campaigns is protected "speech," inaugurating the era of "soft money" in politics—unlimited corporate and union donations to the parties—only partially closed by the McCain-Feingold Campaign Finance Act of 2003. *First National Bank v. Bellotti* (1978) cited *Santa Clara* in invalidating a Massachusetts statute "restricting the use of corporate funds to influence elections." Commenting on these cases in 1981, the *Yale Law Journal* observed, "The renewed vitality of the *Santa Clara* doctrine threatens to resuscitate the spirit of economic due process in new substantive areas." Justice David Souter has warned of "a return to the untenable jurisprudence from which the country extricated itself almost sixty years ago . . . the old judicial pretension discredited and abandoned in 1937." The Rehnquist Court's willingness to wield substantive due process against congressional statutes and state regulation alarmed Souter, who accused the majority in one 2000 case of "adherence to . . . formalistically contrived confines of commerce power" that "in large measure provoked the judicial crisis of 1937." He is not alone in his alarm. Liberal law professors point to conservative judges in the federal appeals courts eager to scrap the New Deal regulatory regime—President George W. Bush's second High Court appointee, Justice Samuel Alito, fits the description. The trend, David Strauss of the University of Chicago Law School told the columnist E. J. Dionne, takes the form of "aggressive interpretation of federal statutes where they pre-empt state regulation" on the

"*. . . old luminaries blazing away*"
The Supreme Court of the United States, 1888. Chief Justice Melville Fuller flanked by Samuel F. Miller on the left and Stephen J. Field on the right.

one hand; and "narrow interpretation" of federal regulations on the other. In short, the jurisprudence of Stephen J. Field.[106]

When the Chicago corporation lawyer Melville W. Fuller took his seat on the bench as chief justice in May 1888, he later recalled, two "giants" occupied the chairs beside him—Samuel Miller on his right, Stephen Field on his left. Putting his own stamp on the Court, Fuller realized, would take time: "No rising sun for me with those old luminaries blazing away with all their ancient fires."[107]

They had been blazing away at *each other,* on crucial issues, since the *Slaughter-House Cases* seventeen years earlier, with Miller drifting toward Field's side in the conflict between state police powers and property rights. "I love Miller," Field once said. "He has so much backbone." In Felix Frankfurter's influential interpretation, the Waite-Field "duel" over federalism and the "social obligations" of private property defined the Waite Court. But Miller v. Field antedated, and (slightly) outlasted, Waite v. Field; and whereas Waite and Field differed on judicial doctrine, the "old luminaries" not only clashed there but on politics and ideology. Indeed, they could have faced each other in the presidential elections of 1880 and 1884, Miller on the Republican ticket, Field on the Democratic.[108]

Both sought nomination; Field campaigned for it. In advance of the 1880 convention in Cincinnati, Field's brothers put money behind his candidacy. They dispatched speakers to talk up his chances, hired southern journalists to boom him with southern delegates, swung New York's Tammany Hall behind him, and rented a railroad car to transport other New York delegates to Cincinnati. There, Field was the only candidate to distribute posters and placards, to print his campaign biography on the front page of the *Cincinnati Commercial,* or to fit out a bandwagon. "A large wagon," a reporter wrote, "draped in national colors and containing a brass band, dispensed music from one end of the city to another this afternoon, and upon banners which hung from the sides of the wagon were the words: 'Stephen J. Field. We must have the Pacific states.' " To one delegate the profusion seemed "an indefensible waste of something which ought to have gone into his own pocket." Another dismissed the Pacific states as a lost cause: "What we do want and must have is New York and Indiana." Field was whispered to be the candidate of the Southern Pacific Railroad and of "capitalist interests in the East." These associations cost him half the California delegation and hurt him outside it. He received only sixty-five of the 728 votes cast for the nomination, which went to Winfield Scott Hancock, the Civil War general.[109]

As for Miller, his name was not placed in nomination at the 1880 Republican convention, but he hoped for the prize. He had won a following with his Granger opinion, along with his dissents in bond default cases pitting midwestern municipalities against the eastern holders of their railroad debt—railroads encouraged with $250,000 in public subsidy capitalized themselves at $500,000 "and sold construction bonds on $500,000 more," leaving towns to pay interest on $1 million. At the convention the Iowa delegation planned to nominate him if General Grant—the candidate of the party "Stalwarts" eager to resume the boodling interrupted by the reform administration of Rutherford B. Hayes—and James G. Blaine of Maine, the two front-runners, deadlocked. They did deadlock, over two days. Then, on the thirty-sixth ballot, before Iowa could act, the Blaine delegates switched to James Garfield, *the* "Dark Horse" candidate in American political history. That mantle, the editor of the *Des Moines Register* later averred, would have fallen on Miller but for the Blaine "stampede."

Four years later Miller and Blaine had an agreement. "If he had failed he would have been for me and I should have been nominated," Miller later said. "What happened to 'my boom'?" he asked in a letter written after the convention nominated Blaine. "Well, as I wrote you last spring, I never permitted it to rise to the dignity of a boom. It was however the nicest and quietest little scheme." According to his son-in-law, "his heart was fixed on it."[110]

Miller, his most recent biographer tells us, wanted to "take back the soul of his party from eastern corporate conservatives."[111] The party of free soil, free men, and free labor had lost its way in the postwar; become what a prelapsarian Republican adjudged "an internally corrupt concern," the political arm of Wall Street financiers like Jay Gould, railroad looter and purchaser of politicians—Garfield, for example, who in the closing days of the 1880 campaign took $150,000 from Gould, enough to buy Indiana and the presidency, promising in exchange to appoint men to the Supreme Court who would overturn *Munn v. Illinois* and strike down the Granger laws in other states; men like Stephen J. Field.[112]

Gould bought the wrong candidate. If elected, Field planned to increase the size of the Court to fourteen justices and appoint "conservative men" to the five new seats. They would overrule the Granger and *Sinking-Fund* decisions and deliver the judicial branch to civilization.

A Field-Miller presidential contest would have placed the inverted Constitution on the ballot. Should the Fourteenth Amendment shelter corporations from regulation, or should state legislatures have the final say? Should the people rule, or judges? Was the Civil War fought to end slavery and secure rights to the freedman, or to secure for New Orleans butchers the right to practice their callings? Not only the Court; the times would have been on the ballot. Miller and Field saw different countries.

For Field, democracy was an invitation to anarchy; for Miller, the only defense against it. Radical leaders were "men of intelligence, speaking and writing many languages," he told a University of Iowa commencement. They heated up into "haters of prosperity and happiness" because society—the courts, business, the parties—rejected their reasonable demands.[113] The threat to democracy from below could be met by "genuine reforms in the fabric of social life as shall tend to ameliorate the hardship of want to prevent needless suffering."[114] More dangerous was the threat from above—from white southerners who stole elections and plutocrats who bought politicians. In his attitudes toward the men whose avarice named the age, Miller had his sharpest difference with Field. "I have met with but few things of a character affecting the public good of the whole country," he wrote a correspondent, "that has shaken my faith in human nature as much as the united, vigorous, and selfish efforts of the capitalists—the class of men who as a distinct class are but recently known in this country." His colleagues' votes for bondholders and against the right of cities like his own Keokuk to get shed of their debts he put down to their professional pasts: "It is vain to contend that judges who have been at the bar for forty years as advocates of railroad companies, and all forms of associated capital, when they are called on to decide cases where such interests are in contest" can be impartial. "All their training, all their feeling are from the start in favor of those who need no influence."[115] Toward the end of his tenure Miller saw new justices coming on the Court, men of the postwar, unable to measure it against memory. For Republicans of the old faith like Miller, the world broke in two: prewar idealism on one side, postwar cynicism on the other.

The war had consumed its moral energies. Slavery and free labor had killed each other off. Investors disgusted Miller because they "did nothing, produced nothing." In fact, they produced the winner, industrial capitalism.

Miller's life witnessed his convictions. Field accepted railroad passes; Miller refused them. Field invested in mines and elevated railways; Miller forbade his wife from investing in Washington real estate "for fear he would be accused of speculation." Field lived comfortably; Miller, obliged to entertain on his $10,000 salary, struggled against debt yet, according to the writer Michael A. Ross, he "turned down an offer to become a consulting attorney for several New York corporations, a job that would have paid him $100,000 a year."[116] What was said of Miller's personality, "His intercourse with his fellows was so cordial and kindly as to endear him to all who came within the sphere of his influence," no man would say of Field's.[117] A plaque on Field's desk read: "My ideal recreation is to keep on working." My motto, the 200-pound Miller quipped, is "Never walk when you can ride, never sit when you can lie down."

Nevertheless, Samuel Miller walked home from the Court. Returned from the 1890 summer recess, on October 10 he stopped by the Court, then set off for his house on Massachusetts Avenue. Within sight of it, he collapsed on the sidewalk, paralyzed on his left side by a stroke.[118] He lingered three days. His doctors found him in characteristic good cheer. Don't talk, they cautioned, it might tax your brain. Miller took that as "a compliment for you must think when I talk I use my brain."[119]

He had settled his debts but left no estate for his wife, who, needing cash, sold his law books. The *American Legal Review* ran an appeal for help. Concerned congressmen wrote a bill awarding her a year of his salary, but nothing came of it.[120]

At the funeral held in the Court chamber, the only sign of mourning was the empty chair, draped in black, to the right of the chief justice's.[121] "He was eminently human and humane," his pastor said of Samuel Miller. The attorney general, William H. H. Miller, in a just eulogy, noted how Justice Miller, "hating the contaminating touch of African slavery," left Kentucky "to seek a new life" in Iowa; how Miller received his commission from President Lincoln, and became his friend. Lincoln seemed further away than ever now. "Alas but that a single strand now connects him with the personality of this court. One member only remains, full of years and honors, discharging the high duties to which he was consecrated by the martyred President."[122]

In 1892 Horace Gray, appointed to the Court by President Arthur in 1881, confided to the chief justice: "Brother Field . . . seems this term to be behaving more like a wild bull than before." Three years later, while the Court debated the constitutionality of the income tax, Justice Harlan told his sons that Field was "act[ing] like a mad man." Yet Field, at eighty, had reason to be content. With Miller gone, and Waite, and more conservative justices replacing them, and the *Munn* "affected with a public interest" regulatory standard undermined by subsequent rulings, and the Court, in the *Minnesota Rate Commission* decision of 1890, finally invoking substantive due process to strike down regulation, Stephen Field had lived into victory. His dissents of the 1870s and 1880s were fast becoming majority opinions. State courts, scything laws made by elected representatives, already treated them that way. The Court, Field would say in his valedictory to it, has "no power to legislate . . . but possesses the power of declaring the law," and "[t]his negative power, the power of resistance, is the only safety of popular government." The courts had to destroy democracy in order to save it. Yet, with legislators balked from enacting the popular will, judicial supremacy left the aggrieved—those going under in the new America—no alternative but extra-political, sometimes violent, protest. Order, beleaguered, still needed Stephen Field.[123]

In Chicago's Haymarket Massacre, a bomb thrown by real anarchists, not Patrons of Husbandry, killed several policemen and touched off a shooting spree by other policemen that killed more of their colleagues. Pittsburgh saw open combat between workers occupying Carnegie's Homestead Steel Works and Pinkerton detectives trying to drive them out. Across the rural South Populist lecturers were radicalizing farmers, their crop prices falling, their tariff-inflated costs rising. Events seemed to be vindicating Field's presentiments. Was America turning into a battleground between "anarchy and civilization"?

That anarchy might be contained by mithridatic doses of reform, the strategy pursued by Progressives as alarmed by disorder as Field, would have seemed a counsel of weakness to him. In an address delivered in New York to mark the 1890 centenary of the Court, he followed the logic of reform to a reactionary conclusion: "[A]s the inequalities in the conditions of men become more and more marked and disturbing—as the enormous aggregation of wealth possessed by some corporations excites uneasiness lest their power should become dominating . . . and thus encroach upon the rights or crush out the business of individuals of small means . . ." The sentence then veers away as if terrified of its own evidence. For those inequalities and that dominating power, far from needing amelioration, must be *protected*. The "as" clauses end in "—it becomes more and more the imperative duty of the court to enforce with a firm hand every guarantee in the constitution. Every decision weakening their restraining power is a blow to the peace of society." That is the credo of ruin-or-rule conservatism, which invites ruin through an excess of rule.[124]

So long as Field could wield the "negative power" of "declaring the law" against the "communist" enemies of inequality and corporate domination, he would not retire. He stayed on the Court past eighty to sanction the Cleveland administration's use of a court injunction to break the Pullman strike, to invoke the Sherman Antitrust Act against unions and declare it unconstitutional against manufacturing corporations, to negate the income tax, and to constitutionalize segregation in *Plessy v. Ferguson.*

Time was running out on Stephen Field, and his internal auditor showed him in arrears on the terms of his election. Am I saved? Am I worthy to be saved? Can I work out my salvation before I die? Is my failing health a sign of God's lost favor? Field may have put away his father's faith. He could not escape its self-scrutiny. He was "more like a wild bull than ever" because time had become terrible to him. Always tetchy, now he shed his dignity at provocation, shouting a profanity over the temperature of a clerk's room, and exploding at a court copyist who brought him water instead of whiskey.[125] He treated pages roughly, though when his colleagues complained about his hectoring of one boy, he said, "I'll make the apology as good as the insult," and made it in the conference room where they must have rubbed their eyes in wonder at the sight. He made few concessions to collegiality within the Court; none to popularity beyond it. Conceding he was "under constant fire" in California for his rulings on Chinese aliens and the Southern Pacific Railroad, he wrote to one of his Ninth Circuit colleagues, "I do not feel disposed . . . to put myself out of the way to please those who thus give me the only return on my labors." His enemies could not know that their enmity was his pleasure.[126]

Rumors of his retirement started as early as 1885, when Grover Cleveland, the first Democrat elected since the war, entered the White House. The California Democratic Party was split between railroad Democrats headed by Field and their anti-monopoly opponents, the Stockton Convention Democrats who read Field out of their party before the 1880 Democratic National Convention. The chief justice swore in Cleveland, but the honor of swearing in the cabinet went to Field. Perhaps that deference to his status in the party encouraged him to believe that he would dispense the California patronage. In any case he lobbied Cleveland to appoint "conservative men" to the cabinet and conservative California Democrats to federal posts in the state. The *New York Times* deplored Field's politicking: a Supreme Court justice "should not soil his robe by becoming an office broker." But to insure defeat of the "Stockton Convention mob," Field wrote an ally, "You and your friends may rest assured that no dainty rules of propriety" would "deter me from such efforts as I may make to thwart their mischievous purposes."[127] When Cleveland nevertheless appointed a Stocktonite as collector of internal revenue for Los Angeles, Field felt betrayed. To Cleveland he denounced the appointee, who'd called Field a hireling of the railroads; and Field slurred the anti-monopolist Democrat whose advice Cleveland had taken in the matter as "a man utterly without principle . . . who has attained a 'bad eminence' in that state for his extreme communistic views."[128] Field had defined "communist" down to Democrat. "I have let them understand," he told one of his California allies, referring to Cleveland and the people around him, "that the question was not whether A or B was appointed. . . . The real contest was between civilization and anarchy." Armageddon hung on one job. Cleveland not only rejected Field's counsel but dodged meeting with Field. "Judge Field called to see me last evening after I was in bed," Representative Samuel Randall wrote Cleveland's secretary. "He is 'wounded.' "[129]

With the years, Field's brown beard whitened and lengthened, supplanting his bald crown as the commanding feature in his photographs. Reading his decisions from the bench in a deep voice that must have echoed off the walls of the old Senate chamber like the voices of Clay and Webster, he put witnesses in mind of "a Hebrew prophet," "Michaelangelo's Moses," even "Raphael's picture of the Creator."[130] "His appearance is awe-inspiring," Arthur Brisbane of the *New York Times* wrote of Field in 1895, engaged in the oral arguments in the income tax case.[131]

If only Brisbane knew what it had cost the old man to be there. A necrotic knee tortured him. And though he joked that "I don't write my opinions with my leg," getting to court was a trial, mounting the platform to the bench an agony. His mind "noticeably feeble," he often "had no perception of the arguments" and forgot how he had voted on cases. From an average of twenty-five opinions a year in his vigor, he managed only nine in 1893, six in 1894, and four in 1895.[132] When Chief Justice Fuller stopped assigning him cases after the 1895 session, he complained plangently: "I do not know and shall not ask the reason that no cases have been assigned to me within the past six months."[133] Days before his "awe-inspiring" appearance on the bench, he wrote Fuller a note at once sad and stirring. "Friends" had suggested he inject carbolic acid into his knee joint and this produced "paroxysms so great that I thought for some time that I should not be able to survive them, and what gave me additional pain was the thought that if I did not survive, our action in regard to the Income Tax case would be defeated."[134] So he got himself to court to cast the deciding vote against the constitutionality of the income tax and, while Justice Harlan delivered his choleric dissent—"it is not possible for this court to have rendered any judgment more to be regretted"—muttered rude comments. "Awe-inspiring" indeed.

After Waite's death Field expected to be named chief justice. His hurt when Cleveland picked Fuller may be guessed from his behavior. Amid rumors of his resignation, he clung to his seat, preventing the president from replacing him with a not so imminently mortal Democrat. Cleveland's return to the presidency in 1893 renewed Field's spite. Affection and ambition, too, counseled staying put. His wife, "my beautiful Sue," was reluctant to forfeit the social nimbus of his position.[135] And there was pride of history. If he could hold on through the summer of 1897, he would succeed John Marshall as the longest-serving member of the Court.

His fellow justices wanted him gone sooner. Years later Justice Harlan told Chief Justice Hughes how they decided to do it. Gently they would remind Field of his service on a committee of justices "which waited on Justice [Robert C.] Grier to suggest his retirement and it was thought that recalling the incident to his memory" might induce Field to retire. Seeing Field "in a state near sleep" on a settee in the robing room "apparently oblivious to his surroundings," Harlan approached him.[136]

Did Justice Field recall his part in the delicate mission to Justice Grier? Harlan inquired. "The old man listened, gradually became alert, and finally, with his eyes blazing with the old fire of youth, he burst out: 'Yes! And a dirtier day's work I never did in my life!' "[137]

Two of the justices were shocked when, calling at his home, he seemed only fitfully aware of their presence. Still, they had come to win his support for their side of a case, so one began to read out his opinion. Field heard something that broke his stupor. "Read that again," he put in. The justice read the passage again. "[N]ot good law," Field declared, and explained why. Law was life to him, and he would not let it go.

Justice Brewer appealed to the Reverend Henry Field, the lone surviving brother, to persuade Stephen to resign. Henry might have failed if Grover Cleveland's term were not up. A month after Cleveland left the White House, Field told Fuller he would resign on December 1. Over the summer, his health rallying, he had a change of heart. "He hopes to come back," Brewer wrote the chief justice. "He intimated that you wish it and expects me to insist upon it as a personal matter." Brewer decided to ignore this last plea, trusting that his uncle would forget he made it.[138] Field's official letter of resignation to the Court was too long, included too many references to his opinions—and in places may have been incoherent. "If he brings to you the letter he read to me," Harlan wrote Fuller, "it will be seen at once that it will not do." Fuller's papers include his heavily inter-lineated copy of Field's original.[139]

Think of it, Field marveled: I sat on the bench with Justice [James M.] Wayne, who sat with Marshall![140] His term, thirty-four years, eight months, and twenty days, exceeded Marshall's by five weeks.[141]

He survived the Court by sixteen months. In his last days, he asked to be baptized, "though some thought he was confused in his mind, and that what he wanted was to make a public confession." His biographer leaves us in ambiguity as to his words but not their meaning, much as Field left those who heard him. Field, if still sentient, wanted to clean the slate. Sought, in the awful privacy of the Puritan conscience, to settle up. Did the social consequences of his opinions show as debits on the ledger? Or was his guilt strictly private—a consciousness of facing his inner capitalist with no possibility of striking an equal bargain? One could disagree with Field's opinions and still respect his judicial integrity if he hadn't sacrificed doctrinal consistency whenever it jeopardized his preferred social outcomes. These came first. So judgment falls on them: on railroads untaxed, monopolies protected, unions broken, farmers extorted, blacks segregated.

Just at the end, Field called his Negro servants to his bedside, apologized for treating them harshly, and asked their forgiveness. Whether they gave it is unknown.[142]

Chapter Seven

ANTI-DEMOCRACY

Thus the majority of human beings, in a condition of eternal tutelage, are predestined by tragic necessity to submit to the dominion of a small minority, and must be content to constitute the pedestal of an oligarchy.
                    —Robert Michels, "The Iron Law of Oligarchy"

Gilded Age politics induces pertinent despair about democracy. Representative government gave way to bought government. Politicians betrayed the public trust. Citizens sold their votes. Dreams faded. Ideals died of their impossibility. Cynicism poisoned hope. The United States in these years took on the lineaments of a Latin American party-state, an oligarchy ratified in rigged elections, girded by bayonets, and given a genial historical gloss by its raffish casting.*

Jay Gould was president. He never ran for office, he never lost office—he *ruled.* He wrote the laws. He interpreted the Constitution. He commanded the army. He staffed the government. He rented politicians, fattening his purse off their favor. He was John D. Rockefeller, James J. Hill, Andrew Carnegie, Tom Scott, and George Pullman; and this was his time—this was his country.

Too busy to take the government in hand themselves, Gould & Company paroled their lawyers to the Gilded Age cabinets. Of the seventy-three men who held cabinet posts between 1868 and 1896, forty-eight either served railroad clients, lobbied for railroads, sat on railroad boards, or had

---

* "Sometime in the late 1870s, a new word entered the political lexicon, 'Mexicanization.' Reflecting a general impression of government in Mexico, where bayonets and stuffed ballot boxes had turned the outward forms of democratic process into false fronts, the term implied that what had become custom among people of an inferior race was turning into standard practice north of the border, too." Mark Wahlgren Summers, *Party Games: Getting, Keeping, and Using Power in Gilded Age Politics* (Chapel Hill: University of North Carolina Press, 2004), p. 161.

railroad-connected relatives. Richard Olney, consecutively secretary of state and attorney general in the second administration of Grover Cleveland, led the field, serving on the boards of the Boston & Maine, the Eastern Railroad, the Chicago, Burlington & Quincy, the Portland and Rochester, and the Philadelphia, Wilmington & Baltimore. While attorney general, Olney remained on the Boston & Maine and Chicago, Burlington boards. Indeed, he was receiving more in compensation from the latter road than his government salary when he used every instrument of federal power except the navy to break the Pullman Strike of 1894,

Jay Gould

which had tied up traffic on the CB&Q. Five of James Garfield's six major cabinet appointees maintained "close links" with railroads; five of six of Chester A. Arthur's. In addition to the Who's Who of the railroad bar, Gilded Age presidents also made affirmative action appointments, choosing the odd Wall Street confectioner, banker, lumber baron, traction magnate, marble company owner, stagecoach line operator, and state party boss. One of the token Confederates, L.Q.C. Lamar, John A. Campbell's cousin, had redeemed himself as a railroad lawyer before becoming senator from Mississippi. Rutherford Hayes's brother-in-law served on the board of a railroad; Hayes's Cincinnati law partner graced another. Hayes invested in railroads: Early in his career one city directory listed his profession as "capitalist." Even the taintless Cleveland, in his Buffalo law practice, had at least two railroads as clients, plus Standard Oil; and from 1889 to 1893, between his presidencies, his New York firm represented J. P. Morgan, the country's leading railroad marriage broker, with whom, in his second term, he "secretly negotiated on unfavorable terms a $65 million gold loan."[1]

As governor of New York, Cleveland incarnated the definition of a reformer as "one who gives to the capitalist for nothing that which the real politician holds for a price" when he vetoed a bill cutting the fare Gould charged New Yorkers to ride on his elevated railways.[2] The president of Cornell praised Cleveland for rising above the "sympathies for the working people" he indulged as mayor of Buffalo by drinking beer with them.[3] The 1884 election (Cleveland versus James G. Blaine) remained undecided for days, and New Yorkers gouged by Gould's transit monopoly feared lest he use his Western Union and his Associated Press monopolies and his newly acquired interest in Greeley's *New York Tribune* to "falsify the election returns." (In fact Gould wrote articles under reporters' bylines and routinely planted stories that enhanced the value of his investments.) While crowds chanting "We'll hang Jay Gould to a sour apple tree" gathered in front of the Western Union Building, he repaired to his yacht in the Hudson.* From there he telegraphed congratulations to Cleveland: "All concede that your Administration as Governor has been wise and conservative, and in the larger field of President, I feel sure that you will do still better, and that the vast business interests of the country will be entirely safe in your hands."[4] Gould's own hands could not have been safer. "No harm shall come to any business interest as the result of administrative policy so long as I am President," Cleveland promised in his inaugural address. Heading a government of railroad lawyers, businessmen, and speculators, Cleveland was a safe bet to keep his word.[5]

Ceding the federal patronage in the states traversed by Northern Pacific Railroad to associates of his "close friend," the Northern's president, James J. Hill, who had a $10,000 stake in Cleveland's victory, and supporting the Huntington-Stanford-Gould confederacy's bribe-loaded petition for lower interest charges on the government's $26 million loan to the Union and Central Pacific, Cleveland vetoed a $10,000 appropriation for seeds to help Texas farmers recover from drought. The message accompanying the veto distilled the ideology of indifference toward those without means to buy their share of government that guided policy from Grant to Theodore Roosevelt:

> I do not believe that the power and duty of the General Government ought to be extended to the relief of individual suffering which is in no manner properly

---

* Get enough distance from Gould and he assumes the shape of an "industrial statesman." To his 1957 biographer, Julius Grodinsky, Gould's objective function as an entrepreneur matters above everything: "As a leader in the railroad industry he built many new roads; he broke down local territorial monopolies, destroyed traffic pools, and wrecked railroad rate structures . . . To Gould, as much as to any other single business leader, goes the credit for that far-reaching reduction in rates that characterized the growth of the American economy in the generation after the Civil War." In the 1880s, this railroad wrecker became a system builder, turning from raiding to managing the industry. Maury Klein, "In Search of Jay Gould," *Business History Review,* vol. 52, no. 2 (Summer 1978), pp. 166–99, quotation is from p. 188. The Klein essay is an antidote to contemporary opinion about Gould. Klein unearths a funny Gould remark. When a former partner shook his finger in Gould's face and vowed that he would live to see Gould earning a living "by going around this street with a hand organ and a monkey," Gould replied: "Maybe you will, Henry . . . And when I want a monkey, Henry, I'll send for you."

related to the public service or benefit. A prevalent tendency to disregard the limited mission of this power and duty should, I think, be steadfastly resisted, to the end that the lesson should constantly be enforced that though the people support the Government the Government should not support the people.[6]

That was the antithesis of Lincoln's philosophy: "The legitimate object of government is to do for a community of people, whatever they need to have done, but can not do, *at all,* or can not so *well* do, for themselves—in their separate, and individual capacities." And it raises a question: Why did the people support a government that on principle refused to support them, that wouldn't spend pennies to save farmers from ruin? Why return to office politicians like Cleveland, who vetoed three times as many bills in one term as all his predecessors combined? What had gone wrong with the Republican experiment in positive government for the country to settle for negative government?

When we catch history repeating itself we turn to first causes, to political culture and national character. What Robert Frost said of poetry applies to American history—it has one subject. For white Americans in the 1870s, 1880s, and 1890s, the active government of the 1860s reeked of race, was borne down by its association with the cause of Negro equality. "Taking a broad view of the matter . . . virtually every aspect of the Democratic Party's rhetorical and programmatic agenda supported white supremacy," the political scientist John Gerring concluded from a quantitative study of the party's convention and campaign speeches from Jackson to Cleveland. "Its opposition to the federal voting rights laws, its all-pervasive anti-statism, its constitutional fundamentalism centered on the tenth amendment . . . its praise of the virtue of tolerance and a pluralistic society, its proto-Marxist critique of capitalism, as well as its embrace of the interests of agriculture all bolstered slavery and Jim Crow." From Reconstruction to the early 1890s, not one Democrat in either house voted for a single civil rights bill. The Democrats were the white man's party in the white man's country. They insisted upon it in their campaign rhetoric, tying the Negro to the Republicans and the Populists. Both suffered from the association, and not just in the South. The domestic liberalism of the 1960s fell into disfavor similarly. Justice Joseph Bradley's words in his majority opinion striking down the Civil Rights Act of 1875, "blacks must cease to be the special favorite of the laws," spoke to two centuries, voiced the political reaction to two Reconstructions, rang out Radical Republicanism and 1960s liberalism alike.[7]

Apart from railroads and tariff-hungry industries, the law's favorite in the Gilded Age was the Civil War veteran. Government supported *him*. By 1900 the Pension Bureau's 6,000 employees directed benefits representing nearly half of the federal budget to 999,446 men, women, and children. With the help of "Corporal" James Tanner, a legless lobbyist, the veterans' pressure group, the Grand Army of the Republic, got what it wanted from a Congress thick with veterans that did little else but pass bills extending or increasing pensions for the totally disabled and the wounded. Right after the war an arm gone at the shoulder merited $18 a month, a lost hand $8; by 1906, even a thumb ($96) got more than that, a hand $360, an arm $432. The unscathed and veterans' dependents eventually received pensions—wives, children, fathers, mothers, brothers, sisters. By 1885, Cleveland administration investigators estimated, a quarter of the 345,000 veterans and survivors owed their pensions to fraudulent claims. During his first term (1885–1888), Cleveland vetoed 233 "private" pension bills, which added individual claimants to the list. A man awarded a pension for chronic diarrhea contracted during his service filed a second claim a few months later to cover a rare complication of that illness. "The ingenuity developed in the constant and persistent attacks upon the public Treasury by those claiming pensions," Cleveland wrote, "and the increase of those already granted is exhibited in bold relief by this attempt to include sore eyes among the results of diarrhea."

In 1888 Cleveland suffered for vetoing pensions for dependents. "Let Grover talk against the tariff tariff tariff / And pensions too," went a Republican campaign song. "We'll give the workingman his due / And pension the boys who wore the blue." The boys who wore the gray got no federal pensions, yet they helped pay for them—through the tariff. After defeating Cleveland in the election, Benjamin Harrison announced that it was "no time to be weighing the claims of old soldiers with apothecary scales"; spending on pensions subsequently increased from an average of $88 million annually under the apothecary Cleveland to $159 million.

The pension lobby and the tariff lobby combined formidably. Pensions "supported the tariff." Every year from 1866 to 1893 the federal government ran a surplus, at least half derived from the tariff. Republicans had to justify this superflux; America's protected industries had to. Shaking it down to the veteran and to his widow and to his orphan (and to his sister) was inspired politics. Assailing a new pension bill as "scheme by which protected interests proposed to use up the surplus and prevent a revision of the tariff," Senator James Breck, a Kentucky Democrat, said that while the Republicans' claimed they wanted to save the veteran from the poorhouse with surplus revenue, "in fact they are really seeking to save the tariff in order to enrich . . . the protected barons . . . making princely fortunes out of it at the expense of the great mass of the people." "The pension system not only disposed of the politically inconvenient surplus," the political scientists Jacob S. Hacker and Paul Pierson observe of this win-win stroke, "but did so in a way that strengthened the business-dominated Republican coalition." "We can stand a pretty big 'steal' in this if we can get railroads in this state." Civil War veterans got *their* railroad.[8]

So did party workers rewarded with patronage jobs. A promise to Jay Gould to appoint justices like Stephen J. Field secured the necessary to leverage Indiana for James Garfield. Yet, surprising in a man who owed his office to a promised job, Garfield was vexed that patronage consumed him in the White House. Months into his term, he wrote Blaine: "I have heretofore been treating of the fundamental principles of government and here I am considering all day whether A or B shall be appointed to this or that office. My God! What is there in this place that a man should ever want to get into it."[9] His assassin could have enlightened him on his duty toward those who campaigned for him. "This is the way politics are run; understand that," Charles Guiteau announced at his murder trial. "You tickle me and I tickle you." The man Guiteau made president, Chester Arthur, saw job-seekers "only" three days a week. Even as government did less—as the percentage of bills Congress passed fell from 22 percent in the 1860s to 10 percent in the 1870s and 1880s to 7 percent in the 1890s—every level of it employed more. The alderman of Jane Addams's ward "boasted" that he had over 2,000 constituents on Chicago's payroll. The Philadelphia Republican machine dispensed between 15,000 to 20,000 jobs, 2,000 on the city gas works. Pennsylvania's counties employed inspectors of flour, lumber, domestic spirits, harness leather, gas, petroleum, and pickled fish. Statewide, Matt Quay, Pennsylvania's Republican "boss," fielded an army of "at least 20,000 regulars"—more men than worked for the Baltimore & Ohio Railroad—costing $24 million a year, two-thirds of the commonwealth's budget for 1888. One of eight voters in New York held local, state, or federal government jobs. The state Republican machine's payroll of 10,000 ate up nearly $20 million annually. The New York City Democratic Party employed four workers—full-time, year-round—for each of the city's 812 voting districts. They had plenty to do; in 1880 the party held seventy-two primaries to nominate candidates for the general election. By the late 1880s New York City elections cost more than $700,000; national campaigns added additional costs. In 1884 it took $14,000 to transport one group of 650 New Yorkers to Chicago to nominate Grover Cleveland; $45,000 to board and feed them for a week; $10,000 to entertain them; and $2,200 to get them drunk at a Hoffman House party. By 1900, the reformer George William Curtis, magnifying the sum out of horror at its dimension, speculated that the parties were spending $30 million on elections.[10]

Today the parties hire pollsters to sample public opinion. In the Gilded Age they deployed battalions to "full poll" swing counties and even swing states—that is, to attempt to survey every voter in the state! In 1892, the Democrats' full poll of Indiana predicted a Cleveland win by 6,000 votes, 482 votes short of Cleveland's total. The thousands who conducted such surveys expected jobs. Little wonder that, between 1870 and 1881, the federal bureaucracy doubled. Garfield's assassination in the latter year by Guiteau, a crazed partisan in the president's feud with Roscoe Conkling over the New York patronage, swung opinion behind civil service reform. However, since the number of employees covered rested with the president, the civil service made slow progress against patronage jobs, which totaled the same in 1900 as in 1883. While Cleveland extended civil service protection to nearly 30,000 federal employees, by the end of his term his "headsman" at the Post Office, Assistant Postmaster General Adlai Stevenson, decapitated 40,000 postmasters. Altogether, loyal Democrats elbowed out two-thirds of the 120,000 federal employees, assumedly Republicans.[11] In turn, within two years of replacing Cleveland, Benjamin Harrison scythed 31,000 Democratic postmasters. The swing from Republican to Democrat to Republican cut through a quarter of a million jobholders. *They* had reason to support, if not the government, then the parties that stocked it with such as them.[12]

And, like Herman Melville, they had reason to kick back a portion of their salary to their party patrons. For twenty years Deputy Inspector No. 75 of the United States Custom Service on the Hudson River Piers, Melville remitted 2 percent of his $4-a-day salary to the New York Republican State Committee and for a stretch in the 1880s the same cut to the national Republican Party. His pride battered by the failure of book after book—at one point he suggested to his publisher that he would be willing to write under another name—he maintained his self-respect against the staining presumption of the age that everyone was on the take by "quietly returning money which has been thrust into his pockets behind his back," his brother-in-law recalled. The parties could not finance their operations solely from assessments on Deputy Inspector No. 75 and his like, so increasingly they squeezed businessmen. As the writer and lawyer Richard Henry Dana explained, "The extension of civil service reform, by cutting off the supply of offices, must tend to increase the demand for and the direct use of money for the support of politicians"—and their exorbitant job machines.

"Neither party has any principles, any distinctive tenets," James Bryce discovered during his fieldwork for *The American Commonwealth* (1893). "Both have traditions. Both claim to have tendencies. . . . All has been lost, except office or the hope for it."*[13]

From the Greenbackers in the late 1870s to the Populists in the early 1890s, the two-party duopoly successfully co-opted insurgencies and either defused anger with "reform" or channeled it into cultural issues.† "Political conflict is not like an intercollegiate debate in which the opponents agree in advance on the definition of the issue," E. E. Schattschneider writes in *The Semisovereign People. "As a matter of fact, the definition of the alternatives is the supreme instrument of power. . . .* He who determines what

* In *The Price of Union*, Herbert Agar saw the era of patronage as a "sign of health" in the party system not of decadence. "The party is intended to be an organization for 'getting or keeping the patronage of government.' Instead of seeking 'principles,' or 'distinctive tenets,' which can only divide a federal union, the party is intended to seek bargains between the regions, the classes, the other interest groups. . . . The members may have nothing in common except a desire for office. . . . They tend to ignore any issue that rouses deep passion. And by doing so they strengthen the Union." The one time the parties polarized over principles "took place between 1850 and 1860" and ended in civil war. Herbert Agar, *The Price of Union* (Boston: Houghton Mifflin, 1966), pp. 689–90. Seen in James L. Sundquist, *Dynamics of the Party System: Alignment and Realignment of the Political Parties in the United States* (Washington, D.C.: Brookings Institution, 1984), pp. 326–27.

† The Greenback-Labor Party uniquely offered a program responsive to the needs of an industrial society and to its injustices: the eight-hour day, an end to child labor, sanitary codes for factories, the regulation of railroads engaged in interstate commerce, a graduated income tax, woman suffrage, and equal voting rights for southern blacks. Organized in 1877 in the worst of the depression, the Greenbackers polled over a million votes and elected fifteen congressmen in 1878, including Hendrick Wright, the Pennsylvanian who called for government loans to homesteaders. A reviving economy hurt the party in 1880, when its presidential candidate, General James B. Weaver, an Iowa congressman, won only 300,000 votes. The Greenbackers wanted to end the resumption of specie payments and to increase the money supply by issuing "fiat money"—greenbacks. See Leonard Dinnerstein, "The Election of 1880," in Arthur M. Schlesinger, Jr., and Fred I. Israel, editors, *History of American Presidential Elections, 1789–1968*, vol. 2 (New York: Chelsea House, 1971), p. 1505; also Richard B. Morris, editor, *Encyclopedia of American History* (New York: Harper & Bros., 1953), pp. 255–56.

politics is about runs the country." As Plato dramatized in the allegory of the cave, power gets to say what counts as real. For southern Democrats, "Negro domination," the specter of Reconstruction resumed, alone counted as real. Politics was about *that,* about keeping the white man's party united against that threat. For Republicans the tariff covered reality. Politics was about protecting protection. Northern Democrats took the bait, championing tariff "reform."[14]

"On the major problems of the day," Leonard Dinnerstein writes, "the major parties had nothing to say." The parties said nothing because the problems with a political valency—deflation in the price of farm commodities, worker exploitation, inequitable taxation—were their funders' opportunities.[15]

Take inequality, once "the problem of rich and poor," increasingly the problem of the rich and the rest, made salient in those terms by the Populist attack on privilege. In "The Owners of the United States," a writer in the *Forum,* extrapolating from the 1880 census, figured that 25,000 people owned half the wealth and 250,000, 75 to 80 percent of it. "Who owns the United States?" he asked. "The USA are practically owned by less than 250,000 persons." Using the 1890 census, a contributor to the *Political Science Quarterly* calculating "The Concentration of Wealth" found that "4,047 families possess as much as do 11,593,887 families." "This result," he wrote, "seems almost incredible."[16]

Policy underwrote that incredible result. Federal taxes had increased six times since 1860 with "the whole of this increase taken out of the relatively poorer classes," who paid 70 to 90 percent of their average annual savings in taxes; the 250,000 "owners" paid 3 to 10 percent. "We tax the tea, the coffee, the sugar, the spices, the poor man uses," Senator John Sherman of Ohio declared in an 1872 speech. "We tax every little thing that is imported from abroad, together with the whiskey that makes him drunk and the beer that cheers him and the tobacco that consoles him," he said, alluding to the excise, liquor, and tariff taxes. "Everything that he consumes we call a luxury and tax it; yet we are afraid to touch the income of Mr. Astor. Is there any justice in that? . . . Why, sir, the income tax is the only one that tends to equalize these burdens between the rich and the poor." In fact during the war Congress had imposed a graduated income tax of 10 percent on incomes above $25,000, and Vincent Astor paid an estimated $1 million under it. By 1872, however, fewer than 100,000 Americans out of 39.5 million paid the income tax, but they lived mainly in the big cities of the big states and they mounted a lobby and they got Congress to abolish the income and inheritance taxes. "Is there any propriety in it?" Sherman asked.[17]

Propriety was too well satisfied by a second policy that transferred income from the whiskey-drinking, tobacco-smoking, tariff-dunned taxpayer to America's 250,000 owners. To finance the war the government borrowed $2 billion from banks and the wealthy, offering favorable terms. Paying off this debt "became one of the most powerful instruments in America for the enrichment of the rentier class, the leading industrialists," according to the tax historian Sidney Ratner. And these rentiers, having purchased the bonds with greenbacks worth 40 cents to the dollar, would take payment in gold only. "Besides collecting their interest in gold (which turned the nominal 6 percent yield into 15 percent)," Kevin Phillips writes, "they could now get a profit on capital of from 100 to 150 percent by being able to cash the bonds for gold rather than the cheaper paper they paid with." Proposals to repay in greenbacks were defeated. The government had borrowed the money promising gold. The national "honor" was at stake. To market its war bonds and handle the issuance of the greenbacks, the Lincoln administration, working with the New York banks, fashioned a system of publicly aided national banks. Their stockholders and officers benefited exceedingly.[18]

The people supported the government and the government supported the corporations and the rentiers with the people's money. And the people did not seem to object, at least not enough of them. "The enormous wealth of a few in this country," concluded the author of "The Owners of the United States," "has been forced upon them by the very masses who have been impoverished for their benefit."

Consider who paid what in state and local property taxes. "Incorporeal values such as bonds and notes escape the burden of taxation," Professor Edwin R. A. Seligman of Columbia, a leading authority on taxation, wrote in an 1894 study of a systemic scandal. By contrast, hogs, horses, and cows could not disguise their corporeality. The tax man included this "personalty" in his assessment of the farmer's realty and taxed both. The stocks and bonds owned by affluent New Yorkers did not moo. While the assessed value of real estate nearly doubled between 1860 and 1880, Seligman reported, the assessed value of personal property *declined;* by 1890 the official value of personal property came to "less than the figure thirty years before." According to the comptroller of New York, owners of personal property in the nation's richest state were $41 million worse off in 1893 than in 1877. Twenty-four New York corporations, a Progressive Era survey found, evaded 96.5 percent "of taxable personalty." A favored method of evasion was bribery of tax assessors; some pulled in $75,000 a year. Lying ran a close second. Addressing an 1889 meeting of Baltimore businessmen, Charles J. Bonaparte, a founder of the National Municipal League and future attorney general, made a revealing confession: "I hope . . . that I have not wholly lost my character as a man of business if I admit that I once, when a young man, told the truth to a tax-gatherer." An author calculated that "the trusts, the corporations, the millionaires of Chicago pay taxes on less than one-tenth of the value of their enormous holdings." Ohio's thinly populated Preble County paid a third more in property taxes than Hamilton County, which included the city of Cincinnati, population 296,000. Seligman's conclusion: "The farmer bears not only his share, but also [that of] the other classes of society." That was sentimental in Seligman. Farmers did what they could to avoid paying their share. New York State farmers, through the rural-dominated legislature, kept their assessments ludicrously low. By 1888 tax evasion had cost Iowa an estimated $1.3 billion.[19]

Ida Tarbell considered the tariff a "defeat of the popular will" (though in 1888, the one presidential election in which the tariff was the central issue, the pro-tariff Republican Benjamin Harrison received 47.8 percent of the popular vote to the tariff-reform Democrat Grover Cleveland's 48.6, suggesting an evenly split electorate on the issue). E. E. Schattschneider documented that defeat in his book on the power that industrial lobbies exerted over Congress in writing the Smoot-Hawley Tariff of 1930: "Economic pressure politics, as seen in this study, is . . . essentially oligarchical and anti-democratic." Yet this undoubtedly correct observation about tariff-setting should be balanced against his assertion that by 1930 the tariff was "firmly established in public favor." Whether the tariff was a triumph of anti-democracy or only an affront to half the electorate, the people as a whole abided with it for decades. The tariff tax they paid swelled the profits of manufacturers of goods from silk to steel. Investors shared in those profits. The 250,000 owners of America *were* those investors. The tariff also supported the government. It disbursed this "external revenue" (along with the internal revenue contributed disproportionately by Americans addicted to drink and tobacco) to veterans and government employees—and, in the early years of the Gilded Age, to railroads, as direct or indirect subsidy. The tariff hurt the railroads, paying the relatively high home market price for rails and equipment. But the railroads got their own back (in land grants, bond guarantees, subsidies, and homesteads) from federal, state, county, and municipal governments. The 250,000 invested in these sweetened railroads, too. Thus, wherever they put their money, the rich benefited from policy, from state capitalism.[20]

In 1895 the Supreme Court rendered agitation for a fairer tax system moot, striking down a 2 percent income tax on incomes above $4,000—including income derived from securities and corporate profits—passed by a Democratic Congress. Dissenting, Justice Henry B. Brown saw in that ruling the "first step toward submergence of the people in a sordid despotism of wealth." Justice Harlan said it amounted to a "judicial revolution" on behalf of "the dominion of aggregated wealth." The income tax case (*Pollock v. Farmer's Loan and Trust Company*) was one of three blows the Court struck for the dominion of wealth in 1895. In *U.S. v. E. J. Knight Company,* it ruled that the Sherman Antitrust Act did not apply to manufacturers like Knight Sugar, which controlled 98 percent of the sugar market. "The effect of the Knight case upon the popular mind," William Howard Taft, the future president and chief justice, wrote in 1915, "and indeed upon Congress as well, was to discourage hope that the statute could be used to accomplish its manifest purpose and curb the great industrial trusts." An article in the *American Law Review* condemned the *Knight* decision as "The most deplorable one . . . in favor of incorporated power and greed against popular rights since the *Dartmouth College Case.*" In the third case, *In re Debs,* the Court upheld the first successful criminal prosecution brought under the Sherman Act—against a *labor union,* the National Railway Union, for "conspiring and combining" to control interstate commerce in the Pullman Strike. "The Federal courts have flagrantly usurped jurisdiction first to protect corporations and perpetuate their many abuses, and, second, to oppress and destroy organized labor," five governors declared of the decision. It was, National Railway Union president Eugene V. Debs reflected, "not the army [nor] any other power" that ended the strike "but simply . . . the United States courts." Oregon governor Sylvester Pennoyer hated judicial review—Field's ruling in *Pennoyer v. Neff* having shorn him of his property. But, assessing the Court's exercise of that power in 1895, he voiced a by no means idiosyncratic opinion: "Our government has been supplanted by a judicial oligarchy."[21]

A survey of editorials on the political influence of business in eleven business journals between 1877 and 1896 found candor on the fact of influence, obliquity as to the means. The journals issued general statements like this from the *Railway Review* in 1890: "Business and politics are now inextricably mixed up"; and assurances like this one from the *Economist* in 1880 that "there was no significant disagreement between the parties on business issues"; and even a warning from *Railway Review* in 1884 that "No legislative body would dare to inaugurate or carry out . . . any measure without first knowing the pleasure of the manufacturing and commercial interests." But they were, the survey's author stipulated, "completely silent about the exchange of bribes for favors in politics . . . one of the primary ways in which some businessmen participated in public life." Silence also fell over the state's promotional role in the economy, responsive as it was to bribery and campaign contributions. The business journals objected to the apparent excess of democracy in Gilded Age government—"too many caucuses, too many elections, too many officers chosen directly by the people"—not of corruption.[22]

The sale of government to business offended Henry Adams; and that is how cultural history has tended to encode Gilded Age corruption—as an incitement to epigrammatic sighs from the species Roscoe Conkling labeled "the man-milliners of reform." Corruption was to public life as filigree to period architecture, an aesthetic travesty, a species of bad taste. That's how it looked from above. Seen from below, seen by its victims, seen through the eyes of the losing class in the class struggle, corruption bought repression.

Late-nineteenth-century presidential campaigns were logistical, manpower, and merchandising feats, and they cost money—money for the 700 different pieces of kitsch produced for the 1888 campaign—for the "match holders, ribbons and handkerchiefs . . . lapel studs and pins, glass and ceramic bric-a-brac . . . caneheads, umbrellas, pocket watches, toys, razors, and clay pipes." Money to depict young Mrs. Cleveland on "song-sheets, posters, playing cards, handkerchiefs, napkins, plates, and . . . tokens." Money to transport, house, and feed the 2,500 Republican orators who gave 10,000 speeches in 1888. Money for the 300,000 flyers casting General Harrison as both "wet" and "dry," for the 300,000 flyers refuting the Democratic calumny that he advocated a dollar-a-day wage, and for the 300,000 lithographed photographs of Harrison—the money spent, the speeches delivered, and the flyers and photographs all distributed in *one* state, Indiana. Businessmen paid for these tools of mobilization, and the parties in power reciprocated by furnishing state militia, federal marshals, and federal troops to break strikes and shoot strikers.[23]

Railway World, the industry mouthpiece, told government what was expected of it during the Great Railroad Strike of 1877. To crush strikers "virtually and actually as wicked and wanton as the portion of Paris which formed . . . the Commune," strikers calling for a reintroduction of "slavery" (forcing corporations to pay higher wages by striking), it was "one of the imperative duties of all governments to enforce this principle [no slavery] . . . even if the drums must beat, the glittering bayonets advance, the breech-loading rifles pour forth death-dealing volleys . . . the Gatling guns mow down crowds of the new champions of slavery, and if heavy artillery must batter down whole towns that become citadels of folly and crime." That appeared in the United States of America.*[24]

Though a Pennsylvania Railroad vice president *wanted* Pittsburgh crowds shelled in 1877, state militia refrained from artillery. Otherwise they took *Railway Age*'s advice as to weapons. Militia account for "The most important single form of domestic violence in American history," according to Richard Hofstadter. Between 1886 and 1895, "to suppress riots consequent upon labor troubles," governors called out the 100,000-man National Guard, successor to the militia after 1880, at least 150 times. Governors were presumed to be beholden to the railroad corporations of their states. When the 1877 strike against the Pennsylvania Railroad broke out, for example, Governor John F. Hartranft was junketing in Wyoming in the private railroad car of Tom Scott, the Pennsylvania's president and puppeteer of the state legislature. Knowing they could count on the Guard, Ernest Crosby, of the Sheet Metal Workers Union contended, "invite[d] employers to hold out against just demands," which goaded strikers into the "riots" that justified Guard intervention. Young men often from the urban middle classes, poorly trained at summer camps, guardsmen provoked riots by panicked firing on strikers, bystanders, policemen, and members of other Guard units. During the Great Railroad Strike of 1877, guardsmen killed at least sixty-nine people and wounded one hundred—few rioters among them—while suffering casualties of three dead and a score wounded. While no strikers were killed in France in the 1890s and only three out of 100,000 injured, in the United States two of every 100,000 strikers were killed and 140 per 100,000 injured.

When local guardsmen refused to use force against their striking neigh-

---

* This passage is symptomatic of ferocious opinion among the selectively civilized. *The Independent*, a journal of religion, sated its sadism with imagined slaughter: "If the club of the policeman, knocking out the brains of the rioter, will answer, then well and good; but if it does not promptly meet the exigency, then bullets and bayonets, cannister and grape—with no sham or pretense, in order to frighten men. . . . Napoleon was right when he said that the way to deal with a mob was to exterminate it." Sven Beckert, *The Monied Metropolis: New York City and the Consolidation of the American Bourgeoisie, 1850–1896* (Cambridge: Cambridge University Press, 2001), p. 233.

bors, as at Pittsburgh in 1877, railroads called in the U.S. Army. "The float-
ing population believes that while the National Guard might hesitate [to
fire]," a New York official observed, " 'them reg'lars are the fellers that
shoot.' "

Deployed in Maryland, Pennsylvania, West Virginia, Indiana, Illinois,
and Missouri in 1877, the regulars broke strikes in the name of restoring
"order." At the request of employers hoping to intimidate strikers into
returning to work on the employers' terms, they sometimes stayed on the
scene after the expiry of their constitutional warrant for being there—to
"suppress Insurrections." General Hancock built "semi-permanent camps"
in the coal region around Scranton ostensibly to deter striking miners
from violence. Yet, asked when the federal occupation would end, Hancock spoke plainly: "It will exist practically until the miners go back to
work." Two months later, they did; and the troops, their mission accomplished, left. During the Pullman Strike of 1894, in Sacramento, Reno, and
Livingston, Montana, "Federal troops used bayonets, gun butts, and
swords to protect train crews and to keep trains moving." In Chicago,
ground zero of the strike, General Nelson Miles conferred regularly with
James Egan, the strike coordinator for the railroad companies, who shared
intelligence gleaned from "labor spies" on the Trainmen's Union plans and
busied Miles with suggestions to shift troops to checkmate the union. "In
almost every instance," Jerry M. Cooper dicovered, "Miles complied with
Egan's requests and many of Miles' reports to Washington not only
reflected Egan's ideas and information but also the latter's memos to the
general."[25]

After the Great Railroad Strike of 1877 put the fear of revolution in
them, the business elite of New York, Chicago, Cleveland, among other
cities, paid for the construction of armories and the arming of local units
of the Guard. To a contemporary observer, Chicago's First Regiment
Armory might have been a stone battleship: "The two upper stories, on
top of the massive masonry of the first floor, are crowned at the angles by
great bastions, from which an enfilade fire may be directed against any
side of the walls." Led by Marshall Field, the Chicago Citizens Association
equipped the police with four twelve-pound cannons, a Gatling gun, 296
breech-loading rifles, and 60,000 bullets. In Manhattan William W. Astor
raised the funds for a "military Gothic" armory for the elite Seventh Regiment situated on East Sixty-sixth Street so as to be "readily accessible"
by the neighborhood's well-born sons "in case of sudden calls," and "so
constructed as to be defensible from all points against mobs." Through

its iron-shuttered rifle loopholes, the tactically astute *New York Evening Express* noted, shooters could "pick off advancing crowds." Alternatively, "two or three Gatling guns could be mounted in the tower and sweep the avenue." Speaking at the groundbreaking ceremony, Secretary of State William Evarts hoped that the "war between labor and capital . . . may be kept within the bounds of peace." Downtown, Mrs. J. P. Morgan did her bit for capital, raising money for the Seventy-first Regiment's medieval fortress on East Thirty-third Street. Jay Gould dispatched his son Edwin to serve as its "inspector of rifle practice." Visiting in the 1890s, a Frenchman had such military redoubts of the upper classes in mind when he observed that American "capitalists have more power than the czar of Russia." But it was a contested power. Their "conception of the world" had not become hegemonic—not yet. "In the 1880s a deep struggle over the meaning of America took place," Herbert G. Gutman reminds us.[26]

The boxcars torched in the 668 railroad strikes between 1881 and 1894 were fiery petitions for redress of grievances, negotiating tactics in what Eric Hobsbawm calls "collective bargaining by riot." Striking trainmen lived as a subject people, under governments as hostile to their aspirations for a better life as the British were to Indian demands for independence. They could vote—but then so could East Germans under communism. Before the introduction of the secret or Australian ballot following the vote-buying scandals of 1888, the parties printed the ballots, "slip tickets," in party-coordinated lengths and colors. ("Big Tim" Sullivan of Tammany Hall perfumed his tickets, "so that they might be tracked to the ballot box by scent, as well as by size, shape, and color.") Inquisitive party hacks manned the polling places. Like the party snoops monitoring East German plebiscites, they knew who voted and how, and who didn't vote. Workingmen could vote—but in company towns like Scranton, Pennsylvania, they had to vote right. "[W]hy do you say the poor men here have not the right of suffrage?" the chairman of a House committee investigating the effects of the long depression of 1873–79 asked a Scranton man. "I do not," he replied, "consider that they have the right of suffrage when a foreman stands at his window and says, as a poor man goes up to cast his ballot, 'There is another of those God-damned short tickets going in; we will have to see that fellow'; and when, a day or two previous to the election, another man is told that the best thing he can do is to keep his mouth closed. In such cases men have the right of suffrage only in name, not in fact."[27]

Elections were fought over middle-class concerns like the civil service, the tariff, and "reform," or over distractions—Samuel Tilden's alleged homosexuality, General Hancock's corset (a "self-maid man"), and Cleveland's "bastard"; Harrison's Irish-slaughtering ancestors, Cleveland's Irish-incensing part in John Bull's free trade plot, and Blaine's Irish-slurring Protestant minister; Garfield's "Morey letter," Cleveland's "Murchison letter," Harrison's "Dudley letter"—planted or leaked documents treated as gospel in the party press, some plausible, others crude beyond credulity. For example, endorsing importation of cheap Chinese labor in a letter to the nonexistent Lynn, Massachusetts, union official Henry L. Morey, James Garfield misspelled his own name. Workers and farmers voted on synthetic or sham issues in corrupt elections that yielded oligarchy mitigated by bunting not representative government.

In at least three states the rules of representation were rigged against majority rule. Politics was turned upside down: The loser always won. The Democrats of Connecticut, Rhode Island, and New Jersey, like the workingmen of Scranton, had "the right of suffrage only in name."

Under a Colonial-era system of town-based as opposed to population-

Minority Rule
Fifteen hundred seventy-eight voters in three tiny Connecticut towns had the same number
of representatives in the state legislature as 188,161 in its three largest cities.
Cartoon from New York World, *1892.*

based voting districts, 14 percent of Connecticut voters could elect a majority of the House of Representatives. Between 1818, when the Connecticut state constitution adopted the town-based standard, and 1910, Hartford's population grew from 6,000 to 98,000, Waterbury's from 2,000 to 73,000, New Haven's from 8,000 to 132,000—*without* additional representation. In 1890 New Haven, population 86,000, sent the same number of representatives to the state legislature as Union, population 431. New Haven's voters were immigrants and Democrats; Union's "native" and Republican. With ethno-religious supremacy at stake, Republicans rose above shame. When a winning candidate for the state legislature failed of a majority, as happened to Democrats with minor party candidates on the ballot, a law passed by a Republican legislature mandated that the Republican legislature should choose the winner. The national Republican Party depended on its Connecticut "rotten borough." Between the 1870s and the 1890s it sent six Republican senators to Washington, where they cast key votes on the tariff and the currency and enabled the GOP to control four different Congresses. Republican-appointed judges on the state Supreme Court rejected attempts to change the formula of Connecticut's anti-democracy, which in weakened strength lasted until ended by the one-man, one-vote court rulings of the early 1960s.

In Rhode Island the Yankee-Protestant minority exercised what one historian calls a "virtual dictatorship" over a state legislature wired for GOP control from 1876 to 1964. Through a one-senator-per-town scheme of representation, Rhode Island's twenty-eight smallest towns representing 8 percent of the population elected 73 percent of the state Senate. This minority legislature passed a property qualification for voting that disfranchised 60 percent of Providence's residents: Any citizen could vote for the Irish-American mayor but only men of property for the Providence City Council, which stymied the mayor, or for local ballot questions on taxes and spending. Rhode Island's Republican boss, Gene C. Brayton, served as chief counsel for the New Haven Railroad and held stock in the Providence Electric Company. Connected corporations like these sluiced money into party-building activities—vote-buying and bribery, "a custom of the country" in Rhode Island, according to the muckraking journalist Lincoln Steffens. ("There would not be an election in Rhode Island . . . without money," a witness told a Senate committee investigating fraud, "any more than a funeral without a corpse.") In return they got a government "pledged to meet their business needs." One, for example, that allowed mill owners to pay the dollar-a-voter registration tax for their employees, herd them to the polls, and guide their pencils down the ballot with them when they got there.

The Republican boss of Connecticut, J. Henry Roraback, a "major stockholder" in state-regulated insurance and utility companies, "did not participate in petty corruption," the *Manchester Evening News* conceded. "Rather than stealing small things, he stole the whole state of Connecticut." He stole it for businesses that subsidized the Republican machine and helped Roraback buy off opposition. When a Democratic ward boss in Hartford won a following for his attacks on the city light company, Roraback pressed Standard Oil to name him general counsel. Labor legislation got nowhere in Connecticut and Rhode Island. In contrast, thanks to its largely population-based voting districts, neighboring Massachusetts pioneered in protective labor laws and business regulation. The majority will registered in Massachusetts. The Republican legislature had to respond.

New Jersey Republicans stayed in power through rules that apportioned one senator to each county. Thus a vote cast in Cape May County had 25 percent more weight than one cast in urban Hudson County. For six consecutive sessions Democrats won a majority of the vote but a minority of seats in the Senate, which frustrated the initiatives of Democratic governors, restricted the franchise for naturalized citizens by passing literacy tests and personal registration laws applying exclusively to Newark and Jersey City, and tortured geography with legislative redistricting diluting the Democratic vote. To ram through the "vicious gerrymander" of 1881 the Republicans passed a gag rule suspending debate and expunged minority protests from the official record, sacrificing "not only the principle of true representative government," one Democrat charged, "but their own sense of decency to make their power perpetual." When the Democrats took over in 1888, they did unto the Republicans what the Republicans had done unto them.[28]

The United States Senate, with at least six senators representing rotten boroughs, deserved the epithet itself. Gilded Age anti-democracy possessed institutional depth. In the ten congressional elections between 1874 and 1892, and in four of the five presidential elections, the Democrats got (slightly) more votes than the Republicans, and in 1880 lost by fewer than 10,000 votes out of more than nine million cast. Yet they could do little to change the policies the Republicans implemented during the Civil War, when southern Democrats were not in Washington to stop them. The postwar Democratic resurgence was checked by the Republican Senate.

The Republicans threw up a majority-proof bastion there by admitting several states (and senators) that did not meet the historical criteria for statehood—West Virginia, Kansas, and Nevada during the war; Nebraska in 1867; Colorado in 1876, just in time to swing the presidential election to Rutherford B. Hayes; and, in a compromise the Republican Senate forced on Grover Cleveland, the "Omnibus states"—North Dakota, South Dakota, Montana, and Washington—in 1889; followed by Idaho and Wyoming in 1890. Excluding West Virginia, of the eleven states admitted between 1861 and 1896 only six equaled "the size of an average congressional district (including Colorado), two were roughly half that size, and Nevada was one-sixth the normal size," Charles Stewart and Barry R. Weingast point out. To admit these smaller states the Republican Senate scrapped the "ratio of representation" standard—arrived at by dividing the population of the country by the size of the House—governing all antebellum state admissions except Oregon in 1859 and under which Nevada would have had to wait until 1970 and Wyoming would still be waiting. "No national electoral majority clearly favored the Republican vision over the Democratic," Stewart and Weingast write in "Stacking the Senate." "Instead the Republicans held on to their policies via manipulating institutions away from majoritarian government. Statehood politics allowed them to create a lock on the Senate by virtue of that body's bias away from population." By 1900 a majority of the country lived in states with only 21 percent of the representation in the upper house.[29]

Aside from Mississippi, where it used mass terror against a black majority, the southern democracy violated democratic norms by suppressing electoral *minorities*—indeed, by Bolshevik-style extirpation of the political opposition, black Republicans and Populists. They threatened a chummy heaven of businessmen and politicians.

The state governments elected after Reconstruction showered tax exemptions on northern railroads and made no fuss over regulation. This Democratic version of the Republican promotional state leveraged a railroad-building boom that opened the South to industry, northern and homegrown. "It was a poor subsidiary of an Eastern railroad that could not find some impoverished brigadier general to lend his name to a letterhead," C. Vann Woodward observes. The chairmen of the Virginia Democratic Party through the 1890s were nearly all railroad presidents or directors, and the northern railroads that obtained Virginia's state railroad system for a song in 1871 controlled the state legislature. The Louisville and Nashville Railroad, with that Wall Street brigadier, Jay Gould, on its board, dominated Kentucky. Tennessee's first Redeemer governor, John C. Brown, was vice president of the Texas and Pacific Railroad; his successor served the Nashville, Chattanooga and St. Louis so well during his two terms that he was elected its president after he left office. The Alabama Democracy waged a successful campaign in 1874 behind the slogan of "White Supremacy" and "Home Rule," but contributions from northern capitalists anxious that Alabama's taxpayers should pay off the $25 million in debt incurred by the Reconstruction governments filled its campaign war chest. The Redeemer of Georgia, Governor Joseph E. Brown, combined office with the presidency of two railroads and two coal companies—worked by state convicts paid 7 cents a day. His successor, General John B. Gordon, provided legal counsel for the Louisville and Nashville, among multifarious business connections. Conservative railroad lawyers led the Democratic Party in Mississippi, which between 1876 and 1890 sent seventeen congressmen to Washington, only seven of whom "sympathized with, worked for, and were approved by the farmers," according to one observer. The Redeemers saved the South from "Negro rule" and for crony capitalism. But what about us? unincorporated southerners, subsidizing railroads and carrying bondholders, had right, and reason, to ask.

"The politician is my shepherd, I shall not want," a Georgia paper wrote in a biblical parody of the new order.

> He leadeth me into the saloon for my vote's sake. He filleth my pockets with five-cent cigars and my beer glass runneth over. He inquireth concerning the health of my family even unto the fourth generation. Yea, though I walk thro the mud and rain to vote for him . . . when he is elected he straightway forgetteth me. Yea, though I meet him in his own office he knoweth me not. Surely the wool has been pulled over my eyes all the days of my life.

No sooner would the wool start to slip off than the Democrats would cry up the black menace and pull it down again. Redemption did not end black voting. Even without their Yankee protectors a majority of southern blacks voted in the 1880 elections, sending seventy-five legislators to southern state capitals and Washington. The restoration of white supremacy had not eliminated the need for extreme measures against black Republicans.[30]

Political violence had gone far to break the northern will to sustain Reconstruction and to put the Redeemers in power. It would help keep them there. Riots and the assassination of Republican candidates made elections a time of terror. The NAACP calculates that between 1889 and

1900, 2,522 blacks were lynched, and evidence suggests that lynchings increased near elections. In Caddo Parish, Louisiana, a black-majority sister of Grant Parish, site of the Colfax Massacre, every election season between 1868 and 1878 witnessed an increase in murders. That they began with Reconstruction and ended with Redemption evidences their political motivation. According to a meticulous study of coroners' reports and other official records, nearly 40 percent of Caddo's white males between eighteen and forty-five killed 10 percent of its black males that age in that decade. The whites killed in death squads, rarely alone. Bands of thirty from Shreveport, fifteen from Atkins Landing, twenty from Bossier Parish, "and a large squad from Red River Parish," for example, converged on Caledonia on the eve of the 1878 election for a "negro hunt" that took twenty lives. In the month before the 1868 election white paramilitaries killed at least 150 blacks, gunning down thirty on the banks of the Red River outside Shreveport, leaving their bodies to the alligators, and shackling nine together in an abandoned structure and burning it down. A posse of over a hundred white men took away all the black men assembled at a Baptist society meeting in Black Bayou; none were seen again.[31]

Political murder, by itself, could not drive blacks away from the polls. In a testament to their belief in a democracy unworthy of it Grant Parish blacks voted in the same numbers as in the presidential election after the Colfax Massacre as they had done in the election before it, a pattern replicated in nine of the twelve southern counties scarred by "riots" during Reconstruction. Terror ("a dead darkey always makes a good Democrat") needed supplementing with voter fraud. In Mississippi, Democratic horses and mules were reputed to have eaten Republican ballot boxes. The governor of Louisiana declared it his duty to "treat the law as a formality and count in the Democrats." The author of Virginia's election law called Virginia elections "crimes against popular government and treason against liberty." Mississippi had not seen an honest election, a white delegate to the state constitutional convention of 1900 admitted, in twenty-five years.

Terror and fraud commanded headlines in Republican newspapers in the North. Pressure mounted on politicians to do something. "A Republican can believe in a tariff reduction or even free trade and still be a Republican," Speaker of the House Thomas B. Reed declared. "But he cannot fail to advocate the Fifteenth Amendment and still be a Republican. . . . Failing to do this the party dishonorably dies." When they regained national power in 1888, the Republicans stirred, coming within one vote of

passing a "Force Bill" sponsored by Senator Henry Cabot Lodge of Massachusetts extending federal supervision of elections to every congressional
district in which at least one hundred voters asked for it to go into effect.
The "old system of pull, drag, buy and knock down," a Memphis paper
reckoned, had proved counterproductive. A legal way to stop blacks from
voting must be found.[32]

That became an imperative of political survival when Populism threatened to split the white vote, possibly allowing black Republicans to take
power. In his *People's Party Paper,* Tom Watson, the Populist congressman
from Georgia, appealed to white and black farmers to meet on common
ground: "You are kept apart that you may be fleeced separately of your
earnings. You are made to hate each other because upon that hatred is
rested the keystone of the arch of the financial despotism which enslaves
you both. You are deceived and blinded that you may not see how this race
antagonism perpetuates a monetary system which beggars both." And:
"There is no reason why the black man should not understand that the law
that hurts me, as a farmer, hurts him, as a farmer; that the law that hurts
me, as a cropper, hurts him, as a cropper." Thousands of blacks attended
Watson's rallies and stood side by side with white farmers, listening and
watching while Watson asked the whites to hold up their hands and promise "to defend the Negro's constitutional rights."* A biracial politics of
"self-interest" was the Democrats' nightmare—it might tear the wool off
the eyes of the white cropper. So might the Populist attack on unrepresentative government. "The professional politicians on both sides are too
intent on their own schemes to give your affairs a passing notice," a Populist speaker told a Louisiana crowd. "If you don't know now you will live
to learn that the farmers and laborers of this country will never get justice
from any party that depends on Eastern capital for campaign boodle,"
Watson wrote.

To neutralize the danger to their "monopoly of power, of place, of
privilege, of wealth, of progress," in their first full-scale electoral contest
against the People's Party in 1892 the Democrats resorted to murder and

---

* This makes Watson's turn to racism—and anti-Semitism and anti-Catholicism—after
the shipwreck of Populism in the 1896 election poignant as well as revolting. He blamed
blacks for the sinking. "The very animals in the stables are not safe from their bestiality,"
he wrote of the black man. And: "In the South we have to lynch him occasionally, and flog
him, to keep him from blaspheming the Almighty, by his conduct, on account of his smell
and color." See C. Vann Woodward, "Tom Watson and Agrarian Politics," *Journal of
Southern History,* vol. 4, no. 1 (February 1938), p. 32.

massive fraud. The Reverend H. S. Doyle, a black minister from Watson's hometown who made over sixty campaign appearances for Watson, was shot at during one speech, the bullet killing a white man behind him. After Doyle was threatened with hanging, hundreds of Winchester-armed white farmers rode all night to Watson's plantation in Thomson to guard him. Doyle survived the campaign, but on election day five black Populists were murdered in the act of voting by men said to be their onetime owners. In Harrison County, Texas, the Democrats met the state requirement that each party be represented on the vote-counting board by appointing "Populists for a day." These stacked boards counted in ballots cast by U.S. Grant, Roscoe Conkling, and James Garfield, among the 3,000 dead and otherwise incommunicative of several species who put the Democrats over the top. James F. "Cyclone" Davis, the Populist candidate for Congress, claimed that at one box a dog named Fido Jenkins voted against him five times. In Georgia, an authority reports: "Negro voters were bought and sold like merchandise and herded to the polls like so many cattle. They were fed at barbecues and made drunk and *penned* up to prevent them from voting if they could not be otherwise controlled." The Democrats unseated Watson by counting twice as many votes from the city of Augusta as there were registered voters. "[A]ll the machinery in the state was against us," Watson reflected. "[A]ll the unseen but terrible cohorts of ignorance and prejudice and sectionalism . . . and all the money."[33]

The South had no monopoly on bought elections. Consent was everywhere a slattern. At all levels of government voters were purchasable and elections purchased. An inquiry in rural Adams County, Ohio, revealed that 85 percent of the electorate had either sold or bought votes between the 1870s and 1910, when a crusading judge and magazine exposés ("The Shame of Ohio") forced a stop. Starting in the early 1890s, party leaders had signed agreements to end the buying only to break them when "the sellers had objected and had given warning that if their votes were not purchased they would vote against the man who first signed the agreement." A Rhode Island investigating committee uncovered voter corruption "almost beyond belief." Newspapers in upstate New York printed quotations on the price of votes—$25 in Ulster County in 1880, $10 to $27 in Elmira in 1885. "Corruption of this sort is spoken of as if it were to be expected, and excites no more comment than would a bad epidemic of the measles," the *Times* noted in dismay. After the introduction of the state-issued secret ballot, the Democratic state chairman admitted that "you cannot any longer tell how a man voted, but if he stays at home you know you have got your money's worth," suggesting that when it no longer made sense to pay people to vote the parties paid them not to. In New Jersey statewide elections, a third of voters received cash; by the turn of the century this boodle amounted to $700,000, with favor-seeking corporations like the Pennsylvania Railroad big givers. Rural "native" voters, not urban immigrants, set the pace. In elections between 1889 and 1906, 41.7 percent of remote Cape May County sold its vote. The *Red Bank Register* guessed that one in four Monmouth County voters, some "well-to-do farmers," were purchasable, including 1,100 of the 1,600 residents of besotted Freehold. "Floaters"—voters for sale to either party—comprised only a sliver of vote-sellers in New Jersey. Instead, most were partisans who still needed a cash incentive to get to the polls. Tellingly, after Progressive reform stanched the traffic in votes, turnout fell ten to twenty points from its 80 to 90 percent peaks of the nineteenth century.[34]

Vote buying was retail fraud. New York's "Boss" Tweed outlined the superior efficiency of wholesale fraud: "The ballots make no result. The counters make the result." In 1868 Tweed manufactured 45,000 votes to keep his machine in power. In Philadelphia, "the most corrupt and most contented" of the municipalities that Lincoln Steffens investigated years later for his "Shame of the Cities" series in *McClure's,* a reformer mailed registered letters to each voter in one of the "ring's" reliable districts. "Sixty-three percent were returned marked 'not at,' 'removed,' 'deceased,' etc." Steffens told of a "ring orator" reminding his hearers that they lived in the same ward as Independence Hall. "[T]hese men, the fathers of American liberty, voted down here once," he said. " 'And,' he added with a catching grin, 'they vote here yet.' " Though the extent of fraud—ballot box stuffing, ballot destroying, serial voting, cadaver voting—can't be documented, it flourished everywhere, inflating those suspiciously high nineteenth-century turnouts.[35]

The turnouts might have been legitimately higher but for the violence that kept unwanted voters away from the polls—and not only in the South. Using "wagon spokes," Democratic election officials in Cincinnati "regularly and severely beat" Negroes trying to vote. The city marked "a quiet election" in 1884 when only eight people were killed. "Never an election goes by" in Philadelphia, a U.S. marshal declared, "without a riot." A midwestern newspaper defined voting as "an arduous task attended by personal danger nearly everywhere in America. Every peaceable man dreads the approach of election day." On the frontier, violence was common. Armed soldiers, often dangerously drunk, brawled among themselves, intimidated voters, and roughly handled poll watchers who dared challenge their fraudulent ballots. Testifying before a congressional committee investigating a disputed 1862 election in Dakota Territory, a farmer told of the goings-on at Hedges store, the voting place at Fort Randall: "I saw a soldier named James Mowder, who was quite drunk . . . , attempt to discharge his musket: Sergeant Crumb, with difficulty wrenched the weapon from him. . . . Isaac Smith, a member of Company A, having heard that Naylor had voted for General Todd, attempted to stab Naylor with a bowie knife, but was prevented by Sergeant Mason, who seized him in the act, and in the scuffle Smith stabbed himself severely in the arm." At the nineteenth-century polling place, Richard F. Bensel writes, "Men placed their bodies in the path of opponents attempting to approach the voting window. They shoved, poked, threatened, grabbed, and sometimes stabbed or shot those they saw as politically damned." In *The American Ballot Box in the Mid-Nineteenth Century* (2004), Bensel documents a "startling paradox" at variance with the received image of the age of mass democracy: "[A]lthough popular voting is the quintessential characteristic of a democratic political system, the polling place, in nineteenth-century America, was often one of the less democratic sites in the nation." In 1889 the editors of the *Journal of United Labor* assayed the quality of consent given in American elections: "Between the bribery of the voters, the intimidation by employers, and the use of fraudulent ballots by corrupt politicians, to say nothing about the opportunity under present methods for stuffing the ballot box by dishonest inspectors . . . the will of the people is oftener outraged than respected." There *were* laws against bribery, Henry George quipped, but they were "of the nature of the Pope's bull against the comet."[36]

Perhaps the Republicans would have triumphed in 1880 and 1888 without buying votes in Indiana and New York, or in 1876 without outbidding the Democrats for the official vote counters in three southern states. But the closeness of elections—Garfield won in 1880 by .1 percent, Cleveland in 1884 by .2 percent—made fraud irresistible. In the last days of the 1880 campaign, a chronicle of "purchased votes, forgery, calumny, and vindictive politics," an Indiana correspondent informed Garfield that "there are 30,000 merchantable votes here . . . which side manages to buy more of them is the question." Representing tariff-mongering industries, the Republicans could buy more of them than the Democrats. In 1888 a letter to party workers from the treasurer of General Harrison's campaign outlined the strategy of vote-buying in Indiana: "Divide the floaters [the purchasable swing vote] into blocks of five and put a trusted man with the necessary funds in charge of these five and make him responsible that none get away and that all vote our ticket." With less than a week to go before the election, Democrats distributed 500,000 copies of the "Dudley letter," which advised Indiana Republicans "to find out who [has] democratic boodle, and steer the democratic workers to them, and make them pay big prices for their own men." To collect what a reporter called "the wages of depravity," the 20,000 floaters merely had to show up at the polls with the right ballot and do their civic duty. Depravity had gone up since the last election; instead of $5, the "boodle man" handed each floater "a brand-new twenty dollar bill." The floater's pocket was the final resting place for who knows how much of the $400,000 the GOP spent carrying Indiana by 2,300 votes out of a half-million cast.

Not that the Democrats wanted for funds. The Democratic National Committee "looked like a railroad board of directors, and there were plenty of representatives of coal interests, too." And if Democratic boodle fell short of Republican boodle in the North, Democratic fraud and intimidation compensated in the South.*

Government "by campaign contributions," Henry D. Lloyd labeled the greenest legacy of Gilded Age politics: "[T]he trusts, and armor-plate contractors, and the whiskey ring, and the subsidized steamship companies, and the street railways and railroads buy the privilege of running [city, state, and national] governments to enrich themselves and send troublesome leaders of the people to jail." The publicity given corruption broadcast the death of hope. Nothing could be done with the unregenerate parties and nothing could be done outside them.[37]

Thomas Wolfe voices posterity's verdict on the postwar presidents in his essay "The Four Lost Men": "For who was Garfield, martyred man, and who had seen him walk the streets of life? Who could believe his footfalls

---

* A Republican fund-raising gambit in 1888 throws light on the business of politics. John Wanamaker, the department store pioneer, sold $10,000 shares in Harrison's victory to businessmen and Republican senators, giving half the money to the campaign and wagering the other half on the outcome, "and after Harrison's victory the contributors redeemed their certificates at a handsome profit." Matthew Josephson, *The Politicos* (New York: Harcourt, 1939), p. 440.

ever sounded on a loud pavement? Who had heard the casual and familiar tones of Chester Arthur? And where was Harrison? Where was Hayes? Which had the whiskers, which the sideburns; which was which?" The relative weakness of the Gilded Age presidency leaps out in housekeeping details. Grant had a staff of three. Not only did the man Hayes asked to serve as his secretary refuse the job but, according to Hayes, he was "hurt that I suggested it to him." Grover Cleveland answered the White House doorbell, and paid the White House bills. "If the President has any great policy in mind or on hand he has no one to help work it out," he complained. The Republicans flanking him, unlike Cleveland wore neither whiskers nor sideburns.[38] Yet far from changing the course set for twenty-five years by the Republicans, the only Democratic president between Buchanan and Wilson confirmed it. Cleveland's second victory, in 1892, elicited this response from Andrew Carnegie, a contributor to Harrison's losing campaign: "Cleveland! Landslide!" he wrote Henry Clay Frick. "Well we have nothing to fear and perhaps it is best. People will now think the *protected* manufacturers are attended to and quit agitating. Cleveland is a pretty good fellow. Off for Venice tomorrow."[39]

The soporific "reform" stilled "agitating." An 1878 measure well characterized by the name of its House sponsor, Richard "Silver Dick" Bland, calmed agitation from inflationists to increase the money supply.[40] On the Senate floor Rhode Island's Nelson Aldrich branded the Interstate Commerce Act of 1887, the upshot of thirty years of agitation over railroad rates, "revolution." Privately he called it "a delusion and a sham. . . . An empty menace to the great, made to answer the clamor of the ignorant and unreasoning."[41] To the president of the Burlington Northern, Attorney General Richard Olney confided that the Interstate Commerce Commission "satisfies the popular clamor for a government supervision of railroads at the same time that the supervision was entirely nominal." Some railroads favored regulation—rate-setting would advantage them competitively; others, like the Burlington Northern, opposed it. The files of the committees that held hearings on the act are "flooded" with petitions from businessmen saying, Yes, regulation is fine, so long as it is "helpful" to my business. A review of this correspondence and committee testimony reveals that "hardly anyone" objected to the act because it violated the tenets of laissez-faire economics or Social Darwinism. "We are not aware that there is the slightest issue of principle involved in the question," *Banker's Magazine* editorialized. "[I]t is one purely of self-interest." The constant was "the desire for economic protection." "It was neither 'the people' nor the 'farmers'—nor even 'businessmen'—who were responsible for government regulation of the railroads," Edward A. Purcell, Jr., concludes from his study of the record. "Rather it was many diverse economic groups in combination throughout the nation which felt threatened by the national economy, and sought to protect their interests through the Federal Government."[42]

A half-century of agitation over "monopoly" succumbed to the Sherman Antitrust Act (1890). Surveying three farm journals that reflexively described corporations as "oppressive," "extortionate," and "tyrannical," Louis Galambos documented the impress of the act on hostile agrarian opinion. In the years immediately before passage "the percentage of unfavorable items increased sharply" while incomes rose; after, unfavorable mentions of corporations fell even as incomes also fell. In its first fifteen years only twenty-three cases were brought under this scourge of the "trusts," which did not hinder the compactions listed by Louis D. Brandeis in *The Curse of Bigness* (1935): the Newspaper Trust, the Writing Paper Trust, the Upper Leather Trust, the Sole Leather Trust, the Woolen Trust, the Paper Bag Trust, the Cordage Trust, the Flour Trust, the Standard Oil Trust, the Steel Trust, the Tobacco Trust, the Sugar Trust, the Rubber Trust, and the Mucilage Trust. Richard Ely, the Progressive economist, thought the Sherman Act stimulated bigness, by encouraging firms to avoid the "soft" combinations vulnerable to prosecution under it in favor of "hard" combinations—mergers. Between 1905 and the New Deal *small* businesses were the target of six out of seven Sherman Act prosecutions. In 1912 Andrew Carnegie shared this revealing piece of insouciance with a House committee investigating U.S. Steel: "Nobody ever mentioned the Sherman Act to me, that I can remember."[43]

The one systemic reform passed by Congress in these years, the establishment of the Federal Civil Service under President Arthur, jeopardized no business interest. On the contrary, it promised relief from exactions by spoilsmen that "burdened the country with debt and taxes, and assisted to prostrate the trade and industry of the nation," in the words of a congressional report on Arthur's pre-presidential operation of the New York Custom House. Every time the "pillar of [the] oligarchy" swayed, the buttress of reform fixed it in place.[44]

What James Bryce "ventured to call the Fatalism of the Multitude" froze the pillar's foundation. In America's democratic society, where "the will of the majority is absolute, always invoked to decide any question, and where the numbers which decide are so vast that one comes to regard them as one regards the largely working forces of nature," Bryce wrote in the second volume of *The American Commonwealth,* "this tendency to acquiescence and submission, this sense of the insignificance of individual effort, this belief that the affairs of men are swayed by large forces whose movement may be studied but cannot be turned" ran deep.

Bryce exposed a paradox of democracy. The forms of democracy—parties, candidates, platforms, primaries, elections, choice—confer agreement on injustices. The political psychology of aggrieved multitudes in democracies might be expressed this way: "We can't rebel; we have the vote. True, the tiny minority that pays for politics rules. But in theory our voices could be heard; our grievances redressed." That theory of the case, the idea of self-rule, can paralyze action to change the fallen reality. With autocracies you get no theories. Government is power, not authority. The idea of the thing sheds no grace on the thing. Injustices that provoke revolutions in autocracies can be platonically legitimated in democracies.

The student of the Gilded Age confronts a mystery: What reverse alchemy transformed mass enthusiasm into policies disfavoring the masses? Put another way, Why, if politics ignored their needs, did roughly 30 percent more Americans than now vote then? A hypothesis consistent with much of the contemporary evidence and with the lore of rule from Roman history to Machiavelli to Karl Rove is the politics of distraction.* The parties exploited sectional, racial, cultural, and religious cleavages to win office, then turned government over to the corporations. Sound familiar? *Vote* to stop abortion; *receive* a rollback in capital gains taxes. . . . *Vote* to get government off our backs; *receive* conglomeration and monopoly everywhere from media to meat-packing. *Vote* to stand tall against terrorists; *receive* a social order in which wealth is more concentrated than

---

* "When in all these thousand of years has there been a time when man has acted only from his own interest," asks Dostoevsky's Underground Man. "What is to be done with the millions of facts that men, consciously, that is fully understanding their own interests, have left them in the background and have rushed headlong on another path, to meet peril and danger, compelled to this course by nobody or nothing, but, as it were, simply disliking the beaten track, and have obstinately, willfully, struck out another difficult, absurd way, seeking it almost in darkness." Feodor Dostoevsky, *Notes from the Underground,* in Constance Garnett, trans., *Three Short Novels of Dostoevsky* (New York: 1960), pp. 196–97, seen in T. Jackson Lears, "The Concept of Cultural Hegemony: Problems and Possibilities," *American Historical Review,* vol. 90, no. 3 (June 1985), p. 584.

ever before in our lifetimes, in which workers have been stripped of power and CEOs are rewarded in a manner beyond imagining." That's Thomas Frank, the contemporary social critic, in *What's the Matter with Kansas? How Conservatives Won the Heart of America* (2004). Working-class voters in Kansas (and America), Frank argues, have been gulled into voting against their economic interests by today's GOP, which, to borrow Ross Perot's lingual felicity, has blinded them with the "gorilla dust" of "social issues" like abortion and gun control.[45]

That attributes a brilliance to GOP politicians not otherwise apparent and a docile dimness to working-class voters. In any case, the politics of distraction did not work like that in the Gilded Age. Scooping up fresh handfuls of gorilla dust to distract voters wasn't necessary. The "Third Party-System," forged in the 1850s structured party competition around section, memory, and ethnocultural division, preventing new "issue-cleavage conflicts" from emerging and blocking the formation of intersectional or cross-cultural coalitions built around economic interests.*

"We rush into politics because politics is the safety-valve," the labor radical Wendell Phillips complained. In their study of the political behavior of Lynn, Massachusetts, shoe workers, the social historians Alan Dawley and Paul Faler conclude that "[d]uring the most critical years of industrialization, the United States was more keenly divided between industrialism and slavery than between industrial workers and industrial capitalists." They cite an 1860 strike by the shoe workers that polarized the city along class lines. The workers organized a Workingmen's Party and in the November elections won "nearly every position in the Lynn city government." But the attack on Fort Sumter ended Lynn's class politics. In

---

* In "What's the Matter with *What's the Matter with Kansas?*," Larry M. Bartels, a Princeton political scientist, surveys National Election Surveys between 1980 and 2004 to test Frank's hypothesis that white working-class voters are "social issue" voters. Bartels "found that less affluent voters attached much *less* weight to social issues than to economic issues, that they attached much less weight to social issues than most affluent voters did, that the apparent weight of social issues increased substantially over the past twenty years among more affluent voters, but *not* among those in the bottom third of the income distribution, and that the apparent weight of economic issues among less affluent voters *increased* rather than decreasing as Frank's account would suggest." Nor have white working-class voters abandoned the Democratic Party. Since 1952, "the Democratic presidential vote share has declined by almost twenty points among southern whites without college degrees. Among non-southern whites without college degrees it has declined by one percentage point. That's it. Fourteen elections, fifty-two years, one percentage point." Larry M. Bartels, "What's the Matter with *What's the Matter with Kansas?*" *Quarterly Journal of Political Science*, vol. 1, 2006, pp. 201–26.

the next election the Republican Party, "dominated by local shoe manufacturers," won for the first time in the city. "[S]oon worker opposition withered away to nothing," Dawley and Faler write. "Literally nothing. Not a single vote was cast against the incumbent Republican mayor in 1863." After the war the politics of section dependably pacified discontent in Lynn.

From the perspective of comparative history, posterity should be grateful to section: It kept the United States off the "Prussian Road" to modernity. Germany embarked on the Prussian Road in 1879 when Otto von Bismarck, the "Iron Chancellor," with a high tariff for industry *and* agriculture, sealed "the marriage of iron and rye" between conservative industrialists and a reactionary Prussian Junker landed class. The Junkers had long opposed tariffs but the American "grain invasion" of the 1870s, which sharply dropped the price of wheat, threatened their economic position. To secure it, they pushed for a tariff on imported wheat, accepting a tariff on manufactured goods as a trade-off. America's cornucopia thus "intensified" the "authoritarian and reactionary trends" in the German polity—militarism, imperialism, anti-liberalism, anti-Semitism— through which the conservative "revolution from above" contained threats from below, ultimately trying "to make reaction popular in the form of fascism," Barrington Moore, Jr., writes in his classic work of comparative political sociology, *The Social Origins of Dictatorship and Democracy.* Bismarck accelerated these reactionary trends, trading protection for Junker support for "a naval build-up, imperial expansion, and a campaign against the Social Democrats."

It could have happened here. Before the Civil War, southern publicists like George Fitzhugh called for a marriage of capital, North and South, against labor, slave and free. "We think that by a kind of alliance, offensive and defensive, with the South, Northern Conservatism may now arrest and turn back the tide of Radicalism and Agrarianism," he wrote in his influential *Sociology of the South.* "Slavery will be everywhere abolished, or everywhere be reinstituted." *That* was Lincoln's nightmare. He had read the appeals in southern newspaper editorials for a marriage of "iron and cotton" against labor, slave and free; his law partner had given him a copy of Fitzhugh's book; and his "House Divided" speech of 1858 stated the issue before the country in Fitzhugh's stark terms: "Either the opponents of slavery will arrest the further spread of it, and place it where the public mind shall rest in the belief that it is in the course of ultimate extinction; or its advocates will push it forward till it shall become alike lawful in all the States, old as well as new, North as well as South." At stake in the struggle over slavery extension was the "white man's charter of freedom," the declaration that "all men are free and equal." On accepting honorary membership in a New York workingman's association, President Lincoln cast the Civil War as a class war: "[T]he existing rebellion means more and tends to more than the perpetuation of African slavery—that it is, in fact, a war upon the rights of all working people."

After the war, "despite flirtations in that direction, no American analogue to the German 'marriage of iron and rye' " emerged, according to Steven Hahn. Bloody-shirt electioneering helped keep northern industrialists and southern planters apart, but politics reflected a deeper schism. "[T]he United States in the late nineteenth century was really two nations joined together by force of arms," Richard F. Bensel observes. "The upper classes of the United States were deeply divided into two branches with almost entirely conflicting interests." Through the tariff and the Civil War pension system for Yankees only, the north fed on the southern taxpayer, making "intersectional redistribution the most important factor in American politics." Dominant in national politics for the first half of the nineteenth century, the planters were eclipsed in the postwar by the new industrial ruling class, which refused to share power. "Between 1865 and 1912 southerners received only 7 of 31 Supreme Court appointments, 2 of 12 House speakerships, 14 of 133 cabinet positions, and excepting the rather unusual case of Andrew Johnson, not even one presidential or vice presidential nomination, let alone an office," Hahn notes. In southern politics it was a different story. "The Populist threat from below helped forge the alliance of industrialists and planters in the South," Jonathan Wiener writes of the "Prussian Road" taken there. "[T]his reactionary coalition intensified the repressive control of labor and struck devastating blows at democracy by disfranchising thousands of blacks and poor whites as well." Thus, in a mixed verdict of history, the Mason-Dixon line blocked intersectional coalitions of the "haves" against the "have nots" as well as the "have nots" against the "haves."

Section trapped Gilded Age voters until the populist revolt of the 1890s created a chance of change. In Colorado, Virginia, Texas, and Minnesota, at Dakota camp meetings and in dirt-floor churches across Alabama, farmers nodded when populist lecturers preached the nineteenth-century version of Thomas Frank's gospel: You've been had by the bloody shirt and the bogey of "Negro domination." Break from section; follow us into interest politics—the producing classes against the capitalists, the Populists urged them. Cast off the values that divide you; rally around the economic interests that unite you—north and south, white and black; vote your hopes not your memories. This way to the twentieth century . . . The farmers nodded—but would they follow and would they go over into the future alone?[46]

The presidential election campaign of 1884 between Grover Cleveland and James G. Blaine might have unfolded today. "Character" dominated. On one side was a man of low public morals; on the other a man of "loose morals," "a rake," "the father of a bastard." Even Cleveland's girth, "a small man everywhere but on the hay scales," drew moralistic comment. The Republicans waved the bloody shirt and assailed the Democrats as "free traders" in John Bull's pay; the Democrats sloganeered over Blaine's "disgraceful record," "Soap, Soap, Blaine's Only Hope" ("soap," paradoxically, was slang for the cash used to incent partisans), and his odious friends, "Blaine, Blaine, Jay Gould Blaine, Continental Liar from the State of Maine." With no clearly delineated issues, nothing hung on the outcome. Yet this nasty void raised a fever of enthusiasm. In New York City Cleveland reviewed a parade of 40,000, Blaine a torchlight procession of 30,000 businessmen including "Wash" Conner, Jay Gould's partner. ("Mr. Gould himself intended to march," the *New York World* dryly noted, "but the nasty dampness dissuaded him.") "You can hardly go out after dark without encountering a torch light procession," a visitor to Maine reported. Five thousand of New Haven's 16,000 registered voters that year belonged to political clubs "or marched in the city's campaign army."[47]

Such reports can mislead political scientists into conjuring a "golden age" of engaged voters. *The World,* a Democratic paper to be sure, applies an astringent to nostalgia: "Many of the organizations" in the Blaine parade, it reported, got a little way up Broadway, ducked into side streets, and rejoined the march beneath new organizational banners. That "humbug" of a parade may have been more like the norm. In Illinois during the 1860 campaign rally goers traveled from town to town staging spontaneous demonstrations. "Local party leaders loaned their activists to the leaders of other towns, expecting payment in kind when they planned their own affairs," Glenn C. Altschuler and Stuart M. Blumin report in a paper complicating the narrative of a nineteenth-century electorate that shames us by its enthusiasm for politics. The 5,000 persons who came out to see Van Amburgh's Menagerie in Greenfield, Massachusetts, that summer far

Mass Politics
This drawing depicts the huge crowd that gathered in New York's Printing House Square to learn who won the 1884 presidential election. Grover Cleveland carried New York state over James G. Blaine by 1,149 votes out of over 1 million cast, giving him a 219–182 electoral college victory. Harper's Weekly, November, 15, 1884.

exceeded the number who turned up at political rallies that fall, when the fate of the Union was on the ballot. The authors see a spectrum of involvement where earlier commentators posited torchlight-to-torchlight commitment. Elites—lawyers, party workers, the party press—often had all they could do to stir disengaged voters, who showed up at rallies for the barbecue and beer, to go up in a balloon, or to hear a brass band. They listened to the speeches with "engaged disbelief."[48]

While much of the fervor betrayed manufacture, the "spectacle campaign" helped to boost turnout in presidential elections to historic highs. Between 1876 and 1892 in the North it *averaged* 82 percent; in 1896, 84 percent, and in five Midwest states—Ohio, Indiana, Illinois, Iowa, and Michigan—95 percent. Nationally, turnout reached its zenith, 78.4 percent, in 1880, yet "a needle could scarcely find a space" between the candidates on the issues, in the representative opinion of one historian. In 1884, observes another, "a voter would have to tax his brain very heavily" to find a substantive difference between the parties. "The fact is," writes yet another, of the 1888 election, "that a voter with an intelligent interest in such questions as civil-service reform, economy in government, or the tariff would have found it difficult to choose between Cleveland and Harrison on the basis of any of these issues." Looking back in 1912, the Yale political economist Henry Crosby Emery testified that many contemporaries felt the same way: "It is more or less true, I think, that the old parties fifteen or twenty years ago stood in the minds of the voters for little more than the question of who should get in and who should stay out."[49]

Gilded Age revisionists have challenged this line of criticism, descended from Lord Bryce and a shibboleth of post–World War II history textbooks. The characterization of the 1888 campaign outlined above, for example, leaves out the "great debate" Cleveland ignited with his 1887 tariff message to Congress. "[T]here was a real difference between the parties," Joanne Reitano writes in *The Tariff Question in the Gilded Age* (1994). "The year 1888 was unique in American history because it was so singularly dedicated to the discussion of ideas." The Democrats assailed the tariff with Smithian political economy. The Republicans countered with the national economy arguments of the German economist Friedrich List, the Pennsylvania manufacturer and social theorist Henry C. Carey, and Henry Clay. "Here was one Gilded Age politician who refused to avoid real issues," Reitano says of Cleveland. "Politics may have failed to deal with the 'real' issues as we may define them," Walter T. K. Nugent cautions, "but the facts of voter participation alone show politics and partisanship made an immense difference to the people of the time." (That begs the question raised above: For many, voting was a job.) Geoffrey Blodgett bears down hard on the condescension lacing the "progressive" derogation of Gilded Age politics: "Either the people did not know what the 'real issues' were, or the whole idea of the 'real issues' versus 'false issues' is intellectually bankrupt." According to H. Wayne Morgan, "Politics was an ever-present, vivid, and meaningful reality to that generation. Men believed fervently that wide differences separated the parties." These revisionists argue that the older historians projected late-twentieth-century assumptions about government onto the Gilded Age. In fact, Vincent P. De Santis tells us, "Government seldom concerned itself with economic and social matters as it does now under the welfare state concept" because "the predominant feeling among Americans then was that the government *should* let well enough alone." The parties faithfully reflected their voters' wish to be let alone. "If there was one thing 19th century parties did well," Keith Ian Polakoff concludes, "it was to represent their constituents." History is argument without end.[50]

A hypothesis consistent with assertions made by both sides is that Gilded Age campaigns were less a clash of "issues" than of identities. In a society of "men in motion," Stephan Thernstrom and Peter R. Knights observe, "[p]arty may have been a substitute for community as a source of personal identity." Catholic immigrants became American by becoming Democrats. Southerners affirmed their whiteness in the "party of the fathers." Through their party Republicans kept touch with the deliquescing glory of the war. In the Ohio of his youth, the journalist Brand Whitlock recalled, Republican "was merely a synonym for patriotism, another name for the nation." Especially in the Midwest religious and ethnic identities overlay party and pumped moral emotion into politics. "Nineteenth-century American partisanship was not rooted in economic distinctions," Paul Kleppner explains in *The Third Electoral System, 1853–1892.* "Partisan identifications mirrored irreconcilably conflicting values emanating from divergent ethnic and religious subcultures." "Catholics," a Wisconsin priest remarked in 1889, "think that one is not a good Catholic if he is a Republican." A Protestant minister wondered how a Christian could go "to the Lord's table on Sunday and vote for Cleveland on Tuesday." The citizens of Hendricks County, Indiana, voted as they prayed. In 1874, 79.7 percent of "liturgicals"—immigrant Catholics and a congeries of high-church Protestants—voted Democratic and 72.3 percent of "pietists"—native-stock Protestants—Republican. Like their co-religionists in similar midwestern counties, Hendricks's liturgicals and pietists voted in the same numbers and as blocs in every presidential election between 1876 and 1908. "In defining their horizons and making their choices," Blodgett writes, "most voters were evidently animated by local issues swirling around schools, saloons, and the Sabbath." Voter attachment to their "political churches" stirred emotions untapped by "issues" lacking ethno-religious content. The "hurrah campaign" invited the "party faithful" to carry their hearts into the streets. Men could drink, whoop, howl, and hate together.

Hoopla fostered in-group solidarity while entertaining the marginally engaged. "What the theater is to the French and the bull-fight to the Spanish, the hustings and the ballot box are to *our* people," a nineteenth-century political anthropologist observed. But the popular "poetry" of campaigning and the special-interest "prose" of governing belonged to different tongues. Politics consumed its purpose in electioneering.[51]

And beneath the froth of partisanship ran the current of business rule. If a single detail can suggest the whole it's this one: Connecticut senator William H. Barnum and Stephen J. Dorsey served as president and secretary respectively of the Bull Domingo Company—and, respectively, as chairman of the Democratic National Committee and secretary of the Republican National Committee in the 1888 election. "[T]he axiom that railroads will not long compete when they can combine is as true of our political machines," Henry George wrote in an 1883 article, "Money in Elections." "Nothing is more common than to find the same combination running both parties and playing with the people the game of 'heads, I win; tails you lose.' Thus freedom of choice is destroyed and, under the forms of popular sovereignty, we are ruled as completely as though our institutions recognized a governing class."[52]

The political scandals of the Gilded Age wore upholstery. "The inquiry commenced under duress, proceeded with as much consideration for the offenders as the circumstances would allow," Ellis Paxon Oberholtzer wrote of the congressional hearings into the bribery of members by the Crédit Mobilier construction finance company, organized by principals of the Union Pacific Railway to siphon off profits from building the road. "As much as could be would be concealed. Investigator and investigated were in a boat together in Congress." The investigation by a bipartisan House committee deserved the headline that greeted its report in the *New York Sun,* which had exposed the scandal: "Whitewash!" Two congressmen—one Republican, one Democrat—were censured and a senator reprimanded for Crédit Mobilier, the signature scandal of the Gilded Age.

Chicago 1894—scene from the Pullman strike. Drawing by Frederic Remington.

Oakes Ames, the Massachusetts Republican censured for seeking to cor-
ruptly influence a roster of GOP lights, from Speaker James G. Blaine to
both of Grant's vice presidents, agreed with the *Sun*. "It's just like the man
in Massachusetts who committed adultery," he told a reporter, "and the
jury brought in a verdict that he was as guilty as the devil but that the
woman was as innocent as an angel. Those fellows are like that woman."[53]

The Star Route scandal of the late 1870s and early 1880s left the GOP
vulnerable to partisan attack. Yet, even though the chairman of the
Republican National Committee was indicted for conspiracy to defraud
the government as a contractor delivering mail in the West, even though
President James Garfield had sent a note soliciting a contribution from
another indictee, even though the assistant attorney general initially
appointed to prosecute had taken $2,500 from a businessman seeking a
contract to deliver mail on one of the so-called Star Routes in the western
states that was under investigation, even though a Washington jury in
a second trial acquitted defendants who had pled guilty in an aborted
first trial, and even though warrants were issued to eight men for
jury-tampering, Cleveland's new postmaster general dropped all charges

against all concerned. The Democrats had *their* contractors to protect. Party competition was subordinated to oligarchic stability.[54]

"[O]n the fundamental question of the time—the role of government in a modern industrial society—the two national parties had no quarrel," James L. Sundquist writes. "Both saw an identity of interest between the government and the great banking, manufacturing, and railroad corporations. . . . Both took for granted the merger of economic and political power." The party of business ruled and with the machinery of government crushed labor.[55]

Chapter Eight

TOM SCOTT, POLITICAL CAPITALIST

He was my great man and all the hero worship that is inherent in youth I showered upon him.

—Andrew Carnegie

American railroads built ahead of demand. Waiting for demand to catch up a railroad borrowed to operate—and build ahead of more (missing) demand. A Pacific-bound road outran settlement between the Mississippi and Missouri rivers but could not pause and wait for economic development to spur demand ahead. It *was* the economic development. It created the demand. Build it and they will come—but when? Speculators got in on the hope and out on the waiting. So much space, so little demand.*

After the war, encouraged by land grants and subsidies, the railroads rapidly overbuilt, spending $1.7 billion on construction between 1868 and 1873.[1] When the most ambitious of them, the Northern Pacific, reached the Missouri in the summer of the latter year, the nation's premier bank, Jay Cooke and Company, which had kept the NP afloat for years, collapsed under the $2 million weight of its patience. Cooke had assured investors of the "intelligence and vigor and economy of the Northern Pacific management." Meanwhile, his partner, Harris Fahnestock, was warning privately, "We know that it has been inefficient, distracted, and extravagant to the last degree." Publicly Cooke extolled the value of the Northern's land grant, but much of it, Fahnestock noted, "was practically valueless either for cultivation or lumbering." Cooke's prospectus promised bondholders a rapid marketing of the land, but as of June 1872 land

---

* "[D]espite a past strewn with disappointment, railroad executives continued to lay tracks where they did not want to build, engage in rate wars they had wished to avoid, and count on a perpetual prosperity that would never come. What seemed to them a series of rational responses added up to an utterly irrational industrial policy that courted danger for large portions of a dependent economy." Robert H. Wiebe, *The Search for Order, 1877–1920* (New York: Hill & Wang, 1967), p. 19.

sales had brought in only $338.76 in cash. Fahnestock saw "discredit if not ruin ahead." "Moneyed men" were ominously absent in the list of Cooke's investors. "Cooke had paid off bankers in country towns to vouch for the safety of the Northern Pacific's bonds," according to Richard White. The banks attracted small investors, reassured by Cooke's patriotic aura as Lincoln's bond salesman during the Civil War. The crunch came when the country banks tried to withdraw funds from Cooke and Company to pay farmers for the fall harvest.[2]

"No one could have been more surprised," the *Philadelphia Inquirer* observed, "if snow had fallen amid the sunshine of a summer noon." "The public, which by Jay Cooke's previous tremendous success had been lulled into believing him invincible, could not understand it," Theodore Dreiser wrote in *The Financier*. "Jay Cooke fail? . . . Suspicion was universal, rumor affected everyone." Financial panic spread as investors took in this object lesson in the risky economics of building ahead of demand. Banks in Virginia, Chicago, and San Francisco failed. Railroad stocks plummeted. "To save the entire 'Street' from utter ruin," its vice chairman announced, the Stock Exchange would close. Businesses shut down. Hundreds of thousands lost jobs—and livelihoods. New York City anticipated that 50,000 would be destitute by December. Cotton rotted in the southern fields. In Iowa that winter farmers burned corn for fuel. "Here was a panic that comprehended the country." Here was the tocsin of five years of depression, an externality of railroad speculation and worldwide overbuilding.[3]

Between 1873 and 1876 wages for Pennsylvania workers fell by more than half; wages for skilled workers in Ohio by nearly a third. One dollar a day, the Ohio Bureau of Labor Statistics estimated, represented "absolute poverty," yet 10,000 Massachusetts textile hands and 60,000 Pennsylvania miners had to live on less. During the first depression winter, a Massachusetts editor saw "[a] drove of poverty-stricken children . . . clad only in one or two ragged and dirty garments down on their hands and knees in the gutters, greedily picking out of the mud and dirt and eating the bits of spoiled and decaying fruit which has been thrown away." In Mississippi, employers held back workers' wages from one to *four* months. Mass layoffs undercut labor's strike weapon and decimated the ranks of unions representing cigar makers, coopers, blacksmiths, and machinists. The Order of Crispins, 50,000 strong in 1871, had ceased to exist by 1878. "In 1877," Samuel Gompers testified years later, "there were not more than 50,000 organized workmen on the American continent."[4]

The engine of the economy, the nation's biggest business and largest employer, stalled. By the end of 1876 half of all railroads were in receivership. Two hundred had defaulted on $814 million in bonds. Revenue for those still operating declined by a third. Construction halted. Railroads laid off workers, cut wages, lengthened trains, and slashed rates. The four east–west trunk lines, the Pennsylvania Railroad, the Baltimore & Ohio, the New York Central, and the Erie, fought a two-year rate war over diminishing traffic. Early in 1877 they reached a truce. Nearly ruined by competition, they tried collusion. They formed a "pool" dividing up the traffic between New York and Chicago. They raised rates; and they announced 10 percent wage cuts to begin in July. The cuts would plunge the bulk of their workforce into "absolute poverty."

Tom Scott, the president of the Pennsylvania Railroad, did not cause the Great Railroad Strike of 1877, the social earthquake of the Gilded Age. But its worst violence bore his signature. When the *New York Times* referred to a certain "Mr. Rockafellow" and Carnegie ascended in obscurity, Scott, forgotten now, was famous, the public face of the largest corporation in the world—the railroad incarnate.[5] Scott left no paper trail in life or death, exerting political influence to prevent the Commonwealth of Pennsylvania from "probating his will publicly." (He left a fortune estimated at $17 million.) Yet R. G. Dun's August 1873 credit report on Scott testified to his reputation in the Gilded Age: "Vice Presdt of the 'Penna RR Co.' + is considered the RR king of this country. . . . Has millions of money at his command + exerts a greater corporative influence than any other man in the U.S. Is about 50 years old, family, self made man. Great ability + looked upon as the muscle + backbone of the 'Penna R.R.' + its tributaries while 'Edgar Thompson' Prest. Is the brain." Scott's life opens the book of the age to the chapter headed Captains of Industry.*[6]

Tom Scott belonged to a species rued by investors—the manager who

---

* T. Lloyd Benson and Trina Rossman, authors of an insightful paper on Scott presented at the Mid-America Conference on History in 1995, found that "although he created major new business structures and was president of what was in its time the largest corporation in the world, our friends in business had never heard of him. And although his company contributed mightily to the growth of Philadelphia, Pittsburgh, Chicago, and Baltimore, among other cities, not one person we have met from any of those places has ever heard of him." Partly because Scott left no papers for them to work with, historians have brushed past him. "For example, Sean Dennis Cashman's survey of the Gilded Age has just three references to Scott in more than two chapters on industry and the 'robber barons'; Albro Martin's recent history of American railroads, *Railroads Triumphant,* has just four brief references to Scott; and Alfred D. Chandler's *Visible Hand* just five brief references." Dr. T. Lloyd Benson and Trina Rossman, "Re-Assessing Tom Scott, the 'Railroad Prince.' " http://facweb.furman.edu/~benson/col-tom.html.

mismanages his company. Andrew Carnegie, his protégé, called him a "genius . . . in his department." That would be political capitalism.[7] Scott had a "genius" for winkling favors out of politicians for the Pennsylvania and allied railroads. "[A]s he trailed his garments across the country," Wendell Phillips said of Scott, "the members of twenty legislatures rustled like dry leaves in a winter wind."[8]

In his company photograph, Scott's pale eyes radiate magnetism. But the Scott persuasion did not rest on charisma, nor on "the charm of . . . personality" to which circumlocutory contemporaries (and naïve commentators) attributed it.[9] Collis P. Huntington, the president of the Southern Pacific, last seen financing Roscoe Conkling's discovery of the corporate person, would have scoffed at that. Lobbying Congress against a Scott lobby for a subsidy to build a road from Texas to the Pacific, Huntington peeled the Scott mystique. "Scott is prepared to pay, or promises to pay, a large amount of money to pass his bill," he wrote an associate as the bidding got under way, "but I do not think he can pass it, although I think this coming session of Congress will be composed of the hungriest set of men ever got together." How far to go to match Scott's bid puzzled Huntington. "Just what effort to make against him is what troubles me. It costs money to fix things so that I know his bill would not pass. I believe with $200,000 I can pass our bill, but I take it that is not worth that much to us."[10]

Congressmen rustled in Scott's garments, swept up in the trailing cloak of his designs. The Texas and Pacific threw off branches to Louisiana, Tennessee, Arkansas, and Missouri. "Each branch represents so many Congressional Districts and so many votes," *The Nation* commented, "and it represents so many thousand tons of steel which are to be manufactured in so many other districts which have so many other votes."[11] When the House stacked the Pacific Railway committee with "Scott men," including the former counsel for the T&P, Huntington despaired: "The Texas Pacific seems to own almost every one in the whole country."[12]

An admirer saw in Scott "one of the most sagacious of politicians," but, among railroad presidents of the land grant–subsidy era, Scott's sagacity stood out only for its pecuniary depth.[13] A study of fifty-three of his peers found that more than half engaged in politics either before or after their tenure, holding eighty-five local, state, or national political jobs.[14] The twentieth century did not invent the "revolving door." Scott himself passed through it, serving as second in command in Lincoln's War Department.

———

Thomas Alexander Scott was born on the highway of life; his father kept an inn on the main road between Harrisburg, Pennsylvania, and Pittsburgh. Sited at the head of the Appalachian Valley, the village of Loudon manufactured the Conestoga wagons that daily rolled by on their way toward the mountain passes beyond. Young Tom Scott, who went to school on his father's cordiality to teamsters, stagecoach passengers, and westering families, looked out on a world in motion, spun by a smile. Thomas Scott died when Tom, the seventh of eleven children, was ten. His mother sent him to live with his older married sister in Chambersburg; he completed his education at her home.

Huntington warned his colleague against underestimating a man who "rose by his own force of character." Character welcomes help. Scott owed his first job in transportation, as a clerk on the State Works, the system of roads, canals, and railroads linking Philadelphia to Pittsburgh, to his brother-in-law, collector of tolls at Columbia. Nepotism opened the first door, aptitude all the others. Scott could add up "three rows of figures at once in his head in less time than his associates could add up one," his celerity undiminished by all-night card games. Rising to chief clerk of the eastern division of the State Works, based in Philadelphia, he became a favorite of his boss, Thomas Given, who had connections on the four-year-old Pennsylvania Railroad. That institution recruited by the "discovery," and Scott's turn came in 1850 when the chief engineer of the western division, J. Edgar Thomson, asked Given if he knew a likely man to run the new station at Duncastle.

Next day, the door of Thomson's Harrisburg office opened and a tall young man "who must have realized the ideal of a Western hero" walked in, his trousers tucked into his boots, a wide-brim slouch hat tipped back on his head, blond hair descending to his shoulders.

"I believe you telegraphed me."

"What's your name?"

"Thomas A. Scott."

A western hero was not what the sober Thomson had in mind for stationmaster in Duncastle. He indicated that to Scott.

"That doesn't make a bit of difference," he came back. "I thought I'd come down here and try you for a month and if I liked you I'd stay, and if I didn't I'd tell you. Good day, sir." Bold words, especially if delivered in a raw version of his mature manner. "When he gets to the end of a sentence his lips close instantly, barely giving the last word time to escape," a reporter later observed, "and he enforces what he has just said with an interval of momentous silence—as a marksman waits to see where his last ball struck before he shoots again."[15]

The ball struck home. "Hold on," Thomson said. "I guess I'll try you for a month." Scott stayed for life.[16]

Childless, Thomson placed his railroad in the hands of young men. He died in 1874; his protégés ran the Pennsylvania until 1909. In this company of the young, Scott rose from station agent to general supervisor of the western division at Pittsburgh in three years. Checking on his trains, Scott haunted the Pittsburgh telegraph office. There, in 1851, *he* discovered Andrew Carnegie, who, with his parents and brother, had emigrated from Scotland three years earlier. Carnegie was one of three people in the country known to be able to translate Morse code into words without first transcribing the dots and dashes. His virtuosity may have given Scott an idea. He obtained Thomson's permission to set up a telegraph office for the Pennsylvania Railroad, and asked Carnegie to manage it.[17] The seventeen-year-old was starstruck. "Mr. Scott was one of the most delightful superiors that anybody could have and I soon became warmly attached to him," Carnegie wrote in his autobiography. "He was my great man and all the hero worship that is inherent in youth I showered upon him."[18]

Hero worship spurs rivalry. Arriving at the office one morning Carnegie discovered that a wreck on the eastern division had stopped traffic in both directions, leaving freight cars in sidings across the state. "Mr. Scott was nowhere to be found." Carnegie "could not resist the temptation to plunge in . . . take the responsibility." Though only the superintendent could issue train orders, Carnegie telegraphed a tattoo of them initialed "TAS" redirecting trains up and down the line. Scott, meanwhile hearing of the wreck, had arrived. We imagine him frantically writing orders for his protégé to telegraph when Carnegie called him off. "He looked in my face for a second. I scarcely dared look at his." Retreating to his desk, Scott said nothing. Carnegie feared he might have overreached, but success pardons presumption, and how could Scott fail to see himself in Carnegie? That night Scott was heard bragging about the exploit of "that little Scotch devil of mine." When that got back to Carnegie, he knew all was forgiven. Secure enough to weather Carnegie's ambition, Scott was no fool. Carnegie noticed that "he came in very regularly and in good time for some mornings after that."[19]

When Thomson appointed Scott general superintendent of the railroad, Carnegie, by now his secretary, accompanied him to its operational headquarters in Altoona. Scott had just lost his first wife and for "many weeks" he and Carnegie shared a room at a railway hotel. "He seemed anxious," Carnegie recalled, "always to have me near him."[20] Yet they had to part for "Mr. Scott's Andy" to fill out the identity of "Andrew Carnegie, Esquire," the thrilling name on the envelope containing his first stock dividend ("Eureka!"), fruit of an investment Scott had chosen and financed. When, in 1860, Scott was promoted to vice president, he urged Thomson to pick Carnegie, twenty-four, to run the western division. How could Scott have foreseen it? While his protégé would become the great industrialist without him, Scott would stumble without *his* mentor.

John Edgar Thomson's taciturnity—he spoke at least twice a day, employees at the Central's Philadelphia headquarters insisted—unsuited him to fight the railroad's public battles.[21] He left them, glory and scars, to the gregarious Scott. When Thomson first told Scott he intended recommending that the board appoint him vice president, Scott demurred: "The person elected to that position must have held at least $10,000 worth of the company's stock for six months before his election and I do not own a single share." "You must be mistaken, Mr. Scott," Thomson replied. "The books show that 200 shares of stock have been registered in your name for more than six months."[22] Sentiment and obligation now impelled Scott, who would name his second son John Edgar, to deliver for Thomson. He had a reputation, in Carnegie's words, as "a great and good man . . . ever mindful of the fact that the spirit of the law was above the letter," and he had promoted Scott to get dirty for him.[23]

Scott's first mission was to lobby the Pennsylvania legislature to lift a barrier to the road's growth. He succeeded, but at a price. Lincoln's secretary of the navy, Gideon Welles, recorded it in his diary, noting another

cabinet member's dismay over Secretary of War Simon Cameron's choice to run his department "with the aid of Tom A. Scott, a corrupt lobby-jobber from Philadelphia."[24]

In chartering the Pennsylvania Railroad in 1846 the state legislature imposed a tax on the tonnage it carried to protect the State Works from competitive injury. When Thomson bought the Main Line of the Public Works from the state, in 1857, the enabling bill included a provision ending a tax the sale robbed of its rationale. But the Pennsylvania Supreme Court struck down that provision on a technicality; for the railroad to escape

Thomas A. Scott

the tax, the constitution mandated repeal of the 1846 legislation that had imposed it. The unpopular Pennsylvania Railroad must abolish a popular tax.[25]

Scott ran the repeal campaign with Machiavellian strategy. To shape public opinion, he planted columns and letters in the newspapers and dangled "huge advertising bonuses" before editors to motivate them to back his bill, "one of the most ingeniously worded measures ever presented to a legislative body," laced with advantages to the railroad disguised as concessions to the state. The bill aimed not at outright repeal, but at "commutation"—that is, in lieu of the tonnage tax the railroad would pay the state a fixed sum for forty years. To win support from key districts, the bill dedicated nearly $1 million, the amount of the tax on interstate commerce Thomson had withheld pending a decision from the courts, toward completing local feeder lines adjacent to the Central's main stem. To keep the issue from entanglement in party politics, Scott persuaded the rival candidates for governor to leave it out of the campaign. Finally, he focused on the legislature.[26]

"If you have anything to say Scott listens intently, looking you full in the eye," a man who met his "steel-blue" gaze recalled. "If he gives you twenty minutes of his time when he is at leisure you are made to feel that you have been the recipient of a social favor. If he devotes five minutes to you when he is busy you are impressed more deeply than you would if another man loaned you a thousand dollars without security. In short the leading fact which Scott's manner impresses you with is that time is money, and that his time in particular is a great deal of money." For the start of the 1861 session, Scott moved to Harrisburg, taking an apartment in the Coverly Hotel, where he is "said to have" handed out reassuring envelopes to wobbly lawmakers, who got Scott's time *and* money.[27]

Opposition to Scott's bill centered in western Pennsylvania. The citizens of Allegheny County had taxed themselves to the limit to pay off bonded railroad debt, and their representatives feared that the state would raise taxes to compensate for the lost tonnage revenue. Also, Pittsburgh's merchants resented that the Central and its tributaries charged less to carry freight from Chicago to Philadelphia than from Chicago to Pittsburgh. Before Pittsburgh's Board of Trade, Scott promised lower rates but refused to commit to charging Pittsburgh freight no more than freight originating beyond Pennsylvania. His partial concession drained away enough western support from the opposition to pass the bill. Victory, however, trailed a bitter wake in Allegheny County, still dependent on a railroad based in Philadelphia, all-powerful in Harrisburg, and with friends in Washington to keep competing interstate roads out of Pittsburgh. Anger over the Central's control of the legislature knew no geography, however. That fall every legislator outside of Philadelphia who had voted with the railroad lost his seat. The attack on Fort Sumter supervened, but the war would not stop the new legislature from investigating what Tom Scott did to the old.[28]

Scott had a controversial war, partly because he fronted for his controversial boss, former senator Simon Cameron, to whom Lincoln's managers at the Chicago convention had promised a cabinet seat in exchange for Pennsylvania's votes. From years of financial buccaneering Cameron earned a reputation as a "man destitute of honor and integrity." He'd reportedly bribed Democratic members of the Pennsylvania legislature to name him to the Senate. Lincoln thought better of tendering him the Treasury. As secretary of war, it was hoped, he would have less scope for peculation.[29]

In that regard Cameron's choice of Scott to serve as assistant secretary of war, the post John A. Campbell held in the Confederate government, appeared unpropitious. Cameron and Scott owned a railroad to which they directed war-related business, doubling its profits for 1861.[30] With the Pennsylvania Railroad, only the Northern Central Railroad linked Washington to the west, so necessity partly excused its owners' patronage. But Cameron's open conflict of interest over "Cameron's road" tapped the worst fears about the secretary of war. Scott would appear to have disguised his conflict in perjury. For, asked by a House committee investigating frauds in war contracts, "Do you own stock in the Northern Central?" Scott, speaking under oath, replied, "I do not."[31]

Scott's *known* conflict of interest lay in the redolent circumstance that he remained vice president of the Pennsylvania Railroad while setting the rates it and other roads charged the army for transporting supplies and men. "How," the *New York Herald* asked, "could Mr. Scott consult the best interests of both the government and his road?" The question arose when it came out that the road levied local, not through, rates on government shipments from Pittsburgh to Philadelphia, a difference of 33 percent in the road's favor. And Scott was not only an officer of the Pennsylvania but a large investor in it. "Cameron and Scott," Matthew Josephson writes, "saw to it that the very troops and horses who rode into battle were carried in their boxcars at exorbitant rates."[32]

It was all a misunderstanding, Scott told the committee. Quartermasters contracting with railroads were supposed to treat his schedule of rates as a statement of the maximum allowable, not as *the* rates. Yet he'd instructed quartermasters, "In making settlements with railroad companies . . . please observe the following as a general basis"—not as a maximum basis. Under Scott's rates the army paid 80 percent more to ship soldiers' baggage than civilians did for their baggage. This scandal fathered the Railroad Act of 1862, which brandished seizure to force the roads to cut rates.[33]

Cameron prodded Scott to route Philadelphia–Baltimore traffic through Harrisburg, a hundred-mile detour to the gain of the Northern Central and the loss of the Philadelphia, Wilmington, and Baltimore. When the president of the PW&B, Samuel M. Felton, raised a storm in the Philadelphia press over Cameron's financial stake in the Northern Central, Cameron dispatched Scott to mollify him. Cameron merely wanted Pennsylvanians to see the Massachusetts regiments detoured through Harrisburg, Scott lamely explained. What did you say to that? a congressman asked Felton. "I said that if that was the reason it seemed a little singular that he should have sent them through a city of 5,000 thereby avoiding a city of 500,000," Felton replied. The report censured these arrangements as "corrupt and dishonorable dealings instigated by the Secretary of War through Mr. Scott," calling his hiring "a grave mistake, if not an act of intentional fraud on the part of the Secretary."[34]

Yet if Cameron had not hired Scott, the author of those words might have fallen into rebel hands. After a copperhead mob attacked the Sixth Massachusetts Militia as it transited Baltimore from one railway station to another, city and state officials, ostensibly to prevent further violence, destroyed the railroad bridges linking Baltimore to the North (a desperate and disloyal act for which the Baltimore police marshal, whose men fired the bridge, was jailed). From April 19, wedged between sullen Maryland and rebellious Virginia, Washington was isolated. With neither rail nor telegraphic connections, only couriers sent through Maryland linked it to the North. A new route had to be opened for the Massachusetts and New York regiments on the way to Washington. With Thomson of the Pennsylvania Central and Felton of the Philadelphia, Wilmington, Scott and Cameron worked out a rail-water-rail route: Troops coming from the north would travel by rail from Philadelphia to Perryville at the mouth of the Susquehanna, by ferry down the Chesapeake below Baltimore to Annapolis, and by rail from there to Washington. Cameron had wanted Scott to come to Washington and manage the Northern Central's route to the city but, its bridge over the Susquehanna having been destroyed, he sent a messenger to Scott asking him to operate the Philadelphia–Annapolis route.[35]

Scott was then in Harrisburg, sent there by Thomson "to assist in the movement of troops from all parts of the State to the camps at the Capital of Pennsylvania, which troops were there to be organized and equipped, and forwarded thence to the National Capital." First, at Governor Andrew G. Curtin's request, he had to reroute Pennsylvania troops dispatched to Washington but, because of the Baltimore riot, hung up between Harrisburg and Baltimore. For thirty-six hours he stayed in an office near the governor's, undoing this bottleneck. He also wired Andrew Carnegie, the superintendent of the Western Division in Pittsburgh, to ship arms and ammunition for the Pennsylvania troops from the Allegheny Arsenal to Harrisburg. The railroad's telegraph line was deemed more secure against rebel wiretapping than the government's direct line, and Carnegie hand delivered the official order—"[F]orward the ammunition by fast train tonight"—to the arsenal commander. "Will all be ready to go . . . without fail," Carnegie sent back, appending the news that 1,100 Ohio troops had arrived in Pittsburgh and had "just gone down to City Hall intending to remain the night." He would "see how soon we can get them off perhaps not till morning." At this juncture a messenger from Cameron delivered a new directive to Scott: "Secure the road between Annapolis and Washington."

Two days later, though warned that going through Wheeling was the safer route, Scott left for Washington via rail to Hagerstown, the faster. Told that southern sympathizers might have sabotaged the tracks around Hagerstown, he "is said to have immediately rejoined that, if anything of that kind had been attempted, Hagerstown should be burned within twenty-four hours." Skirting rebel lines, Scott reached Washington by carriage, having traveled around the clock.[36]

Before leaving Harrisburg, Scott ordered Andrew Carnegie to get down to Annapolis and, with a crew of Pennsylvania Railroad workmen, prepare its single-track railway to serve as the Union's emergency lifeline. Carnegie reported back that he had dispatched eighty men each from Johnstown and Latrobe, Pennsylvania. In Annapolis, Carnegie wrote in his *Autobiography,* he found details from the New York and Massachusetts regiments repairing tracks torn up by rebels. He and his crew fell in with them, working flat-out. Guarded only by the Massachusetts regiment that had suffered forty casualties fighting its way through Baltimore, Washington direly needed these regiments. Pacing alone in the executive office

Lincoln was heard exclaiming, "Why don't they come! Why don't they come!" On Thursday, April 25, General Winfield Scott, the commander of the army, wrote a general order to be sent out the next day testifying to the capital's perceived peril: "From the known assemblage near this city of numerous hostile bodies of troops it is evident that an attack upon it may be expected at any moment." At noon "a mighty shout" from the Sixth Massachusetts camped on Capitol Hill could be heard nearly to the White House. The Massachusetts men were hurrahing a train pulling into the station. Carnegie claimed he was in the cab, his face bleeding from brushing a live telegraph wire; but as David Nasaw, his most recent biographer, discovered, he had not gone to Annapolis, his crew had not worked on the tracks to Washington, and he was not in the cab. He was in Pittsburgh.[37]

Scott next directed Carnegie to lay track from the Baltimore and Ohio depot along Maryland Avenue to a ferry established to transport railcars over the Potomac. "All hands, including Carnegie, worked day and night to accomplish this task," an official from the telegraph office later wrote, "in the remarkably short period of seven days." Using men from the Pennsylvania Central, Scott set up the first telegraphic network in the U.S. Army. "Within a month," Cameron later said, "he could tell the capacity for transportation toward every division of the army." The rebels had destroyed Long Bridge, the main link to Virginia. Scott issued a no-bid contract to a bridge builder to reconstruct it immediately. The House Committee on Government Contracts complained in tranquillity.[38]

Lincoln could tolerate conflicts of interest in the War Department but not incompetence. "What was the last action I took on your case?" the forgetful Cameron asked a caller, who refreshed his memory: "You borrowed my pencil, took a note, put my pencil in your pocket, and lost the paper." Scott compensated for Cameron's intensifying deficiencies. ("What a relief to deal with him," one frustrated claimant for Cameron's attention declared, "with his electric brain and cool, quiet manner.") Nor could Lincoln, who needed God but *had* to have Kentucky, brook Cameron's public advocacy of arming escaped slaves. Mindful of opinion in the slaveholding border states, Lincoln rejected that revolutionary step. After the House, citing details uncovered by the Committee on Government Contracts, censured Cameron, with congressmen flaying him in speeches reflecting on the administration's management of the war, Lincoln decided to get rid of him.

In January 1862 he sent Cameron "a curt dismissal" from the War Department along with a statement that he intended to nominate him as the next minister to Russia. Cameron showed up at Scott's room at midnight carrying Lincoln's note. It was too bluntly worded for publication, bare of praise for his work. It would end his political career. He wept openly. Lincoln had written in haste, Scott assured him. He would see Lincoln that day and have him issue a new note that would preserve Cameron's dignity. In the event, Lincoln released two notes. Given Cameron's interest in taking up a new post, one said, how fortuitous that St. Petersburg had become available. The other, "a generous personal communication," extolled Cameron's "ability, patriotism, and fidelity to the public trust." Scott came through for his friend. Unforgiving to competitors, the businessmen and investors at the top of the Pennsylvania Railroad extended feudal loyalty to one another.[39]

Cameron's replacement, Edwin Stanton, valued Scott's managerial talent and wanted him to stay on, but prudently shifted Scott from making to implementing policy. At Stanton's request, Scott embarked on a six-week, 4,000-mile journey to the far shore of the war, to gauge the western armies' readiness to strike down the Mississippi Valley. From Indianapolis, Springfield, Cairo, St. Louis, Paducah, and, after it fell, Nashville, Scott dispatched prescient appreciations of strategy, the public mood, and men. He was wrapping up an investigation of a procurement scandal at the army post in Cairo when the Pennsylvania legislature subpoenaed him to appear in Harrisburg to answer for corrupting the virgins of the previous legislature. First the sergeant-at-arms and then Scott's chief opponent on the investigating committee went to Washington to bring Scott back for the inquest. Pennsylvania Republicans saw political mischief in it. They urged David Wilmot, elected senator by the same legislature that commuted the tonnage tax, to intercede with Lincoln to protect Scott—and the party. Wilmot met with Lincoln, who, alive to Keystone State politics, sent him to Stanton, who ordered Scott, by then at Fortress Monroe in Virginia, *back* to Cairo. Next morning Scott's pursuer, seeking him at the War Department, was told that Scott had been sent to the Southwest, where transportation problems hindering the army required his immediate attention.

While monitoring the Federal attack on Fort Pillow, Scott fell off his horse. The lapse in communication following this mishap, which coincided with the illness of Scott's secretary, vexed Stanton. Earlier, Stanton had chastised Scott for allegedly giving orders to generals. "Your mission was one for inspection and information, not for command," he wrote. "I have your message of censure," Scott replied. "I have not given orders to any general, nor did not dream of doing so." In a confidential note Scott spoke with an emotional honesty unexpected in so executive a personality: "Your message of yesterday *hurt me.*"

Attacked by confidants of Stanton, including John Garrett, the president of the Baltimore & Ohio Railroad, still rankling over Cameron's— and Scott's—favoritism toward their own railroads in the first months of the war, weakened by the recent release of the House report on government contracts, and requested by president Thomson, who perhaps detected his protégé's unhappiness, to return to his duties with the Pennsylvania Central, Scott resigned as assistant secretary of war on May 10, 1862.

"I have learned with great pain that certain parties have been industriously at work during my absence to injure my character by all kinds of insinuations and charges," he wrote Stanton, "in reply to which permit me to say that amidst all the trials and perplexities of the past year in connection with the organization of the immense army . . . I have endeavored to do my duty faithfully." Defensiveness was not Scott's note. He ended in character: "I shall manage by my future life to live down all such charges and possibly to reward the originators as they deserve." He got right at it, charging that Garrett's B&O was a nest of rebels.[40]

From the end of the war to the Great Strike, Tom Scott seemed a dexterous manager. He attended to the PRR's customers. He forged alliances with potential challengers against settled adversaries, shifted assets from declining to rising markets, welcomed new investors on board, harnessing their self-interest to his, and by skillful public relations won backing for his enterprises from editors and opinion leaders. He pushed responsibility down. He delegated. He empowered. Contemporaries credited him with the Pennsylvania's transformation from "a state-bound route of slightly more than four hundred miles to the largest railroad system in the world, with branches or supporting lines in fifteen states and gross revenues amounting to one-eighth of the entire railroad industry's output," the historians T. Lloyd Benson and Trina Rossman conclude from their research into Scott's career, citing the 1874 obituary of Thomson, in the *U.S. Railroad and Mining Register.* "In the last two or three years, the life of John Edgar Thomson has been of no more importance to the great company and its many roads, than the life of a sleeping partner in a great commercial house is to the business prosperity of the house." Scott, it noted a week later, was responsible for the growth not only of the Pennsylvania "but of a major part of the railway system of the country." In the opinion of *The Road,* an industry paper, "though Thomson was its official head, Mr. Scott . . . was the motive power that propelled its machinery and pushed its conquests." If Scott had devoted this entrepreneurial flair to manufacturing steel the world might never have heard of Andrew Carnegie (who, to be sure, was among the nation's most successful political capitalists, paying the GOP for a high tariff on imported steel).

But, though he invested in the odd silver mine, Tom Scott remained a railroad man, and from the Illinois Central's 1851 land grant to the grants conferred on the Union Pacific, the Northern Pacific, and others in the 1860s, politics led—or leveraged—capital in railroading. The road to Wall Street began in Washington, Harrisburg, Sacramento, and Madison, Wisconsin. With the land grant, a railroad obtained collateral to pay for the land grant. To cadge its 1857 grant from the Wisconsin legislature, for example, the La Crosse and Milwaukee Railroad promised $175,000 in stocks and bonds to thirteen senators and $355,000 to fifty-nine members of the Assembly, $17,000 to the statehouse clerks, $10,000 each to the bank comptroller and the lieutenant governor, $5,000 to the governor's secretary, and $50,000 to the governor, who wisely took it in cash and lit out for Arizona. The *Milwaukee Sentinel* got $10,000 to promote the land grant; the legislator appointed to head an investigation into the bribery came higher—$25,000. With turnover in most state legislatures "almost total every two years," politicians lived by Samuel Pepys's maxim: "It is not the salary of any place that did make a man rich, but the opportunities of getting money while he is in the place." A senator known as "the wicked Gibbs," a reform treatise noted of a cheeky spoilsman, "spent two years in Albany, in which he pursued his 'business' so shamelessly that his constituents refused to send him there again; but he coolly came out a year later and begged for a return to the Assembly on the ground that he was financially embarrassed, and wished to go to the Assembly in order to retrieve his fortunes on the salary of an Assembly-man, which is $1500."[41]

Scott set out to build an empire of his own in rails as this "era of good stealings" was closing fast—bought government giving way to sold government, politicians feeding on industrialists to industrialist-politicians, the wicked Gibbs to Henry C. Payne. A Cleveland oil and railway magnate and father of Standard Oil's treasurer, Payne was elevated to the Senate in 1884 by a legislature "procured . . . by the corrupt use of money," the Ohio Senate charged and the House and governor concurred. One legislator admitted that Oliver Payne, the Standard Oil son, "loaned" him several thousand dollars; others, Henry D. Lloyd wrote, "who were so poor before the election that everything they had was mortgaged . . . [became] so prosperous after their sudden conversion to Payne that they paid off their debts." By 1900 twenty-five multimillionaires had followed Payne into the Senate, many by his method.[42]

Against this background Scott conceived the idea of a Grand Trunk Line—"A national railway system . . . extend[ing] from Washington City in two directions: north to New York and west across the forty-ninth parallel to Seattle, south to Atlanta, and west across the thirty-second parallel to San Diego," writes Scott Reynolds Nelson in *Iron Confederacies*.[43] That scheme drew him into national politics. Pursuing the subsidy needed to realize it, he shifted his lobby from Harrisburg to Capitol Hill. Simultaneously, as a prelude to conquering the West he lay siege to the South, binding first Reconstruction governments, then the successor Redemption governments, to his plan. The presidency became an incident in his ambitions. He used his influence with southern Democrats, many believed, to tip the closest election in history to the Republican candidate. Conveyed to Washington for his inauguration in Scott's luxurious "private car," "Rutherfraud" B. Hayes, Charles A. Dana, editor of the *New York Sun* charged, owed his office to Tom Scott.[44]

Yet all the lucubration devoted to braiding sections and congressmen and a president into his design came too late. Scott mastered political capitalism just as public opinion, sickened by "Tom Scottism," demanded that railroads be cast out of politics and into mere capitalism.

The self-blinded hero entrusts his fate to Fortuna. For a while she saved Tom Scott from falling into the pit. But in the end she abandoned him—or rather John Thomson did, leaving Scott in charge of the Pennsylvania Railroad. On his own, at last, all his ventures failed. Thomson had carried Tom Scott. Even after Thomson was gone, the momentum of success he imparted to the Pennsylvania Railroad held Scott up; and was all that prevented him from destroying it.

The postwar found Scott back at the old well in Harrisburg. "That road comes into these halls and dictates to us what legislation we shall pass . . . and I have made up my mind that it is useless to resist her," a senator from Erie complained during a debate over a Scott bill stripping the charter from a road allied with Garrett's B&O that menaced the Central's stranglehold on Pittsburgh. Resistance seemed futile because "It can declare in seventy-five cases out of a hundred who your Senators and Representatives shall be." With Scott on the floor keeping track, the Senate passed the bill in a midnight vote, after which a senator stood up and inquired, "Mr. Speaker, may we now go Scott free?"[45]

Next Scott turned south. He won a charter to connect the Central's Baltimore terminal to Washington. Then won a contract to build a new bridge across the Potomac. Then another to construct Washington's first Union Station. As in 1861, John Garrett could only fume. He lacked Scott's touch with Congress.

From Washington, Scott launched a years-long campaign to obtain control of the Atlanta & Richmond Air Line, which the Confederacy had commenced building in the Piedmont but did not complete, partly because a third of the slave workforce was shot or maimed trying to escape. Scott was too late for slaves but Georgia spared him from paying wages to construct the section of the line in that state by supplying free black convict labor, badly treated by Scott's contractor, investigated for "whipp[ing] convicts nude for minor offenses."[46] To push his road through, Scott enlisted governors and state legislators of both parties and both colors in four states. To coax Virginia legislators into selling him a key road in his chain, he reportedly stocked Richmond's hotels with "abandoned women" from New York and Philadelphia and, from a parlor in one hotel, presided over two giant punchbowls, one "filled with punch; the other . . . greenbacks," according to a witness. To mask his "Bucktail" takeover of the South's chief highway, he employed "front men" and set up "dummy corporations" and ultimately, with a charter passed as a "personal bill" in Harrisburg, formed the nation's first "holding company" to house these roads under one financial roof. As noted in the 1870 annual report to the directors of the Pennsylvania Railroad, the holding company's purpose was to hide Scott's hand: "Sensible of the prejudice against large corporations since the failure of the United States Bank, the policy of this Company was first directed to the procuring of these connections by securing the organization of independent railway companies, and their construction by such pecuniary assistance as was required." The holding company's name shared prosaic genius with CIA fronts in Latin America during the Cold War—the Southern Railway Securities Company. Its first president was James Roosevelt, FDR's father.[47]

But the Southern comprised only the first leg of the Grand Trunk Line.[48] To complete it Scott needed a railroad with a land grant extending from the South to the Pacific, a railroad heavily invested in Congress, a railroad in straits led by a fool. Such a company existed, and such a fool. The one was the Memphis, El Paso and Pacific Railroad; the other John C. Frémont.

The Pathfinder of the West, blazer of the Oregon Trail in the 1840s, and the first Republican presidential candidate in 1856 ("Free Speech, Free Press, Free Men, Free Labor, Free Territory, and Frémont") retained a prestige unaccountable in a man so prone to error. In July 1861, Lincoln appointed Frémont to command the Western Department of the army in St. Louis; in November Lincoln fired him.[49] Representative Elihu Washburne, who scored Cameron and Scott in the House report on war contracts, knew why. "Our committee labored for two weeks, and our disclosures will astound the world and disgrace us as a nation," he wrote Treasury Secretary Chase from St. Louis. "Such robbery, fraud, extravagance, peculation as have been developed in Frémont's department can hardly be conceived of."[50] Backed by abolitionists for his quickly rescinded proclamation liberating slaves owned by rebel soldiers, Frémont mounted a third-party challenge in 1864, but withdrew his candidacy after the fall of Atlanta in September made Lincoln unbeatable.[51]

War's end found the Pathfinder in reduced circumstances. He had lost much of his 44,000-acre California estate, Mariposa, in costly lawsuits brought by "friends" he'd trusted to run it for him. "He was among friends," an associate remarked. "And he may thank the Lord that he did not fall among thieves." His own lawyers belonged in that category, to judge by the $200,000 David Dudley Field charged to defend Frémont in one (losing) case. "It is rare that a national fame ever rested on such insubstantial foundations," the *San Francisco Bulletin* noted, "or was ever acquired by the exercise of such little ability." Frémont may have courted his reputation for haplessness to cover his larcenies.[52]

In 1848 Frémont had explored a route for a transcontinental railroad between the thirty-seventh and thirty-eight parallels—but the expedition ended in cannibalism after he led his party into New Mexico's Sangre de Cristo range where animals and men alike perished in a blizzard. After the war Frémont renewed his pursuit of a southern route to the Pacific, buying up two Missouri roads as a first step. He did not take another. He constructed only twelve miles of track in a year; he neglected to pay his laborers, who were locked in a boxcar and shipped to St. Louis when they violently objected; and he incurred so much debt that the governor seized both roads to satisfy the creditors.

The Riggs Bank warned the Mexican government against backing Frémont, "a poor and visionary speculator with not very strict morals," in a proposed rail venture in Central America. Loose morals were no disqualification in Texas. Frémont brassed his way into control of the Texas-based Memphis, El Paso and Pacific Railroad Company. The Pathfinder then set out in search of million-acre land grants, blazing a trail littered with French gold, peopled with insatiable congressmen and perfidious lawyers, grazing the White House and the Supreme Court, and leading by way of Tom Scott to Jay Gould.[53]

In the Memphis and El Paso, Frémont saw the makings of a coast-to-coast highway. Gripped by grandiosity, he acquired a 9,000-acre site in San Diego and a tract in Norfolk, Virginia, for its main terminals. To make good on the "Pacific" in the Memphis and El Paso's name, he applied to Congress for a land grant through the territories of New Mexico and Arizona; in 1869, the House obliged.

In a sensational series based on court documents, insider information, and letters from principals and victims, the *New York Sun* revealed how, through "The Greatest Instance of Legislative Corruption in the History of the World," Frémont procured the land grant. With money gleaned from mortgages taken on the road's Texas land grant, the Memphis and El Paso's executive committee, under Frémont's control, amassed a "corruption fund of $11,000,000 of its securities and placed it in the hands of Gen. Frémont to be disbursed for 'Congressional purposes.'" Frémont's agents spread this sum among "about eighty statesmen of every variety, heathen and Christian." The *Sun* named only one, Minnesota Republican Ignatius Donnelly, a Populist tribune in the 1890s, promised $50,000 in cash and $200,000 in stock, but the initiate could guess the names of others on "the list." According to the *Sun*, "*Nearly all the bright lights of the Radical party*" were on it, with others "*bought outright.*" It "would make infinitely more interesting reading than the late Mr. Ames's little book," a reference to an earlier *Sun* exposé: The comparatively trivial sums—343 shares of stock worth $65,000—steered by the Union Pacific's construction company, the Crédit Mobilier, to the dozen congressmen and two vice presidents featured on a list kept by Oakes Ames, the Massachusetts congressman and Union Pacific fixer. Frémont later gave a congressional committee a list, which "rattled the dry bones of the Forty-first Congress," and admitted to giving $290,000 in cash to the men on it.[54]

Frémont could find no takers for Memphis and El Paso bonds in the

United States, where all sentience knew his reputation. But $150,000 persuaded his brother-in-law, a baron serving as the French consul general in New York, to aid in foisting the bonds on a French public fooled by Frémont's celebrity. Frémont's French agents, no better than their principal, sold $5 million in bonds for land the railroad did not own—under the false claim, circulated in lavish pamphlets, that the U.S. government guaranteed 6 percent interest on them. Richard White puts Frémont's scam in context: "In the Gilded Age, the corrupt explored new frontiers; they corrupted information, particularly financial information, on a scale never before possible." Foreigners were acutely vulnerable. In 1876 *Banker's Magazine and Statistical Register* found that whereas 65 percent of U.S. railroad bonds held in Europe defaulted, the default rate for bonds held in the United States was only 14 percent. Frémont's clientele could not tell Texas from a cord of wood.

Through the summer of 1869, Frémont promoted his peccant bonds in Paris. From their sale he took a $500,000 commission, his Paris agents well over $1 million. These were the big-ticket items on a list of expenses—$60,000 in rent and office help, $200,000 in advertising, $60,000 in lawyers' fees—that consumed all but $300,000 of the $5 million. A serpentine American in Paris, John A. C. Gray, an attorney who had once performed legal work for the Pathfinder, heard of Frémont's sting and, the evidence suggests, threatened to expose it in the United States unless Frémont let him buy into the Memphis and El Paso. Gray then conspired with affected parties to attach the road's assets, and had Frémont place the Memphis and El Paso in receivership to shelter them. Gray next persuaded Judge Joseph P. Bradley, newly named to the Supreme Court but still sitting on the Federal Circuit Court in Newark, to appoint *him* receiver. Frémont only slowly realized that brains were necessary in crime and that Gray had foxed him out of the Memphis and El Paso.

During Frémont's stay in Paris the French financial papers caught on to him—he departed Paris "rather hastily." Within three years he would be tried in absentia for fraud and sentenced to five years in prison. Frémont's brother-in-law got three years, his wife dying from grief, or the discovery of a mistress, while the baron served his time.

Enough leaked out about the Memphis and El Paso *a la française* in the United States that Frémont thought it expedient to rename it the Southern Trans-Continental Railway Company. In February 1870 that road applied for a new land grant in the House. The scandal overtook him in the Senate, for the American minister to France was Elihu Washburne. Knowing Frémont's character, he had kept a file of Frémont's bond promotion, along with incriminating documents, letters, clippings from French newspapers, and complaints from French citizens. He sent this material to the State Department, which released it to the Senate. Senator Jacob M. Howard, chairman of the Pacific railroad committee, pounced. "A more stupendous fraud never was committed upon a friendly people," he declared of the Frémont raid on France. Howard was chairman of the subcommittee on Pacific railroads. His speech ended the Pathfinder's Pacific quest—and launched Tom Scott's.

In blocking Frémont, the *Sun* alleged, Howard acted for Scott. "Bonds or stocks" in a new enterprise had been promised to Howard to offset those Frémont promised to *his* senators. Indeed the "Philadelphia interests" personified in Scott *had* submitted a rival bill "praying for" aid to construct a road along the same thirty-second parallel as Frémont's Southern Transcontinental. Scott's Texas and Pacific Railroad Company was a portmanteau held open for the Southern Transcontinental. Desperate for cash Frémont put it in. For $300,000 in Texas and Pacific stock and $300,000 in bonds to cover the cash spent on construction, along with a pledge "to guarantee claims against the old Memphis and El Paso for services in Washington," he relinquished the fata morgana to Scott. Scott also paid off John Gray, who had enlisted with Scott while ostensibly working for Frémont. "Only the wise counsel of my mother," Frank Frémont recalled, "prevented my Father from shooting Gray."[55]

Along with six miles of track, two locomotives, and a Texas land grant, Scott inherited Frémont's goodwill on Capitol Hill. He had a lien on the self-interest of the congressmen on Frémont's "list," who required a show of animation from the venture in order to cash in their bonds. Scott quickly converted these assets into an 18-million-acre land grant to build through the New Mexico and Arizona territories to San Diego. However, Collis P. Huntington had also procured sufficient goodwill on Capitol Hill to cut the Southern Pacific into the Texas and Pacific land grant bill, which authorized the Southern to build south from San Francisco to Los Angeles and then east to the Colorado River, the border with Arizona, where it would meet the Texas and Pacific. Huntington did not intend to stop there. He coveted the whole land grant—he sought to displace the T&P and run the Southern Pacific into the South. "During the whole of my life, I never met a man who was so full of selfishness and so devoid of the commonest principles of fairness and integrity as C. P. Huntington," a Californian who knew the railroad baron wrote in 1896. "[H]e has never knowingly favored a good man or an honest measure. He is the very essence of selfishness, the organization of cruelty and a complete compiled edition of business falsehood." Huntington cultivated this image for its deterrent value. "I have a great many enemies," he once testified at a Senate hearing, "and I am proud of them, for I always hewed to the line and where there were fingers in the way they were pretty sure to be cut." Scott's fingers were in the way.[56]

Bar stagecoach lines, the Southern Pacific monopolized the movement of all persons and goods into and out of California by land, and, after acquiring the California Steam Navigation Company and Pacific Mail Steamship Company, largely by sea. The "Octopus," as cartoonists depicted the Southern, grew by extortion. "They start out their railway track and survey their line near a thriving village," an observer wrote. "They go to the most prominent citizens of the village and say, 'If you will give us so many thousand dollars we will run through here; if you don't we will run by,' and in every instance where the subsidy was not granted, that course was taken, and the effect was just as they said, to kill off the little town." Los Angeles paid out more than $600,000 to avoid extinction. Once a town had the railroad, the railroad had the town. It made shippers sign "special contracts" pledging to ship exclusively with the Southern, which reserved the right to examine their books—to check whether they had smuggled or received goods via another source and if so to refuse their shipments; if the books showed that the shipper could pay more, the railroad charged more. It levied rates double those of eastern railroads, which, though more heavily traveled, netted less profit per mile. Huntington would not let Scott break a suzerainty over California commerce that, by the time he died in 1900, had made him $50 million to $80 million.[57]

Work began on the Texas and Pacific in June 1872. Building west from Marshall, Texas, it had almost reached Fort Worth when the panic halted construction. If he did not resume, Scott would forfeit the Texas land grant, which required the Texas and Pacific to complete so many miles by a looming date certain. He could not borrow from Wall Street, not with the economy in depression. So he applied to Capitol Hill for a $60 million subsidy, *two* times the projected cost of building the railroad.

While Scott wooed southern Democrats, Huntington, seizing on the subsidy issue, made essentially this case to northern Republicans: *Scott wants $60 million in subsidy on top of the land grant. I ask for nothing beyond the grant. The government can have a southern transcontinental for $60 million or for nothing.* That has the ring of a winning argument. Scott, who scaled back his request to $38 million, could not licitly compete with it. Moreover, the Crédit Mobilier scandal had aroused public opinion against aid to railroads. But Scott stuck by the old bonds-for-votes game as if nothing had changed. "The strength of the Scott lobby is almost unbelievable to the student of the period," in the view of one historian, "until the financial, personal, and political connections of the members of the forty-fourth and forty-fifth Congresses are closely scrutinized." Bonds fell "like snow-flakes and dissolv[ed] like dew" on Capitol Hill.[58]

On December 27, 1883, the *New York Sun, Chicago Daily Tribune,* and *San Francisco Chronicle* published the Rosetta stone of bought government, the "Colton Letters," being the letters of Collis P. Huntington to David D. Colton, the financial director of the Central Pacific, covering the years 1874–77 when Huntington and Scott jousted on the field of Congress. On Colton's death in 1878, the Big Four, the Sacramento merchants, Hunting-ton, Leland Stanford, Mark Hopkins, and Charles Crocker, who had founded the Central Pacific in 1861, forced Mrs. Colton to liquidate her husband's holdings on punishing terms, Colton's books having exposed embezzlements. In the ensuing litigation, Huntington's letters to Colton entered the court record, and leaked to the press. They show "[t]he manipulation of Congress and State and Territorial Legislatures, the matching of wits and mendacity by great corporation managers, the in-trigues and contests of the reckless race for wealth, the corruption of the press and of public officials of all kinds," Henry Demarest Lloyd wrote in the *Chicago Tribune.* Trading senator for senator, committee for com-mittee, vote for vote, Huntington and Scott place their bets and spin the wheel.

A Colton sampler:

To checkmate Scott, Huntington sought the help of Arizona.

New York, November 20, 1874: "Friend Colton: Would it not be well for you to send some party down to Arizona to get a bill passed in the Territo-rial Legislature granting the right to build a railroad east from the Col-orado River (leaving the river near Fort Mohave), [and] have the franchise free from taxation . . . ?"

A subsequent letter asks, "Cannot you have [Governor] Safford call the Legislature together and grant such charters as we want at a cost of, say, $25,000? If we could get such a charter as I spoke to you of it would be worth much money to us."

Later, discounting the probity of the legislators, he says that "$5,000" should do the job.

Huntington's focus turns to "MC's"—members of Congress—in a December 1, 1874, letter. "Friend Colton: . . . Has any of our people endeavored to do anything with Low and Frisbee? They are both men that can be convinced. . . . I will see Luttrell when he comes over and talk with him and maybe he and we can work together, but if we can't we can brush him out . . . and then we could . . . get some better material to work with." Apparently Luttrell, a San Francisco MC, wanted too much. "[H]e is a wild hog," Huntington writes five months later. "[D]on't let him come back to Washington . . . it would be well to beat him with a Democrat, but I would defeat him anyway, and if he got the nomination put up another Democrat and run against him, and in that way elect a Republican. Beat him."

To save the Southern the expense of its lobby, Huntington hopes to persuade Scott to stop his road at the California border. He sends Scott a copy of his bill marked up to include that compromise. "We expect to build our road to San Diego, as already pledged to the public to do so. Your suggestions are totally inadmissible," Scott replies.

March 3, 1875: "Have you sent passes and money?"

April 7, 1875: "I have set matters to work in the South that I think will switch most of the South off from Tom Scott's Texas and Pacific bill."

September 23, 1875: "Scott is expecting to make his biggest fight this winter, and as he owes nearly everybody he will have many to help him, as they will think by so doing they will be helping themselves."

January 29, 1876: "Scott has switched Senator Spencer of Alabama . . . this week, but you know they can be switched back with the proper arrangements when they are wanted."

March 4, 1876: "The Railroad Committee of the House was set up for Scott, and it has been a very difficult matter to switch a majority of the committee away from him."

March 22, 1876: "Scott is making a very dirty fight and I shall try very hard to pay him off, and if I do not live to see the grass growing over him I shall be mistaken."

May 1, 1876: "Scott came to my house last Saturday night, and we both agreed to hold off and do nothing. . . . Scott no doubt thinks he will be stronger next winter than now, but I do not think so."

July 5, 1876: "Our payments for materials this month and next will be very large," he writes his financial director, speaking in code, "and you will need to send all the money you well can."

November 11, 1876: "I am glad to learn that you will send to this office $2,000,000 by the 1st of January."

December 25, 1876: "Scott and I had an open break last night. He said he would pass his bill through the committee and I could not prevent it."

And so it goes, the two titans, returning MCs like tennis balls, fighting to a costly draw. Scott's manipulation of reporters with free railroad passes especially vexed Huntington. "Is it not possible to control the agent of the Associated Press in San Francisco?" he asks. Huntington transcribed an interview published in the *New York World* that identified him as "the wealthiest man now living . . . [on] the Pacific Coast" and the Southern as an oppressive monopoly. He did not need to tell Colton that Tom Scott owned the *World*.[59]

Scott might have been running a railroad of his own and perhaps been spared the Texas and Pacific lobby or found a cheaper route to the subsidy except for Andrew Carnegie. In 1868, three years after leaving the Pennsylvania Railroad, Carnegie toted up the value of his investments with a "blunt stub of a pencil" on a scrap of paper: $400,000, or well over $5 million today. One source of Carnegie's wealth derived from a partnership with George Pullman. After the war Carnegie reorganized a sleeping car company that supplied cars to the Pennsylvania Railroad. Unbeknownst to him, as a condition of his 1858 contract to furnish sleepers to the Pennsylvania, Jonah Woodruff, the original owner, was required to steer a one-eighth interest in his business to "another person" whom Scott did not name but Woodruff heard was "a boy then in the superintendent's office." The words are Woodruff's from an 1886 letter to Carnegie correcting his version of the story, in his recently published book *Triumphant Democracy,* "so damaging to your old friend as to merit his rebuke." As Carnegie told it, *he* sold Scott on the idea of the sleeper after meeting Woodruff on a train. Scott and Thomson, David Nasaw surmises, had used Carnegie as a "bagman" to disguise their stake in the Woodruff Sleeping Car Company, offering the "boy" a few shares for his services. All three men nourished their fortunes on kickbacks and conflicts of interest. They preferred to be on both sides of business transactions.[60]

In 1867 the Union Pacific, soon to be the longest road in the country, summoned the handful of sleeping car makers to New York to bid for its custom. Carnegie encountered Pullman on the staircase of their hotel. "Good evening, Mr. Pullman! . . . [A]re we not making a nice couple of fools of ourselves?" he asked his nonplussed competitor. "I explained the situation to him. We were destroying by our rival propositions the very advantages we desired to obtain."[61] Why not join forces instead? Two years later John D. Rockefeller made the same case to Cleveland's competing oil refiners, inviting them to join the nascent Standard Oil Trust, and promising destruction to those who chose to compete. "He expressed scorn for the textbook world of free markets evoked by Adam Smith," Ron Chernow writes in *Titan: The Life of John D. Rockefeller, Sr.* Only "academic Know-Nothings about business," in Rockefeller's view, could believe the economy of big could work like that or society benefit from businesses incessantly "eating each other up." "What a blessing it was that the idea of cooperation, with railroads, with telegraph lines, with steel companies, with oil companies, came in and prevailed," Rockefeller remarked in 1917.*[62]

In early 1871, before Scott wrested control of the Southern Transcontinental from Frémont, Carnegie heard through Pullman that the Union Pacific needed cash. Amos Akerman, the honest Grant attorney general who pressed Klan prosecutions in the South, ruled that the land grant railroads must pay the interest on their government debt semiannually, rather than postpone payment until the bonds matured in thirty years—the germ of the *Sinking Fund Cases* decision of 1879 in which Stephen J. Field saw the Commune. The Union Pacific owed $600,000. Carnegie immediately went to Thomson. "If Thomson would turn over to him enough securities of the Pennsylvania Railroad for him to secure a loan of $600,000 for the Union Pacific," Joseph Frazier Wall writes in his definitive *Andrew Carnegie,* "he and Thomson would then be in a position to dictate their own terms to the directors of the Western road." Thomson agreed. In return the Union Pacific agreed to elect Thomson, Carnegie, and Pullman to its seven-man board—and install Scott as president. The Union Pacific turned over 30,000 shares worth $3 million to Thomson as collateral for the loan, giving the Thomson group the option to buy shares at their current market value of $9. Those shares rose on the news that Congress had authorized the Union Pacific to issue additional bonds to finance the construction of the Omaha Bridge over the Missouri River. Two years later, testifying before a House committee investigating "the affairs of the

---

* Adam Smith unpacked "cooperation" in *The Wealth of Nations*: "People of the same trade seldom meet together, even for merriment and diversion, but the conversation ends in a conspiracy against the public, or in some contrivance to raise prices." On the gain to society from competition: "If . . . capital is divided between two different grocers, their competition will tend to make both sell cheaper, than if they were in the hands of the one only; and if it were divided among twenty, their competition would be so much the greater, and the chance of combining together, in order to raise the price, just so much the less." *The Wealth of Nations* (New York: The Modern Library, 1937), Book 1, Chapter 10, p. 128, and Book 2, Chapter 5, p. 342.

Union Pacific Railroad Company," Scott denied having bribed congressmen for the bridge.[63]

The deal stunned the industry. *The Railroad Gazette* predicted that the Pennsylvania Railroad would "control all the transcontinental traffic for many years to come." And the news that Scott, "generally regarded as one of the most astute railroad managers in the country," would be the new president (backed by the Pennsylvania Railroad) tripled the Union Pacific's share price. Carnegie had placed the stock in his safe and left for London to market the bonds for the Omaha Bridge. On his return he discovered that "Mr. Scott decided to sell our Union Pacific shares." He had given Scott access to his vault but, according to his autobiography, the idea that "our party should lose the splendid position we had acquired with the Union Pacific, never entered my brain."[64]

He must have forgotten sending a telegram Joseph Wall dug up that contradicts him. Writing from London Carnegie asks an associate in New York, "Please place 11,000 shares of Union Pacific which you hold as Trustee for me with Messrs. J. Morgan Sons Bankers." Pullman followed suit. It is unclear whether Thomson and Scott sold their shares. Months later, saying he was "a little embarrassed . . . for want of money," Scott obtained a $60,000 loan from the Union Pacific for the worthless bonds of an Arkansas railroad—and turned the bonds over to James G. Blaine, the Maine congressman and former House speaker, for helping the Texas and Pacific. Carnegie had pocketed over $240,000 on the sale of his Union Pacific shares. Scott might have made as much or more if he had sold his, sparing him the risky expedient of the Union Pacific loan to pay off

Andrew Carnegie

Blaine. On the other hand, by the end of 1871 only 400 shares of Union Pacific stock remained in Carnegie's safe, suggesting that Thomson, said to be "surprised" by Carnegie's cashing in, and Scott cashed in themselves.

The Union Pacific board revolted against its new corporate officers for speculating with their company's collateral. "At the first opportunity we were ignominiously but deservedly expelled from the Union Pacific Board," Carnegie writes. Scott was fired as president. A railroad builder, he stood revealed as a Gould-like railroad looter. Had the cupidity of his protégé undermined his attempt to emerge from the shadow of his mentor? At all events Scott, Wall writes, "was deeply hurt by his public humiliation, and Carnegie was at least correct in saying" that "the transaction marked my first serious difference with a man who up to that time had the greatest influence upon me, the kind and affectionate employer of my youth, Thomas A. Scott."[65]

The breach came two years later, over the Texas and Pacific, by then a Ponzi scheme, with Scott paying the interest on maturing bonds with proceeds from the sales of new bonds. The Panic of September 1873 snuffed out new sales. While waiting for his subsidy, Scott took out short-term loans to finance construction; pinched themselves, his creditors demanded payment. Bankruptcy impended—unless Carnegie could help. The Morgan bank would refinance the debt *if* Carnegie endorsed the notes. On January 12, 1874, Scott sent this telegram to Carnegie in New York: "Please come over tomorrow Monday on 12:30 train and meet me at my house at 4 P.M. If you cannot come over at that time, come over later in the day so I can see you at my house between 10 and 11 P.M. I shall be out early in the evening. Important—please answer." Carnegie made the meeting. Scott asked him for help. "I declined," Carnegie remembered. "It was one of the most trying moments of my life. . . . I told Mr. Scott that I had done my best to prevent him from beginning to construct a great railway before he had secured the necessary capital." Enduring this prim lecture from a young man whose career in capitalism he had nurtured—how galling for Scott! At that same meeting five faithful friends signed notes to cover as much of Scott's shortfall as they could. Thomson alone stood up for nearly $2 million. The Pennsylvania Railroad was a father-and-son operation.

Scott asked Thomson to intercede with Carnegie, whose successive industrial ventures—Union Iron Mills, the Keystone Bridge Company, and the Edgar Thomson Steel Company launched the year before—they had helped finance and with which they had placed Pennsylvania Railroad contracts. "You should tax your friends, if you have not the means yourself" to bail Scott out, he wrote days after Carnegie's declination. "The scheme," he conceded, "has been most wofully mismanaged, Scott having acted upon his faith in his guiding star, instead of sound discretion." Still, "Scott should be carried until his return, and you of all others should lend your helping hand." *You of all others.* But Carnegie was finished playing the son.[66]

"Can a businessman be both good and great?" a recent Carnegie interpreter asks. Greatness "consists of succeeding beyond expectation, beyond

imagination, in the field to which one has elected to devote oneself";
goodness, of "remembering those who have helped you achieve your
goals when you no longer need them." Carnegie believed in his own guiding star, and honoring Scott's role in placing it in his heaven would weaken
his faith in himself. He had begun construction of the Edgar Thomson
steelworks near Pittsburgh. Steel would be his destiny. He must have every
cent to realize it. Andrew Carnegie was a great man.[67]

Tom Scott was a bankrupt; the subvention of his friends had fallen
short of the amount owed his creditors. The California and Texas Construction Company, Scott's financing mechanism for the Texas and Pacific,
failed a month after Carnegie failed Scott. He had persuaded the Pennsylvania company's board to buy $2 million worth of California and Texas
bonds. Gone. Thomson's investment—gone. Disgraced by his default,
Scott submitted his resignation to the board. The board might have
accepted it, but, even though the Pennsylvania's exposure in the Texas and
Pacific had stained him, Thomson would not fire Scott. "If Carnegie wres-
tled with a tortured conscience for letting Scott down in his hour of need,"
Thomson's biographer James A. Ward writes, "then Scott must have been
doubly remorseful because he was primarily to blame for Thomson's
appalling financial losses and perhaps even for his death a few months
later." For his part Thomson "poured out his bitterness at Scott" to his
wife, who would have nothing to do with Scott after her husband's death
in May 1874. Thomson's obituaries noted his rift with Scott—who assumed
the presidency in June, inheriting a damaged crown.[68]

Before the bankruptcy, Scott needed to prove he was Thomson's equal
only to himself; now he had to prove it to the world.

Quickly Scott reorganized the Texas and Pacific, his creditors, rather than
settling for pennies on the dollar, willing to bet on his success. Then he
went on a three-year tear of compensatory audacity, renewing his war
with Huntington, starting a war against John D. Rockefeller, and bargaining the presidency for a railroad.

Historians not only debate Scott's role in the Compromise of 1877 but
whether there *was* a compromise—whether Hayes assumed the presidency through a deal with southern Democrats that restored the South to
"Home Rule." In brief, New York governor Samuel Tilden, the Democratic candidate for president in 1876, defeated Ohio governor Hayes in the
popular vote and was one vote shy of the 185 votes needed for victory in

the electoral college. But circumstances—ranging from his own passivity to his party's chariness over being labeled seditious for prolonging the election crisis—undid Tilden. Commentators then and since have aired the hypothesis that a conspiracy traceable to the era's master plot, the Texas and Pacific Railroad, denied Tilden the presidency. The conspiracy came in two parts. To credit the first you have to believe something improbable about only one man.[69]

Decisive against Tilden was the vote of one member of the electoral commission set up in January by the Republican Senate and the Democratic House to decide which candidate won Florida, South Carolina, and Louisiana, states where the results remained in dispute, with Democrats accusing Republican returning boards—the official vote counters—of fraud and Republicans accusing Democrats of "bulldozing" blacks away from the polls. Both were right: "Democratic violence and republican chicanery so nearly cancelled each other out that historians have not yet been able to determine who really won the election of 1876," C. Vann Woodward wrote in 1951. But, applying the techniques of contemporary social science to the returns in both Louisiana and South Carolina, a careful researcher recently concluded, "it is probable" Hayes won those states and the presidency. At the time, many hoped letting an independent commission decide the election would avert a constitutional collision between the Democratic House, which would award the three states to Tilden, and the Republican Senate, whose president pro-tem, as required by the Twelfth Amendment, would count the electoral ballots and award the states to Hayes. Congress appointed fourteen of the fifteen commissioners: five Democrats and five Republicans from the House and Senate, and four senior Supreme Court Justices, two Republicans and two Democrats. Samuel Miller was one of the Republicans; Stephen J. Field one of the Democrats. The justices would pick the fifteenth member, and all agreed he would be the one independent on the Court, David Davis. But hours after Senate Democrats voted 26–1 to put the election in the hands of the commission, news arrived that the Illinois legislature had elected Davis to the Senate and that he had withdrawn his name from consideration as a commissioner. The four justices chose a Republican justice familiar to us, Joseph P. Bradley, to replace Davis. It was too late for the Democrats to renege. Besides, Bradley had ruled for the *Cruikshank* defendants on the Fifth Circuit Court in New Orleans in 1874, and southern democrats indicated the acceptability of a justice who "saved from punishment . . . the innocent victims of a foul judicial and political conspiracy," in the judgment of the

Nashville Advertiser. For their part, Republicans assured Hayes that Bradley was "safe." And so he proved. Bradley cast the deciding vote for the Hayes electors in the three states, making *Hayes* president by one electoral vote.★[70]

In a tightly argued opinion, Bradley gave his reasons for voting for the Hayes electors. But conspiracists dismiss reasons as rationalizations for motives. One is obvious. Bradley was a Republican appointed by a Republican president—Grant. That answer should have satisfied the most cynical Democrats. But where we reduce politics to "politics," the Gilded Age reduced politics to business. In the editorials of the *New York Sun,* the Texas and Pacific loomed as a Potomac miasma, scandal's breath. In uncovering Crédit Mobilier, the Memphis, El Paso, and other scandals, the *Sun* gained credibility and readers. Under editor Charles A. Dana, Scott's successor as assistant secretary of war and possibly a Scott-hater because of that, circulation tripled in less than a decade buoyed by his partisan passion and slashing style: "It is announced that 'Mrs. Grant will receive every Tuesday afternoon during the winter. . . .' President Grant will receive anytime and anything whenever anything is offered." Dana had been reckless—in a McCarthyite tactic, he did not name the "eighty . . . statesmen" on the "list" of congressman bought by the Memphis and El Paso's "corruption fund"—but substantially right. Set aside the gratuitousness of the question: Was Dana right that Scott bribed—or, through John A. C. Gray, blackmailed—Justice Bradley to decide for Hayes?

"[D]uring the whole of the night [before the commission ruled on the Florida electors], Judge Bradley's house in Washington was surrounded by the carriages of visitors who came to see him apparently about the decision of the Electoral Commission," the *Sun* charged. "These visitors included leading Republicans as well as persons deeply interested in the Texas Pacific

---

★ "In 1877 Justice Bradley concluded that the Commission could not possibly conduct its own detailed inquiry into local election returns and thus had no choice but to accept the findings of local election boards (all Republican) as to who had carried the state. Bradley's position, as [the late Supreme Court chief justice William] Rehnquist argues, was certainly 'reasonable.' Unlike his successors [in *Bush v. Gore*], Bradley did not invent a new constitutional principle (equal protection in the counting of ballots) to reach a pre-determined verdict and then add that the principle applied only in the specific case in hand. Bradley seems to have tried to rise above the immediate political situation, unlike Justice Antonin Scalia, who in 2000 insisted that the Court needed to ensure 'public acceptance' of a Bush presidency." Eric Foner, review of *Centennial Crisis: The Disputed Election of 1876,* in *The Nation,* March 29, 2004. For Bradley's opinion, see Charles Fairman, *Five Justices and the Electoral Commission of 1877* (New York: Macmillan, 1988), pp. 95–106.

Railroad scheme." They arrived in "[s]eventeen carriages, more or less," which "were gathered about [Bradley's] home." No interviews with neighbors corroborating the carriages backed this contention. In the era of the party press, reporting just spoiled the outrage. Instead Dana dissolved questions of current fact in a solution of past innuendo, reprising the *Sun*'s 1875 story about Bradley's undoubtedly suspicious appointment of John A. C. Gray as receiver of the Memphis and El Paso, and his subsequent decision to permit Gray and Frémont to turn it over to Tom Scott.[71]

Justice Joseph P. Bradley

Bradley's appointment of Gray was suspicious because Bradley had apparently been on a list of the original Texas and Pacific incorporators, but the Republican Senate, according to the historian who made this discovery, "refused" to add the newly appointed Supreme Court justice's name to the *official* list. Suspicious because Bradley took the case at the request of his friend, Cortlandt Parker, representing stockholders in the Memphis and El Paso who wanted the road placed under receivership. Suspicious because, even though he was a judge for the U.S. Circuit Court of the Western District of Texas, where the Memphis and El Paso was incorporated, Bradley heard the case in Newark, New Jersey: Gray wanted to circumvent Texas "because the officers of the company would resist the petition, knowing the company was technically solvent," writes the most thorough investigator of the transaction. Suspicious because Bradley agreed to Newark when Gray produced letters from Texas attorneys purporting to represent the road and from an officer of the company—John C. Frémont!—strangely asking for the case to be heard outside of the Texas circuit limits ("The Texas officials of the company," C. Vann Woodward writes, "later claimed that they were not consulted about the matter"). Suspicious, finally, because Bradley ruled for Parker's clients, and appointed another Parker client, Gray, receiver. From that moment, with Gray possessing "little bundles of papers, neatly tied with red tape" that could have Bradley "impeached within five hours," the *Sun* wrote, "Bradley ceased to be his own man and became forever the man of the men who owned him." Bradley was not the "fifth Judge," Dana wrote with Florida decided but Louisiana and South Carolina still to go. "The fifth Judge is John A. C. Gray of New York, assisted by Col. Tom

Scott and Cortlandt Parker. . . . Gray will award the presidency according to his good pleasure, and he will award it to Hayes because Mr. Tilden's inauguration would be very bad for subsidy jobs in general and the Texas-Pacific in particular."[72]

Dana pursued Bradley even after "His Fraudulency" took office. In an August editorial, "An Interesting Historical Fact," Dana alleged that Bradley had read a pro-Tilden opinion to "Judge Clifford and Judge Field, who were likewise members of the Commission," earlier on the evening of the Florida vote, *before* the Republican politicians and Texas and Pacific railroad men, in their seventeen carriages, staged the chariot race from *Ben-Hur* on the streets leading to his I Street house. Asked by a San Francisco reporter to comment on that allegation, Field replied: "Well, sir, all that I care to say with regard to that is that Justice Bradley *read* no opinion to me in advance of the formal submission of opinions to the commission." He added insinuatingly, "Beyond that, I think it would be improper for me to say anything. If I should enter upon the subject, I should probably say a great deal more than I should say."

Bradley refused to answer Dana's "immense gratuitous and unfounded abuse." He'd ignored it in 1875, when the *Sun* rolled his name in the pitch of the Memphis and El Paso. At that time, Cortlandt Parker advised Bradley to say nothing rather than dignify attacks mounted "because [Dana's] paper feeds on libel . . . and because he hates Tom Scott." Bradley, as he wrote years later, "bore these things in silence until it was stated that Judge Field had said . . . that I changed my mind during the sitting of the Commission, and that I had first written an opinion in favor of Tilden and had read it to him and Judge Clifford." He wrote Field "immediately." Field replied that he had not said what he said. Then Bradley turned to Dana.

"The whole thing is a falsehood. Not a single visitor called at my house that evening," he avowed in a long letter to the editor of the *Newark Daily Advertiser.* "The allegation that I read an opinion to Judges Clifford and Field is entirely untrue. I read no opinion to either of them." Then Bradley invited further defamation. "If I did, it could only have been suggestively . . . and not intended as a committal of my final judgement or action." The *Sun* got one thing right thing—he *had* written two opinions: "I wrote and re-wrote the arguments and considerations on both sides as they occurred to me, sometimes being inclined to one view of the subject." Dana crowed over "Bradley's Confession" and called for a congressional investigation, "if the impeachment of Justice Jo Bradley is the only way of reaching the bottom facts of it." To Bradley, Field claimed that he "had said nothing derogatory to my honor and integrity" in his San Francisco interview. To Tilden, Field fanned doubts about Bradley's character: "The language of the letter [in the *Newark Daily Advertiser*] justified some of the comments of the press upon the change of views which the judge experienced shortly before the vote was taken in the Florida case."[73]

Democrats assailed Bradley for "jobbing" the presidency. His name, a Missouri senator declared on the floor, will "never . . . be pronounced without a hiss from all good men of this country." Does he deserve history's hiss? On February 10 William T. Pelton, Tilden's nephew and political fixer, wrote this to his uncle's friend and future biographer, John Bigelow: "It's of vital importance you see Jno. A. C. Gray, and as an old and tried friend advise him to see that Justice Bradley *does right.*" Bigelow called on Gray at his New York home. Gray, he wrote in his diary, "was willing to go to Washington, if he could do any good," but after consulting with Parker decided that "it would irritate Bradley to talk with him about his duty as commissioner." If Gray did not visit Bradley after midnight on February 9, did someone else? "The justice's son remarked at the time that his father, suffering a series of sleepless nights, 'went to bed at eleven and got up at three,'" Keith Ian Polakoff notes. "In short, the Democratic account of Bradley's activities was at least badly garbled and conceivably fabricated out of sheer rage and whole cloth." But the son's testimony cannot be taken as dispositive, considering that Hayes, who owed the presidency to Joseph Bradley, appointed Charles Bradley to a "lucrative" sinecure at the New York Custom House for, Roscoe Conkling charged, "manifest reasons." But Conkling was Hayes's political enemy. One way or another the actors in the Compromise of 1877 are compromised. C. Vann Woodward renders a dappled judgment: "The charge that the influence of Scott and his friends was decisive in determining Bradley's vote on the Electoral Commission was impossible to prove, and in all fairness it should be observed that it was the sort of charge that it is impossible to disprove and difficult to deny effectively."[74]

Bradley had done his worst, but the Democrats still had cards to play. Tilden was gone, they conceded privately. But they would filibuster the counting of the electoral votes in the House, forcing a confrontation with the Republican Senate. Hayes must meet their terms—or enter the White House at bayonet point. "Rifle clubs" were said to be forming among Democrats in northern states. The *Cincinnati Commercial* reported "the existence of a secret political society composed exclusively of Democrats" bent on inaugurating Tilden—"by force, if necessary." A Louisville editor summoned "ten thousand unarmed Kentuckians" to Washington on the day set aside for counting the electoral vote.[75] Democratic newspapers ran headlines threatening "Tilden or War." What force could avert this smash-up of the newly restored Union? Only the svengali of the Texas and Pacific—that conspiracy behind the decade's men and measures. Tom Scott, who had elected governors and named senators, would make a president.

By the end of 1876 Scott still had no subsidy and Rutherford Hayes no way of entering the White House without, it seemed, renewing a small-scale version of the Civil War. Hayes needed support from the South; Scott had it to give. To stimulate enthusiasm the Texas and Pacific had held railroad conventions in the region and thrown out branch lines to St. Louis, Vicksburg, Baton Rouge, New Orleans, and Memphis, joining their citizens in a chorus demanding equal treatment for their region. Congress had subsidized the Pacific railroads; now came the turn of the South. One of the directors of the construction company waiting to build the Memphis connector, Colonel Andrew J. Kellar, put Hayes's need together with Scott's necessity. Kellar, publisher of the *Memphis Avalanche,* enlisted in a cabal of politically connected journalists led by General Henry Van Ness Boynton, the Washington correspondent of the *Chicago Tribune,* who sought to install Hayes with the votes of southern Democrats and draw southern businessmen into the Republican Party. "What we want for practical success," Boynton wrote Hayes's close friend William Henry Smith of the Associated Press, "is thirty or thirty-six votes. West Tennessee, Arkansas, a large Kentucky element, Louisiana, Texas, Mississippi *and Tom Scott* want help for the T&P road."[76] Writing to *Richard* Smith of the *Cincinnati Gazette,* Boynton invoked the Scott persuasion: "He knows *how* to work. I do not know him—have no relations—even indirect—with his lobby. But I know its *power.*" When they met in late January Scott mesmerized him. "Scott will go the whole matter *personally,* & with the skill and discreetness for which he is justly celebrated. . . . From today there will be no lack of help; for Scott's whole powerful machinery will be set in motion at once."[77]

Lukewarm toward this proposition in late December, Hayes cooled in January, having sounded out Carl Schurz, a former Lincoln ally and senator, and keeper of the Republican conscience, on the "Scott plan." "Remember the Credit Mobilier, the Blaine letters, etc.," Schurz advised him. "It looks almost as if a railroad could not come within a hundred miles of a legislative body without corrupting it." Schurz warned against "trying to gain the favor of the Southern people by a bid of such a nature." Hayes agreed. "I am not a believer in the trustworthiness of the forces you hope to rally," he wrote William Henry Smith.[78]

Whatever the degree of Hayes's commitment to it, his people committed him to the "bargain" revealed on February 14 when the *Cincinnati Enquirer* printed the terms of the Compromise of 1877. In exchange for southern votes against the filibuster, "the guarantees to the South are": One or two "Cabinet places"; home rule—that is, the stand-down of the last federal troops in the South, removing federal protection for Republican governors-elect in Louisiana and South Carolina; internal improvements, and "the passage of the Texas Pacific Railroad Bill." In the new House, the Democrats agreed to support a Republican, James Garfield, for speaker. In the event the South got home rule, *one* cabinet appointment—but the postmaster general, wielder of the patronage—and money to repair its levies. It gave away nothing that was not going to happen anyway. On the key filibuster votes only eighteen to twenty-two southerners voted with the Republicans; *northern* Democratic votes, and the rulings against dilatory motions by Samuel Randall of Pennsylvania, the Democratic speaker of the House, killed the filibuster. The Democrats broke their word on Garfield; the Republicans broke theirs on Scott. And the Republican Party broke the hearts of its black constituents in the South. After Hayes ordered the few remaining troops to return to their barracks, a black man from Georgia, B. A. Glenn, wrote him: "How could you betray those who almost fought for your election? O shame that we should thus be dealt with!"

Hayes also betrayed white Republicans. He refused, for example, to give a patronage job to the son of a Republican sheriff in Mississippi, who, along with a teenage son and daughter, was murdered by a mob revenging the killing of a "White Line" terrorist. "Well, you know, I only give appointments to Democrats in the South," Hayes "(kind of laughing)" told the sheriff's widow, who described the scene in a letter to Mississippi's black Republican Senator, Blanche K. Bruce. "The feeling of contempt for Hayes is universal here. It is deep and bitter. Even those holding office under him despise him."[79]

"Scott boasted of controlling vast forces, but in a showdown was unable to deliver them," the historian Allan Peskin writes. "Scott was no power broker, only a hustler, working both sides of the street and hoping to win the gratitude of whomever might wind up in a position to help him." *That* is the job description of a railroad president. Like Jay Gould's old tutor in larceny, Jim Fisk, Scott was a Republican in Republican districts, a Democrat in Democratic districts, and doubtful in doubtful districts, but for his railroad everywhere—in short, a businessman who traded on the mystique of political power to achieve his ends.[80]

As his luxurious car, *Pennsylvania,* bore President-select Hayes from Columbus to Washington, Tom Scott might well have thought that 1877 would be *his* year. He had risen from his financial grave to pay off the bulk of his creditors, the estate of John Edgar Thomson first. Conceding the failure of his plunge into the South, at the behest of the stockholders he had liquidated the Pennsylvania Railroad's holdings in the Southern Railway Securities Company, selling unprofitable lines at a loss before they could drain more capital from the parent company.[81] He had acquired a lattice of lines in the Midwest, securing the Pennsylvania's approaches to Chicago. After a draining rate war, he would soon reach a rate-fixing agreement with his competitors. The wage cuts announced for July 1 would be industry-wide, diffusing employee anger. With Hayes in his corner, the Texas and Pacific would go through at last. From years of fronting for Thomson, and for Cameron, he'd won a reputation for political gamesmanship that he'd turned to his benefit. How many men prolong their defects into advantages? Fortune was with him. Something of that feeling must have motivated his decision to take on John D. Rockefeller and Standard Oil.

Chapter Nine

BREAD OR BLOOD

It was true the $1.00 a day was not enough to support a man and five chil-
dren, if a man would insist on smoking and drinking beer. Was not a dollar a
day enough to buy bread; water costs nothing. [Laughter] Man cannot live by
bread alone but the man who cannot live on bread and water is not fit to live.
[Laughter] A family may live on good bread and water in the morning, water
and bread at midday, and good water and bread at night. [More laughter]
—From a sermon by the Reverend Henry Ward Beecher
delivered at Plymouth Church in Brooklyn on Sunday,
July 22, 1877, as the Great Railroad Strike spread

Tom Scott and John D. Rockefeller shared an infamous patch of business
history. In 1872 they collaborated in what a congressional committee
branded the "most gigantic and daring conspiracy against the free market
ever conceived."[1] That would be the South Improvement Company (SIC),
a plot to escape competition among oil transporters and oil refiners by
effecting a double cartel in rails and oil. Rockefeller called it "a Tom Scott
scheme," and two of his twentieth-century biographers agree, yet also
stipulate that, more than any other episode in his fifty-year business career,
Rockefeller's eager participation in the SIC marked him with the robber
baron stigmata. "There are worse men than John D. Rockefeller," the
Arena, a turn-of-the-century magazine, conceded. "There is probably not
one, however, who in the public mind so typifies the grave and startling
menace to the social order."[2]

The SIC emerged from an accordian charter Scott obtained from the
Pennsylvania legislature conveying the right to form a "holding corporation"—a corporation with holdings in out-of-state corporations. Scott
signed up William Vanderbilt of the New York Central and Jay Gould of
the Erie, mating them with Rockefeller, by then the world's leading
refiner, and his major refining competitors.[3] No longer would the carriers
compete for the lowest bid contract to transport oil from the Pennsylvania

wellheads to the refineries in Cleveland and New York. They would divide up that traffic and double their rates—but offer refiners within the SIC 40 to 50 percent rebates on the listed tariff.

As for the refiners *outside* the SIC, they would be driven out of business by what one Rockefeller biographer calls a "device for the extinction of commerce that was the cruelest and most deadly yet conceived"—the "drawback."[4] Under this rapacious scheme the Standard and the other SIC refiners would get 40 percent rebates on the oil shipped by their independent *competitors*—that is, 40 cents of every dollar the Pennsylvania Railroad charged the independents to carry their oil would go to the SIC. Years later Rockefeller said Scott was "perhaps the most dominant, autocratic power that ever existed, before or since, in the railroad business of our country." But in 1872 Scott's SIC spoke to the autocrat in Rockefeller—and to his detestation of competition. From his near-death experience with price competition after the war, he had learned the foundation truth of Gilded Age capitalism: Competition will break industries with large sunk costs in plant and technology. The SIC was the father of the Standard Oil Trust.

In her *History of the Standard Oil Company* (1904), Ida M. Tarbell says Scott "insisted" on bringing the oil producers into the SIC and penciled that condition into a draft of the contract. But Scott's condition was missing from the final version—"It seems to have been used principally to quiet Tom Scott"—and no one warned the producers that their shipping charges were about to double. The oil region of Pennsylvania, where Tarbell's father operated a hotel, exploded in protest when it found out on February 26.[5] The producers and independent refiners left out of the SIC sent a ninety-four-foot-long petition to Congress demanding an inquiry, besieged the state government in Harrisburg, and mounted "an uprising" in the oil region, destroying Pennsylvania Railroad property and hanging John Rockefeller in effigy. "[H]ad the companies not cancelled the contract which Scott and Vanderbilt and others had entered into," a Venango County lawyer declared at the 1872 constitutional convention, "I venture to say that there would not have been one mile of railroad track left in the County of Venango—the people had come to that pitch of desperation."[*6]

---

* Standard Oil later hired this lawyer, "at a salary equal to that of the President of the United States," Henry Demarest Lloyd reported. "Later, as their counsel, he drafted the famous trust agreement of 1882." Henry D. Lloyd, *Wealth Against Commonwealth* (New York: Harper and Brothers, 1894), p. 55.

When the producers and independents, fighting "monopoly with monopoly," refused to ship oil by the Pennsylvania, Scott wavered. He met with a committee from the counter-monopoly at their Philadelphia hotel, admitted that the SIC contract was "unjust," said he signed it thinking that the SIC refiners "represented the oil industry," and ended with a proposal the committee found "amazing." The Pennsylvania Railroad would make an SIC-like deal with *them,* "the people who *do* represent the oil industry," and turn the tables on Standard Oil! When, as a member recalled during a congressional hearing, the committee objected that they had no "legal authority to do so . . . he said that could easily be fixed because the legislature was then in session, and by going to Harrisburg a charter could be obtained in a very few days."[7] To succeed in business Scott reflexively fell back on politics. Scott's whiplash proposition to the producers substantiates Rockefeller's size-up of his business character as "daring, dare-devil, bold, courageous," capable of a "sledge-hammer stroke" against friends to cut a better deal with enemies.[8]

In 1872 Rockefeller escaped that sledgehammer. In 1877 Scott wielded it over him again. He committed the Pennsylvania Railroad to beat the Standard at its own game—oil-refining. "Companies can pursue two strategies of growth," Alfred Chandler found in his study of the rise and fall of industrial giants in the twentieth century. "Related diversification—related in terms of market and/or technology—allows companies to benefit from their existing learning bases and from the economies of scale and, even more, of scope. . . . The alternative strategy of growth through unrelated diversification is much riskier. When a company moves beyond the industry's competitive arena it loses the protection of that industry's barrier to entry. That puts it at a competitive disadvantage in terms of organizational capabilities. Worse, in the new business, it can't benefit from the interrelated economies of scale and scope built up over decades in its core industry." Nor could Harrisburg's political barriers protect Scott. By this time, as Henry Demarest Lloyd quipped in an *Atlantic Monthly* article, "Story of a Monopoly," "Standard Oil [had] done everything to the Pennsylvania legislature, except refine it." Scott was running the first exclusively *business* risks of his career.[9]

Scott's partner in "unrelated diversification," Joseph Potts, believed they had no alternative. "We reached the conclusion that there were three great divisions in the petroleum business—the production, the carriage of it, and the preparation of it for market," he later testified. Let one party control any one of the three and "they would have a very fair show of controlling the others." Rockefeller was rapidly engrossing refining. Once he monopolized it he could name his rates—or of a whim steer *all* his business to the Pennsylvania's competitors. "Why not do it? Perhaps they would bring the colossus of refining down with a few mighty blows," Allan Nevins imagines their psychology. "And if the Standard was not destroyed, at least Scott and Potts could fight it to a standstill and take a good half of the prize for which the Rockefeller group was reaching."[10]

Potts operated the Empire Transportation Company, a fast-freight shipper with 5,000 cars, 1,500 oil tank cars, pipelines, and oil tanks. The Pennsylvania owned a controlling interest in Empire, and Scott and other Penn officers invested in it: When Empire paid the Pennsylvania to pull its cars, Scott was on both sides of the market. (Scott did not derive his $200,000 a year from his salary.) Potts had barely set up his refinery when Rockefeller put Scott on notice: This means war.[11]

Rockefeller suspended all shipments on the Pennsylvania, carrier of 65 percent of the Standard's business. He slashed the price of kerosene "in all markets reached by the Empire."[12] He commanded his other carriers, the Central, Erie, Baltimore & Ohio, and the Atlantic and Great Western, among others, to start a rate war against Scott's road. By May passenger fares between New York and Chicago fell to $15. To get crude for Potts's refinery, Scott shipped oil "at eight cents a barrel less than nothing."[13] In three months of rate-warring and rate-voiding the Pennsylvania lost $1 million. Scott halted the railroad war in June, when he conspired with his tormentors to raise rates and cut wages. But, still hemorrhaging money on his oil shipments and still resolved to humble Rockefeller, he also decided to double the length of trains without increasing the size of their crews. Wage cuts were announced for June 1; layoffs would hit the Pennsylvania's 20,000-man workforce, without prior announcement, in July.

"We respectfully call your attention to our grievances," the Pennsylvania's workers petitioned management. "Our wages have been from time to time reduced, so that many of us do not earn an average of 75 cents a day." Through the depression the wages of railway workers had indeed fallen—by 2.3 percent—but the wages of nonrailway workers had fallen 15.6 percent, statistics not then available to the railroad to buttress its case in the court of public opinion. The men "sympathized fully" with the company's difficulties, and had "accepted the situation so long as it guaranteed us a bare living; but in the last move was guaranteed to many of us a pauper's grave." Scott met with a committee of thirty, principally engineers, in Philadelphia in late May. The railroad was not "making an iota of profit," he told them. It was run as a charitable venture "simply that men might be employed"—a claim belied by the Pennsylvania's healthy quarterly dividend. Whether moved by their employer's generosity or bowing to the inevitable, the committee accepted the wage cuts. But the engineers did not speak for the Trainmen's Union, which had secretly organized in Pittsburgh to reverse the wage cuts and spread from there. The Trainmen called for a strike on June 27. But on the 25th, the company fired the five representatives who submitted their demands and purged the ranks of suspected members. *That* strike fizzled.

The Great Railroad Strike (judged "the largest strike anywhere in the world in the nineteenth century" by the historian Richard Oestreicher) began on the evening of Monday, July 17, when Baltimore & Ohio trainmen at Martinsburg, West Virginia, who had not yet received their pay for June, uncoupled the engines from trains in the yards. Nothing would move, they told their bosses, until the company paid up *and* rescinded the wage cut. Next day Martinsburg saw the first violence of the strike, when West Virginia militiamen escorting a train traded fire with strikers. The first fatalities came on Friday, when Maryland state militia fired into a Baltimore crowd blocking its armory, killing eleven and wounding forty, most of them bystanders, one a fourteen-year-old newsboy.[14]

The strike reached Pittsburgh on the morning of Thursday, July 19, when an announcement from Robert Pitcairn, who had succeeded Andrew Carnegie as the western division superintendent in 1865, was posted informing the men that all eastbound trains would "henceforth" be double-headers. That is, the length of the trains would be doubled without increasing the size of the crew, costing jobs and endangering train crews. As late as 1890 the railroads successfully lobbied down state attempts to require them to install automatic air brakes, available from 1873, and automatic couplers, or, as in Michigan, ignored laws requiring them. "In the twenty-five years of delay between invention and widespread [adoption]," the historian Walter Licht writes in *Working for the Railroad*, "the lives and physical well-being of tens of thousands of American railwaymen had been imperiled needlessly." Brakemen had to run along the roofs of the cars to turn the brake wheels. "Say, for instance, it is a bad night—what we call a blind night on the road—sleeting, raining, snowing," Augustus Shaw, a veteran brakeman, told a congressional committee investigating accidents. "We hear the call for 'down brakes' . . . we get out on top of the train . . . the top of the cars are completely covered in sleet. In attempting to get at those brakes a great many brakemen lose their lives, slip off the cars." In 1889 slipping off the cars accounted for a fourth of the deaths in the industry. The drinking endemic among trainmen raised the already fearsome risks. The doubleheaders would cost lives.[15]

Shedding responsibility for the strike, Scott later denied knowing anything about the doubleheaders—"a matter of detail management . . . that scarcely ever comes to me at all." That passes belief, though Scott may have left the timing up to Pitcairn. He chose "the wrong time to put on the double-headers, just following the strike in Martinsburg," a Trainmen's Union leader remarked. "That just started the whole thing."[16]

Augustus Harris, a flagman, refused to go out on the first doubleheader. A brakeman joined him. Yardmen joined them. When a brakeman, following his supervisor's orders, started to couple a car to an engine, the strikers threw coupling pins, injuring him, and making him "run for his life." Engineers were warned: Stay away from the trains. "Hice, you have a perfect right to refuse to go out," trainmaster David Garrett told Andrew Hice and a score of strikers, "but you have no right to interfere with others." "It is a question of blood or bread," Hice came back, "and if I can go to the penitentiary I can get bread and water, and that is about all I can get now." After strikers blocked the eastbound switch at the Twenty-eighth Street crossing, all traffic stopped.[17]

Pitcairn had posted his notice and left for Philadelphia, leaving his chief clerk, David Watt, in charge. Watt applied to Mayor William McCarthy for help. McCarthy had no will for that. Squeezing Pittsburgh for decades, the Pennsylvania had incurred its enmity. "From the first commencement of the strike," the *Report of the Committee Appointed to Investigate the Railroad Riots* found, "the strikers had the active sympathy of a large portion of the people of Pittsburgh." If Tom Scott was "the most hated man in Pennsylvania," his stock in Pittsburgh can be imagined. The mayor could spare no police; budget cuts had winnowed his day force to eleven men. Watt could ask for volunteers among the laid-off policemen milling in City Hall awaiting their last paychecks. Ten came forward. Watt led them up Liberty Street toward the switch at the crossing.

Wading into the crowd he declared "I'll turn that switch," and strode toward it. A striker stepped in front of him. Watt took the man by the coat, at which a fist "shot out" and struck Watt in the eye. The police pursued the puncher, the crowd neither resisting nor cooperating. Boys threw stones. Dispatcher Joseph McCabe turned the switch. A freight train pulled out of the yard, the last for three weeks.[18]

In charge at the Philadelphia headquarters of the Pennsylvania Railroad on July 19 was third vice president Alexander Cassatt, a well-born Philadelphian, older brother of the painter Mary Cassatt, husband of Lois Buchanan, President Buchanan's niece, and, at thirty-eight, another Thomson protégé. Reports of the trainmen's walkout reached Cassatt late in the afternoon. After telegraphing Pittsburgh to replace the strikers with "extra conductors and engineers," the National Guard of capital's reserve army of the unemployed, he left not for his townhouse on Broad Street but for Cheswold, the neo-Gothic mansion on the Main Line in Haverford he had commissioned the future architects of Philadelphia's Broad Street Station to build in 1872.[*][19] "One of the attractions of Cheswold for Alexander Cassatt," his biographer explains, "was the space it provided for his horses." And for the relief of bladder and bowel: When most Americans used an outdoor privy during the day and a chamber pot at night and five out of six city dwellers still bathed with pail and sponge, Cheswold boasted seven bathrooms. Cassatt was having dinner with his wife and three children when the stationmaster at Haverford arrived with news that a rough had blacked David Watt's eye and strikers had halted traffic. We picture Cassatt nipping into his mahogany study to fetch talismans of his authority, striding across Cheswold's "vast" walnut entrance hall, accepting his tall white silk hat from one of his dozen servants, then pausing at the threshold for a lingering look at all he had to defend.[20]

Earlier that day Cassatt wired news of the Pittsburgh troubles to Tom Scott, attending a dinner at Andalusia, an estate on the Delaware River eighteen miles away. A descendant of Andrew Jackson's enemy from the

---

[*] "[A] surplus labouring population is a necessary product of accumulation or of the development of wealth on a capitalist basis. . . . It forms a disposable industrial reserve army, that belongs to capital quite as absolutely as if the latter had bred it at its own cost. . . . The overwork of the employed part of the working class swells the ranks of the reserve, whilst conversely the greater pressure that the latter by its competition exerts on the former, forces those to submit to over-work and to subjugation under the dictates of capital. . . . The law, finally, that always equilibrates the relative surplus-population, or industrial reserve army, to the extent and energy of accumulation, this law rivets the labourer to capital more firmly than the wedges of Vulcan did Prometheus to the rock. It establishes an accumulation of misery, corresponding with accumulation of capital. Accumulation of wealth at one pole is, therefore, at the same time accumulation of misery, agony of toil, slavery, ignorance, brutality, mental degradation, at the opposite pole." Karl Marx, *Capital, A Critique of Political Economy* (New York: Modern Library, 1906), pp. 693, 698, 709.

Bank War, Nicholas Biddle, presided over Andalusia. Scott, who had pocketed Cassatt's telegrams unread, kept company with the Philadelphia elite.

On reaching his depot office Thursday evening, Cassatt ordered the railroad's general agent, Charles Pugh, to run a special car to Andalusia and bring Scott back. Cassatt left for Pittsburgh. "When the riots assumed a serious aspect there," Lois Cassatt wrote her children years later, "the President of the Road was away from home, and several of the other officers for reasons best known to themselves, were unable to go to the scene of the action . . . your father, without the slightest hesitation, rushed to Pittsburgh."

At Andalusia, Pugh discovered that Scott was staying nearby, at the home of his son-in-law, Howell Bickley. Pugh got there at ten. Scott, Bickley told him, had retired for the night. Just then Pugh heard Scott's voice harshly instructing Bickley to let Pugh come upstairs. While Scott dressed, Pugh explained. In silence, against the crack and fury of a thunderstorm, they drove by buggy to the waiting car.[21]

Scott got to the Philadelphia depot around midnight. Briefed on the standoff at Pittsburgh, he went to the mattresses, ordering cots to be set up. He then called on every level of government to break the strike his hubris had provoked. Pittsburgh formed the sequel to the anarchic rate-cutting among the trunk lines, to his exorbitant pursuit of the Texas and Pacific mirage—spent manufacturing goodwill in the South and ill will against Coliss Huntington at Washington—and to his race to the bottom on oil rates against John D. Rockefeller.

Swiftly Scott moved to tap his political investments. He summoned the mayor of Philadelphia, William S. Stokley, from his holiday at the Jersey shore. He wired his alarm to Governor John F. Hartranft, off on a six-week junket to Wyoming in Scott's *Pennsylvania*.[22] And he thought out, if he did not dispatch, the first of a battery of telegrams, which the *New York Times* characterized as "peremptory and dictatorial" in tone, to President Hayes at his summer residence at the Soldiers Home in Washington, demanding federal intervention.[23] That, certainly, describes the tone of Scott's wires to Governor Hartranft: "I think it is your imperative duty to return to the state. . . . Will you come? Answer."[24]

Scott knew, or thought he knew, his men. Mayor Stokley, a businessman, was reputedly among the Pennsylvania's largest stockholders.[25] He had "earned a reputation as an upholder of law and a protector of property" by leading a flying wedge of policemen into a march of 400 striking gasworks employees, scattering them, and arresting their leaders. After learning from Scott and the city police chief that railroad firemen hoping to spread the strike to Philadelphia were holding secret meetings, Stokley decided to head off a "riot" by banning meetings. Violating the Constitution written in his city, he suspended the right of assembly and trampled on the freedom of the press, confiscating copies of the *Labor Standard,* a weekly that printed locations where workers could meet. Years later a member of the Committee of Public Safety convened by the mayor to help keep the peace wrote that Stokley also targeted suspected strike leaders for assassination, instructing one of his police captains that "if any riotous action was forced upon him, he should see that the right person or persons were killed." When a group of workers attempted to meet at Fourth and Berks Streets, the police fired fifty shots over their heads, dispersing them, save William McBride, who lay on the ground, shot through the back of the head. The police identified him to the committee as the "ringleader." The Philadelphia papers, which hurled the Commune at the strikers, recalling how "grape and canister" had slaughtered the Communards, reported that a man had died in the affray, without investigating who killed him or why and without giving his age—eighteen.[26]

One recognizes in Governor Hartranft a politician trying to have things both ways, seeking credit for sympathies inconsistent with his acts, mindful that, though elites rule, workingmen vote. Conceding during an earlier wave of disorders that coal miners had been "grievously wronged, and goaded to madness by what they conceive to be the injustice of the law, which seems to protect their employer and leaves them exposed to his caprice or avarice," he repeatedly sent militia to the coal regions to protect their employers in the exercise of their avarice.[27] During the railroad strikes of 1873–74 Hartranft proved his fealty to the Pennsylvania Central by sending troops to Scranton, a pinch-point of the strike, over the protests of residents, who found it "peaceful and orderly."[28] (The Pennsylvania's engineers and firemen struck after the company demanded *they* pay for any engine damage incurred on their runs whether caused by their negligence or not. "If you don't pay the damages," a company official told the engineers, "we'll discharge you.")

As for President Hayes, the *New York Sun* alluded to the hold "railroad chiefs like Scott" had on "the man they inaugurated."[29] Scott could be confident of the cabinet, men who had earned their living from railroads.[30] The secretary of war "represented Iowa and Tom Scott"; Grenville M. Dodge, the builder of the Texas and Pacific, had recommended him for the cabinet.[31] Scott had given a job to the son of the secretary of the navy, the former chief counsel for an Indiana railroad, and a director of the Panama Railroad Company. The postmaster general, David Key, "was the protégé of Texas and Pacific Railroad lobbyist Andrew Kellar, and his selection to the most powerful patronage position in the government was widely viewed as a payoff to . . . the railroad lobby," Roy Morris, Jr., writes in *Fraud of the Century*.[32] The attorney general, a Boston railroad lawyer, had just returned to Washington from a junket through the Pennsylvania coal regions in one of Scott's compromising cars accompanied by the secretary of state, a New York corporation lawyer whose firm represented a Vanderbilt-owned Chicago railroad shut down by the strike.[33] Hayes, we recall, had journeyed to Washington for his inauguration on a "Special car—having in fact two cars of Col. Tom Scott, attached to the regular passenger train," an impressed president-elect specified in his diary.[34]

In Pittsburgh on Thursday the Trainmen's Union voted to send delegates to talk terms with the railroad. A reporter for the *National Labor Tribune* interviewed some of the members. "These men merely want to live—and do not want their wives and little ones to starve, which they must certainly do if they are compelled to accept the terms of the company," he wrote.[35] The union spoke for the strikers but did not represent them, the strike coming as a surprise to its president.[36] The Great Strike was the spontaneous act of un-led men who had taken courage from their anger over the doubleheaders. They had done something hard. They had defied authority; not just a company, but a company-state with a grip on their minds.

Perhaps some of them had learned to read using *Bannan's New Columbian Primer*, published in Philadelphia by Lippincott and adopted by schools in the mining district. It taught the alphabet through lessons sometimes discordant with the animals pictured. The lion, for example, "is the noblest of all beasts, and can be tamed like a cat or dog." "The horse is a useful animal and on account of his docility is loved and petted by his master." *Little Harry's Indestructible Reading Book* for older children featured Blind Harry, victim of a lightning strike but an inspiration to us all, for he is "patient and does not complain. . . . We should learn of him to be patient, and to submit to the will of God in all things." If God worked his will through the Pennsylvania Railroad then it ranks with His most convincing disguises.[37]

Like the black men who fought for the right to vote at the Colfax courthouse, the Pittsburgh strikers asserted their "manliness" against the resignation dinned into them in school and at church. Rejecting the fatalism of the multitude, they broke away from the pedestal beneath business rule. The mainspring of the strike, J. M. Carson of the *Pittsburgh Critic* wrote, "was not so much the [wage] reduction as it was [the railroad] wanted to crush out all the manhood in him, and trample him into the dust." "Few words enjoyed more popularity in the nineteenth century than this honorific," David Montgomery elucidates, "with all its connotations of dignity, respectability, defiant egalitarianism, and patriarchal male supremacy."[38] Men displayed manhood by "refusing to cower before the foreman's glance" or to work at all "when a boss was watching"; by keeping to the "stint," the work pace set by the workers; and by ostracizing the "router," "chaser," "rusher," "runner," "swift," epithets affixed to the "boss's pet." Manliness was the code of a culture in which the categories "employee" and "citizen" did not apply to disjunct realms—when men felt the contradiction between what Samuel Gompers termed "autocracy in the shop and the democracy in political life." The erasure of equality we take for granted in the workplace belongs to the twentieth century.[39]

"The corporations have the law on their side," "own the Legislatures," "control most of the newspapers and manufacture public opinion," the *Reading Daily Eagle* wrote at the height of the Great Strike. "And if the laborers protest in the only way that is left for them to assert their manhood, and contend for the rights of American citizenship, they are branded as rioters, met by force of arms, and then shot dead."[40] Along with the citizenship of the shop, this republicanism of the streets lights up why between 1880 and 1905 6 million workers mounted 36,000 strikes—because they were Americans. The textbooks refer to "labor violence," but that is to blame the victims for the blood spilled in these roughly 1,000 strikes a year. As Richard Hofstadter suggests, "capital violence" or "state violence on behalf of capital" better describes who shot who and why.[41]

The trainmen knew the company knew them. "Troublemakers" went on a "blacklist"—such lists circulated in the industry starting in the 1850s. If they lost the strike, they would lose their jobs, and likely any chance of working on the rails again. Yet these selves hidden under "the mob," these nameless "strikers," rejected what Barrington Moore, Jr., termed the "moral authority of suffering" and stood up for a world more attractive they would never see.[42]

The men had to strike; the railroad officers on the scene had to move the trains. From their comments we know that some, like David Watt, disagreed with the doubleheader decision. Alexander Cassatt had objected to the wage cut: "Why the men cannot buy butter for their bread," he remarked to the road's general manager when the cuts were announced in June. ("What do they want with butter?" came the reply.) But they had a responsibility to do right by bad policy, and they shouldered it.[43]

Around eleven Watt and the railroad's general counsel, John Scott (no relation), roused the sheriff of Allegheny County, Robert H. Fife, from his bed. The city police having failed, the sheriff had to enforce the law. It was up to him, Scott insisted, to order the men blocking the crossing to disperse and to "restore to the company possession of its property." If they refused, local authority would be shown to have failed. General Alfred L. Pearson, commander of the Pittsburgh-based Sixth Division of the Pennsylvania National Guard, would accompany Fife as a reminder of state power. Fife, who had "suffered three severe heart attacks in the past year," left his house and, along with Watt, a deputy, and General Pearson, set off up toward Twenty-eighth Street. Mounting a lumber pile, Fife told the crowd to go home. They told him to go to hell, and "pistol shots were fired into the air." When he hinted he might return with a posse, someone shouted, "Go and bring your posse . . . Mayor McCarthy and his police are with us." Fife gave it up.

John Scott was waiting for him at the Union Depot. Scott, who had served a term in the U.S. Senate "to which he had been named by a quiet order of Tom Scott to the Pennsylvania legislature," observed the legal punctilio. He wrote out a dispatch to Governor Hartranft requesting state militia and had Fife sign it.[44]

John Scott's telegram coincided with Tom Scott's arrival at the West Philadelphia Depot. Earlier that evening, railroad officials had sent for James W. Latta, the state adjutant general whom Hartranft had delegated to command the militia in his absence. "We want troops," they told him. Latta said he needed an official request from the sheriff. Now he had it. Scott, finding Latta "very much disturbed" by his responsibility, lectured him on "the importance of preserving the highways of the country intact." Persuaded, Latta, by this time on his way to Pittsburgh, wired General Pearson to call out the Sixth Regiment.

It's the neutral-seeming concepts that win spontaneous assent. As the strike lengthened, editorial pages adopted the "highway" analogy, the *New York Times* pronouncing railroads "great national highways . . . indispensable to trade and travel."[45]

Highways are public necessities and Scott drew one implication of that in an article in the September issue of the *North American Review* on the lessons of "The Recent Strikes." "The absolute dependence of the whole community upon the great system of railways almost for its very existence as a civilization," he wrote, made *strikes* against railroads crimes against society that the national government, acting under the commerce clause of the Constitution, must suppress.[46] *The New York Journal of Commerce* pointed out a corollary of Scott's argument: "Possibly he does not see that the law desired [placing railroads under federal protection] would be a precedent for quite another kind of interference."[47] If civilization depended on the railroads, how could Congress *not* regulate them? Their tendency in monopoly to charge too much and in competition too little, forcing cutbacks in safety, maintenance, and men; and their treatment of workers upon whose fidelity "civilization" rested: How could profit-seeking corporations be left to decide such matters by themselves? Chief Justice Waite, in the Granger ruling handed down that March, had opened the door to federal regulatory intervention. Like the Chicago grain elevators that *Munn v. Illinois* held lawfully subject to rate regulation, railroads were "businesses affected with a public interest." The Interstate Commerce Commission, toothless in practice but historic in symbolism, Robert V. Bruce writes in *1877: Year of Violence* "was drifting into sight on the political horizon."[48]

When the Trainmen's Union representatives passed their list of demands to Superintendent Pitcairn on the Union Depot platform on Friday morning, he handed it to Alexander Cassatt, now in charge. Cassatt read it—the union wanted the wage cut rescinded and the doubleheaders canceled, mainly—and handed the list back. "Have no further talk with them," he instructed Pitcairn. "They've asked for things we can't grant them at all." Knowing Hartranft had called out the Guard, Cassatt felt no need to bargain. ("We did not think it a thing that affected the men," Cassatt later said of the doubleheaders, "but thought it simply a question of management.") To the men, Pitcairn said, "I can't possibly send such a paper to Mr. Scott."[49]

By late afternoon General Pearson had mustered only 130 men, a force too small, he told Cassatt, to disperse the crowd. A cannonade would do it—he had two artillery pieces—but at an unacceptable cost in lives. Cassatt said he was prepared to accept it. Pearson, a Medal of Honor winner in the Civil War, doubted that his regiment would fire on "their fellow townsmen." Cassatt suggested that Latta "had a good regiment under arms" in Philadelphia; a special train could bring them to Pittsburgh overnight. *They* would shoot, if they had to. Pearson wired Latta that "to avert bloodshed, we should have not less than two thousand troops."[50]

In a decision a Pittsburgh paper branded "insane," Latta called out the

First Division of the Pennsylvania National Guard under Major General Robert M. Brinton.[51] Bad blood between Pittsburgh and Philadelphia extended back decades, to the founding of the Pennsylvania Railroad by "Philadelphia capitalists" and their campaign to keep competitors out of Pittsburgh.[52] How Pittsburghers would react to Philadelphia militia marching through their streets to break a broadly supported strike against the hated Pennsylvania Railroad was foreseeable but not foreseen. That evening the depot thronged with soldiers and their families. Of 1,200 troops in the division, Brinton's summons had reached a little over 600. At 2:00 A.M. they left for Pittsburgh. To his fellow executives Scott remarked that he would finish "this business with the Philadelphia troops."[53]

In cars bearing the marks of stonings by strikers in Harrisburg, Johnstown, and Altoona, the Philadelphia militia pulled past Twenty-eighth Street early Saturday afternoon, their long polished Springfield rifles sticking out the broken windows.[54] The Philadelphians had stopped at the state arsenal in Harrisburg to pick up ammunition, having left Philadelphia too hurriedly to collect it, and two Gatling guns. At the depot Cassatt chafed while they ate sandwiches. He rejected the suggestion made by a steel manufacturer to postpone a confrontation until Monday, when Pittsburgh millmen, who had Saturday afternoon off, would be back at work, thinning a crowd now numbering over 5,000. "We must have our property," Cassatt said. He glanced at his watch. "We have now lost an hour and a half's time."[55]

The Philadelphians were "spoiling for a fight," the *Army Times* later reported, boasting en route they would "clean up Pittsburgh." A *New York Times* reporter who came up from Philadelphia on a later train revealed the source of that mentality: "At Johnstown a mob of 1500 men and boys, many of them armed, stopped the train. Half a dozen of them boarded the engine, and, putting loaded pistols to the engineer's head, told him they would blow his brains out if had brought any soldiers." At Altoona a mob had menaced the militia while they ate sandwiches at the station. Their engineer had been thrown out of his cab, the pin linking the locomotive to the train pulled. As the train finally got under way a man ran up to it and emptied his revolver at the cars. General Brinton knew how his men felt and in his "final briefing" at the depot tempered their impulse to strike back. "No matter what is done to us—even if they spit in our faces— I don't want a shot fired," he said, weakening the admonition by adding:

"But if they attempt any personal violence, we have the right to defend ourselves and we shall do it."

In "fine uniforms of blue or red or grey, one outfit distinguished by black-plumed hats," arrayed in columns of fours, bayonets glittering in the sun, they marched up the tracks toward the crossing, the two Gatlings pulled bumpily along behind. From a parallel street "wild and famished looking women" hissed at them. Alexander Cassatt's tall white hat could be seen bobbing along the tops of the cars on the adjacent track.[56]

Superintendent Pitcairn led the march followed by Sheriff Fife, his deputies, constables, and police. The railroad had got a judge to issue a warrant charging strike leaders with "riot." Pitcairn was to pick out the men; Fife to arrest them. No "riot" had occurred. The strike was the riot.[57]

As they gained the crossing the Philadelphians saw they were marching into a tight spot. A steep hill ran up from the tracks on one side. Four coal cars wedged them in on the other, with "spectators" covering the coal. Spread out on the hill were lawyers and businessmen there out of curiosity, families with small children, trainmen, millmen, miners, and the remnants of the Pittsburgh militia. Ordered to occupy the crossing during the night, by midday some had melted into the crowd; others stacked their arms and sat on the hill with their friends or families. The crowd blocking the tracks numbered "seven to eight thousand." The Philadelphians, having split their force to guard facilities closer to the depot, were 300.

They deployed in a hollow square, facing the Gatlings at the thickest knot of people a few paces down the tracks. A detachment of the "Dark Blues" lowered their rifles and charged the crowd with their bayonets. Men grabbed at the bayonets and tried to pull the rifles away from the soldiers. One "retained his piece by using his bayonet, and my impression is he run the man through," a militiaman recalled. "His piece was rusty the next day." From the hill boys threw stones. From the coal cars came a barrage of coal. Pitcairn, in the center of the square, said coal "clouded the horizon." A soldier "had the whole side of his face taken off by a brick." Others collapsed from sunstroke. "Shoot, you sons of bitches, won't you shoot!" a voice taunted. The crowd surged around the Dark Blues. "At the most, in thirty seconds not a man in our command would have had his piece, they outnumbered us so," a Blue remembered. At least three pistol shots, one from a boy on the hill, rang out. No one gave the order, but up and down the square the militiamen opened fire, at first in all directions, then at the hillside. A reporter for the *Pittsburgh Post* described the scene on the hill: "Women and children rushed frantically about, some seeking safety, others calling for friends and relatives. Strong men halted with fear, and trembling with excitement, rushed madly to and fro, tramping upon the killed and wounded as well as those who had dropped to mother earth to escape injury and death." Five minutes of shooting, two or three shots a second, had left seventeen dead and sixty or seventy wounded. The casualties included at least one woman, a Pittsburgh militiaman, an old man, and a four-year-old girl pulled from the line of fire by a lawyer who tourniqueted her shattered knee with his handkerchief. That night the doctors amputated her leg in vain.[58] The Pittsburgh militiamen on the hill, who "had to be restrained" from firing on the Philadelphians, "tore off their uniforms and flung them on the ground."

"FIRST BLOOD: Seventeen Citizens Shot in Cold Blood by the Roughs of Philadelphia, The Lexington of the Labor Conflict at Hand"— read the headline in the *Sunday Pittsburgh Gazette*. A Pittsburgh grand jury labeled what occurred at the crossing "an unauthorized willful and wanton killing . . . which the inquest can call by no other name than murder." The lawyer who pulled the girl into a ditch, a veteran, condemned the militia for firing without orders. "[T]here was not a particle of discipline," he testified. "[It] was one mob armed against another mob not armed." Yet at least half the Philadelphians were veterans, and one of their officers, conceding the men fired on their own, said "it would not have been half a minute before the command would have been given," adding, "It would have been necessary."*[59]

Rather than stay in the crossing and be overrun by a crowd that swelled as the news of the shooting spread, the Philadelphians took refuge in the Twenty-sixth Street roundhouse, joining the detachment left there earlier. They were fired on throughout the night by rifles and shotguns their attackers had stolen from a local gun shop. At one point the Pittsburghers

* As the lawyer for the British soldiers charged with murder for firing on a Whig mob in the Boston Massacre of 1770, John Adams asked the jurors to consider the circumstances that made the soldiers shoot in self-defense: "[T]he people shouting, huzzaing, and making the mob whistle as they call it, which when a boy makes it in the street, is no formidable thing, but when made by a multitude, is a most hideous shriek . . . the people crying Kill them! Kill them! Knock them over! Heaving snow-balls, oyster-shells, clubs, white birch sticks three inches and a half in diameter, consider yourselves, in this situation, and then judge, whether a reasonable man in the soldier's situation, would not have concluded they were going to kill him." The soldiers were acquitted of the charge. James Grant, *John Adams: Party of One* (New York: Farrar, Straus and Giroux, 2005), p. 97.

brought up one of General Pearson's field pieces and prepared to launch a shell. Before they could fire fifty Philadelphians fired on them, leaving dead and wounded around the gun. When their comrades tried to retrieve the wounded they were shot down. They tried again; and were shot down. A messenger in civilian clothes sent from the roundhouse to Pearson at the depot, Louis D. Baugh, asked what people in the crowd were saying, replied: "They wanted every damned Philadelphia soldier to go home in a box. That they would tear them to pieces." An orderly stationed near the depot Saturday night overheard two men talking. "[T]hey said [Sunday] would be the roughest day's work for the Philadelphia militia . . . that not a damned one would come out alive. . . . They looked to be . . . business-men."[60]

Toward morning rioters ran a burning coke car topped with petroleum into the buildings adjacent to the roundhouse. Its roof caught fire. At the thought of the Philadelphians burning alive the mob let out a "savage, prolonged yell of exultation." Soon men began gagging on the smoke. Before the roof fell in, General Brinton ordered them to evacuate. They left through the office of the burning upholstery shop. They—these factory workers and clerks far from their Philadelphia homes—formed up, one Gatling gun in front, another in the rear, and at a little past eight marched out of the yards.

The sight of the Gatlings panicked the crowd, which rushed for the alleys running off Liberty Street. As the troops passed "pistols blazed at them out of doorways and windows, from behind corners, projecting signs, crates and boxes, from cellars and other places," and even from a police station. Caring people took the wounded into their homes, and lied for them when gunmen, looking for soldiers to kill, rapped on the door. When their pursuers switched to rifles, the Philadelphians fired back, wounding a nonstriking railroad mechanic returning from work, and a plasterer, and killing a saloonkeeper standing in his own door. "Nobody would fire directly at us from a window as we passed along the street—but the firing was after we past, after we got by half a block or a block—then they would let into us," Brigadier General E. DecC. Loud, command-ing the Second Brigade, recalled. Loud noticed a streetcar approaching. "I don't know why, but I was looking at it, wondering whether it was going to try to get through the lines, when the first thing I heard was two rifle shots from the car, and two men of the Sixth regiment fell dead, one on top of the other. The shots were fired by two men apparently lying on their stomachs—lying on the cushions, and firing out the windows." Loud ordered his men to clear out of the way of the Gatling gun, and, just after the driver had uncoupled the horses, the Gatling riddled the car.

They marched on, stalked by "this man they called the bad angel—he would fire and then run into a house, and run back through a yard, and come out again and fire." Loud's friend Lieutenant Ash was hit. "I saw him stagger and fall into the gutter on the north side of the street, and throw up his hand and say, you are not going to leave me." Ash later died. Another military witness remembered that Ash's "bad angel" wore a linen duster: "They said afterwards that the fellow in the duster was the man that had been pegging away at us all night with a rifle that had a bullet in it that exploded when it struck. He kept it up all night when we were in the round-house. They said afterwards that he had lost a brother, and he wanted to be revenged. I am not positive, but I think he was killed—shot." When a fusillade from the windows of a row of houses felled five more of them, the Philadelphians raked the smoking windows with rifle fire, then turned the Gatling on their street-level pursuers. "The moment we commenced firing with that," a soldier said, "we could not see a living thing down the street."[61]

At the Allegheny Arsenal, a major arms depot for the U.S. Army, the Philadelphians were turned away. Afraid that if he harbored Brinton's men the crowd would storm the arsenal and make off with its 36,000 rifles and muskets, its cannon and powder magazine, the commander accepted the wounded only. With his troops low on ammunition and without food or water for twenty-four hours, General Brinton decided not to fight his way to the depot but to march the Philadelphians out of Pittsburgh via the high bridge over the Allegheny to Sharpsburg, camping on the grounds of the local workhouse. That night they ate food sent over to them "through the personal exertions of A. J. Cassatt," the official, and somewhat railroad-friendly report pointed out, and slept in blankets provided "by Colonel Thomas A. Scott, who . . . had been vigilant in looking after the welfare of the men."[62]

The crowd now ruled the city. "Vengeance means retaliation," Barrington Moore, Jr., observes. "It also means a reassertion of human dignity or worth, after injury or damage."[63] Saturday night and Sunday a few outraged Pittsburghers reasserted their dignity against the Pennsylvania Railroad, burning 1,200 of its freight cars, 104 of its engines, forty-six of its passenger cars, and all thirty-nine of its buildings in Pittsburgh, including the Union Depot and hotel. According to Carroll D. Wright, the first United States commissioner of labor, "a great many old freight cars which must soon be replaced by new, were pushed into the fires by agents of the railroad company . . . and of course the loss was included in claims on the county of Allegheny."[64] Scott refused to pay shippers' and merchants' claims against the railroad. Company lawyers adduced the letter Sheriff Fife had sent (and John Scott had written) to General Latta: Allegheny County had asked for the troops; under the riot laws, it was responsible for damages. The tax-paying rioters would have to pay for the riot. A gun shop was looted and sparks briefly ignited lumberyards and shanties near the yards, but no nonrailroad property was deliberately destroyed. The committee investigating the riot found that "the actual destruction was participated in by only thirty to fifty men," though it abased an unspecified number of Pittsburgh women for bringing tea to the "rioters" and for "pillag[ing]." But the goods "taken from the cars"—bacon, hams, liquor, brooms, umbrellas, apronsful of flour—were destined for the flames.[65]

Photographs of the trainyards reveal a wilderness of twisted metal and fallen brick extending two miles, resembling no new Lexington but Berlin circa 1945. "[N]o parallel in the history of the world upon the strength of what we saw," Adjutant General Latta wired Hartranft.[66] "A crowd setting fire to something feels irresistible; so long as the fire spreads, everyone will join in and everything hostile will be destroyed," Elias Canetti writes in *Crowds and Power.* "After the destruction, crowd and fire die away." And so it was in Pittsburgh. "The strike is over," the *Times* correspondent wrote on Sunday night, "for there is nothing here to strike against so far as the Pennsylvania Railroad is concerned."[67]

Late Saturday night Mr. E. B. Godfrey, a Pittsburgh businessman, boarded a darkened passenger car at Union Station—and had to step over thirty Black Hussars huddled on the aisle floor to reach his seat. "Many were wounded," he recalled. They had escaped from the roundhouse, turning their "pantaloons" inside out and throwing away their uniforms to slip through the crowd, and were "in great terror" that they would be discovered and massacred at Twenty-eighth Street. One sat beside a woman passenger and begged her to help him. She threw her shawl over his head, and he crouched down at her feet. At Twenty-eighth Street the train stopped. Armed men came aboard and asked if the passengers had seen "any Philadelphia men." They had piled into the empty car behind. The Pittsburghers were about to open its door when a passenger, with convincing casualness, said, "Oh, there are only a few wounded men in there."[68]

The Roundhouse, July 22, 1877
"No parallel in the history of the world . . ." the commander of the state militia wired
Pennsylvania governor John F. Hartranft after surveying scenes like this.

In Philadelphia that Sunday the Pennsylvania's officers had followed the
Pittsburgh horrors through the electric remove of the Morse code. But
the fear building in the depot all day approached panic at the sight of the
wounded and terrified militiamen emptying from the cars. The crowd of
strikers, curiosity-seekers, and idle youths around the depot, meanwhile,
had grown; from his command post inside, Mayor Stokley ordered the

police to drive them back. Many drifted up the tracks, commandeering a roundhouse and blocking traffic on the road. Stokley's police, doubled in size on funds advanced by Philadelphia businessmen, violently cleared the tracks. These minor disorders Scott magnified into the sack of Rome in a telegram to Governor Hartranft, still en route from Wyoming. "You must not delay a moment about this"—requesting *federal* troops for Philadelphia —"for the destruction of life and property in Philada. and the eastern road of this State greatly exceed what has occurred in Western part of the State last night and today, and which greatly exceeds any thing that has ever occurred in this country."[69]

Hartranft's first telegram to Hayes, sent through Latta, got no response. Neither did a second sent from Wyoming by Hartranft himself. For Hayes stopping "domestic violence" or "quelling mobs," the phrases used by Latta and Hartranft to justify federal intervention, fell short of the constitutionally required standard. "I amend my requisition from the general government," Hartranft, taking the hint, wired from Nebraska, "by adding the words domestic insurrection exists in Pennsylvania which the state authorities are unable to suppress and the Legislature is not in session." Article 1, Section 6 satisfied to the letter, Hayes dispatched a small force to Philadelphia under General Hancock, who had earlier secured order in Baltimore.[70]

The United States Army numbered fewer than 25,000 men strung out along the Texas-Mexico border, pursuing Nez Percé Indians under Chief Joseph in eastern Washington state, and, a year after the Custer massacre, Sioux in the Dakotas. East of the Mississippi the army had only 3,000 troops, fewer than the Pittsburgh mob. Forty soldiers defended the Rock Island Arsenal, twenty the Indianapolis Arsenal and its artillery battery, 25,000 rifles, and 1 million cartridges. Sending the ironclad *Monitor* to protect the Treasury Building in New York, stripping marines from naval bases and ships, handing out rifles to postal employees in Washington, D.C., Hayes strained to guard federal installations—and, worryingly for morale, with soldiers serving without pay. To spike any return to Reconstruction the Democratic House had appropriated no money for the army. A few hundred troops might suffice to check the destruction of railroad property in Philadelphia or picket Pittsburgh's embers but Tom Scott wanted more. He wanted Hayes to emulate Lincoln in 1861 and call out 75,000 volunteers to clear the tracks from New York to St. Louis; to end the "insurrection" disturbing the commerce of the country. After a White House meeting on the strike, two cabinet members told a *New York Sun* reporter that "the railroad wanted to run the government."[71]

During the second week of the strike Scott asked to see Speaker of the House Samuel Randall. "I accepted because I supposed him in trouble," Randall wrote in a private letter. "I soon found out why I was wanted . . . Colonel Scott asked me to write or telegraph 'President' [Randall was a Democrat] Hayes to call out by proclamation a further force. . . . I abruptly and pointedly said I could not and would not do so."[72] Scott was asking for class war. "Tell the President," a Cincinnati man wired Treasury Secretary John Sherman, "a call for volunteers will precipitate a revolution."[73]

Hayes, whose son Ruddy and daughter Emily had passed through Pittsburgh on their way to Columbus twenty-four hours before "the dreadful events of last Sunday," as he characterized them in his diary, did not see "insurrection" in the messages relayed to him by signal corpsmen of the regular army stationed around the country and by officers in the field.[74] While the U.S. marshal in Indianapolis represented the strike there as a riot needing 1,000 deputy marshals to quell, the corpsman on the scene telegraphed Washington "[S]trikers orderly, no indications of violence," and, two days later, "During the night strikers concluded not to hinder the running of passenger trains." "Saw Mr. Scott at Philadelphia last night at twelve," General Hancock wired Hayes from Philadelphia, relating how Scott pushed his plan to militarize the railroads. "The details of the present state of affairs are doubtless better known in Washington than I know them," he ended, "so I leave the matter with the foregoing remarks and *the assertion that everything seems quiet here for the moment.*"[75] Speaking to reporters the day after the Baltimore riot, the president reflected this intelligence in deprecating the view, expressed by the *National Republican,* that the strike "was communism in its purest form." Hayes detected "no spirit of communism" among the strikers, who did not attack "property in general, but merely . . . that of the railroads with which the strikers had difficulty."[76] In an August entry he wrote, "The railroad strikers, as a rule, are good men, sober, intelligent, and industrious."[77] That was more than he would say of Tom Scott in those same pages years later, when the five-times-wounded veteran credited the rumor that while serving as assistant secretary of war Scott had "bought muskets in Vienna at two francs each and sold them to the Government at twelve dollars to fifteen dollars each."[78] Hayes "did not feel beholden to Tom Scott for his election, and even if he had, he would not have altered an administration policy to come to his aid," his most recent biographer surmises. "Restricting himself to keeping the peace when states could not do so, Hayes refused to supply soldiers to operate the railroads and break the strike."[79]

Yet those troops and, more, the spectacle of the national government intervening in the states to uphold state laws, *did* break the strike. Strikers not only feared but respected federal troops, symbols of the nationhood consecrated with the blood of the Union dead. Unlike state governments, everywhere perceived to be serving corporate interests, and state militia, seen as railroad Hessians, the national government possessed authority; it did not have to use force. Not one U.S. soldier killed a striker. Not one was attacked by a mob. Scott never got his thousands of volunteers; they were not needed.

When strikers requested a meeting with Scott to work out a settlement, the editor of the *Pittsburgh Post,* Joseph Barr, ran a supporting editorial, "Why Not Arbitration?," adjuring Scott "to agree to a board of arbitration to present a compromise which will relieve you and labor without disturbing the rights or grievances of either. . . . You have it in your power to restore peace and preserve society." Aware of the dynamics of coercion the federal troops had set in motion, Barr added, "I implore you not to assume the ground that the military can settle anything but defiance of law." Scott spurned him. With 200 federal troops already in the city by noon on Sunday and with General Hancock ordering all troops in transit from the East to other destinations to stop first in Philadelphia, Scott confidently, an historian of the strike writes, "face[d] down a delegation of strikers who met with him later in the afternoon to demand restoration of old wage scales."[80]

As late as August 1 Scott wired Secretary of War George W. McCrary ("who represented Iowa and Tom Scott") that the strikers still blocking the Pittsburgh, Fort Wayne, and Chicago, a subsidiary of his road, were stopping the mails and the shipment of military supplies—charges without independent verification. Even though the governors of Ohio and Indiana had not called on Hayes for troops, McCrary wired Hancock to "use his discretion" in the matter. The two sides at Fort Wayne had been close to an agreement. But the news that troops were coming stiffened the company's terms and the talks collapsed, the company agreeing only to "consider" the workers' grievances. Reaping his political farming, Scott, through McCrary, had usurped the constitutional role of state governors, setting "a very dangerous precedent" (said the *New York Times*) for the Pullman strike.[81]

Another precedent was set by three federal judges on the Seventh Circuit led by Thomas S. Drummond of Chicago. With William B. Ogden, Drummond had promoted and then served on the board of the Galena & Chicago Union Railroad when the financial barriers to entry in the industry were so low that farmers served by a road doubled as its capitalists, when labor scarcity bid up wages—and when launching a railroad had all the innocence of putting on a show. In his nearly forty years on the bench Drummond had "pioneered in the creation of federal receiverships for Midwestern railroads in financial straits."[82] Drummond protected the assets of roads operated by receivers appointed by his court against creditors and striking workers alike. Because railroads were central to "all the relations of society," strikers "commit[ted] as great an offense against the rights of individuals and against the rights of the public, as can well be imagined." Tom Scott could not have stated the "no-right-to-strike-against-the-public" case more concisely. For impeding the operations of *his* roads Drummond charged strikers with contempt of court, fined them heavily, and if they could not pay sentenced them to a month or more in jail.[83] To Attorney General Charles Devens, Drummond and his Seventh Circuit colleagues argued that roads "in the custody of the Court [were] public property for the time being & so claiming protection as such." The Hayes cabinet agreed, sending federal troops and marshals to break strikes on railroads in receivership from Missouri to Pennsylvania. "Hayes set a precedent which was to be used in later years not only for the benefit of receivers, but for all other businessmen as well," Philip S. Foner writes. "Thus the strike injunction, backed by the power of the U.S. Army—one of the most effective weapons to be used against the labor movement—emerged out of the cases in 1877."[84] Stephen J. Field joined the unanimous opinion that upheld the labor injunction ("the Gatling gun on paper") in *In re Debs* (1895). "The strong arm of the national government may be put forth to brush away all obstructions to interstate commerce or to the transportation of the mails," his nephew David Brewer wrote for the Court. "If the emergency arises, the army of the nation, and all its militia, are at the service of the nation to compel obedience to its laws." Between 1880 and 1930 courts issued more than 1,800 injunctions against strikes and boycotts, curtailing strikers' rights of trial by jury, assembly, and speech. Just as liberty of contract blocked reform through legislation, the labor injunction negated self-help through strikes.[85]

A legislative legacy of the strike drastically restricted the economic freedom of American workers. As after other violent upheavals in American history, men asked why. Some interpretations stressed "root causes" like starvation wages; others, the moral degeneracy of strikers and rioters; still others blamed insidious outsiders, "tramps," a word first used by the *New York Times* in 1874 to denote unemployed men traveling to find work. In his annual report to the board, Scott said that local rioters had received reinforcement from "the idle and vicious classes, which exist in all large communities, and which were attracted to the spot by the opportunity for plunder and pillage."[86] In the days before the strike the *Times* credited reports of carloads of tramps arriving in Pittsburgh. Sheriff Fife could not recognize faces in the crowd he addressed on Thursday night, though some there seemed to know him well enough to judge by the shouts of "Go home, you old bald-headed son-of-a-bitch!" "They were the bad elements of society from all parts of the city, and from some parts of the county, in connection with thieves and blackguards from other parts of the country," Fife told the investigating committee. "A great many strangers were there." Superintendent Pitcairn observed no strike ringleaders at the Twenty-eighth Street crossing. Pittsburgh workmen wore dark clothes, but "I saw men in that crowd with light pantaloons, and yellow pantaloons, and two men with velveteen coats on," the lawyer who watched the shooting from the hill told the committee, "and those men seemed to be making the most noise in front of the soldiers. . . . I thought they were tramps."[87]

Were these sportily dressed tramps the match that ignited Pittsburgh? The casualty list lends no support to that hypothesis: Those killed all appeared to be residents of Pittsburgh or its environs. And it elided the Pittsburgh-specific sources of the "riot"—hatred of the Pennsylvania Railroad and rage at the Philadelphia militia for shooting Pittsburgh citizens. But fear, not facts, controlled.

The long depression had set many of the unemployed in motion searching for work. Estimates of the numbers "on the tramp" run as high as 1 million.[88] They slept in city parks, scavenged crops, and broke into farmhouses. In Gore, Ohio, a month before the strike, a tramp murdered a rural family. An "antitramp convention" was held at Bryn Mawr at which Alexander Cassatt and other wealthy men proposed to form a mounted patrol equipped with whistles and flares to bar tramps from their bosky precincts.[89] Tramps were criminally inclined "agitators," vectors of discontent, cousins of the "communist," "Internationalist," and "agrarian." Acting on the "tramps" diagnosis of the riots, states passed "tramp acts" forbidding travel "without visible means of support"—a boon to local employers who did not want the reserve army of the unemployed depleted by migration. By 1896 forty of the forty-four states had tramp acts on the books. In Buffalo more than 2,000 tramps a year were arrested in the 1890s; nearly 5,000 in the peak depression year of 1894. Eighteen-year-old Jack London "rode the rails to see Niagara Falls" and got thirty days at hard labor on bread and water.[90]

History had run backward. The postwar opened with the states of the late Confederacy enacting Black Codes to prevent freed people from moving to better their condition; and closed with "Tramp Laws" against unemployed northern workers doing the same thing.

The unemployed could be jailed for moving to find work. And if they stayed put? Lose your job and you risked the workhouse. Under the anti-vagrancy laws passed or strengthened as the enlightened social policy response to the depression, a man sitting on his front stoop could land in a place designed to "humiliate and abase" him for being idle and make him grateful to work for crumbs when he got out. In New York City police made 1 million vagrancy arrests in 1877 alone. Charities organized the war on vagrancy guided by "political economy" and an experiment conducted by the Freedmen's Bureau, which, by threatening forced labor, had driven former slaves into wage labor. The unemployed, as Samuel Gompers told a congressional committee, were not "workingmen who for a time have become superfluous in society, men rather, whom the employing class have made superfluous," but "lazy" persons needing a semester in a labor camp to teach them the meaning of free labor. "There is . . . nothing which a government has more clearly the right to do than to compel the lazy to work," an 1892 treatise on the criminal law asserted. The state, Amy Dru Stanley writes, gave "moral legitimacy to labor compulsions that came perilously close to slavery."[91] The North had fought the war partly to defend the right to rise, but how could men rise if they couldn't move? And how could they freely contract for their labor if the state held a whip over the transaction?

While tramp and vagrancy laws were abridging the economic freedom of northern workers, thirty years after the Emancipation Proclamation involuntary servitude returned to the South. The Redeemer governments revived the Black Codes banned by the Fourteenth Amendment. To force black families to pick the planters' cotton the new laws criminalized unemployment, "enticement," vagrancy, and breaking labor contracts. Georgia made it a crime to attract a worker "by offering higher wages or in any other way whatever." A Louisiana statute threatened criminal prosecution to "any one who shall persuade or entice away, feed, harbor or secrete any person who leaves his or her employer." These laws endured into the twentieth century. Consider an ad that appeared in the *Caswell Messenger* of Yanceyville, North Carolina: "NOTICE—I forbid any one to hire or harbor Herman Miles, colored, during the year 1939. A. P. Dabbs, Route 1, Yanceyville." Under Florida's "contract-enforcement" laws, "willful disobedience to others," "wanton impudence," or failing to do what the boss told him to do could land a black man in jail. Any (black) Alabama-man convicted of "wandering or strolling about in idleness, who is able to work, and has no property to support him; or any person leading an immoral, profligate life" faced "a $1,000 fine, six months on the state chain gang, or twelve months on the county chain gang." Employers who paid his fine had the free use of that man for a year or more. Labor shortages at harvest time would be met by what a Georgia official described as "wholesale arrests of idle Negroes . . . to scare them back to the farms from which they emanated." Under the convict-lease systems adopted in every state of the Confederacy but Virginia black men sentenced for vagrancy were worked to death laying track for northern-financed railroads and, "through the winter without shoes, standing in water much of the time," mining coal and phosphate. "Of 285 convicts sent to build South Carolina's Greenwood and Augusta Railroad between 1877 and 1880, 128, or 44.9 percent, died," the historian William Cohen calculates. "By way of contrast, the annual death rate in the prisons of New Hampshire, Ohio, Iowa, and Illinois during the period 1881–1885 was slightly more than one percent."

By the 1920s Alabama derived more revenue from convict labor than from taxes. Many convicts worked for out-of-state coal companies that evaded state trials for the injuries caused by on-the-job accidents by invoking *Santa Clara*: Suits between "citizens of different states," the convict and the corporation, must be heard in the more corporate-friendly federal courts. When in 1928, after decades of legal challenge, Alabama abandoned convict-leasing, the death rate among black convicts dropped to 2.5 percent. Convicts, one historian notes, "often housed in movable cages that provided less space per man than would a box 6 × 4 × 4," continued to build the state roads, however—black convicts, like every one of Alabama's 1,089-man road-building crew in September 1932. "Slavery is still in force," a southern editor said to a visitor in the 1930s, "but not generally profitable."[92]

North and South, at the end of the liberal century, for the poor man, the black man, the unemployed, freedom receded.

———

"Please do not be misled by any news of peaceable settlement of existing troubles," Scott wired Hayes on July 31. "The removal of the military in all probability will be followed by renewed outbreaks."[93] Hayes was not misled, noting in his diary for August 5, "The strikers have been put down by *force*." Peace had returned; the trains ran again. It was time to take stock.

The Great Strike had revealed a gulf between the "free labor" ideal that triumphed in the Civil War and the famished facts of wage labor. Writing in the *North American Review*, "A Striker" argued that the "employer has no right to speculate on starvation when he reduces wages below a living figure, saying if we refuse the remuneration there are plenty of starving men out of work that will gladly accept half a loaf instead of no bread."[94] Was he right that employers should not be allowed to use what Henry D. Lloyd called "the generals of supply and demand" to deny fair wages to workers? Or, as Reverend Henry Ward Beecher blithely affirmed, did "the laws of political economy" dictate the wages of starvation? In which case, how could newspaper editors and ministers of conscience justify their moral condemnation of "railroad managers"? Wasn't Tom Scott merely a colonel of supply and demand? Shouldn't railroad workers, in Beecher's words, be "resigned" to "reap the misfortunes of inferiority"? If the laws of political economy were right, how could their lot be "wrong"? How could *any* economic outcome be wrong? Could you, Lloyd asked, "do anything with your fellow man provided you do it in the market?"[95]

Beecher's "bread and water" sermon delivered at the height of the strike—"Man cannot live by bread alone but the man who cannot live on bread and water is not fit to live"—was a gargoyle's version of an orthodoxy taught by economists like Arthur Latham Perry: "Political economy has no concern with questions of personal right. . . . The grounds of Economy and morals are independent and incommensurable." This orthodoxy, Sidney Fine writes in *Laissez Faire and the General-Welfare State,* was shared by "[the majority] of Protestant churchmen." "It is all right to talk and declaim about the dignity of labor," one Protestant journal asserted. "But when all has been said of it, what is labor but a matter of barter and sale." "Be quiet," the Reverend W. D. Wilson advised workingmen. "Whatever your hand finds to do, do it, and be content with your wages. God will take care of the rest." "At bottom," Roswell D. Hitchcock of Union Theological Seminary argued, "it is an immorality to fight against inequality of condition, which simply corresponds with inequality of endowment."

Such gelid ease with injustice was answered from below by a working-class Protestantism that protested what the labor editor George E. McNeill called "the mammonizing interpretation of religious truth." The "elevation of a false god dethrones the real one," the Boston *Daily Evening Voice* editorialized. A writer in the American Federation of Labor's journal demanded *"the real article!*—not a dead Christianity, dreaming of a dead Christ, but live Christians as live Christs, . . . scattering the table of the money changers in the temples, . . . going down in the poverty-stricken alleys of the robbed industrial slaves, and raising up its victims." Use your faith, the *Locomotive Fireman's Magazine* urged its readers, to "beat back to its native hell the theory that . . . laborers . . . are merchandise to be bought and sold as any other commodity—as cattle, mules, swine." Poverty was godly in the gospel according to Beecher, but, the magazine asked, "Do you think it is anything short of insulting to God to pretend to believe He makes ninety-nine paving material for the one to walk into Heaven over?" Working-class spokesmen like these tapped a vital vein of counter-hegemonic feeling. "Preindustrial Christian perfectionism," the labor historian Herbert G. Gutman found in a survey of the Christian spirit in the Gilded Age, "offered . . . absolute values in a time of rapid social change" that "allowed the labor reformer or radical to identify with 'timeless truths' that legitimized his attack on the absolutes of Gilded Age social thought—the determinism of Spencerian [Social Darwinist] dogma, the sanctity of property rights and freedom of contract, and the rigidity of political laissez faire." Secular republicanism was not the only source of cultural resistance to the new industrial capitalism.[96]

It was one thing for a churchman to air brutalist sentiments in religious journals, another to have them delivered publicly by Henry Ward Beecher, whose pursuit of Mrs. Elizabeth Tilton had lately filled newspapers with salacious culls from the court record like, "[S]he said she had been persuaded by him that his very love was proper and not wrong; therefore it followed that the expression of that love whether by the shake of the hand or the kiss of the lips or even bodily intercourse . . . was not wrong"; and "she added that he had many times fondled her to the degree that it required on her part almost bodily resistance to be rid of him"; and "that for years his home had not been a happy one; that his wife had not been a satisfactory wife to him." With even Tom Scott's *New York World* calling his remarks "suicidal and the part of a lunatic"; with shouts of "Put Beecher on a diet!" and "Hang Beecher!" winning ovations at labor rallies; with thirty plainclothesmen nestling up to socialites in his pews and an intimidation of detectives occupying the stoop opposite his church to protect him from his notoriety as the meanest man on earth—with all of that, Beecher took to his platform on the second Sunday of the strike to admonish workers: "If you are being reduced, go down boldly to poverty." Then he left for a two-month vacation in Europe. Beecher put a hideous face on "Beecherism." Social Darwinism, fleetingly, became unfashionable.[97] And while the *New York Graphic* underestimated the staying power of postwar conservatism in asserting, "The laissez-faire policy has been knocked out of men's heads for a generation," it registered an eddy in opinion colloquially put by the *Minneapolis Tribune*. "We want the assistance of Uncle Sam." Calling for a politics of remedy *Harper's* vaulted decades to the Progressive Era: "It is the business of the State, that is, of the people, to prevent disorder of the kind we witnessed in the summer by removing the discontent which is its cause."[98]

Just as the urban riots of the 1960s confronted white America with problems of race and class intractable to the economics of "growth," so the Great Railroad Strike opened men's eyes to the "problem of labor." The *New York Times,* which on July 26 abused the strikers as disaffected elements, "roughs, hoodlums, rioters, mob, suspicious-looking individuals, bad characters, thieves, blacklegs, looters, communists, rabble, labor-reform agitators, a dangerous class of people, gangs, tramps, drunken section-men, law breakers, threatening crowd, bummers, ruffians, loafers, bullies, vagabonds, cowardly mob, bands of worthless fellows, incendiaries, enemies of society, reckless crowd, malcontents, wretched people, loud-mouthed orators, rapscallions, brigands, robbers, riffraff, terrible fellows, felons, and idiots," declared on August 9 that the strike had been "little short of a revelation as to conditions of labor in mining districts and on the railroads."[99] The *Times* responded to the "evidence of hardship, of suffering, of destitution" uncovered by its own correspondent in interviews with Pittsburgh railroad families. How, he asked, could they live on $1.35 a day—and pay rent for the company shack, and for their tiny garden plot, and have fathers buy their own tickets home after taking a one-way trip? It seemed impossible—until he traveled to the mining region around Scranton. Miners there had struck collieries operated by W. W. Scranton, who denied boasting that he "would have miners working for thirty-five cents a day." His miners worked for 50 cents a day. The correspondent entered a two-room, "black-coated shack," where a miner, his wife, and two daughters with faces as black "as if they had worked in the mines," sat around a table. "All were eating potatoes, which, with soda crackers and water, composed their dinner." His eyes staring "wildly" from his black face, the miner "made an ineffectual effort to hide his grimy arms" before telling his story.[100]

For the past year his wages averaged $15 a month. His rent was $4 a month. He bought groceries and supplies at the "truck store" run by the company, which paid him in scrip cashable only at the store, holding him, the correspondent wrote, "in a kind of slavery." The couple could not pay for a doctor to see a sick child, nor afford to bury her when she died that winter, "The mother being unable to get money or credit." "Men say bitterly that 'A funeral is too costly a heritage for the living,' and so they struggle on as a matter of economy," too poor to die. Yet pride survived. "I was shown . . . a man who took [his] dinner pail into a dark shaft" in an "empty pretense . . . for his pail did not contain so much as a crust of bread." And these men, some native-born, others Welsh, Irish, or German immigrants, risked starvation to strike for better wages. The accompanying *Times* editorial condemned "the greed which prompts employers of labor to squeeze out of it . . . the beggarly pittance through the agency of store pay. . . . It is an infamy which the law in any other country has suppressed."[101] It was an infamy soon to be constitutionalized in Pennsylvania as an exercise in "liberty of contract."

The Great Strike exposed the politics of starveling labor in the railroad's grip on government. "Instead of being the creature of States, it has become their master," the *Times* concluded. "It cuts rates and maintains an insensate competition whose penalties fall upon its workmen, and then it calls on federal troops to re-establish the order which its own recklessness imperils." Whatever the short-term results of the strike, which the *Times* considered "a drawn battle," the railroads lost their redoubt on Capitol Hill, where few congressmen would dare be caught doing the bidding before a public roused against them as never before, and it was the end of the line for Tom Scott.[102]

"Between us," the Washington journalist Charles Nordorff wrote a friend, "I think [the Great Strike] finishes Tom Scott, and I shall not be sorry." "Colonel Thomas A. Scott," the *Times* declared, "is no longer a name to conjure by." "Get to your hole, Tom Scott," the *Miners' Journal* advised. The Henry Ward Beecher of railroad arrogance and corruption, Scott had become radioactive. No quantity of the Scott persuasion would rescue the Texas and Pacific subsidy now, though he tried one last time.[103]

"They offered one member of Congress $1,000 cash down, $5,000 when the bill passed, and $10,000 of the bonds when they got them if they would vote for the bill," Huntington reported to Colton about Scott's final push. But the T&P faced an unforeseen obstacle: Rutherford B. Hayes. The Texas and Pacific lobby had all along assumed that Hayes would sign a subsidy bill; it was their understanding of what he'd agreed to in the Compromise. But Hayes did not see it that way. Those who spoke for him had not spoken *with* him. The subsidy undercut his image as a reformer, a Republican immune to "Grantism," and he had given it at best equivocal support. In a December 1877 interview he expressed "grave doubt . . . whether it would be wise to grant aid to the Texas & Pacific road at all or not." The Scott forces cried betrayal. They did not know the half of it.

Years later Huntington explained to H. H. Bancroft, the California historian, how he fooled Scott and the federal government. "He says to me, 'Huntington, we are beating you.' 'Yes,' I said, 'that is the way you should state it, because you are beating me out of nine things and I shall beat you in one . . . in building the road.' He wanted to build a highway to the Pacific. He could not lay a rail every day. We were laying a mile and a half a day. When we were fighting him we were at Los Angeles. We got to Fort Yuma when the next Congress got together. I sent some men over there to work a little." In October Huntington had met with Hayes at the White House to make amends for what those men had done—secretly laid tracks across a bridge spanning the Colorado River, and crossed over from California into the Fort Yuma Indian reservation in Arizona. After Huntington's men and agents for the Texas and Pacific brawled, Secretary of War McCrary had ordered Huntington to stop laying track. While McCrary's soldiers slept, Huntington's crew pressed on across the bridge. Hayes "was a little cross at first," Huntington explained to Colton, but laughed when Huntington told him how they had done it "and said he guessed we meant business." Huntington asked no subsidy, but needed Hayes's permission to lay track through the reservation and across the Arizona Territory. Hayes gave it. Scott's seven-year pursuit of an empire of rails stretching from New York to California ended at that White House meeting.[104]

In August, for the first time in its history, the Pennsylvania Railroad "skipped its dividend, sending its share price tumbling on the stock exchange."[105] It would skip the next five quarterly dividends, funneling earnings to repair the uninsured damage to its property.[106] Desperate for cash, Scott sent Alexander Cassatt to Cleveland to settle with John D. Rockefeller. Scott agreed to get out of the refining business and pay Standard Oil a 10 percent commission on every barrel of oil carried by the

Pennsylvania, whether the Standard's or not; Rockefeller committed to buy the assets of the Empire Transportation Company at fire sale prices.[107] Covering his retreat with bravado, Scott demanded a check for $2.5 million within twenty-four hours. "My brother William raised all the money he could in New York," Rockefeller recalled in a 1918 interview, "and in Cleveland I got into the old buggy and drove from one bank to another. 'I must have all you've got. . . . I must catch the noon train.' " Memories of Scott's surrender kindled magnanimity: "Tom Scott was a great man. I remember how he came into the room in the little hotel in Philadelphia where we made the deal with him—bought out his Empire Transportation Company. I can see him now, with his big soft hat, marching into the room in that little hotel to meet us, not to sweep us away (making a full swing of the right arm) as he had always done, but coming in with a smile, walking right up to the cannon's mouth. 'Well, boys, what will we do?' Then he sat down and signed the papers."[108] He did not swing his right arm because his right side was paralyzed. He had suffered a stroke.[109]

Scott had worn just such a hat when he walked into John Thomson's Harrisburg office on that morning in 1850 when his journey began. He'd met rejection that day with the same brass he showed looking into Rockefeller's cannon—he'd turned Thomson around with it. Thomson had set him a course he could not run alone. To prove himself worthy of the crown he risked the kingdom, stumbled, and fell, crushing his subjects. Convalescing in Europe, he received a handwritten letter from Andrew Carnegie. Since Carnegie had "declined" to endorse a note to cover Scott's Texas and Pacific debt at the 1874 meeting in Scott's house, the two had done business together but no longer as friends. Carnegie regretted failing Scott and even blamed himself for Scott's illness. From "a line in a New York paper picked up here," he wrote from Singapore, he had learned that Scott "had been stricken with paralysis and taken abroad." Now, "[a]ll our miserable differences vanish in a moment—I only reproach myself that they ever existed. This blow reveals that there lay deeper in my heart a chord which still bound me to you in memory of a thousand kindnesses for which I am your debtor—I wish I were near you. . . . If you are not so ill as I fear, & return to work, we can remain apart—If you are still ill & in Europe, I wish to go to you as I pass but in either event rest assured for the future I have nothing but kind thoughts & kind words for you & of you." Scott resigned as president of the Pennsylvania Railroad in May 1880. He died a year later, a month after selling the T&P to Jay Gould, who found him "very much broken up, financially, physically and mentally," for $2 million.[110] Tom Scott was fifty-seven. The headline over the *Times*'s front-page obituary caught his life's struggle in a single word: "A Railroad Prince is Dead."[111]

In the hungry America lit by the fires of the Great Railroad Strike the *New York Sun* discovered want beyond want: Railroad workers' wages were *high* compared to the $5 the textile workers of a Rhode Island mill city received for a six-day week of fourteen-hour days. Nor did the railroads employ "women, boys, and girls": In 1875 two times as many children under twelve worked in the "tariff-made state of Rhode Island," mostly in textile mills, as in 1851. "There is, however, little danger of an outbreak among them," the *Sun* observed. "They live, as a rule, in tenements owned by the company employing them; and when they strike they are at once thrown out in the street. Then they are clubbed by policemen, arrested as vagrants, and sent to the county jail, to be released to take their choice of going to work at the old wages or starving." Recently a man had starved to death—three dogs had been found gnawing on his bones.[112]

Chapter Ten

THE POLITICS OF THE FUTURE

We meet in the midst of a nation brought to the verge of moral, political and material ruin. Corruption dominates the ballot-box, the legislatures, the Congress, and touches even the ermine of the bench. . . . The fruits of the toil of millions are boldly stolen to build up colossal fortunes for a few . . . and the possessors of these, in turn, despise the republic and endanger liberty. From the same prolific womb of governmental injustice we breed the two great classes—tramps and millionaires.

—From the Omaha platform of the
People's Party adopted on July 4, 1892

Populism stirred up quiet people. The cliff-fall in prices depicted in the graph on page 304 made Populists. Drought made them. Fences made them and railroads and the crop lien and the chattel mortgage. The millinery shown in the Montgomery Ward catalogue, a judgment on one-bonnet lives, spread Populism. Despair carried it; and hope. Standing for what they called "the politics of the future," the Populists sought to pull the New Deal through the sleeve of time.

Surveying Populism from the perspective on the era developed in this narrative two themes stand out: oligarchy and economic independence. The Populists rose up against the one to defend the other. Populism emerged from what Supreme Court Justice John Marshall Harlan remembered as a "deep feeling of unrest" among Americans in the late 1880s: "The conviction was universal that the country was in real danger from another kind of slavery . . . that would result from the aggregation of capital in the hands of a few individuals controlling, for their own profit and advantage exclusively, the entire business of the country . . . All felt that it must be met . . . by such statutory regulations as would adequately protect the people against oppression and wrong." Law lagged power; nineteenth-century ideology, the twentieth-century economy.

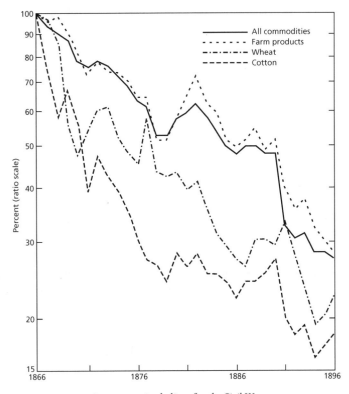

Long-term price decline after the Civil War

The Populists ascribed political causation to economic outcomes—to monopoly, to inequality, to deflation. Where we see forces at work, they saw men. This outlook can seem eccentric to the point of paranoia. In fact, Populism belonged to a tradition of suspicion that infused nineteenth-century American political thought. "Before 1900 inequality was thought to be accomplished by politics," James Huston found in his survey of nineteenth-century American opinion about the distribution of wealth. He calls this bundle of attitudes and rhetoric "the political economy of aristocracy," tracing it to the American revolutionaries' conviction that rule by the few had caused Europe's vicious mal-distribution of wealth. To the revolutionaries, aristocracy, in the words of John Taylor of Caroline, was "an accumulation of wealth by law without industry"—wealth expropriated from labor by government in the pay of avarice. Their template of parasitical aristocracy was the Crown-chartered East India Company and the monopoly prices it charged for its politics-rotten tea. In *Two Letters on the Tea Tax,* John Dickinson spoke for outraged honest labor: "We, our wives and children, together, with the hard earned fruits of our labour, are not *made over* to this almost *bankrupt Company,* to augment their Stock, and to *repair* their *ruined Fortunes.*" Within years of the Revolution, James Madison warned that the National Bank and state-chartered corporations could incubate an American aristocracy. To John C. Calhoun the tariff "was the "means [by] which the fruits of our toil and labour, which on every principle of justice ought to belong to ourselves, are transferred by us to them [northern manufacturers]." To Andrew Jackson, the yeoman farmer and independent artisan could expect to receive the fruits of their labor, Martin A. Lebowitz writes, "only if self-seeking men had not upset the natural balance by obtaining special privileges and other obstructions to justice from government." The political economy of aristocracy, however, rested on more than republican theory. That men sought to accumulate wealth by law without industry was empirical truth in the slave-holding Republic.

The Jacksonian assault on economic privilege bequeathed "populist republicanism" to the Populists. The first (and only) People's Party presidential candidate, James Baird Weaver, deployed it in the 1892 campaign, charging that "[t]he corporations and special interests of every class created during the past twenty-five years by various species of class legislation and favoritism, have grown rich and powerful. . . . The pirate plunders by violence, . . . But the corporation plunders by the permission of or through the agency of the State, and to cut off all hope of redress [corporations] seize upon the courts, which constitute the only hope and refuge of an oppressed people this side of revolution." The "era of class legislation," a reform editor sympathetic to Populism wrote, had sprouted "a mushroom aristocracy of millionaires . . . who, having acquired wealth largely by legislative acts, came to look upon the government as a servant of corporate interests." (Henry Demarest Lloyd counted off "national-bank millionaires, and bond-millionaires, and tariff millionaires, and land-grant millionaires.") In fostering the wealth of monopolists, government stole the "fruits of their labor" from the "producing classes"—John A. Campbell's argument against Louisiana's slaughterhouse monopoly. "Congress has so shaped our laws that the wealth has been legislated out of the pockets of the masses and into the pockets of the classes," the Populists insisted. William A. Peffer, the Populist Senator from Kansas, summed up the era's public life: "Money controls our legislation, it colors our judicial institutions, it manipulates parties, it controls policies."

Still cogent as a critique of Gilded Age political capitalism as late as 1890, populist republicanism was transparently obsolete by 1900. In the decades following the Civil War, the Jacksonian remedies for monopoly—general incorporation, competition, and political laissez-faire—had accelerated the tendency to it. "At the present time . . . monopolies proceed from the nature of industrial society," the Progressive economist Richard Ely contended, "and have for the most part grown up outside the law, and even in spite of the law. . . . It implies a failure to recognize the most obvious social facts to limit the term 'monopoly' to exclusive privileges expressly granted by the legislative branch of government." Using "monopoly" not in its legal sense but as synonym for "corporation" and concentrated wealth, Ely was advancing the twentieth-century view that while government favoritism toward "the busy few" contributes to inequality, the lottery of the market economy creates it without benefit of politicians. Populism was the last protest movement against the "political economy of aristocracy" before the hegemony of the "political economy of capitalism."[1]

The first fall rains were damping the ashes of the Union Depot in Pittsburgh when fourteen men and women meeting in a cabin in remote Lampasas County, Texas, launched the Farmers' Alliance, which Robert A. Caro calls the "greatest mass popular movement in America's history." The alliance eventually recruited nearly half the adult men in Texas and over a quarter of those in the rural South. It reached them through an adult education campaign that lifted the burden of blame from the farmer, telling him what he longed to hear: that he suffered from policy, not his own "overproduction" ("As long as a single cry for bread is heard, it is underproduction and underconsumption"), and from the acts or indifference of a Congress that could "give us a bill in forty-eight hours that would relieve us, but Wall Street says nay," the movement's first national president declared in 1891, adding, "I believe that both parties are afraid of Wall Street. They are not afraid of the people." After education came participation in cooperatives and exchanges that inculcated a "movement culture" based on the vision and practice of self-help. When vested economic power conspired to destroy these institutions failure confirmed the critique the education campaign leveled at the rigged system and set the movement on a course to make the "old parties" afraid of the people.

The Lampasas fourteen were farmers, "comparatively poor," one of them, A. P. Hungate, recalled eighteen years later. They had come together to "more speedily educate ourselves in the science of free government" readying for "the day that is rapidly approaching when all the balance of labor's products becomes concentrated into the hands of a few, there to constitute a power that would enslave posterity." They aimed to build the new Jerusalem in Jay Gould's plundered land—"a grand social and political palace where liberty may dwell and justice be safely domiciled." Hungate's visionary republicanism sprang from years of political education and struggle, and it's unlikely the Lampasans pitched their hopes so high. Rounding up one another's strays and running off rustlers seemed to have been more like the idea.[2]

Still, borrowing the rhetoric and positions of the Greenback-Labor Party, which flared to life in the depression of the 1870s and expired in the prosperity of the early 1880s, Farmers' Alliance leaders sounded Hungate's radical note from the first, striding far ahead of a membership that wanted quotidian relief—seeds for the spring planting, open range for their hogs—toward Hungate's "palace." The "politically ambitious" farmers, doctors, preachers, and journalists comprising the Alliance leadership traced the farmer's troubles, including falling commodity prices and rising railroad and interest rates, to bent government, railroad government, planter government, government for the banker and the bondholder and the land syndicate and the corporation. Populism bit deepest where the evidence for that case was strongest, in states dominated by one party under no competitive pressure to redress farmers' grievances, especially as these were often against the interests protected by the party. Third-party insurgencies break out, a Populist strategist wrote, where governments are seen to be "making bad laws or . . . refusing to legislate on some new issues" and where "all existing parties . . . turn a deaf ear to the demands of the people."[3]

The political etiology of Texas populism illustrates his point. When Thomas L. Nugent, the Populist candidate for governor in 1892, said his party sought office to end "the rule of the ring," Texans knew he was not furnishing a specimen to Richard Hofstadter's "Paranoid Style in American Politics." Texas farmers were not "the innocent pastoral victims of a conspiracy hatched in the distance" but of conspiracies hatched in Austin, one led by Jay Gould, Tom Scott's successor as ringmaster of legislatures.[4]

After buying the Texas and Pacific from the dying Scott, Gould visited Texas to view his property and show his protected person. Death threats came in the mail delivered to his office on Wall Street behind the iron portcullis. A stranger had beaten Gould outside Delmonico's; a betrayed former associate suspended him above an "areaway" and dropped him ("Gould landed on his feet as usual, more's the pity," a Wall Street wag remarked). Gould arrived in Texas just as the legislature was debating whether to establish an independent "Commission of Railroads and Telegraphs" to set rates within parameters established by the legislature but without lobby-driven meddling from politicians. Farmers and shippers had elected legislators pledged to fight for a commission, but Gould, who owned Western Union and controlled the state's major railroads, warned them not to relinquish their authority over rates. He was sanguine about railroad expansion in Texas, he told the *Galveston News,* but "There is one peril—injudicious interference by Congresses and State Legislatures— with business." He blamed the Jay Cooke–induced Panic of 1873 on the "Granger legislation of the Northwest" giving states the power to regulate railroads and grain elevators, legislation that the Waite court had ruled constitutional in *Munn v. Illinois.* Enacting his argument that regulation would chill the business climate, he announced a freeze on construction of a rail link between Fort Worth and Waco until the legislators rejected the independent commission bill. They bent to his will. Between 1881 and 1887 he used like leverage to defeat similar bills. Gould returned in the latter year after the Texas House voted for a commission. Rumors that he had acquired an interest in Standard Oil had lent momentum to commission proponents, the once-fawning *News* calling him "a monopolist masticating a monopoly." However, after the "railroad king" remarked to a Dallas newspaper that "unless there is such legislation as will drive capital away I think that railroad building in Texas will be very active," the Senate interred the commission.[5]

No commission impeded Gould and Collis P. Huntington, in 1885, from fixing their own rates in a no-competition "pool" agreement that the Farmers' Alliance branded a scheme of "arrogant capitalists and powerful corporations" in league with purchasable politicians in Austin. The next year, at Gould's beck, the governor dispatched eight companies of state militia and a company of Texas Rangers to crush the Great Southwest Strike that erupted on the Texas & Pacific and other Gould lines. Gould placed the Knights of Labor strikers on the wrong side of the law by making them federal employees. The leader of the strike, Martin Irons, later claimed that he had been forced at gunpoint to sign a statement attesting to the honesty of the strike vote, then followed for days by an "armed stranger" monitoring his silence. The gunmen, one historian infers, were Gould's agents acting to provoke the strike to break the union. The Knights had struck against Gould successfully in 1885 and his reputation for ruthlessness at stake, he responded by having the T&P default on bonds held by its Gould-owned parent company, the Missouri-

Pacific, and placing the T&P in federal receivership.* Federal judges, following the precedent set by Judge Drummond and his colleagues in 1877, issued injunctions outlawing the strike while state judges deputized Gould's strikebreakers. Workers resisted, sabotaging locomotives and destroying Texas & Pacific property and equipment. "Thousands were indicted, hundreds were jailed, and many were killed," Lawrence Goodwyn writes. The dead and wounded bore out Gould's boast that "I can hire one half of the working class to kill the other half." The strikers, who lost the strike and their jobs, were casualties of "rule of the ring."[6]

So were farmers kept from grazing their livestock on the range by barbed-wire fences strung up by ranchers, cattle companies, and foreign-owned land syndicates. Invented in the 1870s, barbed wire was at first resisted by cattlemen. It might not hold their steers; it might gut them. John "Bet-a-Million" Gates, a wire salesman, silenced those fears in a demonstration in the most famous space in Texas, fencing in the plaza in front of the Alamo, herding steers into it, and stampeding them. After charging the fence a few times, they backed off, huddling together in the plaza center. Gates's showmanship launched a "terrific race to fence in the open range." Taking out high-interest loans from eastern and foreign bankers to buy wire by the carload, cattle barons hung wire across vast areas of public land—a single North Texas ranch strung up 1,500 miles of it. By the late 1880s, from Texas to Wyoming, 10 million acres of the public domain had been fenced in. "Posts every 30 feet and four strands of wire spider-webbed the West," writes an historian of barbed wire.

Farmers and small ranchers counted on the free range. Their cattle and hogs grazed and watered on it, and their economic survival depended on it. In winter storms, their cattle would drift for miles until they found shelter, but the wire stopped them and they froze to death. "I saw drifts of dead cattle along that fence," a Texas cowhand related, "sometimes 400 yards wide, just like they had bedded down." The fences emblemized what Richard Maxwell Brown calls the "Western Civil War of Incorporation," set off by the "consolidating authority of modern capitalistic forces"

---

* The strikers circulated anti-Semitic caricatures of Gould. For decades, anti-Semitism had been an element in Gould's demonization, though Gould, Edward J. Renehan writes, was "an unenthusiastic Presbyterian by birth and a perfunctory Episcopalian by marriage. . . . Gould himself [told] associates that his 'presumed Hebraic origin' could only enhance his reputation as a force against which resistance would prove fatal." Edward J. Renehan, Jr., *Dark Genius of Wall Street: The Misunderstood Life of Jay Gould, King of the Robber Barons* (New York: Basic Books, 2005), p. 3.

in conflict with pre-modern America and Americans. Voicing a resonant sentiment about those forces, the *Wyoming Sentinel* cautioned that, "Some morning we will wake up to find that a corporation has run a wire fence about the boundary line of Wyoming, and all within the same have been notified to move." Eighteen hundred eighty-two saw the outbreak of "fencing wars," fought to defend the grazing economy against incorporation, up and down the wired Plains. In Texas night-riding bands—some made up of Alliancemen—cut wire and tore up fence posts along the farming-ranching frontier in the Cross Timbers region northwest of Austin. Some ranchers found coffins nailed to posts with attached penciled scrawls warning, "This will be your end if you keep fencing." Dozens were shot in confrontations between fence-cutters and fence-defenders. The governor sent the Texas Rangers against the wire-cutters and in January 1884 convened a special session of the legislature, which, in an outrageous display of ring rule, passed a constitutional amendment outlawing the carrying of hidden wirecutters.[7]

In Georgia the planter-dominated Democratic oligarchy passed "stock laws" jeopardizing the economic independence of upcountry farmers. Since the seventeenth century upcountry yeoman with plots of land too small to feed and water hogs had pastured them on the southern range— timberlands and fields often owned by planters or providing concourses to planter land in cultivation. Any fallow or unfenced land was fair pasture for the hog. Some states made it illegal to impede the hog's search for mud or to interfere with the immense hog herds drovers led across the open range, collecting the upcountry farmers' hogs and driving them to coastal markets.[8]

Little the upcountry farmer possessed mattered more than his hog. With it he could be self-sufficient—he did not have to borrow from the furnishing merchant to feed his family; without a hog, he faced debt peonage for food. The hog "could thrive in the Southern uplands or in the lowland canebrakes as long as he could run free, but he could not survive if penned up," the historians Forrest McDonald and Grady McWhiney write in "The South from Self-Sufficiency to Peonage." The pig is "thermo-dynamically ill-adapted" to hot climates, according to the Agricultural Research Council Institute of Animal Physiology: "[A]dult pigs will die if exposed to direct sunlight and air temperatures over 98 degrees." The pig cannot sweat, needing "external moisture" to keep his skin damp. "It prefers to do this by wallowing in fresh clean mud, but it will cover its skin with its own urine and feces if nothing else is available. Below 84 degrees F, pigs kept in pens deposit their excreta away from their sleeping and feeding areas. While above 84 degrees F they begin to excrete indiscriminately throughout the pen." In the antebellum South planters lobbied state and local governments to hold farmers liable for hog-wreaked damage to cotton fields or to force farmers to pen their hogs, but the planters lacked the votes to get their way and the range stayed open. General Sherman's strategic warfare against the southern home front and the incursions of soldiers from both armies decimated the southern hog. By 1880, 2.6 million fewer hogs than in 1860 grazed on a closing range.[9]

Planter and farmer had reached an uneasy modus vivendi in the antebellum economy, "local in character and regulated by custom," but that could not withstand what Steven Hahn calls "the vortex of the [postwar] cotton economy." To prosper in that national volume market, planters (and merchants and farmers with the same interests) moved to bring timberlands and fields into cultivation. Their long conflict with the upcountry farmer entered the endgame.

"The citizens of this county have and always have had the legal, moral, and Bible right to let their stock run at large," a Georgia farmer insisted. Planters disputed the "legal." Insisting on the priority of property rights over social custom, they mounted a puissant campaign for stock laws and fence laws. Backed by the votes of their black sharecroppers, in some counties they could outvote the upcountry farmer and, McDonald and McWhiney note, "through the corrupt influence of their well-heeled Northern connections" easily out-lobby him. County by county, militia district by militia district, the southern range slowly but inexorably closed. Hogs were penned up. Many died; more sickened. Antebellum southerners consumed about 150 pounds of pork and fifty pounds of beef per capita—men, women, and children. That is "five times the amount of *total* protein intake recommended for adult males by the Food and Nutrition Board of the National Research Council in 1978," McDonald and McWhiney wrote in 1980. But on their new diet of fat, pen-fed pork and milled corn, imported from outside the South, the southern "plain folk" consumed little protein and were subject to pellagra and other food-borne diseases. Rather than stay and fall to the black margins of the white caste, in every year of the 1870s, 100,000 farmers and tenants from the southern upcountry scrawled on their cabin doors "GTT" and were "Gone to Texas." But fences followed them.[10]

The Texas fence war, the stock law controversy in the South, introduced an inchoate class politics, a disruptive novelty in a system dedicated to white supremacy. "Where you found the hogs running loose, there were lots of Populists," a Democrat recalled years later, "where you found them penned up, the Democrats were in the majority."[11] And that majority, tethered to office by a Pavlovian manipulation of racist fear, served "Old South" planter and "New South" business interests. Farmers might complain about lien laws giving the planter first call on a bankrupt tenant's chattel and fence laws imperiling their economic independence, but in the one-party South they could be ignored with political impunity.

The hurt and anger expressed by a Texas Populist was not his alone:

> The chairman of our great state democratic executive comeety, call us skunks, anything that has the sent of the plowhandle smells like a polecat to them. (I want to tell you to tell me how in the dickens these God forsakin money mongers know how anything would smell in the nostral of an honest man.) And Judge Terrell went out of his way in his speech at Georgetown to call our wives and little children in their cabbins over the country, spoonds by the wayside, a reglar fish pond off which nabobs feed.

Democrats tended to live in or near towns, and told town jokes about the rural Populists, like this one from the Democratic paper in Lampasas:

> Will you please tell me how I may recognize a soaptail [Populist hick] when I call at his home? I am an agent and am anxious for information on this point.
> Answer: —You can always tell a soaptail by shaking hands with his wife. If her hands are covered with corns and have the appearance of having wielded the ax and held the plow, you may rest assured her husband is a genuine soaptail.[12]

Letters published in the *Southern Mercury*, the journal of the Southern Farmers' Alliance, testify to privation and reveal bruised dignity. "Our lot is cast here in a rough portion of the land," a member of the New Chapel Alliance of Blanco County writes. "But if we do live away up here on the Pedernales River, amid rocks, cliffs, and waterfalls, cedars and wild oaks, we are not varmints, but have hearts just like men." "I never got to school in my life, nor learned my letters till I was 35 years old," sixty-year-old Larkin Landrum wrote. "If this is printed and I can read it I will write once more; for if I can read it I know other people can, who have been to school and worn shoes." The letters plead for help. "[I]t grieves me to chronicle the sad condition of this section," James Blevin reports of the state of morale among Alliancemen in Dripping Springs. "We are worse than lukewarm. We are cold, almost to heart, and unless we can get a remedy soon, we are gone."[13]

Pleas for remedy went unanswered by Democrats in Texas and Republicans in drought-tried Kansas, a quintessence of government for the corporation. "Republican legislatures of Kansas simply obeyed the orders of railroad companies," summed up an aide to the state party boss. It was said that "no candidate could be selected for any office, from township trustee to governor, who was objectionable to the Sante Fe [Railroad]." Overcharged on shipping rates on a scale amounting to "a most gigantic robbery," Kansas farmers suffered from one-party rule, but, pawns of bloody-shirt campaigns against the Democratic opposition led by Senator John J. Ingalls, "the nation's leading Democrat-baiter," kept voting for the party. Prosperity did the rest, solidifying GOP control. The prosperity was precarious, flowing from speculative fever. "Most of us crossed the Mississippi or the Missouri with no money, but with vast wealth of hope," a participant in the action recalled years later. "Haste to get rich . . . made us borrowers, and the borrower has made booms, and booms made men wild, and Kansas became a vast insane asylum covering 80,000 square miles." In the 1880s a half-million people migrated to Kansas drawn by state propaganda printed in four languages, by the boosterism of local newspapers—"In less than a decade the inhabitants of the Ninnescah valley will roll in luxury and wealth," "Eureka! The Eldorado Toward which All the Union is Rapidly Moving. Our Realty Record Shows Conclusively that Wichita . . ."—and by the advertising campaigns of the Santa Fe, the Union Pacific, and the Kansas Pacific. To hold the new Kansans the Kansas legislature created four new counties in 1885, eleven in 1886, and five in 1887. "A new map must be made every week to keep up with the growth of towns in Kansas," the *Chicago Tribune* reported. In Kansas City more real estate sold in April 1886 than in all of 1885. Topeka—"The New Suburb of the Great Metropolis Presents Itself to the Public"—set a record for sales for the month of October 1886; and broke it on a single day the following March. State and local government fueled the boom with bond issues to finance railroad construction: 80 percent of the municipal debt incurred as of 1888 went to aid railroads, which proliferated. A six-week stretch of 1887 saw sixteen new railroad corporations chartered and contracts let for "thirteen new branches of old roads." The increase in Kansas's public debt led the nation in the 1880s; per capita private debt, mostly for farm mortgages, was four times the national average. "I could not loan the money as fast as it came in," the secretary of a western loan company said of the eastern capital being lent at high interest to borrowers the lenders "did not know . . . on land which they had never seen." And why not? Wasn't Kansas, in the words of a Santa Fe ad, "the best thing in the west"? Then the hot winds arrived and blew the Kansas bubble out.[14]

In the early 1880s rainfall beyond the ninety-eighth meridian averaged 21.63 inches, more than the eighteen to twenty inches needed to grow corn and wheat. But a decade of drought began in 1887, with such moisture as the soil captured evaporating in the "hot winds." "Beginning usually in June and lasting through September, blowing from sunrise to sunset, day after day, week after week," the winds withered the corn crop. Only half of that year's corn and wheat survived to be harvested. Nature hit the Plains farmer just as the bottom fell out of the market for his crops. Soon he was selling corn that cost $8.60 an acre to grow for $6.60; and $9.04 wheat for $3.53. An exodus fairly emptied western Kansas. "In God we trusted, in Kansas we busted," read the legend painted on the wagons crossing back over the Missouri.[15]

Farmers who stayed demanded relief—agitated to have interest rates agreed in the boom adjusted downward in the bust, for tax cuts, and railroad rate reductions. Failing that, having assumed chattel mortgages, the farmers would lose everything they had. A new pressure group took up their cause. Missionaries from the Texas Farmers' Alliance, returning home after organizing in Missouri, stopped in Cowley County, Kansas, close to the Oklahoma border. There they contacted the three sons of James Vincent, an abolitionist editor and correspondent for William Lloyd Garrison's *Liberator*. Henry, Leopold, and Cuthbert Vincent had moved to Winfield the year before and with a "thirty-five dollar hand press" started publishing *The American Non-Conformist and Kansas Industrial Liberator*, which in its first issue vowed that "in every struggle it will endeavor to take the side of the underdog." With the Vincents' support a Texan went out among them, organizing sub-alliances in Cowley County in once "Bloody Kansas," scene of guerrilla fighting between southern and northern settlers in the 1850s. The Republican farmers who heard out the Texan speaking in the accent of rebellion could not have guessed it, but he represented the most significant southern invasion of the North since Lee broke into Pennsylvania in the summer of 1863.[16]

To contain the discontent, Republican politicians promised to cut interest rates and adopt other reforms pushed by the independent Union Labor Party, making headway among farmers in the run-up to the 1888 election. "No Republican need leave his party for the purpose of accomplishing any needed reform," a spokesman assured voters after the party's state convention, and for good measure the Republicans waved the bloody shirt: A vote for a third party was a vote for the party of "treason." Though both Kansas senators were corporate officers of "major financial firms" and though the Republicans had campaigned for railroad regulation in 1882 only to betray that commitment in office, the voters believed the GOP would deliver, giving the party thirty-nine of the forty seats in the state Senate and 121 of the 125 in the House. "Our Republicans here, with coats of blue and heads of gray," a farmer wrote in a letter published in the *Kansas Farmer,* have "[t]heir eyes . . . fixed on Topeka, and woe to the man that sells them out."[17]

In Topeka the legislators not only broke their campaign promises, they opposed printing a message from the departing governor reminding his party to keep them. Bank and loan company lobbyists had their way with the senators. During the debate over a law penalizing usury, "One senator declared that he lent money at 24 percent and was assured that he could continue to do so under the new law." The legislature defeated bills shifting more of the tax burden onto railroads, banning alien syndicates from buying up land, restricting the ability of municipalities to issue new railroad bonds, and arming the board of railroad commissioners with the power to check rate discrimination against farmers—in short, the Republicans sold out the voters. Rarely if ever in American history have politicians so brazenly invited their constituents' wrath. William Peffer, the editor of the *Kansas Farmer,* warned the Republicans, "A day of reckoning is coming." Reporting on Alliance meetings for the Lawrence paper, the soon-to-be Populist firebrand Annie Diggs predicted early retirement for the "gullible farmer" cliché. "He is awake."[18]

Sensitive to Republican attacks on the Southern Farmers' Alliance as a "rebel yell" "officered by rebel brigadiers," Kansas organizers forged a State Alliance and affiliated it with the Northern Farmers' Alliance, which, through the 1880s, had organized the Plains states and beyond. From Washington state to Minnesota, farmers, laborers, and miners were being radicalized by vain appeals for relief to governments that plied the politics of distraction to stay in office. In Colorado the Republican machine felt it could ignore not only the "calamity howlers" but the calamities—failing farms and unpaid miners. "In my brief experience in this state," a "stalwart Republican" told delegates to the 1890 state convention, "I have known upon occasion and occasion certain statements were put forth as a plank of the party in our platform that no one thought about after putting the plank in the platform." Promise the voters nothing for a change, he argued, and keep *that* promise. Flourishing the bloody shirt, the *Denver*

Road feebly argued for voters to resist the Populists and stay with the GOP: "The Republican party put down the rebellion, and though that happened possibly before you were born, you are still under obligation to vote as your father did before you."[19] Jay Burrows, leader of the Nebraska State Alliance, had wanted to keep out of politics but changed his mind when, acting for the railroad lobby, the Republicans dropped a "mildly anti-monopoly judge" from their 1889 state ticket and when, after conferencing with railroad officials, Governor John M. Thayer rescinded his call for a special session of the legislature to pressure the roads to offer Nebraska farmers the 30 percent lower "Iowa rates" on wheat shipped to Chicago. "[W]e witness the political machinery of the dominant party used to defeat the will of the people," Burrows declared in June, endorsing the formation of a new party to *"Smash These Machines."* "Having experienced a similar process of conversion," Jeffrey Ostler writes, "nine hundred delegates representing tens of thousands of Nebraska farmers organized the state People's party on 29 July."[20]

In her 1902 novel, *Out of the West,* Elizabeth Higgins portrayed a region in intellectual ferment: "People commenced to think who had never thought before, and people talked who had seldom spoken. . . . Little by little they commenced to theorize upon their condition. Despite the poverty of the country, the books of Henry George, [Edward] Bellamy, and other economic writers were bought up as fast as the dealers could supply them. . . . [The people] discussed income tax and the single tax; they talked of government ownership and the abolition of private property; fiat money and the unity of labor."[21]

In Kansas the people talked through the letters columns of Peffer's *Kansas Farmer;* at neighborhood suppers; and, more and more, at Alliance meetings. By the spring of 1889, twenty sub-alliances were being organized every week.[22] They generated a "movement culture" woven of picnics and parades. Early comers to a parade might stand up in their buckboards and scan the plain for the heralding dust. Slowly, one by one, the white-covered wagons rolled into sight, many hung with evergreens to contrast the Alliance's "living issues" with the desiccated tariff and bloody shirt.[23] As the first wagons mounted a rise families looking back must have felt raised up high atop the long white column. The wagon trains displayed the farmer's strength to himself and to the towns. A six-mile line of 1,500 wagons passed through Wichita. In Medicine Lodge the wagons took an hour to file by the post office (one wagon, full of children, marked "Overproduction").[24] At the picnic grounds there would be lectures and harangues—"it was sometimes necessary to have four orators in operation at one time for all to hear." Brass bands played, the diva of the ninth grade delivered a solo, then all sang together. One ballad, to the tune of "Good-bye, My Lover, Good-bye," became the anthem of the Populist Revolt in Kansas:

GOOD-BYE, MY PARTY, GOOD-BYE
It was no more than a year ago,
Good-bye, my party, good-bye.
That I was in love with my party so,
Good-bye, my party, good-bye . . .
To hear ought else I never would go . . .

I was raised up in the kind of school . . .
That taught how to bow to money rule . . .
And it made of me a "Kansas Fool" . . .
When they found I was a willing tool.

The old party is on the downward track,
Good-bye, my party, good-bye
Picking its teeth with a tariff tack,
Good-bye, my party, good-bye.
With a placard pinned upon his back,
Good-bye, my party, good-bye.
That plainly states, "I will never go back";
Good-bye, my party, good-bye.

To the tune of "Save a Poor Sinner like Me," "The Hayseed" announced the day of reckoning:

I was once a tool of oppression,
And as green as a sucker could be
And monopolies banded together
To beat a poor hayseed like me.

The railroads and old party bosses
Together did sweetly agree:
And they thought there would be little trouble
In working a hayseed like me.

But now I've roused up a little
And their greed and corruption I see,
And the ticket we vote next November
Will be made up of hayseeds like me.[25]

By November, frustrated as a pressure group, the three-year-old Kansas Alliance, in fury at the politicians, had crossed over into politics. It bolted from the party of the fathers after submitting the Alliance platform to the Kansas congressional delegation and receiving the unqualified endorsement of only Senator Preston B. Plumb, and after Senator Ingalls revealed the cynical heart of Gilded Age politics when asked for his thoughts on the clamor for reform in Kansas.[26] "The purification of politics is an iridescent dream," he told the *New York World*. "Government is force. Politics is a battle for supremacy. . . . To defeat the antagonist and expel the party in power is the purpose. . . . This modern cant about the corruption of politics is fatiguing in the extreme. It proceeds from the tea-custard and syllabub dilettantism, the frivolous and desultory sentimentalism of epicenes."[27] "Epicenes"? The "horny-handed sons of toil" in the Mound City sub-alliance? Those farmers who didn't cut their ties to the GOP over Ingalls's Latin expectoration on their manhood could have found fresh provocation in another interview the senator gave. In an articulation of the ideology of indifference worthy of Grover Cleveland, whose veto of the Texas "seeds' bill" to aid stricken farmers made recruits for the Texas Alliance, Ingalls told an editor who advocated "positive legislation" to deal with the crisis on the Kansas farm: "I belong to the school of politicians who think . . . government should interfere as little as possible in the affairs of its citizens. The difficulties in society arise from the fact that Providence has established unequal conditions, making some men wise and others foolish; some men provident and others thriftless; some men industrious and energetic and others idle and self indulgent."[28] Meanwhile farmers in western Kansas, the literary historian Vernon Parrington recalled, sat at night by their kitchen stoves "watching the year's crop go up the chimney."[29] At a "convention of the people" held in Topeka in August 1890 the Alliance founded the People's Party, and nominated candidates to unseat the Republican state legislators who voted in John Ingalls as prelude to unseating "Mr. Republican" himself.[30]

The fall campaign—a "pentacost of politics"—composes a memorable set piece of the Populist revolt. It starred two women orators, Annie Diggs and Mary E. Lease, the "People's Joan of Arc," who, in a voice the *Kansas City Star* called "a pure sweet contralto," telescoped the long fall from Gettysburg in the era's recurring refrain: "It is no longer a government of the people, for the people, by the people, but a government of Wall Street, for Wall Street, and by Wall Street." One of the first women lawyers in Kansas, a campaigner for woman suffrage, prohibition, and freedom for

Mary E. Lease

her ancestral Ireland, a member of the Knights of Labor and the Farmers' Alliance, Lease was a charismatic platform speaker and bruising debater.* A sentence from her debate with a Republican politician in Concordia reads like Dadaist geography but must have sounded like incantatory eloquence: "India rich with every fertility of soil and climate, centralization of wealth, the curse of the money power, the incubus of bonds was loaded on India, and India went down as Persia and Spain, and Greece and Rome, as Turkey and Ireland went down, from the incubus of bonds, the

---

* Lease was also "a fervent exponent of Anglo-Saxon superiority" and a "racist," Walter T. K. Nugent writes. She was "responsible for far more of her share of references to Shylock, Rothschild, Jewish bankers, and British gold, and her prominence in the movement put their ugly onus on the mass of Populists who had never dreamt of such things." Walter T. K. Nugent, *The Tolerant Populists: Kansas Populism and Nativism* (Chicago: University of Chicago Press, 1963), p. 83.

curse of the money power." Though historians assume she did, she did *not* adjure Kansas farmers to "raise less . . . corn and more hell," but regarding it as "a right good bit of advice" accepted the attribution from reporters. Her own words were if anything more inflammatory. "[W]in this ballot with the ballot if possible, but if not that way then with the bayonet," she goaded one audience. If she sheltered "rankly personal" attacks on Republican editors behind her sex, they used it to insult her with impunity, Mr. Lease being at home looking after the four Lease children. The "petticoated smut-mill" earned the "$10 a night . . . this reform People's party" allegedly paid her, a Wellington editor allowed after she spoke there, for her "venomous tongue is the only thing marketable about the old harpy, and we suppose she is justified in selling it where it commands the highest price." Diggs, "a diminutive suffragette who realized that Populism meant woman's rights," sailed against the wind in urging Alliance audiences to admit small merchants as members—"It is no flowery bed of ease to be in the struggle of trade"—but made amends with darts like this: "John J. Ingalls never smelled gunpowder in his life. His war record is confined to court marshalling a chicken thief." Republican papers like the *Walnut Valley Times* mocked her:

> I heard the voice of Anna Diggs
> Across the city park;
> It scared the geese and pigs
> And made the watch dog bark.

The Populist revolt, Diggs reflected in 1901, was rooted less in economic distress than in the people's "discovery that the national machinery of both the Republican and Democratic parties was set to the service of privileged classes and of commercial combinations."

Kansas also witnessed an invasion by a genuine "rebel brigadier," L. L. Polk of North Carolina, the president of the Southern Farmers' Alliance. Addressing a crowd of 6,000 at Winfield on the Fourth of July, Colonel Polk asked "Will you tell me who has a better right in America to go into politics than the farmers?" and then prophesied a fresh line of division in America. "You will see arrayed on one side the great magnates . . . and Wall Street brokers, and the plutocratic power; and on the other you will see the people . . . there shall be no Mason and Dixon line on the Alliance map of the future."[31]

The Populists reached for the politics of the future, but the politics of the past overtook them. The past lay waiting in the South.

By 1892, 40,000 Alliance lecturers swarmed over the rural South speaking at Texas "camps," Georgia "rallies," and Virginia "gatherings." No other radical movement in American history set such store by education. Striking autoworkers sat down. Civil rights activists marched. Alliance farmers learned.[32]

A meeting might open with a didactic anthem from the Alliance songbook. "The Future America" registered an ancient republican fear of concentrated wealth conducing to power, power to privilege, privilege to rule:

> My Country tis of thee
> Land of lost Liberty,
> Of thee I sing.
> Land where the millionaires,
> Who govern our affairs
> Own for themselves and heirs,
> Hail to the King.
>
> Land where the wealthy few
> Can make the many do
> Their royal will,
> And tax for selfish greed
> The toilers till they bleed
> And those not yet weak-kneed.
> Crush down and kill.

Over a third of Alliance leaders had attended college but the lecturer-organizers were usually self-educated and when chronicling the farmers' woes spoke from life. There is a class war, and you are losing it, they told farmers. "[T]here are two distinct and well-defined classes composing society, the producing and non-producing classes," a lecturer informed the producing classes of Natchitoches Parish, Louisiana. "Between these two is an irrepressible conflict." Using William Seward's 1858 phrase for the confrontation between slavery and freedom italicized the conflict between the good people of Natchitoches and "the plutes." Those plutes! They hired politicians to pass laws inimical to the farmer—laws establishing a national banking system, withdrawing greenbacks from circulation, demonitizing silver, and restoring gold; laws parceling out the continent to railroad, mining, cattle, and lumber companies; laws protecting lusty-limbed "infant industries" that taxed the farmer, laws permitting monopolies in manufacturing and transportation that gouged the farmer, laws

restricting mortgages to chattel that impoverished the farmer. Who benefited from these laws? About here the lecturer might name the men
behind the curtain, and Jay Gould, John Rockefeller, Leland Stanford,
Andrew Carnegie, and J. P. Morgan would be execrated to the echo.
"There is something radically wrong at the heart of things," lecturer John
Gardner told a Texas crowd. "[T]he kitchen servant has never been invited
into the parlor of the nation, and until recently has submissively attended
to his scrubbing, while the protected manufacturer and his political pilots
have been playing cards in the drawing room and euchering him out of
the fruit of his sweaty face." To obtain that fruit the farmer had to shuck
his individualism, join the Alliance, and through its "cooperative commonwealth" gain with others what he could not gain alone. And all this
for dues of 25 cents a year. The lecturer would sign up persuaded farmers
(five or more qualified as a sub-alliance); pass out membership forms,
ledgers, and copies of the Alliance constitution and its secret rituals;
pocket his 50-cent "organizing fee"; and leave for the next town.[33]

The lecturers ignited a wildfire. "In spite of all the opposing influences
that could be brought to bear in Wake County," one reported from North
Carolina, "I met the farmers twenty-seven times and twenty-seven times
they organized." By 1891 about every township in Missouri had a sub-
alliance, 4,000 in all. The Alliance, a Grange leader enviously noted,
"swept across Mississippi like a cyclone." For twenty years Alabama farmers had been lost in "inextricable darkness" but now, the president of the
Limestone County Alliance wrote, now "The light of the Alliance was . . .
breaking upon society with healing on its wings." Georgia farmers felt a
loosening of the lien yoke around their necks. "We are going to get out of
debt, we are going to be free and independent people once more," a Georgia Allianceman wrote the *Southern Mercury* in Dallas. "Mr. Editor, we
Georgia people are in earnest."[34]

Once the sub-alliances were set up education resumed indoors.
"Economic tribulation does not necessarily spark political insurgency,"
Steven Hahn observes, "and it dispenses no inherent ideology to its victims." Alliance schools supplied the ideology, in the terms, of Antonio
Gramsci, introduced in chapter one, a counter-hegemonic "conception of
the world." Following a curriculum developed by Dr. Charles Macune, the
major theorist of Populist policies and editor of the *National Economist,* the
Washington-based Southern Alliance paper he founded, the sub-alliances
corrected "miseducation" with reeducation. "Have plenty of music, get
children to speak pieces, and have a short dialogue if convenient," Macune

advised sub-alliance presidents. According to the 1900 census, of the 231 counties in the country with illiteracy rates above 25 percent, 226 were in the South, so Alliance pedagogy stressed oral presentations and many of the farmer-scholars depended on their children to help them in class. Attendance was mandatory.[35]

The first lesson posed this question: "What is the wealth per capita in the United States?" Armed with an estimate of the total wealth and population in 1890, the children chalked their calculations on the blackboard. The answer stung: the "wealth" of farmers—a mule, a mortgaged hog— fell far below the national average. But the lesson also rebutted the tragic view of economic advance shared by Adam Smith, Karl Marx, and John Maynard Keynes that, in Macune's summary, "it is a matter of necessity that some people should suffer, even here." There was more than enough to go around; no one *had* to suffer. A succeeding lesson excavating John D. Rockefeller's fortune drove the point home.[36]

Alliance economics taught the quantity theory of money. In 1868 hogs sold for 10 cents a pound and corn for 45 cents a bushel. Why? There was $50 in currency for every man, woman, and child, the Populists reasoned. In 1889, with only $6 per capita circulating, hogs sold for 3 cents a pound and corn for 10 cents a bushel. The remedy: Increase the money supply to $50 per capita. A new institution, the sub-treasury, would put most of that in farmers' pockets. The sub-treasuries would double as government-run warehouses where farmers could store their crops waiting for a rising market to sell them, and banks. The government would extend a loan to the farmer based on 80 percent value of his crop, and he would pay the loan plus interest back after the government sold his crops. The sub-treasury system would entail the largest government outlays of any domestic program before the New Deal. So it is fitting to note that $50 of currency per capita was not reached until 1940. To reach it in 1892 would have required a $5.4 billion infusion into the economy. According to one analysis, that would have produced "as large an increase in the price level as actually took place from 1890 to 1947 to attain"—an epic inflation. Money was Populism's weak point.[37]

"By controlling the channels of information," two Populist lecturers wrote in Macune's paper, "the capitalist holds your confidence with one hand, while with the other he picks your pocket." History according to the Alliance clashed with the history in school textbooks, which extolled industrialists and the emerging corporate economy of which textbook publishers were a part. Harper Brothers, D. Appleton and Company, and

A. S. Barnes and Company had formed a combination, a "textbook trust," the Alliance asserted, that overcharged for books and monopolized curricula by offering "kickbacks" to state and local school boards. Macune's history lessons, ancient and modern, upended the "Great Man" history of the textbooks, putting bottom rail top: "[O]ur country will be what we, the people, make it; the day of the hero is passed; we are all heroes, or ought to be."[38]

The Alliance had raised chiliastic expectations. Macune identified the Alliance "with the cause of Jesus Christ."[39] "We believe in our hearts that the Alliance is of God the father," the president of Alabama's Limestone County Alliance, rhapsodized, "that he has seen our sorrow and answered our prayers."[40] While laborers could better their condition by striking employers, "The farmer's enemy was not an employer but a *system*," Elizabeth Sanders observes, "—a system of credit, supply, transportation, and marketing."[41] And as soon as Alliance cooperatives started to make a difference in farmers' lives, lowering the cost of purchases by buying in bulk or increasing the farmers' returns by targeted marketing, the system struck back. Fearing "the ill will of a certain class of business men who considered their interests antagonistic to our order," Macune testified, Texas banks refused credit to Alliance schemes to pool members' property and borrow against it.[42] The Texas cotton exchange deemed handling Alliance-bulked cotton unprofitable. Since any loss of sales to Alliance stores impaired their ability to repay wholesalers for goods charged at 18 percent, local merchants pressured manufacturers to boycott Alliance cooperatives. "Mississippi locals could not get farm implements, clubs in North Carolina were denied wholesale prices on shoes, and Texas farmers could not buy flour directly from the mill" while "Virginia railroads refused to give discount shipping rates available to other large customers," an Alliance historian writes. "Not until a co-operative enterprise shows signs of unmistakable victory," Macune lamented, "does the opposition crystallize and unite their whole force to drive it out of existence."[43]

What did he expect? The cooperatives recruited members for the Alliance (though, since one study found only 344 in the eleven leading Populist states, how many is a question), and some succeeded for a time.[44] But they were also bait for a momentous switch. The Alliance radicals had to know that the system exposed by their lecturers would crush the "cooperative commonwealth" in its first stirrings. Either the system's rules must be changed or the system itself changed. Just how was the "cooperative commonwealth" to rub along with corporate capitalism anyway? Or was the idea that it would replace corporate capitalism? Populist agitprop—"Capitalism places property before life, thereby declaring war on humanity"—can leave that impression, though Alliance leaders could not avow that goal without arming the charge that, behind the cornpone and the Christianity, they were "Communards." Even changing the rules of the system would necessitate a massive rearranging of its furniture. Thus, if banks slam their doors on the Alliance and the furnishing merchant won't let the farmer up, we'll get government loans through the sub-treasury. If manufacturers collude to destroy competition, we'll break up the trusts and make the economy safe for the cooperative and the small producer. If the railroads discriminate against rural shippers, we'll follow Europe and nationalize them, freeing up millions of railroad-held acres of free land for farmers. To achieve these "demands" the Alliance had to first capture the state. Voting for "good men" in the old parties wouldn't get it done; as a matter of interests, politics, principle, and history the old parties opposed the demands. Only by forming a third party could the Alliance realize them. The radicals must have suspected that all along, and if they did not build the experience of failure into the "movement culture" to radicalize the farmer, break his loyalty to the old parties, and mobilize him into a new one, they quickly saw the uses of failure. In their history of the Alliance S. O. Daws and W. L. Garvin feed that conjecture when they term "cases of opposition" a "benefit and a great blessing in every way, for they brought the farmer face to face with the evils and wrongs that stand opposed to their interests in marketing their produce. . . . The efforts on the part of the enemies of the Alliance . . . to break the combination of farmers have done so much good for the Order as any one thing." In radical as in party politics elites manipulate "the people" to further their agendas and the left wing of the Southern Alliance to which Daws belonged had argued for a third party all along.[45]

In his first lesson, following the advice to encourage children to speak pieces, Macune warned the sub-alliance presidents to avoid politics like "poison." He drew on sobering experience. Within a year of its founding, having organized throughout North Texas, the Lampasas Alliance had grown big enough to hold a state convention. There it split in two. One faction argued that to ameliorate the land, credit, and transportation problems consigning yeoman farmers to lien-slavery the Alliance had to enter politics as an independent force or align with the radical Greenback-Labor

Party, which alone addressed those issues; another faction warned against taking that "fork in the road." White Texas had just bloodily redeemed the state from Reconstruction, and the Republican Party, with its enfranchised black base still intact, remained potent. To divide the white vote between the "party of the fathers" and a third party invited the return of "Negro domination."

The reconstructed history of Reconstruction reveals nothing approximating that, but to understand why fathers stopped talking to their recreant Populist children, why Populists lost friends, jobs, or customers, we need to see Reconstruction as it looked to its white enemies—to recall John Campbell's revulsion over ex-slaves holding positions of dignity in postwar New Orleans or, to get to the nub, summon up the scene from D. W. Griffith's 1915 film *Birth of a Nation* in which the blond maiden leaps to her death rather than yield her body to a lascivious black pursuer. (Because Griffith's collaborator and the author of the play version of *Birth of a Nation* was a friend of Woodrow Wilson's, it became the first film ever shown at the White House. "It is like writing history with lightning," the Virginia-born, Georgia-bred Wilson said for attribution. "And my only regret is that it's all so terribly true.")[46] White southerners blamed the Negro for the war, the defeat, the humiliation. Above all, "feeling freedom under his feet," they feared where he might go. "For the abolition of slavery, in destroying the rigid fixity of the black at the bottom of the scale," W. J. Cash wrote in *The Mind of the South,* "in throwing open to him at least the legal opportunity to advance, had inevitably opened up to the mind of every Southerner a vista at the end of which stood the overthrow of the . . . absolute taboo on any sexual approach to [the white woman] by the Negro."[47] To their Democratic brothers the Alliancemen voting to endorse the Greenback-Labor Party in the upcoming elections betrayed a higher cause than the Alliance—white supremacy in all its fearful necessity. Third-party politics and race rule splintered the Lampasas Farmers' Alliance and cursed its successor, the Southern Farmers' Alliance. "[T]he argument against the independent political movement in the South," the Populist politician and editor Tom Watson wrote, "may be boiled down into one word—nigger."[48]

To crack the South the Populists simultaneously needed to appeal to white Democrats and black Republicans. Even after Redemption black turnout remained high; in some counties the Republicans got a third of the vote. The Populists had to cut into that vote; or be prepared to fuse—run on a joint ticket—with the Republicans.

A biracial disaffection with unrepresentative government gave the Populists an opening to build a party of the have-nots. One-party southern states were as irresponsive to the stricken farmer as one-party Plains states. The Democrats expected him to wear "the party yoke and vote the ticket even if the monopolist and money sharks write the platform and the devil is made the nominee," a North Carolina Populist complained. At the same time, C. Vann Woodward notes, "The black man was beginning to feel toward his party much the same as the Southern white man was feeling toward his—that his vote was taken for granted and his needs were ignored."[49]

"The Republican party is the ship," Frederick Douglass declaimed at the party's national convention in 1872, "and all else is the sea."[50] But blacks had since been thrown overboard. Bereft over the Republican betrayal of Reconstruction in the Compromise of 1877, despairing over the Republican Supreme Court's negation of the Civil Rights Act ("Blacks must cease to be the special favorite of the laws"), and alarmed at the turn to "Lily White" Republicanism among the up to 20 percent of southern whites who voted for the GOP, southern blacks appeared ready to bolt the party of Lincoln.[51] "The Republicans have deserted them and undertaken to protect the capitalist and the manufacturer of the North," the chairman of the 1890 Colored People's Convention told the *Richmond Dispatch*. "The white Republicans have been traitors to us," affirmed the Negroes' 'Declaration of Independence' issued in Raleigh.[52] The self-help side of Populism attracted black farmers, who needed help: Out of 271 black families in one Georgia district, sixty-one were $100 or more in debt at the end of the year while only five made as much as $100.[53] The Colored Farmers' Alliance ("which," the leading historian of the alliance writes, "may have been the largest Negro organization in American history") enrolled hundreds of thousands of farmers, tenants, and farm laborers within three years of its Houston founding in 1886.[54] It grew in parallel to the Texas and Southern Alliances, which would not admit black men because they admitted white women and heaven and earth might pass away if they attended the same meetings. The Colored Alliance favored a third-party insurgency before the Southern Alliance did, but blacks could line up as easily behind conservative Democrats who bargained for their vote. To win over the black Allianceman leaning toward political heterodoxy, the Populists must convince him that "all God's dangers ain't a white man"— that monopoly and gold and government for the corporation hurt him as a *farmer* and that he should make common cause with the white farmer against these class enemies.[55]

But few southern blacks could imagine a worse danger than the white man at any time and especially in the 1890s. The Populist challenge to the "party of the fathers" lent panic to a frenzy of racial violence; the first appearance of the People's Party on the southern ballot in 1892 coincided with the worst year for lynchings since 1868. Many were "spectacle lynchings," like the February 1893 torture and burning of Henry Smith, "an insane former slave" accused of raping and murdering the three-year-old daughter of a Paris, Texas, policeman who had assaulted him. Captured in Arkansas, returned to Texas by train, Smith was met at the station, in the words of an eyewitness, "by a surging mass of humanity 10,000 strong" who paraded him through town on a float to the "torture platform" where the child's father, brother, and uncles "thrust hot irons into his quivering flesh." "After burning the feet and the legs," the account continues, "the hot irons were rolled up and down Smith's stomach, back and arms. Then the eyes were burnt out and irons were thrust down his throat." And then Henry Smith was burned to ashes. The "black anti-lynching crusader" Ida B. Wells notes in her autobiography that "the mob fought over the ashes for bones, buttons, and teeth for souvenirs." A crude gramophone recorded Smith's cries, which "echoed over the prairie like the wail of a wild animal" and throughout the empire of fear that was the American South for every African-American. The recording may have been the audible lynching played at southern county fairs to sell Edison's "talking machine." In the charged atmosphere of the populist insurgency, spectacle lynchings sent a message: Stay out of any politics that would divide whites and weaken white supremacy. The "plutes" were bad, but did not have a patch on the southern white man.[56]

Yet here he came asking for black votes. What made him different from his kind? The poorer upcountry farmers at the Populist base—weren't they the most dangerous white men, men for whom not being black was one of life's few consolations? ("My name's Sam, I don't give a damn; I'd rather be a nigger than a poor white man," went a black song.) How could *their* leaders be believed when they reached out to the Negro? Having to prove their sincerity to the black farmer while reassuring the "wool hat boys" that a Populist South would be a white man's country still, the Southern Populists walked a political tightrope, swaying now this way, now that.[57]

At their first national convention in Ocala, Florida, the Southern Alliance exchanged fraternal greetings with the Colored Alliance meeting in the same city and the two all but merged—a million white and a million black farmers. But while the Colored Alliance delegates voted unanimously to endorse the Lodge election bill being pushed by Republicans that would range federal judicial power behind black voting rights in the South, the white alliance voted to condemn it, though the Texas and Alabama delegations unanimously dissented.[58] As the 1960s showed, any hope of mobilizing the black voter depended on federal oversight of southern elections to prevent fraud and check intimidation by the ruling Democrats. But an encore of Reconstruction, of "bayonet rule" (under the legislation the president could use military force to defend federal voting monitors from violence), could only end in "Negro Domination." So, between fair elections and white supremacy, the Populists made their choice, "acquiescing in the perpetuation of election frauds in the South that kept them out of power," Robert Saunders acutely observes.[59] Tom Watson, who denounced the "Force Bill," was just the best-known Populist defeated by fraud and fear.* Rueben Kolb, the Populist candidate for governor in Alabama, lost two straight elections to outrages the Lodge bill would have curtailed. "[O]nly 1,031 votes were cast in Wilcox County, yet a majority of over 6000 was returned for the democratic ticket," a Populist remarked of one Black Belt county in the 1894 contest, adding, "The negroes did not register or go to the polls." They mistakenly hoped to deprive the Democrats of votes to steal.[60]

Georgia Populists paid respect to black voters by "going to their homes and sitting up at night in convention on terms of equality with them, all for the sake of their vote." A few black delegates could be seen at Populist state party conventions, where white men heard out black men. There were moving gestures across the divide. When William Warwick of the Virginia Colored Alliance was nominated to serve as an officer of a key meeting at the February 1892 Farmers' Alliance convention in St. Louis, a white Georgian rose to move that the nomination be made unanimous, declaring, "I wish to say that we can stand that down in Georgia." But there was a limit to how much they *could* stand.[61]

---

* The Lodge bill passed the House 155–149 with the Democrats voting 147–0 against. "In the Senate, [it] met with increasing Democratic hostility and Republican apathy. Ultimately, the Democratic members traded votes with pro-silver factions and with Republicans interested in tariff revision and thus won postponement of floor consideration of the bill. Finally, the 51st Congress expired and with it disappeared the last significant attempt to permanently 'reconstruct' the South. . . . The plantation elite controlled the political system of the southern periphery until the passage of a second 'Force Bill,' the Voting Rights Act of 1965." Richard Franklin Bensel, *Sectionalism and American Political Development, 1880–1980* (Madison: University of Wisconsin Press, 1984), p. 79, n. 102.

Judged not by their gestures but by their acts, the southern Populists were friends of convenience to the Negro—for him before the election, against him after. As a Democratic paper out of Louisiana rightly admonished blacks, "Mr. Scipio Africanus ought to know that Mr. Populite loves him less than any other white man on earth, but is willing to go into any deal with him to defeat the Democratic party."[62] In a 1959 essay "The Populist Heritage and the Intellectual," C. Vann Woodward feelingly evoked the biracial promise of Populism: "[T]he most remarkable aspect of the whole Populist movement was the resistance its leaders in the South put up against racism and racist propaganda and the determined effort they made against incredible odds to win back political rights for the Negroes, and defend those rights against brutal aggression, and create among their normally anti-Negro following, even temporarily, a spirit of tolerance in which the two races of the South could work together in one party for the achievement of common ends."[63] More recently historians have tested that thesis against what Populist politicians did in office and what Populist editors said in print. It is a hard test.

The Alliance-dominated Louisiana legislature passed the first Jim Crow bill segregating the races on trains.* In the Georgia legislature one Farmers' Alliance member introduced and his Alliance colleagues supported a similar bill; the Alliancemen "overwhelmingly" backed a change in election laws enabling the "white primary," the key institution of one-race, one-party government until the 1940s; they also voted for bills permitting leased convicts to be whipped, returning the whipping post to the state prison, and mandating that no white prisoner should suffer the shame of being chained to a black prisoner again. [64] In Mississippi, Populists pushed through the poll tax and the literacy test, pioneering black disfranchisement in the South. In Alabama all the Populist legislators voted with all the Democrats for the "Separate but Equal Accommodation Bill" of 1891, "indicat[ing] that there probably were no significant differences between

---

* Southern segregation had a northern precedent. In the North in 1860, Leon Litwack writes, "Negroes found themselves systematically separated from whites. They were either excluded from railway cars, omnibuses, stage coaches, and steamboats or assigned to special 'Jim Crow' sections; they sat, when permitted, in secluded and remote corners of theatres and lecture halls; they could not enter hotels, restaurants, and resorts, except as servants, they prayed in 'Negro pews' in white churches. . . . Moreover, they were often educated in segregated schools, punished in segregated prisons, nursed in segregated hospitals, and buried in segregated cemeteries." Leon Litwack, *North of Slavery: The Negro in the Free States, 1790–1860* (Chicago: University of Chicago Press, 1961), pp. 91–97. Seen in C. Vann Woodward, "Seeds of Failure in Radical Race Policy," *Proceedings of the American Philosophical Society,* vol. 110, no. 1 (February 18, 1966), p. 1.

the Democrats and the Populists on race relations," Sheldon Hackney writes. He finds "no objective difference between the parties on racial policy" generally.[65] Beyond the Deep South, despite their campaign rhetoric, the Populists did no better by the Negro. The North Carolina People's Party, for example, was "avowedly anti-Negro," according to a study of fusion politics in that state. In Virginia the People's Party candidate for governor in 1893 advocated repeal of the Fifteenth Amendment.[66]

"Populist editors sought out achievements of Negroes to praise in their columns," Woodward writes, citing examples.[67] But the same editors, notably Tom Watson in his *People's Party Paper,* pandered to racism at need, keen to refute the calumny that Populists were "nigger lovers and nigger huggers" and turn it against the Democrats who leveled it at them. When the Democratic governor of Virginia held a dinner for visiting Massachusetts lawmakers, a black Massachusetts representative and a black man from Richmond named Mitchell showed up with them at the Governor's Mansion. Watson lit into the governor for allowing his home to be defiled. Why just imagine, he went on, "Mitchell saw, ate and drank along with the Massachusetts delegation, the Governor, and the Governor's wife, just as natural as if he was a human being." A Populist preacher wagged a lubricious finger at Grover Cleveland for hosting a White House dinner for "that leader of niggderdom," Frederick Douglass, and his white wife.[68] North Carolina's future Populist senator, Marion Butler, devoted an edition of his paper, *The Caucasian* [sic], to a rant entitled "Committed to Miscegenation," dilating upon Cleveland's embrace of that abomination.[69] The Populist *Texas Advance,* which praised the People's Party for being open to black participation, greeted news of a Cleveland appointment with this: "Grover Cleveland's nigger, Taylor, desires white lady stenographers for his thirty nigger clerks in the office of recorder of deeds for the District of Columbia. Southern parents desiring good positions for their daughters will endorse Cleveland by applying to Taylor for situations for their girls."[70] In *Blacks and the Populist Movement: Ballots and Bigotry in the New South,* Gerald H. Gaither includes one example after another of that sexual baiting, that playing with fire, that all-justifying provocation to lynching. The 3,442 blacks *reported* lynched by white mobs between 1882 and the 1950s were punished for the murder of white men, for robbery, for self-defense, for insisting on their constitutional rights, even "for expressing sympathy for a lynching victim." But, the political scientist James W. Clarke writes in a 1998 paper, "the imagined and contrived reasons were almost always sexual."[71]

Making allowances for their attempt to forge a biracial coalition of the southerners left behind in the New South of business and industry Gaither gets the Populists right: "All in all, the Populist record in the region is not what its proponents claim it to be, but neither should it be read with complete contempt."[72]

The dramatic scene of hundreds of white farmers roused from their beds by torchlight-bearing horsemen and then riding through the night to Tom Watson's Thomson, Georgia, home to defend a black preacher and his white Populist congressman from a rumored lynch mob—this stirring example of Populism's biracial promise has a downbeat coda. Thomson's mayor had offered Reverend Doyle and Watson "police protection," but, Charles Crowe reported in a 1970 paper in the *Journal of Negro History,* Watson refused, causing the *Macon Telegraph* to wonder if Watson "contrived the incident" to cast himself as a brave defender of a black supporter. Tilting toward his other base, Watson wanted readers of the *People's Party Paper* to know that he directed Doyle "to take up quarters in a Negro house on the lot," though in a 1906 version it was "get in that nigger house." There was no question of his sleeping under the same roof as Mrs. Watson.[73]

"The powers of government should be extended . . . to the end that oppression, injustice, and poverty shall eventually cease in the land."

That Copernican sentence appeared in the preamble to the first platform of the national People's Party. Since the war government had extended its power to protect injustice. In the Gilded Age it was easier to credit the virgin birth than that government could serve the general welfare. Republican government serviced business. The Democrats wanted a weak federal government so that the southern oligarchy could maintain the institutions—lynching, convict labor, fraudulent elections, disfranchisement, racial apartheid—that alone gave it popular legitimacy. The Populist credo—"Equal rights to all, special privileges to none"— challenged the operational maxims of both parties. They had viewed with alarm the rise of the Farmers' Alliance. They had tried to co-opt it. They had waved the bloody shirt in front of it. Yet they could not stop this social movement from birthing a political insurgency. In a fully mobilized electorate blood needn't run in the streets to put bottom rail top. Americans could vote themselves a fairer society. The party of greed and the party of hate now faced a party of hope.

The western Populists and the southern Populists, in Omaha convention assembled, formed up their party and unveiled its platform on July 4, 1892.* They nominated a Union general for president and a one-legged Confederate major for vice president. Although planks in the Omaha platform were calculated to appeal to the northern workingman, the general, the former Greenback presidential candidate James B. Weaver of Iowa, wisely focused his campaign on the regions of agrarian discontent— the West, where he was well received, and the South, where he was not.[74] Democratic papers accused him of wartime cruelties against Tennessee civilians. Mobs harassed and egged him. Mrs. Weaver was made "a regular walking omelet by the Southern chivalry" of Macon, Georgia. That according to Mrs. Lease, who, as the Populists' most gifted orator, stumped with Weaver. Newspapers extended no chivalry to the "short-haired woman" from Kansas with "a nose like an ant-eater and a voice like a cat fight," hinting that she was sleeping with the general if not with both Weavers.[75] After learning that Tom Watson had to be rescued from an Atlanta mob, Weaver canceled the rest of his campaign in the South, and with his retreat ended Populism's dream of erasing the Mason-Dixon line in politics.[76] In November Grover Cleveland swept the "Solid South," Weaver attracting more than a third of the vote only in Alabama. "Stand by your principles," Watson urged white farmers, "and vote for Sally and the babies."[77] But the "wool hat boys" stayed with the "party of the fathers." For all their education, roughly half the members of the Southern Alliance stayed there, too. Blacks, for the most part, either voted for Republicans or for Democrats like William J. Northen, running for governor in Georgia, who promised to pass an anti-lynching bill and increase funding for black schools; and, everywhere blacks were "bulldozed" to the polls and voted by the Democrats.[78]

The election might have turned out differently if Colonel Polk, the Southern Farmers' Alliance president and putative nominee at Omaha, had not died suddenly in June. But Polk, accused by Kansas Republican newspapers of murdering Union prisoners of war "in cold blood," might

* The People's Party became the Populists after an official of the Kansas People's Party complained that while you could refer to someone as a "Republican" or a "Democrat" you would gulp at calling him "a People's." A friendly Democratic leader with a Latin education suggested "Populist." The People's wasn't sure. "I'm afraid of that," he said, "because the newspapers would be calling us 'Pops' within a week." He did not have to wait that long. The *Kansas City Star* used it the next day. John D. Hicks, *The Populist Revolt: A History of the Farmers' Alliance and the People's Party* (Lincoln: University of Nebraska Press, 1961), p. 238, n. 1.

have been cut in the West as badly as Weaver in the South.[79] Senator Lodge's bill might also have helped the Populists; without it Democratic machines from Alabama to Virginia freely engaged in what a witness to it labeled a "bacchanalia of corruption and terrorism" against Populist candidates and voters.[80]

On his way to winning 1 million votes, four states, and twenty-two electoral votes, the best showing for a third-party candidate since 1860, Weaver elected Grover Cleveland. The general took 400,000 votes away from the incumbent Republican president, Benjamin Harrison, in western states carried by him in 1888 and by Cleveland in 1892 by 365,000 votes. The front-page headline the *Topeka Daily Capital* ran the day President Harrison delivered a campaign speech to a "huge gathering" of Union veterans there—"The People's Party is the Scheme of Ex-Rebels"—had proved prophetic.[81]

Politics killed Populism. The Farmers' Alliances either disintegrated when their leaders moved on to the People's Party or disappeared into it. "Hundreds of suballiances were converted into local People's Party clubs, few of which survived the fall campaign," Robert C. McMath, Jr., reports in his *American Populism: A Social History, 1877–1898*.[82] The Alliances might have lived on; the Grange survived its wild youth, evolving from a social movement to a rural social institution. But, with its cooperatives and exchanges destroyed, why would farmers have joined the Alliance? To restore the cooperatives, to save the producer's economy, the Populists had to direct farmers' "pre-political" anger at this merchant or that banker upward, toward the system and its harlot parties. *They* must have looked like pushovers. They stood for nothing. They did nothing for the people. Corrupt, sterile, contemptuous of the voters, the parties were adept at co-optation, at calming the waters, at proposing snake-oil solutions to real problems and making the credulous, the loyal, and the many willing to tolerate injustice to preserve stability suspend their disbelief—for one last time.

Politicians betrayed Populism. A survey of third-party movements in the nineteenth century discerns a common thread in "anti-partyism" during the "party period." The "ignoble enticements of office and power" drew politicians to anti-party movements. The politicians brought experience and organizational skill, "but their self-promotional party-building efforts were at odds with the antiparty promise that had stoked the imaginations of the rank and file," Mark Voss Hubbard found in a study of third parties. A North Carolina Know-Nothing's complaint in the 1850s resonated with those lodged against their leaders by Workingmen's Party activists in the 1830s and Populists in the 1890s: "This struggling and scrambling for office and promotion was one of the very great evils it was the object of our organization to remedy—and yet our success is likely to be jeopardized by the very same evil. The masses are sound but the old party leaders and political hacks, who have come into the order from selfish reasons, will ruin us." In our winner-take-all system a minority party attracting 30 percent of the vote in congressional races does not get 30 percent of the seats. It gets no seats. Invariably third-party leaders are tempted to overcome this hurdle by fusing with the "out" party to defeat the "ins," win offices, and gain a foothold in government. The Populist experience suggests that's a recipe for splitting the leaders from the led. For, Hubbard asks, "[I]f third party movements hoped above all to end politics as usual, how could such high ideals possibly be advanced by fusion with one of the major parties?" True, but "no-fusion," as one Iowa Populist put it, was the strategy of a "no-succeed, no-sense party."[83]

Fusion accepted with the Democrats undermined the People's Party in the West; fusion rejected with the Republicans marginalized it in the South.

The Populist scything of Kansas Republicans in 1890 set Democrats to ruminating on strategy. "So much has been accomplished in the defeat of Ingalls and a general smashing up of the old Republican machine," Thomas Moonlight, a Democratic congressional candidate from Kansas, wrote citizen Grover Cleveland in January 1891.

> We Democrats could not as a party break up the huge machine by reason of the bitter prejudice attaching to the name "Democrat," but another organization with our indirect and almost silent help is doing the work, and I urge our men to aid and assist in the work, and when the smashing process is complete, we will gather up the fragments, and strange as it may seem, they will all come to us. The Alliance in the meantime will *almost* destroy our party . . . [In 1892] our western work must be to cause [Republicans] to lose four or five western Republican states through the power of the Alliance movement. . . . I confess a determination to use it for destructive purposes, and do not fear its future strength.[84]

Moonlight called it correctly. Fusion (varying from joint tickets to silent Democratic help to Populist candidates), besides turning over the White House to the Democrats, not only won four western states for General

Weaver but installed Populist governors, state legislators, congressmen, and senators in Wyoming, Colorado, Nevada, Idaho, Nebraska, and Kansas.[85] In some states, as Democratic votes surged into the Populist column, the Populists almost destroyed the Democrats. But the Populist success was hostage to those Democrats. A national campaign pitting Populists against Democrats would break these state fusions and cost Populist politicians their offices. Fusion at the national level would preserve those gains. Political logic pointed that way. Needed was an umbrella issue.

General Weaver's treatment in the South, the failure of the southern Populists there, fusion with the Democrats in the West, and fusion with Kansas Democrats in the 1892 state elections, sobered Kansas Populists with Republican roots. To demonstrate that the People's Party was disruptive to both national parties—that it was not a "Democratic aid society"—they had evangelized the South. But the Populists *had* aided the Democrats in 1892. "Alliancemen would not believe Republicans two years ago when they told them they were playing into the democracy's hands, but now the evidence is too plain to longer ignore it," the *Mound City Progress* concluded.[86] "In separating from the Republican party, Kansas farmers had no intention of aligning themselves with the enemy whom they have so long opposed and despised," the anti-fusion *Kincaid Kronicle* editorialized. The *Goff Advance* found insupportable the Populist-Democratic nomination of a former Confederate soldier for Congress: "Hereafter we shall be found battling for squatoed, stalwart Republicanism. We would rather belong to the Republican plutocrats than the Southern brigadiers."[87] Southern brigadiers had killed one of Mary Lease's brothers at Fredericksburg, another at Lookout Mountain, and an uncle at Gettysburg. Along with 13,000 of the 45,000 Union prisoners of war held there, her father had died at Andersonville. Fusion betrayed her Union dead. *"I am done with Democrats and fusion,"* she declared. Returning to the party of her father, she campaigned for McKinley in 1896.*[88]

Fearing mass defections at the base, Georgia and Texas Populists rebuffed fusion overtures from Republicans. Fusion would have elected

---

* Her husband, Charles, a Wichita pharmacist, led torchlight parades for William Jennings Bryan. After losing their house for arrears on the mortgage, the Leases were divorced. Mary Lease took the children with her to New York, "where she spent the last thirty years of her life in relative obscurity as a writer for Pulitzer's *New York World*, a lecturer for the New York City Board of Education, and the president of national and international birth control societies." Walter T. K. Nugent, *The Tolerant Populists: Kansas Populism and Nativism* (Chicago: University of Chicago Press, 1963), p. 84.

Populist governors, but the Populist leaders in those states would rather lose the elections of 1892 and 1894 than breach white supremacy. They lost.[89] North Carolina shows how they might have won. On their own the Populists carried three counties in 1892 but thirty-three counties running with the GOP on biracial "Fusion Tickets" in 1894, capturing the state legislature and electing two U.S. senators and a majority of the state's congressmen.[90] Alone in the South, for the four years of Populist-Republican control, North Carolina adopted no disfranchising measures like the poll tax or the literacy test but did enact reforms benefiting blacks and poor whites.[91] In 1896 Texas Populists conducted a stumbling dance of fusion with the Republicans. To win the Populists just had to hold their 1894 vote. But, Gregg Cantrell and D. Scott Barton write, "When a sizeable majority of Texas Populists perceived that they faced a choice between white supremacy and a Populist governor in Austin, they chose white supremacy and doomed the People's party to defeat."[92]

Grover Cleveland furnished the issue that consummated fusion and destroyed the People's Party when he pressured Congress to repeal the Sherman Silver Purchase Act in 1893. President Benjamin Harrison had signed the Sherman bill in 1890 not from any latent financial unorthodoxy—he was a Republican—but as his part of a deal with members of his own party from silver-producing states; in return, these westerners voted for the tumescent "McKinley Tariff," which raised average duties to 48 percent. In the 1892 election, its confidence in Harrison's devotion to gold shaken, Wall Street swung behind Cleveland. *He* had a heart of gold. From the time he denounced the silver bill as a "dangerous and reckless experiment," "[T]he great banking interests of New York," writes Allan Nevins, Cleveland's biographer, promoted his candidacy. They even deputed one of their own, the financier William C. Whitney, to serve as Cleveland's campaign manager.

The Sherman bill committed the Treasury to buying 4.5 million ounces of silver a month and coining more silver currency with it. Anticipating that this increase in the money supply would devalue the dollar, foreign holders of U.S. securities sold them, draining U.S. gold reserves to the suburbs of default. "No more foreign capital comes to the United States and as fast as Europeans can dislodge their holdings in America they take their money away," the *Commercial and Financial Chronicle* reported at the end of 1892. In February, J. P. Morgan told *Harper's Weekly* that repeal of Sherman silver was "essential to the sound financial policy of the government." Cleveland, a former partner in Morgan's law firm, agreed. But repeal would take months. The Treasury would run out of gold in days. Morgan came to the White House with a plan: An international syndicate of bankers would provide $100 million in gold to the Treasury. For this eleventh-hour rescue of the United States from bankruptcy Mary Lease branded Cleveland "the agent of Jewish bankers and British gold."

Although Cleveland warned defectors to expect no patronage, he lost a majority of both southern and western Democrats on the Sherman repeal vote.[93] They had embraced silver partly to offset Populist appeals for an expanded currency, though that did not prevent many silver Democrats from switching to the third party. Populist politicians had been handed an issue that would unite their party and divide the Democrats—and even attract western silver Republicans threatening a bolt if the GOP hewed to gold.

The details of the nineteenth-century specie controversy repel curiosity; only obsession could make them interesting. And on that score, one does well to take James Garfield's warning to heart. "He devoted himself almost exclusively to the study of the currency," Garfield said of a colleague, "became fully entangled with the theories of the subject and became insane." The "currency question" came down to this: Should the U.S. remain on the gold standard, switch to a primarily silver-based currency, or print green paper money backed only by the full faith and credit of the United States, not by either precious metal. Unable to believe that the *composition* of money accounted for the passion it aroused, historians have searched for a deeper source of feeling the currency might have tapped. In "Specie and Species: Race and the Money Question in Nineteenth-Century America," Michael O'Malley ingeniously shows how, in postwar public speech, the language of money overlapped the language of race.* Both rhetorics mediated cultural anxiety over the mutability of standards—over whether money and race could be "negotiated" or were defined by their intrinsic character.

Thus Henry Adams's attack on the Legal Tender Act (under which the

---

* "Before 1865, the vast majority of African Americans were, literally, property, and they served simultaneously as an embodied currency and a labor force. . . . Enslaved black people were not simply likened to money, they were a kind of money. . . . [S]laves were collateral for commercial, speculative, and personal loans." Nell Irvin Painter, "Thinking About the Languages of Money and Race," *American Historical Review*, vol. 99, no. 2 (April 1994), p. 398.

Lincoln administration issued greenbacks to finance the war), as "an attempt by artificial legislation to make something true"—that paper unsecured by specie was money—"that was not true" was mimed by Maryland senator George Vicker's argument that, "no legislation of Congress can elevate or improve the physical, moral or intellectual nature of the negro. We cannot legislate into them any fitness or qualifications which they do not possess." Radical Republicans tended to believe that Congress could make a worthless piece of paper valuable and the freedmen full citizens by "fiat." In the debate over Reconstruction, Conservatives rejected both socially constructed money and rights. Thus Senator August Merrimon of North Carolina maintained, "It would seem that the Almighty had provided these substances [gold and silver]" to serve as currency. Congress might outlaw gold as money but "it would still have value in spite of the statute." By the same token, Congress could not abolish racial differences. "Why did God make our skins white?" Merrimom asked in a later speech. "Why did He make the negro's skin black? . . . I ask Senators, where do they get the authority to change the color God has blessed us with? Where can any authority be found to make my skin black and corrupt my blood?" The currency came to symbolize more than a medium of exchange. "Diluting the money supply diluted the nation's blood," O'Malley observes, "and elevating the freedmen depreciated the value of whiteness."

By the early 1880s the Treasury had accumulated sufficient gold reserves to allow greenbacks to be "redeemed" for gold. In the same years, the South was being "redeemed" from biracial governments led by Yankee "carpetbaggers." That derogative, O'Malley discovered, was first employed before the war in the gamy milieu of "wildcat" banking, when "nearly every specie-basis bank had its carpet-bagger," Congressman William D. "Pig Iron" Kelley recalled, "a fellow it sent out with [dubious] notes by the carpetbag full into some distant State to get them into circulation there." The early Populists called for Congress to bring back "fiat money" as a flexible currency that could expand with economic growth. But gold fetishists had since stigmatized "Greenbackism" as a threat to *all* standards of value. In their Omaha platform, the Populists endorsed a safer alternative than the racially inflected "fiat money"—the "free and unlimited coinage of silver at the present ratio of sixteen to one."[94] In arguing that silver "was a peripheral, an unessential issue, even considered by the early Populists as a fraudulent issue," Peter Argersinger has company among historians. Silver, however, was salient and popular, thanks in part to a best-selling tract,

Coin's Financial School, "Being sold on every railroad train by the newsboys and at every cigar store," a Mississippi congressman informed President Cleveland; and that was enough for the Populist leaders. By retreating from greenbacks and subordinating Omaha's controversial planks—notably the sub-treasury—to silver, they hoped to split the old parties into gold and silver shards, fuse these in the People's Party, and possibly displace either the Democrats or the Republicans in the two-party duopoly.[95]

Over protests from the left wing of the party, the Populist political managers decided to hold their convention after the Democrats' and Republicans' with a view to welcoming defecting delegations from both parties under the big tent of silver Populism. It had the *look* of a sound strategy. The Republicans would not abandon the gold standard. The Cleveland Democracy, under the rule requiring the presidential nominee and platform planks to be ratified by two-thirds of the delegates, would contain the surge to silver and enforce gold on their party. The Populist political managers could not foresee that, in the months leading up to the Democratic National Convention in July, "like a whisper at first, then a half-imperceptible shift in the landscape, and suddenly like a roar, a crash, an irresistible cataclysm," the party would go over to silver; repudiate Cleveland; and, stampeded by his electrifying "Cross of Gold" speech at the Chicago convention, nominate for president former Nebraska congressman William Jennings Bryan. The youngest and most charismatic candidate in either party since the war, he was said to be on "excellent terms" with silver Republicans and silver Populists alike.[96] The issue facing the People's Party delegates who gathered in St. Louis during the last week of July was not how to admit the Democrats wanting to fuse with them. It was whether to fuse with the Democrats by nominating Bryan or to run their own ticket, split the silver vote, elect William McKinley, the GOP nominee, and lose their fused officeholders in the West. Henry Demarest Lloyd put the Populists' dilemma well: "If we fuse we are sunk; if we don't fuse, all the silver [voters] we have will leave us for the more popular Democrats." In *The Populist Response to Industrial America* Norman Pollack may capture the paradoxical truth: "Fusion was both a necessity and an agent of destruction."[97]

For southern Populists especially who advocated sticking to the "middle road" between the major parties and who had suffered at the Democrats' hands, Bryan would be a second betrayal. The first was the Populist leaders' retreat from the Omaha platform to promote silver fusion. "These traitors to the holy cause of the people would have us abandon . . . every aim of our party, in order that we might secure the accession of old party politicians, who, we are coolly informed, are too ignorant or too capitalistic even to endure the mention of all our other reform demands," the Kansas "mid-roader" G. C. Clemens argued in the *St. Louis Post-Dispatch*. Silver was a sham nostrum. The *Southern Mercury*, the voice of Texas middle-roaders, estimated that free silver would increase the money supply by "$1 per capita per year" instead of the $50 per capita in "fiat money" issued directly to the people called for by the sub-treasury plan. Moreover, the star Alliance lecturer Harry Tracy insisted, only an "irredeemable" currency could break the power the "money Kings" possessed over redeemable specie-based currency, whether gold *or* silver. Because the "creditor class" received $1.6 billion in annual interest payments for its holdings in government bonds, it could, in Donna A. Barnes's summary of Tracy's argument, "redeem this sum in gold and withdraw it from circulation if it perceived such action to be in its best interest." In jettisoning the sub-treasury, the People's Party not only sacrificed their core economic doctrine but abandoned the southern farmer to "lien-slavery," the wrong southern populism had been born to right.[98]

To Lloyd, a Christian socialist to the left of the Omaha platform, free silver was "the cow bird of the Reform movement." The cow-bird "waited until the nest had been built by the sacrifices of others, then it laid its eggs in it, pushing out the others which lie smashed on the ground." The Populist leaders—General Weaver, the national chairman, H. E. Taubeneck, and others—were selling out Populism for patronage jobs from the Democrats, the *Kansas Agitator* charged. "Judas betrayed Christ for thirty pieces of silver. Will those Judases who would betray the People's Party (for silver?) still further follow his examples—go and hang themselves?" The mid-roaders spoke for movement Populism but that flame had gone out. Movements can afford purity. Parties can't. Nowhere in the United States had the People's Party received a majority of the vote. In our winner-take-all system, the Populists had to fuse to win, and to fuse they had to dilute Populism.[99]

The party leaders did not follow Judas's example. They did not commit suicide. The party did. For four years party chairman Taubeneck, an Illinois farmer and lawyer, had spoken against fusion. "No fusion with any other party will be tolerated," he said on assuming his post in 1891. "A hen can lay a fresh egg a good deal easier than she can purify a rotten one."

"Fusion means confusion" and "oblivion," he publicly reassured the party before the 1892 convention while secretly arranging fusion tickets with western Democrats. He styled himself a "practical politician" in contrast to the "cranks," "anarchists," and "socialists" among the Populist editors; and apparently felt that role licensed deceit. During the convention, he tried to stampede the delegates into nominating Walter Q. Gresham, a Republican reformer, by reading a "misleading telegram" from Gresham. Mrs. Lease mocked that ploy by claiming that she had received a telegram accepting the People's Party nomination from President Harrison! Blaming the 1892 defeat on "rainbow chasing and endless freaks and foibles," which "drove thousands who are with us heart and soul on the money issue . . . into the ranks of the opposition," Taubeneck wanted "the people's party to get down to a single proposition, namely to the money question, and strip it of all else."

Insisting that "the party will either adopt my policy or we will never succeed as a party," Taubeneck and his claque, Peter Argersinger writes, "manipulated party rules, issued misleading public statements, and . . . secretly discussed fusion plans with Silver Democrats" ahead of the 1896 convention, which Taubeneck salted with delegations receptive to fusion—understood as the Populists absorbing Democratic defectors not the Democratic Party absorbing the Populists. Faced with *that* prospect— which he called "the surrender and destruction of the People's Party organization"—on the eve of the convention Taubeneck tried to engineer the nomination of a silver Republican, Colorado senator Henry Teller, but Teller not only refused to cooperate, he urged "all Populists" to rally behind Bryan. Taubeneck's "practical politics" had betrayed *him*.

As the St. Louis convention fistfights broke out on the floor between mid-roaders and fusionists; pistols were drawn. The Texas delegation, of one mind with the Dallas Populists who wired "Bryan means death," formed a square beneath a mid-road banner to resist fusionists trying to pull them into a Bryan procession. Older Texans wept and one shouted "We will not crucify the People's Party on the cross of the Democracy!" Speaking from the rostrum a black delegate implored the convention to reject union with white supremacy. When the convention chairman and Bryan's friend, Senator William Allen of Nebraska, moved to suspend the rules and nominate Bryan by acclamation, a Washington delegate shouted, "By God, we won't stand it," and the mid-roaders erupted. "Hundreds" stood on their chairs demanding to be heard. On the rostrum behind Allen an Alabama congressman flung himself against the cordon of fusionists protecting the podium while 103 Texans stormed it from the floor. Allen consulted his safety and ordered a roll call.

Three times Harrison Sterling Price "Stump" Ashby, one of the original Texas Populists, interrupted the balloting to formally ask the chairman if he had received a telegram from Bryan stating that he would decline the Populist nomination unless the convention also endorsed his running mate, Maine banker and shipping magnate Arthur Sewall. Earlier the mid-roaders had succeeded in nominating Tom Watson for vice president and if Allen confirmed the Bryan story printed in that morning's St. Louis papers fusion's price—surrender of the complete People's Party ticket to the Democrats—would be unmistakable to the delegates. Enough disillusioned fence-sitters might have joined the mid-roaders to swing the convention against Bryan and nominate a straight Populist ticket of Watson and S. F. Norton, a reform editor and "true mid-roader" on fiat money and the sub-treasury, for president. But three times Allen denied receiving the telegram and three times he lied. Their fears quieted by fusionist-circulated rumors that Sewall had agreed to step aside for Watson and, without knowing if he would deign to accept it, the delegates gave the nomination to William Jennings Bryan, who did not acknowledge receiving it until the People's Party managers officially notified him late in the fall campaign. In his letter of notification, Chairman Marion Butler of North Carolina assured Bryan that he could ignore the People's Party platform. Thus, "[t]here would be no fight for Alliance-Populist principles on a national level in 1896," Barnes writes. "The national leaders of the People's Party had betrayed those principles in their bid for national office."

"Our party, as a party, does not exist any more," Tom Watson wrote. "Fusion has well-nigh killed it." "The largest democratic mass movement in American history," Lawrence Goodwyn writes, "quietly dissolved in the fall of 1896 as the morale of its two million followers collapsed" in the wake of the St. Louis Gethsemane.[100]

American history did not miss the Anti-Masons or the Know-Nothings. It missed the Populists. They spoke to the Texas dirt farmer from Blanco County who had not been to school and did not wear shoes, to people like the St. Louis convention delegates, too poor to afford a train ticket, who'd walked long distances to get there or slept in the city parks so they could buy the "nickel lunch." The *New York Times* compared "this body of 1,400 more or less 'touched' would-be rulers of the country" to "crazy people

THE STORY OF LITTLE RED RIDING HOOD
The Democratic wolf's invitation to the People's Party.

The Democrats woo the Populists in 1896.
Southern Mercury, *October 29, 1896.*

who fancy that some one is always sneaking . . . needles into their hash."*[101] A Republican editor from Kansas described them as "men whose feet stank, and the odor from under whose arms would have knocked down a bull, women with voices like a gong, women with . . . dirty fingernails, women with stockings gone out at the heels. . . . Gray-haired, scrawny, yellow-skinned women appeared upon the stage dressed in hideous or indecent costumes. . . . To wind up the whole thing, delegates were brought up like the hogs they were."[102] To have made such ene-

---

* According to an Associated Press correspondent, "one of the striking things" about the St. Louis convention was "the extraordinary hatred of the Jewish race." He continues, in what Richard Hofstadter terms a "report [that] may have been somewhat overdone," "It is not possible to go into any hotel in the city without hearing the most bitter denunciation of the Jews as a class and of the particular Jews who happen to have prospered in the world." Richard Hofstadter, *The Age of Reform* (New York: Alfred A. Knopf, 1955), p. 89.

mies is Populism's glory. No other party in the century cared to shape its program to the need of Americans with dirty fingernails. Populism was bottom-up in its remedies. Sub-treasury loans would have freed the southern farmer from "lien slavery" and been a tonic to the rural economy. European countries nationalized their railroads and communications systems without the sky falling. It would not have fallen on Kansas. For low commodity prices the Populists put forward a contestable diagnosis. "Was it the appreciation of gold that made the price of potatoes so low in 1895, or was it a crop which exceeded by nearly 900,000 bushels that of any year, with the single exception of 1891, in three decades?" a friendly critic asked in the *Political Science Quarterly.* "The average farm price of wheat for the three years ending with 1894 was about 30 percent less than for the three years ending with 1891. Is the gold standard or an increase of 236,000,000 bushels of wheat in the annual average of the world's supply the more reasonable explanation?"[103] The Farmers' Alliance denied the glut to which its members contributed. While millions went hungry "overproduction" could not exist. The Populist cure for low prices, an expanded currency, was financially plausible but politically problematic. Milton Friedman calculated that the adoption of the 16-to-1 silver standard would have converted the "cumulative deflation" of 14.3 percent between 1889 and 1896 into a cumulative inflation of 16.3 percent.[104] Friedman projected overall prices; farm commodity prices would have risen even more steeply; according to one contemporary estimate free silver would have increased the price of wheat by 35 percent. But that would have made the urban workingman pay more for his bread, one reason Samuel Gompers's American Federation of Labor rejected overtures from the People's Party. The Populists did not erase the Mason-Dixon line in politics. They did not solve the race problem. The weight of the war, the legacy of Emancipation and the southern white rejection of it, bore them down. They could not escape history. Yet they *tried.* They sought a way forward better than what came before *and* after them. Maybe Tom Watson contrived Reverend Doyle's peril. But the white farmers rubbing sleep from their eyes, collecting their rifles, saddling their horses, hitching their teams, and riding through the Georgia night to protect a black comrade from lynching and maybe die doing it—that was real, that was the best of Populism. In all these bitter years you will find nothing so moving.

Chapter Eleven

REVOLUTION FROM ABOVE

[T]here is no evidence that the mass of the population anywhere has wanted an industrial society, and plenty of evidence that they did not. At bottom all forms of industrialization so far have been revolutions from above, the work of a ruthless minority.

—Barrington Moore, Jr.,
*The Social Origins of Dictatorship and Democracy: Lord
and Peasant in the Making of the Modern World*

Politics developed no rhythm after the Civil War, no current in the direction of one party or the other and no realigning issue to replace slavery expansion, which reshaped the electoral universe in the 1850s, melding northern Whigs and Democrats into Republicans and uniting southerners of both parties under the banner of rebellion. The politics of section got a second wind during Reconstruction, which overshadowed the one potentially realigning event, the long depression of the 1870s, from which the Democrats gained a lonely supremacy in the House. Frozen symmetry prevailed, with the Republicans controlling the Senate for seven of the ten Congresses between 1875 and 1895 but the House only twice; the Democrats controlling the House for eight of ten Congresses but the Senate only twice. Between 1876 and 1892 no Republican presidential candidate captured a majority of the popular vote and only one gained a plurality, yet the Republicans elected three presidents. A Democratic presidential candidate won a majority in 1876, others gained pluralities in 1884, 1888, and 1892, yet the Democrats elected only one president, Grover Cleveland, in 1884 and 1892.[1]

In 1890, however, a current swelled by immigrant voters set in toward the Democrats. Attacking the administration of Benjamin Harrison as "a narrow oligarchy in opposition to the needs of the multitude" and the McKinley Tariff as a payoff to the GOP's manufacturing underwriters that raised the cost of living for American families, and assisted by merchant advertising reminding customers to buy *now*, before the tariff went into effect and raised prices, the Democrats swept the congressional elections, unseating chairman of the Ways and Means Committee William McKinley, among seventy-seven other Republicans, and winning state elections from traditionally Republican Wisconsin to primordially Republican Massachusetts. "Iowa will go Democratic when hell goes Methodist," a Republican wag boasted in 1883. In the state elections of 1889, Iowa went Democratic. *The Nation* wondered at the dimensions of "the great political revolution of 1890."[2]

Events broke for the revolution as the 1892 presidential election campaign got under way. No sooner had the Republican convention saluted the tariff as the guarantor of high wages for the American worker than Carnegie Steel, protection's prize child, locked out the 3,800 workers at its Homestead, Pennsylvania, mill after they balked at *lower* wages. "[T]he Homestead Strike," the GOP's Chauncey Depew said, "happened at a crisis and injured us irremediably."[3]

Homestead was an axial event. It portended the end of skilled workers' control over the pace of production, the eclipse of the nineteenth-century entrepreneurial economy, and the triumph of corporate capitalism.

The "new economic history" and the "new labor history" written since the 1960s have unveiled a paradox: Enterprise did not do so well in the Age of Enterprise nor labor so bad. By every measure economic growth declined "with a marked persistence from 1870 to the end of the century," Jeffrey Williamson wrote in the first of several pioneering papers. Significantly, productivity growth fell from 3.2 percent per hour of work in 1874–84 to .6 percent in 1884–94. Yet, thanks to the steady fall in prices, real wages steadily increased. Carroll D. Wright, the respected labor economist, found that "while the prices of 223 commodities entering into consumption" fell by 6 percent between 1860 and 1891, industrial wages rose by nearly 70 percent—in real terms from an average of $375 per year in 1870 to $573 in 1900. That statistical rendering of labor's situation is jarring; the anguish of Pittsburgh railroad workers choosing "blood or bread," the "actual need" of Scranton miners too destitute to bury their dead children, and the privation of "work families" in Rhode Island's mill towns do not square with it.[4]

Equally jarring is the 1889 finding of Edward Atkinson, a Boston economist and manufacturer. Economic historians substantiate his conclusion that, as James Livingston writes in a brilliant 1987 synthesis published in the *American Historical Review,* "the purchasing power of skilled labor had risen about 100 percent since 1865, while the earning power of capital had declined 'absolutely one half and relatively at least 75 percent since 1860.' " The "real" rate of return on railroad bonds, for example, fell from 12.94 percent in 1870 to 4.71 percent in 1891. Capitalists, a University of Pennsylvania economist maintained, "were in danger of becoming public servants." By the late 1880s, with prices falling and real wages rising six times faster than productivity, labor was "expropriating" much of capital's portion of the nation's income. Something must be done about those greedy workers.[5]

Cut their wages to begin with. Make them work harder. To align their interests with their employers, put wage earners on piecework. Above everything, *do* something to stop skilled workers from setting the pace of production and spreading to co-workers their spirit of "manly" resistance to speed-ups. Before the corporate drive for greater productivity revved up in the 1890s, skilled workers could infuse humane—or at least human— touches into the workplace. Printers and cigar rollers would ask literate colleagues to read newspapers and books aloud to them while they worked. Samuel Gompers heard Karl Marx read while working in a New York cigar factory. Coopers struck for free beer at breweries. Many workers stayed home on "Blue Monday" to sleep off lubricated weekends, which lowered the productivity of those who showed up for work. Frederick W. Taylor, whose time-motion studies of workers working earned him renown as "the father of scientific management," described the culture of resistance he encountered as a "gang boss" trying to get more work out of the men in the machine shop of a Pennsylvania steel maker. "[T]he shop was really run by the workmen . . . who carefully planned just how fast each job should be done," he wrote in *The Principles of Scientific Management* (1911). Taylor's men routinely deceived "the boss" by, for example, claiming their machines had broken down from the pace set by the foreman. Sometimes a machine did break—because they had sabotaged it. "Swifts" the men pressured to slow down. Things could go bad for an obdurate—or, from his point of view, ambitious—man. A machinist known as the "big Yankee" who worked for the Hoe Printing Press Company in New York was despised for being a "company man." Nine hundred of his fellow workers joined a citywide strike for shorter hours in 1886—but the big Yankee went to work. When he left the plant for lunch, in David Montgomery's words, "he was viciously beaten by his mates." Taylor, who lived in middle-class respectability "far" from the plant, doubted he could have gotten away with firing "stubborn men" and hiring "green" replacements loyal to him if he had lived in the same neighborhood as the Midvale Steel machinists he did out of their jobs.[6]

Skilled workers could exert control over production because, as late as the 1890s, the artisan tradition survived in industrial work. As the labor journalist John Frey explained: "It is this unique *possession* of craft knowledge and craft skill . . . that is, their *possession* of these things and the employers' ignorance of them, that has enabled the workers to organize and to force better terms from the employers." "The manager's brain," the saying went, "lay under the worker's cap." To raise productivity, the manager had to separate "craft knowledge from craft skill" and glean the knowledge for technology. The goal, as a machinist told a Senate committee, was to organize work so that "The machinery instead of the man is the brains." Andrew Carnegie, watching steel prices decline nearly 19 percent in three years, was among the first industrialists to recognize this problem and the first to solve it. His solution threatened class war.[7]

At Homestead, on the Monongahela River six miles southeast of Pittsburgh, Carnegie worked his men every day of the year except Christmas and the Fourth of July. The workday was twelve hours; the workweek seven days. At thirty-five, men faltered; at forty, they were finished. "The superintendents and foremen are alert to detecting weakness of any sort," a journalist reported, "and if a man fails appreciably, he can expect discharge." The steel puddler's job—to cook molten iron—was "so severe that they have to stop, now and then, in summer, take off their boots, and pour the perspiration out of them." During an 1893 tour of the mills, the novelist Hamlin Garland saw men prodding the deep soaking pits where the ingots glowed in white-hot chambers.

> I saw other men in the hot yellow glare from the furnaces. I saw men measuring the serpentine rosy beams. . . . I saw boys perched high in cages, their shrill voices sounding wild and animal-like in the midst of the uproar; a place into which men went like men going to war for the sake of wives and children, urged on by necessity, blinded and dulled by custom and habit; an inhuman place to spend four-fifths of one's waking hours. . . . Upon such toil rests the splendor of American civilization.

Fifteen to twenty-five men a year died at Homestead. The records of Carnegie Steel's successor, U.S. Steel, include terse notations on workplace accidents at the mill: "Crane chain broke and piece of metal (17500 #

The Homestead Works

gun carriage forging) fell on man," "laddle of molten metal . . . splashed out on a man. . . . Died: 7:47 a.m." As late as 1910 nearly a quarter of all workers in the iron and steel industries suffered injury at least once a year. "You start in to be a man," a Homestead worker confided to Garland, "but you become more and more a machine. . . . It's like any severe labor. It drags you down mentally and morally, just as it does physically."[8]

A third of the Homestead workforce held on to their manhood through the Amalgamated Association of Iron and Steel Workers, with over 20,000 members ostensibly among the country's most powerful unions—but one being undermined by the industry's makeover from iron to steel and by the defection of several of its leaders to management. Perhaps it didn't exercise what Martha Frick Symington terms "a near stranglehold" over her great-grandfather's mill, but that's how management saw it. In the words of the official historian of the Carnegie Homestead Works, "[The] method of apportioning work, of regulating the turns, of altering the machinery, in short every detail of working the great plant, was subject to the interference of some busybody representing the Amalgamated Association." Workplace democracy was inconvenient. "Our principle [*sic*] reason for repudiating the Amalgamated Association at Homestead is the annoyance it puts on us by the mill committee," F. T. Lovejoy, a Carnegie executive, said by way of explaining the lockout. "At all hours we were worried by this committee. We had no power to discharge a man. When we did discharge one, the committee held a so-called investigation, and invariably found that we were wrong. . . . But [now] we have decided to run our Homestead mill ourselves." The union had also bid up wages. A study conducted for Carnegie by William Martin, former editor of the union newspaper, revealed that Carnegie Steel paid close to 50 percent more for skilled labor at Homestead than the industry average. The union had successfully resisted Carnegie's lockout in 1889, winning a three-year contract establishing a sliding scale of tonnage rates it set. To wrest control of the work from the mill's skilled workers, Carnegie first had to destroy the union, redoubt of their self-respect and their resistance.[9]

Politics interposed one obstacle to his plan—labor trouble in an election year might hurt his Republican friends. And the world would know Andrew Carnegie for a hypocrite if he broke the union.

For Carnegie, poor boy risen, was labor's professed friend. "The right of workingmen to combine and to form trade-unions is no less sacred than the right of the manufacturer to enter into associations with his fellows," he'd written in 1883, "and it must sooner or later be conceded." But, as we have seen, moral claims yielded in Carnegie to his cold daemon. "Man must have an idol—The amassing of wealth is one of the worst species of idolatry," he'd privately brooded at thirty-three, confronting his fear that the "debasing . . . worship of money" possessed him. He vowed to retire from business within two years and "choose that life which will be the most elevating in its character," settle in Oxford, perhaps, and "make the acquaintance of literary men," buy a London newspaper, and "take a part in public matters especially those connected with education and improvement of the lower classes." Before his moral personality was destroyed he must break the spell. "To continue much longer overwhelmed by business cares and with most of my thoughts wholly upon the way to make money . . . must degrade me beyond hope of permanent recovery." Driven as few men in history by what Karl Marx called "those passions which are . . . at once the most violent, the basest and the most abominable of which the human breast is capable: the furies of personal interest," Andrew Carnegie never recovered.[10]

Sunlight disagreed with Carnegie's skin. Summers he was off for Scotland and his highland lodge. He left Pittsburgh in May, entrusting the destruction of the union to his new partner, Henry Clay Frick. Having broken unions in the coal fields by bringing in carloads of immigrants (phalanxed by armed guards) to replace striking miners, Frick feared nothing from the charge of hypocrisy. When union representatives asked that wages be kept at the 1889 level, Frick, following Carnegie's orders, demanded a wage *cut,* and laid it on the line: Carnegie Steel would tolerate no more unions. If the men don't agree, Carnegie instructed Frick, lock them out and wait for them to come to their senses. Frick obeyed. For this round Carnegie had targeted only four of the twelve mills comprising the Homestead Works; he had signed new contracts with the workers in the other eight. Yet in solidarity these men walked out when their comrades in the Amalgamated were locked out.[11]

Frick had prepared his defenses like a general of industry. He ringed the mill with a three-mile-long high fence topped with eighteen inches of barbed wire, pocked with rifle ports, and surmounted by light towers housing giant searchlights. He fitted out two armor-plated barges with slits to shoot through. He contracted with the Pinkerton National Detective Agency to put men with Winchesters behind the slits. The barges would float the Pinkertons upriver from Pittsburgh to Homestead, where they would occupy the mill. The Pinkertons numbered 300 but only forty were regular employees; the company had recruited the rest in Philadelphia, New York, and Chicago for an unspecified assignment. They were not told that a town (of 11,000 people) was waiting to kill them if they went ashore nor that a Civil War cannon across the river from the Homestead dock was set to bombard them when still afloat. If a Pinkerton or two died Frick would contain his grief; their blood would justify intervention by the National Guard. "It Is Believed the Firm Are Trying to Hasten a Conflict with the Men So They Can Appeal for State Bayonets to Protect the New Employees," the *New York Herald* headlined a story reporting on Frick's hiring of the Pinkertons.[12]

The Pinkerton Detective Agency, a private army for strikebreaking corporations, recruited men who worked for a dollar a day and the chance to wear a white silver-buttoned blouse marked with the letter "P." The 250-odd recruits put on their uniforms for the first time while the barges floated toward Homestead.

They reached Homestead at dawn. The strikers had occupied the mill; workers and townspeople, many armed, crowded the space between it and the shore. The leader of the Amalgamated, Hugh O'Donnell, pushed to the front. "We have not damaged any property, and we do not intend to," he shouted to the Pinkertons. "In the name of God and humanity don't attempt to land! Don't attempt to enter these works by force!" "We don't wish to shed blood," the Pinkerton captain, Frederick Heinde, came back, "but we are determined to go up there" and take the mill. "If you men don't withdraw, we will mow every one of you down and enter in spite of you." Heinde started across the gangplank. A pistol-carrying worker confronted him. Heinde struck him with his billy club. Both sides opened up. Heinde and the worker, Billy Foy, went down. The battle of Homestead was on.

For twelve hours, pinned down on the barges under the July sun, the Pinkerton "Have-Nots" traded shots through their gun slits with the "Have-Littles" on the bank. At one point the cannon opened fire, blowing a hole in the roof of a barge. A second shot decapitated a twenty-three-year-old worker. The workers fired a raft loaded with oil-soaked lumber and floated it toward the barges. Terrified, many of the recruits made as if to leap overboard but stayed put when a Pinkerton captain threatened to shoot jumpers. The raft flamed out before it reached them. Next, the workers pushed a railroad flatcar loaded with burning barrels down the inclined track between the mill and the dock, but it, too, stopped short of the barges. A reporter for the *St. Louis Post-Dispatch*—one of at least fifteen journalists witnessing the events—described a horror that now ensued on one of the barges. Low on ammunition, unable to retreat since the tug that had pushed the barges from Pittsburgh had abandoned them under fire, the Pinkertons decided against dying for Frick and Carnegie—for the workers, maddened past recall by their losses, intended to kill them every man. At the talk of surrender one hardhead on the barge vowed he'd sooner die fighting than skulk ashore doglike. "You'll come or I'll blow your brains out," a Winchester-carrying veteran warned him. The hold-out turned away in disgust, strode to the stern, drew his Colt, and shot himself in the head, "his brains oozing out on the already blood-soaked boards"—a martyr to the code of manliness and its victim.

Though savage, the battle had still been fought within the code; not so the "carnival of revenge" that followed the Pinkertons' surrender to the workers. In their first fusillade from the barges the Pinkertons' Winchesters cut down thirty men. Altogether, the workers suffered casualties of seven dead and sixty wounded. Their widows and wives had seen their husbands shot for defending their livelihoods. Before the battle, union officials had ordered effigies of Frick and Carnegie taken down. Now the real Carnegie, who had spent the day "being driven behind four superb grays in the most elaborate coach that Scotland had ever seen upon its roads," according to one newspaper, would have been dismembered had he shown up. Led by a union man carrying an American flag followed by a hundred armed strikers, the Pinkertons began filing up the embankment toward the mill yard. Their destination was the town opera house, to be held there for the sheriff, expected to charge them with murder. To reach the mill yard they had to run a quarter-mile-long gauntlet of men, women, and children screaming "Kill the murderers!"

"One [Pinkerton] received a slap from a woman and attempted to strike back," the *Pittsburgh Post* reported. "He was hit at once on the head with a stick and the blood flowed freely. Other women punched the fellows in the ribs with parasols and belabored them with switches." One woman poked out a Pinkerton's eye with her umbrella. "No mercy was shown them. . . . The men were punched by every man that could get a lick at them. . . . They plunged wildly on, begging for mercy." They got none in the town, where widows tore into them in frenzied rushes. One Pinkerton tried to run for his life, but a stout woman overtook him, threw him to the ground, filled his eyes with sand, and beat him with her fists. The strikers had to level their guns at the crowd to stop the bloodletting. "[O]n the walk into town every one of the 300 suffered at least some minor injuries before they reached the sanctity of the village jail," Joseph F. Wall writes in his biography of Carnegie. "Their bright new uniforms had been torn to shreds."

On the docks, meanwhile, "hundreds of women and boys" rushed the barges, pillaged their bedding, mattresses, cups, and pots, then set the heavy wooden vessels afire. "The delight of the onlookers at this finale to the tragic events of the day knew no bounds," the *Post* reporter noted, his description recalling the limbic glee of the Pittsburgh crowd in 1877 at the conflagration of the hated railroad. "They cheered, clapped their hands . . . while the dry wood blazed and crackled, and two huge columns of smoke rose lazily toward the sky and formed clouds overhead."[13]

An artist for *Frank Leslie's Illustrated Weekly* depicted the Pinkertons running the gauntlet in a cover drawing that hurt the union's cause. So did newspaper stories under headlines like "Women and Boys Join in the Horrible Work." Reporters ascribed Hungarian ancestry to the fiercest women. Congressmen investigating Homestead were "loathe to believe that any of these women were native Americans." Yet many were. In *The*

Battle for Homestead, 1880–1892, a rich treatment of the subject, Paul Krause says that the images of the Homestead furies—bottom woman top—shook the patriarchal order. A society that might accept the *idea* of strikers taking over a mill "could not tolerate or even conceptualize" righteously violent women.

A Pittsburgh society reporter who interviewed the widows and the wives of the wounded wrote, "From my heart I wished I could rescue them"—from prostitution, their likely destination. Visiting some years later the British sociologist Beatrice Webb found Homestead's poorer wards abounding with 50-cent prostitutes.[14]

The Pinkertons' ordeal gave Governor Robert Pattison, a Democrat, cover to accede to Frick's entreaties and dispatch 8,500 national guardsmen to restore order and clear the mill so that, notwithstanding Carnegie's Eleventh Commandment, "Thou shalt not take thy neighbor's job," Frick could bring in scabs. Carnegie—"the arch sneak of the age," in the judgment of a Republican congressman—later denied knowing anything about it. Visiting Homestead a year later young Theodore Dreiser saw sullen men loitering on their front stoops or walking the desolate streets while Pinkertons guarded the Polish, Hungarian, and Lithuanian immigrants who had taken their jobs.[15]

"Strikebreakers" earned their name. A study of 2,000 strikes between 1881 and 1894 reveals that employers used "replacement workers" in 40 percent of them, and that labor won only 21 percent of those strikes—but 63 percent of those in which employers did not hire replacements. Nearly two-thirds of the railroad shopmen who struck in 1892, the Bureau of Labor estimated, never got their jobs back and fully three-quarters of those who struck in 1894, the year of the Pullman Strike. For African-Americans, strikebreaking, opening up jobs from which racism otherwise barred them, was a way out of the South, where wages were well below northern levels. Frick, who had experience with racial strikebreaking, recruited experienced black metalworkers from the mills around Richmond to replace strikers at Homestead. That gave the Democrats, saddled with their governor's decision to protect Frick's scab labor, a welcome opportunity to play the race card in the fall election. Their October torchlight parade through Homestead included a float under the slogan "This is Protection"; on it stood "a live sheep painted black and a white man arrayed as a woman." In November, shouting "Let's lynch the nigger sheep!," 2,000 whites, many Eastern European immigrants, attacked the fifty black families living in "Shantytown." They fought back. No one was killed but "several" seriously wounded. Racism, according to Paul Krause, "had always been a part of Homestead," but the workers had "contained" its "most virulent manifestations." Now, with the demoralization of defeat lashing their resentment over scab labor, the immigrants proved their assimilation by joining a lynching party. Not surprisingly nine of the twenty-four most violent strikes between 1880 and 1929 involved African-American strikebreakers. Employers counted on white strikers attacking them to justify calling in the National Guard.*[16]

"No pangs remained of any wound received in my business career save that of Homestead," Carnegie wrote at the end of his life. The British press raked him for hiring a private army; then and later he denied knowledge of it, blaming the Pinkertons on Frick. Yet he knew and approved of them; a July Fourth cable to him from Frick leaves no doubt of that: "Tomorrow night, about 11 o'clock, 300 watchmen from Pinkerton, will leave the cars at Bellevue Station . . . , and take passage on two barges. . . . They will go at once to Homestead. . . . The boats contain the uniforms, the arms, the ammunition." Carnegie got worse press in America. "Count no man happy until he is dead," the *St. Louis Post-Dispatch,* a Democratic paper, wrote:

> Three months ago Andrew Carnegie was a man to be envied. Today he is an object of mingled pity and scorn. . . . One would naturally suppose that if he had a grain of consistency, not to say decency, in his composition, he would favor rather than oppose the organization of a trade union among his own working people at Homestead. . . . If he had a grain of manhood . . . he would at least have been willing to face the consequences of his inconsistency. But what does Carnegie do? Runs off to Scotland. . . . A single word from him might have saved the bloodshed—but the word was never spoken. Ten thousand "Carnegie Public Libraries" would not compensate the country for the direct and indirect evils resulting from the Homestead lockout. Say what you will of Frick, he is a brave man. Say what you will of Carnegie, he is a coward.[17]

After the bloodshed but before Frick replaced the locked-out men, Whitelaw Reid, Harrison's running mate and the editor of the *New York*

---

* Strikebreaking "appealed to many African-Americans because it provided the black man his best opportunity to assume a tough, combative posture in public and to display courage while risking serious injury or even death. Strikebreaking thus allowed African-American men to challenge openly white society's image of them as obsequious, cowardly, and lacking the ability to perform well under pressure." Stephen J. Norwood, *Strikebreaking and Intimidation: Mercenaries and Masculinity in the 20th Century* (Chapel Hill: University of North Carolina Press, 2002), p. 80.

Tribune, appealed to him to compromise with the union. The months-long lockout in the country's most protected industry was a cross to bear for the party of protection. Frick, recovering from stab and bullet wounds inflicted by the anarchist Alexander Berkman, who attacked him in his Pittsburgh office, refused. When a young guardsman protecting the mill cheered the news of Frick's near-assassination, he was hung up by his thumbs until he lost consciousness. "His crime is that of treason," his commanding officer told reporters, ordering the guardsman drummed out of his unit for "aiding, abetting, and giving comfort to our enemy."[18] The citizens of Homestead knew *their* enemy. "This town is bathed in tears today and it is all brought about by one man, who is less respected by the laboring people than any other employer in the world," a Methodist preacher said of Henry Clay Frick at the burial service for three strikers killed in the gun battle with the Pinkertons. "There is no more sensibility in that man than in a toad."

Union men were guarding the mill when General George W. Snowden's soldiers showed up. A union leader served as the town "burgess," or mayor. Homestead, for a few days, had been a "worker's republic." Though the gauntlet gave it a Commune image, order soon prevailed; the worker-citizens even arrested some Pittsburgh anarchists for attempting to hand out revolutionary leaflets. Yet, in his official report, Snowden professed astonishment at "the actual communism of these people," noting, "They believe the works are their's [*sic*] quite as much as Carnegie's."

In this they were like the freedmen who thought their labor gave them right to the planters' land. "Here is where we have toiled nearly all our lives as slaves, and were treated like dumb Driven cattle," Henry Bram, Ishmael Moultrie, and Yates Simpson, spokesmen for the freed people of Edisto Island, South Carolina, wrote in a memorial to President Andrew Johnson in the fall of 1865. "This is our home, we have made These lands what they are. . . . [A]nd if the Government does not make some provision by which our Freedmen can obtain A Homestead, We have Not bettered our condition." Similarly, misled by free labor ideals, the Homestead workers felt they had what a sympathetic Democrat, Senator John A. Palmer of Illinois, called "a moral right" to employment there. The workers echoed John A. Campbell's argument for the New Orleans butchers: As they possessed property rights in their labor, so the Homestead workers' labor, their "sweat equity," created a property right in the mill. Until the consolidation of corporate cultural hegemony after 1900, Americans believed labor was the source of all economic value. As we saw with the Populists, this "producerist's ideology," expressed in the antique phrase

Pay line at Homestead Works around 1908.

"the fruits of labor," was republican doctrine descended from the Revolution and "omnipresent in political rhetoric throughout the 19th century," according to the historian James Huston. Our ancestors pitted republicanism against capitalism, as Senator Palmer did. Holders of property "invested with a public interest" like Homestead, he contended, quoting Chief Justice Waite's opinion in the Granger cases, should "hereafter be regarded as holding their property subject to the correlative rights of those without whose services [such] property would be utterly worthless." The common good trumped private right—pure republicanism. Pure "socialism," the *Pittsburgh Commercial Gazette* labeled it. "[W]orse than a populist," another journal branded Palmer. A southern paper wondered what had happened to the "good old rule" that an owner could "do whatever he pleases with his own." Possessive individualism trumped communal republicanism.

"What is the good of freedom if one has nothing to go on?" a North Carolina freedman asked. Like the Homestead steelworkers, he had yet to take in the lesson of the age of betrayal—that, in the words of a Mississippi planter, "freedom and independence are different things."[19]

Alexander Berkman's assault on Frick killed the strike. The Amalgamated had had nothing to do with Berkman, a demented fanatic. Yet "It would seem that the bullet from Berkman's pistol, failing in its foul intent, went straight through the heart of the Homestead strike," Hugh O'Donnell, the union leader, lamented. Worse, it destroyed the union, not just its Homestead lodge. Frick appeared before public opinion as the target of a bomb-bearing anarchist—Berkman had a capsule of mercury in his teeth—a species made monstrous by the xenophobic reporting given Chicago's Haymarket Riot six years earlier; and the industry tarred the Amalgamated with anarchy by association. Frick's blood mixed with the blood of the Pinkertons to wash unions out of steel for a generation.

That November, angry over "Bloody Homestead" the "rich man's" tariff, the "'employee class' . . . secretly and deceitfully vot[ing] against their employers," in the words of a Republican analyst, turned on the GOP, giving Cleveland a decisive victory in both the popular and electoral vote and electing a Democratic Senate for only the second time since the Civil War. For the first time since *before* the war the Democrats controlled all three branches of the government.[20]

"Grover, Grover," Cleveland's claque at the Democratic National Convention chanted,

> Four more years of Grover;
> In we'll go,
> Out they'll go,
> Then we'll be in clover.

Republican senator Orville Platt of Connecticut doubted that. The Democrats had got in by appealing to "the discontented everywhere" who would expect them to deliver. "Much of the discontent prevailing in the country," he went on, "has foundation in the conduct of the capitalistic classes, and the people whom I have described will not be content with any reasonable correction of existing abuses. They want to cut deep. I think we have got to let the democratic party struggle with this problem a while now. It is little the Government can do about capitalistic abuses."[21]

Two years later, the congressional elections ended in one of "the largest transfer of seats in history," converting a Democratic majority of ninety-one to a Republican majority of 132. Defeated were past and future Democratic leaders, including (in a run for the Senate) William Jennings Bryan, of Nebraska, nationally recognized for his epic speeches against the McKinley Tariff. New England elected only one Democratic congressman—John F. Fitzgerald of Boston, grandfather of John F. Kennedy. A New York City district that had gone Democratic by 8,825 votes in 1892 went Republican by 14,802 in 1894. In the entire Midwest Democrats won only three of eighty-nine races. No Democratic congressman was left standing between Ohio and California.[22]

What happened in the space of two years to reverse Democratic fortunes? Weeks into Cleveland's term the Northern Pacific, the Philadelphia and Reading, the Union Pacific, and the Erie failed. As in 1873, railroad traffic could not service railroad debt piled on by looting or incontinent managements. The stock market spiraled; banks called in loans; the first of over a hundred national banks failed. Here was a nationalizing event, something that occurred everywhere, affected everyone. Not a "capitalistic abuse" but a capitalistic collapse, a panic followed by a depression, the harbinger of incumbent-party defeat.

In January 1894 the *Quarterly Journal of Economics* published a survey based on 1,200 questionnaires sent to municipal officials, relief authorities, and charities in cities from seaboard to seaboard.

The survey, "The Unemployed in American Cities," began in Boston, which had accelerated spending on public works to employ as many as possible of its unemployed, the condition of 40 percent of laborers in thirty-seven different crafts. Providence and Springfield were running "soup houses." In Danbury, Connecticut, the hat manufacturers shut out their workforce, using the distress to break the hatters' union, which appealed in vain to the city to put men to work on city projects. All industry was suspended in Amsterdam, New York, the citizens "approaching beggary." In New York City the unemployed numbered at least 80,000. Public school children were asked to bring a cold potato to school for hungry schoolmates. In East Buffalo, 5,000 Poles faced "imminent danger of starvation." Buffalo itself experienced a "bread riot." Governor Roswell Flowers rejected a public works program for the unemployed, echoing Grover Cleveland's first-term veto of the seeds bill for Texas farmers: "In America the people support the government; it is not the province of the government to support the people." Half of Paterson, New Jersey's, workers were "said to be idle." Washington, D.C., reported "greater destitution than ever before known at this time of year, there being a vast army of the unemployed, and men ["most Negroes"] pleading for food who have never before been compelled to seek aid." Dayton, Ohio, revived "the practice of sweeping the streets by hand." The destitute of Indianapolis subsisted on a weekly ration of 82 cents' worth of food—cornmeal, potatoes, bread, molasses, salt, and pork. Complaints about the want of coffee and sugar got their ration increased 18 cents.

Fifteen hundred people slept in Chicago's City Hall; miles of sleeping men lined the viaducts along the "L" roads. "Famine is in our midst," the chairman of the Relief Committee testified, estimating the number of "starving people" at 2,000 and the number without "food or fuel supplies" at 15,000. The police met all incoming trains, turning back the "hordes of tramps" seeking food in Chicago. With winter nearing, the city permitted the stricken to gather scraps of wood for fires from the plaster and fiber buildings of the White City at the World's Fair, whose "glamour or promise" had drawn thousands of job seekers in May. A year later, during the violent Pullman Strike, a mob spilling out of the adjacent railyards would touch portions of the White City.

To "assist the worthy needy but guard against the impositions of the unworthy," Detroit's 25,000 unemployed underwent "detailed investigation" before they could be entrusted with a bowl of soup. Guided by the dictum of Mrs. Josephine Shaw Lowell, the social work pioneer, that "Relief work, to be a benefit and not an injury, must be continuous, hard and underpaid," cities worked the starving. Baltimore and Pittsburgh sent all applying for relief to a "stone-yard" to break rocks for food. In Denver the path to food went through the wood-yard. Saving its "colored" from demoralization, Kansas City, Missouri, operated a wood-yard, a stone-yard, and a woman's work-room. Kansas governor Lorenzo D. Lewelling issued a "Tramp Circular" that applied the values of his People's Party to the least of the people, declaring the "rock pile abolished in Kansas so long as I am Governor." Men should not be jailed or "made to suffer degradation for no other reason than that they are out of money. It is no crime to be without visible means of support." But, outside of Kansas, it was.[23]

As 1893 ended *Bradstreet's*, the organ of financial analysis, reported a "wave of industrial unrest breaking over the country," with strikes among shoe workers, coal miners, and coke workers in Pennsylvania; iron miners in Minnesota; brick-makers in the Hudson River Valley; shoe and silk workers in New England; and railmen in the western states. Some workers turned violent. When the Detroit Water Board announced that it would no longer offer daily wages for excavation work and instead pay by the yard shoveled, "Five hundred Polish laborers refused to be overawed by the presence of the sheriff, armed deputies, and water board commissioners," David Montgomery writes. "In a bloody encounter, the Poles bludgeoned the sheriff to death, and police gunfire killed eighteen strikers." Dead workers spoke louder than living ones: The board backed down. After Cleveland sent federal troops to suppress the Pullman Strike without Illinois governor John Peter Altgeld requesting them as the Constitution required, the *Arena* accused Cleveland of "Caesarism" and a Williams College professor detected the "virus of tyranny" in the president. Others feared a virus spreading from below. General Nelson Miles, who commanded the troops in Chicago, referring to the strike leader Eugene Debs, recommended forced colonization as the best antidote to "malarial poisons of the Deb's element."[24]

Eighteen ninety-four showed Democrats the danger, in hard times, of being linked to Cleveland's principled negations. "Cleveland might be honest," William Jennings Bryan quipped during a silver debate in the House, "but so were Indian mothers who with misguided zeal threw their children in the Ganges." Cleveland, Jackson Lears observes, "aimed to restore business confidence by making sound money even sounder." Pushing Congress to repeal the Sherman Silver Purchase Act, Cleveland cleansed the currency "of even the smallest taint of silver." Repeal would further contract the money supply, making borrowing even harder; a betrayal of the farmer, for rural Democrats. Throughout 1895 state party conventions from Ohio to California passed resolutions calling for the "free unlimited coinage of silver"—Sherman Silver squared. The Democrats would cure deflation with inflation and tight with easy money. When, at the Democratic National Convention in Chicago, a delegate mentioned Cleveland's name during a debate, "Many of the spectators rose to their feet and cheered"—but not one delegate joined in. Thus the party had gone over to silver well before orator Bryan (who gave "little talks to his playmates from the front steps of his house" starting at age four), arranging to speak last after a row of worthies had stupefied delegates cooking in the heat, let rip his stem-winder, winning the delegates' hearts and their nomination for president.

Bryan had emerged as a leading voice of the anti-Cleveland democracy through congressional speeches that wear better than the "Cross of Gold" speech, which offends our pluralist values. "Today the Democratic party stands between two great forces, each inviting its support," he declared from the floor of the House in 1893.

> On the one side stand the corporate interests of the nation, its moneyed institutions, its aggregations of wealth and capital, imperious, arrogant, and compassionless. They demand special legislation, favors, privileges, and immunities. . . . They demand that the Democratic party become their agent to execute their merciless decrees.
>
> On the other side stands the unnumbered throng which gave a name to the Democratic party and for which it has assumed to speak. Work-worn and dust-begrimed, they make their sad appeal.[25]

If Senator Alben Barkley's voice could "call in the hogs from the next county," what should we say of Bryan's? His biographers claim it could project to 50,000 people. Photographs reveal the chest and neck of a strenuous tenor, and the energy breathed into his words flowed untaxed by doubt or guilt. Certainly he spoke before crowds the size of small cities. In an 18,000-mile rail marathon—the first weeks of which he traveled on regularly scheduled trains—Bryan delivered as many as thirty five-minute speeches a day from the back of his train, from platforms, in town squares and city arenas. He spoke to crowds of 70,000 in Louisville, 50,000 in Columbus, 30,000 in Toledo, and 15,000 in Springfield, Illinois, his voice "reaching for the horizon" every time, rallying "the plain people" to "stand against the encroachments of organized wealth," to stand with *him*. "A rather engaging young man," the *Toledo News* discovered upon inspection, "with a prominent nose, an extremely wide thin-lipped mouth, a smile that was almost a grin, in a black alpaca coat, a 'boil' shirt, a low collar, a string tie." In a torchlight parade Toledo Democrats led him to a square where 30,000 waited for the beardless Democrat; at thirty-six, the youngest presidential candidate ever.[26]

Bryan looms as a historic figure in political history. He led the Democrats out of their thralldom to the enfeebling anti-statism descended from Jefferson and Jackson. Where he led Wilson and FDR followed. In his veto message on the bank, Jackson may have "confronted class reality like no other president," to quote Charles Sellers, but with one eye, seeing class influence on government, blind to class power within society. The rhetoric—"Many of our rich men have not been content with equal protection and equal benefits, but have besought to make themselves richer by act of Congress"—peters out in a piety: "If [government] could confine itself to equal protection, and, as heaven does its rains, shower its favors on the high and the low, the rich and the poor, it would be an unqualified blessing." Government, in this conception, is neutral in the struggle between "the house of Have" and "the house of Want," the class terms used by the Jacksonian historian George Bancroft. In identifying government *favortism* as the enemy of "equal freedom," Jackson left his "farmers, mechanics, and laborers" facing big business alone. Zealous to protect democracy from capitalism, Jacksonianism protected capitalism from democracy. Behind a smoke screen of obeisance to Jefferson and Jackson, which fooled historians into depicting Bryan as a backward-facing pastoralist, he broke with *their* party. Responding to the vacuum of countervailing power created by industrialism, he made the turn from Jackson to FDR, from negative to positive government. "[Those] who have the greatest interests at stake gather around legislative halls and secure legislation that grants them special privileges and then entrench themselves behind the privileges granted," he told the citizens of Ottumwa, Iowa. Behind the "money question" and the "labor question" and "behind the money power stand all those combinations which have been using the Government for public plunder."* Exposing the nexus of power forged by "the busy few"—so far, pure Jackson. But, learning from the Populists, Bryan transcended Jackson's view of government as an indifferent rain. Government must act—but for the "people." Whereas the Republicans believed that if government helped the wealthy "prosperity would leak through on those below," the Bryan democracy held that "legislative action which assists the masses would provide a base for prosperity for all."[27]

---

* Philippic against the "money power" remained a constant of Democratic electioneering. "The masters of the United States are the combined capitalists and manufacturers of the United States," Woodrow Wilson averred. Under Herbert Hoover, FDR charged, the government was "in the hands of one hundred or two hundred all-wise individuals controlling the purse strings of the Nation." Harry Truman declared that the "Republicans want a return to the Wall Street economic dictatorship. . . . The Republican strategy is to divide the farmer and the industrial worker . . . so that big business can grasp the balance of power and take the country over, lock, stock, and barrel." But, to see the difference Bryan made in the history of his party, compare Grover Cleveland's vision—"the Government should not support the people"—to that of the next Democratic president, Woodrow Wilson. "We used to say that the ideal of government was for every man to be left alone and not interfered with," he declared in the 1912 campaign, the "we" being the pre-Bryan democracy. "That was the idea in Jefferson's time. But we are coming now to realize that life is so complicated that we are not dealing with old conditions, and that law has to step in and create new conditions under which we may live." See the remarkable analysis of Democratic convention and campaign speeches in John Gerring, *Party Ideologies in America, 1828–1996* (Cambridge: Cambridge University Press, 1998), pp. 196–205.

Bottom rail first: bad news for government's wards (and masters) those thirty-five years past—the manufacturers who had gotten their tariffs, the bankers their gold standard, the railroads their land grants, the mining companies their mountains, the timber companies their forests, the cattlemen their range, the steamship lines their oceans, the corporate lawyers their "person." If Bryan won, the government would have new owners.

The "People": the Populist deity enters Democratic liturgy with Bryan. Yale students heckled him on the New

William Jennings Bryan

Haven Common but the "plain people" cheered, especially "the struggling masses who are despised and spit upon" beyond the Mississippi. A campaign reporter described Bryan's charismatic bond with his core voters, the farmers, tenants, and farm laborers who named their twins "William" and "Jennings," their triplets "William," "Jennings," and "Bryan," and who buckboarded, some of them, a hundred miles to attend his speakings. "The poor, the weak, the humble, the aged, the infirm," the reporter wrote, "rush forward by the hundreds at the close of Mr. Bryan's speeches, and hold up their hard and wrinkled hands to the young, great orator, as if he were in very truth their promised redeemer from bondage."[28]

Reports like that spoiled breakfasts in Boston and New York. "I do not believe defeat to be possible," Henry Adams wrote in early October, "but it is evident that . . . the last month of Bryan roaring out desperate appeals to hate and envy . . . is having its effect on the dangerous classes." Bryan got his loudest applause in the "Cross of Gold" speech when he said those who charged the silverites with chilling the business climate and harming the businessman "have made the definition of a businessman too limited in its application. The man who is employed for wages is as much a businessman as his employer."[29] Farmers, town merchants, store clerks, and country lawyers were as much "businessmen" as "the few financial magnates who, in a back room, corner the money of the world. . . . We come to speak for the broader class of businessmen." Those businessmen, who swam or sank in the laissez-faire economy the big boys hid from in trusts, wanted political capitalism shut down and competition restored at the top. They *were* dangerous—to the edifice of bought government reared up over them and upon their resignation.

That's why banks reportedly kicked in one-quarter of 1 percent of their capital holdings to defeat Bryan. Why the reaper-maker Cyrus McCormick sent his 7,500 field agents, who talked to scores of farmers and merchants every week and who would spread his words, a letter that said: "If we felt sure the election would go for sound money, and reasonable protection, we should push ahead with our manufacturing. . . . If we thought the country would go for silver, we would run at only half our capacity." Why a Connecticut insurance company declared it would refuse mortgages to farmers in Ohio and Indiana if Bryan won. Why Connecticut General notified *its* 65,000 policyholders that free silver would reduce the value of their insurance. Why contracts were written "to be executed in case Mr. Bryan is defeated, and not otherwise." Why orders placed in Canada were held up "cum McKinley." Why, within two weeks of Bryan's defeat, *Dun's* could report that 383 establishments shut down cum McKinley had reopened in gold's safe sun and another 291 treading water had resumed full production. Why businessmen went frugal for McKinley. "If a man thinks of furnishing his home, or buying anything beyond what he must eat and wear from day to day," *The Nation* reported, "he puts off until after the election." Why organs of metropolitan contumely like *The Nation* and the *Philadelphia Press* charged that Bryan "incarnated the spirit of communism and anarchy"; and that the Chicago platform—which called for a graduated income tax to replace the tariff tax, an end to "government by injunction," an enlargement of the Interstate Commerce Commission's power to regulate railroads, tariff for revenue only, economy in government, and the reduction of "useless offices"—represented "the concrete creed of the mob." Why Mark Hanna, McKinley's Karl Rove, when someone said Bryan might win, sneered: "Do you think we'd let that damned lunatic get into the White House? You know you can hire half of the people of the United States to shoot down the other half if necessary, and we've got the money to hire them."[30]

Scrapping plans for a late-summer cruise off the New England coast, Hanna fought the Bryan tide. "Dollar Mark" mustered money—$250,000 from Standard Oil, $100,000 apiece from Chicago's Big Four meatpackers—employers whipped up fear, Cleveland Democrats bolted, economists flung gold, and newspapers hurled slander. The *New York Times* questioned Bryan's sanity and printed a letter from a psychologist who recognized symptoms of "paranoia querulenta," "graphomania," and "oratorical monomania" in the calculating politician. "Paranoid or Mattoid" (degenerate) read the *Times* headline over two columns of interviews with "alienists" and psychologists who mostly plumped for "Mattoid." By late October, spending $60,000 a day, Mark Hanna, "Promising manna. . . . Pouring out the long green to a million workers," could return a contribution with the note, "It's all over." Grant's uniquely skewed victories aside, McKinley's popular vote margin of 4.4 percent stands as the postwar's largest and costliest, with a national and local GOP campaign fund, topped off with the contributions of the Democrats' corporate and Wall Street investors, approaching $16 million, pitted against Bryan's $600,000, only a fifth contributed by silver interests.[31]

The Republican treasury consummated a new relationship with organized money. Writing in 1900, William E. Chandler, a former Republican National Committee chairman, recognized a historic line had been crossed in 1896: "Four years ago for the first time corporations began to make political contributions directly from their corporate treasuries. Prior to that time no such thing would have been tolerated. In every corporation there were minority directors who would have arrested any such contribution by going to law, if necessary." But, to defeat Bryan, "these democratic minorities in railroad and bank corporations made no objection to contributions to the Republican party taken from the treasuries of the companies." Before, business owners and executives paid for politics; in 1896 corporations bought a controlling stake in the GOP. "All questions in a democracy [are] questions of money," said Mark Hanna, prophet.[32]

Though Democratic publicists framed the race as "son of honest toil" (really the son of prosperous judge) versus "mining and traction magnate," Bryan ran not against Mark Hanna but "Major" William McKinley, to posterity a Hanna-worked puppet. Yet, "To a greater extent than any of his contemporaries," William McKinley "captured the popular fancy," his biographer H. Wayne Morgan writes. "His record as an honest politician, his incessant drumming of the prosperity theme, his personality, his wide travels, the simplicity of his life and views, as well as his refusal to engage in calumny made him the most popular Republican of his day." When Murat Halstead, the editor last seen at a loss for words to convey the roar inside the Wigwam when Lincoln went over the top at the 1860 Republican convention, telephoned McKinley from the Democratic convention in the same city to tell him that Bryan would be the nominee, the major said

"That is rot," and hung up. He couldn't believe the campaign would turn on "this money matter" instead of the tariff: "I am a tariff man, standing on a tariff platform." He rejected Hanna's advice to follow Bryan onto the hustings: "Don't you remember that I announced I would not under any circumstances go on a speechmaking tour? If I should go now, it would be an acknowledgement of weakness. Moreover, I might just as well put up a trapeze on my front lawn and compete with some professional athlete as out speaking against Bryan. I have to *think* when I speak." Instead he turned his home into a Republican shrine for the three-quarters of a million pilgrims—teachers, dockworkers, businessmen, party workers from thirty states—who took special railway cars to Canton, Ohio, to laud in vetted scripts the candidate who bandied pleasantries with them from his front porch, among the most message-laden backdrops in American political history. The Pennsylvania Railroad, now led by Alexander Cassatt, volunteered 1,000 employees for a Canton pilgrimage; Carnegie dispatched a parade of Homestead steelworkers. Even Bryan paid a call, the major churlishly remarking to Bryan's companion, "Silver Dick" Bland, that *he* should have won at Chicago.[33]

Silver *was* the issue of the campaign; Bryan unwisely subordinated platform planks with wider appeal to Democratic voters. Before the Civil War, the United States used a bimetallic currency: sixteen ounces of silver equaled one ounce of gold—the totemic 16 to 1 ratio. After the war, silver so increased in value relative to gold that it was being hoarded. Since the silver dollar was not being used as currency, in the Coinage Act of 1873 Congress dropped it and so demonetized silver. Few realized that the "Crime of '73" had just occurred, but, after silver fell in price and became more abundant following discoveries of new fields in the West, inflationists from the Greenback Party in the 1870s to the Populists in the 1890s shouted it from the rooftops. To contain silver agitation ("Right or wrong, its demonetization is regarded as a grand error if not a crime," Treasury Secretary John Sherman, an architect of the Coinage Act, conceded), Congress partially remonetized silver with the Bland-Allison Act of 1878—but not enough to offset the deflationary drag of a contracted currency. At $30.35 per capita in 1865 and $19.36 by 1880, the money supply lagged the growth of the economy. Between 1879 and 1897 money grew 6 percent and prices fell 1 percent a year. Between 1892 and 1897 it did not grow at all and commodity prices ignited the Populist revolt.

With the Populists, Bryan railed against the Crime of '73 for "assassinat[ing] labor" and subordinating the "toiling masses" to the "interest[s] of avarice and greed"; and he demanded that silver be remonetized at the 1873 ratio of 16 to 1, restoring "the money of the fathers." Bryan wanted the government to coin silver without statutory limit on its amount—hence "free silver"—and to do it unilaterally, without waiting for foreign governments to agree on the "bimetallic ratio" between silver and gold. Although billed as "bimetallism," free silver effectively meant silver monometallism since, as Walter T. K. Nugent explains, "silver coined freely would drive gold out of circulation as long as silver's market price remained considerably below the legal ratio." McKinley, too, advocated bimetallism, but made its adoption in the United States contingent upon its adoption internationally. That was the sound silver position since, unlike free silver, it would not, Nugent writes, "place [the country] at the mercy of foreign creditors who demanded repayment in gold." Given the improbability of its being agreed, however, international bimetallism effectively meant gold monometallism.

In his letter accepting the Republican nomination McKinley attacked silver as a fraud on credulity: "It would not make labor easier, the hours of labor shorter, or the pay better. It would not make farming less laborious, or more profitable. It would create no new occupations. It would add nothing to the comfort of the people, or the wealth of the Nation. . . . It would not conserve values, on the contrary, it would derange all existing values." Milton Friedman demurs. "Adoption of silver by the U.S. would certainly have moderated or eliminated deflationary tendencies here . . . and might have eliminated deflation in the world at large," he and Anna Jacobson Schwartz write in their *Monetary History of the United States.* Deflation was the crux of Bryan's case against gold. In a 1990 paper Friedman advanced even stronger claims for silver. "Silver standard bimetallism would almost surely have avoided what Schwartz and I dubbed 'the disturbed years from 1891 to 1897,' encompassing the very sharp contraction of 1892–94, a brief and mild recovery from 1894 to 1895, followed by another contraction from 1895 to 1896, widespread bank failures plus a banking panic in 1893, and a run on U.S. gold reserves by foreigners fearful that silver agitation would force the U.S. off the gold standard."

In principle Friedman agreed with the Populists and Bryan. "Abandonment of gold . . . would have been highly preferable to the general depression of the 1890's," in part caused by the 11 percent drop in international gold prices between 1891 and 1897, which forced a corresponding drop in

U.S. prices and wages. Bimetallism was feasible *and* desirable—in 1873. But by 1896 "it was almost surely too late to undo the damage: Bryan may have been trying to close the door after the horse had been stolen."[34]

Moreover, citing the "flight from the dollar" touched off by Bryan's nomination, Friedman agreed with McKinley that in the context of the depression silver "would not restore business confidence, but its direct effect would be to destroy the little which yet remains." Ironically, thanks in part to the discovery of gold fields in the Yukon and elsewhere, the prosperity beginning with the McKinley era was transfused by a 7.5 percent yearly increase in the money supply, which between 1897 and 1914 enabled a 2 percent yearly increase in prices, just what Bryan and the Populists predicted more money in circulation would accomplish.

While compelling to economists able to abstract the debate from its environing context, weighing the merits of gold versus silver clouds *our* rearward look. Richard Hofstadter captures it, finding "something genuinely tragic in the clash of the two hypnotic dogmatisms," reminding us that the "battle of the standards" unfolded in the midst of "economic misery" magical metals could not relieve. More than at any other time between the Civil War and the Great Depression, the nation needed the politics of remedy, not one more churn of the politics of distraction.[35]

"I have borne the sins of Grover Cleveland," Bryan said, explaining his defeat. Imagine if, instead of renominating Herbert Hoover in 1932, the Republicans had put up another candidate who blamed Hoover's policies for the Depression. Bryan was in that candidate's position in 1896. The Depression occurred on a Democratic president's watch and with the Democrats, between 1892 and 1894, leading both houses of Congress. Although Cleveland's gold Democrats bolted the party when it nominated Bryan, the Republicans tagged him as the candidate of "the party of depression," which "in full and unrestricted control of the government . . . for the first time since the Civil War," the Republican platform charged, "precipitated panic, blighted industry and trade with prolonged depression, closed factories, reduced work and wages, halted enterprise and crippled American production, while stimulating foreign products for the American market."

Bryan committed his own sins against victory, pitching his campaign, rhetoric, and remedies, to rural, white, evangelical Protestant America. "Burn down *your* cities and leave our farms and your cities will spring up again as if by magic; but destroy our farms and the grass will grow in the streets of every city in the country," he declaimed in his "Cross of Gold" speech at the Chicago convention. As he shouted the last words—"You shall not crucify mankind on a cross of gold!"—he extended his arms out from his shoulders in imitation of Christ crucified. Some delegates picked up on that icon's subtext, chanting "Down with gold! Down with the hooknose shylocks of Wall Street! Down with Christ-killing gold bugs!" Fortuitously for McKinley, to avoid offending either Catholics or Protestants, a rabbi had delivered the opening prayer at the GOP convention in St. Louis.[36]

The religious heat he gave off hurt Bryan in cities everywhere except in the mountain West. "The people here think if a man talks like Bryan he is *nutty*," a Philadelphian remarked. Though the Irish stayed with Bryan (he was a Democrat), ethno-religious politics proved stronger than his economic populism. The evangelical vesture of his campaign widened the social divide between farmer and worker, and his unifying message—that government worked for "the money power," not the "plain people"— foundered on his silver solution.[37]

The 70 percent fall in commodity prices since 1865 had proved a deliverance to straitened urban workers, who, until their wages caught up, would be hurt by the currency inflation—and higher prices—that would help farmers. "The rise in prices, by increasing the cost of living," a fair-minded critic wrote, "would undoubtedly curtail for many years the consuming power of the wages receiving class." For that reason the Socialist Workers Party attacked free silver. Bryan reached out to the industrial worker— "Labor Unions All Right: One of the Few Things in This Country Mr. Bryan Likes," the *Times* headlined—advocating immigration restriction, a union cause. And he proffered the solidarity of the Populist farm: "Wherever there has been an effort on the part of laboring men to secure any legislation on their behalf, where have they found their friends?" he asked at Hornellsville, New York. "They found their friends on the farm, and not in Wall Street among the advocates of the gold standard." But he seemed uncomprehending of the nature of industrial society when, in speeches in Lynn, Massachusetts, and elsewhere, he described wage workers in free labor terms as independent producers, a "jarringly anachronistic perception," in Paul Kleppner's words. "Bryan's campaign polarized sentiment on what, for his purposes, was the wrong basis," James L. Sundquist observes in his study of realignment. "He did not set class against class; he set rural against urban."[38]

Poster for William McKinley's 1896 presidential campaign.

While some employers pressured their workers to reject Bryan and a few fired vocal Bryanites, coercion cannot account for the dimension of Bryan's defeat in Democratic cities. In 1892 Cleveland carried New York by 76,000 votes, Chicago by 35,000, and Boston by 10,000; four years later Bryan lost New York by 21,000—the first Democrat since 1848 who failed to carry Kings County—Chicago by 56,000, and Boston, where 75,000 "howling, good-natured" people had gathered on the Common to hear his September 26 speech, by 18,000. While Cleveland won San Francisco by 6,600 votes, Bryan lost California by 392 votes because he lost San Francisco, his pietistic supporters having anathematized "the city of Sin and Syringes." In eighty-five Midwest cities Cleveland's plurality totaled 162,000; McKinley's 464,000. Despite the GOP platform's endorsement of a literacy test for new immigrants, Chicago's Germans and Scandinavians went strongly for McKinley, and the Republican vote increased by 21 percent in Polish and Bohemian wards, leaving the Irish wards alone in their 90 percent ardor for the Democracy. Of 10,000 factory workers surveyed in downstate Illinois, only 15 percent supported Bryan, 81 percent McKinley. Among 3,500 railroad workers, 11 percent were for Bryan, 86 percent for McKinley. By 1896 men could vote their conscience with the secret ballot. For the most part urban workers freely rejected William Jennings Bryan. And McKinley gave them something to vote *for.* The Democrats had trimmed the McKinley tariff's 49 percent rate to 41 percent—and the economy fell into depression. McKinley pledged to raise the tariff. Protection would restore prosperity.[39]

According to Josephus Daniels, Bryan's colleague from the Wilson cabinet, Bryan "never doubted" he won, though he lost by 569,748 votes. Bryan calculated that a change of 19,446 votes in the right places, and he'd have taken office. He did not contest the election, Daniels said, afraid civil war might follow.[40]

Politics is the struggle for control of the state between the "house of Want" and the "house of Have." After the Civil War "the house of Have" launched a revolution from above, which a party system still organized along the sectional axis of competition established in the 1850s protected against a counterrevolution from below. "The takeoff phase of industrialization has been a brutal and exploitive process everywhere, whether managed by capitalists or commissars," the political scientist Walter Dean Burnham wrote in his influential interpretation of late-nineteenth- and early-twentieth-century voting behavior cited in chapter one. "A vital functional political need during this phase is to provide adequate insulation of the industrializing elites from mass pressures, and to prevent their displacement by a coalition of those who are damaged by the processes of capital accumulation." Small farmers and urban laborers headed the casualty list of accumulation in the United States—and they could vote. Joined politically, they might have captured the state from the house of Have and fashioned an early New Deal—allowing industrialization to proceed but under new rules cushioning society against its brutalities. During the depression of 1893–97, plunging agricultural prices and mass unemployment in the cities made "industrializers and their intellectual and legal spokesmen . . . acutely conscious that these two profoundly alienated groups might coalesce."

Instead, "The Democratic-Populist effort to create a coalition of the dispossessed . . . created the most enduringly sectional political alignment in American history." In 1892 Cleveland carried Connecticut, Delaware, Maryland, New Jersey, New York, Kentucky, West Virginia, Wisconsin, North Dakota, Illinois, and Indiana; Bryan lost every one, improving on Cleveland only in the silver West. The Democrats were back to 1860 in presidential elections—a party of the South. Excluding 1912, when a split in the GOP magnified the Democrats' national appeal, 84.5 percent of their electoral votes between 1896 and 1928 came from southern and border states. The Republicans, more than ever, were the party of the North and decisively of the president-making Midwest. That political geography endured until 1932 when the economics of depression overrode sectional and cultural divisions, and the two wings of the house of Want united in the New Deal coalition.[41]

It had been a near-run thing, and three months after the election the New York elite celebrated, ringing out the Gilded Age with a "charity ball" of criminal opulence that occupied half the space in the Waldorf Hotel—ballrooms, restaurants, private dressing rooms—and all of its 700 servants. Competition as well as charity motivated Bradley and Cornelia Martin, he a prominent lawyer, she the inheritor of nearly $7 million, to give the ball. Mrs. Martin, the *New York Times* reported, had vowed to top the $100,000 the then Mrs. Alva Vanderbilt spent on an 1883 ball to christen her new $3 million mansion on Fifth Avenue, an event to which Alva's sister-in-law Alice came "dressed as The Electric Light in an evening gown fitted with gas jets that periodically spouted flames." Having since traded in one millionaire for another, the now Mrs. Alva Belmont was Mrs. Martin's rival in the contest to be the social queen of New York. To provide work for local dressmakers and milliners—the charity aspect—Mrs. Martin mailed the invitations late, so that her guests would not have time to send to Paris for finery. She requested they wear costumes from the court of Louis XV (1715–1774), famous for "hunting women and foxes." One of the former, Madame de Pompadour, spoke prophetically when she said, "Après nous le déluge." A dozen women came dressed as Marie Antoinette, Louis XVI's wife, who lost her head in the deluge.

Fear stalked the fete. The Reverend Dr. William S. Rainsford, rector of St. George's Episcopal Church, warned his wealthy congregants to think twice about attending. "[S]uch a display at this time is ill-advised," he told the *Times*. It would only increase the "widespread discontent expressed in the National election by the casting of 6 million votes against existing social conditions." Threatening letters from the discontented could not cow the Bradley Martins; others were not so brave. At any rate, of 1,200 invited, only 600 showed up. But they included *names:* Astor, Fish, Harriman, Morgan, Drexel, Cunard, and Rockefeller. John Jacob Astor attended, dressed in purple tights as Henry of Navarre, carrying a diamond-studded sword. J. P. Morgan wore a "Molière costume." His daughter Anne—in leather dress, leggings, and a feathered headdress—appeared as Pocahontas. Two George Washingtons represented the American Republic. Caroline Astor had $250,000 worth of gems sewn through her dress. To dispel any confusion on the point, Mrs. William Astor wanted it known that she had never before been in a hotel. Mrs. Astor's concession to novelty put Cornelia Martin one up on her rival.

The guests processed into the grand ballroom, which had been tarted up to resemble Versailles, and where, from a mock throne under a velvet canopy, Cornelia Martin received them. Beside her sat a powdered apparition in pink satin, white breeches, and red shoes with diamond buckles that was Bradley Martin. Overdoing the doomed-royalty note, Cornelia not only wore a ruby necklace that had once belonged to Marie Antoinette but a dress worn by Mary Stuart. It is not recorded whether any of America's aristos winced when, as their equipages passed in the street, an onlooker shouted, "Off with his head!"

"No Such Social Function Ever Before Seen in America," the *Times* headlined its story on the ball, which began on page one and filled two inside pages. No detail was beneath its notice ("The eye scarcely knew where to look or what to study"). The society reporter got tipsy in air perfumed by 35,000 "galax, that rich dark leaf gathered in South Carolina from the hillsides," by the "royal asparagus vines," by the 5,000 roses, and by the 3,000 orchids and the "long-stemmed pink roses intertwined with the most lavish abandon, and forming a floral screen in front of the balcony." By turns awestruck and amused at the spectacle of men dancing the cotillion "with swords at their sides . . . for the first time in the history of balls in this city since colonial times," the reporter noted that great was the "merriment caused by the awkwardness of many in handling so unfamiliar an appendage of high dress." And he seemed overcome by the sight of Miss Lena Goodrich wearing "[a] dainty Louis XV dress, the skirt of watermelon corded silk trimmed with lace flounces, over dress of Pompadour silk with Watteau and paniers edged with wide lace . . . lace and chiffon around the low neck, with clusters of roses half hidden [by] elbow sleeves finished by lace ruffles . . . the front of the bodice . . . embroidered with jewels and little pink bows finished the trimming at the front." She was one of the number of revelers, arranged by alphabetical order, given a sartorial box score. Marinating in the splendor, the *Times* reporter felt as if "some fairy godmother, in a dream, had revived the glories of the past for one's special enjoyment, and that one was mingling with the dignitaries of ancient regimes, so perfect was the illusion."

Outside the Waldorf, Deputy Police Chief Cartwright looked to the disposition of his 250 men who, with a "hired army" of Pinkertons, protected the sportive rulers of the age of capital from "thieves or men of socialistic tendencies," though no self-respecting socialist could keep down his Terrapène decossee à la Baltimore in that company. "As a further precaution," Sven Beckert relates in *The Monied Metropolis,* "the first-floor windows of the Waldorf were nailed shut."[42]

Chapter Twelve

MISSISSIPPI AND THE AMERICAN WAY

> If the stronger and cleverer race is free to impose its will upon "new-caught, sullen peoples" on the other side of the globe, why not in South Carolina . . . ? The advocates of the "shotgun policy" are quite as sincere, and we are inclined to think as unselfish, as the advocates of "benevolent assimilation." The two phrases, in fact, are two names for the same thing.
>
> —1901 editorial in *The Atlantic Monthly*,
> on white supremacy in the Philippines and the South[1]

Visiting the United States in the early 1900s, a land-poor aristocrat on the scout for an American "dollar princess" like Cornelia Martin's daughter (landed by the Earl of Craven), might have thought Bryan had won in 1896. Although in the 1890s Theodore Roosevelt had called for Populist leaders to be "taken out and shot," after succeeding to the presidency following McKinley's assassination in 1901 he championed an urban middle-class version of Populist reform, appealing to a mood and movement known as Progressivism. In the Kansas editor William Allen White's rendering, the Progressives "caught the Populists in swimming and stole all of their clothing except the frayed underdrawers of free silver." They also borrowed the Populists' indignant perception that America had taken a wrong turn since the Civil War. The depression of the early 1890s revealed depths of want and alienation in the new industrial civilization. What had happened? Who was to blame? Seventy-five years after Andrew Jackson framed the issue presented by the Second Bank as whether the people were "to govern through representatives chosen by their own unbiased suffrages" or by "the money and power of a great corporation," Progressive reformers were battling the same enemy.[2] Blaming the malady of the times on business rule, they targeted the "corporate arrogance" of daily life. They found it "in an unprotected railway crossing where children were killed as they came home from school or in the refusal of an impoverished water company to make improvements needed to provide the healthful water which could stop the epidemics of typhoid fever," David P. Thelen writes. "Such incidents made the corporation look like a killer." He cites the arrogance of the Milwaukee streetcar and electric light monopoly, which raised its fares, got a court to prevent the city from lowering them, rejected arbitration with its striking employees, and, through the guile of its general manager, the Republican boss of Wisconsin, lobbied the state legislature to halve its taxes and kill legislation requiring it to stop fouling the air. A cross-class, pan-ideological coalition spanning the Chamber of Commerce and the Socialist Party fought to take back their city.[3]

As muckraking exposés and legislative investigations between 1904 and 1907 uncovered the pervasive corruption of politics by business, articulate opinion recoiled. It would no longer stand a steal as the price of government promotion of industry. In its investigation of corruption by the insurance industry, the New York State legislature heard from Senator Chauncey Depew, who admitted under oath that Equitable Insurance paid him "a substantial annual retainer." His Senate colleague Thomas C. Platt testified that he received "tens of thousands" in cash from the insurance companies before every election. The investigation moved New York to ban corporate contributions and changed state politics, propelling the chief counsel of the legislative investigating committee, Charles Evans Hughes, into the governor's office.[4]

In "How I Was Converted—Politically," an anonymous "Kansas Progressive Republican" described his "awakening" to the costs of corruption. When he first entered politics, in the early 1890s, "Three great railway systems governed [the state]. This was a matter of common knowledge, but nobody objected or was in any way outraged by it"— nobody except the Populists. Riding their railroads, Kansans, like most Americans in the Gilded Age, tolerated bought government. Then as Theodore Roosevelt, damaged by the revelation of business contributions to *his* 1904 presidential campaign, "pounded away" at corruption, Kansans pushed for change. When railroad lobbying aborted reform "it began to dawn on" the Kansan "that railroad contributions to campaign funds were part of the general game. I saw they were in politics to run things as they pleased." Kansans weren't going to take it anymore: "We have got our eyes open now . . . we have seen that the old sort of politics was used to promote all sorts of private ends, and we have got the idea that the new politics can be used to promote the general interest." Nebraskans had their eyes opened, too. "They see the shameless debauchery of the primaries by railroad tools," the *Lincoln Call* wrote. "They see the rape of the highest tribunal of the State by a convention packed with cheap hirelings carried to the convention hall on passes and bought by the dozen in the back rooms. They see the conspiracy between the railroad managers and a subsidized press." *Americans* weren't going to take it anymore.[5]

The new politics pushed through a federal ban on corporate campaign contributions and legislation in the states banning legislators from accepting free railroad passes, a habitual and extensive custom: Pennsylvania legislators of the 1870s "received as many as thirty passes in addition to their own."[*][6] Yet "the structural power of business in a federal system" frustrated broader social reform: Businesses could vote against unemployment or old-age insurance with their feet—by leaving the state. "State policymakers' fears of placing their state at a competitive disadvantage permeates social policy discourse during this period," Jacob S. Hacker and Paul Pierson found. Minimum wage legislation for women passed in fifteen nonindustrial states, but in only one industrial state—Massachusetts—and there in gelded form. Business's structural power vetoed unemployment insurance—no state enacted it before 1929. Workman's compensation laws passed "but none of the systems adopted posed a threat to the profitability of local businesses even if other states had failed to act." As for publicly funded old-age assistance, "In the entire county, there were roughly 1,000 recipients . . . in 1929." Social reform escaped the "prison" of interstate competition only with the New Deal, which federalized social welfare policy, overriding the business veto in the states (except in the South: Southern Democrats excluded agricultural and domestic workers from the social insurance system, categories encompassing three-fifths of African-Americans).[7] For industrial workers the right to rise depended on the right to organize, but that, too, awaited the New Deal. Partly bowing to the structural power of business, "When class divisions were drawn in labor disputes," William E. Leuchtenburg writes, "progressives frequently aligned themselves against the unions."[8] Milwaukee's Socialist Party could

---

[*] Decades later, at a hearing of the U.S. Senate Commerce Committee on the combustible issue of railroad rebates, Iowa governor Albert B. Cummins realized that he "was the only man in that large room who had not gone there on the invitation of the railroads and on a free pass." While the chairman was "probing" Cummins, "there sat by his side the general attorney for all the railroads in the United States . . . passing to the chairman question after question to embarrass me." Seen in Kevin Phillips, *Wealth and Democracy: A Political History of the American Rich* (New York: Broadway Books, 2001), p. 243.

unite with the Chamber of Commerce to fight the streetcar monopoly, where their interests coincided; but such alliances broke down over labor issues, where class interests clashed. And the National Guard continued to break strikes, its heyday as a corporate constabulary coming as late as the 1920s, when the use of the labor injunction, wielded against 25 percent of all strikes and 46 percent of sympathy strikes, peaked.[9] Only the "Constitutional Revolution of 1937" ended the Supreme Court's forty-year disposition to put property rights before democracy and human rights.*

In the Gilded Age, corruption abridged democracy; in the Progressive Era *reform*. Alongside the corporation, the fully mobilized electorate of the Gilded Age took the onus for corruption. Henry George foresaw this reaction in the 1880s. He conceded the worst: "That democratic government is with us becoming a failure is clear; that we are driving toward oligarchy and Caesarism in a new form may be seen by whoever will look." But, he insisted, "they are weak and foolish who say that democracy is therefore condemned, or that universal suffrage must be abandoned." Bryan, quoting Wendell Phillips, insisted on that point: "If corruption seems rolling over us like a flood, it is not the corruption of the humbler classes—it is millionaires, who steal banks, mills and railways; it is defaulters, who live in palaces and make away with millions; it is money kings, who buy up Congress. . . . I believe in the people, in universal suffrage." Mark the contrast with Carter Glass, a Virginia Progressive, voicing the anti-democratic ambitions of reform: "Nothing can be more dangerous to our republican institutions than to see hordes of ignorant and worthless men marching to the polls and putting in their ballots against the intelligence and worth of the land." In the one-party South after 1900 intelligence and worth had the polls pretty much to themselves.[10]

Beginning with Mississippi in 1890 and ending with Oklahoma in 1910, southern states adopted new constitutions that disfranchised blacks using poll taxes, registration requirements, and literacy tests to annul the

---

* Altogether the agrarian Populist clothes proved too big for the urban Progressive frame. James Edward Wright draws the essential contrast: "The Progressives wanted to combat corporate power by democratizing the political process—initiative, referendum, judicial recall, direct primary, popular election of United States senators. The Populists sought substantive economic legislation: corporate power could be curtailed, they believed, only by moving against the corporation itself, through government ownership or legislation directly restricting corrupt corporate practices." In short, while the Progressives "would block the political power of corporations; the Populists aimed at restricting their economic power." James Edward Wright, *The Politics of Populism: Dissent in Colorado* (New Haven: Yale University Press, 1974), p. 260.

Fifteenth Amendment that Samuel Miller, having confined the protection offered by the Fourteenth Amendment to the high seas, looked to as the one remaining way blacks could defend themselves in the post-Reconstruction South. Energized by elite anxiety over the black-white politics of class introduced into the South by the Populists, the anti-democracy movement not only disfranchised nearly all blacks, driving black registration in Louisiana from 93 percent in 1896 to 1.1 percent in 1904, but most poor whites as well—in South Carolina, for example, half of all white voters lost their right to vote when the Negro lost his. Disfranchisement, the *Charlotte Observer* wrote, represents "the struggle of the white people of North Carolina to rid themselves of the dangers of the rule of negroes and lower class whites." So anodyne a reform as the substitution of the publicly printed Australian or secret ballot for the party-printed slip ticket discouraged illiterates, a majority of southern blacks in seven states and close to a fifth of whites, from undergoing the ordeal described in the lyrics of an Arkansas Democratic campaign song:

> The Australian Ballot works like a charm
> It makes them think and scratch
> And when a Negro gets a ballot
> He has certainly got his match.

The ballot included the names of major and minor office seekers often arranged by office rather than party—in short, a maze to men cleft of their written tongue by states that renounced the Reconstruction governments' support of public education. "The Australian ballot demanded not merely literacy, but fluency," notes the political historian J. Morgan Kousser. In 1901 Maryland passed a law forbidding poll workers from assisting illiterate voters with the Australian ballot, though Tennessee allowed help to "any person who could have voted in 1857"—before Negro enfranchisement. The Tennessee law, rammed through the legislature in 1888 by Democrats fearing a northern backlash against the fraud and violence used to suppress the Republican vote, confined the Australian ballot to counties where Republicans were strongest. It worked as hoped. Statewide, turnout fell by a third in 1890, an off-year election, but by two-thirds in counties using the secret ballot. In Nashville and Memphis the black vote plummeted by 25 to 30 percent in the 1892 and 1896 elections.*

---

* The congressional architects of the Fifteenth Amendment had deliberately left the door open to the imposition of literacy or educational tests on voters. "Such tests were already

When Virginia adopted the Australian ballot, an advocate of disfranchisement acknowledged, "great numbers of our white people were too sensitive to go to the polls, because they had to ask a judge of election or a constable to fix the ticket." A Republican watching Virginia mountain people waiting to be questioned by a voting registrar found it "painful and pitiful to see the horror and dread visible on the faces of the illiterate poor white men who were waiting to take their turn before the inquisition. . . . [H]orrible to see the marks of humiliation and despair that were stamped on the faces of honest but poor white men who had been refused registration and . . . robbed of their citizenship without cause."[11]

Reformers led a similar purification of the ballot in the North. Historians and political scientists debate whether they intended to disfranchise urban working-class and immigrant voters or whether disfranchisement was a "side effect" of election laws passed in reaction to the vote-buying scandals of the Gilded Age by "the forces of good government." These reforms included the secret ballot, adopted in thirty-eight states by 1900, to eliminate the incentive to "buy" votes, residence requirements, literacy tests in states from Maine to Wyoming, above all personal registration laws to deter "repeaters" and prevent voting by residents of other states or localities. In the nineteenth century either government registrars compiled lists of eligible voters and registered them automatically or voters registered in person once and for life. After 1900 many rural-dominated state legislatures required big cities to adopt personal registration, a process, two political scientists wrote in 1924, "expensive [because workers had to take time out from their jobs to register], burdensome and inconvenient to the voter," and in some cities *periodic* personal registration. In New Jersey, voters could register only four workdays a year, with policemen standing by to challenge voter eligibility. The political scientists found three times as many Chicagoans unable to vote because they had not registered as registered voters who failed to vote. A New Yorker interviewed outside a voting registrar's office in 1964 spoke for generations of the disfranchised: "I sure do want to vote against that man [Barry Goldwater] but I don't think I hate him enough to stand in that line all day long."[12]

Northern politicians, like their southern counterparts, "constructed" the electorate, and northern political scientists did not repine over the

in existence in Massachusetts and other Northern states, and the debate made it perfectly apparent what might be expected to happen later in the South." C. Vann Woodward, "Seeds of Failure in Radical Race Policy," *Proceedings of the American Philosophical Society,* vol. 110, no. 1 (February 18, 1966), p. 7.

consequences, intended or not. "There is not the slightest doubt in my mind," Columbia's John D. Burgess averred, "that our prodigality with the suffrage has been the chief source of corruption of our elections." Surveying attitudes toward voting among political scientists in 1918, when the United States was fighting "to make the world safe for democracy," two Yale researchers discovered that "the theory that every man has a natural right to vote no longer commands the support of students of political science." In elections in twenty-six nonsouthern states, turnout in 1916—before woman suffrage expanded the potential size of the electorate—fell by 15 to 20 percent from its 1896 high in the industrial states, for which the good side of reform, stopping wholesale vote-selling, was only fractionally responsible. Legal impediments made voting harder just as the extinction of electoral competition in the Democratic South and its eclipse in the Republican North made it meaningless. Paul Kleppner attributes as much as a third of the drop-off in early-twentieth-century voting to this latter factor. The drop-off was dramatic. Average turnout in presidential elections in the South fell from 69.4 percent in 1868–80 to 24.7 percent in 1920–48, and in the North from 85.4 percent in 1884–96 to 60.6 percent in 1920–32. "The Mississippi Plan," in C. Vann Woodward's words, had become "the American way."[13]

Erecting barriers to lower-class voting outside the South—in New Jersey among foreign-born voters turnout fell twenty points between 1896 and 1916, while black turnout fell thirty-two points from its 1888 high—and the exile of virtually all black and many poor white voters from the southern electorate tilted politics to the right. Today's electoral universe, with its 100-million-member "party of nonvoters," took shape after 1896 and from its sequel—the demobilization of the mass electorate of the nineteenth century. The legal barriers to voting imposed then have since come down, though not the major procedural one: The United States, one study found, "is almost alone among major democracies in requiring citizen-initiated registration to vote." But American politics still rests on the arch-stone set in the era of disfranchisement—a class-skewed electorate. Nearly nine out of ten Americans earning $75,000 or above vote compared to half of those earning $15,000. "As a consequence of this disproportionate abstention, an electorate that was already strongly class-skewed four decades ago has become markedly more unrepresentative socioeconomically," concludes a political scientist investigating declining turnout between 1960 and 2000. The party of nonvoters haunts democracy. "[T]he present situation perpetuates a standing danger that the half of the American electorate which is now more or less entirely outside the universe of active politics may someday be mobilized in substantial degree by totalitarian or quasi-totalitarian appeals," Walter Dean Burnham warns. Strong attachments to party tend to "immunize" voters against extremist appeals. Less-partisan or independent voters are more exposed. Nonvoters are ripe for contagion. Burnham uncovered that pattern in an analysis of the behavior of independents, weak partisans, and white working-class nonvoters drawn into the electorate in 1968 by the presidential candidacy of the segregationist governor of Alabama, George C. Wallace. Events in another democracy disclosed the same pattern—in the context of social polarization, weak partisans and nonvoters rallying to an extremist party. In one sample constituency the percentage of nonvoters fell from 43.2 in one election to 28 in the next to 7.1 in the last—a 36 percent surge that went almost totally to the extremists. The elections took place in 1928, 1930, and 1933. The constituency was the town of Westerstede in Oldenburg. The democracy was Weimar Germany. The extremist party was the Nazis.[14]

Realignment shifted onto the Republicans the burden of economic recovery that had broken the Democrats. In control of all three branches of government for the next fourteen years, they had to fill "McKinley's dinner pail." Cornelia Martin threw her Waldorf party, she told the *Times,* to jump-start the McKinley boom. Bryan's defeat lightened the hearts of investors and businessmen, but they still needed capital and customers to spur recovery, which would not fully arrive for three years. "Business is at a standstill, and will remain so," the *Portland Oregonian* observed, "until something happens."[15] On the evening of February 15, 1898, something happened in Havana harbor.

Homestead steelworkers had rolled the armor plate for the stricken battleship *Maine.* In *Triumphant Democracy,* published in 1886, Carnegie had written, "It is one of the chief glories of the Republic that she spends her money for better ends and has nothing worthy to rank as a ship of war." But Carnegie's pacifism was no match for his greed. After his friend James G. Blaine became Benjamin Harrison's secretary of state, Carnegie confided in one of his partners, "There may be millions for us in armor." There were. According to Paul Krause, "Blaine virtually delivered to him enormous foreign naval contracts." Doubtless inside connections with the Navy Department helped Carnegie win contracts to armor two cruisers, the *Raleigh* and the *Cincinnati,* and two battleships, the *Texas* and the *Maine.* He facilely squared the warships with his professed hatred of war: The armor was for their *defense.* He would armor more ships in the expanded Homestead Works soon to rise on the 400-acre site of the City Poor Farm, land worth over $1 million that, through "extralegal collusion" with Pittsburgh's Republican "boss," Carnegie acquired for $370,000 in what the Democratic *Pittsburgh Post* pilloried as an "outrageous swindle." Carnegie owed his fortune to political capitalism. The country's foremost protectionist erected his steel empire behind high tariff walls. Just when a glut in the civilian market threatened his profits, political capitalism landed him government contracts. It should come as no surprise that, two years after the lockout, four Homestead steelworkers blew the whistle on a scheme by Carnegie Steel to defraud the Navy Department "by supplying it with defective armor plate."[16] By this time Carnegie had no defenses against himself. Marx diagnosed his moral defect and at the same time extenuated it—the "capitalist" is "personified capital." Yet, Marx goes on, "Fanatically bent on making value expand itself, he ruthlessly forces . . . the development of the productive powers of society, and creates those material conditions, which alone can form the real basis of a higher form of society, a society in which the full and free development of every individual forms the ruling principle." It takes a lot of dialectic to redeem Andrew Carnegie.[17]

In 1896 all three party platforms had expressed sympathy for the rebels fighting to free Cuba from Spain but only humanitarians and businessmen with interests on the island urged intervention. After the *Maine* blew up, a Missouri resident reported that "patriotism . . . ooz[ed] out of every boy old enough to pack feed to the pigs," and New York theatergoers "cheered, stamped, and wept" at the playing of "The Star-Spangled Banner." "I know that to threaten war for political reasons is a crime," Senator Henry Cabot Lodge wrote Theodore Roosevelt in March. "But to sacrifice a great party and bring free silver upon the country . . . is hardly less odious. . . . If we should have a war we will not hear much of the currency question in the elections."[18] War, declared on April 11, provided a distraction not only from silver but from a revolution in business, for 1898, Richard Hofstadter points out, was "the year in which the modern trust-forming period really dates its beginning."[19] By 1904, 1,800 companies had been compacted into 157 behemoths in the steel, oil, tobacco, and copper industries and in gas, traction, and electric utilities, "transforming [the United States] overnight from a nation of freely competing, individually owned enterprises into a nation dominated by a small number of giant corporations."[*][20]

Consolidation was the legacy of Homestead. Overcoming the crisis in productivity by squeezing workers sparked violence. A safer answer to the falling return on capital lay on the demand side. "A large part of the friction that has existed between capital and labor causing strikes, lockouts, and riots, was the result, in part, of overproduction," the vice chairman of the Chicago Conference on Trusts reasoned. "The product was unloaded at a loss, the owners tried to recompense themselves by cutting the wages of their workmen." There were too many producers. "[T]he waste of competition . . . which comes from the inability of adapting one's plants and output to the market . . . can be partly saved by combination of many manufacturing establishments in one industry under one management," the Cornell economist Jeremiah Jencks argued, expressing a view fast forming among industrialists.[21] Bryan's "broader class of businessman"—the sole proprietor in his shop, the small producer—would have to go. He was cumbering the economy. He was also becoming an ideological embarrassment, prating of competition's virtues when competition had glutted the economy and stoked a zero-sum war between labor and capital. Increasing the money supply, Bryan's silver solution, would only encourage small producers to take bigger entrepreneurial risks. More competition was the last thing companies with large sunk costs in plant and equipment wanted.

John D. Rockefeller had unveiled the future. Integrate backward into supply and forward into distribution, invest heavily in technology, and manage work to increase production. Frederick W. Taylor underscored how in italics. "It is only through *enforced* standardization of methods, *enforced* adoption of the best implements and working conditions, and *enforced* cooperation that . . . faster work can be assured," he wrote in his *Principles of Scientific Management*. "And the duty of enforcing the adoption of standards and enforcing this cooperation rests with *management*

---

* Scale and scope production helped these giants endure. "In 1917, 22 of the largest 200 companies were in the petroleum business. In 1973, 22 of the largest 200 were still in petroleum. For the most part, they were the same 22. . . . In 1917, 5 of the largest 200 companies were in the rubber business. In 1973, 5 of the largest 200 were still in rubber. Four of these were the same (Goodyear, Goodrich, Firestone, Uniroyal). The fifth, Fisk, merged with Uniroyal—then called United States Rubber. . . . In 1917, 20 of the largest companies were in the machinery business. In 1973, 18 of the largest 200 were still in machinery. For the most part, they were the same companies." Thomas K. McCraw, *Prophets of Regulation* (Cambridge: Harvard University Press, 1984), p. 75.

alone."[22] Finally, against the evil day when the Sherman Act should be enforced, don't consolidate in trusts or monopolies; instead form oligopolies—let two or three or, to be safe, three or four, firms dominate each industry. Control production, control the market, and name your own price (but, following Rockefeller's example, don't be greedy). Here was the twentieth-century solution to the crisis of nineteenth-century entrepreneurial capitalism. As a dividend, with the money saved from costly price wars, the great industrial corporation could invest in the machinery and management expertise to de-skill its skilled workers—*and* pay higher wages. There was one catch.

"We are surrounded by conditions that will permit us to pay two or three times as much wages as our foreign competitors and still meet successfully their competition," Frank Vanderlip, vice president of the National City Bank of New York, wrote in 1903 as the merger wave neared its crest. But, he continued, "we cannot, in addition to that handicap, of high wages, permit the workers to limit production and hope for a successful outcome in a world contest." Carnegie had been too rough. Still, look what breaking his union, seizing control of production from his skilled workers, cutting tonnage rates, extending the twelve-hour day to more workers, and replacing 500 men with new machinery—look what resolving the productivity crisis had done for Carnegie! From $4 million in 1892 (before the Homestead strike), his bottom line showed profits of $40 million in 1900. "Ashamed to tell you profits these days," he wrote a friend. "Prodigious!"[23]

By the McKinley-Bryan rematch, in 1900, the war to free Cuba had screened a grab for empire across the Pacific (also in Cuba and Puerto Rico). The United States, William James cried out, had "puke[d] up its ancient soul, and the only thing that gave it eminence among nations," betraying its revolutionary birthright by making ignoble war upon the Filipino rebels who had risen up to free their islands from Spain only to be occupied by their American liberators. "Our conduct there has been one protracted infamy toward the Islanders," James wrote, "and one protracted lie towards ourselves."[24] The infamy included the deaths of 700,000 Filipino civilians from American attacks on their villages, the destruction of their crops, and war-spread disease. The lie to ourselves began with the president, who couldn't find the Philippine Islands on a map and said our mission there was to "to uplift and . . . Christianize" a people largely Roman Catholic for 300 years.

"The fervent Methodists, at the beginning of the war, resolved that it was going to be a righteous and holy war," the anti-imperialist E. L. Godkin wrote in *The Nation*, "because it would destroy 'Romish superstition' in the Spanish West Indies." The Methodists were "the most powerful propagandists for McKinley's wars," he added, after McKinley annexed the Philippines. Meeting at the White House with a group of Methodist leaders, McKinley said that when the Philippines "had dropped in our laps I confess I did not know what to do with them. . . . [N]ight after night until midnight," he had paced "the floor of the White House; and I am not ashamed to tell you, gentlemen, that I bent down on my knees and prayed to Almighty God for light and guidance." One night, light descended. It revealed that "there was nothing left for us to do but to take them . . . and to educate the Filipinos, and uplift and civilize and Christianize them . . . And then I went to bed, and went to sleep, and slept soundly."

God was a white Anglo-Saxon Protestant, probably an American. It was the "divine right of the Caucasian to govern the inferior races," in the view of Senator John L. McLaurin of South Carolina. The South had shown the way. After the Supreme Court upheld disfranchisement in Mississippi, *The Nation* called it "an interesting coincidence that this important decision is rendered at a time when we are taking in an assortment of inferior races . . . which, of course, could not be allowed to vote." Long divided by the race issue at home, North and South could unite in bearing the white man's burden abroad. The *Boston Evening Transcript* might regret that "the Administration of the very party which carried the country into and through a civil war to free the slave" had adopted a colonial policy inspired by the "Southern way." But Columbia's John Burgess, "an ex-Confederate soldier who started to a little Southern college with a box of books, a box of tallow candles and a Negro boy" in the words of W.E.B. Du Bois, argued that "imposing the sovereignty of the United States upon eight millions of Asiatics" would change Republican views about disfranchisement and Jim Crow. Trying to make white men out of that dingy swarm would teach northerners to never "again give themselves over to the vain imagination of the political equality of all men."[25]

Besides God's revelation to McKinley of the destiny of the American branch of the "Anglo-Saxon race" to rule over "weaker races," industrial capitalism drove expansion. The second industrial revolution harnessing science to production was under way. The "home market" could not soak up the overspill. Meeting in Cincinnati in September 1895, scores of industrialists formed the National Association of Manufacturers to lobby for government help in opening foreign markets. Plundering Africa and Asia for customers and raw materials, the European powers showed brooding-class Americans they had company in fearing confinement—and in seeing trade as a hedge against unemployment and discontent at home, and imperialism as a solvent for radicalism. New markets must be found "if American operatives and artisans are to be kept employed the year around," a State Department paper affirmed. "We escape the menace and peril of socialism and agrarianism, as England has escaped them, by a policy of colonization and conquest," Henry Watterson, the editor of the *Louisville Courier-Journal,* told a New York reporter the month Teddy Roosevelt and his Rough Riders charged up San Juan Hill.[26] Oozing patriotism and blood, farm boys were safe from Populism.

In April 1897, in a widely reprinted speech delivered in Boston, a thirty-six-year-old lawyer and soon to be Republican senator from Indiana, Albert Beveridge, summoned American families to be ready to sacrifice their sons for the imperatives of a resource-dependent economy: "America's factories are making more than the American people can use; America's soil is producing more than they can consume. Fate has written her policies for us; the trade of the world shall be ours. . . . And American law, American order, American civilization and the American flag will plant themselves on shores bloody and benighted."

Who were we to keep the America of the 1890s, with its 250,000 owners, its one-eyed Pinkertons, its starving Hoosiers, its disfranchised and terrorized and impoverished southern blacks chained to the plantation thirty years after Emancipation—who were we to keep what William Dean Howells was calling "our deeply incorporated civilization" to ourselves? The world deserved America and America deserved the world.[27]

RETROSPECT

Immanuel Kant's "crooked timber of humanity" offers material for crooked works only, for achievements scarred by their hard birth. In the preface to his 1953 biography of John D. Rockefeller, Allan Nevins maintained that, in the light of their recent history, Americans should reconsider their disdain for the men identified with America's industrial preeminence. "Everyone who looks at the record of industry and commerce from the Civil War to the First World War sees that the economy underwent the most sweeping transformation," he wrote. "This transformation involved a long process of destruction and reconstruction." Historians of an earlier era played up the destructive side, called "the leaders in this process . . . 'robber barons' and the process itself the 'great barbecue.' " Even those who looked beyond personalities and corruption to the historic success of American industrialism regretted its pace: "Down to 1910 it could be said with great apparent force that even if the transformation of our economy was inevitable, it had proceeded much too fast." But, from the perspective of 1953, "this view appears dubious." After all, "had our pace been slower and our achievement weaker, had we not created so swiftly our powerful industrial units in steel, oil, textiles, chemicals, electricity and the automotive vehicles, the free world might have lost the First World War and most certainly would have lost the Second."

On the eve of his inauguration, Woodrow Wilson may have sensed his war coming. It would be "an irony of fate," he said, if foreign affairs should divert him from his domestic agenda—to implement measures first championed by Bryan and the Populists. But the world was at peace when he took the oath of office on March 4, 1913, and in his inaugural address Wilson looked inward and backward toward the un-receding past, asking Americans to pause with him and take the measure of the years since glory.

"We have been proud of our industrial achievements," he said, "but we have not hitherto stopped thoughtfully enough to count the human cost, the cost of lives snuffed out, of energies overtaxed and broken, the fearful physical and social cost to the men and women and children upon whom the dead weight and burden of it all has fallen piteously the years through. The groans and agony of it all had not reached our ears, the solemn, moving undertone of life, coming out of our mines and factories and out of every home where the struggle had its intimate and familiar seat."

Acknowledgments

The Alfred P. Sloan Foundation generously supported my early work on this project. Special thanks to program director Doron Weber. I can't thank David and Judy Kennedy enough for their hospitality and for bringing me to the attention of the Media Fellows program at the Hoover Institution at Stanford University. The deputy director of the institution, David Brady, and the Media Fellows program assistant, Mandy MacCalla, welcomed and regaled me during my two productive sojourns there.

At the *Atlantic Monthly*, thanks to Katie Bacon, my former editor, and her successor, Sage Stossel. The late Michael Kelly, killed while covering the U.S. invasion of Iraq, set my mind at ease for spending so much *Atlantic* time on this book. I hope Cullen Murphy, who replaced Michael at the helm of the *Atlantic*, knows how grateful I am to *him*.

My debt to WBUR, the public radio station where I have worked going on two decades, exceeds calculation. I am obliged to Jane Christo, the former general manager of WBUR, for offering me the chance to work on a new show, *On Point*; and to Sam Fleming, the news director and a professional in broadcast journalism. Warm thanks to my *On Point* colleagues—Eileen Imada, Karen Shiffman, Meghna Chakrabarti, Stefano Kotsonis, Hillary Barngrove McQuilkin, Julie Diop, Christina Russo, James Ross, Tania Ralli, and Philip Martin. Graham Griffith, the senior producer of *On Point*, invented the program over one weekend in September 2001, and has charted its course with intelligence, professionalism, and effective leadership. I'm proud to work with him. The same goes for our host, Tom Ashbrook. His commitment to truth, his questioning of power, his omnivorous curiosity, and above all his will to make *On Point* a forum for "national conversation," make Tom a daily inspiration.

I am grateful to the staff of Dartmouth's Baker Library, a superb place to do historical research, for numerous helps. Thanks to my fellow author and Henry James biographer, Sheldon Nowick, for inviting me to deliver a version of "The Inverted Constitution" to his class at the Vermont Law School. A student whose name I did not write down said I started to put him to sleep—then he got caught up in the lives of the characters and stayed awake. His comment meant everything to me. My editor at Knopf, Jonathan Segal, matched his reputation for taste, tact, and care. I am grateful to the Knopf copy editor, Fred Chase, for his fine eye. Also thanks to Rob Grover and Kyle Mccarthy, Jonathan's assistants, for their time-consuming and thorough work in obtaining permissions for the illustrations. My agent Rafe Sagalyn started me on the road to book writing twenty-five years ago, believed in me when I didn't, and has helped me keep going ever since.

Thanks to our Upper Valley friends for the pleasure of their company—Kevin and Lynne O'Hara, Gerry Bergstein, and Gail Boyajian, the much-missed Sue Miller and Doug Bauer, Kathy and Bill Craig, Ed and Kathy Kimball, Kristine, Hernan, and Alexandra Laca, the best neighbors we ever had. I'm grateful to Michael Mufson for suffering my complaints and for the profit of his mind. Sarah Cook took a day out of her life to calm my computer panic. Thank you, Sarah.

In thirty years of marriage my wife, Lois, has given me her counsel, her wit, her style, her grammar, her candor, her patience, her impatience, and her love, which I return. The dedication is to Aaron Beatty—my friend, and my beloved son.

Notes

Introduction

1. Matthew Josephson, *The Politicos, 1865–1896* (New York: Harcourt Brace, 1938), pp. 426–33; Henry Adams, *The Education of Henry Adams* (New York: Library of America, 1990), p. 299.

2. David W. Blight, *Race and Reunion: The Civil War in American Memory* (Cambridge: Harvard University Press, 2001), pp. 188–89, 202–3.

3. Lewis L. Gould, *Grand Old Party: A History of the Republicans* (New York: Random House, 2003), p. 57; Roy Morris, Jr., *Fraud of the Century: Rutherford B. Hayes, Samuel Tilden, and the Stolen Election of 1876* (New York: Simon & Schuster, 2003), p. 141.

4. Ellis Paxson Oberholtzer, *A History of the United States Since the Civil War*, vol. 4 (New York: Macmillan, 1931), p. 92. For Garfield, see Stanley P. Hirshson, *Farewell to the Bloody Shirt: Northern Republicans and the Southern Negro, 1877–1893* (Bloomington: Indiana University Press, 1962), p. 23.

5. *Chicago Tribune*, 7/2/1888. For commander of the Grand Army of the Republic, see Richard Jensen, *The Winning of the Midwest: Social and Political Conflict, 1888–1896* (Chicago: University of Chicago Press, 1971), p. 24. For last campaign, see Joanne Reitano, *The Tariff Question in the Gilded Age: The Great Tariff Debate of 1888* (University Park: Pennsylvania State University Press, 1994), p. 109.

6. *Atlanta Constitution*, 7/2/1888.

7. Eric Foner, *Reconstruction: America's Unfinished Revolution, 1863–1877* (New York: Harper & Row, 1989), pp. 297–98. Foner comments (p. 298, n. 33): "Longstreet's decision to join the Republican party made him an 'object of hatred' among Southern democrats for the rest of his life. When he died in 1903, the United Daughters of the Confederacy voted not to send flowers to his funeral, and unlike other Confederate generals, no statues of Longstreet graced the Southern landscape."

8. James M. McPherson, *Battle Cry of Freedom: The Civil War Era* (New York: Oxford University Press, 1988), pp. 651–61. "My heart was heavy," Longstreet wrote years later. "I could see the desperate and hopeless nature of the charge and the hopeless slaughter it would cause. . . . That day at Gettysburg was one of the saddest of my life" (p. 661). For Lee, see ibid., p. 655, n. 42. *New York Tribune*, 7/3/1888.

9. *Chicago Tribune*, 7/3/1888.

10. McPherson, *Battle Cry of Freedom*, p. 660; Blight, *Race and Reunion*, p. 95. For Twain, see Rebecca Edwards, *New Spirits: Americans in the Gilded Age, 1865–1905* (New York: Oxford University Press, 2006), p. 4.

11. *Chicago Tribune*, 7/3/1888. For Gordon, see Eric Foner, *Forever Free: The Story of Emancipation and Reconstruction* (New York: Alfred A. Knopf, 2005), p. 174. For more on Gordon, see William F. Holmes, "The Southern Farmers' Alliance and the

Georgia Senatorial Election of 1890," *Journal of Southern History,* vol. 50, no. 3 (May 1984), pp. 197–224.

12. Ari Hoogenboom, *Rutherford B. Hayes: Warrior and President* (Lawrence: University of Kansas Press, 1995), pp. 493–95.

13. David Cay Johnston, "Richest Are Leaving Even the Rich Far Behind," in *Class Matters* (New York: Times Books, 2005), p. 186. For Mississippi congressman, see Edwards, *New Spirits: Americans in the Gilded Age,* p. 28. For the diamond hunt, see Andrew Delbanco, *Melville: His World and Work* (New York: Alfred A. Knopf, 2005), p. 305. For the *Economist,* see Arnaud de Borchgrave, "America's Class-Based Society," *Washington Times,* 1/10/2005. For the polling data and the quotation from Ornstein and Mann, see Peter Beinart, *The Good Fight: Why Liberals—and Only Liberals—Can Win the War on Terror and Make America Great Again* (New York: HarperCollins, 2006), pp. 203–5. Also see endnotes for p. 204 on p. 274. "American Democracy in an Age of Rising Inequality," Task Force on Inequality and American Democracy, American Political Science Association, 2004, at http://www.apsanet .org/imgtest/taskforcereport.pdf; Paul Krugman, "The Big Disconnect," *New York Times,* September 9/1/2006, p. A19.

14. For Weaver, see Peter H. Argersinger, "No Rights on This Floor: Third Parties and the Institutionalization of Congress," *Journal of Interdisciplinary History,* vol. 22, no. 4 (Spring 1992), p. 663. Geoffrey Barraclough, *An Introduction to Contemporary History* (New York: Basic Books, 1964), p. 12.

Chapter One: Annihilating Space

1. The information in this and the previous paragraphs is taken from Michael O'Malley, *Keeping Watch: A History of American Time* (New York: Viking, 1990), pp. 58–136; John E. Stover, *American Railroads* (Chicago: University of Chicago Press, 1997), pp. 157–58; John R. Stilgoe, *Metropolitian Corridor Railroads and the American Scene* (New Haven: Yale University Press, 1983), pp. 203–5; Carlton J. Corliss, *The Day of Two Noons* (Washington: Association of American Railroads, 1951), pp. 5–16; and Ian R. Bartky, "The Adoption of Standard Time," *Technology and Culture,* vol. 30, no. 1 (January 1989), pp. 25–56. Also from the *New York Times, Chicago Tribune, Washington Post, New York Tribune,* for 11/18/1883 and the days following; also the *Boston Evening Transcript,* 10/25/1883.

2. O'Malley, *Keeping Watch,* p. 109.

3. Ibid., p. 113.

4. For Britain, see *Washington Post,* 10/29/1883, p. 1. For jewelers, see *New York Times,* 10/17/1883, p. 1.

5. For the attorney general, see *New York Tribune,* 10/17/1883, p. 1.

6. Barbara Young Welke, *Recasting American Liberty: Gender, Race, Law and the Railroad Revolution, 1865–1920* (Cambridge: Harvard University Press, 2001), pp. 40, 157–58; James A. Ward, *Railroads and the Character of American Life* (Knoxville: University of Kentucky Press, 1986), p. 108. For more on George Beard, see Linda Simon, *Dark Light: Electricity and Anxiety from the Telegraph to the X-Ray* (New York: Harcourt, 2004), especially pp. 97–167.

7. O'Malley, *Keeping Watch,* p. 146.

8. *New York Times,* 2/23/1889, p. 1.

9. O'Malley, *Keeping Watch,* p. 132.

10. Ibid., p. 129.

11. Ibid., pp. 134, 145.

12. Ward, *Railroads and the Character of American Life,* pp. 111–12.

13. O'Malley, *Keeping Watch,* p. 128.

14. For Greeley, see David E. Nye, *America as Second Creation* (Cambridge: MIT Press, 2003), p. 157; Ward, *Railroads and the Character of American Life,* p. 82.

15. Ward, *Railroads and the Character of American Life,* p. 81; Ralph Waldo Emerson, "The Young American," in *Emerson: Essays and Lectures* (New York: Library of America, 1983), p. 213.

16. Gustavus Myers, *The Great Fortunes,* vol. 2 (Chicago: C. H. Kerr, 1910), p. 44.

17. Seen in Alfred D. Chandler, Jr., Thomas K. McCraw, Richard S. Tedlow, *Management: Past and Present* (Cincinnati: South-Western Publishers, 1996), Case 2, p. 38. Said of Jay Gould by fellow swindler James R. Keene; also, O'Malley, *Keeping Watch,* p. 191.

18. Henry Adams, *History of the United States During the Administration of Thomas Jefferson,* vol. 1 (New York: A. & C. Boni, 1930), pp. 7, 8. 83.

19. Tedlow et al., *Management,* Case 1, p. 54.

20. Adams, *History of the United States,* vol. 1, p. 14.

21. Winifred B. Rosenberg, "The Market and Massachusetts Farmers, 1750–1855," *Journal of Economic History,* vol. 41 (1981), p. 30.

22. Jeremy Atack and Peter Passell, *A New Economic View of American History* (New York: W. W. Norton, 1994), p. 147.

23. George Rogers Taylor, *The Transportation Revolution, 1815–1860* (New York: Rinehart, 1960), p. 5.

24. Richard Wade, *The Urban Frontier: The Rise of Western Cities, 1790–1830* (Cambridge: Harvard University Press, 1959), p. 40.

25. Atack and Passell, *A New Economic View of American History,* p. 156.

26. Lance Davis et al., editors, *American Economic Growth* (New York: Harper & Row, 1972), p. 486.

27. Pauline Maier, Merritt Roe Smith, Alexander Keysar, Daniel J. Kevles, *Inventing America: A History of the United States,* vol. 1 (New York: W. W. Norton, 2003), p. 29.

28. Harvey H. Siegel, "Canals and American Economic Development," in Carter Goodrich, editor, *Canals and American Economic Development* (New York: Columbia University Press, 1961), pp. 221, 218.

29. Ibid., p. 218.

30. Ibid., p. 27.

31. For Tocqueville, see Carter Goodrich, *Government Promotion of Canals and Railroads* (New York: Columbia University Press, 1960), p. 55.

32. Thomas A. Bailey, David M. Kennedy, Lizabeth Cohen, *The American Pageant: A History of the Republic,* vol. 1 (Boston: Houghton Mifflin, 1998), p. 320.

33. Ibid.

34. Siegel, "Canals and American Economic Development," pp. 227–28, 231.

35. Nye, *America as Second Creation,* p. 152.

36. Maier et al., *Inventing America,* p. 352.

37. Goodrich, *Government and the Promotion of Canals and Railroads,* p. 8.

38. Arthur M. Johnson and Barry E. Supple, *Boston Capitalists and Western Railroads* (Cambridge: Harvard University Press, 1967), p. 75.

39. William G. Roy, *Socializing Capital: The Rise of the Large Industrial Corporation in America* (Princeton: Princeton University Press, 1997), p. 74.

40. 288 US Reports 548. For an argument that the resistance to corporations was based on "republican" principles, see "Incorporating the Republic: The Corporation in Antebellum Political Culture," *Harvard Law Review,* vol. 102, no. 8 (June 1989), pp.

1883–1903. For James Harrington, see James L. Huston, "The American Revolution-aries, the Political Economy of Aristocracy, and the American Concept of the Distribution of Wealth, 1765–1900," *American Historical Review*, vol. 98, no. 4 (October 1993), pp. 1079–1105. For the fear of privilege and power, see Bernard Bailyn, *Faces of the Revolution: Personalities and Themes in the Struggle for American Independence* (New York: Alfred A. Knopf, 1990), p. 220.

41. Richard Hofstadter, *The American Political Tradition and the Men Who Made It* (New York: Vintage, 1948), p. 73; Charles Sellers, *The Market Revolution: Jacksonian America, 1815–1846* (New York: Oxford University Press, 1991), p. 312. Also Morton J. Horwitz, *The Transformation of American Law, 1760–1860* (New York: Oxford University Press, 1977), p. 112.

42. Robert V. Rimini, *Andrew Jackson and the Course of American Freedom, 1822–1832* (New York: Harper & Row, 1981), pp. 228–29. For Jackson's inauguration, see Sean Wilentz, *The Rise of American Democracy: Jefferson to Lincoln* (New York: W. W. Norton, 2005), pp. 424, 308–9. Also see Richard P. McCormick, "New Perspectives on Jacksonian Politics," *American Historical Review*, vol. 65, no. 2 (January 1960), pp. 288–301. For franchise restrictions prior to 1824, see Richard P. McCormick, "Suffrage Classes and Party Alignment: A Study in Voter Behavior," *Mississippi Valley Historical Review*, vol. 46, no. 3 (December 1959), pp. 397–411, and Richard P. McCormick, "Political Development and the Second Party System," in William Nisbet Chambers and Walter Dean Burnham, editors, *The American Party Systems: Stages of Political Development* (New York: Oxford University Press, 1967), pp. 108–9. The details on the Bank War are from Major L. Wilson, "The 'Country' Versus the 'Court': A Republican Consensus and Party Debate in the Bank War," *Journal of the Early Republic*, vol. 15, no. 4 (Winter 1995), pp. 619–47.

43. Hofstadter, *The American Political Tradition*, p. 64.

44. Sellers, *The Market Revolution*, p. 352.

45. For "mere license," see Horwitz, *The Transformation of American Law*, p. 137. For cost of incorporation see "The Report on the Machinery of the United States 1855" as printed in Nathan Rosenberg, editor, *The American System of Manufactures* (Edinburgh: Edinburgh University Press, 1969), p. 339. For analogy of the corporation to the flashy son-in-law, see Marvin Meyers, *The Jacksonian Persuasion: Politics and Belief* (Stanford: Stanford University Press, 1960), p. 266.

46. Douglas C. North, *The Economic Growth of the United States, 1790–1860* (New York: W. W. Norton, 1966), pp. 69–70.

47. Alfred D. Chandler, Jr., "The Railroads: The First Modern Business Enterprises, 1850's–1860's," in Jack Beatty, editor, *Colossus: How the Corporation Changed America* (New York: Broadway Books, 2001), pp. 97–99.

48. Albert Fishlow, *American Railroads and the Transformation of the Antebellum Economy* (Cambridge: Harvard University Press, 1965), p. 12.

49. Chandler, "The Railroads."

50. Ibid., p. 107.

51. Sellers, *The Market Revolution*, p. 133.

52. Alfred D. Chandler, Jr., *The Visible Hand: The Managerial Revolution in American Business* (Cambridge: Harvard University Press, 1977), pp. 64, 65.

53. Ibid., pp. 67–68.

54. Ibid., pp. 98, 103, 104.

55. Alexis de Tocqueville, *Democracy in America*, vol. 2 (New York: Random House, 1990), p. 160.

56. For railroad casualties, see Alan Trachtenberg, *The Incorporation of America* (New York: Hill & Wang, 1982), p. 91. For railroad lobbying, see Nye, *America as Second Creation*, pp. 189–90; also see Beatty, *Colossus*, p. 138.

57. The paragraphs on industrialism closely follow Walter Dean Burnham, "The Changing Shape of the Political Universe," "Theory and Voting Research," "Party Systems and the Political Process," collected in Walter Dean Burnham, *The Current Crisis in American Politics* (New York: Oxford University Press, 1980), pp. 3–117. The characterization of industrialism as a structure of power is from Walter Dean Burnham, "The System of 1896: An Analysis," in Paul Kleppner et al., editors, *The Evolution of American Electoral Systems* (Westport: Greenwood Press, 1981), p. 162. Andrew Martin, "Political Constraints on Economic Strategies in Advanced Industrial Societies," *Comparative Political Studies*, vol. 10, no. 3 (October 1977), pp. 323–45; Andrew Martin, *The Politics of Economic Policy in the United States* (Beverly Hills: Sage, 1973); and Andrew Martin, "Is Democratic Control of Capitalist Economies Possible?," in Leon N. Linberg et al., editors, *Stress and Contradiction in Modern Capitalism: Public Policy and the Theory of the State* (Lexington: Lexington Books, 1975), pp. 13–53. For Sombart, see Sidney Pollard, "Factory Discipline in the Industrial Revolution," *Economic History Review*, new series, vol. 16, no. 2 (1963), p. 254. For the Duchess of Sutherland, see Karl Marx, *Capital: A Critique of Political Economy* (New York: Modern Library, 1906), pp. 801–2, n. 1. For six laborers for every job, see Richard Sennett, *The Culture of the New Capitalism* (New Haven: Yale University Press, 2006), pp. 84–85. Also, Karl Polanyi, *The Great Transformation: The Political and Economic Origins of Our Time* (Boston: Beacon Press, 1957), pp. 78, 117, 224–25. For capital formation, see Clark Kerr, John T. Dunlop, Frederick S. Harbison, and Charles A. Myers, *Industrialism and Industrial Man* (Cambridge: Harvard University Press, 1960), p. 99. For the restricted franchise in Canada, Britain, and other countries, see Ballard Campbell, "Comparative Perspectives on the Gilded Age and the Progressive Era," *Journal of the Gilded Age and Progressive Era*, vol. 1, no. 2 (2000), p. 7. For the debate over the trade-off model, see Jeffrey C. Williamson, *Inequality, Poverty, and History: The Kuznets Memorial Lectures* (Cambridge: Harvard University Press, 1991), especially pp. 66–103, quotation on p. 20 is from *Inequality*, p. 69. For the effect of immigration on wages, see Ashley S. Timmer and Jeffrey G. Williams, "Immigration Policy Prior to the 1930's: Labor Markets, Policy Interactions, and Globalization Backlash," *Population and Development Review*, vol. 24, no. 4 (December 1998), pp. 739–71, especially Fig. 2 on p. 750. Also E. J. Hobsbawm, *Labouring Men* (London: Weidenfeld & Nicolson, 1964), p. 106; E. P. Thompson, *The Making of the English Working Class* (New York: Vintage, 1963), pp. 198–99, 211–12; also, E. P. Thompson, "Time, Work-Discipline, and Industrial Capitalism," *Past and Present*, no. 38 (December 1967), pp. 56–97. S. Pollard, "Investment, Consumption, and the Industrial Revolution," *Economic History Review*, vol. 11, no. 2 (1958), pp. 215–26. For a view of the Confederacy as the instrument of "a state-imposed modernization of the sort that occurred in Bismarck's Germany," see Lawrence N. Powell, "The Prussians Are Coming," *Georgia Historical Quarterly*, vol. 71, no. 4 (Winter 1987), p. 664. For Lynn shoe workers, see Alan Dawley and Paul Fraler, "Working-Class Culture and Politics in the Industrial Revolution: Sources of Loyalism and Rebellion," *Journal of Social History*, vol. 9 (June 1976), pp. 466-80. For the Melville story, see Herman Melville, *The Piazza Tales and Other Prose Pieces, 1839–1860*, in vol. 9 of *The Writings of Herman Melville* (Evanston: Northwestern University Press, 1987), pp. 323–35, quotations are from pp. 328, 333, 334. Hobsbawm on industrialism's first

generation seen in Herbert G. Gutman, "Protestantism and the American Labor Movement: The Christian Spirit in the Gilded Age," *American Historical Review*, vol. 72, no. 1 (October 1966), p. 96, n. 93. For the Toledo bulb works, see the moving account in David Montgomery, *The Fall of the House of Labor: The Workplace, the State, and American Labor Activism, 1865–1925* (New York: Cambridge University Press, 1987), pp. 112–14. For the New York elite's assault on the franchise, see Sven Beckert, *The Monied Metropolis: New York City and the Consolidation of the American Bourgeoisie, 1850–1896* (New York: Cambridge University Press, 2001), pp. 218–24. For the Kansas Populist, see Peter H. Argersinger, *Populism and Politics: William Alfred Peffer and the People's Party* (Lexington: University of Kentucky Press, 1974), p. 308. For "cultural hegemony," see T. J. Jackson Lears, "The Concept of Cultural Hegemony: Problems and Possibilities," *American Historical Review*, vol. 90, no. 3 (June 1985). For public relations campaigns, see Roland Marchand, *Creating the Corporate Soul: The Rise of Public Relations and Corporate Imagery in American Big Business* (Berkeley: University of California Press, 1998), especially pp. 1–47. For counterhegemonic opposition, see Leon Fink, "The New Labor History and the Powers of Historical Pessimism," *Journal of American History*, vol. 75, no. 1 (June 1988), p. 123. For the contrast between France and the United States, see Gerald Friedman, "Strike Success and Union Ideology: The United States and France, 1880–1914," *Journal of Economic History*, vol. 48, no. 1 (March 1988), pp. 1–25. For "domestic militarism," see Michael Mann, *The Rise of Classes and Nation-States, 1760–1914* (New York: Cambridge University Press, 1993), pp. 644–55. For the revolt from below, see Lawrence Goodwyn, *The Populist Moment: The Agrarian Revolt in the United States* (New York: Oxford University Press, 1978).

Chapter Two: Rome of the Railroads

1. Lance Davis et al., *American Economic Growth* (New York: Harper & Row, 1972), pp. 487–97; Albert Fishlow, *American Railroads and the Transformation of the Ante-Bellum Economy* (Cambridge: Harvard University Press, 1965), pp. 6–8.

2. John Moses, *History of Chicago* (Chicago: Munsell, 1895), pp. 60–65; Bessie Louise Pierce, *A History of Chicago*, vol. 1 (New York: Alfred A. Knopf, 1937), pp. 22–28. For early history of Chicago, also see Edwin O. Gale, "Chicago as It Is and Was," in *Transactions of the Illinois State Historical Society*, no. 3, 1908, p. 140; J. Seymour Currey, *Chicago and Its Builders*, vol. 1 (Chicago: S. J. Clarke, 1912), pp. 77–84. Fishlow, *American Railroads*, p. 201.

3. Moses, *History of Chicago*, p. 119.

4. Robert G. Spinney, *City of Big Shoulders: A History of Chicago* (DeKalb: Northern Illinois University Press, 2000), p. 31.

5. Harriet Martineau, essay in Mabel McIlvaine, *Reminiscences of Chicago During the Forties and Fifties* (Chicago: R. R. Donnelley, 1913), p. 29.

6. Joseph Kirkland, *The Story of Chicago* (Chicago: Dibble, 1892), p. 168.

7. William Cronon, *Nature's Metropolis: Chicago and the Great West* (New York: W. W. Norton, 1991), p. 30; Moses, *History of Chicago*, p. 105; Charles Fenno Hoffman, essay in McIlvaine, *Reminiscences of Chicago*, p. 14. For cups, see Spinney, *City of Big Shoulders*, p. 250.

8. Moses, *History of Chicago*, p. 81; Allan Nevins, *Ordeal of the Union: A House Dividing, 1852–1857* (New York: Scribners, 1947), p. 223.

9. Martineau, in McIlvaine, *Reminiscences of Chicago*, p. 29. For "sixty days straight," see Moses, *History of Chicago*, p. 65.

10. Earnest Elmo Calkins, *Genesis of a Railroad* (Chicago: R. R. Donnelly, 1939), p. 44. For slough, see McIlvaine, *Reminiscences of Chicago,* p. 40. For "quagmires" and cattle, see Gale "Chicago as It Is and Was," pp. 43, 59.

11. Judson Fiske Lee, "Transportation as a Factor in the Development of Northern Illinois Previous to 1860," in *Journal of the Illinois State Historical Society,* vol. 10, no. 1 (April 1917), p. 23.

12. Spinney, *City of Big Shoulders,* pp. 43–44.

13. Arthur M. Johnson and Barry E. Supple, *Boston Capitalists and Western Railroads* (Cambridge: Harvard University Press, 1967), p. 81.

14. Alfred T. Andreas, *History of Chicago from the Earliest Period to the Present Time,* vol. 3 (Chicago: A. T. Andreas, 1884–1886). p. 247ff.

15. Cronon, *Nature's Metropolis,* p. 66.

16. Kirkland, *The Story of Chicago,* p. 249.

17. Robert J. Casey and W.A.S. Douglas, *Pioneer Railroad: The Story of the Chicago and Northwestern System* (New York: Whittlesey House, 1948), p. 55.

18. Ibid., p. 53. Cronon, *Nature's Metropolis,* p. 405, n. 47. Andreas, *History of Chicago,* vol. 3, p. 247; Kirkland, *The Story of Chicago,* p. 144; Casey and Douglas, *Pioneer Railroad,* p. 250.

19. Daniel J. Boorstin, "The Businessman as an American Institution," in Alexander Callow, editor, *American Urban History* (New York: Oxford University Press, 1969), pp. 136–39.

20. Peter F. Drucker, *Innovation and Entrepreneurship* (New York: Harper & Row, 1985), p. 21.

21. Boorstin, "The Businessman as an American Institution," p. 138. For more on Ogden, see Dumas Malone, editor, *Dictionary of American Biography* (New York: Scribners, 1934), pp. 644–45.

22. Casey and Douglas, *Pioneer Railroad,* p. 59; Pierce, *A History of Chicago,* p. 35.

23. Casey and Douglas, *Pioneer Railroad,* p. 35.

24. Lee, "Transportation as a Factor in the Development of Northern Illinois," p. 409. Boorstin, "The Businessman as an American Institution," p. 139.

25. Jackson's second vice president, Martin Van Buren, was the source of "a busy few." See Arthur M. Schlesinger, Jr., *The Cycles of American History* (Boston: Houghton Mifflin, 1986), p. 228. For the figures on local debt and the accompanying quotation, see Charles W. McCurdy, "Justice Field and the Jurisprudence of Government-Business Relations: Some Parameters of Laissez-Faire Constitutionalism, 1863–1897," *Journal of American History,* vol. 61 (1976), pp. 970–1005.

26. David M. Potter, *The Impending Crisis, 1848–1861* (New York: Harper & Row, 1976), p. 342.

27. Ibid., p. 152. The comparison between the Compromise and the railroad is made in Robert W. Johannsen, *Stephen A. Douglas* (New York: Oxford University Press, 1973), p. 306. Jefferson Davis gave Douglas chief credit for the Compromise: "If any man has a right to be proud of the success of their measures, it is the Senator from Illinois." After reviewing the debate, a twentieth-century historian agrees: "It is evident that the Compromise of 1850 was chiefly the work of Douglas." F. H. Hodder, "The Authorship of the Compromise of 1850," *Mississippi Valley Historical Review,* vol. 22, no. 4 (March 1936), pp. 525–41.

28. Johannsen, *Stephen A. Douglas,* pp. 306–12.

29. Paul W. Gates, *The Illinois Central Railroad and Its Colonization Program* (Cambridge: Harvard University Press, 1934), pp. 31–35. Ibid., p. 68.

30. Ibid., p. 313.

31. Ibid., pp. 54–65.

32. Johnson and Supple, *Boston Capitalists and Western Railroads*, pp. 134–35.

33. Gates, *The Illinois Central Railroad*, pp. 124–27.

34. William E. Dodd, "The Fight for the Northwest, 1860," *American Historical Review*, vol. 16, no. 4 (July 1911), pp. 774–88; Gates, *The Illinois Central Railroad*, pp. 169, 241; Johnson and Supple, *Boston Capitalists and Western Railroads*, p. 128.

35. Moses, *History of Chicago*, p. 122.

36. Gates, *The Illinois Central Railroad*, p. 86.

37. Ibid., p. 96.

38. Ibid., pp. 185–87.

39. Ibid., p. 216.

40. Ibid., p. 226; Richard C. Overton, *Burlington West: A Colonization History of the Burlington Railroad* (Cambridge: Harvard University Press, 1941), p. 161; Gates, *The Illinois Central Railroad*, p. 224.

41. Overton, *Burlington West*, p. 71; Allan Nevins, *A House Dividing, 1852–1857* (New York: Scribners, 1947), p. 231; Cronon, *Nature's Metropolis*, pp. 109–16.

42. Ibid., pp. 51, 48.

43. Norris quotation is from the frontispiece in ibid.

44. Spinney, *City of Big Shoulders*, p. 50.

45. Theodore J. Karamanski, *Rally 'Round the Flag, Boys: Chicago and the Civil War* (Chicago: Nelson-Hall, 1993), p. 3; Cronon, *Nature's Metropolis*, p. 104.

46. Johannsen, *Stephen A. Douglas*, p. 266; Howard Copeland, "The Development of Chicago as a Center of the Meat Packing Industry," *Mississippi Valley Historical Review* vol. 10, no. 3 (1923–24), p. 273.

47. For "mad," see Carl Abbot, *Boosters and Businessmen* (Wesport: Greenwood, 1981), p. 133. For preacher, see William S. Patterson, "Kipling's First Visit to Chicago," *Journal of the Illinois Historical Society*, vol. 63, no. 3 (Autumn 1970), p. 293.

48. Karamanski, *Rally 'Round the Flag, Boys*, p. 41. Robert Kanigel, *The One Best Way: Frederick Winslow Taylor and the Enigma of Efficiency* (New York: Viking, 1997), p. 495.

49. Cronon, *Nature's Metropolis*, p. 205.

50. Patterson, "Kipling's First Visit to Chicago," p. 293ff.

51. Cronon, *Nature's Metropolis*, p. 12.

52. Ibid., pp. 229, 249, 250.

53. Ibid., p. 251.

54. Alfred D. Chandler, Jr., *Scale and Scope: The Dynamics of Industrial Capitalism* (Cambridge: Harvard University Press, 1990), pp. 14–46, especially pp. 24–26.

55. Cronon, *Nature's Metropolis*, pp. 210–11, 230.

56. Ibid.

57. Ibid., p. 259.

58. Potter, *The Impending Crisis*, p. 422; Karamanski, *Rally 'Round the Flag, Boys*, p. 9.

59. Arthur C. Cole, *Lincoln's "House Divided" Speech: Did It Reflect a Doctrine of Class Struggle?*, (Chicago: University of Chicago Press, 1923), p. 11.

60. Potter, *The Impending Crisis*, p. 427; James M. McPherson, *Battle Cry of Freedom: The Civil War Era* (New York: Oxford University Press, 1988), p. 219.

61. Carl Sandburg, *Abraham Lincoln: The Prairie Years and the War Years* (New York: Harcourt, 1954), pp. 168–70.

62. David Donald, *Lincoln* (New York: Simon & Schuster, 1996), p. 248; Karamanski, *Rally 'Round the Flag, Boys*, pp. 6, 27.

63. Karamanski, *Rally 'Round the Flag, Boys*, p. 18.

64. Fred Harvey Harrington, *Fighting Politician: Major General N. P. Banks* (Philadelphia: University of Pennsylvania Press, 1948), pp. 1–13.

65. Steven R. Weisman, *The Great Tax Wars: Lincoln to Wilson—The Fierce Battles over Money and Power That Transformed the Nation* (New York: Simon & Schuster, 2002), p. 16; Christopher Lasch seen in Mattson, "The Historian as Social Critic: Christopher Lasch and the Uses of History," *The History Teacher*, vol. 36, no. 3 (May 2003), p. 7.

66. David Montgomery, *Beyond Equality: Labor and the Radical Republicans, 1862–1872* (New York: Alfred A. Knopf, 1967), p. 14.

67. Cole, *Lincoln's "House Divided" Speech*, p. 19.

68. Cronon, *Nature's Metropolis*, pp. 242–43.

69. For an estimate of self-employment, see Richard Sennett, *The Culture of the New Capitalism* (New Haven: Yale University Press, 2006), p. 141: "[T]he rate of full-time self-employment in the United States . . . has held steady at about 8.5% for the last forty years."

70. Eric Foner, *Free Soil, Free Labor, Free Men: The Ideology of the Republican Party Before the Civil War* (New York: Oxford University Press, 1970), p. 17. For New York constitutional convention, see Rowland Berthoff, "Conventional Mentality: Free Blacks, Women, and Business Corporations as Unequal Persons, 1820–1870" *Journal of American History*, vol. 76, no. 3 (December 1989), p. 760. For McNeill and working-class republicanism, see Richard Oestreicher, "Urban Working-Class Political Behavior and Theories of American Electoral Politics, 1870–1940" *Journal of American History*, vol. 74, no. 4 (March 1988), pp. 1251–57.

71. *The Liberator*, March 19, 1847, seen in Philip S. Foner and Herbert Shapiro, editors, *Northern Labor and Antislavery: A Documentary History* (Westport: Greenwood Press, 1994), p. 61; W.E.B. Du Bois, *Black Reconstruction in America: An Essay Toward a History of the Part Black Folks Played in the Attempt to Reconstruct Democracy in America, 1860–1880* (New York: Russell & Russell, 1935), p. 10.

72. Nevins, *A House Dividing*, pp. 11, 334–35.

73. Barrington Moore, Jr., *The Social Origins of Dictatorship and Democracy: Lord and Peasant in the Making of the Modern World* (Boston: Beacon, 1966), p. 144; Nevins, *A House Dividing*, p. 269.

74. Moore, *The Social Origins of Dictatorship and Democracy*, pp. 111–55; Weisman, *The Great Tax Wars*, p. 33; Douglas C. North, *The Economic Growth of the United States, 1790–1860* (New York: W. W. Norton, 1966), pp. 204–6. For southerners, see James M. McPherson, *Abraham Lincoln and the Second American Revolution* (New York: Oxford University Press, 1991), pp. 12–13.

75. For Greeley, see Reinhard H. Luthin, "Abraham Lincoln and the Tariff" *American Historical Society*, vol. 49, no. 4 (July 1944), pp. 609–21. Moore, *The Social Origins of Dictatorship and Democracy*, p. 130.

76. For Wilmot, see Charles B. Goring, *David Wilmot, Free-Soiler* (New York: Appleton, 1924), p. 528.

77. Halstead, seen in ibid, p. 57.

78. Potter, *The Impending Crisis*, p. 428.

79. Ibid., pp. 428–29; John G. Nicolay and John Hay, *Abraham Lincoln: A History* (New York: The Century Company, 1890), p. 277.

80. Karamanski, *Rally 'Round the Flag, Boys*, p. 15; Donald, *Lincoln*, p. 245 for blush.

81. For the fence rails, see Nicolay and Hay, *Abraham Lincoln*, p. 284 and Karamanski, *Rally 'Round the Flag, Boys*, p. 15.

82. Karmanski, *Rally 'Round the Flag, Boys*, p. 31. For cannonade, see *New York Times*, May 20, 1860.

Chapter Three: "Vote Yourself a Tariff"

1. Alfred E. Eckes, *Opening America's Markets: U.S. Trade Policy Since 1776* (Chapel Hill: University of North Carolina Press, 1995), p. 286.

2. James M. McPherson, *Battle Cry of Freedom: The Civil War Era* (New York: Oxford University Press, 1988), p. 854.

3. Ibid., p. 619, n. 53; Claudia Goldin and Frank Lewis, "The Economic Cost of the American Civil War: Estimates and Implications" *Journal of Economic History*, vol. 35, no. 2 (June 1975), p. 316. E. Merton Coulter, *The South During Reconstruction, 1865–1877* (Baton Rouge: Louisiana State University Press, 1947), p. 14.

4. Stanley L. Engerman, "The Economic Impact of the Civil War," *Explorations in Economic History*, vol. 3, no. 3 (Spring/Summer 1966), p. 196; Richard F. Wacht, "A Note on the Cocoran Thesis and the Small Arms Industry in the Civil War" *Explorations in Entreprenurial History*, vol. 4, no. 1 (Fall 1966), pp. 57–62. Thomas C. Cochran, "Did the Civil War Retard Industrialization?," *Mississippi Valley Historical Review*, vol. 58, no. 2 (September 1961), pp. 197–210; Douglass C. North, *The Economic Growth of the United States, 1790–1860* (New York: W. W. Norton, 1966), p. 215; James Ford Rhodes, *A History of the United States from the Compromise of 1850*, vol. 5 (New York: Harper & Brothers, 1904), p. 207; Allan Nevins, *The War for the Union*, vol. 4, *The Organized War, 1863–1864* (New York: Scribners, 1971), pp. 229–30; Wacht, "A Note on the Cochoran Thesis," pp. 57–62. The author estimates that 66,000 tons of domestic iron went into the making of 1.6 million muskets and 32,000 repeating rifles. Also see Ralph Andreano, editor, *Economic Change in the Civil War Era* (Cambridge: Harvard University Press, 1967).

5. Goldin and Lewis, "The Economic Cost of the American Civil War," p. 302.

6. Nevins, *The Organized War*, pp. 217–70. Also see Harry N. Schreiber, "Economic Change in the Civil War: An Analysis of Recent Studies," *Civil War Quarterly*, vol. 2, no. 4 (1965), pp. 396–441; John Steele Gordon, *An Empire of Wealth: The Epic History of American Economic Power* (New York: HarperCollins, 2004), p. 199; Steven R. Weisman, *The Great Tax Wars: Lincoln to Wilson—The Fierce Battles over Money and Power That Transformed the Nation* (New York: Simon & Schuster, 2002), p. 81.

7. Rhodes, *A History of the United States*, pp. 212–20; Weisman, *The Great Tax Wars*, p. 79.

8. Rhodes, *A History of the United States*, pp. 212–20. James Sellers, "The Economic Incidence of the Civil War in the South," *Mississippi Valley Historical Review*, vol. 14, no. 2 (September 1927), pp. 179, 180–81.

9. J. T. Trowbridge, *The South: A Tour of Its Battlefields and Ruined Cities* (Hartford: L. Stebbins, 1866), excerpted in John Richard Dennett, editor, *The South as It Is, 1865–1866* (Athens: University of Georgia Press, 1965), p. 180; Rhodes, *A History of the United States*, p. 644; McPherson, *Battle Cry of Freedom*, p. 829; John Samuel Ezell, *The South Since 1865* (New York: MacMillan, 1963), pp. 26–28. For Grant, see Carol Bundy, *The Nature of Sacrifice: A Biography of Charles Russell Lowell, Jr.* (New York: Farrar, Straus & Giroux, 2005), p. 404; Coulter, *The South During Reconstruction*, p. 16.

10. Sellers, "The Economic Incidence of the Civil War in the South," pp. 180–89; Morton Keller, *Affairs of State: Public Life in Late Nineteenth Century America* (Cambridge: Harvard University Press, 1977), pp. 198–99, 220–21, 232–33.

11. For Southern elites and terror, see Eric Foner, *Reconstruction: America's Unfinished Revolution, 1863–1877* (New York: Harper & Row, 1988), pp. 425–37; C. Vann Wood-

ward, *Origins of the New South, 1877–1913* (Baton Rouge: Louisiana State University Press, 1971), pp. 310, 115, 307, 224–25, 319. For details of the South's ambivalent pursuit of northern investment, see James Tice Moore, "Redeemers Reconsidered: Change and Continuity in the Democratic South, 1870–1900," *Journal of Southern History*, vol. 44, no. 3 (August 1978), pp. 357–78. For North Carolina labor laws, see Richard Franklin Bensel, *The Political Economy of American Industrialization, 1877–1900* (Cambridge, Eng.: Cambridge University Press, 2000), pp. 208, n. 6, 214–15. Edward L. Ayers, *The Promise of the New South: Life After Reconstruction* (New York: Oxford University Press, 1992), pp. 9–13, 106.

12. Foner, *Reconstruction*, p. 23. For pensions, see Theda Skocpol, *Protecting Soldiers and Mothers: The Political Origins of Social Policy in the United States* (Cambridge: Harvard University Press, 1992), p. 128. Steven Hahn, "Class and State in Postemancipation Societies: Southern Planters in Comparative Perspective," *American Historical Review*, vol. 95, no. 11 (February 1990), p. 92. For Republican pamphlet, see Joel H. Silbey, "The American Political Experience from Andrew Jackson to the Civil War," in Byron E. Shafer and Anthony J. Badger, editors, *Contested Democracy: Substance and Structure in American Political History, 1775–2000* (Lawrence: University of Kansas Press, 2001), p. 85.

13. Heather Cox Richardson, *The Greatest Nation of the Earth: Republican Economic Policies During the Civil War* (Cambridge: Harvard University Press, 1997), p. 143; Leonard P. Curry, *Blueprint for Modern America: Non-Military Legislation of the First Civil War Congress* (Nashville: Vanderbilt University Press, 1968). For bills passed, see Keller, *Affairs of State*, Table 1, p. 23.

14. On the tariff, see Jeffrey G. Williamson, "Watersheds and Turning Points: Conjectures on the Long-Term Impact of Civil War Financing," *Journal of Economic History*, vol. 34, no. 3 (September 1973), pp. 636–61: Robert J. Morrison, "Henry C. Carey and American Economic Development," *Explorations in Economic History*, vol. 5, no. 2 (Winter 1967).

15. Sidney Ratner, *The Tariff in American History* (New York: Van Nostrand, 1972), p. 29. The Republicans quoted in the paragraph above are taken from Charles W. Calhoun, "Political Economy in the Gilded Age: The Republican Party's Industrial Policy," *Journal of Policy History*, vol. 8, no. 3 (November 1996), pp. 291–309. This is the outstanding paper on the subject.

16. For views of the business elite, see John P. Roche, "Entrepreneurial Liberty and the Commerce Power: Expansion, Contraction, and Casuistry in the Age of Enterprise," *University of Chicago Law Review*, vol. 30, no. 4 (Summer 1963), p. 681.

17. For William Pitt, see Robert L. Heilbroner, *The Worldly Philosophers: The Lives, Times, and Ideas of the Great Economic Thinkers* (New York: Simon & Schuster, 1989), p. 74.

18. Eckes, *Opening America's Markets*, p. xiii; Weisman, *The Great Tax Wars*, p. 21. For Wilson, see Joanne Reitano, *The Tariff Question in the Gilded Age: The Great Debate of 1888* (University Park: Pennsylvania State University Press, 1994), p. 127; Richard Franklin Bensel, *Sectionalism and American Political Development, 1880–1980* (Madison: University of Wisconsin Press, 1984), p. 62. For tax on exports, see Douglas A. Irwin, "Tariff Incidence in the Gilded Age," www.dartmouth.edu/~dirwin/papers.htm, March 2006, p. 16. William Belmont Parker, *The Life and Public Service of Justin Smith Morrill* (Boston: Houghton Mifflin, 1924), p. 111.

19. For David A. Wells, see Douglas A. Irwin, "Could the U.S. Iron Industry Have Survived Free Trade after the Civil War?" and for clashing views, see Irwin's "Tariffs

and Growth in Late Nineteenth-Century America," June 2000, at www.dartmouth .edu/~dirwin/papers.htm. Also see Tom E. Terrill, "David A. Wells, the Democracy, and Tariff Reduction, 1877–1894," *Journal of American History,* vol. 56, no. 3 (December 1969), pp. 540–55; and Bennett D. Baack and Edward John Ray, "Tariff Policy and Comparative Advantage in Iron and Steel Industry: 1870–1929," *Explorations in Economic History,* vol. 11, no. 1 (Fall 1973), pp. 3–23. James Fallows, *Looking at the Sun: The Rise of the New East Asian Economic and Political Systems* (New York: Pantheon, 1994), pp. 198, 180, 477, 193. For Wharton, see Sidney Fine, *Laissez Faire and the General-Welfare State* (Ann Arbor: University of Michigan Press, 1956), p. 113, n. 58. Paul Bairoch, *Economics and World History: Myths and Paradoxes* (Chicago: University of Chicago Press, 1993), p. 52. William D. "Pig Iron" Kelley, a Philadelphia congressman, expressed the prevailing view of the Republican Party in Pennsylvania and in the Congress: " '[I]t became apparent to me, not only that Political Economy was not a science, but that it was impossible to frame a system of abstract economic propositions which would be universally applicable and beneficent.' Fortunately, 'the intimate relations of many . . . students with the industries and people of the country render the scholasticisms of their teachers harmless.' " Keller, *Affairs of State,* p. 163. For a contemporary critique of economics as divorced from the real world, see Robert Heilbroner and William Milberg, *The Crisis of Vision in Modern Economic Thought* (New York: Cambridge University Press, 1995).

20. For Grant, see Ha-Joon Chang, "Kicking Away the Ladder: Infant Industry Protection in Historical Perspective," *Oxford Development Studies,* vol. 31, no. 1 (2003), pp. 25–26. "What the British advocates of laissez-faire neglected to talk about was the role that a system of national power had played in creating conditions for Britain to embark on its dynamic development path." Also see, Mehdi Shafaeddin, "How Did Developed Countries Industrialize? The History of Trade and Industrial Policy: The Cases of Great Britain and the USA," UNCTAD Discussion Papers, No. 139 (December 1998), pp. 1–25.

21. Eckes, *Opening America's Markets,* Table 2.2, p. 50, and Table 2.6, p. 54.

22. Kevin O'Rourke, "Tariffs and Late 19th Century Growth," *Economic Journal,* vol. 110 (April 2000), pp. 456–83, especially pp. 466, 473, 468. For two key papers on the positive late-twentieth-century correlation between free trade and growth, see D. Sachs and A. Warner, "Economic Reform and the Process of Global Integration" *Brookings Papers on Economic Activity,* vol. 1995, no. 1 (1995), pp. 1–118; Lee J. W., "International Trade, Distortions, and Long-Run Economic Growth," IMF Staff Papers, vol. 40, no. 2 (June 1993), pp. 299–328.

23. Eckes, *Opening America's Markets,* Table 2.3, p. 54, plus last line on page; O'Rourke, "Tariffs and Late 19th Century Growth," p. 474. Also see G. R. Hawke, "The United States Tariff and Industrial Protection in the Late 19th Century," *Economic History Review,* vol. 28, no. 1 (February 1975), pp. 84–97.

24. Frank W. Taussig, *Some Aspects of the Tariff Question* (Cambridge: Harvard University Press, 1918), pp. 19–34, 141, 115–18. This last is a surprising conclusion for Professor Taussig, described as "[a] man who ascribed positive moral virtues to a 'natural' (that is, free free-market equilibrium) pattern of international specialization and trade." P. A. David, "Learning by Doing: A Reconsideration of the Case of the Ante-Bellum U.S. Cotton Textile Industry," *Journal of Economic History,* vol. 30, no. 3 (September 1970), p. 528. See also Robert Allen, "International Competition in Iron and Steel, 1850–1913," *Journal of Economic History,* vol. 39, no. 4 (December 1979), pp. 911–37. For background on tariff making, see Edward Stanwood, *American Tariff*

Controversies in the Nineteenth Century (Boston: Houghton Mifflin, 1903). For Senator Stewart, see Calhoun, "Political Economy in the Gilded Age," p. 301.

25. Thomas K. McCraw, "Mercantilism and the Market," in Claude E. Barfield and William A. Schambra, editors, *The Politics of Industrial Policy* (Washington, D.C.: American Enterprise Institute, 1984), pp. 33–62; quotation is from p. 53.

26. Eckes, *Opening America's Markets,* for wages, p. 35, for Wilson, p. 43, for McKinley, p. 33. Richard B. Freeman, "Toward an Apartheid Economy?," *Harvard Business Review,* September–October 1996. For background on the new departure in trade after World War II, see Michael A. Clemens and Jeffrey G. Williamson, "Why Did the Tariff-Growth Correlation Change After 1950?," *Journal of Economic Growth,* vol. 9, no. 1 (March 2004), p. 5ff; Lester Thurow, *Head to Head: The Coming Economic Battles Among Japan, Europe, and America* (New York: William Morrow, 1992), p. 82.

27. Eckes, *Opening America's Markets,* p. 35. Weisman, *The Great Tax Wars,* p. 138.

28. Ratner, *The Tariff in American History,* p. 119. Ida M. Tarbell, *The Tariff in Our Times* (New York: Macmillan, 1911), pp. 161, 338–49. For Democrats against the tariff, see Reitano, *The Tariff Question in the Gilded Age,* p. 76.

29. Fred A. Shannon, *The Farmer's Last Frontier: Agriculture, 1860–1897* (White Plains: M. E. Sharpe, 1972), p. 195.

30. Theodore Saloutos, "The Agricultural Problem and 19th Century Industrialism," *Agricultural History,* vol. 22, no. 1 (January 1948), pp. 162–65; Tarbell, *The Tariff in Our Times,* p. 89.

Chapter Four: "Vote Yourself a Farm"

1. The scene recaptured by Colonel Higginson appears in Rebecca Edwards, *New Spirits: Americans in the Gilded Age, 1865–1905* (New York: Oxford University Press, 2006), p. 11. This book provides a superb panorama on the era. For Lord Bryce, see Richard Hofstadter, *The American Political Tradition and the Men Who Made It* (New York: Vintage, 1948), p. 169. For Adams, see Eric Foner, *Free Soil, Free Labor, Free Men: The Ideology of the Republican Party Before the Civil War* (New York: Oxford University Press, 1970), p. 34. Louis W. Koenig, *Bryan: A Political Biography* (New York: Putnam, 1991), p. 334; Paolo E. Coletta, *William Jennings Bryan, Political Evangelist, 1860–1908,* vol. 1 (Lincoln: University of Nebraska Press, 1964), p. 193.

2. Eric Foner, *Reconstruction: America's Unfinished Revolution, 1863–1877* (New York: Harper & Row, 1988), p. 523.

3. Ibid., p. 610.

4. For letter from ex-slave, see Jonathan M. Wiener, "Class Structure and Economic Development in the American South, 1865–1955," *Journal of American History,* vol. 84, no. 4 (October 1979), p. 976. For Yorktown, see Eric Foner, "Rights and the Constitution in Black Life During the Civil War and Reconstruction," *Journal of American History,* vol. 74, no. 3 (December 1987), p. 871.

5. Patrick W. Riddleberger, "George W. Julian: Abolitionist Land Reformer," *Agricultural History,* vol. 29, no. 4 (July 1955), pp. 108–10. In his memoirs Julian said that some of his fellow Radicals, fearing Lincoln's lenience toward the postwar South, saw the president's death as "a godsend to the country." Kenneth M. Stampp, *The Era of Reconstruction, 1865–1877* (New York: Alfred A. Knopf, 1966), p. 50.

6. Stampp, *The Era of Reconstruction,* pp. 41–42.

7. Foner, *Reconstruction,* pp. 70–71. For a discerning discussion of Foner's contribution to historians' understanding of Reconstruction, see Steven Hahn, "The Other

American Revolution," a review of Eric Foner, *Forever Free: The Story of Emancipation and Reconstruction* (New York: Alfred A. Knopf, 2005) in *The New Republic*, vol. 235, August 7, 2006, pp. 23–29.

8. W.E.B. Du Bois, *Black Reconstruction in America: An Essay Toward a History of the Part Which Black Folk Played in the Attempt to Reconstruct Democracy in America, 1860–1880* (New York: Russell & Russell, 1935), p. 206. For "masters" see Foner, *Reconstruction*, p. 246. Jay R. Mandle, "Continuity and Change: The Use of Black Labor After the Civil War," *Journal of Black Studies*, vol. 21, no. 4 (June 1991), p. 419. James Tice Moore, "Redeemers Reconsidered: Change and Continuity in the Democratic South, 1870–1900," *Journal of Southern History*, vol. 44, no. 3 (August 1978), p. 367.

9. For "gang labor," see Eric Foner, *Nothing but Freedom: Emancipation and Its Legacy* (Baton Rouge: Louisiana State University Press, 1983), pp. 4, 45, 86. Du Bois, *Black Reconstruction in America*, p. 671.

10. W. E. Burghardt Du Bois, "Reconstruction and Its Benefits," *American Historical Review*, vol. 15, no. 4 (July 1910), pp. 781–99, quotes historian John W. Burgess on p. 784; Foner, *Reconstruction*, p. 199.

11. Du Bois, *Black Reconstruction*, p. 136.

12. For Georgia plantation, see Eric Foner, *Nothing But Freedom*, p. 83. Joseph D. Reid, Jr., "Sharecropping as an Understandable Market Response: The Post-Bellum South," *Journal of Economic History*, vol. 33, no. 1 (March 1973), p. 110. Foner, *Reconstruction*, pp. 70–71; Foner, *Nothing but Freedom*, pp. 86, 45.

13. Reid, "Sharecropping," p. 112. Sven Beckert, "Emancipation and Empire: Reconstructing the Worldwide Web of Cotton Production in the Age of the American Civil War," *American Historical Review*, vol. 109, issue 5 (December 2004), pp. 1–42, taken from the History Cooperative, http://www.historycooperative.org.

14. Gilbert C. Fite, "Southern Agriculture Since the Civil War," *Agricultural History*, vol. 53, no. 1 (January 1979), p. 6.

15. Fred A. Shannon, *The Farmer's Last Frontier: Agriculture, 1860–1897* (White Plains: M. E. Sharpe, 1945), p. 88.

16. Ibid., p. 99.

17. Fite, "Southern Agriculture," pp. 3–21. Harold D. Woodman writes, "Sharecro[pping] was strongly associated with race: blacks more often became sharecroppers than did whites, who tended to be small landowners and tenants." Harold D. Woodman, "Comments," *American Historical Review*, vol. 84, no. 4 (October 1979), p. 1001. For figures on the antebellum agricultural ladder, see Lacy K. Ford, Jr., "Frontier Democracy: The Turner Thesis Revisited," *Journal of the Early Republic*, vol. 13, no. 2 (Summer 1993), pp. 152–53.

18. Roger Ransom and Richard Sutch, "The Ex-Slave in the Post-Bellum South: A Study of the Economic Impact of Racism in a Market Environment," *Journal of Economic History*, vol. 33, no. 1 (March 1973), p. 135.

19. Roger Ransom and Richard Sutch, "Debt Peonage in the Cotton South After the Civil War," *Journal of Economic History*, vol. 32, no. 3 (September 1972), p. 644. For banks, see Theodore R. Mitchell, *Political Education in the Southern Farmers' Alliance, 1887–1900* (Madison: University of Wisconsin Press, 1987), p. 28.

20. Ransom and Sutch, "The Ex-Slave," p. 144.

21. Ibid., p. 142. Jay Mandle, "Continuity and Change: The Use of Black Labor After the Civil War," *Journal of Black Studies*, vol. 21, no. 4 (June 1991), p. 42.

22. Peter Temin, "Post-Bellum Recovery of the South and the Cost of the Civil War," *Journal of Economic History*, vol. 36, no. 1 (December 1976), p. 904.

23. Roger Ransom and Richard Sutch, "The Impact of the Civil War and of Emancipation on Southern Agriculture," *Explorations in Economic History*, vol. 12, no. 1 (January 1975), p. 14.

24. Fite, "Southern Agriculture," pp. 10–11.

25. C. Vann Woodward, *Origins of the New South, 1877–1913* (Baton Rouge: Louisiana State University Press, 1971), pp. 180–85; Ransom and Sutch, "Debt Peonage," p. 665; Thomas D. Clark, "The Furnishing and Supply System in Southern Agriculture Since 1865," *Journal of Southern History*, vol. 12 (February 1946), pp. 24–44. For the quotations from contemporary observers, see Michael Schwartz, *Radical Protest and Social Structure: The Southern Farmers' Alliance and Cotton Tenancy, 1880–1890* (New York: Academic Press, 1976), pp. 36–39.

26. Ransom and Sutch, "Debt Peonage," p. 656.

27. For planters, see Jonathan M. Wiener, "Class Structure and Economic Development in the American South, 1865–1955," *American Historical Review*, vol. 84, no. 4 (October 1919), p. 989; David M. Kennedy, *Freedom from Fear: The American People in Depression and War, 1929–1945* (New York: Oxford University Press, 1999), p. 192.

28. Fite, "Southern Agriculture," p. 15. George B. Tindall, *The Emergence of the New South, 1913–1945* (Baton Rouge: Louisiana State University Press, 1967), p. 409.

29. Kennedy, *Freedom from Fear,* p. 208.

30. Du Bois, *Black Reconstruction,* p. 298.

31. Ibid., pp. 73–74.

32. Shannon, *The Farmer's Last Frontier,* p. 84.

33. For an account of the plantations at Davis Bend and for "Emperor of Russia," see Stampp, *The Era of Reconstruction,* p. 126; Du Bois, *Black Reconstruction,* p. 673, and Stephen Joseph Rosi, "Freed Soil, Freed Labor, Freed Men: Joseph Eaton and the Davis Bend Experiment," *Journal of Southern History*, vol. 44, no. 2 (May 1972), pp. 213–32.

34. Du Bois, *Black Reconstruction,* pp. 197–98.

35. Stephan Thernstrom, *Poverty and Progress: Social Mobility in a Nineteenth Century City* (Cambridge: Harvard University Press, 1964), pp. 161–65; Herbert C. Gutman, "The Reality of the Rags-to-Riches 'Myth,' " in *Work, Culture and Society in Industrializing America* (New York: Vintage, 1977), pp. 214–15. Richard White does not let "mobility" slide by. In his spirited history of the American West, he lays bare the assumption built into the concept: "Historians can only recover labels, farm laborer, carpenter, etc. A western carpenter, for example, may have worked his whole life, raised a family, and obtained the respect of his fellows. He might consider his life a success. A historian, however, might dismiss the same life as a failure because the carpenter began life as a carpenter and ended it as a carpenter. He never got a 'better' job; he never advanced up the class ladder. When we attempt to measure something like social mobility we assume all workers would change jobs in order to advance to more rewarding prestigious work." Richard White, *"It's Your Misfortune and None of My Own," A History of the American West* (Norman: University of Oklahoma Press, 1991), pp. 284–85.

36. Edward Pessen, *Riches, Class and Power Before the Civil War* (Lexington: D. C. Heath, 1973), p. 77; Alan Trachtenberg, *The Incorporation of America: Culture and Society in the Gilded Age* (New York: Hill & Wang, 1984), p. 79.

37. Edward Pessen, *The Log Cabin Myth* (New Haven: Yale University Press, 1984), pp. 25, 26, 173.

38. Richard S. Tedlow, *Giants of Enterprise: Seven Business Innovators and the Empires They*

Built (New York: HarperCollins, 2001), pp. 26–37. For Reverend Smyth, see Stephan Thernstrom, *The Other Bostonians: Poverty and Progress in the American Metropolis, 1880–1970* (Cambridge: Harvard University Press, 1973), pp. 45–46.

39. Fred A. Shannon, "The Homestead Act and the Labor Surplus," *American Historical Review*, vol. 41, no. 2 (July 1936), p. 639.

40. Willa Cather, *O Pioneers!* (New York: Vintage, 1992), pp. 11–12.

41. Shannon, *The Farmer's Last Frontier*, p. 54.

42. Trachtenberg, *The Incorporation of America*, pp. 78–79.

43. David M. Potter, *People of Plenty: Economic Abundance and the American Character* (Chicago: University of Chicago Press, 1954), p. 101. Karl Marx, *Capital: A Critique of Political Economy* (New York: Modern Library, 1906), p. 389. For teacher, see p. 398, n. 1.

44. Pessen, *The Log Cabin Myth*, pp. 25–26, 173.

45. Marx, *Capital*, pp. 298, 307, n. 1.

46. For the 1890 census, see Robert Wiebe, *Self-Rule: A Cultural History of American Democracy* (Chicago: University of Chicago Press, 1995), p. 121; for a textured discussion of the two-class class system, see pp. 113–37. Michael B. Katz, "Social Class in North American Urban History," *Journal of Interdisciplinary History*, vol. 2, no. 4 (Spring 1981), pp. 579–605. Herbert G. Gutman, "Class, Status, and Community Power in a Nineteenth-Century American Industrial City, Paterson, New Jersey: A Case Study," in *Work, Culture and Society in Industrializing America*, pp. 282–83. According to Gutman, in 1880, 49 percent of all the boys in Paterson and 52.1 percent of all the girls "had occupations listed by name." See Charles Perrow, "A Society of Organizations," *Theory and Society*, vol. 20 (1991), p. 743. Charles Sellers, *The Market Revolution: Jacksonian America, 1815–1846* (New York: Oxford University Press, 1991), p. 368.

47. Adam Smith, *The Wealth of Nations* (New York: Modern Library, 2000), p. 840; Fred A. Shannon, "A Post-Mortem on the Labor Surplus," *Mississippi Valley Historical Review*, vol. 32, no. 1 (January 1945), p. 31. "[L]et an outlet be formed that will carry off our superabundant labor to the . . . West. . . . The labor market will thus be eased of the present distressing competition, and those who remain, as well those who migrate, will have the opportunity of realizing a comfortable living." *The Working Man's Advocate*, July 1844.

48. Shannon, "A Post-Mortem on the Labor Surplus."

49. Ray Allen Billington, *Frederick Jackson Turner: Historian, Scholar, Teacher* (New York: Oxford University Press, 1973), p. 459.

50. G.W.F. Hegel, *Philosophy of History* (New York: P. F. Collier & Son, 1900), pp. 141–42; Carter Goodrich and Sol Davison, "The Wage Earner in the Westward Movement," *Political Science Quarterly*, vol. 51, no. 2 (January 1935), pp. 165, 174.

51. Greeley, a member of the platform committee, said he "fixed" the Homestead plank, "exactly to my own liking." Foner, *Free Soil*, p. 28. Roy Marvin Robbins, "Horace Greeley: Land Reform and Unemployment, 1837–1862," *Agricultural History*, vol. 7, no. 1 (January 1933), p. 41.

52. Foner, *Free Soil*, p. 27; Goodrich and Davison, "The Wage Earner," p. 178.

53. *New York Times*, 6/12/1862; *New York Tribune*, 6/25/1862.

54. Henry George, *Progress and Poverty*, p. 388; Dayton Duncan, *Miles from Nowhere, Tales from America's Contemporary Frontier* (New York: Viking, 1993), pp. 3–6; Lee Benson, "The Social Background of Turner's Frontier Essay," *Agricultural History*, vol. 25, no. 2 (April 1951), p. 77. The contemporary "frontier, defined as 'a region

with less than two inhabitants to a square mile," the standard used by the 1890 census, comprises 13 percent of the nation's contiguous landmass—401,781 square miles, an area a little larger than everything east of the Mississippi River." Duncan, *Miles from Nowhere,* p. 7.

55. Paul W. Gates, "The Homestead Act in an Incongruous Land System," *American Historical Review,* vol. 41, no. 4 (July 1936), p. 653. For Senator Stewart, see Calhoun, "Political Economy in the Gilded Age," p. 301.

56. White, *"It's Your Misfortune and None of My Own,"* p. 184.

57. Carl N. Degler, *Out of Our Past: The Forces That Shaped America* (New York: Harper-Perennial, 1984), pp. 335–36.

58. Arthur M. Schlesinger, Sr., "The City in American History," *Mississippi Valley Historical Review,* vol. 27, no. 1 (June 1940), pp. 58–62.

59. Billington, *Frederick Jackson Turner,* p. 450.

60. For Turner, see Malcolm J. Rohrbrough, "Frederick Jackson Turner and the Significance of the Public Domain in American History," *Journal of the Early Republic,* vol. 13, no. 2 (Summer 1993), pp. 179–93. "His inquiries were preliminary, almost fragmentary, broad brush summaries with sweeping generalizations that fitted his overall themes of frontier and section," Rohrbrough writes of Turner's treatment of the public lands (p. 193).

61. Frederick Jackson Turner, *The Frontier in American History* (New York: N. H. Holmes, 1920), p. 274.

62. Goodrich and Davison, "The Wage Earner," p. 184.

63. Fred A. Shannon quoted in Ellen Von Naroff, "The American Frontier as Safety Valve—The Life, Death, Reincarnation, and Justification of a Theory," *Agricultural History,* vol. 36, no. 5 (July 1962), p. 131.

64. Goodrich and Davison, "The Wage Earner," pp. 161–85.

65. Ibid., p. 86ff.

66. Turner, *The Frontier in American History,* pp. 37, 1: Richard Hofstadter, *The Progressive Historians: Turner, Parrington, and Beard* (New York: Alfred A. Knopf, 1968), pp. 122–23; Billington, *Frederick Jackson Turner,* pp. 452–56. In a letter written a few months before his death, Turner spoke of the availability of free land on the frontier as "a key" to American history, a shift from his earlier "the one key."

67. Marion Clawson, *The Land System of the United States: An Introduction to the Theory and Practice of Land Use and Land Tenure* (Lincoln: University of Nebraska Press, 1968), p. 51.

68. Turner, *The Frontier in American History,* p. 12. For population figures, see Arthur M. Schlesinger, Sr., "The City in American History," *Mississippi Valley Historical Review,* vol. 27, no. 1 (June 1940), pp. 58–62. For Boston, see Stephan Thernstrom and Peter R. Knights, "Men in Motion: Some Data and Speculations about Urban Population Mobility in Nineteenth-Century America," *Journal of Interdisciplinary History,* vol. 1, no. 1 (Autumn 1970), p. 22. White, "It's Your Misfortune and None of My Own," p. 184.

69. Paul W. Gates, *Landlords and Tenants on the Prairie Frontier: Studies in American Land Policy* (Ithaca: Cornell University Press, 1973), p. 311.

70. Everett Dick, *The Sod-House Frontier, 1865–1890: A Social History of the Northern Plains from the Creation of Kansas and Nebraska to the Admission of the Dakotas* (New York: D. Appleton Century, 1937), pp. 126–27.

71. Gates, *Landlords and Tenants,* p. 150.

72. Ibid., pp. 155–56; White, *"It's Your Misfortune and None of My Own,"* p. 141.

73. Gates, *Landlords and Tenants*, p. 154.

74. Ibid., p. 322.

75. Ibid., pp. 83–84. In the 1930s, W. Averell Harriman, the president of the Union Pacific Railroad, "paid a little more than $1 an acre [for 3881 acres] to Ernest Bass, a rancher who had lost his cattle to poisonous larkspur weeds and his sheep to the plummeting prices of the Depression." In this way Harriman purchased Sun Valley. See Hal Rothman, "Tourism as Colonial Economy: Power and Place in Western Tourism," in Richard White and John M. Findlay, editors, *Power and Place in the North American West* (Seattle: Center for the Study of the Pacific Northwest, 1992), pp. 182–83.

76. Gates, *Landlords and Tenants*, p. 58.

77. Paul W. Gates, *Agriculture and the Civil War* (New York: Alfred A. Knopf, 1965), p. 283.

78. Gates, *Landlords and Tenants*, p. 146.

79. Barrington Moore, Jr., *Social Origins of Democracy and Dictatorship: Lord and Peasant in the Making of the Modern World* (Boston: Beacon, 1966), p. 130.

80. Shannon, "The Homestead Act and the Labor Surplus," pp. 645–46, 651; Fred A. Shannon, "The Status of the Midwestern Farmer in 1900," *Mississippi Valley Historical Review,* vol. 38 (1950–1951), p. 496.

81. Shannon, "The Homestead Act and the Labor Surplus," p. 641.

82. William F. Deverell, "To Loosen the Safety-Valve," *Western Historical Quarterly,* vol. 19, no. 3 (August 1986), pp. 274–80; Morton Keller, *Affairs of State: Public Life in Nineteenth Century America* (Cambridge: Harvard University Press, 1977), pp. 186, 189, 165.

83. David M. Ellis, "Homestead Clause in Railroad Land Grants," in David M. Ellis, editor, *American Development: Essays in Honor of Paul Wallace Gates* (Ithaca: Cornell University Press: 1969), pp. 48–53.

84. White, *"It's Your Misfortune and None of My Own,"* p. 247.

85. Wallace D. Farnham, "The Pacific Railroad Act of 1862," *Nebraska History,* vol. 43, no. 3 (September 1962), p. 160.

86. White, *"It's Your Misfortune and None of My Own,"* pp. 145–46.

87. Gates, "The Homestead Act in an Incongruous Land System," p. 663.

88. Robert A. Caro, *The Years of Lyndon Johnson: The Path to Power* (New York: Alfred A. Knopf, 1982), p. 308. The city, of course, bred its own loneliness. "You may be separated from your next neighbor by only a few inches," the clergyman Josiah Strong noted, "and yet never see his face or learn his name. Mere proximity does not imply social touch. . . . [T]he first thing that is impressed on them [new arrivals from the country] is their . . . utter loneliness, which often seems unendurable." Degler, *Out of Our Past,* p. 347.

89. Richard White, "Frederick Jackson Turner," in John R. Wunder, editor, *Historians of the American Frontier: A Bio-Bibliographical Sourcebook* (Westport: Greenwood, 1988), pp. 677–78.

90. Shannon, "The Homestead Act and the Labor Surplus," p. 638.

91. Ibid., pp. 646–47.

92. Paul W. Gates, *Jeffersonian Dream: Studies in the History of American Land Policy and Development* (Albuquerque: University of New Mexico Press, 1996), p. 108.

93. Leslie E. Decker, " 'The Great Speculation': An Interpretation of Mid-Continent Pioneering," in David M. Ellis, editor, *The Frontier in American Development* (Ithaca: Cornell University Press, 1969), p. 386.

94. Dick, *The Sod-House Frontier,* p. 128.

95. Ibid., pp. 35–37, 128.

96. Decker, " 'The Great Speculation,' " p. 377.

97. White, *"It's Your Misfortune and None of My Own,"* pp. 137–38.

98. Ian Frazier, *Great Plains* (New York: Penguin, 1989), p. 72.

99. White, *"It's Your Misfortune and None of My Own,"* p. 145.

100. C. F. Emerick, "An Analysis of Agricultural Discontent, ii, The Significance of the Increase in Farm Mortgages and Farm Tenants," *Political Science Quarterly,* vol. 2, no. 4 (December 1896), p. 607.

101. White, *"It's Your Misfortune and None of My Own,"* pp. 152–53.

102. Paul Wallace Gates, "Federal Land Policy in the South, 1866–1888," *Journal of Southern History,* vol. 6, no. 3 (August 1940), p. 328.

103. Ibid., pp. 318, 305, 328, 325.

104. Paul W. Gates, "Homestead Centennial Symposium," *Agricultural History,* vol. 36, no. 4 (October 1962), pp. 222–24.

105. Clawson, *The Land System of the United States,* p. 95.

106. Gates, "The Homestead Act in an Incongruous Land System," pp. 677–78, 665.

107. Shannon, *The Farmer's Last Frontier,* p. 62.

108. Gifford Pinchot, "How Conservation Began in the United States," *Agricultural History,* vol. ii, no. 4 (October 1937), pp. 260–61.

109. Shannon, *The Farmer's Last Frontier,* p. 63.

110. Pinchot, "How Conservation Began in the United States," p. 260.

111. Shannon, *The Farmer's Last Frontier,* pp. 69–70.

112. Gates, "The Homestead Act in an Incongruous Land System," p. 665.

113. See R. S. Henry, "The Railroad Land Grant Legend in American History Texts," *Mississippi Valley Historical Review,* vol. 32, no. 2 (September 1945), and the responses to it by David Maldwyn Ellis, Richard C. Overton, Robert E. Riegel, Herbert O. Brayer, Chester McArthur Destler, Stanley Pargellis, Fred A. Shannon, and Edward C. Kirkland, *Mississippi Valley Historical Review,* vol. 32, no. 4 (March 1946), pp. 557–76. See also David Maldwyn Ellis, "The Forfeiture of Railroad Land Grants, 1867–1894" *Mississippi Valley Historical Review,* vol. 33, no. 1 (June 1946), pp. 27–60. For Cleveland, see Thomas A. Bailey, David M. Kennedy, and Lizabeth Cohen, *The American Pageant,* vol. 2, *Since 1865* (Boston: Houghton Mifflin, 1998), p. 537. Henry's 1945 paper put the savings on rates to the federal government at $900 million and gave a low estimate to the size of the land grants; several of his critics, citing objective sources, correct him on both counts. While a reputable scholar, Henry was also an assistant to the president of the Association of American Railroads, which was lobbying Congress to end the discount for government shipments.

114. Henry, "The Railroad Land Grant Legend," p. 185. For "inescapable fact," see Ellis, "The Forfeiture of Railroad Land Grants," p. 558.

115. Dick, *The Sod-House Frontier,* pp. 36–363.

116. Gates, "The Homestead Act in an Incongruous Land System," p. 677ff; *Report of the Commissioner of the General Land Office,* Forty-ninth Congress, First Session, House Executive Document, no. 1, vol. 2, pt. 5., Serial 2378 (Washington, D.C., 1886), p. 155.

117. *Report of the Commissioner of the General Land Office,* p. 179.

118. Ellis, "Homestead Clause in Railroad Land Grants," pp. 32–33.

119. *Report of the Commissioner of the General Land Office,* p. 205.

120. Ibid., p. 204.

121. Ibid., p. 179.

122. Ibid., pp. 210–12.

123. Gates, "The Homestead Act in an Incongruous Land System," pp. 680–81.

124. John D. Hicks, *The Populist Revolt: A History of the Farmers' Alliance and the People's Party* (Lincoln: University of Nebraska Press, 1961), pp. 11–15.

125. Dick, *The Sod-House Frontier*, pp. 48–49. For Dakota boosters, see Robert C. McMath, Jr., *American Populism, A Social History 1877–1898* (New York: Hill & Wang, 1993), p. 23.

126. Von Naroff, "The American Frontier as Safety Valve," pp. 133–35.

127. Ibid., pp. 104, 184; Billington, *Frederick Jackson Turner*, pp. 459–60; Richard B. Morris, *Encyclopedia of American History* (New York: Harper & Brothers, 1953), p. 434.

128. Pinchot, "How Conservation Began to the United States," p. 264.

129. White, *"It's Your Misfortune and None of My Own,"* p. 59. My claim that "in some basic way," the federal government created the West follows Naomi R. Lamoreaux, "Did Insecure Property Rights Slow Economic Development? Some Lessons from Economic History," *Journal of Policy History*, vol. 18, no. 1 (2006), p. 159.

130. Dick, *The Sod-House Frontier*, p. 205.

131. Ibid., pp. 205–10.

132. Ibid., p. 216.

133. Theodore Roosevelt, *An Autobiography* (New York: Library of America, 2004), p. 364.

134. Dick, *The Sod-House Frontier*, p. 126.

135. Frazier, *Great Plains*, pp. 63–64.

136. Dick, *The Sod-House Frontier*, p. 212.

137. White, *"It's Your Misfortune and None of My Own,"* pp. 113–15.

138. Dick, *The Sod-House Frontier*, pp. 164–84.

139. Degler, *Out of Our Past*, p. 354.

140. Ibid., p. 349.

141. Jeremy Atack and Peter Passell, *A New Economic View of American History* (New York: W. W. Norton, 1994), p. 402.

142. Degler, *Out of Our Past*, p. 354.

143. Ibid., pp. 350–51.

144. Shannon, *The Farmer's Last Frontier*, p. 145. Also see Sidney Ratner, James H. Soltow, and Richard Sylla, *The Evolution of the American Economy: Growth, Welfare, and Decision Making* (New York: Basic Books, 1979), pp. 266–67 and David R. Mayhew, *Electoral Realignments: A Critique of an American Genre* (New Haven: Yale University Press, 2002), p. 132. I borrow Mayhew's hypothesis that, where it existed, farm prosperity served as a "firewall" against Populism.

145. Atack and Passell, *A New Economic View*, p. 415.

146. Degler, *Out of Our Past*, p. 352.

147. C. F. Emerick, "An Analysis of Agricultural Discontent in the United States, Part 1," *Political Science Quarterly*, vol. 2, no. 3 (September 1896), p. 435.

148. Degler, *Out of Our Past*, p. 352.

149. Emerick, "An Analysis of Agricultural Discontent in the United States, Part 1." p. 433.

150. Ibid., p. 456.

151. Degler, *Out of Our Past*, p. 352.

152. Gates, "Agriculture and the Civil War," p. 436.

153. Theodore Saloutos, "The Agricultural Problem and 19th Century Industrialism," *Agricultural History*, vol. 22, no. 1 (January 1948), p. 162.

154. Lee Bensen, "The Social Background of Turner's Frontier Essay," *Agricultural History*, vol. 25, no. 2 (April 1951), pp. 63–64.

155. Gates, "Agriculture and the Civil War," p. 454.

156. C. F. Emerick, "An Analysis of Agricultural Discontent in the United States, Part 3:

Four Remedies for the Agricultural Depression Considered," *Political Science Quarterly,* vol. 2, no. 1 (March 1897), p. 100.

157. Shannon, *The Farmer's Last Frontier,* p. 291.

158. C. F. Emerick, "An Analysis of Agricultural Discontent in the United States, Part 2: The Significance of the Increase of Farm Mortgages and Farm Tenants," *Political Science Quarterly,* vol. 2, no. 4 (December 1896), p. 601.

159. Fred A. Shannon, "A Post-Mortem on the Labor Safety Valve Theory," *Agricultural History,* vol. 19, no. 1 (January 1945), p. 37.

160. Gavin Wright, "American Agriculture and the Labor Market: What Happened to Proletarianization?," *Agricultural History,* vol. 62, no. 1 (Summer 1988), p. 184.

161. La Wanda Cox, "The American Agricultural Wage Earner, 1865–1900," *Agricultural History,* vol. 23, no. 2 (April 1948), p. 97.

162. Wright, "American Agriculture and the Labor Market," pp. 196–98; Cox, "The American Agricultural Wage Earner," p. 114.

163. Ibid., p. 97.

164. Hiram M. Drache, *The Days of the Bonanza: A History of Bonanza Farming in the Red River Valley of the North* (Fargo: North Dakota Institute for Regional Study, 1964), pp. 38, 52, 111.

165. Cox, "The American Agricultural Wage Earner," p. 114: "Farm labor was approaching the essential nature of industrial labor."

166. Ibid., p. 107.

167. Ibid., p. 110.

168. Fred A. Shannon, "The Status of the Midwestern Farmer in 1900," pp. 496–500.

169. Wright, "American Agriculture and the Labor Market," p. 183.

170. Shannon, *The Farmer's Last Frontier,* p. 298.

171. Robert A. McGuire, "Economic Causes of Nineteenth Century Unrest: New Evidence," *Journal of Economic History,* vol. 41, no. 4 (December 1981), p. 849; Robert Higgs, "Railroad Rates and the Populist Uprising," *Agricultural History,* vol. 62, no. 3 (July 1978), pp. 291–97.

172. C. F. Emerick, "An Analysis of Agricultural Discontent in the United States, Part 3," *Political Science Quarterly,* vol. 12, no. 1 (March 1897), p. 121. For Country Life Commission, see Degler, *Out of Our Past,* pp. 355–56.

173. New words entered the American vocabulary in the Gilded Age: "hayseed" and "old-time." To be "country was to be outside the currents of modern history, to be backward, ludicrous." Edward L. Ayres, *The Promise of the New South: Life After Reconstruction* (New York: Oxford University Press, 1992), p. 213.

Chapter Five: The Inverted Constitution

1. Eric Foner, *Reconstruction: America's Unfinished Revolution, 1863–1877* (New York: Harper & Row, 1988), p. 587; Michael J. Horan, "Political Economy and Sociological Theory as Influences Upon Judicial Policy-Making," *American Journal of Legal History,* vol. 56, no. 1 (January 1972), pp. 71–87. Horan characterizes the Court's ruling in the "Civil Rights Cases" as the judicial complement to the Compromise of 1877, and praises the decision as an antidote to "the strong centralizing tendencies" of early postwar "governance." The country, Kentucky's John Marshall Harlan wrote in his dissent, was entering "an era of constitutional law, when the rights of freedom and American citizenship cannot receive . . . that efficient protection which heretofore was unhesitatingly accorded to slavery."

2. Paul Kens, *Stephen J. Field: Shaping Liberty from the Gold Rush to the Gilded Age* (Lawrence: University of Kansas Press, 1997), p. 241.

3. Robert Kaczoworski, "The Inverted Constitution," in Sandra VanBurkleo, Kermit L. Hall, and Robert J. Kaczorowski, editors, *Constitutionalism and American Culture: Writing the New Constitutional History* (Lawrence: University of Kansas Press, 2002), p. 29ff.

4. Avian Soifer, "The Paradox of Paternalism and Laissez-Faire Constitutionalism: The United States Supreme Court, 1888–1921," in Warren J. Samuels and Arthur S. Miller, editors, *Corporations and Society: Power and Responsibility* (Westport: Greenwood, 1987), p. 162.

5. Morton J. Horwitz, *The Transformation of American Law: The Crisis of Legal Orthodoxy, 1870–1960* (New York: Oxford University Press, 1992), pp. 66–67.

6. 118 US Reports 395–422.

7. "We can endure it," Hegel says of the demoralizing spectacle of unreason in history—the "violence, evil, and vice . . . associated *especially* with good designs and righteous aims"—"and strengthen ourselves against it only by thinking that this is the way it had to be—it is fate; nothing can be done." G.W.F. Hegel, *Philosophy of History* (New York: P. F. Collier & Son, 1920), pp. 65–66.

8. Charles Warren, *The Supreme Court in United States History*, vol. 2 (Boston: Little, Brown, 1926), p. 319; James M. McPherson, *Battle Cry of Freedom* (New York: Oxford University Press, 1988), p. 725.

9. McPherson, *Battle Cry of Freedom*, p. 179.

10. Ibid., pp. 170–81.

11. Charles Fairman, *Reconstruction and Reunion, 1864–1888: Part One* (New York: Macmillan, 1971), p. 26.

12. Carl B. Swisher, *The Taney Period, 1836–1864* (New York: Macmillan, 1974), pp. 741, 648, 970.

13. Howard Jay Graham, *Everyman's Constitution: Historical Essays on the Fourteenth Amendment, the "Conspiracy Theory," and American Constitutionalism* (Madison: University of Wisconsin Press, 1968), p. 20.

14. Charles Fairman, *Reconstruction and Reunion, 1864–1888, Part Two* (New York: Macmillan, 1987), p. 1396. For Wagner Act, see David M. Kennedy, *Freedom from Fear: The American People in Depression and War, 1929–1945* (New York: Oxford University Press, 1999), pp. 335–37.

15. Richard Rubin, "The Colfax Riot," *Atlantic Monthly*, July–August 2003.

16. Ted Tunnell, editor, *Carpetbagger from Vermont: The Autobiography of Marshal Harvey Twitchell* (Baton Rouge: Louisiana State University Press, 1989), p. 133. A marker erected on the front lawn of the Colfax courthouse at the close of the Jim Crow era drapes political magnolia over the carnage's racial motives: "On this site occurred the Colfax Riot in which three white men and 150 negroes were slain. This event on April 13, 1873 marked the end of carpetbag misrule in the South."

17. William Gillette, *Retreat from Reconstruction, 1869–1879* (Baton Rouge: Louisiana State University Press, 1979), p. 111. Nicholas Lemann, *Redemption: The Last Battle of the Civil War* (New York: Farrar, Straus, and Giroux, 2006), p. 13. Lemann's twenty-nine page prologue is the most fully researched and powerful account of the Colfax Massacre extant.

18. Ibid., pp. 112–15.

19. *Report of Committee of the House, 1874–1875*, Forty-third Congress, Second Session, pp. 409–22. Details of the massacre are from this testimony unless otherwise indi-

cated; also see Joe Gray Taylor, *Louisiana Reconstructed, 1863–1877* (Baton Rouge: Louisiana State University Press, 1974), pp. 267–70; Gillette, *Retreat from Reconstruction*, pp. 115–16.

20. Foner, *Reconstruction*, p. 530. "Between 1868 and 1876 lethal riots of considerable consequence took place in Opelousas, Louisiana, Clinton, Vicksburg, and Yazoo City, Mississippi, Laurens, South Carolina, Pine Bluff, Arkansas and Hamburg, South Carolina." Richard Hofstadter, "Reflections on Violence in the United States," in Richard Hofstadter and Michael Wallace, editors, *American Violence: A Documentary History* (New York: Alfred A. Knopf, 1970), p. 16.

21. *Report of the Committee of the House 1874–1875*, p. 413.

22. For cholera, see Howard Markel, *How Germs Travel: Six Major Epidemics That Have Invaded America Since 1900 and the Fears They Have Unleashed* (New York: Pantheon, 2004), pp. 196–99. Herbert Hovenkamp, *Enterprise and American Law, 1836–1937* (Cambridge: Harvard University Press, 1991), p. 119; Michael A. Ross, "Justice Miller's Reconstruction: The Slaughter-House Cases, Health Codes, and Civil Rights in New Orleans, 1861–1873," *Journal of Southern History*, vol. 44, no. 4 (November 1998), pp. 655–59; also see Michael A. Ross, "Obstructing Reconstruction: John Archibald Campbell and the Legal Campaign Against Louisiana's Republican Government," *Civil War History*, September 2003; Mitchell Franklin, "The Foundations and Meaning of the Slaughter-House Cases," *Tulane Law Review*, vol. 10, no. 18 (October 1943), pp. 1–10. For details on the epidemics, see Ronald M. Labbe and Jonathan Lurie, *The Slaughterhouse Cases: Regulation, Reconstruction, and the Fourteenth Amendment* (Lawrence: University of Kansas Press, 2003), pp. 17–37.

23. Ross, "Justice Miller's Reconstruction," p. 662.

24. Fairman, *Reconstruction and Reunion, Part Two*, p. 1322.

25. Foner, *Reconstruction*, p. xx.

26. Hovenkamp, *Enterprise and American Law*, p. 117. For a more critical perspective on lobbying, see Labbe and Lurie, *The Slaughterhouse Cases*, pp. 71–102.

27. Ross, "Justice Miller's Reconstruction," p. 655.

28. Ibid., p. 659.

29. Ibid., p. 663.

30. Fairman, *Reconstruction and Reunion, Part Two*, p. 1325.

31. Swisher, *The Taney Period*, p. 244. For black officeholders, see Kenneth M. Stampp, *The Era of Reconstruction, 1865–1877* (New York: Alfred A. Knopf, 1966), p. 107. "Of Judge Campbell of Alabama, there is nothing to be said, except that on the subject in question he is more fanatical than the fanatics, more Southern than the extreme South from which he comes. A judicial . . . decision from him, where slavery is concerned, is of no more value than the cawing of a raven. He is a middle-aged, middle-size man, bald, and possessed of middling talents." *New York Tribune*, 5/17/1857.

32. Ludwell H. Johnson, "Fort Sumter and Confederate Diplomacy," *Journal of Southern History*, vol. 26 (1960), p. 446.

33. McPherson, *Battle Cry of Freedom*, p. 269.

34. Robert Saunders, Jr., *John Archibald Campbell: Southern Moderate, 1811–1889* (Tuscaloosa: University of Alabama Press, 1997), p. 147, McPherson, *Battle Cry of Freedom*, pp. 266–68.

35. Glyndon G. Van Deusen, *William Henry Seward* (New York: Oxford University Press, 1967), pp. 276–77; Taylor, *Louisiana Reconstructed*, p. 154. Traveling through the South that spring, William H. Russell, of the London *Times*, found "not the least indication of Union sentiment or of the attachment for the Union which Mr.

Seward always assumes to exist in the South. . . . On the contrary, I met everywhere with but one feeling. . . . To a man the people went with their States and had
but one battle cry, 'state-rights, and death to those who make war against them!' "
James Ford Rhodes, *History of the United States from the Compromise of 1850*, vol. 3,
1860–1862 (New York: Harper & Brothers, 1895), p. 407, footnote. For Haig, see Lou
Cannon, *President Reagan: The Role of a Lifetime* (New York: Simon & Schuster,
1991), p. 199.

36. Saunders, *John Archibald Campbell*, p. 147.
37. Johnson, "Fort Sumter and Confederate Diplomacy," p. 449ff.
38. John M. Taylor, *William Henry Seward: Lincoln's Right Hand* (New York: Harper-
     Collins, 1991), p. 148.
39. Saunders, *John Archibald Campbell*, p. 149; Allan Nevins, *The War for the Union*, vol. 1,
     The Improvised War, 1861–1862 (New York: Scribners, 1959), p. 50.
40. Saunders, *John Archibald Campbell*, pp. 140–41. For letter to Lamar, see James Mur-
     phy, "Notes and Documents: Justice John Archibald Campbell on Secession,"
     Alabama Review, January 1975, pp. 56, 53.
41. Saunders, *John Archibald Campbell*, pp. 146, 148.
42. Ibid., p. 146. For dissembling, see Johnson, "Fort Sumter and Confederate Diplo-
     macy," p. 466.
43. Johnson, "Fort Sumter and Confederate Diplomacy," p. 465–66.
44. Ibid.; David Herbert Donald, *Lincoln* (New York: Simon & Schuster, 1995), p. 293.
45. Saunders, *John Archibald Campbell*, p. 152.
46. Ibid.
47. McPherson, *Battle Cry of Freedom*, pp. 269–70.
48. William Gillette, "John A. Campbell," in Leon Friedman and Fred L. Israel, editors,
     *The Justices of the United States Supreme Court, 1789–1969: Their Lives and Major Opin-
     ions* (New York: Chelsea House, 1969), p. 936. For Stanton, see Charles Warren, *The
     Supreme Court in United States History*, vol. 2 (Boston: Little Brown, 1926), p. 375, n. 1.
49. Van Deusen, *William Henry Seward*, p. 281; Taylor, *William Henry Seward*, pp. 150–51;
     McPherson, *Battle Cry of Freedom*, p. 270.
50. Taylor, *William Henry Seward*, p. 236.
51. McPherson, *Battle Cry of Freedom*, p. 846.
52. Ibid., p. 847. For a piquant account of Lincoln's visit—and the controversy sur-
     rounding its commemoration in 2003—see Andrew Ferguson, "When Lincoln
     Returned to Richmond," *Weekly Standard*, December 29, 2003, pp. 21–39.
53. McPherson, *Battle Cry of Freedom*, p. 823.
54. Saunders, *John Archibald Campbell*, p. 184.
55. Ibid., p. 182.
56. Ibid., p. 185.
57. J. T. Dorris, "Pardoning Leaders of the Confederacy," *Mississippi Valley Historical
     Review*, vol. 15, no. 1 (June 1928), pp. 10–14.
58. Saunders, *John Archibald Campbell*, pp. 185–89.
59. Ibid., p. 190.
60. Eric Foner, *Nothing but Freedom: Emancipation and Its Legacy* (Baton Rouge:
     Louisiana State University Press, 1983), p. 6. Foner, *Reconstruction*, pp. 9, 255.
61. David W. Blight, *Race and Reunion: The Civil War in American Memory* (Cambridge:
     Harvard University Press, 2001), p. 407.
62. Michael A. Ross, "Obstructing Reconstruction," p. 4.
63. Blight, *Race and Reunion*, p. 110.
64. Ibid., pp. 114, 118.

65. Michael A. Ross, *Justice of Shattered Dreams: Samuel F. Miller and the Supreme Court During the Civil War Era* (Baton Rouge: Louisiana State University Press, 2003), p. 263; Saunders, *John Archibald Campbell*, p. 195; Tunnell, *Carpetbagger from Vermont*, pp. 103–06. For Miller's appointment, see Charles Noble Gregory, "Samuel F. Miller Associate Justice of the Supreme Court," *Yale Law Journal*, vol. 17, no. 1 (April 1908), pp. 424–42.

66. Ross, "Justice Miller's Reconstruction," p. 655.

67. Foner, *Reconstruction*, p. 590.

68. Ross, "Obstructing Reconstruction," pp. 1–17.

69. Ross, "Justice Miller's Reconstruction," p. 664.

70. Saunders, *John Archibald Campbell*, 1875 photograph of Campbell, p. 175; his eyes, p. 41; Fairman, *Reconstruction and Reunion, Part Two*, p. 1356.

71. Saunders, *John Archibald Campbell*, p. 215.

72. Charles Fried, *Saying What the Law Is: The Constitution in the Supreme Court* (Cambridge: Harvard University Press, 2004), p. 196.

73. Don Fehrenbacher, *Slavery, Law, and Politics: The Dred Scott Case, Its Significance in American Politics* (New York: Oxford University Press, 1981), p. 2.

74. Ibid., p. 206.

75. Donald Grier Stephenson, Jr., *The Waite Court: Justices, Rulings, and Leaders* (Santa Barbara: ABC-CLIO, 2003), p. 122. The novelty of substantive due process remains in dispute. In *The Transformation of American Law, 1870–1960*, Morton Horwitz calls it "a fabrication of progressive thought, designed to delegitimate the *Lochner* Court by arguing that it had taken a completely unprecedented turn in the late 19th century." The doctrine is "not very different from those that had developed under the contracts clause or state just compensation provisions." In the *Dartmouth College Case*, which conferred immortality on corporations, Daniel Webster traced due process—"the law of the land"—to Magna Carta, and defined it as follows: "That every citizen shall hold his life, liberty, and property . . . under the protection of the general rules that govern society. Everything which may pass under the form [of legislative] enactment is not to be considered the law of the land." Before the Civil War abolitionists mounted due process arguments against federal enforcement of the Fugitive Slave Law; and some state courts used it to strike down laws that placed "special burdens" on railroad companies. "Despite these preliminary manifestations of substantive due process," Arnold Paul writes, "the great weight of judicial precedent prior to the 1870's still favored a strictly procedural interpretation." See Horwitz, *The Transformation of American Law*, p. 158; Edward S. Corwin, "The Doctrine of Due Process of Law Before the Civil War," *Harvard Law Review*, vol. 60 (1910–1911); and Arnold Paul, *Conservative Crisis and the Rule of Law: Attitudes of Bar and Bench, 1887–1895* (Ithaca: Cornell University Press, 1960), p. 7.

76. Ross, "Justice Miller's Reconstruction," p. 667. For opera houses, see Mitchell Franklin, "The Foundation and Meaning of the Slaughter-House Cases, Part 2," *Tulane Law Review*, (December 1943), pp. 28–29.

77. Foner, *Reconstruction*, p. 240; Morton Keller, *Affairs of State: Public Life in Nineteenth Century America* (Cambridge: Harvard University Press, 1977), pp. 99, 144. Johnson played on sexual fears in his veto of the Civil Rights Act: "[I]f Congress can abrogate all State laws of discrimination between the two races in the matter of real estate, of suits, and of contracts generally Congress may . . . also repeal State laws as to the contract of marriage between the two races." Keller, *Affairs of State*, p. 65.

78. For the statements of Julian and Boutwell as well as a discussion of northern resistance to black equality, see C. Vann Woodward, "Seeds of Failure in Radical Race

Policy," *Proceedings of the American Philosophical Society*, vol. 110, no. 1 (February 18, 1960), pp. 1–9. Foner, *Reconstruction*, p. 251; Fairman, *Reconstruction and Reunion, Part Two*, p. 1298.

79. Fairman, *Reconstruction and Reunion, Part Two*, p. 1347.
80. Ross, *Justice of Shattered Dreams*, pp. 10, 11.
81. Ibid., p. 31.
82. William Gillette, "Samuel Miller," in Friedman and Israel, editors, *The Justices of the United States Supreme Court*, p. 1012.
83. Ross, "Justice Miller's Reconstruction," pp. 669–70.
84. Charles Fairman, *Mr. Justice Miller and the Supreme Court, 1862–1890* (Cambridge: Harvard University Press, 1939), pp. 192–93.
85. For *Commonwealth v. Alger*, see Labbe and Lurie, *The Slaughterhouse Cases*, pp. 42–43. Barry Crouch, "A Spirit of Lawlessness; White Violence; Texas Blacks, 1865–1868," *Journal of Social History*, vol. 18, no. 2 (Winter 1984), pp. 217–29. In a letter to Senator Zachariah Chandler, of Michigan, George Custer told of a "loyal white man" who, after he ran the Stars and Stripes over his home, was warned by a committee of neighbors, "We are willing to acknowledge ourselves whipped, but raising the stars and stripes is a little too d——d strong." He refused to take the flag down; and he was killed. George M. Blackburn, "Radical Republican Motivation: A Case History," *Journal of Negro History*, vol. 54, no. 2 (April 1969), p. 120; Ross, "Obstructing Reconstruction," p. 10.
86. Fairman, *Reconstruction and Reunion, Part Two*, p. 1026.
87. Gillette, *Samuel Miller*, p. 1027.
88. Fairman, *Reconstruction and Reunion, Part Two*, p. 1027.
89. Foner, *Reconstruction*, pp. 198–201.
90. Gillette, "Samuel Miller," p. 1031 (from Miller's opinion).
91. 303 US Reports 90 (1938).
92. Gillette, "Samuel Miller," p. 1029.
93. Foner, *Reconstruction*, p. 529.
94. Michael Les Benedict, "Preserving Federalism: Reconstruction and the Waite Court," 1979/University of Chicago/www.utdallas.edu/-jfg)021000/benedict.html; Fairman, *Mr. Justice Miller*, p. 60.
95. C. Peter McGrath, *Morrison R. Waite: The Triumph of Character* (New York: Macmillan, 1963), p. 117.
96. Graham, *Everyman's Constitution*, p. 132; Foner, *Reconstruction*, p. 529.
97. *Report of the Committee of the House, 1874–1875*, p. 413; Joel M. Sipress, "From the Barrel of a Gun: The Politics of Murder in Grant Parish," *Louisiana History*, vol. 42, no. 3 (Summer 2001), pp. 303–4.
98. Tunnell, *Carpetbagger from Vermont*, pp. 133–34.
99. Foner, *Reconstruction*, p. 528; McGrath, *Morrison R. Waite*, p. 130; Robert J. Kaczorowski, *The Politics of Judicial Interpretation: The Federal Courts, Department of Justice and Civil Rights, 1866–1876* (Dobbs Ferry, N.Y.: Oceana, 1985), p. 176. Williams rose above economy in his own perquisites. He had the Department of Justice buy "an elegant landaulet"—a convertible carriage—manned by liveries to lend pomp to his comings and goings and he dipped into department funds for personal expenses. After a congressional investigation ventilated his largesse, the press stamped him "Landaulet Williams" and Grant withdrew his name for nomination as the new chief justice to replace Salmon P. Chase, who died in May 1873. McGrath, *Morrison R. Waite*, pp. 10–11.

100. Saunders, *John Archibald Campbell,* p. 221.

101. Taylor, *Louisiana Reconstructed,* p. 271. For "White version" of Nash's escape, see Lemann, *Redemption,* p. 24.

102. Kaczorowski, *The Politics of Judicial Interpretation,* pp. 178–80.

103. McGrath, *Morrison R. Waite,* p. 167.

104. Kaczorowski, *The Politics of Judicial Interpretation,* p. 177.

105. Ibid., p. 179. For Marr, see J. Morgan Kousser, *Colorblind Justice: Minority Voting Rights and the Undoing of the Second Reconstruction* (Chapel Hill: University of North Carolina Press, 1999), p. 50.

106. McGrath, *Morrison R. Waite,* p. 121.

107. Graham, *Everyman's Constitution,* p. 183.

108. Kaczorowski, *The Politics of Judicial Interpretation,* p. 183; Grant Gilmore, *The Ages of American Law* (New Haven: Yale University Press, 1977), p. 60. For Beckwith's views on Bradley, see Everette Swinney, "Enforcing the Fifteenth Amendment," *Journal of Southern History,* vol. 28, no. 3 (May 1962), p. 208.

109. For Colfax celebration, see Lemann, *Redemption,* p. 25; Tunnell, *Carpetbagger from Vermont,* p. 144.

110. Kaczorowski, *The Politics of Judicial Interpretation,* pp. 188–91.

111. For Klan anthem, see David M. Oshinsky, "Worse Than Slavery: Parchman Farm and the Ordeal of Jim Crow Justice," http://www.history isaweapon.org/defcon1/oshinsky.html, pp. 15–16; Tunnell, *Carpetbagger from Vermont,* p. 155.

112. McGrath, *Morrison R. Waite,* p. 125.

113. Ibid.

114. Ross, "Justice of Shattered Dreams," p. 200. For Miller, see Labbie and Lurie, *The Slaughterhouse Cases,* p. 14.

115. McGrath, *Morrison R. Waite,* pp. 75–77.

116. Ibid., p. 16.

117. Ibid., p. 107.

118. Ibid., p. 2. Contrast theses dismissive judgments a priori with the *Chicago Tribune*'s obituary of Waite after his eighteen years as chief justice (1874–88) had revealed his qualities: "In freedom from prejudice, justness of decision, as well as in the personal dignity with which he presided, and in his courtesy to practitioners, he was the peer of his six predecessors in his exalted office if not the equal of some of them in ability. Those who doubted his ability have since promptly conceded it." McGrath, *Morrison R. Waite,* pp. 318–19.

119. Fairman, *Mr. Justice Miller,* p. 273.

120. Fairman, *Reconstruction and Reunion,* p. 221; Kaczorowski, *Politics of Judicial Interpretation,* p. 208; McGrath, *Morrison R. Waite,* p. 129.

121. James T. Patterson, *Grand Expectations: The United States, 1945–1974* (New York: Oxford University Press, 1996), p. 389. For Waite, see Swinney, "Enforcing the Fifteenth Amendment," pp. 203–18, especially p. 208.

122. McGrath, *Morrison R. Waite,* pp. 130, 131, 129.

123. Keller, *Affairs of State,* pp. 30, 44, 161.

124. Foner, *Reconstruction,* pp. 554, 467; J. G. Randall, *The Civil War and Reconstruction* (Boston: D. C. Heath, 1937), pp. 821, 848, 849, 850; Charles F. Adams and Henry Adams, *Chapters of Erie and Other Essays* (Ithaca, N.Y.: Great Seal Books, 1956), p. 134; Randall, *The Civil War and Reconstruction,* pp. 848, 849, 850; Stampp, *The Era of Reconstruction,* p. 184.

125. William B. Hesseltine, "Economic Factors in the Abandonment of Reconstruc-

tion," *Mississippi Valley Historical Review*, vol. 22 (1936), pp. 203–6; Foner, *Reconstruction*, pp. 518–20; Richard Hofstadter, *The American Political Tradition* (New York: Vintage, 1948), p. 170.

126. Howard K. Beale, "The Tariff and Reconstruction," *American Historical Review*, vol. 35, no. 2 (January 1935), pp. 276–94. For clashing views of Radical motives, see La Wanda Cox and John Cox, "Negro Suffrage and Republican Politics: The Problem of Motivation in Reconstruction Historiography," *Journal of Southern History*, vol. 33, no. 3, (August 1967), pp. 303–30; C. Vann Woodward, *The Burden of Southern History* (New York: Mentor, 1968), p. 75.

127. For "more influential," see Vincent P. DeSantis's review of Stanley P. Hirshon, *Farewell to the Bloody Shirt: Northern Republicans and the Southern Negro, 1877–1893*, in *American Historical Review*, vol. 68, no. 2 (January 1963), pp. 486–87; Peter Kolchin, "The Business Press and Reconstruction, 1865–1868," *Journal of Southern History*, vol. 33, no. 2 (May 1967), pp. 183–96; Glenn M. Linden, " 'Radicals' and Economic Policies: The Senate, 1861–1873," *Journal of Southern History*, vol. 32 (1966), pp. 189–99.

128. Foner, *Reconstruction*, p. 602; Blight, *Race and Reunion*, p. 237.

129. Blight, *Race and Reunion*, pp. 228, 252, 355.

130. Foner, *Reconstruction*, p. 523.

131. W. J. Cash, *The Mind of the South* (New York: Vintage 1991), p. 113.

132. Tunnell, *Carpetbagger from Vermont*, p. 159.

133. McGrath, *Morrison R. Waite*, pp. 132–33.

Chapter Six: The Scandal of Santa Clara

1. Arnold M. Paul, *Conservative Crisis and the Rule of Law: Attitudes of Bar and Bench, 1887–1895* (Ithaca: Cornell University Press, 1960), pp. 55–56. F. W. Maitland, "Moral Personality and Legal Personality," *Collected Papers*, H.A.L. Fisher, editor (Cambridge: Cambridge University Press, 1911), p. 307.

2. Robert G. McCloskey, *American Conservatism in the Age of Enterprise: A Study of William Graham Sumner, Stephen J. Field, and Andrew Carnegie* (Cambridge: Harvard University Press, 1951), p. 87.

3. Carl Brent Swisher, *Stephen J. Field: Craftsman of the Law* (Washington, D.C.: Brookings Institution, 1930), p. 10.

4. Ibid., p. 11.

5. McCloskey, *American Conservatism*, p. 88.

6. Jackson Lears, *No Place of Grace: Antimodernism and the Transformation of American Culture, 1880–1920* (New York: Pantheon, 1981), p. 43; C. Peter McGrath, *Morrison R. Waite: The Triumph of Character* (New York: Macmillan, 1963), p. 257; Allen F. Westin, "Stephen J. Field and the Headnote to *O'Neil v. Vermont*," *Yale Law Journal*, vol. 67, no. 3 (January 1958), p. 363. Field schemed to have one of his colleagues on the Ninth Circuit removed. See Christian G. Fritz, *Federal Judge in California: The Court of Ogden Hoffman, 1851–1891* (Lincoln: University of Nebraska Press, 1991).

7. Swisher, *Stephen J. Field*, p. 12; Richard B. Morris, *Encyclopedia of American History* (New York: Harper & Bros., 1953), p. 658.

8. McCloskey, *American Conservatism*, p. 91.

9. Ibid., pp. 88, 106. "Education in this country was largely under clerical influence up to the end of the 19th century. . . . Generally the college president was also professor of philosophy. The dominant philosophy throughout the 19th century here was Scottish intuitionism, in which every human dogma was elevated to an eternal intuition of the human mind. It was in this climate of opinion that the var-

ious doctrines as to the nature of constitutional law spread and took root . . . not uninfluenced, of course, by the fact that [they] lifted issues out of . . . politics, where the votes of the majority could decide, into the forum of law where those who could hire the ablest lawyers had a distinct advantage." Morris R. Cohen, *The Faith of a Liberal: Selected Essays of Morris R. Cohen* (New York: Henry Holt, 1946), p. 191.

10. Swisher, *Stephen J. Field,* p. 23. For 4,000 died, see Andrew Delbanco, *Melville: His World and Work* (New York: Alfred A. Knopf, 2005), p. 107.

11. David Riesman, *The Lonely Crowd* (New Haven: Yale University Press, 1961), p. 120.

12. Peter J. Blodgett, *Land of Golden Dreams: California in the Gold Rush Decades, 1848–1858* (San Marino: Huntington Library, 1999), pp. 32–33; James M. McPherson, *Battle Cry of Freedom: The Civil War Era* (New York: Oxford University Press, 1988), p. 51; Hubert Howe Bancroft, *History of California,* vol. 5 (Santa Barbara: W. Hebberd, 1963), p. 344; Robert Wiebe, *The Search for Order, 1877–1920* (New York: Hill & Wang, 1967), p. 46; Kevin Starr, *America and the California Dream* (New York: Oxford University Press, 1973).

13. Swisher, *Stephen J. Field,* pp. 27–28; Paul Kens, *Stephen J. Field: Shaping Liberty from the Gold Rush to the Gilded Age* (Lawrence: University of Kansas Press, 1997), p. 22.

14. Kens, *Stephen J. Field,* p. 29.

15. Swisher, *Stephen J. Field,* pp. 35, 40.

16. For the Terry shooting, see Paul Kens, "The Incident at Lathrop Station," *Journal of Supreme Court History,* vol. 30, no. 2 (2005), pp. 85–105.

17. Andrew Delbanco and Alan Heimert, editors, *The Puritans in America: A Narrative Anthology* (Cambridge: Harvard University Press, 1985), p. 382.

18. Max Weber, *General Economic History* (New York: Collier Books, 1961), p. 270.

19. Delbanco and Heimert, *The Puritans in America,* p. 150.

20. Howard Jay Graham, *Everyman's Constitution: Historical Essays on the Fourteenth Amendment, the "Conspiracy Theory," and American Constitutionalism* (Madison: University of Wisconsin Press, 1968), p. 115. For two thorough—and damning—reviews of Field's distortions in *Pennoyer,* see Wendy C. Perdue, "Sin, Scandal, and Substantive Due Process," *Washington Law Review,* vol. 62 (1997), pp. 479–587, and Adrian M. Tocklin, *"Pennoyer v. Neff:* The Hidden Agenda of Stephen J. Field," *Seton Hall Law Review,* vol. 28, no. 1 (1997–1998), pp. 75–141. Pennoyer, "a cornerstone of American law," is as much a scandal as *Santa Clara.* "The reality of existing attachment law," Tocklin writes, "was erased from the legal culture by simply ignoring it, as any Stalinist effort to erase history in the U.S.S.R." (pp. 94, 136).

21. Swisher, *Stephen J. Field,* p. 110.

22. Graham, *Everyman's Constitution,* p. 115.

23. McCloskey, *American Conservatism,* p. 114; Swisher, *Stephen J. Field,* pp. 101–3.

24. Graham, *Everyman's Constitution,* p. 115.

25. Ibid., pp. 124–25.

26. Ibid., pp. 113, 129.

27. Edmund Wilson, *To the Finland Station: A Study in the Writing and Acting of History* (New York: Doubleday Anchor, 1953), p. 32; Duncan Townson, *Dictionary of Modern History, 1789–1945* (London: Penguin, 1994), pp. 284–85; Graham, *Everyman's Constitution,* p. 124, n. 58; Neill Irvin Painter, *Standing at Armeggedon: The United States 1877–1919* (New York: W. W. Norton, 1987), pp. 18–19.

28. Graham, *Everyman's Constitution,* pp. 124–25.

29. According to Frederick Busi, the most radical reform the Commune implemented was the "abolition of night bakeries." Frederick Busi, "The Failure of Revolution,"

Massachusetts Review, vol. 12, no. 3 (Summer 1971), pp. 400–403. Samuel Bernstein, *Essays in Political and Intellectual History* (New York: Paine Whitman, 1955), pp. 169–72. For Chicago Fire see, James Green, *Death in the Haymarket: A Story of Chicago, the First Labor Movement, and the Bombing That Divided Gilded Age America* (New York: Pantheon Books, 2006), p. 44.

30. For the treatment of the unemployed, see Herbert G. Gutman, "The Failure of the Movement by the Unemployed for Public Works in 1873," *Political Science Quarterly,* vol. 80, no. 2 (June 1965), pp. 254–70, and Samuel Rezneck, "Distress, Relief, and Discontent in the United States During the Depression of 1873–78," *Journal of Political Economy,* vol. 58, no. 6 (December 1950), pp. 494–512.

31. Graham, *Everyman's Constitution,* pp. 125–28.

32. Ibid., p. 127, n. 67.

33. Kens, *Stephen J. Field,* p. 245. For the Big Four, see Richard White, *"It's Your Misfortune and None of My Own": A History of the American West* (Norman: University of Oklahoma Press, 1991), p. 249. The other two were Charles Crocker and Mark Hopkins. Swisher, *Stephen J. Field,* p. 245.

34. Graham, *Everyman's Constitution,* pp. 121–22.

35. Swisher, *Stephen J. Field,* pp. 121–22.

36. Graham, *Everyman's Constitution,* p. 113.

37. McGrath, *Morrison R. Waite,* pp. 219, 175.

38. Ibid., p. 178; Swisher, *Stephen J. Field,* pp. 370–84.

39. Graham, *Everyman's Constitution,* p. 113; Swisher, *Stephen J. Field,* p. 123.

40. Graham, *Everyman's Constitution,* p. 100, n. 136.

41. Michael A. Ross, *Justice of Shattered Dreams: Samuel Freeman Miller and the Supreme Court During the Civil War Era* (Baton Rouge: Louisiana State University Press), p. 124. For the Field brothers' difference of opinion over the Wilmot Proviso, see Manuel Cachan, "Justice Stephen Field and Free Soil, Free Labor Constitutionalism: Reconsidering Revisionism," *Law and History Review,* vol. 20 (2002), p. 551. For "Satan," see Tocklin, *"Pennoyer v. Neff,"* p. 109.

42. Graham, *Everyman's Constitution,* p. 140. Kens, "The Incident at Lathrop Station," p. 102. For details on the convention, see R. Hal Williams, *The Democratic Party and California Politics, 1880–1896* (Stanford: Stanford University Press, 1973), pp. 48–51.

43. Graham, *Everyman's Constitution,* p. 144, n. 113. For Field's letter, see Williams, *The Democratic Party and California Politics,* p. 54.

44. For Brewer, see Paul, *Conservative Crisis,* pp. 70–71. Thomas T. Lewis and Richard L. Wilson, editors, *The Encyclopedia of The Supreme Court,* vol. 1 (Pasadena: Salem, 2001), p. 100. Brewer wrote the majority opinion in *In re Debs* (1895) upholding the use of a federal injunction to end the 1894 Pullman Strike, sanctioning strikebreaking by injunction. For a portrait of Brewer as a principled believer in the Court's "counter-majoritarian" role in our system, see Owen M. Fiss, "David J. Brewer: The Judge as Missionary," in Philip J. Bergan, Owen M. Fiss, and Charles W. McCurdy, editors, *The Fields and the Law: Essays* (San Francisco: Federal Bar Council, 1986). For Field's Pensacola inconsistency, see Cachan, "Justice Stephen Field and Free Soil, Free Labor Constitutionalism," pp. 541–71. For the Adam Smith note, see Field's dissent, US Reports Wallace 83, 110, n (1873), For "artisan republicanism," see Sean Wilentz, *Chants Democratic: New York City and the Rise of the American Working Class, 1788–1850* (New York: Oxford University Press, 1984), pp. 61–103, also p. 242.

45. Charles Fried, *Saying What the Law Is: The Constitution in the Supreme Court* (Cambridge: Harvard University Press, 2004), pp. 175–76.

46. For Fuller, see Barry Cushman, *Rethinking the New Deal Court: The Structure of a Constitutional Revolution* (New York: Oxford University Press, 1988), p. 140. For Tiedeman, see Paul, *Conservative Crisis*, pp. 17, 25. Roscoe Pound, "Liberty of Contract," *Yale Law Journal,* vol. 18, no. 7 (May 1909), pp. 454–87. The link between *In re Jacobs* and the AFL's rejection of political action is made by William E. Forbath, "The Shaping of the American Labor Movement," *Harvard Law Review,* vol. 102, no. 6 (April 1989), pp. 1134–41, 1145.

47. Pound, "Liberty of Contract." For "breaker boys," see Grant Gilmore, *The Ages of American Law* (New Haven: Yale University Press, 1977), p. 130, n. 33.

48. Robert G. McCloskey, *The American Supreme Court* (Chicago: University of Chicago Press, 1960), p. 101.

49. Jane Addams, "Trade Unions and Public Duty," *American Sociological Review,* vol. 13 (1899), p. 466. For Colorado miners, see Forbath, "The Shaping of the American Labor Movement," pp. 1138–41.

50. Michael J. Phillips, *The Lochner Court, Myth and Reality: Substantive Due Process from the 1890's to the 1930's* (Westport: Greenwood, 2001), p. 25, n. 20. For "a symbol," see Morton J. Horwitz, "Republicanism and Liberalism in American Constitutional Thought," *William and Mary Law Quarterly,* vol. 29 (1987), p. 59. For Peckham, see the entry under his name by Paul Kens in Kermit L. Hall, editor, *The Oxford Companion to the United States Supreme Court* (New York: Oxford University Press, 1992), pp. 626–27. For the Louisiana case, see the entry for *Allgeyer v. Louisiana* in the same volume by Michael Les Benedict, p. 28. For background, see Walton H. Hamilton, "The Path of Due Process of Law," *Ethics,* Vol. 48, no. 3 (April 1938), pp. 269–96.

51. Charles Fried, *Saying What the Law Is,* p. 173; Barbara H. Fried, *The Progressive Assault on Laissez Faire: Robert Hale and the First Law and Economics Movement* (Cambridge: Harvard University Press, 1998), pp. 32–33, 67; Benjamin Twiss, *Lawyers and the Constitution: How Laissez-Faire Came to the Supreme Court* (Princeton: Princeton University Press, 1942), pp. 141, 158. For Laughlin, see Sidney Fine, *Laissez Faire and the General-Welfare State: A Study of Conflict in American Thought, 1865–1901* (Ann Arbor: University of Michigan Press, 1956), p. 57, also pp. 48–51, 95; Pound, "Liberty of Contract," p. 467. As Barbara Fried points out, had Pound's fifty years of law students read Book V, "On the Influence of Government," they would have encountered the side of Mill that made *Principles of Political Economy* "a bible for later generations of progressives." While the economic laws governing production have the "character of physical laws," Mill wrote, not so the laws of distribution: "[T]he distribution of wealth . . . is a matter of human institution solely. The things once there, mankind, individually or collectively, can do with them as they like. They can place them at the disposal of whomsoever they please, and on whatever terms. . . . Even what a person has produced, by his individual toil, unaided by any one, he cannot keep, unless by permission of society." Also, "[T]here is scarcely anything, really important to the general interest, which it may not be desirable, or even necessary, that the government should take upon itself, not because private individuals cannot effectually perform it, but because they will not." Barbara Fried, *The Progressive Assault on Laissez Faire,* pp. 77–78; Fine, *Laissez Faire and the General-Welfare State,* p. 57, n. 31. For more on the complicated social outlook of John W. Burgess, see Daniel Rodgers, *Contested Truths: Keywords in American Politics Since Independence* (New York: Basic Books, 1987), pp. 157–70.

52. Graham, *Everyman's Constitution,* p. 92, n. 86, p. 378.

53. Ibid., p. 420.

54. Ibid., p. 24. For *In re Ah Fong*, see *3 Sawyer 144* (1874)

55. Graham, *Everyman's Constitution*, pp. 144–45; 337 US Reports 578, n; Thomas Wuil Joo, "New 'Conspiracy Theory' of the Fourteenth Amendment: Nineteenth-Century Chinese Civil Rights Cases and the Development of Substantive Due Process Jurisprudence," *University of San Francisco Law Review*, vol. 29 (1994–1995), pp. 373–75, also p. 374, n. 162.

56. Graham, *Everyman's Constitution*, p. 371.

57. La Wanda Cox, "The American Agricultural Wage Earner, 1865–1900," *Agricultural History*, vol. 23, no. 2 (April 1948), pp. 97–103; T. H. Watkins, *California: An Illustrated History* (Palo Alto: American West, 1973), pp. 182–83; Carl Brent Swisher, "Motivation and Political Technique" in *The California Constitutional Convention, 1878–79* (New York: Da Capo, 1969), p. 7. For quartz, see White, *"It's My Business and None of Your Own,"* p. 280; Watkins, *California: An Illustrated History*, pp. 204–8. For the Chinese laborers, see David Montgomery, *The Fall of the House of Labor: The Workplace, the State, and American Labor Activism, 1865–1925* (Cambridge: Cambridge University Press, 1987), p. 67.

58. For Henry Demarest Lloyd, see "California Cornered," *Chicago Tribune*, 10/8/1883. Swisher, "Motivation and Political Technique," p. 78. For Field's 1879 interview on Chinese exclusion, see Owen M. Fiss, "David J. Brewer," in Bergan, Fiss, McCurdy, editors, *The Fields and the Law*, p. 67, note 12.

59. For "Terry," see Kens, "The Incident at Lathrop Station," pp. 101–2.

60. Williams, *The Democratic Party and California Politics*, pp. 34–36. Eric Foner, *Reconstruction: America's Unfinished Revolution, 1863–1877* (New York: Harper & Row, 1988), p. 555.

61. Kens, "The Incident at Lathrop Station," pp. 237–39.

62. Graham, *Everyman's Constitution*, p. 404.

63. Ibid., p. 24.

64. Ibid., p. 404.

65. See the *Railroad Tax Cases: County of San Mateo v. Southern Pacific Railroad Co (1882) 8 Sawyer 238*, pp. 9, 10, 13, 15, 16, 19 (LexisNexis: 13 F. 722; 1882 U. S. App. LEXIS 2045); Ross, *Justice of Shattered Dreams*, p. 51. For the three theories of corporate personhood, see Morton J. Horwitz, *The Transformation of American Law, 1870–1960* (New York: Oxford University Press, 1992), pp. 69–107; and Phillip I. Brumberg, "The Corporate Personality in American Law: A Summary Review," *American Journal of Comparative Law*, vol. 38, supplement (1990), pp. 49–69. For "group person," see John Dewey, "The Historical Background of Corporate Legal Personality," *Yale Law Journal*, vol. 35 (1926), pp. 655–73. For the formulation "things specifically allowed by its charter," see Gregory A. Mark, "Personification of the Business Corporation in American Law," *University of Chicago Law Review*, vol. 54 (1987), pp. 1441–83, quotation is from p. 1455. Also see Larry E. Ribstein, "The Constitutional Conception of the Corporation," *Supreme Court Economic Review*, vol. 4 (1995), pp. 95–140.

66. McGrath, *Morrison R. Waite*, p. 219.

67. Graham, *Everyman's Constitution*, p. 397.

68. Ibid., pp. 16, 417, 597.

69. For "no contemporary evidence," see Kenneth Stampp, *The Era of Reconstruction, 1865–1877* (New York: Alfred A. Knopf, 1966), p. 136.

70. McGrath, *Morrison R. Waite*, p. 220. Conkling's presentation gave rise to a Progres-

sive bugbear—the "Conspiracy Theory of the 14th Amendment" given influential circulation by Charles and Mary Beard in *The Rise of American Civilization* (1927). The Beards took Conkling at his doubtful word, treating his quotations from the "Journal of the Joint Committee" as veracious—proof of a Republican–big business conspiracy; a "capitalist joke." "Republican law makers," they wrote, "restored to the Constitution the protection for property which the Jacksonians had whittled away [in the *Charles River Bridge* case] and made it more sweeping in its scope by forbidding states . . . 'to deprive any person of life, liberty, or property without due process of law.' By a few words *skillfully chosen* every act of every state and local government which touched adversely the right of persons and property was made subject to review and annulment by the Supreme Court at Washington." See Howard Jay Graham, "The 'Conspiracy Theory' of the Fourteenth Amendment," *Yale Law Journal*. vol. 47, no. 3 (January 1938). 373. In this and a subsequent paper Graham exposed Conkling's dissimulation and demolished the conspiracy theory. For Conkling's day in court, see Louis B. Boudin, "Truth and Fiction About the Fourteenth Amendment," *New York University Law Quarterly*, vol. 82 (1938–39), pp. 19–82, especially p. 31, n. 9. For Conkling's declination of Chester A. Arthur's nomination, see the entry under his name by Judith K. Schafer in Hall, editor, *The Oxford Companion to the Supreme Court of the United States*, p. 178.

71. McGrath, *Morrison R. Waite*, p. 260; also for dinner at Chamberlin's.
72. Graham, *Everyman's Constitution*, pp. 410–11, n. 155.
73. Swisher, "Motivation and Political Technique," p. 113. Graham, *Everyman's Constitution*, p. 428, offers a different account.
74. Swisher, "Motivation and Political Technique," p. 113.
75. Kens, *Stephen J. Field*, pp. 247, 245.
76. Graham, *Everyman's Constitution*, p. 567, n. 220.
77. Westin, "Stephen J. Field and the Headnote to *O'Neil v. Vermont*," p. 379.
78. McGrath, *Morrison R. Waite*, p. 253.
79. 118 US Reports (1886) 394–95.
80. Thom Hartmann, "The Deciding Moment," Chapter 6 of *Unequal Protection*, www.thomhartmann.com. Hartman's original analysis has informed my treatment of *Santa Clara* throughout.
81. McGrath, *Morrison R. Waite*, pp. 223–24.
82. 118 US Reports 412–17.
83. 118 US Reports 395.
84. 118 US Reports 410.
85. 118 US Reports 422–23.
86. 337 US Reports 542 (1949). Graham, *Everyman's Constitution*, p. 387, n. 68.
87. 99 US Reports 719.
88. McGrath, *Morrison R. Waite*, pp. 222–24.
89. Charles Warren, *The Supreme Court in United States History*, vol. II (Boston: Little, Brown, 1926), p. 596.
90. 118 US Reports 356.
91. Graham, *Everyman's Constitution*, p. 569.
92. Ibid., p. 424. Its framers wanted the amendment's protection to extend to white Republicans and other "loyal white men," so they used "persons" rather than "persons of the Negro race" in the wording. In his concurrence in *San Mateo*, Ninth Circuit Court judge Lorenzo Sawyer emphasized that, as history would show, elastic ambiguity: "I apprehend it would have struck the world with some amazement

when this amendment was proposed to the people of the United States for adoption, if it had read 'Nor shall any state deprive any person of the *negro* race of life, liberty, and property without due process of law.' " Seen in Andrew C. McLaughlin, "The Court, the Corporation, and Conkling," *American Historical Review,* vol. 46, no. 1 (October 1940), p. 47.

93. Graham, *Everyman's Constitution,* p. 385. This reading of *Barbier v. Connolly* follows Charles J. McClain, *In Search of Equality: The Chinese Struggle Against Discrimination in Nineteenth-Century America* (Berkeley: University of California Press, 1994), pp. 110–111. For text, see 113 US Reports 31.

94. McGrath, *Morrison R. Waite,* pp. 272–74. Felix Frankfurter, *The Commerce Clause Under Marshall, Taney, and Waite* (Chapel Hill: University of North Carolina Press, 1937), pp. 95, 110.

95. For Marx interview, *Chicago Tribune,* January 5, 1879, Marx-Engels Internet Archive. Willard L. King, *Melville Weston Fuller, Chief Justice of the United States* (New York: Macmillan, 1950), p. 110. For Marx's attitude toward the state, see Isaiah Berlin, *The Sense of Reality: Studies in Ideas and Their History* (New York: Viking, 1996), pp. 103–4, 142–45.

96. 118 US Reports 161–80; King, *Melville Weston Fuller,* p. 230.

97. Graham, *Everyman's Constitution,* p. 578.

98. Westin, "Stephen J. Field and the Headnote to *O'Neil v. Vermont,*" pp. 368, 369, 370, 379.

99. Waite's friend, Rutherford B. Hayes, recorded this tribute in his diary shortly after hearing of his death: "He was great-hearted, warm-hearted, and of generous, just and noble sentiments and feelings. . . . He was always cheerful, easily made happy by others, and with amazing powers and a never-failing disposition to make others happy. He was the best-beloved man that ever lived in this part of the U.S." McGrath, *Morrison R. Waite,* pp. 310–11. Felix Frankfurter's judgment on Waite offers a standard to judge Field: "Like Taney before him and [Oliver Wendell] Holmes in our own time, Waite illustrates that judicial self-limitation be the most significant aspect of judicial action in the American constitutional system." Frankfurter, *The Commerce Clause Under Marshall, Taney, and Waite,* p. 95.

100. 125 US Reports 181–89; headnotes, p. 181; Field's Fourteenth Amendment interpolation, p. 184; his dictum, p. 189.

101. Graham, *Everyman's Constitution,* p. 24.

102. 337 US Reports 562.

103. 303 US Reports 87–88; Graham, *Everyman's Constitution,* p. 386.

104. 13 Federal Cases 67, no. 7. For an excellent brief account of the "Constitutional Revolution of 1937," see David M. Kennedy, *Freedom from Fear: The American People in Depression and War, 1929–1945* (New York: Oxford University Press, 1999), pp. 334–37. For the debate over its "internal" and "external" sources, see the *American Historical Review* forum published in 2005: Laura Kalman, "The Constitution, the Supreme Court, and the New Deal," William E. Leuchtenburg's "Comment on Laura Kalman's Article," and G. Edward White's rejoinder to both, "Constitutional Change and the New Deal: The Internalist/Externalist Debate," *American Historical Review,* vol 110, no. 4 (June 2005). The Leuchtenburg quotations are from his "Comment" as well as one of the quotations from Justice Souter. Also see William E. Leuchtenburg, *The FDR Years: On Roosevelt and His Legacy* (New York: Columbia University Press, 1999), pp. 221–23. For Hughes, see Boudin, "Truth and Fiction," p. 81.

105. For Douglas, see William O. Douglas, "Stare Decisis," *Columbia Law Review,* vol. 49, no. 6 (June 1949), pp. 735–58.

106. For a survey of conservative jurisprudence, see "The Corporation and the Constitution: Economic Due Process and Corporate Speech," note, *Yale Law Journal,* vol. 90, no. 7 (June 1981), p. 1860; E. J. Dionne, *Stand Up and Fight* (New York: Simon & Schuster, 2004), pp. 186–89.

107. Ross, *Justice of Shattered Dreams,* p. 241.

108. Richard Franklin Bensel, *The Political Economy of American Industrialization, 1877–1900* (Cambridge, Eng.: Cambridge University Press, 2000), p. 347. Swisher, *Stephen J. Field,* pp. 288–97; Frankfurter, *The Commerce Clause Under Marshall, Taney, and Waite,* p. 110.

109. For details of the 1880 GOP convention, see Matthew Josephson, *The Politicos, 1865–1896* (New York: Harcourt, 1938), pp. 285–86.

110. Ross, *Justice of Shattered Dreams,* p. 237; Richard Hoftsadter, *The American Political Tradition* (New York: Viking, 1948), p. 170. Charles Fairman, *Mr. Justice Miller and the Supreme Court, 1862–1890* (Cambridge: Harvard University Press, 1939), p. 374. For railroad bonds, see Lawrence Goodwyn, *Democratic Promise: The Populist Moment in America* (New York: Oxford University Press, 1976), p. 117.

111. Ross, *Justice of Shattered Dreams,* p. 237.

112. McGrath, *Morrison R. Waite,* pp. 235–47. "Indiana had been put down on the books always as a state that might be carried by close and perfect organization and a great deal of ——— (laughter). I see the reporters are present; therefore I will simply say that everybody showed a great deal of interest in the occasion and distributed tracts and political documents all through the state." Garfield's vice president elect, Chester A. Arthur, speaking at a victory dinner held at Delmonico's restaurant in New York. McGrath, *Morrison R. Waite,* p. 243.

113. Ross, *Justice of Shattered Dreams,* p. 243.

114. Ibid., pp. 246–47.

115. Ibid., p. 224.

116. Ibid., pp. 225–26.

117. 137 US Reports 707.

118. Charles Fairman, *Mr. Justice Miller,* p. 439.

119. Ross, *Justice of Shattered Dreams,* p. 256.

120. Ibid.

121. *New York Times,* 10/14/1890.

122. 137 US Reports In Memoriam 704–7.

123. King, *Melville Weston Fuller,* p. 222; for Harlan, see Paul, *Conservative Crisis,* p. 205, n. 50. The new justices included Rufus W. Peckham, who wrote the *Lochner* opinion, who as a justice of the New York State Supreme Court wrote a Fieldian dissent to an 1889 ruling that sustained a law setting maximum prices for warehouses and grain elevators situated along the Erie Canal: "The legislation under consideration is not only vicious in its nature, communistic in its tendency, wholly inefficient to permanently attain the result aimed at, but . . . is an illegal effort to interfere with the lawful privilege of the individual to seek and obtain such compensation as he can for the use of his own property." As *Budd v. New York* the case reached the Supreme Court in 1892; constrained by the *Munn* standard—business "affected with a public interest"—the Court voted 6–3, with Field in the minority, to sustain the decision of the New York Supreme Court. Justice Brewer's dissent drew a comment from Seymour D. Thompson, the editor of the *American Legal Review,* that

crystallized the Progressive case against judge-made law: "His opinion is more rhetorical than judicial, and, like some of his associates, he is evidently laboring under the hallucination that he is a legislator instead of merely being a judge. He indulges in such sentences as this: 'The paternal theory of government is to me odious.' What if it is? He was not put there to decide constitutional questions according to his whims, or according to what was or was not odious to him personally."

124. Paul, *Conservative Crisis*, pp. 73–74, n. 31. Graham, *Everyman's Constitution*, p. 114.

125. Swisher, *Stephen J. Field*, p. 439.

126. McGrath, *Morrison R. Waite*, p. 257.

127. Swisher, *Stephen J. Field*, p. 312.

128. Ibid., pp. 316–19.

129. Graham, *Everyman's Constitution*, p. 140. For Field and Cleveland, see Williams, *The Democratic Party and California Politics*, pp. 72–81.

130. Swisher, *Stephen J. Field*, p. 430.

131. Ibid., p. 410.

132. King, *Melville Weston Fuller*, p. 224.

133. James G. Ely, Jr., *The Chief Justiceship of Melville W. Fuller, 1888–1910* (Columbia: University of South Carolina Press, 1995), p. 48.

134. King, *Melville Weston Fuller*, p. 217. For Field's "rude comments," see Linda Przybyszewski, *The Republic According to John Marshall Harlan* (Chapel Hill: University of North Carolina Press, 1999), p. 177.

135. Swisher, *Stephen J. Field*, p. 441.

136. Ely, *The Chief Justiceship of Melville W. Fuller*, p. 48.

137. Swisher, *Stephen J. Field*, pp. 443–44.

138. King, *Melville Weston Fuller*, pp. 244–45.

139. Loren P. Beth, *John Marshall Harlan* (Lexington: University of Kentucky Press, 1992), p. 163. Justice Douglas, who served from 1939 to 1975, exceeded Field's record in 1973.

140. King, *Melville Weston Fuller*, p. 227.

141. *New York Times*, 4/4/1899.

142. Swisher, *Stephen J. Field*, p. 448.

Chapter Seven: Anti-Democracy

1. For the information on railroad men in the era's cabinets, see Philip H. Burch, Jr., *Elites in American History*, vol. 2, *The Civil War to the New Deal* (New York: Holmes & Meir, 1981), pp. 69–103; for the numbers see the charts in Appendix A of that volume beginning on p. 327. Also see Horace Samuel Merrill, *Bourbon Democracy of the Middle West, 1865–1896* (Seattle: University of Washington Press, 1967), p. 182; Matthew Josephson, *The Politicos* (New York: Harcourt, 1939), p. 376; C. Vann Woodward, *Origins of the New South, 1877–1913* (Baton Rouge: Louisiana State University Press, 1971), p. 18. For Garfield and Arthur, see Sven Beckert, *The Monied Metropolis: New York City and the Consolidation of the American Bourgoisie, 1850–1896* (New York: Cambridge University Press, 2001), p. 309. For Cleveland's secret negotiation with Morgan, see James L. Sundquist, *Dynamics of the Party System: Alignment and Realignment of Political Parties in the United States* (Washington, D.C.: Brookings Institution, 1983), p. 150.

2. Josephson, *The Politicos*, p. 354.

3. Ibid., pp. 353–54. Also, Steve Fraser, *Every Man a Speculator: A History of Wall Street in American Life* (New York: HarperCollins, 2005), p. 107.

4. Josephson, *The Politicos,* p. 375.

5. For Cleveland, see Morton Keller, *Affairs of State: Public Life in Late Nineteenth Century America* (Cambridge: Harvard University Press, 1977), p. 299. For Gould, see Richard White, "Information, Markets, and Corruption: Transcontinental Railroads in the Gilded Age," *Journal of American History,* vol. 90, no. 1 (June 2003), pp. 44–76.

6. Josephson, *The Politicos,* pp. 390–91; Merrill, *Bourbon Democracy of the Middle West,* pp. 186–87. For Hill's $10,000, see Mark Wahlgren Summers, *Party Games: Getting, Keeping, and Using Power in Gilded Age Politics* (Chapel Hill: University of North Carolina Press, 2004), p. 158.

7. John Gerring, "A Chapter in the History of American Party Ideology," *Polity,* vol. 26, no. 4 (Summer 1994), pp. 729–68; quotation is on p. 735. For the fate of domestic liberalism after the Civil Rights Acts, see Allen J. Matusow, *The Unraveling of America: A History of Liberalism in the 1960's* (New York: Harper & Row, 1984); Thomas Bryne Edsall and Mary D. Edsall, *Chain Reaction: The Impact of Race, Rights, and Taxes on American Politics* (New York: W. W. Norton, 1992); James T. Patterson, *Grand Expectations: The United States, 1945–1974* (New York: Oxford University Press, 1996), especially chapter 21, "Rights Polarization, and Backlash, 1966–1967." Robert Dallek, *Flawed Giant: Lyndon Johnson and His Times, 1961–1975* (New York: Oxford University Press, 1998). Dallek quotes Johnson (p. 120), after signing the Civil Rights Act of 1964, telling his aide, Bill Moyers, "I think we just delivered the South to the Republican party for a long time to come."

8. For details on the pension system, see Theda Skocpol, *Protecting Soldiers and Mothers: The Origins of Social Policy in the United States* (Cambridge: Harvard University Press, 1992), pp. 102–51; Keller, *Affairs of State,* pp. 307–10; David Montgomery, *Citizen Worker: The Experience of Workers in the United States with Democracy and the Free Market During the Nineteenth Century* (New York: Cambridge University Press, 1993), pp. 80–81. For Cleveland quotation, see John Gerring, *Party Ideologies in America, 1828–1996* (New York: Cambridge University Press, 1998), p. 169; for Cleveland, Harrison, and Senator Breck, see Richard Franklin Bensel, *Sectionalism and American Political Development, 1880–1980* (Madison: University of Wisconsin Press, 1984), pp. 65–70.

9. Josephson, *The Politicos,* pp. 312–13; Jacob S. Hacker and Paul Pierson, "Business Power and Social Policy: Employers and the Formation of the American Welfare State," *Politics and Society,* vol. 30, no. 2 (June 2002), p. 289.

10. Keller, *Affairs of State,* pp. 306, 239; also see Glenn C. Altschuler and Stuart M. Blumin, *Rude Republic: Americans and Their Politics in the Nineteenth Century* (Princeton: Princeton University Press, 2000), p. 255. For Arthur, see Michael Schudson, *The Good Citizen: A History of American Civic Life* (New York: Free Press, 1998), p. 149, also pp. 152, 156. For details on Pennsylvania and New York, as well as for the dollar amounts, see C. K. Yearley, *The Money Machines: The Breakdown and Reform of Governmental and Party Finance in the North, 1860–1920* (Albany: State University Press of New York, 1970), pp. 104–6.

11. Josephson, *The Politicos,* p. 310. For "full poll," see Robert D. Marcus, *Grand Old Party: Political Structure in the Gilded Age, 1880–1896* (New York: Oxford University Press, 1971), pp. 11–12.

12. Josephson, *The Politicos,* p. 382.

13. Ibid., p. 439. For Melville, see Andrew Delbanco, *Melville: His World and Work* (New York: Alfred A. Knopf, 2005), pp. 275, 296. For the comment of his brother-in-law, see C. Vann Woodward, *The Burden of Southern History* (New York: Mentor, 1968), p. 84. For change in the sources of funding after civil service, see Josephson, *The*

Politicos, pp. 276–77, 219–323; James Bryce, *The American Commonwealth*, vol. 1 (New York: Macmillan, 1907), p. 21.

14. E. E. Schattschneider, *The Semisovereign People: A Realist's View of Democracy in America* (New York: Holt, Rinehart & Winston, 1960), p. 68.

15. Leonard Dinnerstein, "The Election of 1880," in Arthur M. Schlesinger, Jr., and Fred I. Israel, editors, *History of American Presidential Elections, 1789–1968*, vol. 2 (New York: Chelsea House, 1971).

16. George K. Holmes, "The Concentration of Wealth," *Political Science Quarterly*, vol. 8, no. 4 (December 1897), pp. 560–89; Thomas G. Shearman, "The Owners of the United States," *Forum*, November 1889. In fact the richest 1 percent owned 26 percent of the wealth; the richest 10 percent, 72 percent. "Not only was the nineteenth century distribution of economic rewards unequal, there appears to have been a trend toward more inequality as the century progressed." Clayne Pope, "Inequality in the Nineteenth Century," in Stanley L. Engerman and Robert E. Gallman, editors, *The Cambridge Economic History of the United States*, vol. 2, *The Long Nineteenth Century* (Cambridge: Cambridge University Press, 1946), pp. 132–37.

17. Steven R. Weisman, *The Great Tax Wars: Lincoln to Wilson—The Fierce Battles over Money and Power That Transformed the Nation* (New York: Simon & Schuster, 2002), chapter 4, "There Is No Tax More Equal," pp. 75–104.

18. Eric Foner, *Reconstruction: America's Unfinished Revolution, 1863–1877* (New York: Harper & Row, 1988), pp. 22–23; Weisman, *The Great Tax Wars*, p. 101. Kevin Phillips, *Wealth and Democracy: A Political History of the American Rich* (New York: Broadway Books, 2001), p. 34.

19. See C. F. Emerick, "An Analysis of Agricultural Discontent in the United States Part 2," *Political Science Quarterly*, vol. 2, no. 4 (December 1896), pp. 601–39. For Charles J. Bonaparte and tax evasion in New York and Iowa, see Yearley, *The Money Machines*, pp. 63–74.

20. For "Tarbell," see Ida M. Tarbell, *The Tariff in Our Times* (New York: Macmillan, 1911), pp. vii, 21. For Harrison-Cleveland, see Douglas A. Irwin, "Tariff Incidence in America's Gilded Age," March 21, 2006, draft of paper available on the author's website at Department of Economics, Dartmouth College. Also, E. E. Schattschneider, *Politics, Pressures and the Tariff: A Study of Free Enterprise in Pressure Politics, as Shown in the 1929–1930 Revision of the Tariff* (New York: Prentice-Hall, 1935), pp. 212, 283.

21. For the 1895 decisions, see Alan Furman Westin, "The Supreme Court, the Populist Movement, and the Campaign of 1896," *Journal of Politics*, vol. 15, no. 1 (February 1953), pp. 3–41. For *Debs* and background of government by injunction, see William E. Forbath, "The Shaping of the American Labor Movement," *Harvard Law Review*, vol. 102, no. 6 (April 1989), pp. 1109–1258, especially pp. 1160–62. For Pennoyer, see his note in the *American Law Review*, vol. 29 (1895), pp. 550–55. Also Emerick, "An Analysis of Agricultural Discontent," p. 627.

22. William C. Reuter, "Business Journals and Gilded Age Politics," *The Historian*, vol. 56, no. 1 (Autumn 1993), p. 55ff.

23. For Indiana, see Richard Jensen, *The Winning of the Midwest: Social and Political Conflict, 1888–1896* (Chicago: University of Chicago Press, 1971), p. 12. For 700 "pieces of kitsch," see Joanne Reitano, *The Tariff Question in the Gilded Age: The Great Debate of 1888* (University Park: Pennsylvania State University Press, 1994), p. 125.

24. For the quotation from *Railway World*, see Beckert, *The Monied Metropolis*, pp. 232–33.

25. Richard Hofstadter and Michael Wallace, editors, *American Violence: A Documentary History* (New York: Alfred A. Knopf, 1970), p. 9; Robert Reinders, "Militia and Public Order in 19th Century America," *Journal of American Studies*, vol. 11, no. 1 (April 1977), p. 98. Philip Foner, *The Great Labor Uprising of 1877* (New York: Monad, 1977), pp. 47–48, 63–64, 672–73, 76, 90, 118. For New York official, see Barton C. Hacker, "The United States Army as a National Police Force: The Federal Policing of Labor Disputes, 1877–1898," *Military Affairs*, vol. 33, no. 1 (April 1969), p. 260. Jerry M. Cooper, "The Army as Strikebreaker—The Railroad Strikes of 1877 and 1894," *Labor History*, vol. 18, no. 2 (Spring 1977), pp. 181–96.

26. For details on the National Guard, see James Green, *Death in the Haymarket: A Story of Chicago, the First Labor Movement, and the Bombing That Divided Gilded Age America* (New York: Pantheon, 2006), p. 80, and Beckert, *The Monied Metropolis*, pp. 293–98. Herbert G. Gutman, *Power & Culture: Essays on the American Working Class* (New York: Pantheon Books, 1987), p. 338.

27. Hobsbawm seen in Charles Tilly, Louise Tilly, and Richard Tilly, *The Rebellious Century, 1830–1930* (Cambridge: Harvard University Press, 1975), pp. 1–16, 289; Sheldon Stromquist, *A Generation of Boomers: The Pattern of Labor Conflict in Nineteenth Century America* (Urbana: University of Illinois Press, 1987), p. 25; Louis M. Hacker and Benjamin B. Kendrick, *The United States Since 1865* (New York: F. S. Crofts, 1932), pp. 233–39. For "slip tickets," see James Bryce, *The American Commonwealth*, vol. 2 (New York: Macmillan, 1916), pp. 146–48. For federal patronage after the civil service, see Mark Lawrence Kornbluh, *Why America Stopped Voting: The Decline of Participatory Democracy and the Emergence of Modern American Politics* (New York: New York University Press, 2000), p. 52, also for the figures on patronage in Chicago and Philadelphia.

28. See the striking original research by Peter H. Argersinger, "The Value of the Vote: Political Representation in the Gilded Age," *Journal of American History*, vol. 76 (June 1989), pp. 59–90, which builds on John D. Buenker, "The Politics of Resistance: The Rural-Based Yankee Republican Machines of Connecticut and Rhode Island," *New England Quarterly*, vol. 47, no. 2 (June 1974), pp. 212–37. Also, Schudson, *The Good Citizen*, p. 162.

29. Charles Stewart and Barry R. Weingast, "Stacking the Senate, Changing the Nation: Republican Rotten Boroughs, Statehood Politics, and American Political Development," *Studies in American Political Development*, vol. 6, no. 2 (Fall 1992), pp. 223–71. For statistics on elections, see Joel H. Silbey, *The American Political Nation, 1838–1893* (Stanford: Stanford University Press, 1991), p. 219.

30. Woodward, *Origins of the New South*, pp. 1–22; Edward L. Ayers, *The Promise of the New South: Life After Reconstruction* (New York: Oxford University Press, 1992), p. 37. For Blaine's southern vote, see James M. McPherson, "The Antislavery Legacy: From Reconstruction to the NAACP," in Barton L. Bernstein, editor, *Towards a New Past: Dissenting Essays in American History* (New York: Vintage, 1969), p. 144.

31. Gilles Vandal, "The Policy of Violence in Caddo Parish, 1865–1884," *Louisiana History*, vol. 32, no. 2 (Spring 1991), pp. 159–82. The NAACP estimates that 2,522 African-Americans were lynched between 1889 and 1900. For a study linking lynching to intensified political competition, see Sarah A. Soule, "Populism and Black Lynching, 1890–1900," *Social Forces*, vol. 71, no. 2 (December 1992), pp. 431–49.

32. J. Morgan Kousser, "The Voting Rights Act and the Two Reconstructions," in Bernard Grofman and Chandler Davidson, editors, *Controversies in Minority Voting* (Washington, D.C.: Brookings Institution, 1992), pp. 135–75, especially pp. 143–44.

For Reed, see J. Morgan Kousser, *The Shaping of Southern Politics: Suffrage, Redistricting, and the Establishment of the One-Party South, 1880–1910* (New Haven: Yale University Press, 1974), p. 20.

33. Quotations are taken from, Ayers, *The Promise of the New South*, pp. 37, 53, 267, 272, 276, 277, 278. Also see C. Vann Woodward, *Tom Watson: Agrarian Rebel* (New York: Oxford University Press, 1963), pp. 186–209; the Woodward quotation is from C. Vann Woodward, "Tom Watson and the Negro in Agrarian Politics," *Journal of Southern History*, vol. 4, no. 1 (February 1938), p. 22. Lawrence C. Goodwyn, "Populist Dreams and Negro Rights: East Texas as a Case Study," *American Historical Review*, vol. 76, no. 4 (December 1971), pp. 1435–56. Also Worth Robert Miller, "Harrison County Methods: Election Fraud in Late 19th Century Texas," *Locus*, vol. 7, no. 2 (Spring 1995), pp. 111–28, and Gerald H. Gaither, *Blacks and the Populist Movement: Ballots and Bigotry in the New South* (Tuscaloosa: University of Alabama Press, 2005), pp. 145–46.

34. Genevieve B. Gist, "Progressive Reform in a Rural Community: The Adams County Vote-Fraud Case," *Mississippi Valley Historical Review*, vol. 48, no. 1 (June 1961), pp. 60–77; John Reynolds, " 'The Silent Dollar': Vote Buying in New Jersey," *New Jersey History*, vol. 98, nos. 3 and 4 (Fall–Winter 1980), pp. 191–211. Peter H. Argersinger, "New Perspectives on Election Fraud in the Gilded Age," *Political Science Quarterly*, vol. 100, no. 4 (Winter 1985), pp. 673–82; Gary W. Cox and J. Morgan Kousser, "Turnout and Rural Corruption in New York," *American Journal of Political Science*, vol. 25, no. 4 (November 1981), pp. 654–56.

35. Lincoln Steffens, *The Shame of the Cities* (New York: Hill & Wang, 1957), pp. 136–39.

36. Argersinger, "New Perspectives on Election Fraud"; Henry George, "Money in Elections," *North American Review*, Vol. 86 (March 1983), pp. 201–12. Richard Franklin Bensel, *The American Ballot Box in the Mid-Nineteenth Century* (New York: Cambridge University Press, 2004), pp. 194–95, 290.

37. Dinnerstein, "The Election of 1880," p. 1510; Josephson, *The Politicos*, pp. 299–301, 430–33, 545, 641–709; C. Vann Woodward, *Reunion and Reaction: The Compromise of 1877 and the End of Reconstruction* (Boston: Little, Brown, 1966), pp. 154–65. "The Election of 1888," in Schlesinger and Israel, editors, *History of American Presidential Elections*, Vol. 2, p. 1637; Keller, *Affairs of State*, p. 523; Jensen, *The Winning of the Midwest*, pp. 29; 269, n. 2; 275. For Lloyd, see Chester McArthur Destler, *American Radicalism, 1865–1901* (Chicago: Quadrangle, 1966), p. 198.

38. Keller, *Affairs of State*, p. 544; David Madden, editor, *Thomas Wolfe's Civil War* (Tuscaloosa: University of Alabama Press, 2004), pp. 122–43. For housekeeping, see Peter H. Argersinger, "The Transformation of American Politics, 1865–1910," in Byron E. Shafer and Anthony J. Badger, editors, *Contesting Democracy: Substance & Structure in American Political History* (Lawrence: University of Kansas Press, 2001), p. 120.

39. Josephson, *The Politicos*, p. 617. The quotation on Bland-Allison is from Allen Weinstein, *Prelude to Populism: Origins of the Silver Issue, 1867–1878* (New Haven: Yale University Press, 1970), p. 356.

40. Rendig Fels, "The Long-Wave Depression, 1873–79," *Review of Economics and Statistics*, vol. 31, no. 1 (February 1949), pp. 69–73.

41. Josephson, *The Politicos*, p. 393.

42. Ibid., pp. 574–75. Also, Louis Galambos, "The Agrarian Image of the Large Corporation, 1879–1920: A Study in Social Accommodation," *Journal of Economic History*, vol. 28, no. 3 (September 1968), pp. 341–62. Passage of the Hepburn Act, the Mann-Elkins Act, and the Supreme Court's breakup of the Standard Oil monopoly also

correlated with less negative and finally neutral assessments of big business. For committee records, see Edward A. Purcell, Jr., "Ideas and Interests: Businessmen and the Interstate Commerce Act," *Journal of American History*, vol. 54, no. 3 (December 1967), pp. 561–78.

43. Thomas K. McCraw, "Mercantilism and the Market," in Claude E. Barfield and William A. Schambra, editors, *The Politics of Industrial Policy* (Washington, D.C.: American Enterprise Institute, 1986), pp. 33–62; Louis D. Brandeis, *The Curse of Bigness: The Miscellaneous Papers of Louis D. Brandeis* (New York: Viking, 1935), p. 117; Richard Hofstadter, "What Happened to the Anti-Trust Movement?," in *The Paranoid Style in American Politics and Other Essays* (New York: Alfred A. Knopf, 1965), pp. 188–237; Thurman Arnold, *The Folklore of Capitalism* (New Haven: Yale University Press, 1937), p. 212. For Carnegie, see Richard Franklin Bensel, *The Political Economy of American Industrialization, 1877–1900* (Cambridge, Eng.: Cambridge University Press, 2000), p. 344. Hofstadter points out that the Sherman Act was unlikely to resolve the perennial problem of antitrust—that Americans fear bigness in theory but have long since accepted it in practice, "a perfect illustration of how the problems of the past are not solved but outgrown" (p. 223).

44. Josephson, *The Politicos*, pp. 246–47; Ellis Paxson Oberholtzer, *A History of the United States Since the Civil War*, Vol. 3, *1872–1878* (New York: Macmillan, 1926), p. 341.

45. Thomas Frank, *What's the Matter with Kansas? How Conservatives Won the Heart of America* (New York: Henry Holt, 2004), p. 7.

46. Larry M. Bartels, "What's the Matter with *What's the Matter with Kansas?*," *Quarterly Journal of Political Science*, vol. 1, 2006), pp. 201–26. For *Kansas Gazette* and Hamlin Garland, see Sundquist, *Dynamics of the Party System*, p. 136, n. 8. For class politics in Lynn, see Alan Dawley and Paul Fraler, "Working-Class Culture and Politics in the Industrial Revolution: Sources of Loyalism and Rebellion," *Journal of Social History*, vol. 9 (June 1976), pp. 475–76. For Prussian Road, see Barrington Moore, Jr., *The Social Origins of Dictatorship and Democracy: Lord and Peasant in the Making of the Modern World* (Boston: Beacon, 1966), pp. 433–52. Moore does not use the phrase. Also, Lawrence Powell, "The Prussians Are Coming," *Georgia Historical Quarterly*, vol. 71, no. 4 (Winter 1987), pp. 638–67. For Fitzhugh and Lincoln, see Arthur C. Cole, *Lincoln's "House Divided" Speech: Did It Reflect a Doctrine of Class Struggle?* (Chicago: University of Chicago Press, 1923), pp. 1–36. Steven Hahn, "Class and State in Postemancipation Societies: Southern Planters in a Comparative Perspective," *American Historical Review*, vol. 95, no. 1 (February 1990), pp. 75–98, quotation is from p. 93. For comparative political analysis with Germany, see Peter Alexis Gourevitch, "International Trade, Domestic Coalitions, and Liberty: Comparative Responses to the Crisis of 1873–1896," *Journal of Interdisciplinary History*, vol. 8, no. 2 (Autumn 1977), pp. 281–313, quotation is from p. 312. Also see Richard Franklin Bensel, *Yankee Leviathan: The Origins of Central State Authority, 1859–1877* (New York: Cambridge University Press, 1990), p. 425, and by the same author, *The Political Economy of American Industrialization*, p. 526. Jonathan M. Wiener, "Class Structure and Economic Development in the American South, 1865–1955," *American Historical Review*, vol. 84, no. 4 (October 1979), pp. 970–92, quotation is from p. 98. Also see the critical responses to Wiener, by Robert Higgs and Harold Woodman, pp. 993–1001. For a case study of planter-led modernization, see John J. Beck, "Building the New South: A Revolution from Above in Piedmont County," *Journal of Southern History*, vol. 53, no. 3 (August 1987), pp. 441–70. For Schattschneider and issue-cleavage conflicts, see John Gerring, "Culture Versus Economics: An American Dilemma," *Social Science History*, vol. 23, no. 2 (Summer 1999), pp. 129–30. Gerring

argues convincingly that the national parties have avoided divisive cultural issues in favor of economic issues. They may have done so in their party platforms, but in the Gilded Age section ruled in electioneeering.

47. Ellis Paxson Oberholtzer, *A History of the United States Since the Civil War,* vol. 4 (New York: Macmillan, 1926), pp. 202–5. For details on campaign distractions, see the index in Summers, *Party Games.*

48. Glenn C. Altschuler and Stuart M. Blumin, "Limits of Political Engagement in Antebellum America: A New Look at the Golden Age of Participatory Democracy," *Journal of American History,* vol. 84, no. 3 (December 1997), pp. 855–85.

49. Michael McGeer, *The Decline of Popular Politics: The American North, 1865–1922* (New York: Oxford University Press, 1986), pp. 7, 26, 106; Jensen, *The Winning of the Midwest,* pp. 2, 3. For issue polarities, see Dinnerstein, "The Election of 1880," in Schlesinger and Israel, editors, *History of American Presidential Elections,* vol 2, p. 1495, and in the same volume Mark D. Hirsch, "The Election of 1884," pp. 1571, 1580. For Emery, see Schudson, *The Good Citizen,* p. 186.

50. Selections from the debate over Gilded Age politics are taken from Vincent P. De Santis, "The Political Life of the Gilded Age: A Review of the Recent Literature," *History Teacher,* Vol. 9, no. 1 (November 1975), pp. 73–106. For 1888, see Reitano, *The Tariff Question in the Gilded Age,* pp. xvi, 8.

51. For self-identification, see Mark Wahlgren Summers, "Party Games: The Art of Stealing Elections in the Late Nineteenth Century United States," *Journal of American History,* vol. 88, no. 2 (September 2001), pp. 424–36. For party as a substitute for community, see Stephan Thernstrom and Peter R. Knights, "Men in Motion: Some Data and Speculations about Urban Population Mobility in Nineteenth-Century America," *Journal of Interdisciplinary History,* vol. 1, no. 1 (Autumn 1970), p. 35. For Brand Whitlock, see Sundquist, *Dynamics of the Party System,* p. 105. For ethno-religious differences, see the summary in Paul Kleppner, "Voters and Parties in the Western States," *Western Historical Quarterly,* vol. 14, no. 1 (January 1983), p. 193. For Wisconsin priest and Protestant minister, see Richard Oestreicher, "Urban Working-Class Political Behavior and Theories of American Electoral Politics, 1870–1940," *Journal of American History,* vol. 74, no. 4 (March 1988), pp. 1262–263. For Hendricks County, see Jensen, *The Winning of the Midwest,* pp. 59–60. For presidential voting in Hendricks, see Walter Dean Burnham, "Theory and Voting Research," in *The Current Crisis in American Politics* (New York: Oxford University Press, 1982), pp. 84–85. Geoffrey Blodgett, "The Mugwump Reputation: 1870 to the Present," *Journal of American History,* vol. 66, no. 4 (March 1980), p. 878.

52. Oberholtzer, *A History of the United States,* vol. 4, pp. 178–212; Harry J. Sievers, *Benjamin Harrison, Hoosier Statesman,* (Chicago: Regnery, 1952), p. 180, n. 89; Summers, *Party Games,* pp. 8–12. Henry George, "Money in Elections," *North American Review,* Vol. 76, (March 1883), pp. 201–12,

53. Oberholtzer, *A History of the United States,* vol. 3, p. 71. For Crédit Mobilier, see David Haward Bain, *Empire Express: Building the First Transcontinental Railroad* (New York: Viking, 1999), pp. 666–705.

54. J. Martin Klotske, "The Star Route Cases," *Mississippi Valley Historical Review,* vol. 22, no. 3 (December 1935), pp. 413–17. Also see *The Independent,* 4/28/1884, p. 15, and the *Christian Union,* 3/20/1884, which noted: "The prosecutions were pressed with vigor more apparent than real."

55. Sundquist, *Dynamics of the Party System,* p. 154.

Chapter Eight: Tom Scott, Political Capitalist

1. Ellis Paxson Oberholtzer, *A History of the United States Since the Civil War*, vol. 3, *1872–78* (New York: Macmillan, 1926), p. 83.

2. Henrietta M. Larson, *Jay Cooke: Private Banker* (Cambridge: Harvard University Press, 1936), pp. 406–11; also Richard White, "Information, Markets, and Corruption: Transcontinental Railroads in the Gilded Age," *Journal of American History*, vol. 90, no. 1 (June 2003), pp. 44–76.

3. Oberholtzer, *A History of the United States*, vol. 3, pp. 90, 97; Theodore Dreiser, *The Financier* (New York: Meridian, 1967), p. 437.

4. Samuel Bernstein, "Labor During the Long Depression," in *Science and Society* vol. 20, (1956), pp. 59–83. For Massachusetts editor, see Rebecca Edwards, *New Spirits: Americans in the Gilded Age, 1865–1905* (New York: Oxford University Press, 2006), p. 100.

5. Ron Chernow, *Titan: The Life of John D. Rockefeller, Sr.* (New York: Random House, 1998), p. 142.

6. For Dun's report on Scott, see Dr. T. Lloyd Benson and Trina Rossman, "Reassessing Tom Scott, the 'Railroad Prince,'" a paper for the Mid-America Conference on History, September 16, 1995. Paper available at http://facweb.furman.edu/~benson/col-tom.html. For Thomas A. Scott, see James A. Ward, *J. Edgar Thomson: Master of the Pennsylvania* (Westport: Greenwood, 1980), especially pp. 204–8; James A. Ward, "J. Edgar Thomson and Thomas A. Scott: A Symbiotic Partnership?," *Pennsylvania Magazine of History and Biography*, vol. 100, no. 1 (January 1976), pp. 37–62; Richard S. Tedlow, *Giants of Enterprise: Seven Business Innovators and the Empires They Built* (New York: HarperCollins, 2001), pp. 32–54; Chernow, *Titan*, pp. 129–42, 200–205; Allan Nevins, *Study in Power: John D. Rockefeller Industrialist and Philanthropist* (New York: Scribners, 1953), especially chapter 13, "War with the Pennsylvania"; Patricia T. Davis, *End of the Line: Alexander D. Cassatt and the Pennsylvania Railroad* (New York: Neal Watson, 1978); Joseph S. Clark, "The Railroad Struggle for Pittsburgh," *Pennsylvania Magazine of History and Biography*, vol. 48, no. 1 (April 1924), pp. 1–37; Philip English Mackey, "Law and Order, 1877: Philadelphia's Response to the Railroad Riots," *Pennsylvania Magazine of History and Biography*, vol. 46 (April 1975), pp. 183–200; *New York World*, 2/20/1877, 7/24/1877. Also see Thomas A. Scott, "The Recent Strikes," *North American Review*, vol. 125, no. 258 (September 1877), pp. 351–63.

7. I borrow "political capitalism" from Gabriel Kolko, *The Triumph of Conservatism: A Reinterpretation of American History, 1900–1916* (New York: Free Press, 1963), especially chapter 3, "Theodore Roosevelt and the Foundations of Political Capitalism." Whereas Kolko uses the term "political capitalism" to characterize "big business control of politics set in the context of the political regulation of the economy," I use the term to mean crony capitalism, government favors to business in return for business favors to politicians. Andrew Carnegie, *Autobiography* (New York: Houghton Mifflin, 1920), p. 63; Tedlow, *Giants of Enterprise*, p. 32.

8. Chernow, *Titan*, p. 135.

9. See, for example, Clark, "The Railroad Struggle for Pittsburgh," p. 23.

10. C. Vann Woodward, *Reunion and Reaction: The Compromise of 1877 and the End of Reconstruction* (Boston: Little, Brown, 1966), p. 95

11. Ibid., p. 90.

12. Ibid., p. 95.

13. Ward, "J. Edgar Thomson and Thomas A. Scott," p. 41.

14. Barbara Crandall, "American Railroad Presidents in the 1870's: Their Background and Careers," *Explorations in Entrepreneurial History,* vol. 2, no. 5 (July 1950), pp. 282–89.

15. See the obituaries in the *Chicago Tribune, New York Tribune,* and *New York Times,* 5/22/1881.

16. *New York Times,* 5/22/1881.

17. Tedlow, *Giants of Enterprise,* pp. 36, 260.

18. Carnegie, *Autobiography,* p. 70.

19. Ibid., pp. 71–73; Tedlow, *Giants of Enterprise,* p. 37

20. Carnegie, *Autobiography,* p. 84.

21. Ward, *J. Edgar Thomson,* p. 3; Samuel R. Kamm, *The Civil War Career of Thomas A. Scott* (Philadelphia: University of Pennsylvania Press, 1940), p. 3.

22. *New York Times,* 5/22/1881.

23. Carnegie, *Autobiography,* p. 117.

24. Kamm, *The Civil War Career of Thomas A. Scott,* p. 47, n. 8.

25. Clark "The Railroad Struggle for Pittsburgh," p. 22.

26. Ibid., p. 13.

27. Ibid., pp. 13–15.

28. Ibid., p. 18.

29. Allan Nevins, *War for the Union: The Organized War, 1863–1864* (New York: Scribners, 1971), p. 288; James M. McPherson, *Battle Cry of Freedom: The Era of the Civil War* (New York: Oxford University Press, 1988), p. 260.

30. Kamm, *The Civil War Career of Thomas A. Scott,* pp. 9–12.

31. *House Reports of Committees,* Thirty-seventh Congress, Second Session (1142), vol. 1, p. 566.

32. Josephson, *The Politicos* (New York: Harcourt, 1939), pp. 77–78.

33. George Edgar Turner, *Victory Rode the Rails: The Strategic Place of Railroads in the Civil War* (Indianapolis: Bobbs-Merrill, 1953), p. 55; Robert G. Angevin, *The Railroads and the State: War, Politics, and Technology in Nineteenth Century America* (Stanford: Stanford University Press, 2004), pp. 131–34. In *The Civil War Career of Thomas A. Scott,* Samuel R. Kamm argues that Scott's rate schedule was more innocent than it looked to Congress. "Enough has been written in this study to show that Scott was merely following the action of the eastern railroads concerning rates for government service taken before and at the outset of the war" (p. 188).

34. Nevins, *War for the Union,* pp. 85, 86, 396–97, n. Turner, *Victory Rode the Rails,* p. 66; *House Reports of Committees,* Thirty-seventh Congress, Second Session (1142), vol. 1, pp. 696, 625ff. Thomas Weber, *The Northern Railroads and the Civil War 1861–1865* (New York: King's Crown Press, 1952), pp, 24–41; Kamm, *The Civil War Career of Thomas A. Scott,* p. 34; Joseph Frazier Wall, *Andrew Carnegie* (New York: Oxford University Press, 1970), p. 108; Andrew Carnegie, *Autobiography,* p. 100.

35. Kamm, *The Civil War Career of Thomas A. Scott,* pp. 72–73; James Ford Rhodes, *History of the United States from the Compromise of 1850,* vol. 3, 1860–1862 (New York: Macmillan, 1895), p. 366; Nevins, *War for the Union,* pp. 81–85, footnote on 85; Weber, *The Northern Railroads and the Civil War,* pp. 25–27.

36. For Carnegie and Scott, see David Nasaw, *Andrew Carnegie* (New York: Penguin Press, 2006), p. 72. Nevins, *War for the Union,* pp. 408–9; Rhodes, *History of the United States,* p. 577. Kamm, *The Civil War Career of Thomas A. Scott,* pp. 122–23.

37. Kamm, *The Civil War Career of Thomas A. Scott,* pp. 124–26. Nasaw, *Andrew Carnegie,* pp. 69–71.

38. Ibid., p. 97.

39. For Cameron, see Joel Sibley, *The American Political Nation, 1838–1893* (Stanford: Stanford University Press, 1991), p. 128. Rhodes, *History of the United States*, p. 576. For "frustrated claimant," see Nevins, *War for the Union*, p. 415.

40. Kamm, *The Civil War Career of Thomas A. Scott*, p. 131.

41. Rhodes, *History of the United States*, p. 61, n. 1. Mark W. Summers, *The Plundering Generation: Corruption and the Crisis of the Union, 1849–1861* (New York: Oxford University Press, 1987), pp. 100–113, 98; James Bryce, *The American Commonwealth*, vol. 1 (New York: Macmillan, 1907), p. 543, n. 2.

42. For Scott's reputation, see Benson and Rossman, "Re-Assessing Tom Scott," at http://facweb.furman.edu/~benson/col-tom.html. Josephson, *The Politicos,* pp. 444–45. For Payne, see Henry Demarest Lloyd, *Wealth Against Commonwealth* (New York: Harper & Brothers, 1894), pp. 373–85.

43. Scott Reynolds Nelson, *Iron Confederacies: Southern Railways, Klan Violence, and Reconstruction* (Chapel Hill: University of North Carolina Press, 1999), pp. 73–75.

44. Ari Hoogenboom, *Rutherford B. Hayes, Warrior and President* (Lawrence: University of Kansas Press, 1995), p. 295.

45. Clark, "The Railroad Struggle for Pittsburgh," pp. 1–37.

46. Nelson, *Iron Confederacies,* pp. 74, 76.

47. Ibid., pp. 78–79.

48. Ibid., p. 86

49. Rhodes, *History of the United States*, p. 466ff. For Frémont's campaign slogan, see Sean Wilentz, *The Rise of American Democracy: Jefferson to Lincoln* (New York: W. W. Norton, 2005), p. 696.

50. Rhodes, *History of the United States*, p. 482

51. McPherson, *Battle Cry of Freedom*, pp. 715–16, 776; Allan Nevins, *John C. Frémont: The West's Great Adventurer,* vol. 2 (New York: Harper & Brothers, 1939), p. 669ff.

52. For Mariposa, see Nevins, *John C. Frémont,* pp. 619, 675, 687. Andrew Rolle, *John Charles Frémont, Character as Destiny* (Norman: University of Oklahoma Press, 1991), p. 238ff.

53. Cardinal Goodwin, *John Charles Frémont: An Explanation of His Career* (Stanford: Stanford University Press, 1930), pp. 160–67.

54. *New York Sun,* 2/1, 3, 11, 13, 15, 22, 1875; Albert V. House, "Post Civil War Precedents for Recent Railroad Reorganization," *Mississippi Valley Historical Review,* vol. 25, no. 4 (March 1939), pp. 505–22; David Haward Bain, *Empire Express: Building the First Transcontinental* (New York: Viking Press, 1999), pp. 677–80; Martin Ridge, *Ignatius Donnelley: The Portrait of a Politician* (Chicago: University of Chicago Press, 1962), p. 124; Josephson, *The Politicos,* p. 181. For "Frémont later gave," see Virginia H. Taylor, *The Franco-Texan Land Company* (Austin: University of Texas Press, 1969), p. 107.

55. Goodwin, *John Charles Frémont,* p. 248: "Of course he knew the content of the pamphlet. There is no evidence that he ever attempted to prevent the information from circulating." Compare Nevins, *John C. Frémont,* p. 685: "It is impossible to think of a man of his high honor consenting to an improper act." Scott never fully paid Frémont as promised, and the Pathfinder was in straits. His friends in Congress got him appointed governor of Arizona Territory in 1878, but he was "driven out by intelligent public opinion" two years later. In 1884, when it was proposed to retire him as a major general on a pension of $10,000 a year, the *Galveston Daily News* asked why the "people of the United States [should] be taxed to pay $10,000 a year to a wild, visionary, perverted, creature." Taylor, *The Franco-Texan Land Company,* p. 137; For Gray, see Taylor throughout; also House, "Post Civil War Precedents,"

pp. 512–13. White, "Information, Markets, and Corruption," see p. 27. For "my mother," see Rolle, *John Charles Frémont*, p. 241. For Huntington's fortune, see Gustavus Myers, *History of the Great American Fortunes* (New York: Modern Library, 1937), p. 528.

56. For Huntington quotations above, see R. Hal Williams, *The Democratic Party and California Politics 1880–1896* (Stanford: Stanford University Press, 1973), p. 11, for railroad, p. 10. Also, *New York Sun*, 2/13/1875. For details on the Southern's method of fixing rates, see T. H. Watkins, *California: An Illustrated History* (Palo Alto: American West Publishing, 1973), p. 232.

57. For details of the land grant, see Lloyd J. Mercer, *Railroads and Land Grant Policy: A Study in Government Intervention* (New York: Academic Press, 1982), pp. 43–44. *Chicago Tribune*, 10/8/1883; Chester McArthur Destler, *Henry Demarest Lloyd and the Empire of Reform* (Philadelphia: University of Pennsylvania Press, 1963), p. 117.

58. House, "Post Civil War Precedents," p. 52.

59. *Chicago Tribune*, 12/27/1883; Julius Grodinsky, *Jay Gould: His Business Career 1867–1892* (Philadelphia: University of Pennsylvania Press, 1957), p. 320.

60. Wall, *Andrew Carnegie*, pp. 138–43. Wall's monumental biography was the first to publish Woodruff's letter, earlier biographers having "accepted [Carnegie's] story in every detail," Nasaw, *Andrew Carnegie*, pp. 61–62.

61. Peter Krass, *Carnegie* (New York: Wiley, 2002), pp. 108–9; Wall, *Andrew Carnegie*, p. 286.

62. Chernow, *Titan*, p. xviii; *John D. Rockefeller Interviews 1917–1920*, conducted by William Inglis (Westport: Meckler Publishers, text-fiche ed., 1984).

63. Wall, *Andrew Carnegie*, pp. 285–91. Nasaw, *Andrew Carnegie*, pp. 123–24.

64. Krass, *Carnegie*, pp. 108–10; Ward, *J. Edgar Thomson*, pp. 201–4; Oberholtzer, *A History of the United States*, vol. 3, pp. 262–63; vol. 4, p. 189. For the financing of Edgar Thomson Steel, see Thomas J. Misa, *A Nation of Steel: The Making of Modern America, 1865–1925* (Baltimore: Johns Hopkins University Press, 1995), chapter 3, "Developing the Technology."

65. Wall, *Andrew Carnegie*, pp. 302–3.

66. Ward, *J. Edgar Thomson*, pp. 206–7, 213–15. For telegram, see Nasaw, *Andrew Carnegie*, pp. 154–55.

67. Tedlow, *Giants of Enterprise*, pp. 427–28.

68. Ward, *J. Edgar Thomson*, p. 215.

69. For undecided historians, see Peskin, "Was There a Compromise of 1877?" *Journal of American History*, vol. 60, no. 1 (June 1973), pp. 63–75; for Electoral Commission, see Woodward, *Reunion and Reaction*, pp. 150–51; Charles Fairman, *Five Justices and the Electoral Commission of 1877* (New York: Macmillan, 1988), p. 124. For an excellent account of the crisis, see Michael W. McConnell, "The Forgotten Constitutional Moment," *Constitutional Commentary* 11, vol. 2, no. 1 (Winter 1994), pp. 115–46.

70. See Woodward, *Reunion and Reaction*, and Woodward, "Yes, There Was," *Journal of American History*, vol. 60, no. 1 (June 1973), pp. 215–19; Michael Les Benedict, "Southern Democrats in the Crisis of 1876–1877: A Reinterpretation of Reunion and Reaction," *Journal of Southern History*, vol. 46, no. 4 (November 1980), pp. 489–524; Peskin, "Was There a Compromise of 1877?," pp. 63–75; and also see the relevant pages in Roy Morris, Jr., *Fraud of the Century: Rutherford B. Hayes, Samuel Tilden, and the Stolen Election of 1876* (New York: Simon & Schuster, 2003); Harry Barnard, *Rutherford B. Hayes and His America* (Indianapolis: Bobbs-Merrill, 1954); Charles

Richard Williams, *The Life of Rutherford Birchard Hayes,* vol. 2 (Boston: Houghton Mifflin, 1914); Hoogenboom, *Rutherford B. Hayes;* Rhodes, *History of the United States,* pp. 230–90. For a convincing social science investigation of the vote in Lousiana and South Carolina, see Ronald F. King, "A Most Corrupt Election: Lousiana in 1876," *Studies in American Political Development,* vol. 15 (Fall 2001), pp. 123–37, and Ronald F. King, "Counting the Votes: South Carolina's Stolen Election of 1876," *Journal of Interdisciplinary History,* vol. 32, no. 2 (Autumn 2001), pp. 169–91.

71. For Dana, see Mark Wahlgren Summers, *The Press Gang: Newspapers and Politics, 1865–1878* (Chapel Hill: University of North Carolina Press, 1994), pp. 62–64. *New York Sun,* 2/20/1877. For details of the receivership, see Woodward, *Reunion and Reaction,* pp. 157–58; and Fairman, *Five Justices,* pp. 140–41; and Taylor, *The Franco-Texan Land Company,* p. 66. Also see House, "Post Civil War Precedents," pp. 513–14. House writes: "The sketch of Justice Bradley by E. S. Corwin in *Dictionary of American Biography* (New York: Scribners, 1928–1936), II, 571, is very suggestive of such questionable activities as are revealed by this receivership." Nothing in Corwin's portrait supports that construal of it.

72. *New York Sun,* 2/20/1877, 8/4/1877, 9/1/1877, 9/6/1877; Woodward, *Reunion and Reaction;* Morris, *Fraud of the Century,* p. 223; Taylor, *The Franco-Texan Land Company,* p. 130, n. 90.

73. Fairman, *Five Justices,* pp. 123, 141–42, n. 34, 168. For Bradley's thoughts, see Charles Bradley, editor, *Miscellaneous Writings of the Late Hon. Joseph P. Bradley* (Newark: L. J. Hardham, 1902), p. 223. In July, after the *Sun* accused him of doing the bidding of the "Pennsylvania Railroad and other corporations" and the Grant administration in the *Legal Tender Cases* (1870–71), Bradley poured out his resentment to his friend Thomas T. Kinney, editor of the *Newark Daily Advertiser.* "[T]o charge *me* with mingling in politics, who have abstained from every thing of the kind—*me* who sits by the side of a Judge that is in the inmost councils of the Democratic Party at all times!" He meant Field. Fairman, *Five Justices,* pp. 126–27. "Of a nervous and sensitive nature [Bradley] keenly regretted that the choice had fallen on him; he was expected to sink all political differences and be an impartial arbitrator while his brothers on the bench had been chosen because of their political predilections." Rhodes, *History of the United States,* p. 264.

74. For Bigelow, see Fairman, *Five Justices,* pp. 140–42. Keith Ian Polakoff, *The Politics of Inertia: The Election of 1876 and the End of Reconstruction* (Baton Rouge: Louisiana State University Press, 1973), p. 290; Woodward, *Reunion and Reaction,* p. 162. For Conkling, see Hoogenboom, *Rutherford B. Hayes,* p. 381. Writing nearly forty years after Woodward, Charles Fairman entered a cogent brief in defense of Justice Bradley, dismissing Dana's assertions about the "seventeen carriages" as malicious invention. Woodward indulged a second account of Bradley's perfidy given by Abram Hewitt, chairman of the Democratic Committee, in Allan Nevins, *Abram S. Hewitt, With Some Account of Peter Cooper* (New York: Harper & Bros., 1935). Fairman demolishes the claims made about Bradley in Hewitt's "Secret History of the Disputed Election, 1876–1877," published for the first time by Nevins. Nevins, and Woodward after him, gave unwonted credit to the self-interested testimony of an old man given to fabulation. See Nevins's *Abram S. Hewitt* and the "Secret History" in Fairman, *Five Justices,* pp. 159–96.

75. Woodward, *Reunion and Reaction,* pp. 110–11.

76. Polakoff, *The Politics of Inertia,* pp. 253, 256; also Woodward, *Reunion and Reaction,* pp. 24–30.

77. Woodward, *Reunion and Reaction,* pp. 167–68.

78. Hoogenboom, *Rutherford B. Hayes,* pp. 283–84.

79. See Les Benedict, "Southern Democrats in the Crisis of 1876–1877," pp. 489–524; and Hoogenboom, *Rutherford B. Hayes,* pp. 293–94. Vincent P. De Santis, "The Republican Party and the Southern Negro, 1877–1897," *Journal of Negro History,* vol. 45, no. 2 (April 1960), p. 80. For white sheriff, see Nicholas Lemann, *Redemption: The Last Battle of the Civil War* (New York: Farrar, Straus, and Giroux, 2006), pp. 182–83.

80. Peskin, "Was There a Compromise of 1877?," p. 70; Polakoff, *The Politics of Inertia,* p. 290.

81. Mark W. Summers, *Railroads, Reconstruction, and the Gospel of Prosperity: And under the Radical Republicans, 1865–1877* (Princeton: Princeton University Press, 1984), p. 277.

Chapter Nine: Bread or Blood

1. Ron Chernow, *Titan: The Life of John D. Rockefeller, Sr.* (New York: Random House, 1998), p. 142.

2. John T. Flynn, "The Muckrakers," in Earl Latham, editor, *John D. Rockefeller: Robber Baron or Industrial Statesman?* (Boston: Heath, 1949), p. 3.

3. Chernow, *Titan,* p. 112.

4. Allan Nevins, *Study in Power: John D. Rockefeller, Industrialist and Philanthropist,* vol. 1 (New York: Scribners, 1953), p. 107.

5. Chernow, *Titan,* pp. 138–42.

6. Henry Demarest Lloyd, *Wealth Against Commonwealth* (New York: Harper & Brothers, 1894), pp. 55, 8.

7. Ida Minerva Tarbell, *History of the Standard Oil Company* (New York: P. Smith, 1904), pp. 90–91.

8. John D. Rockefeller interview, 1917–20, conducted by William O. Inglis (Westport: Meckler, text-fiche edition, 1984), p. 1307.

9. Alfred D. Chandler, Jr., *Shaping the Industrial Century: The Remarkable Story of the Evolution of the Modern Chemical and Pharmaceutical Industries* (Cambridge: Harvard University Press, 2005), pp. 283–312; also author interview with Professor Chandler conducted on 3/29/2005. For Lloyd, see "Story of a Monopoly," *The Atlantic Monthly,* March 1881.

10. Nevins, *Study in Power,* p. 236.

11. Ibid., p. 233.

12. Ibid., p. 239.

13. Lloyd, *Wealth Against Commonwealth,* p. 88.

14. Philip S. Foner, *The Great Labor Uprising of 1877* (New York: Monad, 1977), p. 47. Richard Oestreicher, "Urban Working-Class Political Behavior and Theories of American Electoral Politics, 1870–1940," *Journal of American History,* vol. 74, no. 4 (March 1988), p. 1260.

15. Ibid., p. 56. For a detailed discussion of job safety, see Walter Licht, *Working for the Railroad: The Organization of Work in the Nineteenth Century* (Princeton: Princeton University Press, 1983), pp. 164–215; the quotation from Augustus Shaw is on 183; the Licht quotation is on p. 190; the wage statistics are from the table on p. 128; the drinking is on p. 100.

16. For details of the strike, see *Report of the Committee Appointed to Investigate the Railroad Riots in July, 1877* (Harrisburg: 1878); Foner, *The Great Labor Uprising of 1877;* Robert V. Bruce, *1877: Year of Violence* (Indianapolis: Bobbs-Merrill, 1959); Patricia T. Davis, *End of the Line: Alexander J. Cassatt and the Pennsylvania Railroad* (New York:

Neale Watson, 1978); Philip English Mackey, "Law and Order, 1877: Philadelphia's Response to the Railroad Riots," *Pennsylvania Magazine of History and Biography*, vol. 46 (April 1972), pp. 183–202; Frederick Howe, editor, "President Hayes Notes of Four Cabinet Meetings," *American Historical Review*, vol. 37 (January 1932), pp. 287–89; T. Harry Williams, editor, *Hayes: The Diary of a President, 1875–1881* (New York: D. McKay, 1964); *New York Times*, 7/16–8/6/1877; *New York World*, 7/20–7/30/1877.

17. Foner, *The Great Labor Uprising of 1877*, p. 57.

18. *Report of the Committee Appointed to Investigate the Railroad Riots*, p. 18; Bruce, *1877*, pp. 122–23; for "most hated man," see Virginia Taylor, *The Franco-Texan Land Company* (Austin: University of Texas Press, 1969), p. 46.

19. Davis, *End of the Line*, pp. 34–44, 49; Daniel E. Sutherland, *The Expansion of Everyday Life, 1860–1876* (New York: Harper & Row, 1989), pp. 37–38.

20. Davis, *End of the Line*, p. 50.

21. Ibid., pp. 50–51.

22. Bruce, *1877*, p. 73; Mackey, "Law and Order, 1877," p. 186.

23. *New York Times*, 7/24/1877; Howe, editor, "President Hayes Notes," p. 56.

24. George Edward Reed, L.L.D., *Pennsylvania's Archives, 4th Series, Papers of Governors, 1871–1883* (Harrisburg: 1902), pp. 616–17.

25. Bruce, *1877*, p. 195.

26. Mackey, "Law and Order, 1877," especially pp. 197–98. The member of the Committee of Public Safety was Alexander K. McClure. See his *Old Time Notes of Pennsylvania*, vol. 2 (Philadelphia: John C. Winston, 1905), pp. 456–59.

27. Bruce, *1877*, pp. 18, 304; Anthony F. C. Wallace, *St. Clair: A Nineteenth-Century Coal Town's Experience with a Disaster-Prone Industry* (Ithaca: Cornell University Press, 1988), p. 247.

28. Herbert G. Gutman, "Trouble on the Railroads in 1873–1874: Prelude to the 1877 Crisis?" *Labor History*, vol. 2 (Spring 1961), p. 58. Asked by the legislative committee investigating the riot if the PRR had experienced any strikes before then, Scott recalled one in 1860 but "I believe we had no strike or trouble with our people from that time up to the occurrences last summer." *Report of the Committee Appointed to Investigate the Railroad Riots*, p. 927.

29. Bruce, *1877*, p. 213.

30. Gerald G. Eggert, *Railroad Labor Disputes: The Beginnings of Federal Strike Policy* (Ann Arbor: University of Michigan Press, 1967), p. 29.

31. Bruce, *1877*, p. 210.

32. Roy Morris, Jr., *Fraud of the Century: Rutherford B. Hayes, Samuel Tilden, and the Stolen Election of 1876* (New York: Simon & Schuster, 2003), p. 243.

33. Bruce, *1877*, pp. 210–12; Eggert, *Railroad Labor Disputes*, p. 28.

34. Williams, editor, *Hayes: The Diary of a President*, p. 79.

35. Foner, *The Great Labor Uprising of 1877*, p. 58.

36. Bruce, *1877*, p. 117.

37. Wallace, *St. Clair*, pp. 408–9.

38. *Report of the Committee Appointed to Investigate the Railroad Riots*, p. 821; David Montgomery, *Beyond Equality: Labor and the Radical Republicans, 1862–1872* (New York: Alfred A. Knopf, 1967), p. 238.

39. David Montgomery, *Workers' Control in America: Studies in the History of Work, Technology, and Labor Struggles* (New York: Cambridge University Press, 1979), pp. 12–13.

40. Foner, *The Great Labor Uprising of 1877*, p. 71.

41. David Montgomery, "Strikes in Nineteenth Century America," *Social Science His-*

tory, vol. 4, no. 2 (Spring 1980), pp. 89–92; and Martin Shefter, "Trade Unions and Political Machines: The Organization and Disorganization of the American Working Class in the Late Nineteenth Century," in Ira Katznelson and Aristide R. Zolberg, editors, *Working-Class Formation: Nineteenth-Century Patterns in Western Europe and the United States* (Princeton: Princeton University Press, 1986), pp. 203–4, 211–20; Richard Hofstadter and Michael Wallace, editors, *Violence in America: A Documentary History* (New York: Alfred A. Knopf, 1970), p. 39.

42. See Barrington Moore, Jr., *Injustice: The Social Bases of Obedience and Revolt* (White Plains: M. E. Sharpe, 1978), especially chapter 2, "The Moral Authority of Suffering and Injustice," for a discussion of this constant of the human condition. For blacklist, see Licht, *Working for the Railroad*, pp. 123–24.

43. Williams, editor, *Hayes: The Diary of a President*, p. 59.

44. Bruce, *1877*, pp. 131–34; *Report of the Committee Appointed to Investigate the Railroad Riots*, pp. 79, 809.

45. Eggert, *Railroad Labor Disputes*, p. 9.

46. Thomas A. Scott, "The Recent Strikes," *North American Review*, vol. 125, no. 258, (September–October 1877), pp. 351–63.

47. Bruce, *1877*, p. 315.

48. Ibid., p. 316.

49. Davis, *End of the Line*, p. 52ff; *Report of the Committee Appointed to Investigate the Railroad Riots*, pp. 698–99.

50. Davis, *End of the Line*, pp. 136–38. For Pearson, see p. 621 of the report cited in n. 49. Davis writes, "Cassatt vehemently denied ever applying to the state authorities for protection and insisted that this step had been taken by Fife before his arrival" (p. 53).

51. Foner, *The Great Labor Uprising of 1877*, p. 60.

52. Bruce, *1877*, p. 138; Foner, *The Great Labor Uprising of 1877*, p. 60.

53. Foner, *The Great Labor Uprising of 1877*, pp. 60, 138; Mackey, "Law and Order, 1877," p. 186.

54. *New York Times*, 7/22/1877.

55. Davis, *End of the Line*, p. 54.

56. *New York Times*, 7/22/1877.

57. Foner, *The Great Labor Uprising of 1877*, p. 62.

58. *Report of the Committee Appointed to Investigate the Railroad Riots*, pp. 214, 992.

59. Foner, *The Great Labor Uprising of 1877*, p. 63; *Report of the Committee Appointed to Investigate the Railroad Riots*, pp. 216, 963.

60. *New York Times*, 7/23/1877. For damages, see Dr. T. Lloyd Benson and Trina Rossman, "Re-Assessing Tom Scott, the 'Railroad Prince,'" a paper for the Mid-America Conference on History, September 16, 1995. Paper available at http://facweb.furman.edu/~benson/col-tom.html.

61. *Report of the Committee Appointed to Investigate the Railroad Riots*, pp. 972, 964–66, 975, 988, 855.

62. Bruce, *1877*, pp. 151, 166–67; *Report of the Committee Appointed to Investigate the Railroad Riots*, p. 15.

63. Moore, *Injustice*, p. 17.

64. Gustavus Myers, *History of the Great American Fortunes* (New York: Modern Library, 1937), p. 138; Bruce, *1877*, p. 173.

65. Foner, *The Great Labor Uprising of 1877*, p. 64; *Report of the Committee Appointed to Investigate the Railroad Riots*, p. 15.

66. Pennsylvania State Archives, Fourth Series, vol. 9, *Papers of the Governors, 1871–1883* (Harrisburg: The State of Pennsylvania, 1902), p. 622.

67. Elias Canetti, *Crowds and Power* (New York: Viking, 1966), pp. 20–22. New York Times, 7/25/1877.

68. *New York Sun*, 7/23/1877.

69. Mackey, "Law and Order, 1877," p. 190, n. 16: "Scott must have forgotten about his telegram eight months later when he averred, under oath, that there had not been 'any trouble at any time' during the Philadelphia disturbances."

70. Ibid., pp. 31–32.

71. Bruce, *1877*, pp. 88–89, 218–20, 210.

72. Ibid., p. 279.

73. Ari Hoogenboom, *Rutherford B. Hayes: Warrior and President* (Lawrence: University of Kansas Press, 1995), p. 332.

74. Williams, editor, *Hayes: The Diary of a President*, p. 92.

75. Eggert, *Railroad Labor Disputes*, p. 49.

76. Hoogenboom, *Rutherford B. Hayes*, p. 331.

77. Williams, editor, *Hayes: The Diary of a President*, p. 93.

78. Hoogenboom, *Rutherford B. Hayes*, pp. 585–86, n. 7.

79. Ibid., p. 330.

80. Foner, *The Great Labor Uprising of 1877*, p. 67.

81. *New York Times*, 8/1, 8/2, 8/3/1877

82. Eggert, *Railroad Labor Disputes*, pp. 35–41.

83. Bruce, *1877*, p. 309.

84. Foner, *The Great Labor Uprising of 1877*, p. 196.

85. Leon Fink, in "Labor, Liberty, and Law: Trade Unionism and the Problem of American Constitutional Order," *Journal of American History*, vol. 74, no. 3 (December 1987), counts "more than 1800 labor injunctions between 1880 and 1931" (p. 711). David Montgomery, *Citizen Worker: The Experience of Workers in the United States with Democracy and the Free Market During the Nineteenth Century* (New York: Cambridge University Press, 1993), pp. 150–51. For Gatling gun, see Joshua Freeman and Nelson Lichtenstein et al., editors, *Who Built America? Working People and the Nation's Economy, Politics, Culture and Society*, vol. 2 (New York: Pantheon, 1992), p. 125. In an Albany speech the year before the Pullman Strike Brewer had taken an alarmed view of the revolutionary danger of the union movement. "The first shot fired by the regular soldiers at the mobs here will be the signal for a civil war . . . 90 per cent of the people of the United States will be arrayed against the other 10 per cent . . . I do not say this as an alarmist, but calmly and thoughtfully"—as if a calm and thoughtful call for class war was possible. See Owen Fiss, "Troubled Beginnings of the Modern State, 1888–1910," in *The Oliver Wendell Holmes Devise History of the Supreme Court of the United States* (New York: Macmillan, 1993), pp. 53–74. For statistics on the labor injunctions, see William Forbath, "The Shaping of the American Labor Movement," *Harvard Law Review*, vol. 102, no. 6 (April 1989), pp. 1151–52.

86. H. W. Schotter, *The Growth and Development of the Pennsylvania Railroad Company* (Philadelphia: Allen, Lane & Scott, 1927), p. 176.

87. *Report of the Committee Appointed to Investigate the Railroad Riots*, pp. 176–77, 215; Bruce, *1877*, p. 143.

88. Bruce, *1877*, p. 27.

89. Ibid., pp. 68–69.

90. Sidney L. Harring, "Class Conflict and the Suppression of Tramps in Buffalo, 1892–1894," *Law and Society Review*, vol. 11, no. 5 (Summer 1977), pp. 873–911; Montgomery, *Citizen Worker*, pp. 86–89.

91. Montgomery, *Citizen Worker*, pp. 88–89; Amy Dru Stanley, "Beggars Can't Be

Choosers: Compulsion and Contract in Post-Bellum America," *Journal of American History*, vol. 78, no. 4 (March 1992), pp. 1265–93

92. William Cohen, "Negro Involuntary Servitude in the South, 1865–1940: A Preliminary Analysis," *Journal of Southern History*, vol. 42, no. 1 (February 1976), pp. 31–60. C. Vann Woodward, *Origins of the New South* (Baton Rouge: Louisiana State University Press, 1971), p. 214. For Alabama and the *Santa Clara* connection, see Steve Suitts, *Hugo Black of Alabama: How His Roots and Early Career Shaped the Great Champion of the Constitution* (Montgomery: New South Books, 2005), p. 377ff.

93. Bruce, *1877*, p. 291.

94. "Fair Wages," *North American Review*, vol. 125, no. 258 (September–October 1877), pp. 322–27.

95. Bruce, *1877*, pp. 313–14. Henry Demarest Lloyd, "The New Conscience," *North American Review*, vol. 147, no. 3 (September 1888), p. 336.

96. Sidney Fine, *Laissez Faire and the General-Welfare State: A Study of Conflict in American Thought, 1865–1901* (Ann Arbor: University of Michigan Press, 1956), pp. 120–24. Herbert G. Gutman, "Protestantism and the American Labor Movement: The Christian Spirit in the Gilded Age," *American Historical Review*, vol. 72, no. 1 (October 1966), pp. 74–101. Gutman contrasts his working-class "labor evangelists" to the ministers and reformers who promulgated the much better known "Social Gospel." He quotes Henry May's *Protestant Churches and Industrial America* (New York: Harper, 1949), on the difference between them, pp. 99–100: "The Social Gospel of the American nineteenth century . . . did not grow out of actual suffering but rather out of moral and intellectual dissatisfaction with the suffering of others. It originated not with the 'disinherited' but rather with the educated and pious middle class. It grew through argument, not through agitation; it pleaded for conversion, not revolt or withdrawal." Of course, many labor evangelists did not speak out of an experience of "actual suffering," either.

97. *New York Sun*, 7/30/1877. Bruce, *1877*, p. 313. William Vanderbilt, the president of the New York Central, stood beside Beecher in the dock of public derision for this statement: "Our men feel that, although I . . . may have my millions and they the rewards of their daily toil, still we are about equal. If they suffer, I suffer, and if I suffer they cannot escape." His gift of $100,000 to his employees for their "loyalty and faithfulness during the strike," Charles Francis Adams, Jr., likened to "a shilling thrown to a tramp." Scott could find only $3,000 worth of loyal employees. Bruce, *1877*, p. 302.

98. Bruce, *1877*, p. 314.

99. Foner, *The Great Labor Uprising of 1877*, p. 82.

100. *New York Times*, 7/30/1877. The *Irish World* "accused national guardsmen in Scranton of preventing an alderman from arresting W. W. Scranton, the city's most eminent businessman, on murder charges, after he led vigilantes through the streets during the strike to shoot at assembled groups of people." Montgomery, *Citizen Worker*, p. 101.

101. *New York Times*, 7/30/1877.

102. *New York Times*, 8/4/1877.

103. Bruce, *1877*, p. 301; *New York Times*, 8/5/1877.

104. Colton letters, *Chicago Tribune*, 12/27/1883; Woodward, *Reunion and Reaction*, pp. 235–36. For interview with Bancroft, see Lewis B. Lesley, "A Southern Transcontinental Railroad into California: Texas and Pacific Versus Southern Pacific, 1865–1885," *Pacific Historical Review*, vol. 5, no. 1 (1936), p. 58.

105. Chernow, *Titan*, p. 202.

106. James A. Ward, "Power and Accountability on the Pennsylvania Railroad, 1846–1878," *Business History Review*, Spring 1975, p. 56.

107. Lloyd, *Wealth Against Commonwealth*, p. 89; Nevins, *Study in Power*, p. 249.

108. Chernow, *Titan*, pp. 202–3; Rockefeller interview, p. 232; Williams, *End of the Line*, p. 69.

109. Nevins, *Study in Power*, p. 231; C. Vann Woodward, "Yes, There Was," *Journal of American History*, vol. 60, no. 1 (June 1973), p. 219.

110. Bruce, *1877*, p. 301; George H. Burgess and Miles C. Kennedy, *Centennial History of the Pennsylvania Railroad Company, 1846–1946* (Philadelphia: Pennsylvania Railroad Co., 1949), p. 383. For Gould, see Virginia Taylor, *The Franco-Texan Land Company* (Austin: University of Texas Press, 1969), p. 176.

111. *New York Times*, 5/22/1881. For Carnegie letter, see David Nasaw, *Andrew Carnegie* (New York: Penguin Press, 2006), pp. 155–56. For Gould, see Matthew Josephson, *The Robber Barons* (New York: Harcourt, 1962), p. 194.

112. *New York Sun*, 7/30/1877. For number of children employed in Rhode Island, see Charles Perrow, "A Society of Organizations," *Theory and Society*, vol. 20 (1991), p. 743.

Chapter Ten: The Politics of the Future

1. These paragraphs follow the arguments made by Thomas Goebel, "The Political Economy of American Populism from Jackson to the New Deal," *Studies in American Political Development*, vol. 2 (Spring 1997), pp. 109–48, and James L. Huston, "The American Revolutionaries, the Political Economy of Aristocracy, and the American Concept of Wealth Distribution, 1765–1900," *American Historical Review*, vol. 98, no. 4 (October 1993), pp. 1079–1105. For Justice Harlan, see Richard Jensen, "Democracy, Republicanism, and Efficiency, 1885–1930," in Byron E. Shafer and Anthony J. Badger, editors, *Contesting Democracy: Substance and Structure in American Political History, 1775–2000* (Lawrence: University of Kansas Press, 2001), p. 155. For the roots of conspiracy thinking, see Gordon S. Wood, "Conspiracy and the Paranoid Style: Causality and Deceit in the Eighteenth Century," *William and Mary Quarterly*, 3d ser., 39 (July 1982), pp. 401–41. For the Jacksonian view of inequality, see Martin A. Lebowitz, "The Jacksonians: Paradox Lost?" in Barton J. Bernstein, editor, *Towards a New Past: Dissenting Essays in American History* (New York: Vintage, 1969), p. 72. For Senator Peffer, see Richard J. Ellis, "Rival Visions of Equality in American Political Culture," *Review of Politics*, vol. 54, no. 2 (Spring 1992), p. 269. For Sarah Emery, see Jeffrey Ostler, "The Rhetoric of Conspiracy in the Formation of Kansas Populism," *Agricultural History*, vol. 69, no. 1 (Winter 1995), pp. 1–27. Ostler agrees with Lawrence Goodwyn that "the world of populism constructed by [Richard] Hofstadter now languishes in ruins," but argues that "anti-revisionists" like Goodwyn have scanted the role of conspiracy in the Populist persuasion to avoid the sins of Hofstadter, who, in the still-revered *The Age of Reform: From Bryan to F.D.R.* (New York: Alfred A. Knopf, 1955), reduced Populism to its most paranoid rhetoric— tanamount to a future historian writing the history of today's Republican Party off Patrick Buchanan's books and Jerry Falwell's speeches. For excellent accounts of how and why Hofstadter got Populism wrong, treating it as continous with McCarthyism, see David S. Brown, *Richard Hofstadter: An Intellectual Biography* (Chicago: University of Chicago Press, 2006), especially pp. 97–160; Robert M.

Collins, "The Originality Trap: Richard Hofstadter on Populism," *Journal of American History*, vol. 76, no. 1 (June 1989), pp. 150–67; Walter T. K. Nugent, *The Tolerant Populists: Kansas Populism and Nativism* (Chicago: University of Chicago Press, 1963); and C. Vann Woodward, "The Populist Heritage and the Intellectual," in *The Burden of Southern History* (New York: Mentor, 1968).

2. See "Lampasas County QuickFacts from the U.S. Census Bureau," also the essay on Lampasas County in the *Handbook of Texas Online*. http://www.tsha.utexas.edu/handbook/online/articles/LL/hc13.html. For Hungate, see Lawrence Goodwyn, *Democratic Promise: The Populist Moment in America* (New York: Oxford University Press, 1976), pp. 33 and 620, notes 14 and 16. Also Robert A. Caro, *The Years of Lyndon Johnson: The Path to Power* (New York: Alfred A. Knopf, 1982), pp. 8–21, 25. Robert C. McMath, Jr., *American Populism: A Social History, 1877–1898* (New York: Hill & Wang, 1993), p. 67. Also see Robert C. McMath, Jr., "Sandy Land and Hogs in the Timber: Agricultural Origins of the Farmers' Alliance in Texas," in Steven Hahn and Jonathan Prude, editors, *The Countryside in the Age of Capitalist Transformation: Essays in the Social History of Rural America* (Chapel Hill: University of North Carolina Press, 1985), p. 211; Benjamin Heber Johnson, "Red Populism? T. A. Bland, Agrarian Radicalism, and the Debate Over the Dawes Act," in Catherine McNicol Stock and Robert D. Johnston, editors, *The Countryside in the Age of the Modern American State: Political Histories of Rural America* (Ithaca: Cornell University Press, 2001), p. 15; Elizabeth Sanders, *Roots of Reform: Farmers, Workers, and the American State, 1877–1917* (Chicago: University of Chicago Press, 1999), p. 123. The total membership of the Southern Farmers' Alliance is in dispute, with estimates ranging from 940,000 to 2 million. The percentages cited are based on the lower figure. See Michael Schwartz, "An Estimate of the Size of the Southern Farmers' Alliance and Cotton Tenancy, 1880–1890," *Agricultural History*, vol. 51 (1977), p. 768. For underproduction, see Lawrence Goodwyn, *The Populist Moment: A Short History of the Agrarian Revolt in America* (New York: Oxford University Press, 1978), p. 134. The leader was L. L. Polk, the editor of the North Carolina–based *Progressive Farmer*.

3. For a discussion of where Populism gained traction and where it didn't and why, see Jeffrey Ostler, "Why the Populist Party Was Strong in Kansas and Nebraska but Weak in Iowa," *Western Historical Quarterly*, vol. 23, no. 4, pp. 451–74. For the "Populist strategist," see Peter H. Argersinger, "Taubeneck's Laws: Third Parties in American Politics in the Late Nineteenth Century," *American Nineteenth Century History*, vol. 3, no. 2 (Summer 2002), p. 98.

4. For Nugent, see Mark Voss-Hubbard, "The 'Third Party Tradition' Reconsidered: Third Parties and American Public Life, 1830–1900," *Journal of American History*, vol. 86, no. 1 (June 1999), p. 130. The "innocent pastoral victims" appear in Hofstadter, *The Age of Reform*, as cited by Goodwyn, *The Populist Moment*, p. 335

5. For Gould's office, see Steve Fraser, *Every Man a Speculator: A History of Wall Street in American Life* (New York: HarperCollins, 2005), pp. 107–18. For his being dropped, see Robert V. Bruce, *1877: Year of Violence* (Indianapolis: Bobbs-Merrill, 1959), p. 310.

6. For Gould's remarks in Texas, see "Hazardous Business: Industry, Regulation, and the Texas Railroad Commission, in Texas State Library and Archives Commission, http://www.tsl.state.tx.us/exhibits/railroad/intro.html. For fuller context, see Robert L. Peterson, "Jay Gould and the Texas Railroad Commission of Texas," *Southwestern Historical Quarterly*, vol. 58, no. 3 (January 1955), pp. 422–25; also James R. Novell, "The Railroad Commission of Texas Its Origin and History, *Southwestern Historical Review*, vol. 68, no. 4 (April 1965), pp. 465–80. For details of the strike, see Goodwyn, *Democratic Promise*, pp. 52–54. Also, see the contemporary article by

F. W. Taussing, "The South-Western Strike of 1886," *Quarterly Journal of Economics,* vol. 1, no. 2 (January 1887), pp. 184–222. For different interpretations of Iron's claim that he was coerced at gunpoint to approve the strike, see Gerald N. Grob, *Workers and Utopia: A Study of Ideological Conflict in the American Labor Movement, 1865–1900* (New York: Quadrangle Books, 1961), p. 67. Irons's letters to the Union president, Terrence Powderly, "fully authenticate one of the strangest affairs in the annals of American labor," according to Grob. But Michael J. Cassity, "Modernization and Social Crisis: The Knights of Labor and a Midwest Community, 1885–1886," *Journal of American History,* vol. 66, no. 1 (June 1979), p. 54, n. 36, has doubts: "Whether this interpretation is an accurate description of the origins of the strike or merely an excuse that Irons fabricated to diminish his own responsibility in the dismal outcome of the strike, cannot be resolved."

7. McMath, *American Populism,* pp. 51–72; also McMath, "Sandy Land and Hogs in the Timber," especially pp. 217–21. For fences, see Otto Wolfgang, "How the Wild West Was Fenced In," *Cattleman,* vol. 53, no. III (August 1966). Richard Maxwell Brown, "Western Violence: Structure, Values, Myth," *Western Historical Quarterly,* vol. 24, no. 1 (February 1994), pp. 4–20. Also, W. Eugene Hollon, *Frontier Violence: Another Look* (New York: Oxford University Press, 1974), pp. 167–71.

8. See Forrest McDonald and Grady McWhiney, "The Antebellum Southern Herdsman: A Reinterpretation," *Journal of Southern History,* vol. 41, no. 2 (May 1975), pp. 158, 162.

9. Forrest McDonald and Grady McWhiney, "The South from Self-Sufficiency to Peonage: An Interpretation," *American Historical Review,* vol. 85, no. 5 (December 1980), pp. 1095–1118, especially pp. 111–18.

10. This paragraph reduces to outline elements of the thesis complexly developed by Steven Hahn in *The Roots of Southern Populism: Yeoman Farmers and the Transformation of the Southern Upcountry, 1850–1890* (New York: Oxford University Press, 1983). The quotations are from pp. 180, 33, and chapter 4. Also Theodore R. Mitchell, *Political Education in the Southern Farmers' Alliance, 1887–1900* (Madison: University of Wisconsin Press, 1987), p. 27. For an argument against Hahn's thesis, see Shawn Everett Kantor and J. Morgan Kousser, "Common-Sense or Commonwealth? The Fence Law and Institutional Change in the Postbellum South," *Journal of Southern History,* vol. 51, no. 2 (May 1993), pp. 201–42; also see Hahn's reply, "A Response: Common Cents or Historical Sense?," *Journal of Southern History,* vol. 59, no. 2 (May 1993), pp. 243–58, and Kantor's and Kousser's "Rejoinder: Two Visions of History," *Journal of Southern History,* vol. 59, no. 2 (May 1993), pp. 259–66. McDonald and McWhiney, "The South from Self-Sufficiency to Peonage," pp. 1115–17. For merchant-planter alliance, see Lacy K. Ford, "Rednecks and Merchants: Economic Development and Social Tension in the South Carolina Upcountry, 1865–1900," *Journal of American History,* vol. 71, no. 2 (September 1984), pp. 294–318.

11. McMath, *American Populism,* p. 56.

12. James Turner, "Understanding the Populists," *Journal of American History,* vol. 67, no. 2 (September 1983), p. 371.

13. For letters, see Caro, *The Path to Power,* pp. 34–35.

14. Quotations are from Peter H. Argersinger, *Populism and Politics: William Alfred Peffer and the People's Party* (Lexington: University of Kentucky Press, 1974), pp. 7, 4. "No candidate" is from Hallie Farmer, "The Economic Background of Frontier Populism," *Mississippi Valley Historical Review,* vol. 10, no. 4 (March 1924), p. 424. For local boosterism, see Raymond C. Miller, "The Background of Populism in Kansas," *Mississippi Valley Historical Review,* vol. 11, no. 4 (March 1925), pp. 4–5. For

railroad promotion and details on Kansas real estate, see Farmer, "The Economic Background of Frontier Populism," pp. 406–27. For debt, see Argersinger, *Populism and Politics,* p. 11.

15. Farmer, "The Economic Background of Frontier Populism," pp. 416–19; Miller, "The Background of Populism in Kansas," p. 477.

16. This account follows Goodwyn, *Populist Moment,* pp. 60–63, and Goodwyn, *Democratic Promise,* pp. 99–102, and p. 630, n. 24. In "The Populist Uprising," her contribution to the *History of Kansas* (1928), Elizabeth Barr offers a different account of how the Texas Farmers' Alliance reached Kansas, dating the first contact to August 1888, and changing its direction. "It was brought by the Vincent brothers, publishers of the *Non-Conformist* in Winfield. They went to Texas, were initiated, and returned to organize." Seen in Scott G. McNall, *The Road to Rebellion: Class Formation and Kansas Populism, 1865–1900* (Chicago: University of Chicago Press, 1988), pp. 191–92.

17. Argersinger, *Populism and Politics,* pp. 1–21.

18. Ibid., pp. 15–18. For Annie Diggs, see Goodwyn, *Democratic Promise,* p. 184.

19. James Edward Wright, *The Politics of Populism: Dissent in Colorado* (New Haven: Yale University Press, 1974), p. 110ff.

20. For "anti-monopoly" candidate, see Voss-Hubbard, "The 'Third Party Tradition' Reconsidered," p. 130; Ostler, "Why the Populist Party Was Strong," pp. 471–72.

21. John D. Hicks, *The Populist Revolt: A History of the Farmers' Alliance and the People's Party* (Lincoln: University of Nebraska Press, 1961), p. 132.

22. McMath, *American Populism,* p. 196.

23. Goodwyn, *Democratic Promise,* pp. 194–95.

24. McNall, *The Road to Rebellion,* pp. 193–94.

25. Hicks, *The Populist Revolt,* pp. 168–70.

26. Gene Clanton, *Populism: The Humane Preference in America, 1890–1900* (Boston: Twayne, 1991), p. 32.

27. Argersinger, *Populism and Politics,* pp. 30–31.

28. Clanton, *Populism,* p. 29.

29. Goodwyn, *Populist Moment,* p. 129; Goodwyn, *Democratic Promise,* p. 195.

30. Stanley B. Parsons, Karen Toombs Parsons, Walter Killilae, and Beverly Borgers, "The Role of Cooperatives in the Development of the Movement Culture of Populism," *Journal of American History,* vol. 69, no. 4 (March 1983), p. 883.

31. For Lease and Diggs quotations, see McNall, *The Road to Rebellion,* pp. 214–15, and Argersinger, *Populism and Politics,* pp. 43, 307. For the Lease sentence, see Nugent, *The Tolerant Populists,* p. 82. For Polk, see Goodwyn, *Populist Moment,* p. 134. For Lease on "less . . . corn and more hell," see Clanton, *Populism,* pp. 43–44. For the campaign, see the accounts in Goodwyn, *Democratic Promise;* Argersinger, *Populism and Politics;* Clanton, *Populism;* Hicks, *The Populist Revolt;* and McNall, *The Road to Rebellion.* For the vituperation Mrs. Lease inspired, see C. Robert Haywood, "Populist Humor: The Fame of Their Own Effigy," *Kansas Quarterly,* vol. 16, no. 1 (Spring 1993), pp. 35–36.

32. Mitchell, *Political Education in the Southern Farmers' Alliance,* p. 57.

33. Ibid, pp. 50–58. For the elite background of National Alliance leaders, see Schwartz, *Radical Protest and Social Structure,* pp. 115–18. The leaders of the Texas Alliance were hardly elite, as Mitchell, *Political Education in the Southern Farmers' Alliance,* p. 61, points out: "Of the twenty Alliance leaders for whom education data are available, only five received more than a common-school education." The list of laws follows Sanders, *Roots of Reform,* p. 109.

34. For North Carolina, Mississippi, and Georgia see Goodwyn, *The Populist Moment,*

pp. 58–59. For Missouri, see Homer Clevenger, "The Teaching Techniques of the Farmers' Alliance: An Experiment in Adult Education," *Journal of Southern History,* vol. 2, no. 4 (November 1945), p. 509. For Alabama, see Richard C. Goode, "The Godly Insurrection in Limestone County: Social Gospel, Populism, and Southern Culture in the Late Nineteenth Century," *Religion and American Culture,* vol. 3, no. 2 (Summer 1993), p. 161.

35. For Hahn, see Mitchell, *Political Education in the Southern Farmers' Alliance,* pp. 112–14, 55; for attendance, see Clevenger, "The Teaching Techniques of the Farmers' Alliance," p. 509.

36. Mitchell, *Political Education in the Southern Farmers' Alliance,* pp. 112–14.

37. Clevenger, "The Teaching Techniques of the Farmers' Alliance," p. 515. For corn, see Goodwyn, *The Populist Moment,* pp. 69–70. For inflation, see William P. Yohe, "An Economic Appraisal of the Sub-Treasury Plan," in Goodwyn, *Democratic Promise,* pp. 576, 580.

38. Mitchell, *Political Education in the Southern Farmers' Alliance,* pp. 119, 128–29.

39. Ibid., p. 69.

40. Goode, "The Godly Insurrection in Limestone County," p. 161.

41. Sanders, *Roots of Reform,* p. 101.

42. Donna A. Barnes, *Farmers in Rebellion: The Rise and Fall of the Southern Farmers' Alliance and People's Party in Texas* (Austin: University of Texas Press, 1984), pp. 69–70; Goodwyn, *The Populist Moment,* pp. 75–76.

43. Sanders, *Roots of Reform,* p. 101. Goodwyn, *The Populist Moment,* pp. 55–92; Barnes, *Farmers in Rebellion,* pp. 51–99; Schwartz, *Radical Protest and Social Structure,* pp. 201–15, quotation is on p. 210.

44. Parsons et al., "The Role of Cooperatives," p. 872.

45. For "capitalism," see Schwartz, *Radical Protest and Social Structure,* p. 275. For Daws and Garvin, see Barnes, *Farmers in Rebellion,* pp. 69–70. For a nuanced discussion of the complicated subject of Populism and capitalism, see Bruce Palmer, *"Man over Money": The Southern Populist Critique of American Capitalism* (Chapel Hill: University of North Carolina Press, 1980), quotation is from p. 203. See Schwartz's discussion of oligarchy in the Farmers' Alliance on pp. 102–4 and 270–77. For an argument against Schwartz's leader vs. member reading of the "Cleburne Demands" (the manifesto of Texas Populism), see Barnes, *Farmers in Rebellion,* pp. 76–77. See also Goodwyn's analysis of Daws's and Garvin's position on independent political action as early as Cleburne: "Daws's solution . . . was sufficiently conservative in its appearance and sufficiently radical in its specific uses as to constitute an entirely new definition of the order's relationship to the political process. It became the tactical foundation upon which third-party radicals thereafter rested their case" (pp. 66–70). Goodwyn writes: "To describe the origins of populism in one sentence, the cooperative movement recruited American farmers, and their subsequent experience within the cooperatives radically altered their political consciousness" (*Democratic Promise,* p. xviii). Parsons et al. argue on the basis of statistical evidence that there were too few cooperatives operating at any one time in the South—448 is their high count—to have their collapse be a radicalizing experience for farmer-members (The Role of Cooperatives"). Details on the business counterreaction are taken from Schwartz, *Radical Protest and Social Structure,* pp. 201–15.

46. For Texas violence during early Reconstruction, see Gregg Cantrell, "Racial Violence and Reconstruction Politics in Texas, 1867–1868," *Southwestern Historical Quarterly,* vol. 93, no. 3 (January 1990), pp. 333–55. Also Barry Crouch, "A Spirit of Lawlessness: White Violence; Texas Blacks, 1865–1868," *Journal of Southern History,*

vol. 18, (Winter 1984), pp. 217–32. W.E.B. Du Bois writes: "The editors of the four-teenth edition of the *Encyclopedia Britannica* asked me for an article on the history of the American Negro. From my manuscript they cut out all my references to Reconstruction. I insisted on including the following statement: White historians have ascribed the faults and failures of Reconstruction to Negro ignorance and cor-ruption. But the Negro insists that it was Negro loyalty and the Negro vote alone that restored the South to the Union; established the new democracy, both for white and black, and instituted the public schools." "The Propaganda of History," *ChickenBones: A Journal for Literary and Artistic African-American Themes,* http://www.nathanielturner.com/propagandaofhistorydubois.htm, p. 4. For Wilson and *Birth of a Nation,* see the account in Jack Beatty, *The Rascal King: The Life and Times of James Michael Curley, 1874–1958* (Boston: Addison-Wesley, 1992), pp. 179–80.

47. For "freedom under his feet," see David M. Oshinsky, "Worse Than Slavery: Parch-man Farm and the Ordeal of Jim Crow Justice," chapter 1, "Emancipation," p. 6, http://www.historyisaweapon.org/defcon1/oshinsky. W. J. Cash, *The Mind of the South* (New York: Vintage, 1991), p. 116.

48. Gerald H. Gaither, *Blacks and the Populist Movement: Ballots and Bigotry in the New South* (Tuscaloosa: University of Alabama Press, 2005), p. 101.

49. For North Carolina Populist, see Argersinger, "Taubeneck's Laws," p. 97. C. Vann Woodward, *Origins of the New South, 1877–1913* (Baton Rouge: Louisiana State Uni-versity Press, 1971), p. 220.

50. Gaither, *Blacks and the Populist Movement,* p. 51.

51. Ibid., p. 55.

52. Woodward, *Origins of the New South,* pp. 218–19.

53. Jack Abramowitz, "The Negro in the Populist Movement," *Journal of Negro History,* vol. 24, no. 2 (April 1950), p. 89.

54. William F. Holmes, "The Leflore County Massacre and the Demise of the Colored Farmers' Alliance," *Phylon* (1960–), vol. 34, no. 3 (3rd Qtr., 1973), p. 268. Also see William F. Holmes, "The Arkansas Cotton Pickers Strike of 1891 and the Demise of the Colored Farmers' Alliance," *Arkansas Historical Quarterly,* vol. 32, no. 2 (Sum-mer 1973), pp. 107–19, and William F. Holmes, "The Demise of the Colored Farm-ers' Alliance," *Journal of Southern History,* vol. 41, no. 2 (May 1975), pp. 187–200.

55. Seen in Barry Crouch, "Self-Determination and Local Black Leaders in Texas," *Phy-lon* vol. 39, no. 4 (4th Qtr., 1978), p. 355. "All God's dangers" is from Theodore Rosen-garten, *All God's Dangers: The Life of Nate Shaw* (New York: Alfred A. Knopf, 1974), p. 223. It is a saying of Nate Shaw, the former black sharecropper who is the subject of the book.

56. See Gaither, *Blacks and the Populist Movement,* p. 31; David Brion Davis, *Inhuman Bondage: The Rise and Fall of Slavery in the New World* (New Haven: Yale University Press, 2006), p. 29; Orlando Patterson, "Rituals of Blood: Sacrificial Murders in the Postbellum South," *Journal of Blacks in Higher Education,* vol. 23 (Spring 1999), pp. 123–27; James W. Clarke, "Without Fear or Shame: Lynching, Capital Punishment and the Subculture of Violence in the American South," *British Journal of Political Science,* vol. 28, no. 2 (April 1998), p. 278.

57. Gaither, *Blacks and the Populist Movement,* pp. 202, 101.

58. Goodwyn, *Democratic Promise,* pp. 227–28.

59. Robert Saunders, "Southern Populists and the Negro, 1893–1895," *Journal of Negro History,* vol. 54, no. 3 (June 1969), p. 243.

60. Jack Abramowitz, "The Negro in the Populist Movement," *Journal of Negro History,*

vol. 38, no. 3 (July 1953), p. 281; Joseph H. Taylor, "Populism and Disfranchisement in Alabama," *Journal of Negro History*, vol. 34, no. 4 (October 1949), pp. 410–27.

61. Woodward, *Origins of the New South*, pp. 256–57.

62. Gaither, *Blacks in the Populist Movement*, p. 69.

63. C. Vann Woodward, *The Burden of Southern History* (New York: Mentor, 1966), p. 114; Gaither, *Blacks and the Populist Movement*, p. 97. Woodward later conceded that "Populist gains in interracial cooperation were limited." See Robert C. McMath, Jr., "C. Vann Woodward and the Burden of Southern Populism," *Journal of Southern History*, vol. 67, no. 4 (November 2001), pp. 741–68; quotation is on p. 756. Also see J. Morgan Kousser and James M. McPherson, "C. Vann Woodward: An Assessment of His Work and Influence," in *Region, Race, and Reconstruction: Essays in Honor of C. Vann Woodward* (New York: Oxford University Press, 1982).

64. For Louisiana, see Floyd J. Miller, "Black Protest and White Leadership: A Note on the Colored Farmers' Alliance," *Phylon* (1960–), vol. 33, no. 2 (2nd Qtr., 1972), p. 172. For Georgia, see Charles Crowe, "Tom Watson, Populists, and Blacks Reconsidered," *Journal of Negro History*, vol. 55, no. 2 (April 1970), p. 109.

65. Seen in Crowe, "Tom Watson," p. 102.

66. For North Carolina, see Palmer, "*Man over Money*," p. 153. For Virginia, see William Edward Spriggs, "The Virginia Colored Farmer's Alliance: A Case Study of Race and Class Identity," *Journal of Negro History*, vol. 64, no. 3 (Summer 1970), p. 201.

67. Seen in Gaither, *Blacks and the Populist Movement*, p. 108.

68. Ibid., p. 104.

69. Saunders, "Southern Populists and the Negro," p. 250.

70. Palmer, "*Man over Money*," p. 55; Gaither, *Blacks and the Populist Movement*, p. 110.

71. Clarke, "Without Fear or Shame," pp. 271, 280, n. 34; Gaither, *Blacks and the Populist Movement*, pp. 66–78. For Twain, see Rebecca Edwards, *New Spirits: Americans in the Gilded Age, 1865–1905* (New York: Oxford University Press, 2006), p. 245.

72. Gaither, *Blacks and the Populist Movement*, p. 106.

73. Palmer, "*Man over Money*," p. 66; Crowe, "Tom Watson," pp. 107, 115, n. 13.

74. Clanton, *Populism*, p. 83.

75. Hicks, *The Populist Revolt*, p. 244; Clanton, *Populism*, p. 98.

76. McMath, *American Populism* p. 177.

77. Edward L. Ayers, *The Promise of the New South: Life After Reconstruction* (New York: Oxford University Press, 1992), p. 262.

78. Crowe, "Tom Watson," p. 110; Clanton, *Populism*, p. 96.

79. Clanton, *Populism*, p. 99; Argersinger, *Populism and Politics*, p. 45.

80. Woodward, *Origins of the New South*, p. 259.

81. Argersinger, *Populism and Politics*, p. 45.

82. McMath, *American Populism*, p. 178.

83. Voss-Hubbard, "The 'Third Party Tradition' Reconsidered," pp. 145–46. Also see Steven J. Rosenstone, Roy L. Behr, and Edward H. Lazarus, *Third Parties in America: Citizens' Response to Major Party Failure* (Princeton: Princeton University Press, 1984), especially pp. 63–80. For "Iowa Populist," see Agersinger, "Taubeneck's Laws," p. 103.

84. Argersinger, *Populism and Politics*, p. 121.

85. Goodwyn, *Democratic Promise*, pp. 119–20.

86. Argersinger, *Populism and Politics*, p. 142.

87. Ibid., p. 144.

88. Ibid., pp. 168–69. For more on Mrs. Lease's Civil War, see Nugent, *The Tolerant Pop-*

ulists, p. 81. For Andersonville deaths, see James M. McPherson, *Battle Cry of Freedom: The Civil War Era* (New York: Oxford University Press, 1988), p. 796.

89. For Georgia, see Crowe, "Tom Watson," p. 110. For Texas, see Saunders, "Southern Populists and the Negro," p. 257; also Clanton, *Populism*, p. 143.

90. Gaither, *Blacks and the Populist Movement*, pp. 125–26.

91. Crowe, "Tom Watson," p. 110. However, 1898 saw a violent reaction to fusion by the Democrats.

92. Gregg Cantrell and D. Scott Barton, "Texas Populists and the Failure of Biracial Politics," *Journal of Southern History*, vol. 55, no. 4 (November 1989), pp. 659–92, quotation is from p. 660.

93. James L. Sundquist, *Dynamics of the Party System: Alignment and Realignment of Politcal Parties in the United States* (Washington, D.C.: Brookings Institution, 1983), pp. 145–48. The Cleveland-Morgan rescue follows the account in Jean Strouse, *Morgan: American Financier* (New York: Random House, 1999), pp. 304–7, 342–46.

94. Michael O'Malley, "Specie and Species: Race and the Money Question in Nineteenth-Century America," *American Historical Review*, vol. 99, no. 2 (April 1994), pp. 369–95. Also see the response by Nell Irvin Painter, "Thinking About the Languages of Money and Race: A Response to Michael O'Malley, 'Specie and Species,' " *American Historical Review*, vol. 99, no. 2 (April 1994), pp. 396–404. For background on the currency, see Milton Friedman and Anna Jacobson Schwartz, *A Monetary History of the United States* (Princeton: Princeton University Press, 1963), pp. 134, 91–93; Milton Friedman, "Bimetallism Revisted," *Journal of Economic Perspectives*, vol. 4, no. 4 (Autumn 1990), pp. 85–104; Milton Friedman, "The Crime of 1873," *Journal of Political Economy*, vol. 98, no. 6 (December 1990), pp. 1159–94. For figures on the per capita supply of money, see Sanders, *Roots of Reform*, p. 109. Hicks, *The Populist Revolt*, p. 442.

95. Argersinger, *Populism and Politics* , p. 264; Goodwyn, *Democratic Promise*, pp. 388–502. For another view of what Goodwyn terms "the shadow movement" of silver Populism, see Robert W. Cherny, "Lawrence Goodwyn and Nebraska Populism: A Review Essay," *Great Plains Quarterly*, vol. 1, no. 3 (Summer 1981), pp. 181–94. For *Coin's Financial School*, see Richard Hofstadter, *The Paranoid Style in American Politics* (New York: Alfred A. Knopf, 1965), p. 241.

96. Nevins seen in Robert F. Durden, "The 'Cow-bird' Grounded: The Populist Nomination of Bryan and Tom Watson in 1896," *Mississippi Valley Historical Review*, vol. 50, no. 3 (December 1963), p. 409. Elmer Ellis, "The Silver Republicans in the Election of 1896," *Mississippi Valley Historical Review*, vol. 18, no. 4 (March 1932), p. 529.

97. For Pollack, see Norman Pollack, *The Populist Response to Industrial America* (New York: W. W. Norton, 1966), pp. 103–4. Argersinger, *Populism and Politics*, pp. 235–36, 263, 246. Also see Michael Kazin, *A Godly Hero: The Life of William Jennings Bryan* (New York: Alfred A. Knopf, 2006), p. 64.

98. Argersinger, *Populism and Politics*, pp. 257–58. For the "money Kings," see Barnes, *Farmers in Rebellion*, p. 164.

99. Argersinger, "Taubeneck's Rules," pp. 105–7.

100. For details on the convention, see Goodwyn, *Democratic Promise*, pp. 483–92, and Goodwyn, *The Populist Moment*, p. 285. Also see the divergent accounts in Durden, "The 'Cow-bird' Grounded," Pollack, *The Populist Response to Industrial America*, and Argersinger, *Populism and Politics*. For Dallas Populists, see Cantrell and Barton, "Texas Populists," p. 675. For Bryan's delay in acknowledging the nomination, see Pollack, *The Populist Response to Industrial America*, p. 126. For the rumor of Sewall's

withdrawal, see Barnes, *Farmers in Rebellion,* p. 177; quotation from Barnes is on p. 188.

101. Durden, "The 'Cow-bird' Grounded," p. 410.

102. Clanton, *Populism,* pp. 155–56.

103. C. F. Emerick, "An Analysis of Agricultural Discontent in the United States," *Political Science Quarterly,* vol. 12, no. 1 (September 1896), pp. 433–63.

104. For Milton Friedman see Jeffrey A. Frieden, "Monetary Populism in Nineteenth-Century America: An Open Economy Interpretation," *Journal of Economic History,* vol. 57, no. 2 (June 1997), p. 371.

Chapter Eleven: Revolution from Above

1. On the politics of stalemate, see Paul Kleppner, *The Cross of Culture: A Social Analysis of Midwestern Politics, 1850–1900* (New York: Free Press, 1970), pp. 5–6; Samuel T. McSeveney, *The Politics of Depression: Political Behavior in the Northeast, 1893–1896* (New York: Oxford University Press, 1972), pp. 3–31. For a succinct outline of realignment theory, see V. O. Key, Jr., "A Theory of Critical Elections," *Journal of Politics,* vol. 17 (February 1955), pp. 3–18; for its application, see Lee Benson, Joel H. Sibley, and Phyllis Field, "Toward a Theory of Stability and Change in American Voting Patterns: New York State, 1792–1970," in Joel H. Sibley et al., editors, *The History of American Political Behavior* (Princeton: Princeton University Press, 1978), pp. 78–105. For a thoughtful argument against the concept of realignment, see David R. Mayhew, *Electoral Realignments: A Critique of an American Genre* (New Haven: Yale University Press, 2002).

2. For merchants, see Richard Franklin Bensel, *The Political Economy of American Industrialization, 1877–1900* (Cambridge, Eng.: Cambridge University Press, 2000), p. 478. Robert D. Marcus, *Grand Old Party: Party Structure in the Gilded Age, 1880–1896* (New York: Oxford University Press, 1971), pp. 159–60. For "ethnocultural legislation," see Peter H. Argersinger, "The Transformation of American Politics, 1865–1910," in Byron E. Shafer and Anthony J. Badger, *Contesting Democracy: Substance & Structure in American Political History 1775–2000* (Lawrence: University of Kansas Press, 2001), p. 131. For hell-going Methodist, see Paul Kleppner, *The Third Electoral System, 1853–1892: Parties, Voters, and Political Cultures* (Chapel Hill: University of North Carolina Press, 1979), p. 298.

3. Joseph Frazier Wall, *Andrew Carnegie* (New York: Oxford University Press, 1970), p. 567.

4. James Livingston, "The Social Analysis of Economic History and Theory: Conjectures on Late Nineteenth-Century American Development," *American Historical Review,* vol. 92, no. 1 (February 1987), pp. 69–95. For the "new labor history," see David Montgomery, *The Fall of the House of Labor: The Workplace, the State, and American Labor Activism, 1865–1925* (New York: Cambridge University Press, 1987), introduction and chapter 1; also David Montgomery, "The Shuttle and the Cross: Weavers and Artisans in the Kensington Riots of 1844," *Journal of Social History,* vol. 5, no. 4 (Summer 1972), pp. 411–39; Melvyn Dubofsky, "The Origins of Western Working-Class Radicalism, 1890–1905," *Labor History,* vol. 7 (1966), pp. 131–54. Also, Jeffrey Williamson, "Late Nineteenth-Century American Retardation: A Neo-Classical Analysis," *Journal of Economic History,* vol. 33, no. 3 (September 1973), pp. 582–607.

5. Livingston, "The Social Analysis of Economic History and Theory," table 2, p. 585.

6. Montgomery, *The Fall of the House of Labor*, pp. 189–91. For Gompers, see James Green, *Death in the Haymarket: A Story of Chicago, the First Labor Movement and the Bombing That Divided Gilded Age America* (New York: Pantheon, 2006), p. 108.

7. Livingston, "The Social Analysis of Economic History and Theory."

8. For details on work at the Homestead mill, see William Serrin, *Homestead: The Glory and Tragedy of an American Steel Town* (New York: Vintage, 1993), pp. 54–95; the Hamlin Garland passage is on p. 58. Also see Alan Trachtenberg, *The Incorporation of America: Culture and Society in the Gilded Age* (New York: Hill & Wang, 1982), pp. 77, 87. For injuries in iron and steel industries, see Charles Perrow, "A Society of Organizations," *Theory and Society*, vol. 20 (1991), p. 791. Also, see Les Standiford, *Meet You in Hell: Andrew Carnegie, Henry Clay Frick, and the Partnership That Transformed America* (New York: Crown, 2005), p. 117. This book includes a vivid account of the strike.

9. Martha Frick Symington Sanger, *Henry Clay Frick: An Intimate Portrait* (New York: Abbeville, 1998), p. 169. For official historian, see Livingston, "The Social Analysis of Economic History and Theory." p. 79. For union numbers, see Montgomery, *The Fall of the House of Labor*, p. 35. For Lovejoy, see Paul Krause, *The Battle for Homestead, 1880–1892: Politics, Culture, and Steel* (Pittsburgh: University of Pittsburgh Press, 1992), pp. 294, 290.

10. For Carnegie's self-inventory, see Wall, *Andrew Carnegie*, pp. 224–25.

11. For Carnegie's skin, see Sanger, *Henry Clay Frick*, p. 170. For mills of Homestead, see Linda Schneider, "The Citizen Striker: Ideology in the Homestead Strike of 1892," *Labor History*, vol. 23 (Winter 1882), p. 50.

12. For barges, see Montgomery, *The Fall of the House of Labor*, p. 37, For Pinkertons, see Krause, *The Battle for Homestead*, p. 3ff, for headline, see p. 312.

13. For the battle, see the accounts in Serrin, *Homestead*, pp. 76–81; in Wall, *Andrew Carnegie*, pp. 537–61; Sanger, *Henry Clay Frick*, pp. 184–85; and Krause, *The Battle for Homestead*, pp. 3–43. For suicide, see Standiford, *Meet You in Hell*, p. 175. For Carnegie in Scotland, see David Nasaw, *Andrew Carnegie* (New York: Penguin Press, 2006), p. 428. The dialogue between O'Donnell and Heinde is in Nasaw, *Andrew Carnegie*, p. 421.

14. For society reporter, see Krause, *The Battle for Homestead*, pp. 325–26. For Beatrice Webb, see S. J. Kleinberg, *The Shadow of the Mills: Working-Class Families in Pittsburgh, 1870–1907* (Pittsburgh: University of Pittsburgh Press, 1989), p. 168.

15. Wall, *Andrew Carnegie*, pp. 541, 568, 570. For Dreiser, see Jerome Loving, *The Last Titan: A Life of Theodore Dreiser* (Berkeley: University of California Press, 2005), pp. 77–78.

16. Joshua L. Rosenbloom, "Strikebreaking and the Labor Market in the United States," *Journal of Economic History*, vol. 58, no. 1 (March 1998), pp. 183–205; Montgomery, *The Fall of the House of Labor*, pp. 209, 42; Krause, *The Battle for Homestead*, p. 346. For statistics on African-Americans involved in strikebreaking, see Warren C. Whatley, "African-American Strikebreaking from the Civil War to the New Deal," *Social Science History*, vol. 17, no. 4 (Winter 1993), pp. 525–58. In a "gross underestimation" based on secondary sources, Whatley counts 111 incidents of African-American strikebreaking between 1880 and 1929, including "nearly all" the major strikes of the period. See also Eric Arnesen, "Specter of the Black Strikebreaker: Race, Employment, and Labor Activism in the Industrial Era," *Labor History*, vol. 44, no. 3 (2003), pp. 319–35. Arnesen writes: "[F]or many black workers, not all workplace issues were primarily racial issues; that is, everything experienced in

the labor market could not be reduced to a matter of race. Like whites, black workers objected to low wages, intolerable working conditions, abusive managers, and
workplace humiliation." Once the racist barriers to joining white unions began to
come down, blacks joined unions to fight such conditions.

17. For Frick cable, see Nasaw, *Andrew Carnegie,* p. 419. For *St. Louis Post-Dispatch,* see
Jack Beatty, editor, *Colossus: How the Corporation Changed America* (New York:
Broadway Books, 2001), p. 175.

18. Krause, *The Battle for Homestead,* p. 355. For Methodist preacher, see Herbert G. Gutman, "Protestantism and the American Labor Movement: The Christian Spirit in
the Gilded Age," *American Historical Review,* vol. 72, no. 1 (October 1966), p. 99, n. 102.

19. The quotations are from Krause, *The Battle for Homestead,* pp. 340–41, whose discus-
sion of the issues they raise is searching and profound. Also see Schneider, "The
Citizen Striker," pp. 47–66. For republicanism and the labor theory of value, see
James L. Huston, "The American Revolutionaries, the Political Economy of Aris-
tocracy, and the American Concept of the Distribution of Wealth, 1765–1900,"
American Historical Review, vol. 98, no. 4 (October 1993), pp. 1079–1105. For the quo-
tations from freedmen, see Steven Hahn, "Extravagant Expectations of Freedom,"
Past and Present, no. 157 (November 1997), pp. 144–45, 142, 151. For "the public good,"
see Gordon S. Wood, *The Creation of the American Republic, 1776–1787* (Chapel Hill:
University of North Carolina Press, 1969), chapter 11, "Republicanism," pp. 46–83.
For the vogue of republicanism in historical scholarship, see Daniel T. Rodgers,
"Republicanism: The Career of a Concept," *Journal of American History,* vol. 79,
no. 1 (June 1992), pp. 11–38; Joyce Appleby, "Republicanism and Ideology," *American
Quarterly,* vol. 37, no. 4 (Autumn 1985), pp. 461–73. "The wild fire popularity of
republicanism indicates how keenly historians feel the need to talk about the ineffa-
ble aspects of the past," Appleby comments. The wildfire began with Gordon S.
Wood's book and with J.G.A. Pocock's *The Machiavellian Moment: Florentine Political
Thought and the Atlantic Republican Tradition* (Princeton: Princeton University Press,
1975), especially chapter 15, "The Americanization of Virtue"; also see J.G.A.
Pocock's "Virtue and Commerce in the Eighteenth Century," *Journal of Interdisciplinary History,* vol. 3 (Summer 1972), pp. 119–34. Also Rowland Berthoff, "Indepen-
dence and Attachment, Virtue and Interest: From Republican Citizenship to Free
Enterprise," in his *Republic of the Dispossessed,* (New York: Columbia University
Press, 1997), pp. 131–54.

20. Donald Marquand Dozer, "Benjamin Harrison and the Presidential Campaign of
1892," *American Historical Review,* vol. 54, no. 1 (October 1948), pp. 49–77.

21. H. Wayne Morgan, *From Hayes to McKinley: National Party Politics, 1877–1896* (Syracuse: Syracuse University Press, 1969), p. 417. For Platt, see Marcus, *Grand Old Party,*
pp. 192–93.

22. Carl N. Degler, "American Political Parties and the Rise of the City," *Journal of
American History,* vol. 51, no. 1 (June 1964), p. 47. For New England and Midwest, see
Mark Lawrence Kornbluh, *Why America Stopped Voting: The Decline of Participatory
Democracy and the Emergence of Modern American Politics* (New York: New York Uni-
versity Press, 2000), p. 72. For New York City and Ohio, see Marcus, *Grand Old
Party,* pp. 196–97. For Bryan, see Michael Kazin, *A Godly Hero: The Life of William Jen-
nings Bryan* (New York: Alfred A. Knopf, 2006), p. 42.

23. Carlos C. Clossum, Jr., "The Unemployed in American Cities," *Quarterly Journal of
Economics,* vol. 8, no. 3 (January 1994), pp. 168–217. Samuel Rezneck, "Unemployment, Unrest, and Relief in the United States During the Depression of 1893–97,"

Journal of Political Economy, vol. 61, no. 4 (August 1953), pp. 328–45. Charles Hoffmann, "The Depression of the Nineties," *Journal of Economic History,* vol. 16, no. 2
(June 1956), pp. 137–64. Albert C. Stevens, "Analysis of the Phenomena of the Panic
in 1893," *Quarterly Journal of Economics,* vol. 8, no. 3 (January 1894), pp. 117–42. For
miles of men sleeping on Chicago's viaducts, see Chester McArthur Destler, *American Radicalism, 1865–1901* (Chicago: Quandrangle, 1966), p. 177. For the White City
being torched, see Worth Robert Miller, "Farmers and Third-Party Politics in Nineteenth Century America," originally published in Charles W. Calhoun, editor, *The
Gilded Age: Essays on the Origins of Modern America* (Wilmington, Del.: Scholarly
Resources, 1996) and taken from http://history.missouristate.edu/wrmiller/
Populism/texts/farmers_and_third_partypolitics..htmn.

24. Rezneck, "Unemployment, Unrest, and Relief," pp. 334–38; Montgomery, *The Fall of
the House of Labor,* pp. 92–93.

25. Morgan, *From Hayes to McKinley,* p. 454; James A. Barnes, "Myths of the Bryan Cam-
paign, *Mississippi Valley Historical Review,* vol. 34, no. 3 (December 1947), pp. 367–404.
Also Jackson Lears, "When Jesus Was a Democrat," a review of Kazin, *A Godly
Hero, New Republic,* April 10, 2006, pp. 21–28. For silent delegates, see Harry
Thurston Peck, "The First Bryan Campaign, How Bryan was Nominated," in *Great
Epochs of American History,* www.usgennet.org/usa/topic/preservation/epochs/
vol10/pg108.htm. For the Bryan speech, see James L. Sundquist, *Dynamics of the
Party System: Alignment and Realignment of Political Parties in the United States* (Wash-
ington, D.C.: Brookings Institution, 1983), pp. 137–38. For vote on Cleveland at the
Chicago convention, see Sundquist, *Dynamics of the Party System,* p. 151.

26. Paxton Hibbard, *The Peerless Leader: William Jennings Bryan* (New York: Farrar, Rinehart, 1929), p. 197; Paolo E. Coletta, *William Jennings Bryan, Political Evangelist,
1860–1908,* vol. 1 (Lincoln: University of Nebraska Press, 1964), pp. 140, 177; Gilbert
Fite, "The Election of 1896," in Arthur M. Schlesinger, Jr., and Fred Israel, editors,
History of American Presidential Elections (New York: Chelsea House, 1971), vol. 2,
p. 1815.

27. For Bryan as the Moses of the New Deal, see John Gerring, *Party Ideologies in America, 1828–1996* (New York: Cambridge University Press, 1998), pp. 187–231. For Jackson, see Charles Sellers, *The Market Revolution: Jacksonian America, 1815–1846* (New
York: Oxford University Press, 1991), p. 325. For Bancroft, see Arthur M. Schlesinger,
Jr., *The Age of Jackson* (Boston: Little, Brown, 1945), p. 163. For Bryan quotation, see
Coletta, *William Jennings Bryan,* vol. 1, pp. 175–77. "Democrats subscribed to the
original sin theory of government: The state was evil in and of itself, and the most
it could do for its citizens was to restrain its greed." John Gerring, "A Chapter in the
History of American Party Ideology: The Nineteenth Century Democratic Party,
1828–1892," *Politics,* vol. 26, no. 4 (Summer 1994), pp. 740–41.

28. Barnes, "Myths of the Bryan Campaign," p. 395.

29. Coletta, *William Jennings Bryan,* vol. 1, pp. 187, 123–24; Barnes, "Myths of the Bryan
Campaign," pp. 401–2.

30. McSeveney, *The Politics of Depression,* pp. 184–85; Barnes, "Myths of the Bryan Campaign," pp. 389, 388, 390, 391, 400; Coletta, *William Jennings Bryan,* vol. 1, p. 175; Stanley L. Jones, *The Presidential Election of 1896* (Madison: University of Wisconsin
Press, 1964), p. 315. For heaving floors, see Kazin, *A Godly Hero,* p. 60.

31. For *New York Times,* see Coletta, *William Jennings Bryan,* p. 193. For Hanna, Paolo E.
Coletta, "The Bryan Campaign of 1896," in Paul W. Glad, editor, *William Jennings
Bryan: A Profile* (New York: Hill & Wang, 1968), p. 19, for campaign spending, see

p. 22. For a summary of Bryan's positions on the issues, see John A. Garraty, "A Leader of the People," in ibid. For "manna," see Vachel Lindsay, "Bryan, Bryan, Bryan, Bryan," in *Collected Poems* (New York: Macmillan, 1923), pp. 97–105. For Bryan's opportunism, see Richard Hofstadter, *The American Political Tradition and the Men Who Made It* (New York: Vintage, 1948), p. 190.

32. For Chandler, see Marcus, *Grand Old Party*, p. 247.

33. Matthew Josephson, *The Politicos* (New York: Harcourt, 1939), pp. 700–706. To be sure, "intimidation worked both ways," H. Wayne Morgan writes. "White Democrats and Populists obviously kept Negroes from voting. Bribery, threats, and force were no strangers to Democratic city machines." *From Hayes to McKinley*, p. 523. Coletta, *William Jennings Bryan*, vol. 1, pp. 192–94; Morgan, *From Hayes to McKinley*, p. 516; Fite, "The Election of 1896," p. 1816; Herbert Croly, *Marcus Alonzo Hanna: His Life and Work* (New York: Macmillan, 1923), p. 215. For visits by Homestead and Pennsylvania Railroad workers, see Sanders, *Roots of Reform*, p. 141. For Bryan's visit, see Hibbard, *The Peerless Leader*, pp. 189, 197.

34. For information on this and the above paragraph, see Milton Friedman and Anna Jacobson Schwartz, *A Monetary History of the United States* (Princeton: Princeton University Press, 1963), pp. 134, 91–93; Milton Friedman, "Bimetallism Revisted," *Journal of Economic Perspectives*, vol. 4, no. 4 (Autumn 1990), pp. 85–104; Milton Friedman, "The Crime of 1873," *Journal of Political Economy*, vol. 98, no. 6 (December 1990), pp. 1159–94. For Bryan on the Crime of '73, see Paul Kleppner, *Continuity and Change in Electoral Politics, 1893–1988* (Westport: Greenwood, 1987), p. 173. Also see Walter T. K. Nugent, *Money and American Society, 1865–1880* (New York: Free Press, 1968), chapter 15, "Ideology: The Emergence of International Bimetallism and Free Silver." For background, see Allen Weinstein, *Prelude to Populism: Origins of the Silver Issue, 1867–1878* (New Haven: Yale University Press, 1970). The quotation from John Sherman is on p. 362. Also, Richard Hofstadter, "Free Silver and the Mind of 'Coin' Harvey," in *The Paranoid Style in American Politics and Other Essays* (New York: Alfred A. Knopf, 1965), p. 286.

35. Hofstadter, "Free Silver and the Mind of 'Coin' Harvey," p. 286.

36. Fite, "The Election of 1896," p. 1813, Coletta, *William Jennings Bryan*, vol. 1, p. 190; McSeveney, *The Politics of Depression*, pp. 185, 187.

37. Coletta, *William Jennings Bryan*, vol. 1, pp. 3–6.

38. McSeveney, *The Politics of Depression*, p. 181; Coletta, *William Jennings Bryan*, vol. 1, p. 172. For Kleppner, see Sundquist, *Dynamics of the Party System*, p. 164. Sundquist quotation also on p. 164.

39. McSeveney, *The Politics of Depression*, p. 198; Richard Jensen, *The Winning of the Midwest: Social and Political Conflict, 1888–1896* (Chicago: University of Chicago Press, 1971), pp. 269–308. For election statistics, see Morton Keller, *Affairs of State: Public Life in Late Nineteenth-Century America* (Cambridge: Harvard University Press, 1977), p. 585, and Jensen, *The Winning of the Midwest*, pp. 58, 301 n. 55, 297, table 20. For the San Francisco vote, see R. Hal Williams, *The Democratic Party and California Politics, 1880–1896* (Stanford: Stanford University Press, 1973), pp. 252–53. For McKinley and the tariff, see Richard Jensen, "Democracy, Republicanism, and Efficiency, 1885–1930," in Bryron E. Shafer and Anthony J. Badger, *Contesting Democracy: Substance and Structure in American Political History, 1775–2000* (Lawrence: University of Kansas Press, 2001), p. 154. For literacy test, see Eric Rauchway, "William McKinley and Us," *Journal of the Gilded Age and Progressive Era*, vol. 4, no. 3 (July 2004), p. 6.

40. C. F. Emerick, "An Analysis of Agricultural Discontent," *Political Science Quarterly*, vol. 2, no. 4 (December 1896), p. 632.

41. Walter Dean Burnham, "The Changing Shape of the American Political Universe," in *The Current Crisis in American Politics* (New York: Oxford University Press, 1982), pp. 25–53. For the Democrats' electoral votes, see Walter Dean Burnham, "Party Systems and the Political Process," in Walter Nisbet Chambers and Walter Dean Burnham, editors, *The American Party Systems: Stages of Political Development* (New York: Oxford University Press, 1967), p. 300. Also see Thomas Ferguson, *Golden Rule: The Investment Theory of Party Competition and the Logic of Money-Driven Political Systems* (Chicago: University of Chicago Press, 1995), pp. 67–79. For a criticism of the "Burnham thesis," see Richard L. McCormick, "Walter Dean Burnham and 'The System of 1896,'" *Social Science History*, vol. 10, no. 3 (Autumn 1986), pp., 245–62; also see Burnham's rejoinder, "Periodization Schemes and Party Systems: The 'System of 1896' as a Case in Point," *Social Science History*, vol. 10, no. 3 (Autumn 1986), pp. 263–314. For industrializing elites, see Clark Kerr, et al., *Industrialism and Industrial Man: The Problem of Labor and Management in Economic Growth* (Cambridge: Harvard University Press, 1960), especially pp. 99–109. For accumulation, see S. Pollard, "Investment, Consumption, and the Industrial Revolution," *Economic History Review*, 2nd Series, Vol. 11, no. 2 (1958), pp. 215–226. For price decline, see Coletta, "The Bryan Campaign of 1896," p. 30, also 21. Political scientists continue to debate whether 1896 was, as Schattschneider wrote, "one of the decisive elections in American history." For a view that 1896 "has a good deal less immediate impact than the elections of 1912, 1832 and 1972," see Larry M. Bartels, "Electoral Continuity and Change," *Electoral Studies*, vol. 17 (September 1998), pp. 301–26. Also see the essays gathered in Byron R. Shafer, editor, *The End of Realignment: Interpreting American Electoral Eras* (Madison: University of Wisconsin Press, 1991), which includes an essay by Burnham responding to his critics. The book ends with a thirty-two page bibliography of writings about realignment, a testament to a fruitful contribution to political science.

42. Details of the Waldorf party are taken from the voluminous account in the *New York Times*, 2/10 and 2/11/1897; and from among the best books about Gilded Age America, Sven Beckert, *The Monied Metropolis: New York City and the Consolidation of the American Bourgeoisie, 1850–1896* (New York: Cambridge University Press, 2001), pp. 1–2, 334. Also see Robert Muccigrosso, "New York Has a Ball: The Bradley Martin Extravaganza," *New York History*, vol. 75, no. 3 (July 1994), pp. 297–313, a deftly understated account; and Michael McGeer, *A Fierce Discontent: The Rise and Fall of the Progressive Movement 1870–1920* (New York: Free Press, 2003), pp. 4–6. For Louis XV, see Norman Davies, *Europe: A History* (New York: Oxford University Press, 1996), pp. 627–28. For Mrs. Vanderbilt's 1883 ball, see Rebecca Edwards, *New Spirits: Americans in the Gilded Age, 1865–1905* (New York: Oxford University Press, 2006), pp. 97–98.

Chapter Twelve: Mississippi and the American Way

1. C. Vann Woodward, *Origins of the New South, 1877–1913* (Baton Rouge: Louisiana State University Press, 1971), p. 325.

2. For Countess Craven, see Robert Muccigrosso, "New York Has A Ball: The Bradley Martin Extravaganza," *New York History*, vol. 75, no. 3 (July 1994), p. 302. Major L. Wilson, "The 'Country' Versus the 'Court': A Republican Consensus and Party

Debate in the Bank War," *Journal of the Early Republic*, vol. 15, no. 4 (Winter 1995), p. 630. For William Allen White, see Kevin Phillips, *Wealth and Democracy: A Political History of the American Rich* (New York: Broadway Books, 2002), p. 48.

3. David P. Thelen, "Social Tensions and the Origins of Progressivism," *Journal of American History*, vol. 56, no. 2 (September 1969), pp. 323–41. For an account of clashing interpretations of the Progressive Era see David M. Kennedy, "Overview: The Progressive Era," *The Historian*, vol. 37, no. 3 (May 1975), pp. 453–69. Also, Martin J. Sklar, "Periodization and Historiography: Studying American Political Development in the Progressive Era, 1890's–1916," *Studies in American Political Development*, vol. 5 (Fall 1991), pp. 173–213, and see the response by Steven Hahn. Linda Gordon participated in a conference on Progressivism at which both the "arch-conservative legal scholar Richard Epstein" and the arch-liberal Arthur Schlesinger, Jr., defined Progressivism "identically: state regulation of the economy." Linda Gordon, "If the Progressives Were Advising Us Today, Should We Listen?," *Journal of the Gilded Age and Progressive Era*, vol. 1, no. 2 (April 2002).

4. Richard L. McCormick, *The Party Period and Public Policy: American Politics from the Age of Jackson to the Progressive Era* (New York: Oxford University Press, 1986), pp. 304–5.

5. Richard L. McCormick, "The Discovery That Business Corrupts Politics: A Reappraisal of the Origins of Progressivism," *American Historical Review*, vol. 86, no. 2 (April 1983), pp. 247–74. For Nebraskans, see front-page story headlined "War in the Horizon, Intense Hatred of the Union Pacific in Nebraska, A Rotten Corporation," *Chicago Tribune*, 2/1/1890.

6. For railroad passes, see Mahlon H. Hellerich, "Railroad Regulation in the Constitutional Convention of 1873," *Pennsylvania History*, vol. 26, no. 1 (January 1959), pp. 35–53.

7. Jacob S. Hacker and Paul Pierson, "Business Power and Social Policy: Employers and the Formation of the American Welfare State," *Politics and Society*, vol. 30, no. 2 (June 2002), pp. 277–325.

8. For Progressives and unions, see William E. Leuchtenburg, *The FDR Years: On Roosevelt and His Legacy* (New York: Columbia University Press, 1999), p. 38.

9. For statistics on the labor injunction, see William Forbath, "The Shaping of the American Labor Movement," *Harvard Law Review*, vol. 102, no. 6 (April 1989), p. 1152.

10. Henry George, "Money in Elections," *North American Review*, vol. 86 (March 1883), pp. 201–12. For Bryan, see John Gerring, *Party Ideologies in America, 1828–1996* (New York: Cambridge University Press, 1998), p. 196. For Glass, see J. Morgan Kousser, *The Shaping of Southern Politics: Suffrage Restrictions and the Establishment of the One-Party-South, 1880–1910* (New Haven: Yale University Press, 1974), p. 262.

11. Eric Foner, *Reconstruction: America's Unfinished Revolution 1863–1877* (New York: Harper & Row, 1988), p. 593. For "disfranchisement," see chapter 12, "The Mississippi Plan as the American Way," in Woodward, *Origins of the New South*, pp. 321–49. The moving vingette of voters defeated by literacy test and other details are from the powerful Kousser, *The Shaping of Southern Politics*, pp. 262–64, 92, 163, 54, 51, 252. For Maryland's law, see Michael Schudson, *The Good Citzen: A History of American Civic Life* (New York: Free Press, 1998), p. 184. Details on the Tennessee statute are from J. Morgan Kousser, "Post-Reconstruction Restrictions in Tennessee: A New Look at the V. O. Key Thesis," *Political Science Quarterly*, vol. 88, no. 4 (December 1993), pp. 665, 678–79.

12. For "side effect" and "the forces of good government," see Philip E. Converse, "Change in the American Electorate," quoted in Kousser, *The Shaping of Southern Politics,* p. 51, n. 12; and Richard Ayres, William C. Bowen, and Stanley Kelley, Jr., "Registration and Voting: Putting First Things First," *American Political Science Review,* vol. 61, no. 2 (June 1967), pp. 359.

13. For the debate on disfranchisement in the North, see Walter Dean Burnham, "Theory and Voting Research," *American Political Science Review,* vol. 68, no. 3 (September 1974), pp. 1002–23, and the responses to the "Burnham Theory" by Philip E. Converse, "Comments on Burnham's 'Theory and Voting Research,' " *American Political Science Review,* vol. 68, no. 3 (September 1974), pp. 1024–27, and Jerrold Rusk, "Comment: The American Political Universe: Speculation and Evidence," *American Political Science Review,* vol. 68, no. 3 (September 1974), pp. 1028–49, and Burnham's reply. For turnout, see Walter Dean Burnham, "The Changing Shape of the Political Universe," in *The Current Crisis in American Politics* (New York: Oxford University Press, 1982), table 2, p. 30; and Thomas Ferguson, *Golden Rule: The Investment Theory of Party Competition and the Logic of Money-Driven Political Systems* (Chicago: University of Chicago Press, 1995), table 1.1, p. 74. For turnout in 1916, see Walter Dean Burnham, *Critical Elections and the Mainspring of American Politics* (New York: W. W. Norton, 1970), p. 84. For Mississippi voting in 1920, see Richard Franklin Bensel, *Sectionalism and American Political Development, 1880–1980* (Madison: University of Wisconsin Press, 1984), p. 81. For nineteenth-century registration procedures and for Paul Kleppner's estimate of the effects of waning competition on voting, see Mark Lawrence Kornbluh, *Why America Stopped Voting: The Decline of Participatory Democracy and the Emergence of Modern American Politics* (New York: New York University Press, 2000), pp. 133–34, 148. For Mississippi, see Woodward, *Origins of the New South,* p. 321.

14. For the conservative consequences of excluding southern blacks from the electorate from the 1890s to the 1960s, see Eric Foner, "Rights and the Constitution in Black Life During the Civil War and Reconstruction," *Journal of American History,* vol. 74, no. 3 (December 1987), p. 883. Speaking with National Public Radio's Scott Simon on the fortieth anniversary of the Voting Rights Act, former Atlanta mayor and U.N. ambassador Andrew Young said that shortly after completing the examination required to practice dentistry in Louisiana in two rather than the four days allowed, his brother, a college and dentistry school graduate and former naval officer, went to register to vote. He was told he could not vote because he had failed the literacy test. For New Jersey turnout, see Kornbluh, *Why America Stopped Voting,* p. 109. For "totalitarianism," see Burnham, "The Changing Shape of the American Political Universe," pp. 52–53; for "system of 1896" see p. 46. Also, Walter Dean Burnham, "Political Immunization and Political Confessionalism: The United States and Weimar Germany," *Journal of Interdisciplinary History,* vol. III, no. 1 (Summer 1972), pp. 1–30. For the class skew in the electorate, see various authors, "American Democracy in an Age of Rising Inequality," the Task Force on Inequality and American Democracy, the American Political Science Association, at http://www.apsanet.org/imgtest/taskforcereport.pdf. The quotation on registration is from Richard B. Freeman, "What, Me Vote?," National Bureau of Economic Research, Working Paper 9896, http://www.nber.org/papers. w9896. The study on declining turnout is from David Darmofal, "Socioeconomic Bias, Turnout Decline, and the Puzzle of Participation," p. 20, people.cas.sc.edu/darmofal.

15. Seen in Samuel Rezneck, "Unemployment, Unrest, and Relief in the United States

During the Depression of 1893–97," *Journal of Political Economy*, vol. 61, no. 4 (August 1953), p. 345. For Cornelia Martin's countercyclical party, see Sven Beckert, *The Monied Metropolis* (New York: Cambridge University Press, 2001), p. 1. For recovery, see Charles Hoffmann, "The Depression of the Nineties," *Journal of Economic History*, vol. 16, no. 2 (June 1956), pp. 117–42.

16. Paul Krause, *The Battle for Homestead, 1860–1892* (Pittsburgh: University of Pittsburgh Press, 1992), pp. 269–83.

17. Karl Marx, *A Critique of Political Economy* (New York: Modern Library, 1906), pp. 648–49.

18. Robert Dallek, *The American Style of Foreign Policy: Cultural Politics and Foreign Affairs* (New York: Alfred A. Knopf, 1983), pp. 12–13.

19. Richard Hofstadter, *The Age of Reform: From Bryan to F.D.R.* (New York: Alfred A. Knopf, 1955), p. 14, and Richard Hofstadter, "Cuba, the Philippines, and Manifest Destiny," in *The Paranoid Style in American Politics* (New York: Alfred A. Knopf, 1965), p. 162.

20. Naomi R. Lamoreaux, *The Great Merger Movement in American Business, 1895–1904* (New York: Cambridge University Press, 1985), pp. 1–2.

21. James Livingston, "The Social Analysis of Economic History: Conjectures on Late Nineteenth-Century American Development," *American Historical Review*, vol. 92, no. 1 (February 1987), p. 75.

22. David Montgomery, *The Fall of the House of Labor* (New York: Cambridge University Press, 1987), p. 229.

23. Ibid., pp. 41–42.

24. Hofstadter, "Cuba, the Philippines, and Manifest Destiny," pp. 169, 180–181, 128. For William James, see Frank Freidel, "Dissent in the Spanish-American War and the Philippine Insurrection," in Samuel Eliot Morison, Frederick Merk, and Frank Freidel, editors, *Dissent in Three American Wars* (Cambridge: Harvard University Press, 1971), pp. 90–91.

25. For McKinley, God, and the map, see Stanley Karnow, *In Our Image: America's Empire in the Philippines* (New York: Random House, 1989), p. 11. For war casualties, see Michael Addas, *Dominance by Design: Technological Imperatives and America's Civilizing Mission* (Cambridge: Harvard University Press, 2005), p. 134. For the "Southern way," see Woodward, *Origins of the New South*, pp. 324–25. Also see William Appleman Williams, *The Tragedy of American Diplomacy* (New York: Delta, 1962), pp. 18–50. For God, Methodism, and McKinley, see Edward J. Blum, *Reforging the White Republic: Race, Religion, and American Nationalism, 1865–1898* (Baton Rouge: Louisiana State University Press, 2005), pp. 209–49, especially p. 229. For McKinley's statement to the Methodist leaders, see Thomas Bender, *A Nation Among Nations: America's Place in World History* (New York: Hill & Wang, 2006), p. 221. For Burgess and his "Negro boy," see W.E.B. Du Bois, "The Propaganda of History," *ChickenBones: A Journal for Literary and Artistic African American Themes*, http://www.nathanielturner.com/propagandaofhistorydubois.htm, p. 9.

26. Hofstadter, "Cuba, the Philippines, and Manifest Destiny," pp. 180–81. Bensel, *Sectionalism and American Political Development*, p. 96.

27. Beveridge seen in Rezneck, "Unemployment, Unrest, and Relief," p. 345. For Howells, see Alan Trachtenberg, *The Incorporation of America: Culture and Society in the Gilded Age* (New York: Hill & Wang, 1982), p. 230.

Index

Illustrations Credits

Printed in the United States
by Baker & Taylor Publisher Services